LET'S

■ PAGES PACKED WITH ESSENTIAL INFORMATION

"Value-packed, unbeatable, accurate, and comprehensive."

—The Los Angeles Times

"The guides are aimed not only at young budget travelers but at the independent traveler; a sort of streetwise cookbook for traveling alone."

—The New York Times

"Unbeatable; good sight-seeing advice; up-to-date info on restaurants, hotels, and inns; a commitment to money-saving travel; and a wry style that brightens nearly every page."

—The Washington Post

■ THE BEST TRAVEL BARGAINS IN YOUR BUDGET

"All the dirt, dirt cheap."

—People

"Let's Go follows the creed that you don't have to toss your life's savings to the wind to travel—unless you want to."

—The Salt Lake Tribune

■ REAL ADVICE FOR REAL EXPERIENCES

"The writers seem to have experienced every rooster-packed bus and lunar-surfaced mattress about which they write."

—The New York Times

"[Let's Go's] devoted updaters really walk the walk (and thumb the ride, and trek the trail). Learn how to fish, haggle, find work—anywhere."

—Food & Wine

"A world-wise traveling companion—always ready with friendly advice and helpful hints, all sprinkled with a bit of wit."

—The Philadelphia Inquirer

■ A GUIDE WITH A SPIRIT AND A SOCIAL CONSCIENCE

"Lighthearted and sophisticated, informative and fun to read. [Let's Go] helps the novice traveler navigate like a knowledgeable old hand."

—Atlanta Journal-Constitution

"The serious mission at the book's core reveals itself in exhortations to respect the culture and the environment—and, if possible, to visit as a volunteer, a student, or a teacher rather than a tourist."

—San Francisco Chronicle

LET'S GO PUBLICATIONS

TRAVEL GUIDES

Australia 9th edition
Austria & Switzerland 12th edition
Brazil 1st edition
Britain 2008
California 10th edition
Central America 9th edition
Chile 2nd edition
China 5th edition
Costa Rica 3rd edition
Eastern Europe 13th edition
Ecuador 1st edition
Egypt 2nd edition
Europe 2008
France 2008
Germany 13th edition
Greece 9th edition
Hawaii 4th edition
India & Nepal 8th edition
Ireland 13th edition
Israel 4th edition
Italy 2008
Japan 1st edition
Mexico 22nd edition
New Zealand 8th edition
Peru 1st edition
Puerto Rico 3rd edition
Southeast Asia 9th edition
Spain & Portugal 2008
Thailand 3rd edition
USA 24th edition
Vietnam 2nd edition
Western Europe 2008

ROADTRIP GUIDE

Roadtripping USA 2nd edition

ADVENTURE GUIDES

Alaska 1st edition
Pacific Northwest 1st edition
Southwest USA 3rd edition

CITY GUIDES

Amsterdam 5th edition
Barcelona 3rd edition
Boston 4th edition
London 16th edition
New York City 16th edition
Paris 14th edition
Rome 12th edition
San Francisco 4th edition
Washington, D.C. 13th edition

POCKET CITY GUIDES

Amsterdam
Berlin
Boston
Chicago
London
New York City
Paris
San Francisco
Venice
Washington, D.C.

LET'S GO

PUERTO RICO

NOGA LEAH RAVID EDITOR

RESEARCHER-WRITERS
PAUL G. HAMM
SARAH REA

MAISIE CLARK MAP EDITOR
CALINA CIOBANU MANAGING EDITOR

ST. MARTIN'S PRESS ✹ NEW YORK

HELPING LET'S GO. If you want to share your discoveries, suggestions, or corrections, please drop us a line. We read every piece of correspondence, whether a postcard, a 10-page email, or a coconut. **Address mail to:**

Let's Go: Puerto Rico
67 Mount Auburn St.
Cambridge, MA 02138
USA

Visit Let's Go at **http://www.letsgo.com,** or send email to:

feedback@letsgo.com
Subject: "Let's Go: Puerto Rico"

In addition to the invaluable travel advice our readers share with us, many are kind enough to offer their services as researchers or editors. Unfortunately, our charter enables us to employ only currently enrolled Harvard students.

Maps by David Lindroth copyright © 2008 by St. Martin's Press.

Distributed outside the USA and Canada by Macmillan.

ISBN-13: 978-0-312-37447-1
ISBN-10: 0-312-37447-X
Third edition
10 9 8 7 6 5 4 3 2 1

Let's Go: Puerto Rico is written by Let's Go Publications, 67 Mount Auburn St., Cambridge, MA 02138, USA.

Let's Go® and the LG logo are trademarks of Let's Go, Inc.

CONTENTS

HOW TO USE THIS BOOK

COVERAGE LAYOUT. *Let's Go: Puerto Rico* launches out of **San Juan.** From this bustling capital city, venture to the **Northeast** for trips to the rainforest and beautiful beaches. Head all the way to the east coast for the city of Fajardo and transportation to the idyllic Caribbean islands of **Vieques** and **Culebra.** Back on the mainland, the journey continues through the sleepy coastal towns of the undiscovered **Southeast,** ending in Puerto Rico's southern jewel, Ponce. Next, trek west through the cactus forests and salt flats of the **Southwest** for relaxed ocean fun, with a brief foray to the isolated reserve of Isla Mona. Then, head north into the rugged karst landscape of the **Northwest** for world-class surfing. Lastly, travel through the seldom-visited, mountainous center of the island on the winding series of roads called the **Ruta Panorámica.**

TRANSPORTATION INFO. For making connections between destinations, information is generally listed under both the arrival and departure cities. Parentheticals usually provide the trip duration followed by the frequency, then the price. Travelers to Puerto Rico must choose between driving and going by *carros públicos* (public cars). For more information on this and on general travel concerns, consult **Essentials** (p. 9).

COVERING THE BASICS. The first chapter, **Discover Puerto Rico** (p. 1), contains highlights of the island, complete with **Suggested Itineraries.** The **Essentials** (p. 9) section contains practical information on planning a budget, making reservations, and other useful tips for traveling in Puerto Rico. Take some time to peruse the **Life and Times** section, which briefly sums up the history, culture, and customs of Puerto Rico. The **Appendix** (p. 309) has climate information, as well as a Spanish pronunciation guide and glossary. For study abroad and volunteer opportunities in Puerto Rico, **Beyond Tourism** (p. 81) is all you need.

PRICE DIVERSITY. Our researchers list establishments in order of value from best to worst, with absolute favorites denoted by the *Let's Go* thumbs-up (🕮). Since the cheapest price does not always mean the best value, we have incorporated a system of price ranges for food and accommodations; see p. viii.

SCHOLARLY ARTICLES. Four contributors with unique local insight wrote articles for *Let's Go: Puerto Rico.* **María Pilar Barreto** discusses her experience volunteering in a San Juan public library (p. 83). Education policy specialist **Adrián Cerezo** explains Puerto Rico's unusual public transportation system (p. 80). Harvard PhD **Camille Lizarribar** explores Puerto Rico's traditional Roman Catholic icons, *santos y palos* (p. 72). Harvard PhD candidate **Iliana Pagán Teitelbaum** discusses Puerto Rico's complicated political relationship with the US (p. 60).

PHONE CODES AND TELEPHONE NUMBERS. The area code for all of Puerto Rico is ☎**787.** Phone numbers in text are preceded by the ☎ icon.

A NOTE TO OUR READERS. The information for this book was gathered by *Let's Go* researchers from May through August of 2007. Each listing is based on one researcher's opinion, formed during his or her visit at a particular time. Those traveling at other times may have different experiences since prices, dates, hours, and conditions are always subject to change. You are urged to check the facts presented in this book beforehand to avoid inconvenience and surprises.

Puerto Rico Chapter Divisions

Atlantic Ocean

Culebra
- Dewey
- Culebra **pp. 186-199**

Vieques
- Isabel Segunda
- Vieques **pp. 170-185**

- Luquillo
- Fajardo
- **The Northeast pp. 150-169**
- Naguabo

- Loíza
- San Juan
- Guaynabo
- **San Juan pp. 89-149**
- Caguas

- Dorado Cataño
- Bayamón
- Barranquitas
- Aibonito
- **The Southeast pp. 200-223**
- Guayama
- Arroyo
- Salinas

- Manatí

- Jayuya
- **La Rua Panorámica pp. 290-308**

- Arecibo
- Utuado
- **The Northwest pp. 258-289**
- Adjuntas
- Maricao

- Ponce

- Isabela
- Aguadilla
- Rincón
- Mayagüez
- San Germán
- **The Southwest pp. 224-257**
- Cabo Rojo
- Boquerón
- La Paguera
- Guánica
- *Cabo Rojo*

Caribbean Sea

RESEARCHER-WRITERS

Paul G. Hamm
Northwest, Southwest, Ruta Panorámica

Veteran Let's Go researcher Paul Hamm *(Let's Go: Hawaii 2007)* returned this year for some more island hopping, making his way out west to discover the unplumbed depths and unclimbed heights of Puerto Rico's pristine coast and rugged central mountains. A sturdy outdoorsman with a keen sense of fun and an appreciation for creative facial hair, Paul hiked, camped, and surfed his way through Puerto Rico. Between busy days of research he still managed to find time to fish, spelunk, attend the odd basball game and wedding, and brush up on his Spanish—all the while sending back comprehensive and entertaining prose.

Sarah Rea
Culebra, Northeast, San Juan, Southeast, Vieques

This sunny Toronto native brought her sense of adventure and solo travel smarts to the sprawling metropolis of San Juan and more secluded areas of the Southeast. Sarah braved sea urchins, packed roads, and a waterlogged cell phone to get the low down on everything from sangria and salsaing in San Juan to snorkeling off the white sand coast of Culebra, befriending everyone in her path. With a good eye for interesting stories and great deals, Sarah infused new life into the East Coast coverage.

CONTRIBUTING WRITERS

María Pilar Barreto is a native of Guaynabo. She has completed a BA in Latin American Studies at Harvard University and hopes to enter a career in diplomacy.

Adrián Cerezo directs the Community-Based Education Center at Sacred Heart University in San Juan. He has a BA in clinical psychology from Sacred Heart and received a Distinguished Alumni Award in 1998 for his contributions to the field of education.

Camille Lizarribar has a PhD in Comparative Literature from Harvard University and a JD from Harvard Law. She most recently worked as a clerk for a judge at the Federal district court in San Juan.

Iliana Pagán Teitelbaum received her BA in Latin American Studies from the University of Puerto Rico. She expects to receive a PhD in Romance Languages and Literatures from Harvard University.

ACKNOWLEDGMENTS

LET'S GO

NOGA THANKS: Paul and Sarah for their sense of adventure, their stories, and their ▨determination. Calina, probably the best ME around, for her support, fondness for mongeese (touch them, yes), and all her dedication and help throughout this process. Vicki, Prod Queen Supreme, back rubber extraordinaire, general good cookie. Thanks to Calina and Vicki both for being lovely housemates. To Maisie for her humor and patience and spectacular maps. To Cooonroy, Miss Molly, and Anne for making this (physically) freezing pod a true delight to be in. To Molly for snorting, to Matt for making her snort. Who's judging? No one, but I'm counting. To Eff and Torito, mutually, separately, for squeezes. And of course, much gratitude and love to Mummy, Daddy, Yinon, and Jonathan for their humor and faith; you're the best, best.

MAISIE THANKS: Sarah for not being afraid to call me on the phone. Paul for his friendly map notes. Noga for her patience with my newbness. Beenanz Farrar for google-chatting with me when times got rough. And of course, Martha and Peter Clark. You are the best parents in the whole world!

Publishing Director
Jennifer Q. Wong
Editor-in-Chief
Silvia Gonzalez Killingsworth
Production Manager
Victoria Esquivel-Korsiak
Cartography Manager
Thomas MacDonald Barron
Editorial Managers
Anne Bensson, Calina Ciobanu, Rachel Nolan
Financial Manager
Sara Culver
Business and Marketing Manager
Julie Vodhanel
Personnel Manager
Victoria Norelid
Production Associate
Jansen A. S. Thurmer
Director of E-Commerce & IT
Patrick Carroll
Website Manager
Kathryne A. Bevilacqua
Office Coordinators
Juan L. Peña, Bradley J. Jones

Director of Advertising Sales
Hunter McDonald
Senior Advertising Associate
Daniel Loo

Editor
Noga Leah Ravid
Managing Editor
Calina Ciobanu
Map Editor
Maisie Clark
Typesetter
Nathaniel Brooks

President
William Hauser
General Managers
Bob Rombauer, Jim McKellar

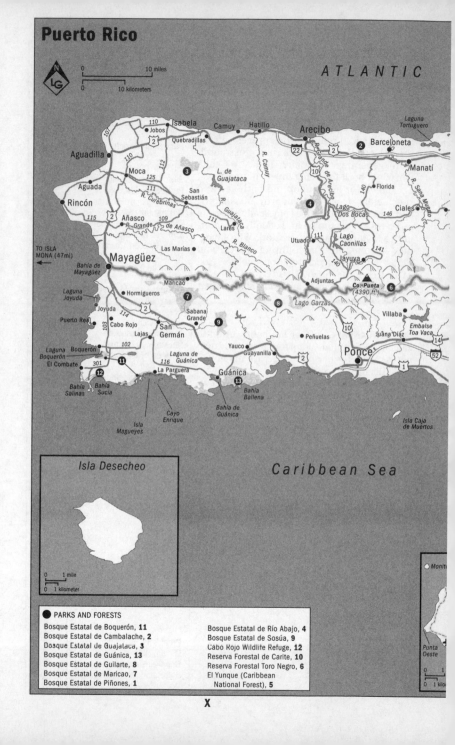

Puerto Rico

ATLANTIC

0   10 miles
0   10 kilometers

Laguna
Tortuguero

Isabela   Camuy   Hatillo   Arecibo   Barceloneta
Jobos
Quebradillas   Manatí
Aguadilla
Moca   L. de   Florida
Aguada   Guajataca   Lago
Rincón   San   Dos Bocas   Ciales
Añasco   Sebastián
Mayagüez   Lares   Utuado   Lago
Las Marías   Caonillas
Jayuya
TO ISLA
MONA (47mi)   Adjuntas   Co. Punta
Bahía de   (4390 ft.)
Mayagüez   Maricao
Laguna   Lago Garzas   Villaba
Joyuda   Hormigueros
Sabana   Embalse
Joyuda   Grande   Toa Vaca
Puerto Real   Juana Díaz
Cabo Rojo   San   Yauco   Peñuelas
Lajas   Germán   Guayanilla   Ponce
Laguna de
Laguna   Boquerón   Guánica   Yauco   52
Boquerón
El Combate   La Parguera   Guánica
Bahía   Bahía   Bahía
Salinas Sucia   Ballena
Cayo   Bahía de
Enrique   Guánica   Isla Caja
Isla   de Muertos
Magueyes

Caribbean Sea

Isla Desecheo

0   1 mile
0   1 kilometer

Monit

Punta
Oeste
0
0   1 kilo

● PARKS AND FORESTS
Bosque Estatal de Boquerón, 11   Bosque Estatal de Río Abajo, 4
Bosque Estatal de Cambalache, 2   Bosque Estatal de Sosúa, 9
Bosque Estatal de Guajataca, 3   Cabo Rojo Wildlife Refuge, 12
Bosque Estatal de Guánica, 13   Reserva Forestal de Carite, 10
Bosque Estatal de Guilarte, 8   Reserva Forestal Toro Negro, 6
Bosque Estatal de Maricao, 7   El Yunque (Caribbean
Bosque Estatal de Piñones, 1   National Forest), 5

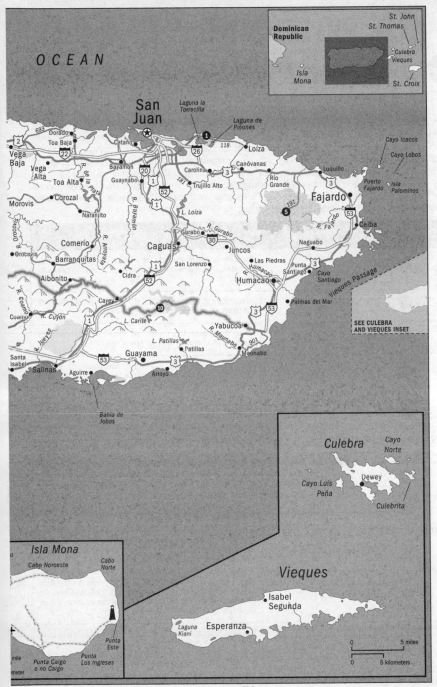

OCEAN

San Juan

Dominican Republic

St. John
St. Thomas
Culebra
Vieques
St. Croix
Isla Mona

Laguna la Torrecilla
Laguna de Piñones

693
Dorado
Toa Baja
Cataño
118
Loíza
Cayo Icacos
Cayo Lobos

2
Vega Baja
Vega Alta
Toa Alta
Bayamón
Carolina
Canóvanas
Luquillo

22
Guaynabo
Trujillo Alto
Río Grande
Puerto Fajardo
Isla Palominos

20
181
3
Fajardo

Morovis
Corozal
52
L. Loíza
191
53
Ceiba

Naranjito
Comerío
Gurabo
R. Gurabo
Naguabo

Orocovis
Barranquitas
Caguas
30
Juncos
R. Fajardo

Aibonito
Cidra
San Lorenzo
Las Piedras
Punta Santiago
Cayo Santiago

Cayey
Humacao
Vieques Passage

Coamo
10
Palmas del Mar
SEE CULEBRA AND VIEQUES INSET

R. Cuyón
L. Carite
Yabucoa
3
53

Santa Isabel
L. Patillas
Patillas
R. Maunabo
901
Maunabo

Salinas
Aguirre
Guayama
3
Arroyo

Bahía de Jobos

Culebra
Cayo Norte

Cayo Luis Peña
Dewey
Culebrita

Isla Mona

Cabo Noroeste
Cabo Norte

Vieques

Isabel Segunda
Esperanza

Laguna Kiani

Punta Este

Punta Caigo o no Caigo
Punta Los Ingleses

0   5 miles
0   5 kilometers

XI

PRICE RANGES ③ ④
① ② PUERTO RICO ⑤

Our researchers list establishments in order of value from best to worst; our favorites are denoted by the Let's Go thumbs-up (✍). However, because the best value is not always the cheapest price, we have also incorporated a system of price ranges, based on a rough expectation of what you'll spend. For **accommodations,** we base our range on the cheapest price for which a single traveler can stay for one night. For **restaurants** and other dining establishments, we estimate the average amount a traveler will spend. The table tells you what you'll *typically* find in Puerto Rico at the corresponding price range; keep in mind that no system can allow for every individual establishment's quirks, and you'll typically get more for your money in larger cities. In other words: expect anything.

ACCOMMODATIONS	RANGE	WHAT YOU'RE *LIKELY* TO FIND
①	under $40	Primarily campgrounds or fields in which you can pitch a tent. Include toilets, water, and often showers. Some have security guards.
②	$40-60	Inexpensive guesthouses, as well as rustic cabins and villas for larger groups. You may have a private bathroom.
③	$61-89	Small, independent hotels. Rooms should have private bath and decent amenities, such as phone and TV.
④	$90-130	Nicer guesthouses, small hotels, and most *paradores*. Similar to 3, but may have more amenities or be in a more highly touristed or conveniently located area.
⑤	above $130	Large hotels, upscale chains, and realtor-owned vacation rentals. If it's a 5 and it doesn't have the perks you want, you've paid too much.
FOOD	RANGE	WHAT YOU'RE *LIKELY* TO FIND
①	under $6	*Panaderías* and *cafeterías* serving sandwiches and typical Puerto Rican food. Usually only open for lunch. No tips.
②	$6-10	Inexpensive sit-down restaurants with waitstaff and relatively expensive *cafeterías* serving dinner.
③	$11-15	Entrées are more expensive, but chances are, you're paying for decor and ambience. You'll probably have a waiter or waitress, so the tip will bump you up a few dollars.
④	$16-20	Most seafood restaurants. As in 3, higher prices are probably related to better service, but in these restaurants, the food will tend to be fancier or more elaborate, or the location will be especially convenient or historical.
⑤	above $20	The best restaurants in Puerto Rico. Your meal might cost more than your room, but there's a reason—it's something fabulous or famous, or both, and you'll probably need to wear something other than sandals and a T-shirt.

DISCOVER PUERTO RICO

From the rumble of reggaeton to the beat of *bomba*, life on Puerto Rico is a pulsing blur of sound and movement. Hordes of cars weave across the island, commerce bustles at the pace of a developed metropolis, and seemingly incessant *fiestas* ensure that nobody ever lacks a reason to celebrate. Sights, too, fill the island: Puerto Rico is remarkable for the sheer amount of stuff squeezed onto a plot of land the size of Connecticut. In addition to its four million people, Puerto Rico is home to some of the world's most beautiful beaches, the only tropical rainforest in the US, acres of coral reef, the world's third-largest underground cave system, seven protected nature reserves, and species of wildlife not found anywhere else on the planet.

It is no wonder, then, that *puertorriqueños* are so widely known for their deep national pride, a sentiment most immediately evident in the ubiquitous Puerto Rican flags and "Borinquén Querida" bumper stickers. Puerto Rico stands at the intersection of the cultural and economic worlds of the United States and Latin America: the language is Spanish and the culture decidedly Latin, but Americanization and commercial development have penetrated most of its cities. Instead of choosing between these two worlds, Puerto Ricans have unified their diverse heritage—Taíno, African, and Spanish—to create a vibrant identity that is uniquely Puerto Rican, or more accurately, Boricua. The island's original Taíno name still serves as a password for the lively spirit that is Puerto Rico.

FACTS AND FIGURES

OFFICIAL NAME: Estado Libre Asociado de Puerto Rico (Free Associated State of Puerto Rico).

CAPITAL: San Juan.

POPULATION DENSITY: 1127 people per sq. mi.

PER CAPITA GDP: $19,300.

PERCENTAGE OF US RUM PRODUCED IN PUERTO RICO: 70.

POPULATION OF PUERTO RICANS IN THE US: 3.9 million.

NUMBER OF CITIES THAT CLAIM COLUMBUS LANDED THERE: 5 (Combate, Guayanilla, Mayagüez, Boquerón, Añasco).

WHEN TO GO

Most travelers escape to Puerto Rico between December and April when the weather up north is miserable and the island's climate is at its prime. As a result, hotels in San Juan, Culebra, and Vieques raise their rates during this season. If you want to travel during this time, the best solution is to go to parts of the island that are less frequented by foreigners, such as the southern and western coasts, or the central mountains. The high season on these parts of the island is from May to November. Puerto Ricans travel during school vacations—primarily Christmas (late Dec.), *Semana Santa* (the week before Easter), and summer (June-Aug.)—filling up accommodations and beaches nearly everywhere outside of San Juan. It may be best not to make travel plans during these times, but if you do, make reservations in advance. During the summer, Puerto Rico is at its hottest and most humid. **Hurricane season** officially lasts from June to November, but most storms are in August and September. Traveling during this time is risky: a hurricane will almost certainly ruin any vacation, but if there is no hurricane (most of the time) travelers will enjoy empty beaches and major hotel discounts. **Surf season** in Puerto Rico runs from November to mid-April.

WHAT TO DO

Puerto Rico easily has enough cultural and natural attractions to keep anyone busy for weeks. Whether you're looking for a taste of Latin culture and Caribbean history, an outdoor adventure, or just a relaxing vacation on the beach, Puerto Rico will not disappoint.

IN THE SEA

Puerto Rico is a great place to swim with sharks, turtles, manatees, barracudas, dolphins, whales, lobsters, and hundreds of brightly colored fish. Everyone agrees that Puerto Rico's best diving is at **Isla Mona** (p. 246), which boasts hundreds of dive sites and visibility up to 180 ft. However, the 4hr. journey takes a lot of planning and even more money. For a similar but more accessible option, try Rincón, where boats leave almost daily for **Isla Desecheo** (p. 287), an offshore island surrounded by thriving reefs. A completely different dive experience awaits off the southwestern coast of Puerto Rico. Six miles offshore, a dramatic sea wall starts at 60 ft. and then seems to disappear completely as a sheer cliff descends to over 150 ft. The best place to access "The Wall" is the spirited *pueblo* of **La Parguera** (p. 230). One of Puerto Rico's most bizarre dive spots can be found just off the coast of **Aguadilla** (p. 271), where hundreds of old tires have been transformed into an artificial reef. Visitors who want a slightly cheaper glimpse of the island's underwater world are in luck—some of the best snorkeling opportunities can be found off the coasts of **Vieques** (p. 170), **La Parguera** (p. 230), and **Isla Caja de Muertos** (p. 214). Culebra (p. 186), Isabela (p. 271), Isla Mona (p. 246), Rincón (p. 279), San Juan (p. 89), and La Cordillera off the northeastern coast (p. 165) also offer snorkeling spots of varying quality.

ON THE SAND

If it's beaches you're after, you've come to the right place. From Culebra to San Juan to Isla Mona, Puerto Rico has some of the most gorgeous beaches in the world. The best of the best is **Playa Flamenco** (p. 194), Culebra's public beach. With an enormous crescent of white sand, aquamarine water, and medium-sized waves, Flamenco is the stuff of Caribbean dreams. Culebra's other beaches are equally, if not more, stunning, but a bit more difficult to reach. The many beaches of **Vieques** (p. 170) come in a close second. Back on the mainland, prized patches of sand can be found in southwest Puerto Rico. **Balneario Boquerón** (p. 242) and **El Combate** (p. 240) could all tempt you to extend your vacation. Luquillo's **Balneario Monserrate** (p. 157) deservedly receives a lot of public acclaim, but it must share the spotlight with fellow north coast all-star beaches **Balneario Seven Seas** (p. 165), **Balneario Cerro Gordo** (p. 142), and **Balneario Puerto Nuevo** (p. 264). In terms of aesthetics alone, the dramatic coastline of northwest Puerto Rico is incomparable, although the rough waves in the area make it difficult to swim. Almost any northern coastline drive will reveal spectacular beaches, but easily accessible areas include **Playa Jobos** (p. 275) in Isabela; **Piñones** (p. 142) near San Juan; and **Las Ruínas** (p. 275) near Aguadilla. And, of course, if you're looking for one of the best metropolitan beaches in the world, the coastline around **San Juan** (p. 89) cannot be beat.

IN DA CLUB

This island knows how to party—on Friday and Saturday nights, San Juan's nightlife competes with the best in the world. Traffic slows to a crawl as thousands of young *sanjuaneros* prowl the streets for the biggest and best party. **Old San Juan** (p. 135), Calle San Sebastián in particular, is without a doubt the hippest scene on the island. If it's big clubs you're after, **Old San Juan** and **Isla Verde** (p. 140) offer anything and everything: salsa, reggae, pop, gay, straight, ritzy, and low-key. But San Juan is not the exclusive home of Puerto Rico's nightlife. **Ponce** (p. 201) has a lively bar scene, and, during the surf season, **Rincón** (p. 279) and **Playa Jobos** (p. 277) host a good party any night of the week. University students liven things up in **Mayagüez** (p. 252) on weeknights and head out to the coastal towns of **La Parguera** (p. 230) and **Boquerón** (p. 242) on weekends. Only in Vieques, Culebra, and La Ruta Panorámica will you have trouble finding hopping nightlife.

BACK THROUGH TIME

Over the course of its history, Puerto Rico has served as a home to the Taíno people, an early Spanish colony, and a melting pot of cultures and traditions; the island's varied past has left it with a legacy of great historical sights. If you can tear yourself away from the beach, take the opportunity to wander down to the dungeon of the 16th-century Spanish fort **Castillo San Cristóbal** (p. 117) in Old San Juan. In the same part of town, **Museo de Las Américas** (p. 126) and **Museo de la Raíz Africana** (p. 126) offer visitors a peek at the Spanish and African heritage that has shaped Puerto Rican art, crafts, music, and religion today. Outside of San Juan, the first stop for history buffs is the city of **Ponce** (p. 201), which has a variety of museums, including the **Museo de la Música Puertorriqueña,** which takes visitors through the history of Puerto Rico's musical beats. Last but not least is the remarkable collection of religious paintings and *santos* in the centuries-old **Porta Coeli Chapel and Museum of Religious Art** (p. 239) in San Germán.

TOP 10 FESTIVALS

In Puerto Rico, there's always something to celebrate:

1. Festival San Juan Bautista, San Juan (p. 134). San Juan's patron saint festival includes music, beachside bonfires, and a traditional dip in the water.

2. Festival de Santiago Apóstol, Loíza (p. 146), features *vejigante* masks (colorful masks with horns) and live *bomba* music.

3. Festival de la Calle San Sebastián, San Juan (p. 133), draws crowds with an artisan craft fair and, after dark, the island's biggest street party.

4. Festival de las Flores, Aibonito (p. 296). Home-grown flowers line the streets during this beautiful harvest festival.

5. Carnaval, Ponce (p. 212). This pre-Lent party offers parades, *vejigantes*, and a good time.

6. Festival de las Máscaras, Hatillo (p. 270). Spanish-influenced masks and costumes animate the sleepy town of Hatillo.

7. Bacardí Feria de Artesanía, Cataño (p. 134). This giant artisan festival offers more than just world-famous rum.

8. Casals Festival, San Juan (p. 134). A celebration of classical music featuring musicians from Puerto Rico and abroad.

9. Fiesta del Café, Maricao (p. 307). Coffee-lovers will be the first in line for free samples at this bean-filled party.

10. Festival de Platos Típicos, Luquillo (p. 157). For all the fried plantains you can eat, try this festival of typical dishes.

IN THE WILD

Find San Juan a bit tame? Is Vieques too "laid-back" for your vacation? Never fear; Puerto Rico has some first-rate adventures that offer an all-natural adrenaline rush. Start your engines and head to Arecibo's **Camuy Caves** (p. 268), a system of undergrounds caves and rivers. Several tour operators lead expeditions that kick the action up a notch with spelunking, rappelling, rafting, and hiking. For an entirely different wild side of Puerto Rico, arrange a trip out to the deserted island of **Isla Mona** (p. 246), where enormous iguanas and hordes of hermit crabs greet visitors. Puerto Rico's rugged **Ruta Panorámica** (p. 290) is the gateway to many of the island's isolated nature reserves, where you can have the call of the *coquí* and the mountain views all to yourself. The rough road may require some crafty driving skills, but the panoramic views, ample hiking, and numerous lakes make the trip worthwhile. For a shorter stint in Puerto Rico's wilds, try the beautiful **El Yunque** forest (p. 150), where you can summit a mountain in an afternoon

⚅LET'S GO PICKS

BEST PLACE TO SALSA THE NIGHT AWAY: San Juan's many glitzy dance clubs, especially **Rumba** (p. 135) and **Nuyorican Café** (p. 135).

BEST PLACE TO BE AWE-INSPIRED BY NATURE: The peak of **El Yunque Mountain** (p. 153), where on a clear day the views extend to the Caribbean Ocean; **Isla Mona** (p. 246) where animals still rule the roost; and **Cabo Rojo Lighthouse** (p. 241), where earth meets land in the most dramatic way possible.

BEST WAY TO GLOW IN THE DARK: Swimming in the bioluminescent bays of **Vieques** (p. 183), **Fajardo** (p. 167), and **La Parguera** (p. 233).

BEST PLACE TO HANG TEN: The popular surf breaks off the coast of **Jobos** (p. 275) and **Rincón** (p. 286).

BEST SUNSETS: The lighthouse at **Rincón** (p. 284), the coastline of **Boquerón** (p. 242), or, if you're in the mood for adventure, Playa Sardinera on **Isla Mona** (p. 246).

BEST PLACE TO LOSE $10 BUCKS AND GAIN LOCAL CREDIBILITY: Betting on a cockfight with the *sanjuaneros* at Isla Verde's **Club Gallístico** (p. 132).

BEST PLACE TO GET SLOSHED: San Juan's **Festival de la Calle San Sebastián** (p. 133), where the drinking never seems to stop.

BEST PLACE TO SEE MACHO PUERTO RICAN MEN WEAR DRESSES: Ponce's **Carnaval** (p. 212), where machismo takes a backseat to tradition.

BEST LOCAL FLAVOR: The fresh fruit and even fresher *batidas* in Isla Verde's **Plaza del Mercado** (p. 122).

BEST PLACE TO HAVE A FENDER-BENDER: Highway 3, the highly congested road that connects San Juan to Fajardo. Or perhaps Hwy. 2, or maybe Hwy. 5...or just about anywhere.

BEST PLACE TO RECUPERATE FROM STRENUOUS DRIVING: The traffic-free white sand beaches of **Culebra** (p. 186) or its surrounding **cays** (p. 165).

SUGGESTED ITINERARIES

BEST OF PUERTO RICO (4 WEEKS)

DISCOVER

Bosque Estatal de Guajataca (1 day)
Karstic scenery, caves, a fishing lake, and forest trails await (p. 277).

San Juan (5 days)
Don't miss the museums, nightlife, art, and markets of this diverse metropolis (p. 89).

Bosque Estatal de Cambalache (1 day)
Come here for hiking and biking trails, as well as the elusive caimans (p. 261).

El Yunque (1 day)
Allow a morning to brave the traffic en route to El Yunque before an afternoon of hiking and splashing under waterfalls (p. 150).

Rincón (3 days)
Surf's up! Join the beach bums and test out the waves at the former sites of the World Surfing Championships (p. 279).

Arecibo (2 days)
Stop on your way out west to see the amazing Camuy Caves and the world's largest radio telescope at the Arecibo Observatory (p. 264).

Culebra (2 days)
Peer through some of Puerto Rico's clearest waters for snorkeling and diving (p. 186).

START

END

San Germán (1 day)
Take a break from the beach to see historic houses and museums (p. 236).

Toro Negro (1 day)
Gaze across the island from the tallest peak in Puerto Rico's central mountains, or simply walk through the woods (p. 299).

Bosque de Guánica (2 days)
Hike isolated acres of dry forest in the dramatic southern landscape (p. 224).

Utuado (1 day)
Visit the Parque Indígena Caguana and travel back in time to an age when Taínos ruled the island (p. 304).

Reserva Forestal de Carite (2 days)
Hike in the forest or volunteer to help preserve it at Las Casa de la Selva in Carite (p. 291).

Ponce (3 days)
Stroll through the plaza amid 19th-century houses, or visit museums, a preserved sugar cane and coffee plantation, and a deserted island in the shape of a coffin (p. 201).

Vieques (3 days)
The bioluminescent bay, deserted beaches, and unique accommodations of this island merit a little extra time (p. 170).

WHIRLWIND TOUR (1 WEEK)

Arecibo (1 day)
Rent a car and head out to the Camuy Caves; the adventurous can book a tour for tubing or rapelling. Don't miss the famous Arecibo Observatory (p. 264).

Old San Juan (2 days)
Explore the colonial forts, many museums, upscale restaurants, and hopping nightlife in Puerto Rico's capital city (p. 124).

Culebra (2 days)
Allow a few hours for the ferry and get ready to enjoy superb beaches, snorkeling, and swimming on this laid-back island, which boasts only six stop signs (p. 186).

El Yunque (½ day)
Head east for an afternoon of hiking in a tropical rainforest (p. 150).

Utuado (½ day)
Start the day early at Utuado's Parque Indígena Caguana to see the drawings that the island's early residents left behind (p. 304).

Luquillo (½ day)
Enjoy eats from the food stands on the beautiful public beach of Luquillo (p. 157).

Fajardo (½ day)
Catch a nighttime tour of a bioluminescent bay in Fajardo (p. 160).

THE GREAT OUTDOORS (2 WEEKS)

Bosque Estatal de Guajataca (1 day)
Explore the caves and well-maintained trails of the forest, or try your hand at fishing in the lake (p. 277).

Bosque Estatal de Cambalache (1 day)
Enjoy the hiking and mountain biking trails. If you're lucky, you may catch a glimpse of the caimans (p. 261).

El Yunque (2 days)
Warm up your walking legs in the tropical rainforest by hiking to the top of El Yunque mountain, camping with the *coquís*, or trying the National Recreation Trail (p. 150).

Isla Mona (3 days)
This deserted island reserve, with its giant iguanas and tiny hermit crabs, is the highlight of the tour. (p. 246).

Toro Negro (2 days)
Check out the trails and look down from the highest point in Puerto Rico (p. 299).

Bosque Estatal de Carite (2 days)
Save Puerto Rico's forest with the volunteers at Las Casas de la Selva in Carite (p. 291).

Bosque de Guánica (2 days)
Wander in the cactus forests of the south or stick to the shore for beaches and diving (p. 224).

Cañón San Cristóbal (1 day)
Descend into this dramatic canyon with a guide (p. 294).

PUERTO RICO BY SEA (8 DAYS)

Isla Desecheo (1 day)
Chase after angelfish, sea turtles, and sting rays in waters with 100 ft. visibility, where diving and snorkeling are both good options (p. 287).

Aguadilla (1 day)
Explore Playa Crash Boat's walk-in dive and snorkeling area, where old dock pilings covered with colorful sponges host a wide variety of marine life (p. 271).

Culebra (2 days)
End your trip at Culebra's acclaimed beaches, with mild currents and excellent underwater visibility, or travel to Isla Culebrita y Faro for a more remote dive site (p. 186).

Rincón (2 days)
Get above water for for a couple of days in this renowned surf haven, and try catching some waves topside (p. 279).

La Parguera (2 days)
Start out your tour of Puerto Rico's watery domains with a dive to the La Parguera Wall, a 150 ft. cliff filled with trenches, valleys, and thousands of tropical fish (p. 230).

Fajardo (1 day)
Cross the island and venture off this east coast hub to the remote cays of Icacos, Diablo, Palominos, and Palomonitos for crystal-clear snorkeling and quiet beaches (p. 160).

SAN JUAN (5 DAYS)

Old San Juan (2 days)
Walkable Old San Juan has a wide variety of museums and historical sights, with restaurants conveniently placed for hungry sightseers (p. 124).

Isla Verde (1 day)
Catch rays at the beaches of Isla Verde. Ocean Park and Condado also offer accessible alternatives (p. 106).

Bosque Estatal de Piñones (1 day)
Take the B40 bus or hire a *público* to Piñones, where you can rent a bike to traverse the forest. Check out the budget-friendly food stands and secluded beaches before heading home (p. 142).

Cataño (½ day)
Catch the ferry over to the Bacardi Rum factory for a tour and free samples (p. 141).

Río Piedras (½ day)
Hit Plaza del Mercado and Paseo de Diego for some unbeatable bargains on fresh food and outlet clothing (p. 138).

You'd rather be traveling.

LET'S GO
BUDGET TRAVEL GUIDES
www.letsgo.com

ESSENTIALS

PLANNING YOUR TRIP

ENTRANCE REQUIREMENTS

Passport (p. 10). Required for citizens of every country except the US (US citizens should bring government-issued identification to prove citizenship).

Visa (p. 12). Required for citizens of every country except the US, Canada, Bermuda, or one of the 27 countries participating in the US Visa Waiver Program.

Inoculations (p. 21). Recommended up-to-date on DTaP (diphtheria, tetanus, and pertussis), *Haemophilus influenzae* B, Hepatitis B, MMR (measles, mumps, and rubella), and polio booster.

Work Permit (p. 11). Required for all foreigners planning to work in Puerto Rico.

EMBASSIES AND CONSULATES

US CONSULAR SERVICES ABROAD

For immigration purposes, Puerto Rico is treated as part of the US. Contact the nearest US embassy or consulate for information regarding visas to Puerto Rico. The **US State Department** provides contact info for **US embassies and consulates abroad** at http://usembassy.state.gov.

Australia: Moonah Pl., Yarralumla (Canberra), ACT 2600 (☎+61 02 6214 5600; fax 6214 5970; http://canberra.usembassy.gov). **Consulates:** 553 St. Kilda Rd., Melbourne, VIC 3004 (☎+61 03 9526 5900; fax 9510 4646; http://melbourne.usconsulate.gov); 16 St. George's Terr., 4th fl., Perth, WA 6000 (☎+61 08 9202 1224; fax 9231 9444; http://perth.usconsulate.gov); MLC Centre, 19-29 Martin Pl., 59th fl., Sydney, NSW 2000 (☎+61 02 9373 9200; fax 9373 9184; http://sydney.usconsulate.gov).

Canada: 490 Promenade Sussex Dr., Ottawa, ON K1N 1G8 (☎+61 613-688-5335; fax 688-3091; http://canada.usembassy.gov). **Consulates:** 615 Macleod Trail SE, Rm. 1000, Calgary, AB T2G 4T8 (☎+1 403-266-8962; fax 264-6630); Purdy's Wharf Tower II, Ste. 904, 1969 Upper Water St., Halifax, NS B3J 3R7 (☎+1 902-429-2480; fax 423-6861); 1155 Saint Alexandre St., Montreal, QC H3B 1Z1 (☎+1 514-398-9695; fax 398-9748); 2 Place Terrasse Dufferin, Québec City, QC G1R 4T9 (☎+1 418-692-2095; fax 692-4640); 360 University Ave., Toronto, ON M5G 1S4 (☎+1 416-595-1700; fax 595-6501); 1095 W. Pender St., Vancouver, BC V6E 2M6 (☎+1 604-685-4311; fax 685-7175); 201 Portage Ave., Ste. 860, Winnipeg, MB R3B 3K6 (☎+1 204-940-1800; fax 940-1809).

Ireland: 42 Elgin Rd., Ballsbridge, Dublin 4 (☎+1 353 1 668 8777; fax 353 1 668 9946; http://dublin.usembassy.gov).

New Zealand: 29 Fitzherbert Terr., Thorndon, Wellington (☎+64 4 462 6000; fax 499 0490; http://wellington.usembassy.gov). **Consulates:** Citibank Building, 23 Customs St., 3rd fl., Auckland (☎+64 9 303 2724, ext. 2842; fax 366 0870).

UK: 24 Grosvenor Sq., London W1A 1AE (☎+44 20 7499 9000; fax 7894 0020; http://london.usembassy.gov). **Consulates:** Danesfort House, 223 Stranmills Rd., Belfast, N. Ireland BT9 5GR (☎+44 28 9038 6100; fax 9068 1301); 3 Regent Terr., Edinburgh, Scotland EH7 5BW (☎+44 131 556 8315; fax 557 6023).

CONSULAR SERVICES IN PUERTO RICO

Of the above countries, only Canada has consulates in Puerto Rico. Other countries have embassies in Washington, D.C., which serve travelers in Puerto Rico.

Australia: 1601 Massachusetts Ave., Washington, D.C. 20036 USA (☎202-797-3000; fax 797-3168; www.austemb.org).

Canada: 501 Pennsylvania Ave., NW, Washington, D.C. 20001, USA (☎202-682-1740; fax 682 7619; www.canadianembassy.org). **Consulates:** Hato Rey Center, Av. Ponce de León 268, Ste. 802, San Juan, 00918 PR (☎759-6629).

Ireland: 2234 Massachusetts Ave., NW, Washington, D.C. 20008, USA (☎202-462-3939; fax 232-5993; www.irelandemb.org).

New Zealand: 37 Observatory Circle, NW, Washington, D.C. 20008, USA (☎202-328-4800; fax 667-5227; www.nzemb.org).

UK: 3100 Massachusetts Ave., Washington, D.C., 20008 USA (☎202-588-7800; fax 588-7850; www.britain-info.org)

TOURIST OFFICES

The **Puerto Rican Tourism Company** (**PRTC;** ☎800-866-7827; www.gotopuertorico.com), the island's official tourist center, has offices in Aguadilla (p. 271), Boquerón (p. 242), Ponce (p. 201), and San Juan (p. 89). In addition, there are regional offices in countries around the world. Any office will send you a complimentary issue of *¡Qué Pasa!* magazine (p. 49). Most municipal Alcaldías (Mayor's Offices), located on or near the plazas of municipal centers, can provide packets of historical information about the municipality.

Canada: 41-43 Colbourne St., Ste. 301, Toronto, ON M5E 1E3 (☎+1 416-368-2680, in Canada 800-667-0394).

UK: 67a High St., 2nd fl., Walton-on-Thames, Surrey, KT 12 1DJ (☎+44 1932 253 302; puertoricouk@aol.com).

US: 3575 W. Cahuenga Blvd., Ste. 405, Los Angeles, CA 90068 (☎323-874-5991; 800-874-1230, ext. 10); 901 Ponce de León Blvd., Ste. 101, Coral Gables, FL 33134 (☎305-445-9112 or 800-815-7391); 666 Fifth Ave., 15th fl., New York, NY 10103 (☎212-586-6262 or 800-223-6530).

DOCUMENTS AND FORMALITIES

PASSPORTS

REQUIREMENTS

Citizens of all countries except the US need valid passports to enter Puerto Rico and to re-enter their home countries. Puerto Rico does not allow entrance if the holder's passport expires in under six months; returning home with an expired passport is illegal and may result in a fine. US citizens need to carry valid government ID, such as a driver's license, to prove their citizenship.

NEW PASSPORTS

Citizens of Australia, Canada, Ireland, New Zealand, the UK, and the US can apply for a passport at any passport office or at selected post offices and courts of law. Citizens of these countries may also download passport applications from the official website of their country's government or passport office. Any new passport or renewal applications must be filed well in advance of the departure date, though most passport offices offer rush services for a very steep fee. Note, however, that "rushed" passports still take up to two weeks to arrive.

PASSPORT MAINTENANCE

Photocopy the page of your passport with your photo, as well as your visas, traveler's check serial numbers, and any other important documents. Carry one set of copies in a safe place, apart from the originals, and leave another set at home. Consulates also recommend that you carry an expired passport or an official copy of your birth certificate in a part of your baggage separate from other documents.

If you lose your passport, immediately notify the local police and the nearest embassy or consulate of your home government. To expedite its replacement, you must show ID and proof of citizenship; it also helps to know all information previously recorded in the passport. In some cases, a replacement may take weeks to process, and it may be valid only for a limited time. Any visas stamped in your old passport will be irretrievably lost. In an emergency, ask for immediate temporary traveling papers that will permit you to re-enter your home country.

VISAS, INVITATIONS, AND WORK PERMITS

VISAS

US citizens do not need a passport or visa to enter Puerto Rico, just proof of citizenship. As of August 2007, citizens of Canada, Bermuda, and countries participating in the US Visa Waiver Program (see www.travel.state.gov for a list of these countries) can enter the Puerto Rico without a visa, provided they present a valid passport, are traveling only for business or pleasure, and are staying for less than 90 days. In addition, travelers under the Visa Waiver Program must provide proof of intent to leave (such as a return plane ticket) and complete an I-94 form (provided to travelers at their port of entry). If you lose your I-94 form, you must replace it through **US Citizenship and Immigration Services (USCIS;** ☎ 800-375-5283; www.uscis.gov).

Travelers not from the US, Canada, Bermuda, or Visa Waiver Program countries must obtain a visa before traveling to Puerto Rico. The 90-day nonimmigrant visa allows visitors temporary entrance into the US and Puerto Rico, and can be obtained through an online application (http://evisaforms.state.gov/). With the exception of US citizens, all travelers planning to spend longer than 90 days in Puerto Rico must receive a visa from a US embassy or consulate in their home country before traveling to the island (to locate a US embassy or consulate, visit http://usembassy.state.gov). Visas cost around $100 and usually allow business or pleasure travelers to spend six months to a year in Puerto Rico. Visa extensions can sometimes be obtained by filing an I-539 form with the USCIS. Call the forms request line at ☎ 800-870-3676 for more details.

Double-check entrance requirements at the nearest embassy or consulate of the United States (see **US Consular Services Abroad,** p. 9) for up-to-date info before departure. US citizens can also consult http://travel.state.gov.

WORK PERMITS

Admission as a visitor does not include the right to work, which is authorized only by a work permit. US citizens can work in Puerto Rico without any type of work permit or visa. If you are not a US citizen, you need a work permit or "green card" to work in Puerto Rico. Normally you must have a job offer before you can obtain the permit. First, your potential employer in Puerto Rico must file an I-129 Petition for Nonimmigrant Worker with the USCIS and receive a notice of approval. In order to obtain approval, your employer will usually have to demonstrate that you have skills that locals lack. Next, you must apply for a temporary worker visa by filing a DS-156 and submitting the approval form received by your employer to the US embassy or consulate in your home country. You must also provide a passport, photograph, and I-797 form. Temporary work visas cost around $100. Visit http://travel.state.gov/visa/temp/types/types_1271.html for more details. Obtaining a work visa may seem complex, but it's critical that you go through the proper channels—the alternative is potential deportation. Travelers who wish to work on a cruise ship must obtain a US C1-D visa from the nearest US consulate.

IDENTIFICATION

When you travel, always carry at least two forms of identification on your person, including a photo ID; a passport and a driver's license or birth certificate is usually an adequate combination. Never carry all of your IDs together; split them up in case of theft or loss, and keep photocopies of all of them in your luggage and at home.

STUDENT, TEACHER, AND YOUTH IDENTIFICATION

The **International Student Identity Card (ISIC),** the most widely accepted form of student ID, provides discounts on some sights, accommodations, food, and transportation; access to a 24hr. emergency helpline; and insurance benefits for US cardholders. Applicants must be full-time secondary or post-secondary school students at least 12 years of age. Because of the proliferation of fake ISICs, some services (particularly airlines) require additional proof of student identity.

The **International Teacher Identity Card (ITIC)** offers teachers the same insurance coverage as the ISIC and similar but limited discounts. To qualify for the card, teachers must be currently employed and have worked a minimum of 18hr. per week for at least one school year. For travelers who are under 26 years old but are not students, the **International Youth Travel Card (IYTC)** also offers many of the same benefits as the ISIC. Each of these identity cards costs $22. ISICs, ITICS, and IYTCs are valid for one year from the date of issue. To learn more about ISICs, ITICs, and IYTCs, try www.myisic.com. Many student travel agencies (p. 24) issue the cards; for a list of issuing agencies or more information, see the **International Student Travel Confederation (ISTC)** website (www.istc.org).

The **International Student Exchange Card (ISE Card)** is a similar identification card available to students, faculty, and youths aged 12 to 26. The card provides discounts, medical benefits, access to a 24hr. emergency helpline, and the ability to purchase student airfares. An ISE Card costs $25; call ☎800-255-8000 (in North America) or ☎480-951-1177 (from all other continents) for more info, or visit www.isecard.com.

CUSTOMS

Upon entering Puerto Rico you must declare certain items from abroad and pay a duty on those articles if their value exceeds $10,000. Upon returning home, you must declare all articles acquired abroad and pay a duty on the value of articles in excess of your home country's allowance. In order to expedite your return, make a list of any valuables brought from home and register them with customs before traveling abroad, and be sure to keep receipts for all goods acquired abroad. If you are flying back through the US, your baggage will be inspected by the US Department of Agriculture. You are allowed to take avocado, papaya, coconut, and plantain through the US, but not mango, soursop, passion fruit, or potted plants.

MONEY

CURRENCY AND EXCHANGE

The currency chart below is based on August 2007 exchange rates between local currency and Australian dollars (AUS$), Canadian dollars (CDN$), European Union euro (EUR€), New Zealand dollars (NZ$), British pounds (UK£), and US dollars (US$). Check the currency converter on websites like www.xe.com or www.bloomberg.com, or a large newspaper for the latest exchange rates.

CURRENCY		
AUS$1 = US$0.85	US$1 = AUS$1.67
CDN$1 = US$0.95	US$1 = CDN$1.05
EUR€1 = US$1.37	US$1 = EUR€0.72
NZ$1 = US$0.76	US$1 = NZ$1.31
UK£1 = US$2.02	US$1 = UK£0.49

As a general rule, it's cheaper to convert money in Puerto Rico than at home. While currency exchange will probably be available in your arrival airport, it's wise to bring enough foreign currency for the first 24 to 72 hours of your trip.

When changing money abroad, try to go to banks that have at most a 5% margin between their buy and sell prices. In Puerto Rico, the ubiquitous **Banco Popular** usually offers competitive rates. Since you lose money with every transaction, **convert large sums** (unless the currency is depreciating rapidly), but **no more than you'll need.** However, there is little need to convert foreign currency in Puerto Rico as traveler's checks and credit cards are widely accepted and ATMs are everywhere.

If you use traveler's checks or bills, carry some in small denominations (the equivalent of US$50 or less) for times when you are forced to exchange money at disadvantageous rates, but bring a range of denominations since charges may be levied per check cashed. Store your money in a variety of forms; ideally, at any given time you will be carrying some cash, some traveler's checks, and an ATM and/or credit card.

TRAVELER'S CHECKS

Traveler's checks are one of the safest and least troublesome means of carrying funds. American Express and Visa are the most recognized brands. Many banks and agencies sell them for a small commission. Check issuers provide refunds if the checks are lost or stolen, and many provide additional services, such as toll-free refund hotlines abroad, emergency message services, and assistance with lost and stolen credit cards or passports. Traveler's checks are readily accepted in most tourist areas of Puerto Rico, such as San Juan and other big cities. They are less useful in the rural areas and usually not accepted at small establishments. Ask about toll-free refund hotlines and the location of refund centers when purchasing checks, and always carry emergency cash.

American Express: Checks available with commission at select banks, at all AmEx offices, and online (www.americanexpress.com; US residents only). American Express cardholders can also purchase checks by phone (☎800-528-4800). Checks available in Australian, British, Canadian, European, Japanese, and US currencies, among others. American Express also offers the Travelers Cheque Card, a prepaid reloadable card. Cheques for Two can be signed by either of 2 people traveling together. For purchase locations or more information, contact AmEx's service centers: in Australia ☎29 271 8666, in New Zealand 93 674 567, in the UK 1 273 696 933, in the US and Canada 800-221-7282; elsewhere, call the US collect at 1 336 393 1111.

Travelex: Visa TravelMoney prepaid cash card and Visa traveler's checks available. For information about Thomas Cook MasterCard in Canada and the US call ☎800-223-7373, in the UK 0800 622 101; elsewhere call the UK collect at +44 1733 318 950. For information about Interpayment Visa in the US and Canada call ☎800-732-1322, in the UK 0800 515 884; elsewhere call the UK collect at +44 1733 318 949. For more information, visit www.travelex.com.

Visa: Checks available (generally with commission) at banks worldwide. For the location of the nearest office, call the Visa Travelers Cheque Global Refund and Assistance Center: in the UK ☎0800 895 078, in the US 800-227-6811; elsewhere, call the UK collect at +44 2079 378 091. Checks available in British, Canadian, European, Japanese, and US currencies, among others. Visa also offers TravelMoney, a prepaid debit card that can be reloaded online or by phone. For more information on Visa travel services, see http://usa.visa.com/personal/using_visa/travel_with_visa.html.

CREDIT, DEBIT, AND ATM CARDS

Credit cards are widely accepted throughout Puerto Rico, although small establishments only accept cash. Major credit cards—**MasterCard** (including its European counterpart **EuroCard**) and **Visa** (including its European counterpart **Carte Bleue**)—are the most prevalent. **American Express** is slightly less common, followed by **Discover** and **Diner's Club.**

Where they are accepted, credit cards often offer superior exchange rates—up to 5% better than the retail rate used by banks and other currency exchange establishments. Credit cards may also offer services such as insurance or emergency help, and are sometimes required to reserve hotel rooms or rental cars.

The use of ATM cards is widespread in Puerto Rico. Depending on the system that your home bank uses, you can most likely access your personal bank account from abroad. ATMs get the same wholesale exchange rate as credit cards, but there is often a limit on the amount of money you can withdraw per day (usually around US$500). There is typically also a surcharge of US$1-5 per withdrawal.

Debit cards are as convenient as credit cards but withdraw money directly from the holder's checking account. A debit card can be used wherever its associated credit card company (usually MasterCard or Visa) is accepted. Debit cards often also function as ATM cards and can be used to withdraw cash from associated banks and ATMs throughout Puerto Rico.

The two major international money networks are **MasterCard/Maestro/Cirrus** (for ATM locations ☎800-424-7787 or www.mastercard.com) and **Visa/PLUS** (for ATM locations ☎800-847-2911 or www.visa.com). Most ATMs charge a transaction fee that is paid to the bank that owns the ATM.

GETTING MONEY FROM HOME

If you run out of money while traveling, the easiest and cheapest solution is to have someone back home make a deposit to your bank account. Failing that, consider one of the following options.

WIRING MONEY

It is possible to arrange a **bank money transfer,** which means asking a bank back home to wire money to a bank in Puerto Rico. This is the cheapest way to transfer cash, but it's also the slowest, usually taking several days or more. Note that some banks may only release your funds in local currency, potentially sticking you with a poor exchange rate; inquire about this in advance. Money transfer services like **Western Union** are faster and more convenient than bank transfers—but also much pricier. Western Union can be found in almost every **Pueblo** supermarket in Puerto Rico. To find locations worldwide, visit www.westernunion.com, or call in Australia ☎ 1800 173 833, in Canada and the US 800-325-6000, and in the UK 0800 833 833. To wire money using a credit card (Discover, MasterCard, Visa), call in Canada, the US, and Puerto Rico ☎ 800-CALL-CASH, in the UK 0800 833 833.

COSTS

The cost of your trip will vary considerably depending on where you go, how you travel, and where you stay. The most significant expenses will likely be your round-trip **airfare** to Puerto Rico (see **Getting to Puerto Rico: By Plane,** p. 24), **accommodations,** and **car rental.** Before you go, spend some time calculating a reasonable daily **budget.**

STAYING ON A BUDGET

Your budget in Puerto Rico will vary depending on whether you stay in a large city, like San Juan, or in rural areas where it is possible to camp. To give you a general idea, a bare-bones day in San Juan (sleeping in cheaper guesthouses, buying food at supermarkets) would cost around $55-65; a slightly more comfortable day (sleeping in guesthouses and the occasional budget hotel, eating one meal per day at a restaurant, going out at night) would cost $90-100; for a luxurious day, the sky's the limit.

In rural areas, a modest day (camping and buying food at supermarkets) would cost about $25-35; a more comfortable day (staying at guesthouses or vacation centers, eating one meal per day at a restaurant, and catching some nightlife) would cost $100-110; and for a luxurious day, you can spend just as much as you would in any major city. Don't forget to factor emergency reserve funds (at least $200) into your budget.

TIPS FOR SAVING MONEY

Some simple ways to save include splitting accommodation and food costs with trustworthy fellow travelers, buying food in supermarkets rather than eating out, and doing your **laundry** in the sink (unless you're explicitly prohibited from doing so). Also, try staying in *paradores* that include meals, laundry, and Internet. Museums often have certain days per week or month when admission is free; information on such discounts is included in listings throughout the book so you can plan accordingly. San Juan also has frequent **festivals** with free live music and entertainment (see p. 133).

TOP 10 WAYS TO SAVE IN PUERTO RICO

Puerto Rico is one of the cheapest Caribbean vacation destinations. Here are some ways to sweeten the deal.

1. Buy food at grocery stores and open-air markets instead of eating at a restaurant. Many guesthouses and *paradores* have kitchenettes for cooking.

2. Camp. You can't beat $10-per-night accommodations in the heart of the Puerto Rican forest.

3. Be on the lookout for days when you can get into sights and museums free. In San Juan, this is pretty much every day.

4. Drink tap water. It's safe and the savings add up fast.

5. Buy beer and liquor at markets instead of bars.

6. Take *públicos* or walk as much as possible.

7. Choose accommodations in less-touristed urban centers. Use them as a base to explore the surrounding area. Examples include Hatillo in the west and Fajardo in the east, just a short drive from popular attractions.

8. Find free Internet access in libraries and universities, or stay at hotels where Wi-Fi is included.

9. Bring your own snorkel and dive equipment. It may take up precious luggage space, but rental prices are steep.

10. Build the outdoors into your itinerary. Entrance to most Puerto Rican reserves and public beaches is free.

Wise travelers **pay close attention to high season.** The high season in San Juan and the eastern islands is from November to May. Hotels in these areas typically raise their rates during this time. West coast hotels, on the other hand, charge more from June to October, the high season on that part of the island. The weather is pleasant year-round throughout Puerto Rico, though, so choose your destination accordingly. Travelers willing to brave the risk of hurricane season will find that everything gets cheaper in September and October. Of course, **camping** is by far the most budget-friendly option. Culebra and Vieques have exceptionally nice campgrounds.

Don't forget about walking—you can learn a lot about a city by seeing it on foot. Old San Juan is especially pedestrian-friendly. Budget travelers with flexible schedules and travel plans may consider traveling by **públicos**—informal public vans that carry passengers between town centers for about $1-5—instead of renting a car. *Público* drivers wait for passengers in public squares starting around 6am, but don't leave until their vans are full, making departure times somewhat irregular. Visitors who plan to travel by *público* should note that these vans do not normally take passengers outside of town centers to sights, beaches, or nature reserves.

With bottles of water priced around $1, staying hydrated can add up quickly. Cut costs by filling **water bottles** in hotel sinks or potable water cisterns and requesting **agua de pluma** (tap water) in restaurants. Drinking at bars and clubs can also become expensive. It's cheaper to buy alcohol at a supermarket and make your own *cuba libres* before going out. That said, don't go overboard. You shouldn't pinch pennies at the expense of your health or a great travel experience.

TIPPING AND BARGAINING

In Puerto Rico, it is customary to tip waitstaff and cab drivers 15-20% (at your discretion). Tips are usually not included in restaurant bills. It is unnecessary to tip at most *cafeterías, panaderías,* and other small eateries where you pick up food at the counter. Porters expect at least $1 per bag. Though not obligatory, it is also nice to give *público* drivers a small tip; about 10% should suffice. **Bargaining** is generally frowned upon and fruitless in Puerto Rico, but it does not hurt to ask hotel or guest house owners if they can offer a discount—many will lower rates if they are not full.

TAXES

Get ready to shop; Puerto Rico has **no sales tax, restaurant tax,** or **value added tax.** There is a 9% **accommodations tax,** but unofficial guesthouses frequently do not charge it. *Let's Go* indicates if tax is included in most accommodations listings.

PACKING

Pack lightly: Lay out only what you absolutely need, then take half the clothes and twice the money. The Travelite FAQ (www.travelite.org) is a good resource for tips on traveling light. The online **Universal Packing List** (http://upl.codeq.info) will generate a customized list of suggested items based on your trip length, the expected climate, your planned activities, and other factors. If you plan to do a lot of hiking, also consult **The Great Outdoors,** .

Luggage: If you plan to cover most of your itinerary by foot, a sturdy **frame backpack** is unbeatable. (For the basics on buying a pack, see p. 43.) Toting a **suitcase** or **trunk** is fine if you plan to live in 1 or 2 cities and explore from there, but not a great idea if you plan to move around frequently. In addition to your main piece of luggage, a **daypack** (a small backpack or courier bag) is useful.

Clothing: No matter when you're traveling, it's a good idea to bring a rain jacket (Gore-Tex® is both waterproof and breathable), sturdy shoes or hiking boots, and thick socks. Flip-flops or waterproof sandals are must-haves for grubby guesthouse showers, and extra socks are always a good idea. If you plan to visit religious or cultural sites, remember that you will need modest and respectful dress. In Puerto Rico's mild climate, jeans paired with a tank top (women) or light button-down shirt (men) are everyday dress. No matter how steamy the weather gets, Puerto Rican locals will not wear shorts—wearing them will mark you as a tourist. A long-sleeved T-shirt or a light jacket may come in handy for cooler nights in the mountains, though during the summer it's almost never needed. Puerto Ricans dress up to go out—women wear tight pants (usually jeans) with shirts that redefine scandalous, and men wear slacks and button-down shirts. You may want to bring a nicer outfit for going out, along with a nice pair of shoes.

Converters and Adapters: In Puerto Rico, as in the rest of the US, electricity is 110 volts AC. 220/240V electrical appliances will likely self-destruct when plugged into 110V current. Visit a hardware store for an adapter (which changes the shape of the plug) and a converter (which changes the voltage; about $20). Don't make the mistake of using only an adapter, unless appliance instructions explicitly state otherwise. For more on all things adaptable, check out http://kropla.com/electric.htm.

Toiletries: Condoms, deodorant, razors, tampons, and toothbrushes are often available, but it may be difficult to find your preferred brand; bring extras. Contact lenses are likely to be expensive and difficult to find, so bring enough extra pairs and solution for your entire trip. Also bring your glasses and a copy of your prescription in case you need emergency replacements.

First-Aid Kit: For a basic first-aid kit, pack bandages, a pain reliever, antibiotic cream, a thermometer, a multifunction pocketknife, tweezers, moleskin, decongestant, motion-sickness remedy, diarrhea or upset-stomach medication (Pepto Bismol® or Imodium®), an antihistamine, sunscreen, insect repellent, and burn ointment.

Film: Film and developing in Puerto Rico are slightly more expensive than elsewhere (about $5 to purchase a roll of 24 color exposures), so consider bringing along enough film for your entire trip and developing it at home. Airport security X-rays can fog film, so buy a lead-lined pouch at a camera store or ask security to hand-inspect it. Always pack film in your carry-on luggage, since higher-intensity X-rays are used on checked luggage. If you don't want to bother with film, consider using a digital camera. Although it requires a steep initial investment, a digital camera means you never have to buy film again. Just be sure to bring along a large enough memory card and extra (or rechargeable) batteries. For more info on digital cameras, visit www.short-courses.com/choosing/contents.htm.

Other Useful Items: For safety purposes, you should bring a **money belt** and a small **padlock**. Basic **outdoors equipment** (plastic water bottle, compass, waterproof matches, pocketknife, sunglasses, sunscreen, hat) may also prove useful. **Quick repairs** of torn garments can be done on the road with a needle and thread; also consider bringing electrical tape for patching tears. If you want to do laundry by hand, bring detergent, a small rubber ball to stop up the sink, and string for a makeshift clothes line. Other things you're liable to forget include: an umbrella, sealable **plastic bags** (for damp clothes, soap, food, shampoo, and other spillables), an **alarm clock,** safety pins, rubber bands, a flashlight, earplugs, garbage bags, and a small calculator. A **cell phone** can be a lifesaver (literally) on the road; see **Cellular Phones** (p. 36) for information on acquiring one that will work in Puerto Rico.

Important Documents: Don't forget your passport, traveler's checks, ATM and/or credit cards, adequate ID, and photocopies of all of the aforementioned in case these documents are lost or stolen. Also check that you have any of the following that might apply to you: a driver's license (p. 12); travel insurance forms; ISIC (p. 12).

SAFETY AND HEALTH

GENERAL ADVICE

In any type of crisis situation, the most important thing to do is **stay calm.** Your country's embassy abroad (p. 9) is usually your best resource when things go wrong; registering with that embassy upon arrival in the country is often a good idea. The government offices listed in the **Travel Advisories** box (p. 19) can provide information on the services they offer their citizens in case of emergencies abroad.

LOCAL LAWS AND POLICE

In an emergency, the Puerto Rican police are good resource for help. To reach them or other emergency personnel anywhere in Puerto Rico, dial ☎**911.** In a few remote areas 911 may not work. If it does not, the Puerto Rico police department phone number is listed in every practical information section of this guide; it is generally the regional prefix plus 2020.

IN CASE OF EMERGENCY, DIAL ☎911.

DRUGS AND ALCOHOL

The legal drinking age in Puerto Rico is 18, although many establishments do not ask for identification. Let's Go does not recommend underage drinking. It is illegal to drive with a blood alcohol level over 0.8%. Some cities have specific rules about drinking in public. It is illegal to drink in the streets of Old San Juan and some other Puerto Rican cities. It is also illegal to drink out of a bottle on the street in many cities. Narcotics such as marijuana, heroin, and cocaine are highly illegal in Puerto Rico, and this prohibition is strictly enforced. If you carry prescription drugs while traveling, keep a copy of the prescription with you.

SPECIFIC CONCERNS

HURRICANES

Hurricane season in Puerto Rico officially runs from June 1 to November 30, but poses the most significant threat from August to October. On average, a hurricane brushes by San Juan every 3.85 years. Travelers should be aware that hurricanes sometimes cause serious flooding and take lives. In the event of a hurricane, travelers should stay tuned to radio and TV stations for warnings from the US National Weather Service (NWS). If instructed to remain where they are, travelers should wait out the storm indoors and away from windows. Travelers may be advised to stock up on cash, water, and canned food before a hurricane arrives. For more advice, visit http://www.nws.noaa.gov.

TERRORISM

In light of the September 11, 2001 terrorist attacks in the eastern US, the US government frequently puts the nation, and its territories, on an elevated terrorism alert. Puerto Rico has not had any attacks—or threats of attacks—but like the rest of the US, the island has taken precautions. Monitor developments in the news and stay on top of any local, state, or federal terrorist warnings. The box on **travel advisories** lists offices to contact and webpages to visit to get the most updated list of your home country's government's advisories about travel.

TRAVEL ADVISORIES. The following government offices provide travel information and advisories by telephone, by fax, or via the web:

Australian Department of Foreign Affairs and Trade: ☎+61 1300 555 135; www.dfat.gov.au.

Canadian Department of Foreign Affairs and International Trade (DFAIT): ☎800-267-8376; www.dfait-maeci.gc.ca. Call for their free booklet, *Bon Voyage...But.*

New Zealand Ministry of Foreign Affairs: ☎+64 044 398 000; www.mft.govt.nz/travel/index.html.

United Kingdom Foreign and Commonwealth Office: ☎+1 020 7008 1500; www.fco.gov.uk.

PERSONAL SAFETY

EXPLORING AND TRAVELING

To avoid unwanted attention, try to blend in as much as possible. Respecting local customs (in many cases, dressing more conservatively than you would at home) may placate would-be hecklers. Familiarize yourself with your surroundings before setting out, and carry yourself with confidence. Check maps in shops and restaurants rather than on the street. If you are traveling alone, be sure someone at home knows your itinerary, and never tell anyone you meet that you're by yourself. When walking at night, stick to busy, well-lit streets and avoid dark alleyways. If you ever feel uncomfortable, leave the area as quickly and directly as you can.

San Juan has its share of crime, but it's no less safe than other metropolitan areas such as London or New York. Most incidents are limited to specific areas; travelers often feel most comfortable in Old San Juan, Condado, Ocean Park, and Isla Verde. It is best not to be out alone, especially at night, in the neighborhoods of Santurce, Hato Rey, and Río Piedras. Travelers should also take caution in the metropolitan areas of Ponce, Mayagüez, Arecibo, Fajardo, and Aguadilla. Unlike other major tourist destinations, Puerto Rico does not have a history of crime specifically targeting foreigners; the biggest problem is being in the wrong place at the wrong time.

There is no sure-fire way to avoid all the threatening situations you might encounter while traveling, but a good **self-defense course** will give you concrete ways to react to unwanted advances. **Impact, Prepare,** and **Model Mugging** can refer you to local self-defense courses in Australia, Canada, Switzerland and the US. Visit the website at www.modelmugging.org for a list of nearby chapters.

If you are using a **car,** learn local driving signals and wear a seat belt. Children under 40 lbs. should ride only in specially designed carseats, available for a small fee from most car rental agencies. Study route maps before you hit the road, and if you plan on spending a lot of time driving, consider bringing spare parts. For long drives in desolate areas, invest in a cellular phone and a roadside assistance program (see p. 32). Park your vehicle in a garage or well-traveled area, and use a steering wheel locking device in larger cities. **Sleeping in your car** is the most dangerous way to get your rest, and it's also illegal in many countries. For info on the perils of **hitchhiking,** see p. 34.

POSSESSIONS AND VALUABLES

Never leave your belongings unattended; crime occurs in even the most safe-looking guesthouse or hotel. Always lock your hotel room. Carry your backpack in front of you where you can see it, especially on public transportation.

There are a few steps you can take to minimize the financial risk associated with traveling. First, **bring as little with you as possible.** Second, buy a few combination **padlocks** to secure your belongings either in your pack or in a hostel or train station locker. Third, **carry as little cash as possible.** Keep your traveler's checks and ATM/credit cards in a **money belt**—not a "fanny pack"—along with your passport and ID cards. Fourth, **keep a small cash reserve separate from your primary stash.** This should be about $50 sewn into or stored in the depths of your pack, along with your traveler's check numbers and photocopies of your passport, your birth certificate, and other important documents.

Unfortunately, petty thieves in Puerto Rico have learned that travelers like to swim in the ocean and leave all of their valuables on the beach. Do not take anything valuable to the beach. This includes wallets, cell phones, cash, and jewelry. If you are traveling with a group, have one person stay on the beach and watch your stuff while the others swim. If you are traveling alone, the best thing to do is to put your hotel/car key in a waterproof bag, keep it with you when you enter the water, and leave absolutely nothing valuable on the beach. Another option is to ask a nearby beachgoer to watch your stuff while you swim, but this requires a bit of trust and a lot of luck. Less-frequented beaches have become targets for carjackings, especially along the north coast. When parking at the beach, do not leave anything in sight in your car or store valuables in your trunk.

If you will be traveling with electronic devices, such as a laptop computer or a PDA, check whether your homeowner's insurance covers loss, theft, or damage when you travel. If not, you might consider purchasing a low-cost separate insurance policy. **Safeware** (☎800-800-1492; www.safeware.com) specializes in covering computers and charges $90 for 90-day comprehensive international travel coverage up to $4000.

PRE-DEPARTURE HEALTH

In your **passport,** write the names of any people you wish to be contacted in case of a medical emergency, and list any allergies or medical conditions. Matching a prescription to a foreign equivalent is not always easy or safe, so if you take prescription drugs, consider carrying up-to-date, legible prescriptions or a statement from your doctor stating the medication's trade name, manufacturer, chemical name, and dosage. While traveling, be sure to keep all medication with you in your carry-on luggage. For tips on packing a **first-aid kit** and other health essentials, see p. 17.

The names in Puerto Rico for common drugs are:

DRUG NAME IN ENGLISH	SPANISH TRANSLATION
acetaminophen	acetaminofén
antihistamine	antihistimíno
aspirin	aspirina
antibiotic ointment	crema antibiotica
ibuprofen	ibuprofén
penicillin	penicilina

IMMUNIZATIONS AND PRECAUTIONS

There are no required inoculations for entry into Puerto Rico, but travelers over two years old should make sure that the following vaccines are up to date: MMR (measles, mumps, and rubella); DTaP (diphtheria, tetanus, and pertussis); IPV (polio); Hib (*Haemophilus influenza* B); and HepB (Hepatitis B). For recommendations on immunizations and prophylaxis, consult the CDC (see below) in the US or the equivalent in your home country, and check with a doctor for guidance.

USEFUL ORGANIZATIONS AND PUBLICATIONS

The American **Centers for Disease Control and Prevention** (**CDC;** ☎877-FYI-TRIP; www.cdc.gov/travel) maintains an international travelers' hotline and an informative website. Consult the appropriate government agency of your home country for consular information sheets on health, entry requirements, and other issues for various countries (see the listings in the box on **Travel Advisories,**). For quick information on health and other travel warnings, call the **Overseas Citizens Services** (M-F 8am-8pm from US ☎888-407-4747, from overseas 202-501-4444), or contact a passport agency, embassy, or consulate abroad. For information on medical evacuation services and travel insurance firms, see the US government's website at http://travel.state.gov/travel/abroad_health.html or the **British Foreign and Commonwealth Office** (www.fco.gov.uk). For general health information, contact the **American Red Cross** (☎202-303-4498; www.redcross.org).

STAYING HEALTHY

Common sense is the simplest prescription for good health while you travel. Drink lots of fluids to prevent dehydration and constipation, and wear sturdy, broken-in shoes and clean socks.

ONCE IN PUERTO RICO

ENVIRONMENTAL HAZARDS

To avoid **heat exhaustion and dehydration,** take extra precautions when hiking in Puerto Rico's central mountains and visiting the island's many beaches. Heat exhaustion leads to nausea, excessive thirst, headaches, and dizziness. Avoid it by drinking plenty of fluids, eating salty foods (e.g., crackers), abstaining from dehydrating beverages (e.g., alcohol and caffeinated beverages), and always wearing sunscreen. Continuous heat stress can eventually lead to heatstroke, characterized by a rising temperature, severe headache, delirium, and cessation of sweating. Victims should be cooled off with wet towels and taken to a doctor. Visitors should be especially careful to avoid **sunburn,** a common problem for travelers in Puerto Rico. Always wear sunscreen (SPF 30 is or higher) when spending time outdoors. If you get sunburned, drink more fluids than usual and apply an aloe-based lotion. Severe sunburns can lead to sun poisoning, a condition that affects the entire body, causing fever, chills, nausea, and vomiting. Sun poisoning should always be treated by a doctor.

INSECT-BORNE DISEASES

Many diseases are transmitted by insects—mainly mosquitoes, fleas, ticks, and lice. Be aware of insects in wet or forested areas, especially while hiking and camping; wear long pants and long sleeves, tuck your pants into your socks, and use a mosquito net. Use insect repellents such as DEET and soak or spray your gear with permethrin (licensed in the US only for use on clothing). **Mosquitoes**—responsible for diseases including **dengue fever**—can be particularly dangerous in wet, swampy, or wooded areas, which exist in rural areas of Puerto Rico. Dengue fever is transmitted by *Aedes* mosquitoes, which bite during the day rather than at night. The incubation period is 3-14 days, though usually 4-7 days. Early symptoms include a high fever, severe headaches, swollen lymph nodes, and muscle aches. Many patients also suffer from nausea, vomiting, and a pink rash. If you experience these symptoms, see a doctor immediately, drink plenty of liquids, and take fever-reducing medication such as acetaminophen (Tylenol). *Never take aspirin to treat dengue fever.* There is no vaccine available for dengue fever. **Ticks**—which can carry Lyme disease, among others— can be particularly bad in rural and forested regions, such as the central mountains and national forests of Puerto Rico.

FOOD- AND WATER-BORNE DISEASES

Prevention is the best medicine: be sure that your food is properly cooked and the water you drink is clean. Watch out for food from markets or street vendors that may have been cooked in unhygienic conditions. Other culprits are raw shellfish, unpasteurized milk, and sauces containing raw eggs. Always wash your hands before eating or bring a quick-drying, purifying liquid hand cleaner.

Traveler's diarrhea: Results from drinking fecally contaminated water or eating uncooked and contaminated foods. Symptoms include nausea, bloating, and urgency. Try quick-energy, non-sugary foods with protein and carbohydrates to keep your strength up. Over-the-counter anti-diarrheals (e.g., Imodium) may counteract the problem. The most dangerous side effect is dehydration; drink 8 oz. of water with ½ tsp. of sugar or honey and a pinch of salt, try uncaffeinated soft drinks, or eat salted crackers. If you develop a fever or your symptoms don't go away after 4-5 days, consult a doctor. Consult a doctor immediately for treatment of diarrhea in children.

Hepatitis A: A viral infection of the liver acquired through contaminated water or shellfish from contaminated water. Symptoms include fatigue, fever, loss of appetite, nausea, dark urine, jaundice, vomiting, aches and pains, and light stools. The risk is highest in rural areas and the countryside, but it is also present in urban areas. Ask your doctor about the Hepatitis A vaccine or an injection of immune globulin.

Giardiasis: Transmitted through parasites and acquired by drinking untreated water from streams or lakes. Symptoms include diarrhea, cramps, bloating, fatigue, weight loss, and nausea. If untreated, it can lead to severe dehydration. Giardiasis occurs worldwide.

Schistosomiasis: Also known as bilharzia; a parasitic disease caused when the larvae of flatworm penetrate unbroken skin. Symptoms include an itchy localized rash, followed in 4-6 weeks by fever, fatigue, painful urination, diarrhea, loss of appetite, and night sweats. To avoid it, try not to swim in fresh water; if exposed to untreated water, rub the area vigorously with a towel and apply rubbing alcohol.

OTHER INFECTIOUS DISEASES

The following diseases exist in every part of the world. Travelers should know how to recognize them and what to do if they suspect they have been infected.

Rabies: Transmitted through the saliva of infected animals; fatal if untreated. By the time symptoms (thirst and muscle spasms) appear, the disease is in its terminal stage. If you are bitten, wash the wound, seek immediate medical care, and try to have the animal located. A rabies vaccine, which consists of 3 shots given over a 21-day period, is available and recommended for developing world travel, but is only semi-effective.

AIDS and HIV: For detailed information on Acquired Immune Deficiency Syndrome (AIDS) in Puerto Rico, call the US Centers for Disease Control's 24hr. hotline at ☎800-

342-2437, or contact the Joint United Nations Programme on HIV/AIDS (UNAIDS), 20 Ave. Appia, CH-1211 Geneva 27, Switzerland (☎+41 22 791 3666; fax 22 791 4187).

Sexually transmitted infections (STIs): Gonorrhea, chlamydia, genital warts, syphilis, herpes, and other STIs are easier to catch than HIV and can be just as deadly. **Hepatitis B** and **Hepatitis C** can also be transmitted sexually. Though condoms may protect you from some STIs, oral or even tactile contact can lead to transmission. If you think you may have contracted an STI, see a doctor immediately.

OTHER HEALTH CONCERNS

MEDICAL CARE ON THE ROAD

Puerto Rico has one of the best medical systems in the Caribbean. Every municipal center has some kind of health clinic or hospital, and all large cities have major hospitals with 24hr. emergency rooms. Travelers who have a minor medical problem in Puerto Rico can visit any hospital **clinic** and wait to see a doctor. Most hospitals have English-speaking doctors; smaller hospitals that do not should be able to find a translator. In an emergency, dial ☎911 from any phone and an operator will send out paramedics, a fire brigade, or the police as needed. Alternatively, go directly to the nearest emergency room for immediate service. Puerto Rican hospitals take many American medical insurance plans, but other travelers will have to pay for medical service. Almost all cities and towns have standard pharmacies. Culebra has much more limited medical services and in a real emergency you will have to be evacuated to Fajardo. Isla Mona has no medical services and is very remote.

If you are concerned about obtaining medical assistance while traveling, you may wish to employ special support services. The *MedPass* from **GlobalCare, Inc.,** 6875 Shiloh Rd. East, Alpharetta, GA 30005, USA (☎800-860-1111; www.globalcare.net), provides 24hr. international medical assistance, support, and medical evacuation resources. The **International Association for Medical Assistance to Travelers (IAMAT;** US ☎716-754-4883, Canada +1 519-836-0102; www.iamat.org) has free membership, lists English-speaking doctors worldwide, and offers detailed info on immunization requirements and sanitation. If your regular policy does not cover travel abroad, you may wish to purchase additional coverage.

Those with medical conditions (such as diabetes, allergies to antibiotics, epilepsy, or heart conditions) may want to obtain a **MedicAlert** membership (US$40 per year), which includes among other things a stainless steel ID tag and a 24hr. collect-call number. Contact the MedicAlert Foundation International, 2323 Colorado Ave., Turlock, CA 95382, USA (☎888-633-4298, outside US ☎209-668-3333; www.medicalert.org.)

WOMEN'S HEALTH

Women traveling in unsanitary conditions are vulnerable to **urinary tract (including bladder and kidney) infections.** Over-the-counter medicines can sometimes alleviate symptoms, but if they persist, see a doctor. **Vaginal yeast infections** may flare up in hot and humid climates. Wearing loosely fitting trousers or a skirt and cotton underwear will help, as will remedies like Monostat or Gynelotrimin. Bring supplies from home if you are prone to infection, as they may be difficult to find on the road. **Tampons, pads,** and reliable **contraceptive devices** are widely available in Puerto Rico, though your favorite brand may not be stocked—bring extras of anything you can't live without. **Abortion** is legal in Puerto Rico. Planned Parenthood's affiliate in Puerto Rico is PRO-FAMILIA, Urbanización El Vedado, Calle Padre Las Casas 117, Hato Rey, San Juan, PR 00919 (☎787-765-7373; www.profamiliapr.org).

ESSENTIALS

GETTING TO PUERTO RICO

BY PLANE

When it comes to airfare, a little effort can save you a bundle. Courier fares are the cheapest for those whose plans are flexible enough to deal with the restrictions. Tickets sold by consolidators and standby seating are also good deals, but last-minute specials, airfare wars, and charter flights often beat these fares. The key is to hunt around, be flexible, and ask about discounts. Students, seniors, and those under 26 should never pay full price for a ticket.

AIRFARES

Puerto Rico is the airline hub of the Caribbean and flights are relatively inexpensive year-round, especially from the US east coast. Only San Juan's Luis Muñoz Marín International Airport has flights to destinations outside of the US. Most travelers will end up connecting somewhere on the US east coast, though **Iberia** also offers direct flights to Madrid.

Airfares to Puerto Rico peak between December and April; holidays are also expensive. The cheapest times to travel are September and October, during the height of hurricane season. Midweek (M-Th morning) round-trip flights run $40-50 cheaper than weekend flights, but they are generally more crowded and less likely to permit frequent-flier upgrades. Not fixing a return date ("open return") or arriving in and departing from different cities ("open-jaw") can be pricier than round-trip flights. Patching one-way flights together is the most expensive way to travel.

If Puerto Rico is only one stop on a more extensive globe-hop, consider a round-the-world (RTW) ticket. Tickets usually include at least five stops and are valid for about a year; prices range $1200-5000. Try **Northwest Airlines/KLM** (☎ 800-225-2525; www.nwa.com) or **Star Alliance,** a consortium of 16 airlines including United Airlines (www.staralliance.com).

Fares for roundtrip flights to San Juan from the US or Canadian east coast cost $250-600 in the high season (Nov.-May) and $250-500 in the low season (June-Oct.); from the US or Canadian west coast US$700-900/US$600-800; from the UK, UK£550-650/UK£500-550; from Australia AUS$3000-3400/AUS$2300-2600; from New Zealand NZ$2800-3300/NZ$2600-2800.

BUDGET AND STUDENT TRAVEL AGENCIES

While knowledgeable agents specializing in flights to Puerto Rico can make your life easy and help you save, they may not spend the time to find you the lowest possible fare—they get paid on commission. Travelers holding **ISICs** and **IYTCs** (see p. 12) qualify for big discounts from student travel agencies. Most flights from budget agencies are on major airlines, but in peak season some may sell seats on less reliable chartered aircraft.

CTS Travel, 30 Rathbone Pl., London W1T 1GQ, UK (☎+44 020 7447 5000; www.ctstravel.co.uk). A British student travel agent with offices in 39 countries including the US, Empire State Building, 350 Fifth Ave., Ste. 7813, New York, NY 10118 (☎877-287-6665; www.ctstravelusa.com).

STA Travel, 5900 Wilshire Blvd., Ste. 900, Los Angeles, CA 90036, USA (24hr. reservations and info ☎800-781-4040; www.statravel.com). A student and youth travel organization with over 150 offices worldwide (check their website for a listing of all their offices), including US offices in Boston, Chicago, Los Angeles, New York, Seattle, San

Francisco, and Washington, D.C. Ticket booking, travel insurance, railpasses, and more. Walk-in offices are located throughout Australia (☎+61 03 9207 5900), New Zealand (☎+64 09 309 9723), and the UK (☎+44 08701 630 026).

Travel CUTS (Canadian Universities Travel Services Limited), 187 College St., Toronto, ON M5T 1P7, Canada (☎888-592-2887; www.travelcuts.com). Offices across Canada and the US including Los Angeles, New York, Seattle, and San Francisco.

USIT, 19-21 Aston Quay, Dublin 2, Ireland (☎+353 01 602 1904; www.usit.ie), Ireland's leading student/budget travel agency has 20 offices throughout Northern Ireland and the Republic of Ireland. Offers programs to work, study, and volunteer worldwide.

FLIGHT PLANNING ON THE INTERNET. The Internet may be the budget traveler's dream when it comes to finding and booking bargain fares, but the array of options can be overwhelming. Many airline sites offer special last-minute deals on the Web. **STA** (www.statravel.com) and **StudentUniverse** (www.studentuniverse.com) provide quotes on student tickets, while **Orbitz** (www.orbitz.com), **Expedia** (www.expedia.com), and **Travelocity** (www.travelocity.com) offer full travel services. **Priceline** (www.priceline.com) lets you specify a price, and obligates you to buy any ticket that meets or beats it; **Hotwire** (www.hotwire.com) offers bargain fares, but won't reveal the airline or flight times until you buy. Other sites that compile deals include www.bestfares.com, www.flights.com, www.lowestfare.com, www.onetravel.com, and www.travelzoo.com. **SideStep** (www.sidestep.com) and **Booking Buddy** (www.bookingbuddy.com) are online tools that can help sift through multiple offers; these two let you enter your trip information once and search multiple sites. **Air Traveler's Handbook** (www.faqs.org/faqs/travel/air/handbook) is an indispensable resource on the Internet; it has a comprehensive listing of links to everything you need to know before you board a plane.

COMMERCIAL AIRLINES

The commercial airlines' lowest regular offer is the **APEX** (Advance Purchase Excursion) fare, which provides confirmed reservations and allows "open-jaw" tickets. Generally, reservations must be made seven to 21 days ahead of departure, with seven- to 14-day minimum-stay and up to 90-day maximum-stay restrictions. These fares carry hefty cancellation and change penalties (fees rise in summer). Book peak-season APEX fares early. Use **Expedia** (www.expedia.com) or **Travelocity** (www.travelocity.com) to get an idea of the lowest published fares, then use the resources outlined here to try to beat those fares. Low-season fares should be appreciably cheaper than the **high-season** (Nov.-May) ones listed here.

Note that flights to cities other than San Juan (such as Mayagüez, Aguadilla, and Ponce) occur on an intermittent schedule. Standard commercial carriers like American and United will probably offer the most convenient flights, but they may not be the cheapest, unless you manage to snag a special promotion. You will likely find flying "discount" airlines like Jet Blue Airlines, Song Airlines, or Spirit Airlines a better deal, if any of their limited departure points is convenient for you.

American Airlines (☎800-433-7300; www.aa.com), is the largest airline flying out of San Juan. Flights go throughout North America, as well as to Scotland, England, and New Zealand and Australia. In the Caribbean flies to Mayagüez, Santo Domingo, Tortola, St. Thomas, St. Maarten, St. Lucia, St. Kitts, and St. Croix.

Continental Airlines (☎800-523-3273; www.continental.com), has direct flights to Houston and Newark, where connections to North America, the UK, and Ireland can be made.

Copa (☎800-359-2672; www.copaair.com), flies to a variety of destinations in Central and South America.

Delta Airlines (☎800-221-1212; www.delta.com), flies direct to Atlanta, New York, and Orlando, where connections to North America and New Zealand can be made. Connections to Europe are offered on a seasonal basis.

Iberia (☎800-772-4642; www.iberia.com), has direct flights to Madrid with connections to cities throughout Europe.

Jet Blue Airlines (☎800-538-2583; www.jetblue.com). This budget airline offers great deals to major cities across the US.

Song Airlines (☎800-359-7664; www.flysong.com), is Delta's budget spin-off. Flights from San Juan go to Boston, New York, and Orlando, with US connections.

Spirit Airlines (☎800-772-7117; www.spiritair.com). This budget airline flies directly to Fort Lauderdale and Orlando, with US connections.

United Airlines (☎800-864-8331; www.ual.com), flies direct to Chicago and Philadelphia, with connections to other US cities, Australia, Europe, and New Zealand.

US Airways (☎800-428-4322; www.usair.com), flies to Newark, New York and Philadelphia, with connections to Australia, Europe, New Zealand, and the US.

STANDBY FLIGHTS

Traveling standby requires considerable flexibility in arrival and departure dates. Companies dealing in standby flights sell vouchers rather than tickets, along with the promise to get you to your destination (or near your destination) within a certain window of time (typically 1-5 days). You call in before your specific window of time to hear your flight options and the probability that you will be able to board each flight. You can then decide which flights you want to try to catch, show up at the appropriate airport at the appropriate time, present your voucher, and board if space is available. Vouchers can usually be bought for both one-way and round-trip travel. You may receive a monetary refund only if every available flight within your date range is full; if you opt not to take an available (but perhaps less convenient) flight, you can only get credit toward future travel. Carefully read agreements with any company offering standby flights, as tricky fine print can leave you in the lurch. To check on a company's service record in the US, contact the Better Business Bureau (☎703-276-0100; www.bbb.org). It is difficult to receive refunds, and clients' vouchers will not be honored when an airline fails to receive payment in time.

TICKET CONSOLIDATORS

Ticket consolidators, or **"bucket shops,"** buy unsold tickets in bulk from commercial airlines and sell them at discounted rates. The best place to look is in the Sunday travel section of any major newspaper, where many bucket shops place tiny ads. Call quickly, as availability is extremely limited. Not all bucket shops are reliable, so insist on a receipt that gives complete information about restrictions, refunds, and tickets, and pay by credit card (in spite of the 2-5% fee) so you can stop payment if you never receive your tickets. For more info, see www.travel-library.com/air-travel/consolidators.html. Some consolidators worth trying are **Rebel** (☎800-732-3588; www.rebeltours.com), **Cheap Tickets** (www.cheaptickets.com), **Flights.com** (www.flights.com), and **TravelHUB** (www.travelhub.com). Let's Go does not endorse any of these agencies; be cautious and research companies before you hand over your credit card number.

CHARTER FLIGHTS

Tour operators contract charter flights with airlines in order to fly extra loads of passengers during peak season. These flights are not hassle free: they occur less frequently than major airlines, make refunds particularly difficult, and are almost always fully booked. Their scheduled times may change or they may be cancelled at the last moment—some times as late as 48hr. before the trip, and without offering a full refund. And although check-in, boarding, and baggage claim for charter flights are often much slower, they can also be much cheaper. Discount clubs and fare brokers offer members savings on last-minute charter and tour deals. Study contracts closely; you don't want to end up with an unwanted overnight layover.

BY BOAT

FERRIES

Unfortunately, no public boats make the trip between Puerto Rico and the Virgin Islands. However, there is a private ferry between Mayagüez, Puerto Rico and Santo Domingo, Dominican Republic. For more information see **Mayagüez**, p. 252.

CRUISE SHIPS

Every year hundreds of cruise ships drop off travelers in the San Juan bay to spend the day wandering the streets of Old San Juan. Cruises generally depart from a major port (such as New York, Miami, or Fort Lauderdale) and spend four to seven days traveling throughout the Caribbean. Some cruise ships depart from European ports to head to the Caribbean, but these are much more expensive. Nights, and some days, are spent onboard the ship, while most days are spent at various destination islands. All of the major online travel agents (www.expedia.com, www.orbitz.com, and www.travelocity.com) offer highly discounted cruise prices (four-night cruises $400-900, seven-night cruises $500-1200). The individual cruise ship sites list regular fares with the occasional super-special thrown in. Typically a cruise price includes accommodations, onboard meals and entertainment, and port taxes. However, travelers have to pay for their own transportation to the port of departure, meals and entertainment in the port city, casinos, gratuities, and alcoholic beverages. Price also varies with the type of accommodation: a suite or a cabin with a window is much more expensive than an interior cabin.

Carnival (www.carnival.com) and **Royal Caribbean** (www.rccl.com) use San Juan as a home port year-round. **Princess** (www.princess.com) uses San Juan as a home port only during the high season. The other major cruise lines that stop in San Juan include: **Celebrity** (www.celebrity.com), **Costa Cruises** (www.costacruise.com), **Cunard** (www.cunard.com), **Holland America** (www.hollandamerica.com), **Norwegian Cruise Line** (www.ncl.com), **P&O Cruises** (www.pocruises.com), **Radisson Seven Seas Cruises** (www.rssc.com), **Seabourn** (www.seabourn.com), **Silversea** (www.silversea.com), and **Windstar Cruises** (www.windstarcruises.com). The following websites also sell discounted cruises: www.bestpricecruises.com, www.1-800-cruises.com, www.cruisehotfares.com, www.beatanycruiseprice.com, www.caribbean-on-line.com, and www.acruise2go.com.

ESSENTIALS

GETTING AROUND PUERTO RICO
BY PLANE

ONE-WAY TICKET TO PARADISE. There are several options for getting to the offshore islands of Vieques and Culebra. The fastest route is to fly directly from San Juan's Luis Muñoz Marín International Airport, but this is also the most expensive (one-way $75). Slightly cheaper is to fly from Isla Grande airport, just outside Puerta de Tierra (one-way $45). Larger groups may find it convenient to take a taxi from San Juan to Fajardo ($65 for four people), then either fly to an island ($35-40) or take the ferry ($2-2.25). By far the most economical option is to take a *público* from Río Piedras to Fajardo ($3.50), then hop on the ferry. Allow at least 4hr. for the ride from Río Piedras to Fajardo. Ask the driver to take you all the way to *la lancha* (the dock).

Most of Puerto Rico's internal flights connect Culebra, Fajardo, San Juan, and Vieques. All of the airlines flying to the Spanish Virgin Islands use tiny planes and charge similar rates. Note that flying into San Juan's international airport is significantly more expensive than flying into San Juan Isla Grande Airport. For information about flights see **Culebra** (p. 186), **Fajardo** (p. 160), **Mayagüez** (p. 252), **Ponce** (p. 201), **San Juan** (p. 92), or **Vieques** (p. 170). Unless you're in a big hurry, it's much more economical to rent a car or take a *público* than it is to fly.

BY PÚBLICO

There is no island-wide bus or train service. Instead, Puerto Ricans travel on *carros públicos* (also called *guaguas públicas*), private vehicles that transport groups of people between city centers. It is possible, albeit difficult, to travel to many cities using *públicos* alone, as long as you get used to the system. Be prepared to spend several hours each day waiting for a bus to your destination city and do not plan on visiting sights or parks outside of city centers.

On one hand, *públicos* are cheap; the longest ride shouldn't cost more than $10. On the other hand, they are extremely slow, they have no schedule, and vehicles may not keep to quality standards. Generally *públicos* wait either by a town's central plaza or in a *público* terminal starting early in the morning, then leave when they are full. This means that travelers have to wake up at the crack of dawn, then sit in a stuffy van waiting for enough people to show up so they can leave. Drivers usually leave for the day when passengers stop showing up, but this time varies; if you come after 10am, however, all vehicles may be gone.

The system is time-consuming and frustrating but relatively comprehensive. *Públicos* leave from almost every municipal center and travel to adjacent municipalities and smaller *barrios* within the municipality. The destination of the vehicle is usually written on the front of the windshield. For a higher price, most *público* drivers will act as taxi drivers and take you wherever you want to go, but beware that if a *público* drops you off at the beach, you may end up stranded. It is also possible to flag down a *público* mid-route, especially along Hwy. 3 (*públicos* traveling between San Juan and Fajardo) and Hwy. 2 (*públicos* traveling between San Juan and Arecibo). The best strategy is to wait at one of the big cement benches on the side of the road. It is polite to tip a *público* driver at least 10% per person and more if you have bags.

Let's Go lists *público* routes in the transportation section of each town, but information changes frequently, so it's a good idea to stop by the *público* station the night before you leave to get an update. The transport times listed in *Let's Go*

Puerto Rico on Public Transportation

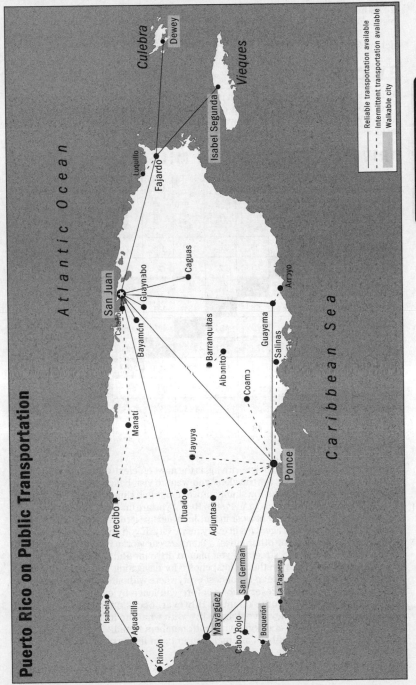

Reliable transportation available
Intermittent transportation available
Walkable city

Atlantic Ocean

Caribbean Sea

Culebra
Dewey
Vieques
Isabel Segunda
Luquillo
Fajardo
Caguas
Arroyo
San Juan
Guaynabo
Cataño
Bayamón
Guayama
Barranquitas
Salinas
Aibonito
Coamo
Manatí
Jayuya
Ponce
Arecibo
Utuado
Adjuntas
San Germán
La Paguera
Isabela
Mayagüez
Aguadilla
Cabo Rojo
Boquerón
Rincón

are estimates provided by *público* drivers and they are almost always overly optimistic. For instance, it theoretically takes 1hr. to get from San Juan to Fajardo, but on a *público* it can take up to 4hr. when you include traffic and frequent stops to pick up additional passengers. Do not take a *público* when you are in a hurry.

BY CAR

Driving is the favorite transportation method for most locals and visitors in Puerto Rico. Roads are usually paved, but often poorly maintained and extremely congested. Watch out for narrow and washed-out roads in the central mountains and reckless drivers just about everywhere. (See **On The Road**, p. 32.)

DRIVING DISTANCES (IN MILES)

	Aguadilla	Aibonito	Arecibo	Cabo Rojo	Fajardo	Luquillo	Mayagüez	Ponce	San Germán	San Juan
Aguadilla		95	33	26	112	108	17	63	31	81
Aibonito	95		61	72	59	62	78	32	66	42
Arecibo	33	61		58	79	73	49	52	62	48
Cabo Rojo	26	72	58		131	131	9	41	7	111
Fajardo	112	59	79	131		7	129	89	125	34
Luquillo	108	62	73	131	7		124	90	124	28
Mayagüez	17	78	49	9	129	124		46	14	98
Ponce	63	32	52	41	89	90	46		34	70
San Germán	31	66	62	7	125	124	14	34		104
San Juan	81	42	48	111	34	28	31	98	70	

RENTING

Though car rental can be expensive, driving is the most efficient way to get around in Puerto Rico. A car is a must for travelers who want to visit beaches outside the city center, hike in national parks, or simply move about in a timely manner. Unfortunately, it is impossible to rent a car in Puerto Rico if you are under 21 and pricey to do so at any age. Most travelers rent a car in San Juan and use it to get around the island, though there are car rental agencies in every major city. If you will be spending most of your time in San Juan or other cities, a compact car works best to navigate the island's narrow, congested streets. If you plan to drive the Ruta Panorámica, a car with four-wheel drive may be the optimal choice for navigating the sharp turns and steep hills, though it's possible to get almost everywhere without four-wheel drive.

You can generally make reservations before you leave by calling major international offices in your home country. However, occasionally the price and availability information they give doesn't jive with what the local offices in your country will tell you. Try checking with both numbers to make sure you get the best price. Local desk numbers are included in town listings; for home-country numbers, call your toll-free directory.

To rent a car in Puerto Rico, you must be at least 21 years old. Some agencies require renters to be 25, and most charge those aged 21-24 an additional insurance fee (around $5-10 per day). Policies and prices vary from agency to agency. Occasionally, small local operations rent to people under 21, but this is not a predictable or reliable service; be sure to ask about the insurance coverage and deductible, and always check the fine print.

INTERNATIONAL AGENCIES
All of the following rental agencies have offices at the Luis Muñoz Marín Airport.

Alamo: ☎800-462-5266, Puerto Rico 787-791-1805; www.alamo.com.

Avis: ☎800-331-1212, Puerto Rico 787-791-2500; www.avis.com.

Budget: ☎800-527-0700, Puerto Rico 787-791-3685; www.budget.com.

Dollar: ☎800-800-4000, Puerto Rico 787-791-5500; www.dollar.com.

Hertz: ☎800-654-3131, Puerto Rico 787-791-0840; www.hertz.com.

National: ☎800-227-7368, Puerto Rico 787-791-1805; www.nationalcar.com.

Payless Car Rental: ☎800-729-5377, Puerto Rico 787-625-8880; www.paylesscarrental.com.

Thrifty: ☎800-847-4398, Puerto Rico 787-253-2525; www.thrifty.com.

PUERTO RICAN AGENCIES

AAA Car Rental: ☎787-726-7350 or 787-726-7355; www.aaacarrentalpr.com.

Charlie Car Rental: ☎800-289-1227, Puerto Rico 800-289-1227; www.charliecars.com.

L&M Car Rental: ☎800-666-0807, Puerto Rico 787-791-1160; www.lmcarrental.com.

COSTS AND INSURANCE
Rental car prices start at around $40 a day from national companies, $30 from local agencies. Expect to pay more for larger cars and for four-wheel drive. Cars with **automatic transmission** can cost up to $10 a day more than cars with manual transmission (stick shift), and in some places, automatic transmission is hard to find. Moreover, it is often difficult to find an automatic four-wheel drive.

Many rental packages offer unlimited miles, while others offer a limited number of miles per day with a surcharge per mile after that. Return the car with a full tank of gasoline (petrol) to avoid high fuel charges at the end. Be sure to ask whether the price includes **insurance** against theft and collision, tax, and special airport fees. Remember that if you are driving a conventional vehicle on an **unpaved road** in a rental car, you are almost never covered by insurance; ask about this before leaving the rental agency. Be aware that cars rented on an **American Express, Visa,** or **MasterCard Gold** or **Platinum** credit card in Puerto Rico might *not* carry the automatic insurance that they would in other countries; check with your credit card company. Insurance plans from rental companies almost always come with a **deductible** of around $500 for conventional vehicles; the excess ranges up to around $800 for younger drivers and for four-wheel drive. This means that the insurance bought from the rental company only applies to damages over the excess; damages up to that amount must be covered by your existing insurance plan. Some rental companies in Puerto Rico require you to buy a **Collision Damage Waiver (CDW),** which will waive the excess in the case of a collision. **Loss Damage Waivers (LDWs)** do the same in the case of theft or vandalism.

National chains often allow one-way rentals (picking up in one city and dropping off in another). There is usually a minimum hire period and sometimes an extra drop-off charge of several hundred dollars.

ESSENTIALS

DRIVING PERMITS AND CAR INSURANCE

INTERNATIONAL DRIVING PERMIT (IDP)

If you plan to drive a car while in Puerto Rico, you must be 18. Puerto Rico accepts unexpired International Driving Permits or driver's licenses from any country that imposes requirements similar to Puerto Rico (including the US, Canada, and many European countries) for up to 120 days. Visitors staying longer than 120 days must apply for a Puerto Rican license.

Your International Driver's Permit, valid for one year, must be issued in your own country before you depart. An application for an IDP usually requires one or two photos, a current local license, an additional form of identification, and a fee. It may be a good idea to get an IDP, in case you're in a situation (e.g., an accident or stranded in a small town) where the police do not know English; information on the IDP is printed in 11 languages, including Spanish. To apply, contact your home country's automobile association. Be careful when purchasing an IDP online or anywhere other than your home automobile association. Many vendors sell permits of questionable legitimacy for higher prices.

CAR INSURANCE

Most credit cards cover standard insurance. If you rent, lease, or borrow a car, you will need a **Green Card,** or an **International Insurance Certificate,** to certify that you have liability insurance and that it applies abroad. Green cards can be obtained at car rental agencies, car dealerships, some travel agents, and some border crossings. Rental agencies may require you to purchase theft insurance in countries that they consider to have a high risk of auto theft.

ON THE ROAD

Puerto Rican drivers can be classified somewhere between confident and reckless. Traffic is heavy; many people disregard speed limits, neglect to signal turns, and cut off other cars. Markers such as stop signs are treated more like suggestions than laws. Aggressive urban drivers will feel right at home.

NO HABLO ESPAÑOL. It seems that everyone in Puerto Rico speaks English—until you hit the road. All Puerto Rican road signs are in Spanish and if you get pulled over, the cop probably won't speak English either. However, this doesn't prevent English-speakers from driving. Most road signs have the same design that you'll find in the US or Europe—an 8-sided red sign isn't hard to decipher in any language. However, it's a good idea to brush up on your Spanish vocabulary before you get on the road. See the **Phrasebook,** p. 310.

Puerto Rico's road system is very similar to that of the US. In this book "Rte." (as in "Rte. 1") refers to small, one-lane roads, and "Hwy." (as in "Hwy. 7") to highways and expressways; Puerto Ricans call almost all roads *carreteras*. Roads are fairly easy to navigate, though signage varies. In San Juan, remember that all signs pointing to "San Juan" eventually lead to Old San Juan. Puerto Rico has several good road maps, available for sale at most gas stations and drug stores. Hwy. 22, Hwy. 30, Hwy. 52, and Hwy. 53 are the island's only **toll roads.** These freeways have intermittent toll booths charging $0.30-1. Use the lane with the green "C" if you have correct change and the lane with the red "A" if you do not.

One confusing aspect of Puerto Rico's road system is the use of the **metric system** alongside the **imperial system.** Gas is measured in liters and the distance markers on the side of the road measure kilometers traveled. However, the speed limit is posted in miles per hour. Gasoline (petrol) prices vary, but average about $0.50 per liter in cities and from $0.55 per liter in outlying areas.

Carjackings are common in Puerto Rico, especially in big cities. If you are in a big city hotel without a parking lot, it's a good idea to put your car in a garage. Ask the hotel receptionist for regional advice. Never leave anything visible in your car; people have been known to break in for something as small as a couple of tapes. Carjackings frequently occur at beaches, especially deserted beaches. When driving, keep doors locked. To help drivers avoid nighttime carjackings, Puerto Rico has passed a law that cars are not required to stop at red lights between midnight and 6am. While driving, be sure to buckle up—seat belts are required by law in Puerto Rico. The speed limit varies from region to region. Most highways have a limit of 65 mph, while residential areas may post limits as low as 20 mph.

DRIVING PRECAUTIONS. When traveling in the summer or in the desert, bring substantial amounts of water (a suggested 5 liters of **water** per person per day) for drinking and for the radiator. For long drives to unpopulated areas, register with police before beginning the trek and again upon arrival at the destination. Check with the local automobile club for details. When traveling for long distances, make sure tires are in good condition and have enough air, and get good maps. A **compass** and a **car manual** can also be very useful. You should always carry a **spare tire** and **jack, jumper cables, extra oil, flares,** a **flashlight,** and **heavy blankets** (in case your car breaks down at night or in the winter). If you don't know how to **change a tire,** learn before heading out, especially if you are planning on traveling in deserted areas. Blowouts on dirt roads are very common. If your car breaks down, **stay in your vehicle;** if you wander off, there's less likelihood trackers will find you.

DANGERS
Central mountain roads tend to be narrow with sharp curves, poor visibility, and frequent one-lane washouts. Throughout the island, most roads are paved, though many are poorly maintained and have accumulated their share of potholes. Never drive in the mountains at night or during a rainstorm. Perhaps the greatest danger are the local drivers, who often use the whole road in narrow spots and drive at high speeds around sharp turns. Drivers are also reckless on the roads around large cities such as San Juan, where signaling turns is uncommon practice and speed limits are frequently exceeded.

CAR ASSISTANCE
Most automobile clubs offer free towing, emergency roadside assistance, and travel-related discounts in exchange for a modest membership fee. US or Canadian residents traveling to Puerto Rico should consider contacting the **American Automobile Association (AAA; ☎** 800-564-6222 roadside assistance 787-620-7805; www.aaa.com), which offers service in Puerto Rico. Membership costs vary depending on which branch you join ($50-60 for the first year; less for renewals and additional family members).

BY TAXI
All major Puerto Rican cities have taxi services, which are listed in the **Practical Information** sections. Puerto Rican taxi drivers usually give passengers a fair deal, but they rarely use a meter. Agree on a price before you get in the cab just to be certain. San Juan taxis use regulated fares; see p. 94 for more information.

BY BICYCLE
Some travelers harbor romantic visions of biking around a Caribbean island, but that is much more feasible on less-developed islands. Heavy traffic and a mountain range running through the center of Puerto Rico make it difficult to ride anywhere,

unless you're interested in mountaing biking. While the best place to ride is on the southern half of the island where there are flat roads with less traffic, the only bike rental stores are in San Juan and on Vieques and Culebra. Many travelers try to get around Culebra and Vieques on bikes, but both islands have mountains (or at least large hills) in the middle. In Puerto Rico, it is advisable to use bikes as a form of recreation rather than a mode of transportation.

BY THUMB

Let's Go never recommends hitchhiking as a safe means of transportation, and none of the information presented here is intended to do so.

Let's Go strongly urges you to consider the risks before you choose to hitchhike. Hitchhiking means entrusting your life to a stranger and risking assault, sexual harassment, theft, and unsafe driving. For women traveling alone (or even in pairs), hitching is just too dangerous. A man and a woman are a less dangerous combination; two men will have a harder time getting a lift, while three men will go nowhere. Hitchhiking in Puerto Rico is dangerous and seldom done.

KEEPING IN TOUCH

BY EMAIL AND INTERNET

Internet access is widespread in Puerto Rico. Cybercafes have even sprung up in the small towns of Puerto Rico's central mountains. Logging on will usually cost about $1 per 10min. Though in some places it's possible to forge a remote link with your home server, in most cases this is a much slower (and thus more expensive) option than taking advantage of free **web-based email accounts** (e.g., www.gmail.com, www.hotmail.com). **Internet cafes** and the occasional free Internet terminal at a public library or university are listed in the **Practical Information** sections of major cities. For a list of additional cybercafes in Puerto Rico, check out www.netcafeguide.com.

Increasingly, travelers find that taking their **laptop computers** on the road can be a convenient option for staying connected. Laptop users can call an Internet service provider via a modem using long-distance phone cards specifically intended for such calls. They may also find Internet cafes that allow them to connect their laptops to the Internet. And most excitingly, travelers with wireless-enabled computers may be able to take advantage of an increasing number of Internet "hot spots,"where they can get online for free or for a small fee. Newer computers can detect these hot

WARY WI-FI. Wireless hot spots make Internet access possible in public and remote places. Unfortunately, they also pose **security risks.** Hot spots are public, open networks that use unencrypted, unsecured connections. They are susceptible to hacks and "packet sniffing"—ways of stealing passwords and other private information. To prevent problems, disable ad hoc mode, turn off file sharing, turn off network discovery, encrypt your e-mail, turn on your firewall, beware of phony networks, and watch for over-the-shoulder creeps. Ask the establishment whose wireless you're using for the name of the network so you know you're on the right one. If you are in the vicinity and do not plan to access the Internet, turn off your wireless adapter completely.

spots automatically; otherwise, websites like www.jiwire.com, www.wififrees-pot.com, and www.wi-fihotspotlist.com can help you find them. For information on insuring your laptop while traveling, see . Travelers should be aware that the extreme heat and humidity in Puerto Rico can damage laptops.

BY TELEPHONE

PLACING INTERNATIONAL CALLS. To call Puerto Rico from home or to call home from Puerto Rico, dial:

1. The **International dialing prefix.** To call from **Australia,** dial 0011; **Canada** or the **US,** 011; **Ireland, New Zealand,** or the **UK,** 00; **Puerto Rico,** 011.
2. The **country code** of the country you want to call. To call **Australia,** dial 61; **Canada** or the **US,** 1; **Ireland,** 353; **New Zealand,** 64; the **UK,** 44; **Puerto Rico,** 1.
3. The **city/area code.** The area code for the entirety of **Puerto Rico** is ☎ 787.
4. The **local number.**

CALLING HOME FROM PUERTO RICO

You can usually make **direct international calls** from pay phones, but if you aren't using a phone card, you may need to drop your coins as quickly as your words. **Prepaid phone cards** are a common and relatively inexpensive means of calling abroad. Each one comes with a Personal Identification Number (PIN) and a toll-free access number. To purchase prepaid phone cards, check online for the best rates; www.callingcards.com is a good place to start. Online providers generally send your access number and PIN via email, with no actual "card" involved. You can also call home with prepaid phone cards purchased in Puerto Rico (see below).

Another option is to purchase a **calling card,** linked to a major national telecommunications service in your home country. Calls are billed collect or to your account. To obtain a calling card, contact the appropriate company listed below. Where available, there are often advantages to purchasing calling cards online, including better rates and immediate access to your account. To call home with a calling card, contact the operator for your service provider in Puerto Rico by dialing the appropriate toll-free access number (listed below in the third column).

COMPANY	TO OBTAIN A CARD:	TO CALL ABROAD:
AT&T (US)	800-364-9292 or www.att.com	800-225-5288
Canada Direct	800-561-8868 or www.infocanadadirect.com	800-496-7123
MCI (US)	800-777-5000 or www.minutepass.com	800-888-8000
Telecom New Zealand Direct.	www.telecom.co.nz	ATT 800-248-0064; MCI 800-666-5494; Sprint 800-659-0064
Telstra Australia	1800 676 638 or www.telstra.com	MCI 888-343-5067; Sprint 888-311-9050

Placing a **collect call** through an international operator can be expensive, but may be necessary in case of an emergency. You can frequently call collect without even possessing a company's calling card just by calling its access number and following the instructions.

CALLING WITHIN PUERTO RICO

There are several different phone areas on the island, meaning that calling from the east coast to the west coast (or from San Juan to either coast) is long-distance. The simplest way to call within the country is to use a coin-operated phone. Puerto Rican pay phones cost $0.50 for local calls, and start at $1 for long-distance calls. **Prepaid phone cards**—available at newspaper kiosks, convenience stores, and drugstores—which carry a certain amount of phone time depending on the card's denomination, usually save time and money in the long run. The computerized phone will tell you how much time, in units, you have left on your card. Another kind of prepaid telephone card comes with a PIN and a toll-free access number. Instead of inserting the card into the phone, you call the access number and follow the directions on the card. These cards can be used to make international as well as domestic calls. Phone rates typically tend to be highest in the morning, lower in the evening, and lowest on Sunday and late at night.

> **AREA CODE.** You must use the area code (☎ 787) before dialing any number in Puerto Rico, local or long-distance. For directory assistance call ☎ 511.

CELLULAR PHONES

Although cell phones have spotty service in Puerto Rico's central mountains, they have fairly consistent reception in coastal regions and can be a useful emergency communication tool for drivers. However, cell phones are not as cost-effective as phone cards. They probably don't make sense for visitors who will not be making frequent calls or using a cell phone as a safety precaution when traveling by car. Travelers who own cell phones with coverage in the US will likely also have Puerto Rico included in their calling plan; check with your carrier before traveling.

The international standard for cell phones is **Global System for Mobile Communication (GSM).** To make and receive calls in Puerto Rico you will need a **GSM-compatible phone** and a **SIM (Subscriber Identity Module) card,** a country-specific, thumbnail-sized chip that gives you a local phone number and plugs you into the local network. However, most **phones available for sale in Puerto Rico are not GSM-compatible** so if you are planning to make calls to places other than the US or Canada, you must make certain you are purchasing a GSM-compatible phone. It may be easiest to purchase one before you leave your home country. Many SIM cards are **prepaid,** meaning that they come with calling time included and you don't need to sign up for a monthly service plan. Incoming calls are frequently free. When you use up the prepaid time, you can buy additional cards or vouchers (usually available at convenience stores) to get more. For more information on GSM phones, check out www.telestial.com, www.orange.co.uk, www.roadpost.com, or www.planetomni.com. Companies like **Cellular Abroad** (www.cellularabroad.com) rent cell phones that work in a variety of destinations around the world, providing a simpler option than picking up a phone in-country.

> **GSM PHONES.** Just having a GSM phone doesn't mean you're necessarily good to go when you travel abroad. The majority of GSM phones sold in the United States operate on a different **frequency** (1900) than international phones (900/1800) and will not work abroad. Tri-band phones work on all three frequencies (900/1800/1900) and will operate through most of the world. Additionally, some GSM phones are **SIM-locked** and will only accept SIM cards from a single carrier. You'll need a **SIM-unlocked** phone to use a SIM card from a local carrier when you travel.

TIME DIFFERENCES

Puerto Rico is 4hr. behind Greenwich Mean Time (GMT), and does not observe Daylight Savings Time.

The following table applies from late October to early April.

4AM	5AM	6AM	7AM	8AM	NOON	10PM
Vancouver Seattle San Francisco Los Angeles	Denver	Chicago	New York Toronto	**SAN JUAN** New Brunswick	London	Sydney Canberra Melbourne

This table is applicable from early April to late October.

4AM	5AM	6AM	7AM	8AM	NOON	9PM
Vancouver Seattle San Francisco Los Angeles	Denver	Chicago	**SAN JUAN** New York Toronto	New Brunswick	London	Sydney Canberra Melbourne

BY MAIL

Sending a postcard within Puerto Rico costs $0.25, while sending letters (up to 1 oz) domestically costs $0.39 and requires about 6 days.

SENDING MAIL HOME FROM PUERTO RICO

Airmail is the best way to send mail home from Puerto Rico. **Aerogrammes,** printed sheets that fold into envelopes and travel via airmail, are available at post offices. Write "airmail," "par avion," or "por avión" on the front. Most post offices will charge exorbitant fees or simply refuse to send aerogrammes with enclosures. **Surface mail** is by far the cheapest and slowest way to send mail. It takes one to two months to cross the Atlantic and one to three to cross the Pacific—good for heavy items you won't need for a while, such as souvenirs or other articles you've acquired along the way that are weighing you down.

SENDING MAIL TO PUERTO RICO

To ensure timely delivery, mark envelopes "airmail," "par avion," or "por avión." In addition to the standard postage system whose rates are listed below, **Federal Express** (www.fedex.com; Australia ☎ +61 13 26 10, Canada and the US 800-463-3339, Ireland +353 1800 535 800, New Zealand +64 0800 733 339, the UK + 44 0800 123 800) handles express mail services from most countries to Puerto Rico. Mail is more reliable in large metropolitan areas; allow extra time for mail to reach rural areas.

There are several ways to arrange pick-up of letters sent to you while you are abroad. Mail can be sent via **General Delivery** or **Lista de Correos** in almost any city or town in Puerto Rico with a post office, and it is somewhat reliable (your best bet is to send packages as "certified mail"). Address General Delivery letters like so:

Ricky MARTIN
General Delivery
City, PR POSTAL CODE

The mail will go to a special desk in the central post office, unless you specify a post office by street address or postal code. It's best to use the largest post office, since mail may be sent there regardless. It is usually safer and quicker, though more expensive, to send mail express or registered. Bring your passport (or other photo ID) for pick up. If the clerks insist that there is nothing for you, have them check under your first name as well. *Let's Go* lists post offices in the **Practical Information** section for each city and most towns.

ESSENTIALS

ACCOMMODATIONS

With the exception of a couple of dorm-style rooms in Rincón, there are no youth hostels in Puerto Rico. Most travelers will end up staying in a combination of hotels, guesthouses, and *paradores*. Groups of visitors staying in one place for a week or more can save money by contacting a realtor for vacation homes.

GUESTHOUSES

Guesthouses are usually the most affordable type of accommodation in Puerto Rico, with a single room costing about $60-100, depending on the region. Generally owned by a private individual (as opposed to a company or chain), guesthouses range from ramshackle rooms rented out on the second floor of a residence to charming hotel-style accommodations complete with a reception area and complimentary breakfast. Most accommodations of this type do not have 24hr. reception, so it is best to have a reservation if you plan to arrive late. Guesthouse rooms almost always have private bathrooms with hot water, but the furniture may be old or mismatched and the room itself may be aged. Guesthouse rooms rarely have daily maid service; instead, rooms are cleaned after a guest leaves. The most important quality in a guesthouse is safety; even though locks are standard, you will still be trusting your life, and all your possessions, to the owner. Rooms are typically priced by the number of beds instead of the number of occupants, so a single person will pay the same as two people staying in one double bed and two people staying in separate beds will have to pay the price of a quad. Few guesthouses accept credit cards. Guesthouses are not always endorsed by the government, and thus they do not always charge the 9% accommodations tax.

PARADORES

Not found in major cities, *paradores* (roughly translated as "country inns") are small, independent hotels that are endorsed by the Puerto Rican Tourism Company (PRTC). A single room usually runs about $50-75 and the PRTC dictates that rates cannot change by season, making west coast *paradores* an excellent bargain during summer months (the high season on that part of the island). *Paradores* usually have 24hr. reception, daily maid service, an English-speaking staff, a restaurant, and corporate discounts; some offer tours, and most also have a pool. Located primarily in the central mountains and on the west coast, *paradores* are very popular vacation destinations for Puerto Ricans. The Puerto Rican Tourism Company web site (www.gotopuertorico.com) and *¡Qué Pasa!* magazine both have a complete list of *paradores*.

ACCOMMODATIONS FOR GROUPS

VACATION RENTALS

Travelers staying for at least three days should consider consulting a realtor for information about vacation rentals. Most vacation rentals are either winter homes that the owners rent out during the rest of the year or permanent vacation homes that realtors rent out on a rotating basis. These units range from timeshare condos in San Juan to luxurious houses on Culebra and Vieques. Most vacation rentals are quite classy and come with bedding, linens, and a fully equipped kitchen. Some also have air conditioning, pools, cable TV, and hot tubs. Always make sure you know exactly what amenities are included before reserving a vacation home, as units vary greatly and it is usually impossible to see a unit before reserving. Prices range between $100-$500 per day for anywhere from 2-6 beds. Vacation rentals rarely have daily maid service, but usually offer unparalleled privacy and a remarkably good deal for larger groups. *Let's Go* includes realtor information in San Juan, Luquillo, Vieques, Culebra, and Rincón. Many properties are also listed on the web. Try the following web sites: www.vacationhomes.com, www.prwest.com, www.surf-sun.com, and www.10kvacationrentals.com.

CABINS AND VACATION CENTERS

When Puerto Ricans travel, they frequently take the whole extended family. Several no-frills accommodations cater directly to these large groups. The Puerto Rican **Compañía de Parques Nacionales (CPN)** sponsors **centros vacacionales** (vacation centers) at beaches in Añasco, Arroyo (p. 220), Boquerón (p. 242), and Humacao, and in the forest near Maricao (p. 307). These vacation centers usually have two types of cabins. **Cabañas** are basic concrete structures with two bedrooms, bunk beds, a tiny kitchen area, no air conditioning, and no hot water. **Villas** have a similar structure, but are slightly more expensive and come with air conditioning and hot water. Almost all vacation center structures accommodate six people in a very small space. In addition to rooms, most complexes also contain a pool, basketball courts, and a large beach. These are a great bargain for groups of travelers who plan to spend most of their time outside and don't mind cramped quarters. All villas and cabins come with a full kitchen, but do not include sheets, towels, or kitchen supplies. In 2005 the National Parks Company charged $65 per night for *cabañas* or $110 for *villas* plus 9% tax, with occasional promotional discounts. During low season on the west coast (Nov.-May), it is usually possible to show up and get a room, but during major holidays (*Semana Santa* and Christmas) and summer (May-Aug.) you must reserve well in advance either at the specific vacation center or at the San Juan office of the CPN, Apartado 9022089, San Juan, PR 00902-2089 (☎787-622-5200; fax 982-2107; www.parquesnacionale-spr.com). Several private individuals have opened *cabañas* with a similar design; again, travelers must bring their own towels, linens, and kitchen equipment.

OTHER TYPES OF ACCOMMODATIONS

HOTELS

When Puerto Ricans refer to hotels, they typically mean the large American chains. These hotels are not listed in *Let's Go*, but if you feel like shelling out, most major chains have web sites with full information. **Hotel singles** in Puerto Rico cost about $200 per night, doubles $300. However, many offer discounts for military personnel, businesses, AAA members, frequent fliers, and a variety of other groups.

There are also a few **small hotels** in most urban areas (and quite a few in San Juan) that charge much more reasonable rates (singles $65-140 per night). These hotels usually have the regular amenities—bathrooms, daily maid service, 24hr. reception, sometimes continental breakfast—but few of the perks, like casinos and pools. These small hotels can fill up fast, so it is best to reserve in advance, especially during high season. Hotel employees almost always speak some English.

UNIVERSITY DORMS

Many **colleges** and **universities** open their residence halls to travelers when school is not in session; some do so even term-time. Getting a room may take a couple of phone calls and require advanced planning, but rates tend to be low and many offer free local calls and Internet access. For more information contact the University of Puerto Rico (In San Juan ☎787-764-0000, www.uprrp.edu;

Aguadilla ☎ 787-890-2681, www.uprm.edu; Bayamón ☎ 787-786-2885; Cayey ☎ 787-738-2161; Mayagüez ☎ 787-832-4040, www.uprm.edu; Ponce ☎ 787-844-8181; Utuado ☎ 787-894-2828, http://upr-utuado.upr.clu.edu), which has campuses in most major Puerto Rican cities.

HOME EXCHANGES AND HOSPITALITY CLUBS

Home exchange offers the traveler lodging in various types of homes (houses, apartments, condominiums, villas, and even castles), plus the opportunity to live like a native and to cut down on accommodation fees. For more information, contact HomeExchange.Com, P.O. Box 787, Hermosa Beach, CA 90254, USA (☎ 800-877-8723; www.homeexchange.com).

Hospitality clubs link their members with individuals or families abroad who are willing to host travelers for free or for a small fee to promote cultural exchange and general good karma. In exchange, members usually must be willing to host travelers in their own homes; a small membership fee may also be required. **GlobalFreeloaders.com** (www.globalfreeloaders.com) and **The Hospitality Club** (www.hospitalityclub.org) are good places to start. **Servas** (www.servas.org) is an established, more formal, peace-based organization, and requires a fee and an interview to join. An Internet search will find many similar organizations, some of which cater to special interests (e.g., women, GLBT travelers, or members of certain professions). As always, use common sense when planning to stay with or host someone you do not know.

LONG-TERM ACCOMMODATIONS

Travelers planning to stay in Puerto Rico for extended periods of time may find it most cost-effective to rent an apartment. A basic one-bedroom (or studio) apartment in San Juan will range $1000-1300 per month. Besides the rent itself, prospective tenants usually are also required to front a security deposit (frequently one month's rent) and the last month's rent.

There are no special requirements for foreigners renting an apartment in Puerto Rico. Because the island is a major tourist destination, almost every rental group is used to dealing with foreign renters. However, the sublet and rental markets are geared toward tourists looking for a vacation rental by the sea; it takes a little extra work to find cheaper, hole-in-the wall accommodations.

You can start your apartment search at http://puertorico.craigslist.org, www.yellowpages-caribbean.com/Countries/Puerto_Rico, or in the classifieds of Puerto Rican newspapers, such as the *Puerto Rico Herald*. Many vacation rental and real estate agencies (listed at the beginning of each major city) rent out vacation properties by the month ($1500-2000 for one bedroom) during the low season.

CAMPING

Camping in Puerto Rico can be a rewarding way to slash travel costs. Camping areas are generally in beautiful locations, either steps from the beach or deep in a tropical forest, and often offer the same views as 5-star hotels. Puerto Rico's temperate climate makes camping feasible year-round. During the winter months (Nov.-May) very few Puerto Ricans go on vacation and most of the campgrounds are completely empty. The exceptions are major holidays, such as Christmas and *Semana Santa*. During the summer months, Puerto Ricans flock to campgrounds around the island and it is advisable to make reservations in advance.

Women and solo travelers may feel less comfortable camping and should consider picking campgrounds with guards or other security measures. Camping with trusted fellow travelers is ideal. All campers should be sure to park their cars in a visible location, lock up valuables, and carry cash reserves in several places. There are two principal organizations that maintain camping areas in Puerto Rico. The **Departamento de Recursos Naturales y Ambientales** operates campgrounds at reserves primarily in the Cordillera Central, while the **Compañía de Parques Nacionales** allows camping at several of the public beaches *(balnearios)* throughout the island (see below). Puerto Rico has very few private campgrounds and those that do exist tend to be more expensive and have fewer amenities than public camping areas. There are no camping sites in the San Juan region, though some people have been known to camp illegally in the Piñones area. For more information on outdoor activities in Puerto Rico, see **The Great Outdoors**, p. 42.

DEPARTAMENTO DE RECURSOS NATURALES Y AMBIENTALES (DRNA).

Puerto Rico's DRNA operates camping areas in **Cambalache, Carite, Guajataca, Guilarte, Isla Mona, Lago Luchetti, Río Abajo, Sosúa,** and **Toro Negro.** Good news first: most DRNA campgrounds are relatively safe, well-located, and well-equipped with a gate, rustic showers, flush toilets (bring your own toilet paper), running water, covered picnic tables, outdoor grills, and trash cans. The bad news is that the camping process is enormously bureaucratic. Campers must first **get a permit** and **make a reservation** with a regional DRNA office (see list below). To get a permit, you must pay $4 per person and provide the exact dates you want to camp. DRNA officials ask that campers reserve at least two weeks in advance, but they sometimes make exceptions during low season. After obtaining a permit, campers need to check into the reserve's office during opening hours (usually M-F 7am-3:30pm) to get a key; campgrounds do not have attendants and campers use their own key for the front gate and the bathrooms. A car is required to access most DRNA camping areas. Finally, few DRNA officers speak English. If you can handle the runaround, most campgrounds are gorgeous and peaceful, especially in the slow winter months. The main DRNA office is located in **San Juan** (☎999-2200; www.gobierno.pr/drna) next to the Club Náutico on Puerta de Tierra (p. 131). Regional offices are in: **Aguadilla** (p. 271), **Arecibo** (p. 264), **Mayagüez** (p. 252), and **Ponce** (p. 201). For complete information (in Spanish), check the DRNA web site at www.gobierno.pr/drna.

COMPAÑÍA DE PARQUES NACIONALES (CPN).

The National Parks Company's oceanfront campgrounds afford travelers the opportunity to enjoy a million-dollar view for a few bucks. The CPN allows camping at seven public beaches around Puerto Rico, including **Cerro Gordo** (near Dorado), **La Monserrate** (in Luquillo), **Seven Seas** (in Fajardo), **Punta Guilarte** (near Arroyo), **Tres Hermanos** (near Añasco), **Cavernas de Camuy** (Camuy); there are also incredible beach campgrounds on **Vieques.** These campgrounds almost always consist of big grassy fields that are transformed into a sea of tents during big holidays. Camping areas usually have some type of picnic tables, outdoor showers, and flush toilets, though some bathrooms are not cleaned regularly. Only some CPN camping areas have 24hr. surveillance and unfortunately some of the others (Cerro Gordo and La Monserrate) have reputations for being less than safe. **Never camp alone at a camping area without a guard.** The CPN charges campers $10 per tent for up to six people, except at Playa Flamenco in Culebra, where prices are now $20 per tent. Fortunately, the CPN is much less bureaucratic than the DRNA and travelers can usually arrive any time and camp without a reservation. For more information contact the CPN main office in San Juan, Apartado 9022089, San Juan, PR 00902-2089 (☎787-622-5200; fax 982-2173). Spanish speakers can find additional information on the CPN web site at www.parquesnacionalespr.com.

ESSENTIALS

THE GREAT OUTDOORS

The **Great Outdoor Recreation Page** (www.gorp.com) provides excellent general information for travelers planning on camping or spending time in the outdoors.

LEAVE NO TRACE. Let's Go encourages travelers to embrace the "Leave No Trace" ethic, minimizing their impact on natural environments and protecting them for future generations. Trekkers and wilderness enthusiasts should set up camp on durable surfaces, use cookstoves instead of campfires, bury human waste away from water supplies, bag trash and carry it out with them, and respect wildlife and natural objects. For more detailed information, contact the **Leave No Trace Center for Outdoor Ethics,** P.O. Box 997, Boulder, CO 80306 (☎ 800-332-4100 or 303-442-8222; www.lnt.org).

USEFUL RESOURCES

A variety of publishing companies offer hiking guidebooks to meet the educational needs of novice or expert. For information about camping, hiking, and biking, write or call the publishers listed below to receive a free catalog.

Family Campers and RVers, 4804 Transit Rd., Bldg. #2, Depew, NY 14043, USA (☎ 800-245-9755; www.fcrv.org). Membership (US$25) includes *Camping Today* magazine.

National Geographic Society, P.O. Box 6916, Hanover, PA 17331, USA (US or Canada ☎ 800-437-5521, elsewhere 717-633-3319; www.nationalgeographic.com). Carries a selection of books and maps on the Caribbean, Puerto Rico included.

Sierra Club Books, 85 Second St., 2nd fl., San Francisco, CA 94105, USA (☎ 415-977-5500; www.sierraclub.org). Publishes general resource books ($14-20) on hiking and camping.

The Mountaineers Books, 1001 SW Klickitat Way, Ste. 201, Seattle, WA 98134, USA (☎ 206-223-6303; www.mountaineersbooks.org). Over 600 titles on hiking, biking, mountaineering, natural history, and conservation.

Woodall Publications Corporation, 2575 Vista Del Mar Dr., Ventura, CA 93001, USA (☎ 877-680-6155; www.woodalls.com). Annually updates campground directories.

NATIONAL PARKS

Puerto Rico has a system of *Bosques Estatales* (State Forests), and **El Yunque** is part of the US National Park system. The entire island of Isla Mona is a nature preserve and research center. These parks and reserves preserve Puerto Rico's amazing tropical rainforests and unique wildlife. Unfortunately, the Puerto Rican government does not have the financial resources to maintain extensive trail networks for tourists. Visitors to parks—with the exception of El Yunque, which has several well-groomed trails—must choose between sticking to a few short, paved routes or hiring a guide to take them deeper into the forest. The good news is that visitors face few environmental hazards—the biggest risk is getting lost.

There are no entrance fees for national parks, although tours and camping require small fees. The **DRNA** (p. 41) is in charge of administrating state parks and some campgrounds. The **US Fish & Wildlife Service** (www.fws.gov/southeast) is in charge of national parks.

WILDERNESS SAFETY

Staying **warm, dry,** and **well-hydrated** is key to a happy and safe wilderness experience. For any hike, prepare yourself for an emergency by packing a first-aid kit, a reflector, a whistle, high-energy food, extra water, raingear, a hat, mittens, and extra socks. Cotton is a bad choice for clothing as it dries painfully slowly.

Check **weather forecasts** often and pay attention to the skies when hiking, as weather patterns can change suddenly. Always let someone—a friend, your guest-house owner, a park ranger, or a local hiking organization—know when and where you are going. Know your physical limits and do not attempt a hike beyond your ability. See **Safety and Health,** p. 18, for information on outdoor medical concerns.

WILDLIFE

LAND ANIMALS. Puerto Rico is lucky to have very few dangerous animals. There are no poisonous snakes and the most threatening land animal is the **rabid mongoose.** This species was originally imported to control the rat population and now runs wild, especially in El Yunque. If you see a small, furry, weasel-like animal, chances are it's a mongoose. Simply walk away as quickly as possible. **Mosquitoes** and other flying nuisances are especially bothersome in rural areas of Puerto Rico and may carry tropical diseases. Insects reach peak annoyance levels between May and November and travelers will probably want to bring bug repellent containing **DEET.**

CREATURES OF THE SEA. Jellyfish and sea lice populate the seas around Puerto Rico, but few have fatal stings. To protect yourself from jellyfish stings, wear protective clothing (a wet suit or lycra) when spending extensive amounts of time in the water. The Portuguese Man-of-War has been known to inhabit Caribbean waters. Purplish-blue in color with tentacles up to 30 ft. long, the Portuguese Man-of-War also has a painful and potentially dangerous sting, which can cause anaphylactic shock, interference with heart and lung function, and even death. If you are stung by a Portuguese Man-of-War, rinse the sting with salt or fresh water and apply a cold compress to the affected area. If pain persists or if breathing difficulty develops, consult a medical professional. Shark attacks in Puerto Rico are extremely rare—Puerto Rico has had eight unprovoked shark attacks since 1749, and only two were fatal. Still, sharks—especially small nurse sharks—do patrol the Caribbean. Surfers and spearfishers are at greatest risk; swimmers are advised to stay out of the water at dawn and dusk when sharks move toward shore to feed. Experts also advise against wearing high-contrast clothing or shiny jewelry and to avoid excessive splashing, all of which can attract sharks.

CAMPING AND HIKING EQUIPMENT

WHAT TO BUY

Good camping equipment is both sturdy and light. North American suppliers tend to offer the most competitive prices.

Sleeping Bags: Most sleeping bags are rated by season; "summer" means 30-40°F (around 0°C) at night; "four-season" or "winter" often means below 0°F (-17°C). Bags are made of **down** (warm and light, but expensive, and miserable when wet) or of **synthetic** material (heavy, durable, and warm when wet). Prices range $50-250 for a summer synthetic to $200-300 for a good down winter bag. **Sleeping bag pads** include foam pads ($10-30), air mattresses ($15-50), and self-inflating mats ($30-120). Bring a **stuff sack** to store your bag and keep it dry.

Tents: The best tents are free-standing (with their own frames and suspension systems), set up quickly, and only require staking in high winds. Low-profile dome tents are the best all-around. Worthy 2-person tents start at $100, 4-person tents start at $160. Make sure your tent has a rain fly and seal its seams with waterproofer. Other useful accessories include a **battery-operated lantern,** a plastic **groundcloth,** and a nylon **tarp.**

Backpacks: Internal-frame packs mold well to your back, keep a lower center of gravity, and flex adequately to allow you to hike difficult trails, while **external-frame packs** are more comfortable for long hikes over even terrain, as they carry weight higher and distribute it more evenly. Make sure your pack has a strong, padded hip-belt to transfer weight to your legs. There are models designed specifically for women. Any serious backpacking requires a pack of at least 4000 cu. in. (16,000cc), plus 500 cu. in. for sleeping bags in internal-frame packs. Sturdy backpacks cost anywhere from $125 to 420—your pack is an area where it doesn't pay to economize. On your hunt for the perfect pack, fill up prospective models with something heavy, strap it on correctly, and walk around the store to get a sense of how the model distributes weight. Either buy a **rain cover** ($10-20) or store all of your belongings in plastic bags inside your pack.

Boots: Be sure to wear hiking boots with good **ankle support.** They should fit snugly and comfortably over 1-2 pairs of **wool socks** and a pair of thin **liner socks.** Break in boots over several weeks before you go to spare yourself blisters.

Other Necessities: Synthetic layers, like those made of polypropylene or polyester, and a pile jacket will keep you warm even when wet. A **space blanket** ($5-15) will help you to retain body heat and doubles as a groundcloth. Plastic **water bottles** are vital; look for shatter- and leak-resistant models. Carry **water-purification tablets** for when you can't boil water. Although most campgrounds provide campfire sites, you may want to bring a small **metal grate** or **grill.** For those places that forbid fires or the gathering of firewood, you'll need a **camp stove** (the classic Coleman starts at $50) and a propane-filled **fuel bottle** to operate it. Also bring a **first-aid kit, pocketknife, insect repellent,** and **waterproof matches** or a **lighter.**

WHERE TO BUY IT

The online and mail-order companies listed below offer lower prices than many retail stores. A visit to a local camping or outdoors store will give you a good sense of the look and weight of certain items before you buy.

Campmor, 400 Corporate Dr., P.O. Box 680, Mahwah, NJ 07430, USA (☎800-525-4784; www.campmor.com).

Cotswold Outdoor, Unit 11 Kemble Business Park, Crudwell, Malmesbury Wiltshire, SN16 9SH, UK (☎+44 08704 427 755; www.cotswoldoutdoor.com).

Discount Camping, 833 Main North Rd., Pooraka, South Australia 5095, Australia (☎+61 618 8262 3399; www.discountcamping.com.au).

Eastern Mountain Sports (EMS), 1 Vose Farm Rd., Peterborough, 03458 NH, USA (☎888-463-6367; www.ems.com).

Gear-Zone, 8 Burnet Rd., Sweetbriar Rd. Industrial Estate, Norwich, NR3 2BS, UK (☎+44 1603 410 108; www.gear-zone.co.uk).

L.L. Bean, Freeport, ME 04033, USA (US and Canada ☎800-441-5713; UK +44 0800 891 297; www.llbean.com).

Mountain Designs, 443a Nudgee Rd., Hendra, Queensland 4011, Australia (☎+617 3114 4300; www.mountaindesigns.com).

Recreational Equipment, Inc. (REI), Sumner, WA 98352, USA (US and Canada ☎800-426-4840, elsewhere 253-891-2500; www.rei.com).

ORGANIZED ADVENTURE TRIPS

Organized adventure tours offer another way of exploring the wild. Activities include hiking, biking, skiing, canoeing, kayaking, rafting, climbing, photo safaris, and archaeological digs. Tourism bureaus often can suggest parks, trails, and outfitters. Organizations that specialize in camping and outdoor equipment like REI and EMS (see above) also are good sources for information. One of the greatest adventures in Puerto Rico is exploring the limestone caves along the northern coast, either by foot, in a kayak, or by rapelling. See **Parque de las Cavernas del Río Camuy,** p. 268, for more information. Tours endorsed by the **Puerto Rico Tourism Company** (www.gotopuerto.com) are listed on its website. *Let's Go* also lists local tours in the **Practical Information** section in each town.

ACAMPA (☎787-706-0695; www.acampapr.com). Camping, hiking, backpacking, caving, rapelling, and customized nature tours around the island. Also offers expeditions to Isla Mona. Day tours from $85.

Adventuras Tierra Adentro, (☎787-766-0470; www.aventuraspr.com). Daytrips canyoning in El Yunque and caving in Río Camuy. $160 per person, group rates available.

AdvenTours (☎787-530-8311; www.adventourspr.com). Offers a variety of tours leaving from San Juan, Mayagüez, and Luquillo and traveling throughout the island. Activities include city tours, hiking, kayaking, biking, bird-watching, and backpacking. Also offers ecotours, and Hatha Yoga, and specialty tours to coffee plantations. Guides available in English, French, German, and sign language. Prices range $200-1000 depending on the number of days.

Caradonna Dive Adventures (☎800-328-2288; www.caradonna.com). Offers 7-night scuba dive packages at several resorts around the island for $740-1200.

Expediciones Palenique (☎787-823-4354; www.expedicionespalenque.com). Has 1-day trips to Adjuntas, Arecibo, Camuy, Ciales, Jayuya, and Utuado ($80-90), as well as 3- to 5-day backpacking and rock climbing trips ($180-250).

Las Tortugas Adventures (☎787-809-0253; www.kayak-pr.com). One of the island's most comprehensive kayak tour operators. Offers daytrips to Río Espíritu Santo, Laguna de Piñones, Fajardo's bioluminescent bay, and La Cordillera Islands. Trips cost around $40-70. Also has multi-day and snorkeling packages.

SPECIFIC CONCERNS

SUSTAINABLE TRAVEL

As the number of travelers on the road continues to rise, the detrimental effect they can have on natural environments becomes an increasing concern. With this in mind, Let's Go promotes the philosophy of **sustainable travel.** Through a sensitivity to issues of ecology and sustainability, today's travelers can be a powerful force in preserving as well as restoring the places they visit. **Ecotourism,** a rising trend in sustainable travel, focuses on the conservation of natural habitats and how to use them to build up the economy without exploitation or overdevelopment. Travelers can make a difference by doing research in advance and by supporting organizations and establishments that pay attention to their impact on their natural surroundings and that strive to be environmentally friendly.

The best way to become involved in preserving Puerto Rico's unique species of flora and fauna is to volunteer with one of the organizations listed in the **Beyond Tourism** chapter (p. 81). In general, travelers should avoid driving off-road and use public transportation or travel on foot whenever possible. Also, avoid visiting Culebra's beaches at night during turtle breeding season.

Although many companies and nonprofits in Puerto Rico claim that their activities are "ecotourism," Puerto Rico has yet to decide on a formal definition for the word. According to the Puerto Rico Tourism Company's ecotourism manager, only **Casa Pueblo** (p. 84) and the **Cabo Rojo Committee for Health & the Environment** qualify by international standards. Check out the organizations below general information on ecotourism in Puerto Rico.

ESSENTIALS

Caribbean Alliance for Sustainable Tourism, 1000 Av. Ponce de León, 5th fl., San Juan, PR 00907 (☎787-725-9139; www.cha-cast.com/). Nonprofit working with hotel and tourism sectors to reduce waste and improve land use. Lists establishments certified as "green globe."
Caribbean Conservation Corporation, 4424 NW 13th St., Ste. B-11, Gainesville, FL 32609, USA (☎800-678-7853 or 352-373-6441; http://cccturtle.org). Mainly concerned with preserving sea turtle species in the Caribbean.
Fideicomiso de Conservación (Conservation Trust), Casa Ramón Power y Giralt, 155 C. Tetuán, San Juan Antiguo, PR 00901 (☎787-722-5834; www.fideicomiso.org). A Puerto Rican private nonprofit dedicated to preserving natural land areas.

 ECOTOURISM RESOURCES. For more information on environmentally responsible tourism, contact one of the organizations below:
Conservation International, 2011 Crystal Dr., Ste. 500, Arlington, VA 22202, USA (☎800-406-2306 or 703-341-2400; www.conservation.org).
Green Globe, Green Globe vof, Verbenalaan 1, 2111 ZL Aerdenhout, The Netherlands (☎+31 23 544 0306; www.greenglobe.com).
International Ecotourism Society, 1333 H St., NW, Ste. 300E, Washington, D.C. 20005, USA (☎202-347-9203; www.ecotourism.org).
United Nations Environment Program (UNEP), 39-43 Quai André Citroën, 75739 Paris Cedex 15, France (☎+33 1 44 37 14 50; www.uneptie.org/pc/tourism).

RESPONSIBLE TRAVEL

The impact of tourist dollars on the destinations you visit should not be underestimated. The choices you make during your trip can have powerful effects on local communities—for better or for worse. Travelers who care about the destinations and environments they explore should make themselves aware of the social and cultural implications of the choices they make when they travel. Simple decisions such as buying local products instead of globally available ones, paying fair prices for products or services, and attempting to say a few words in Spanish can have a strong, positive effect on the community.

Community-based tourism aims to channel tourist dollars into the local economy by emphasizing tours and cultural programs that are run by members of the host community and that often benefit disadvantaged groups. This type of tourism also benefits travelers themselves, taking them beyond conventional tours of the region. The coastal regions of Puerto Rico and the eastern islands are heavily dependent upon tourism, particularly tours of natural areas. In general, travelers should look for tours offered by local guides, such as Tanamá Expeditions (p. 304) or Las Casas de la Selva (p. 292), rather than those run out of large hotels and resorts. The *Ethical Travel Guide* (UK£13), a project of **Tourism Concern** (☎+44 020 7133 3330; www.tourismconcern.org.uk), is an excellent resource for information on community-based travel with a directory of 300 establishments in 60 countries.

TRAVELING ALONE

There are many benefits to traveling alone, including independence and a greater opportunity to connect with locals. On the other hand, solo travelers are more vulnerable targets of harassment and street theft. If you are traveling alone, look confident, try not to stand out as a tourist, and be especially careful in deserted or very crowded areas. Stay away from areas that are not well lit. If questioned, never admit that you are traveling alone. Maintain regular contact with someone at home who knows your itinerary, and always research your destination before traveling. For more tips, pick up *Traveling Solo* by Eleanor Berman (Globe Pequot Press, US$18), visit www.travelaloneandloveit.com, or subscribe to **Connecting: Solo Travel Network,** 689 Park Rd., Unit 6, Gibsons, BC V0N 1V7, Canada (☎+1 604-886-9099; www.cstn.org; membership US$30-48).

WOMEN TRAVELERS

Women exploring on their own inevitably face some additional safety concerns, but it's easy to be adventurous without taking undue risks. If you are concerned, consider staying in hostels which offer single rooms that lock from the inside or in religious organizations with single-sex rooms. Stick to centrally located accommodations and avoid solitary late-night treks or metro rides.

Always carry extra cash for a phone call, bus, or taxi. **Hitchhiking** is never safe for lone women, or even for two women traveling together. Look as if you know where you're going and approach older women or couples for directions if you're lost or uncomfortable.

Generally, the less you look like a tourist, the better off you'll be. Dress conservatively, especially in rural areas. Wearing a conspicuous **wedding band** sometimes helps to prevent unwanted advances.

Your best answer to verbal harassment and kissing noises—both common in Puerto Rico—is no answer at all; feigning deafness, sitting motionless, and staring straight ahead at nothing in particular will do a world of good that reactions usually don't achieve. The extremely persistent can sometimes be dissuaded by a firm, loud, and very public "¡Déjeme en paz!" (Leave me alone!). Don't hesitate to seek out a police officer or a passerby if you are being harassed. Memorize the emergency numbers in places you visit, and consider carrying a whistle on your keychain. A self-defense course will both prepare you for a potential attack and raise your level of awareness of your surroundings (see **Personal Safety,** p. 19). Be sure you are aware of the health concerns that women face when traveling (p. 23).

GLBT TRAVELERS

Puerto Rico is one of the Caribbean's premier GLBT destinations. GLBT travelers should have no problems traveling throughout the island, though urban areas are more accustomed to alternative sexuality than rural areas. For the latest info on Puerto Rico's gay scene, do not miss **Puerto Rico Breeze,** a Spanish/English newsletter that includes articles, advertisements, and a calendar of events related to the island's gay scene (available at most gay-friendly establishments in San Juan). Online, check out www.orgulloboricua.net for updates on events and a forum for Puerto Rico's GLBT community. Listed below are contact organizations, mail-order bookstores, and publishers that offer related materials. **Out and About** (www.planetout.com) offers a bi-weekly newsletter and a comprehensive web site addressing gay travel concerns. The online newspaper **365gay.com** also has a travel section (www.365gay.com/travel/travelchannel.htm).

Gay's the Word, 66 Marchmont St., London WC1N 1AB, UK (☎+44 020 7278 7654; http://freespace.virgin.net/gays.theword/). The largest gay and lesbian bookshop in the UK, with both fiction and non-fiction titles. Mail-order service available.

Giovanni's Room, 345 South 12th St., Philadelphia, PA 19107, USA (☎215-923-2960; www.queerbooks.com). An international lesbian and gay bookstore with mail-order service (carries many of the publications listed below).

International Lesbian and Gay Association (ILGA), Avenue des Villas 34, 1060 Brussels, Belgium (☎+32 2 502 2471; www.ilga.org). Provides political information, such as homosexuality laws of individual countries.

ESSENTIALS

ESSENTIALS

 ADDITIONAL RESOURCES: GLBT

Spartacus 2005-2006: International Gay Guide. Bruno Gmunder Verlag (US$33). *Damron Men's Travel Guide, Damron Road Atlas, Damron Accommodations Guide, Damron City Guide,* and *Damron Women's Traveller.* Damron Travel Guides (US$18-24). For info, call ☎800-462-6654 or visit www.damron.com. *The Gay Vacation Guide: The Best Trips and How to Plan Them,* Mark Chesnut. Kensington Books (US$15). *Gayellow Pages USA/Canada,* Frances Green. Gayellow Pages (US$20). They also publish smaller regional editions. Visit Gayellow pages online at http://gayellowpages.com.

TRAVELERS WITH DISABILITIES

Puerto Rico is just as accessible to travelers with disabilities as the rest of the US. In big cities, most hotels and restaurants are wheelchair-accessible, though this may not be the case in smaller towns or rural areas. All hotels endorsed by the Puerto Rican Tourism Company (listed in *¡Qué Pasa!*) are required to have at least one wheelchair-accessible room. However, these hotels tend to be more expensive than guesthouses. Also, handicapped visitors will likely have to rent a car, as the *público* system does not accommodate such passengers, making travel around Puerto Rico more expensive. Those with disabilities should inform airlines and hotels of their disabilities when making reservations; some time may be needed to prepare special accommodations. Call ahead to restaurants, museums, and other facilities to find out if they are wheelchair-accessible. **Guide dog owners** should inquire as to the quarantine policies of each destination country.

USEFUL ORGANIZATIONS

Accessible Journeys, 35 West Sellers Ave., Ridley Park, PA 19078, USA (☎800-846-4537; www.disabilitytravel.com). Designs tours for wheelchair users and slow walkers. The site has tips and forums for all travelers.

Flying Wheels Travel, 143 W. Bridge St., Owatonna, MN 55060, USA (☎507-451-5005; www.flyingwheelstravel.com). Specializes in escorted trips to Europe for people with physical disabilities; plans custom trips worldwide.

Mobility International USA (MIUSA), P.O. Box 10767, Eugene, OR 97440, USA (☎541-343-1284; www.miusa.org). Provides a variety of books and other publications containing information for travelers with disabilities.

Society for Accessible Travel and Hospitality (SATH), 347 Fifth Ave., Ste. 610, New York, NY 10016, USA (☎212-447-7284; www.sath.org). An advocacy group that publishes free online travel information. Annual membership US$49, students and seniors US$29.

MINORITY TRAVELERS

Because the vast majority of Puerto Ricans have darker skin and are of mixed Taíno, African, and European ancestry, there is relatively little discrimination on the island. Minority travelers will most likely not experience hostility or outright discrimination, but some minor harassment is not unheard of. Most likely, minority travelers will experience more curiosity than aggressiveness.

DIETARY CONCERNS

Vegetarians will not find it easy to survive on Puerto Rican food. Traditional island food centers around meat, beans cooked with lard, and sandwiches filled with chicken, beef, or pork. In San Juan the tourist-oriented restaurants will usually have at least one vegetarian option; unfortunately, there's not much variety and these restaurants tend to be more expensive. Outside of San Juan, some options include *mofongo* without meat inside, pizza *empanadillas*, and cheese sandwiches. Most major cities have at least one vegetarian *cafetería*, but these are typically only open for lunch. Those who abstain from meat but eat fish are in luck—a variety of seafood options are available in many restaurants. Memorizing the phrases "sin carne" (without meat) and "soy vegetariano(a)" (I am a vegetarian) or "No como carne" (I do not eat meat) may also be helpful.

The travel section of the The Vegetarian Resource Group's website, at www.vrg.org/travel, has a comprehensive list of organizations and websites that are geared toward helping vegetarians and vegans traveling abroad. They also provide an online restaurant guide. For more information, visit your local bookstore or health food store, and consult *The Vegetarian Traveler: Where to Stay if You're Vegetarian, Vegan, Environmentally Sensitive*, by Jed and Susan Civic (Larson Publications; US$16). Vegetarians will also find numerous resources on the web; try www.vegdining.com, www.happycow.net, and www.vegetariansabroad.com, for starters.

Travelers who keep kosher should contact synagogues in larger cities for information on kosher restaurants. Your own synagogue or college Hillel should have access to lists of Jewish institutions across the nation. If you are strict in your observance, you may have to prepare your own food on the road. A good resource is the *Jewish Travel Guide*, edited by Michael Zaidner (Vallentine Mitchell; US$18). Travelers looking for halal restaurants may find www.zabihah.com a useful resource.

OTHER RESOURCES

Let's Go tries to cover all aspects of budget travel, but we can't put *everything* in our guides. Listed below are books and websites that can serve as jumping-off points for your own research.

USEFUL PUBLICATIONS

The following publications are available in Puerto Rico.

- ▨ **¡Qué Pasa!** (☎800-246-8677; www.gotopuertorico.com). The official publication of the Puerto Rican Tourism Company (PRTC) includes accommodations, restaurants, nightlife options, feature articles, and maps. Call to have a copy mailed home or pick up a copy at any tourist office or hotel. Free. The PRTC also publishes **Go To Puerto Rico,** another magazine describing hotels and restaurants throughout the island. Free.

- **The San Juan Star.** It may not be the best newspaper in Puerto Rico, but *The San Juan Star* is the only island paper to come out with a daily English edition. Also has a Spanish-language version. $0.45.

- **Places to Go** (www.coral-publications.com). Puerto Ricans' favorite travel guide is a color brochure listing hotels and restaurants in every city on the island. Available in English and Spanish at most tourist businesses and offices on the island. Also publishes the less-popular *Bienvenidos* magazine. Free.

- **El Boricua** (www.elboricua.com). A monthly bilingual publication on Puerto Rican cultural and current events. Publishes the work of Puerto Rican poets.

- **Puerto Rican Telephone Tourist Quick Guide** (www.superpagespr.com). It's hard to find, but this is one of Puerto Rico's most helpful publications. Includes tourism-related articles and an abbreviated version of the Yellow Pages designed for tourists. Free.

ESSENTIALS

WORLD WIDE WEB

Almost every aspect of budget travel is accessible via the web. Listed here are some regional and travel-related sites to start off your surfing; other relevant websites are listed throughout the book. Because website turnover is high, use search engines (e.g., www.google.com) to strike out on your own.

 WWW.LETSGO.COM Our website features extensive content from our guides; a community forum where travelers can connect with each other, ask questions or advice, and share stories and tips; and expanded resources to help you plan your trip. Visit us to browse by destination and to find information about ordering our titles.

THE ART OF TRAVEL

BootsnAll.com: www.bootsnall.com. Numerous resources for independent travelers, from planning your trip to reporting on it when you get back.

How to See the World: www.artoftravel.com. A compendium of great travel tips, from cheap flights to self defense to interacting with local culture.

Travel Intelligence: www.travelintelligence.net. A large collection of travel writing by distinguished travel writers.

Travel Library: www.travel-library.com. A fantastic set of links for general information and personal travelogues.

World Hum: www.worldhum.com. An independently produced collection of "travel dispatches from a shrinking planet."

INFORMATION ON PUERTO RICO

Caribbean National Forest: www.southernregion.fs.fed.us/caribbean/index.htm. The official web site of El Yunque, with flora and fauna descriptions, forest facts, and recreation information.

CIA World Factbook: www.odci.gov/cia/publications/factbook/index.html. Tons of vital statistics on Puerto Rico's geography, government, economy, and people.

Escape to Puerto Rico: http://escape.topuertorico.com. A variety of island-specific info, including a current events discussion forum, Puerto Rico e-cards, a search engine for island restaurants, and a history quiz.

Geographia: www.geographia.com. Highlights, culture, and people of Puerto Rico.

Music of Puerto Rico: www.musicofpuertorico.com. The ultimate site for anything you ever wanted to know about Puerto Rican music, including sound clips of popular songs in every genre.

PlanetRider: www.planetrider.com. A subjective list of links to the "best" websites covering the culture and tourist attractions of Puerto Rico.

Puerto Rico Herald: www.puertorico-herald.org. The island's only online English-language newspaper. A great source for current events.

Puerto Rico Magazine: www.prmag.com. Puerto Rico's first online travel magazine. Includes photos, maps, travel tips, island info, travel stores, and an online chat room.

Super Pages: www.superpagespr.com. Puerto Rico's Yellow Pages search engine.

US State Department: www.state.gov. Information about the current governmental initiatives in the US (of which Puerto Rico is a commonwealth) as well as passports, visas, and other entrance requirements.

World Travel Guide: www.travel-guides.com. Helpful practical info.

LIFE AND TIMES

Puerto Rico's history is a lesson in absorption, a brilliant mosaic of the cultures that have influenced its traditions for nearly two millennia. The **Igneri** people were among the first to populate the island, migrating upward from Venezuela; later on, the Native American **Taíno** civilization gave the island the name of **Borikén**, the origin of the modern-day term *Borinquén*, an affectionate name for Puerto Rico. West Africans, who came to Puerto Rico both as slaves and free persons, introduced the beat of **bomba y plena** and the religious tradition of **Santería**. Perhaps the most influential people to inhabit Puerto Rico were the Spanish colonists, who forcefully left the island with the legacy of the **Spanish** language, **Roman Catholicism**, the music of **danza** and **décima**, and traditional Spanish foods, such as **flan** and **bistec empanado**. The perceived importance of Puerto Rico's Hispanic heritage is one of the reasons Puerto Ricans have consistently voted against becoming a US state. Despite their diverse heritage, Puerto Ricans are clearly united by their love of *Borinquén Querida* (beloved Puerto Rico) and are happy to introduce visitors to the wonders of their island home.

LAND

The island of Puerto Rico lies where the Caribbean Sea meets the Atlantic Ocean, 123 mi. southeast of Florida, between the **Greater Antilles** to the west and the smaller islands of the **Lesser Antilles** to the east. Besides the main island, four smaller islands are also included in Puerto Rico's land area—**Isla Mona** and **Isla Desecheo** to the west and **Vieques** and **Culebra** to the east. While the main island only measures 100 mi. east to west and 35 mi. north to south, it has a whopping 700 mi. of coastline—good news for visitors seeking sand and surf.

Three primary geographic regions cover Puerto Rico: the mountainous interior, the coastal plains, and the northern plateau (karst country). The mountainous **interior,** dominated by the **Cordillera Central,** occupies 75% of the island's land area and includes Puerto Rico's highest peak, **Cerro de Punta** (1388m). It is surrounded by **coastal plains**—the most fertile land on the island. In the past, most crops were grown in this area; however, only 5% of the island is arable and today less than 1% of the island's gross domestic product (GDP) comes from agriculture. Northern Puerto Rico is studded with rugged **karst country,** where water has dissolved limestone to form a series of narrow canyons and deep **caves** (p. 268). In this environment, the underground **Río Camuy** has created the third-largest system of subterranean caves in the world (p. 268). In contrast, the south and southwest coasts feature a dry, desert terrain.

Puerto Rico contains over 1000 **streams** and 45 **rivers,** but they are all relatively small and unnavigable. No significant natural lakes exist on the island, but several rivers have been dammed to create artificial reservoirs. As a result of its strategic position at the mouth of the Caribbean, Puerto Rico (literally "rich port") has several shipping **ports;** Ponce and Mayagüez are among the largest.

CLIMATE

It's not hard to guess why many North Americans spend the winter here. The mild, **tropical climate** is pretty much perfect year-round. The locals start grumbling when the temperature falls below 70°F. Even winter cold fronts, called

nortes, only drop to about 60°F. The temperature does vary slightly around the island; temperatures in the mountains usually hover about 5-9°F lower than those on the coast (see **Climate Chart,** p. 309). Northeasterly trade winds drop all of the rain on the northern side of the island before clouds hit the mountains, leaving the south relatively arid and dry. Officially, the **dry season** runs from November to March, although on most of the island there is no distinguishable difference between the two seasons. It can rain all year round, usually in fifteen- to twenty-minute spurts at a time.

The more important season to keep in mind is **hurricane season,** which officially runs from June 1 to November 30 but only poses a significant threat from August to October. Hurricanes have plagued Puerto Rico throughout its history, destroying crops and taking lives—in fact, the word "hurricane" derives from the Taíno name for the god of winds and destruction, Jurakán. On average, a hurricane brushes by San Juan every 3.85 years. Hurricane Georges, the worst storm in recent history, hit on September 21, 1998, and caused almost $2 billion in damage.

FLORA AND FAUNA

PLANTS

PLANT HABITATS. Due to industrialization, the vast majority of primary forest on Puerto Rico has been destroyed; however, much of it has been recultivated and **national reserves** now protect a full 5% of Puerto Rican land. **El Yunque** (p. 150) contains 75% of the island's scant virgin forest, including orchids, giant ferns, bamboo, and 240 species of trees. The reserve has both a high altitude cloud forest and a slightly lower altitude **rainforest,** consisting of sierra palms and epiphytes, plants that use other plants to climb high into the canopy. **Subtropical wet forests** abound at even lower elevations and, strangely, on mountains above 3000 feet. This vegetation, including open-crowned and canopy trees, can be found at **Reserva Forestal Toro Negro** (p. 299) and **Bosque Estatal de Guilarte** (p. 306). At an even lower elevation, **subtropical moist forest**—most adapted to flooding caused by hurricanes—is the most common type of vegetation on the island; it can be found in **Bosque Estatal de Guajataca** (p. 277). Southwest Puerto Rico is covered by an entirely different dry forest, defined by low rainfall and arid vegetation, including bunch grass and many varieties of cacti. Although it's not indigenous, the brightly colored **flamboyán tree** is one of the most famous plants on the island. The flowering tree blooms from June to August at elevations below 2000 ft., especially along the **Ruta Panorámica** (p. 290). Several types of **mangroves** grow on the calm waters around the southwest coast, the east coast, and Vieques. Mangroves develop extensive root systems that attract corals, sponges, oysters, and many fish.

ENDANGERED PLANTS. Puerto Rico is home to over 40 species of endangered trees, ferns, cacti, and orchids. However, it is often difficult to identify endangered species, which are only distinguishable from their relatives by subtle physical variations. One of the easiest endangered plants to identify is the **Higo Chumbo** cactus. Now found only on the islands of Mona, Monito, and Desecheo, it is a narrow, night-blooming cactus that produces green, cone-shaped flowers.

ANIMALS

COMMON ANIMALS. Don't come looking for lions, tigers, and bears—because of Puerto Rico's volcanic origins, most animals reached the island by swimming, flying, or floating. The most famous animal in Puerto Rico is the **coquí**, a one-inch-long tree frog famous for its loud, distinct "ko-kee" call. Of the 16 species of *coquí*, 13 are endemic to Puerto Rico. The *coquí* is quite a tease—the first syllable of the famous *coquí* call serves as a warning for other frogs to go away, but the second sound, the "kee," serves as an invitation for females to come reproduce. Puerto Ricans love their little mascot, and the *coquí*'s image appears on merchandise throughout the island. The frogs themselves reside in any forest area. Beyond that, Puerto Rico is home to hundreds of bird species and a variety of reptiles native to the island's various habitats.

Many of Puerto Rico's unique animals do not make their home on the island itself. The seas around Puerto Rico are teeming with manta rays, octopi, barracudas, bananafish, and nurse sharks, among others. The **coral reefs** that surround the island make for lively underwater communities of fish, crustaceans, and echinoderms—perfect for travelers interested in snorkeling and diving. In Vieques, Fajardo, and La Parguera, mangroves support populations of tiny, luminescent creatures called **dinoflagellates;** when the water is disturbed by a boat or swimmer, these critters make the seawater around them glow (see **Swimming in Stardust,** p. 183). Farther offshore, **humpback whales** are often sighted en route to their breeding grounds in the Virgin Islands between December and May.

Puerto Rico's most incredible wildlife is found on small **Isla Mona,** 50 mi. west of the mainland. This uninhabited island is home to an astounding 700 species of animals, including the 4 ft. **Mona iguana** and **Isla Mona boa,** neither of which is found anywhere else in the world. The island is often referred to as the Galapagos of the Caribbean (p. 246).

ENDANGERED ANIMALS. One bird of note, the **Puerto Rican parrot,** is among the 10 most endangered species in the world—the population once dropped as low as 14 parrots. Scientists have been working for 40 years to save the species, which initially declined due to deforestation and intense human population growth. Initial results have been moderately successful; in 2006 alone, 42 new birds were born in captivity and approximately 20 were released into the wild from captivity breeding programs. The Puerto Rican parrot—identifiable by its bright green body, red forehead, wide white eye-rings, and its noisy squawks and squeals—can be found in El Yunque. On the island of Culebra, endangered **leatherback** and **hawksbill sea turtles** come ashore to lay their eggs. Leatherbacks are the largest variety of sea turtles, reaching up to six feet in length and weighing close to a ton. Hawksbills are slightly smaller, weighing in at about 300 pounds, and can be identified by their beak-like mouths and colorful, patterned shells. Visitors should never disturb turtle nests and should not visit the beaches at night.

DANGEROUS ANIMALS. Travelers are advised to be wary of **mongeese**—small, furry mammals that look like weasels—as they have been known to carry **rabies. Tarantulas, scorpions,** and **centipedes** found in the forest may sting, but are only harmful to travelers with allergies to these creatures. There are no poisonous snakes in Puerto Rico.

A non-dangerous but certainly pesky creature prevalent on Puerto Rican beaches is the **sand flea.** These tiny, remarkably mobile insects emerge around dusk and leave behind a myriad of itchy bites as unsolicited souvenirs of your sunny day. Cover your legs and leave beaches before dark to avoid them. Other seaside bothers include small jellyfish.

LIFE AND TIMES

HISTORY

BEFORE THE SPANISH (PRE-1493)

AD 300
The Igneri populate the island.

AD 1000
The Taínos refer to their island home as "Borikén," which means "land of the lords."

1300s
The violent Caribs land on Puerto Rico, threatening the Taínos' lordship.

1492
Christopher Columbus first sails the ocean blue.

The first inhabitants of the area now known as Puerto Rico, the Arcaicos, likely came to the island from North America and settled around Loíza. They were soon followed by the Igneri people, who came up from Venezuela around AD 300 and inhabited the coastal areas. However, the Ostinoids replaced both of these tribes; by AD 1000, the Ostinoids had evolved into the Taíno civilization, the most influential group in the island's ancient history. Known for making grinding tools and jewelry, this peaceful people lived in communities of 300 to 600 inhabitants, governed by one *cacique* (chief). Their name for the island, Boriquén (Borinquén, or Borikén), is a term still used proudly and affectionately by Puerto Ricans today. After nearly 500 years alone on the island, the Taínos were attacked by the **Caribs** of South America. This invasion sent many Taínos scrambling to the central mountains in retreat, a precursor to the more lasting invasions that the near future would hold.

THE SPANISH EMPIRE IN THE NEW WORLD (1493-1835)

1493
After a successful first try, Columbus takes another crack at it—this time prepared for colonization with 17 ships and 1500 men. He happens on Puerto Rico.

1508
Juan Ponce de León gives up on the fountain of youth and settles for *La Isla Encantadora.*

1510
Taíno chief Urayoán commands his warriors to drown Spaniard Diego Salcedo to determine if the Taínos' Spanish conquerors are immortal. As it turns out, they are not.

1518
Portuguese and Dutch ships bring the slave trade to Puerto Rico.

CARIBBEAN TREASURE: A RICH PORT. Puerto Rico changed forever on November 19, 1493, when **Christopher Columbus,** representing the Spanish government, landed on the island during his second exploratory trip to the New World. After dubbing the island "San Juan Bautista," Columbus promptly moved on in search of greater treasures. One man on this initial voyage, however, didn't dismiss the island so quickly: the famed **Juan Ponce de León** returned in July 1508 to settle down for good. The Taínos, possibly looking for allies against the Caribs (or possibly living up to their peaceful reputation) were hospitable to Ponce de León and allowed him to explore the northern coast in search of gold. On August 12, 1508, the Spaniard established the first European settlement on the island, **Caparra.**

This peaceful arrangement did not last. Under the auspices of the *Repartimiento de Indos* (Distribution of Indians) ordinance, Ponce de León instituted a system to control the native population by selecting an *hidalgo* (aristocrat) to control each village, encouraging intermarriage between Europeans and Taínos, and converting the local population to **Catholicism.** This plan was intended to civilize the Taínos and prepare them to be slaves for the Spaniards. Needless to say, the island's 30,000 Taínos did not find the arrangement nearly as agreeable as the Spanish did—a sentiment that only deepened when the natives began dying from **smallpox, whooping cough,** and other European diseases. In 1511, the Taínos joined with their erstwhile enemies, the Caribs, to rebel against the Spaniards. However, they could not hold out against the European pistols, and by 1550 the few indigenous peoples who remained retreated to the central mountains.

MORE TROUBLE IN PARADISE. Meanwhile, the Spaniards were facing their own problems confronting the difficulties of life in the yet-undeveloped Caribbean. The island was plagued by persistent disease, unreliable crops, and hurricanes. Soon, too, the Spanish discovered that the flat, swampy terrain of the Caparra settlement exposed residents to both malaria-carrying mosquitoes and human attacks. They therefore moved the capital to an island in front of a large, protected bay—the future San Juan. (In an unexplained mix-up, the capital city took the island's name and the island became "Puerto Rico.")

When the Spaniards realized that other European powers might attack the island in an attempt to disrupt Spanish trade, they constructed several forts, including **La Fortaleza** (p. 117), **El Morro** (p. 116), and **San Cristóbal** (p. 117). This foresight prepared the Spanish for strikes by French, English, and Dutch forces. Most of the attackers didn't get beyond the forts of San Juan; those with the ingenuity to attack other spots on the island were quickly conquered by tropical diseases. At this time the Spanish also began importing West African slaves to replace the labor of the rapidly dwindling native population.

THE EMERGENCE OF A PEOPLE. Bound by the rules of a mercantile economy, Puerto Rican islanders traded only with the Spanish, sending raw materials to Spain and receiving finished goods in return. Because the Spanish levied heavy taxes on Puerto Rican products, the Spanish profited while the islanders lived in poverty. To remedy the situation, inhabitants outside of San Juan, hidden from the watchful eye of the Spanish, began clandestine trade with other nations. When Spanish royalty got wind of this illegal trade in the 1760s, it sent Irish-born Spaniard **Alejandro O'Reilly** to put an end to it. Upon arrival, O'Reilly found a population of 50,000 people with no government infrastructure. He responded by lowering taxes, building roads and schools, and developing the sugar cane industry. The changes were a success: within 50 years the population tripled and a Puerto Rican identity began to develop.

A REVOLUTIONARY WORLD. In the late eighteenth century, the eruption of revolutions all over Latin America would irrevocably, though indirectly, shape Puerto Rico's future. A 1791 slave rebellion on the nearby island of Hispaniola caused foreign nations to turn to Puerto Rico for sugar and rum imports; this marked the beginning of the island's close relationship with the US. By 1830 the population had soared to 330,000, and Puerto Rico and Cuba were the only two remaining Spanish colonies. The Spanish monarchy's fear of losing the islands prompted a series of reforms. In 1809 Puerto Rico was officially allowed to send a non-voting representative to the Spanish *Cortes* (Parliament), and the mercantilist trade system slowly came to an end as Spain cut tariffs and opened ports to foreign trade. Many white Spaniards migrated to the island and developed an agricultural industry, with large haciendas producing the cash crops of **sugar cane, coffee,** and **tobacco.**

LIFE AND TIMES

1522
Iglesia San José is founded. It is now the oldest church still in use in the US.

1533
The Spaniards begin constructing La Fortaleza to protect the island from English, Dutch, and French invaders—but construct it too far inland.

1539
The Spaniards realize their mistake and begin constructing El Morro.

1600-1785
Twelve hurricanes strike the island.

1809
Puerto Rico finally gets a representative in the Spanish *Cortes* (parliament).

1835
For the first time, Puerto Ricans lead a minor revolution against Spanish rule.

1873
Slavery is abolished in Puerto Rico.

1897
Luis Muñoz Rivera requests Puerto Rico's independence—and his wish is granted. Who knew all he had do was ask?

1898
Puerto Rican members of the Cuban revolutionary movement correspond with President McKinley in hopes of being included in US plans to attack Spanish colonies.

1898
The US wins the Spanish-American war and takes control of Puerto Rico.

FROM COLONY TO PROVINCE TO NATION TO COLONY (1835-1898)

REVOLUTIONARY PUERTO RICO. In spite of these preventative measures, a minor revolution erupted in 1835, and three years later native islander **Buenaventura Quiñones** was exiled for planning a second revolution. An uprising initiated in the town of Lares in September 1868 declared the island a republic and elected a president, but failed to gain popular support and faded after a month and a half. Perhaps the most lasting contribution of the movement was the rallying cry "Viva Puerto Rico Libre!" which became known as the **Grita de Lares** (Cry of Lares). These revolutions failed, but changes came about nonetheless. In late September 1868, the Spanish military overthrew the monarchy and a civil war broke out in Cuba. Consequently, Madrid felt the call to improve its relationship with Puerto Rico. Over the next 20 years, Puerto Ricans were granted the right to participate in the Spanish parliament, to form municipal councils, and to develop political parties. Moreover, the island finally achieved the status of a "province."

A TEMPORARY VICTORY. In 1881, the election of the liberal **Práxedes Mateo Sagasta** as prime minister of Spain marked a new era in the country's governance. Taking advantage of this opportunity, Puerto Rican **Luis Muñoz Rivera,** leader of the Autonomist Party, went to Madrid to politely ask for Puerto Rico's independence. In 1897, Mateo Sagasta granted Puerto Rico political and administrative autonomy but retained a military presence on the island. For the next year, Puerto Rico enjoyed a brief stint as a relatively independent state.

ENTER THE US. Meanwhile, Spain was battling rebel forces in Cuba and their supporters in Puerto Rico. Independence fighters looked to the increasingly powerful US for assistance and began corresponding with US President **William McKinley.** On February 15, 1898, the **US battleship Maine** mysteriously exploded in Havana's harbor. Although the accident remained a mystery, American journalists blamed the Spanish and public opinion persuaded McKinley to press for war. McKinley requested that Spain withdraw immediately from Cuba, and on April 20, 1898 the US Congress authorized the use of force in the Caribbean.

US troops attacked San Juan on May 12, 1898 with limited success, but within three months the Spanish forces surrendered in Cuba and the war was essentially over. When US troops landed at Guánica on July 25, the Spaniards barely put up a fight. Consequently, on December 10, 1898, Spain signed the **Treaty of Paris,** which granted Cuba independence and ceded Puerto Rico and Guam to the US. Puerto Rico was subject to outside government once again.

SUGARVILLE, USA (1898-1942)

A ROCKY START. The first two years of American control were a difficult time for the Puerto Ricans. Inhabitants of the island who had hoped for greater liberty under US control were disappointed when the US government placed Puerto Rico under **military rule** and limited free speech in the press. Additional problems ensued when the Americans mandated that Puerto Rico separate the **Catholic Church** from the state, which in turn necessitated a complete restructuring of the religion-based educational system. On the economic front, American corporations bought out local businessmen in hopes of taking over the sugar and tobacco industries. To make matters worse, a hurricane devastated crucial coffee crops in 1899. The Americans did provide food, import new vaccines, and build a network of roads on the island, but the first two years of US rule were as rough as any the island had previously experienced.

THE BOOM... This tenuous situation could not last, and in 1900 the US passed the **Foraker Act,** which formally established a governor for the island, appointed by the US president, who would control a house of delegates (with elected representatives) and an upper legislature (with appointed officials). Residents of Puerto Rico would be taxed according to US laws, but they would not be considered American citizens. The 1917 **Jones Act** expanded the legislature to two houses of elected representatives and gave Puerto Ricans American citizenship—coincidentally, just before they would be eligible for the WWI draft.

At this time, the island experienced an economic boom. As a result of the fact that Puerto Rican industry was not taxed or charged duties for trading with the US, American investment increased. The Puerto Rican sugar industry grew, and by 1920 75% of islanders depended on sugar for their livelihood. Wages rose, disease decreased, education expanded, the government spent $50 billion on developing roads, and the population was increasing rapidly.

...AND THE BUST. Everything came crashing to a halt in the 1930s. Devastating hurricanes in 1928 and 1932 ruined the agricultural income; then, the Great Depression came rolling onto the island. As unemployment rose to 65%, many Puerto Ricans attempted to solve their problems by migrating to the US. Others became increasingly dissatisfied with US control and joined the independence movement. The **Puerto Rican Nationalist Party** (Partido Nacionalista Puertorriqueño; PNP), headed by **Pedro Albizu Campos,** led protests for Puerto Rican independence. In 1936, the party was set back when four members were killed and others were jailed for murdering a chief of police, but the demonstrations continued. A year later, at the **Masacre de Ponce,** 19 people were killed at a PNP protest.

A more peaceful solution to the island's problems emerged in 1938 when **Luis Muñoz Marín** (grandson of revolutionary

1900
The US government appoints Puerto Rico's first governor.

1903
The Universidad de Puerto Rico is founded.

1917-1919
20,000 Puerto Ricans fight under the US flag in WWI.

1929
The Great Depression sends Puerto Rico's economy into a tailspin.

1934
The US mandates that Puerto Rican sugar production must be cut in half—a bitter pill to swallow.

1938
Luis Muñoz Marín founds the Popular Democratic Party, which later favors commonwealth status.

LIFE AND TIMES

1940s
President Franklin Delano Roosevelt encourages economic development in Puerto Rico with Operation Bootstrap.

1948
Puerto Rico participates in its first Olympic games with its own team but with the US flag as its banner. The resulting controversy spurs the commonwealth to choose a Puerto Rican flag.

1952
Puerto Rico officially becomes a commonwealth of the US.

1954
In the name of independence, several Puerto Ricans open fire in the US House of Representatives.

1967
For the first time, Puerto Ricans are allowed to vote on their status—and the majority chooses a commonwealth.

Luis Muñoz Riviera; see p. 56) founded the **Popular Democratic Party** (Partido Popular Democrático; PPD). Marín was less concerned with the status of the island as a colony than he was about improving the quality of life for Puerto Ricans. This plan was well received; in 1940, the PPD won control of the legislature and Muñoz Marín became president of the senate. With this position he attempted to end the sugar monopolies and diversify the economy. Though Muñoz Marín took the first steps toward reviving the economy, it would take a powerful outsider to finish the job.

OPERATION SAVE PUERTO RICO (1942-1999)

LET THE GOOD TIMES ROLL. In the early 1940s a few changes permanently transformed Puerto Rico, "the poorhouse of the Caribbean," into a developed area. The first was that Americans began to drink rum when WWII cut off their whiskey supply. Suddenly rum became a major Puerto Rican export. The second, much more significant change, came when American President **Franklin Delano Roosevelt** devised a plan to shift the island's economy away from agriculture toward the more lucrative manufacturing and tourism industries. This was **Operation Bootstrap,** the most successful economic revival campaign in the island's history. The American government encouraged US manufacturers to move to Puerto Rico, where revenue was partially free from US income tax and cheap labor was available. By 1964, over 2000 American companies had relocated to Puerto Rico. Net income per capita soared from $121 in 1940 to $1900 in the early 1970s. **Tourism** boomed and Puerto Rico entered the fast lane.

OFFICIAL STATUS AT LAST. Political improvements soon followed. In 1948, the US offered the island a constitutional government that Puerto Ricans approved in a 1951 vote, and in 1952 Puerto Rico became an official **commonwealth of the US.** As a commonwealth, Puerto Rico was similar to a US state, but residents could not vote in presidential elections, were not represented in Congress, and did not pay income taxes. Many Puerto Ricans, especially *independentistas* (supporters of independence), protested the island's new status. These opponents attempted to assassinate both Muñoz Marín and US President **Harry Truman** by opening fire on the governor's mansion on the day the bill was signed, July 25, 1952. Two years later, they started shooting in the US House of Representatives, reviving the old Cry of Lares as they shouted "Viva Puerto Rico Libre!" The attack wounded five American legislators.

The violence subsided, but the issue continued to loom large in Puerto Rican politics as two parties competed for power. The **New Progressive Party** (Partido Nuevo Progresista; PNP), founded in 1968, advocated for statehood; the PPD supported the commonwealth; and a small but vocal minority continued to argue for independence. In 1962, responding to this controversy, Muñoz Marín and US President **John F.**

Kennedy created a **"three-point program"** that would first study the benefits of the options and then allow Puerto Ricans to vote on the issue. In July 1967, with voter turnout lowered to 65.8% by *independentista* boycotts, 60.5% of Puerto Ricans voted to maintain commonwealth status, 38.9% cast their ballots for statehood, and .06% voted for independence.

During this time, Operation Bootstrap continued to support Puerto Rico's economy, generating improvements in education, literacy, life expectancy, and wages. Combined with a growing tourism industry of 100,000 visitors per year, this made the 1960s a time of plenty in Puerto Rico.

THE SHIFTY SEVENTIES. Puerto Rico's economic health declined throughout the 1970s as the US recession increased the cost of imported fuels and consumer goods. Unemployment on the island rose to an astounding 25% in 1975.

TERROR AND TRAGEDY. Controversy wracked the island in 1978 when two alleged terrorists, both under 25 years old, were shot and killed by policemen on the mountaintop of **Cerro Maravilla** (p. 300) as they were attempting to blow up a television tower as a sign of support for independence. In his 1980 reelection campaign, governor Carlos Romero Barceló called the policemen who were involved heroes and used the incident to further his political agenda, but an investigation later uncovered that the boys had surrendered and were kneeling when the police shot them. Ten members of the Puerto Rican police were convicted and many regard the event, though tragic, as a triumph of the Puerto Rican legal system.

ENVIRONMENTAL AND MILITARY CONCERNS. Environmental issues became prominent due to continued population growth and industrial pollution. New organizations developed around these issues, such as the **Conservation Trust of Puerto Rico,** a nonprofit created to protect the island's natural resources, and the **Departamento de Recursos Naturales y Ambientaloo (DRNA),** a government run organization that oversees most of the island's nature reserves and protected areas.

The foremost issue of the 1980s became the US military presence on the island. Puerto Rico's strategic position at the edge of the Greater Antilles and its proximity to Cuba made it an ideal site for the American military. The two most prominent bases were the **Roosevelt Roads Naval Station,** located on the eastern coast, and the enormous naval base that occupied two-thirds of **Vieques** until 2003. Puerto Ricans protested the bases from the start, and alarm grew throughout the 1980s when nuclear weapons were placed on the island.

MORE VICTORIES FOR THE COMMONWEALTH. In March 1998, the US House of Representatives narrowly passed a bill finally allowing Puerto Rico to have a federally authorized binding referendum on statehood status—if the advocates of statehood won, then Puerto Rico would be admitted into the Union. However, on December 13, 1998, when the vote was held, almost 80% of the population turned up to vote and 51% chose to retain commonwealth status.

1971
The US Army takes over the much of the island of Culebra for training and testing purposes.

1998
Hurricane Georges devastates Puerto Rico, causing $2 billion in damage.

1999
A stray naval bomb on Vieques accidentally kills civilian guard David Sanes, spurring public unrest.

2000
Sila Calderón is elected the first female governor of Puerto Rico.

2006
Puerto Rico takes the Miss Universe title—again.

2007
Congress calls for a plebiscite on the issue of commonwealth status.

LIFE AND TIMES

commonwealth or colony

Puerto Rico's Convoluted Relationship with the US

Tourists are often surprised to hear Spanish spoken on the streets of Puerto Rico. Puerto Ricans, patriotically known as Boricuas (for the indigenous name of the island, Borikén) are US citizens, but many identify themselves as part of a Latin American nation that is divided between support of the status quo, statehood, and independence. The political status issue brings Puerto Ricans to an intense debate—elections regularly draw 80% voter participation.

In its 1952 constitution, Puerto Rico was labeled a Commonwealth or, as it is called in Spanish, *Estado Libre Asociado* (ELA; Free Associated State). To many, the ELA is a misnomer; Puerto Rico—an unincorporated territory of the US since 1898 and one of the longest standing colonies on earth—is neither free nor a state, and it lacks the power of a true "associate." Puerto Rico's economic dependency on the US interferes with the resolution of the ever-present political status problem.

Both the right-wing statehooders (who want Puerto Rico to become the 51st US state) and the left-wing *independentistas* (who favor Puerto Rico becoming an independent country) denounce the exploitation brought on by the colonial status of the island. Statehooders and the center-right status quo supporters differ only in their conception of the degree of political autonomy to be surrendered in exchange for US economic benefits. In their campaigns, all three groups emphasize the preservation of Puerto Rican nationality and culture, including the Spanish language, the Puerto Rican flag, and Puerto Rican representation in the Olympics and the Miss Universe pageant.

After four centuries under Spanish rule and one century under US influence, Puerto Ricans (on the island and in the US) are proud of their resistance and of their flexibility as a people. The Puerto Rican celebration of American Independence Day on July 4th can seem particularly confusing to outsiders. Some Puerto Ricans cheer for the US liberation from British colonial domination, while others demand the same freedom for Puerto Rico.

The environmental and economic effects of interactions with the US have been devastating. While multinational corporations profit $26 billion annually from the island, 60% of Puerto Ricans live in poverty. Additionally, the per capita income is a third of the US average, or half that of the poorest state in the US. Many US industries have polluted the land and water with impurities. Fertile agricultural lands have been paved over in order to build giant car lots, shopping malls, and housing developments. Puerto Rico has been forced to rely on imports, and town centers are dying out as local merchants fail to compete with Wal-Mart.

With no vote in the US Congress or the UN, Puerto Rico has been repeatedly utilized as an "Experimental Island." In places like Vieques and El Yunque Rainforest, the US military has experimented with live artillery, napalm, and uranium.

> ## "Puerto Ricans are proud of their resistance and their flexibility as a people."

After decades of being not-quite-equal "associates" with the US, Puerto Ricans remain divided to this day as to what the best political alternative is. The historical tension of a US-Puerto Rico relationship that seems unjust to some, but convenient or indispensable to others, has become part of daily life for Puerto Ricans.

The outcome of this struggle for definition remains to be seen. The Puerto Rico Democracy act of 2007 calls for a new plebiscite on the question of Puerto Rican independence, to be held by 2009.

Iliana Pagán Teitelbaum received her BA in Latin American Studies from the University of Puerto Rico. She is currently finishing her dissertation and expects to receive a PhD in Romance Languages and Literatures from Harvard University.

PUERTO RICO TODAY

In 2000, Puerto Ricans elected the island's first female governor, **Sila Calderón,** who focused her campaign on the US military presence in Puerto Rico and especially on the island of Vieques. In April 1999 a bombing accident on the island accidentally killed a Puerto Rican security guard, prompting extensive protests. Finally, in June 2001, US President **George W. Bush** announced that the Navy would leave **Vieques** by May 2003. The Navy kept its end of the bargain, but chose in 2004 to also close the **Roosevelt Roads Navy Base,** dealing a tough blow to the island's economy with the loss of 6000 jobs. The unexploded bombs and other environmental hazards left on Vieques prompted Calderón to call for the former bombing range to be placed on the US **Environmental Protection Agency (EPA)** Superfund National Priorities list of most hazardous waste sites. In 2005, the EPA took this step, and a clean-up of the former Navy sites is in progress.

In the 2004 elections, former Puerto Rican Congressman **Aníbal Acevedo Vilá** of the PPD defeated former Governor Pedro Rosselló of the PNP to assume the Governor's seat. The excruciatingly narrow margin of victory, 0.2% of the vote, produced a politically contentious recount. In the same election, the PNP party was given a majority in the Puerto Rican legislature, splitting control of the government. Under Acevedo Vilá's watch, the US Congress passed the **Puerto Rico Democracy Act of 2007,** calling for a plebiscite to be held on the question of Puerto Rican independence no later than December 1, 2009. In this vote, Puerto Ricans will choose between continued territorial status for Puerto Rico or pursuit of a path toward non-territorial status as a US state or its own sovereign nation. The revival of this question, combined with upcoming gubernatorial elections and an **unemployment rate** still hovering around 10%, shows that Puerto Rico has many domestic issues to confront as it looks toward the future.

GOVERNMENT

On July 25, 1952, Puerto Rico officially became a commonwealth of the United States. Ever since, people have been asking, "What does that mean?" In many ways Puerto Rico resembles a state: the national American government handles foreign relations, defense, the postal service, and customs; Puerto Ricans are US citizens who are eligible for the draft; and the commonwealth is led by a **governor** who is popularly elected to a four-year term. Like the US's, the Puerto Rican government is divided into **executive, legislative,** and **judicial branches,** with the executive governor choosing a cabinet and the judicial branch consisting of one supreme and many superior courts. However, some crucial differences fuel the intense debate over potential statehood status. Although Puerto Rico sends a representative to the US House of Representatives (until 2008 the seat will be held by **Luis G. Fortuño** of the PNP, now a candidate in the 2008 gubernatorial election), this representative cannot vote. While Puerto Ricans are citizens, they cannot vote in US presidential elections and they don't have to pay federal taxes.

Additional aspects of Puerto Rico's government differ from a US state more in details and name than in functionality. The legislative branch of the government consists of two houses elected to four-year terms on the same cycle as the governor. In an interesting quirk, at least one-third of the legislators must be from the minority party. If that does not happen, the houses are enlarged to make space for more representatives. Until November 2008, **the PNP will control both houses of the legislature;** this may change after the November elections. On a more local level, the island is divided into 78 municipalities, each with a mayor and an assembly.

LIFE AND TIMES

THE POLITICAL PARTIES OF PUERTO RICO. When conversing with locals, knowledge of the Puerto Rican political parties will quickly prove that you're the most educated tourist around. And it ain't that hard:
New Progressive Party (*Partido Nuevo Progresista*; PNP). Endorses statehood.
Popular Democratic Party (*Partido Popular Democrático*; PPD). Supports comonwealth status.
Puerto Rican Independence Party (*Partido Independentisto Puertorriqueño*; PIP). Endorses independence.

ECONOMY

Puerto Rico is the economic success story of Latin America, thanks to Operation Bootstrap. Within 60 years, Puerto Rico transformed from one of the poorest islands in the Caribbean, with a single-crop agricultural economy, to one of the most prosperous, with a diversified industrial economy. The US is by far the island's largest trading partner and major exports include apparel, electronics, rum, and pharmaceuticals—Puerto Rico produces 50% of US pharmaceuticals. Today, the $74.9 billion GDP breaks down as 54% services, 45% industry, and 1% agriculture. Increasing tourism has also played an important role in Puerto Rico's economic success.

But life on the island isn't all peachy. With a **per capita GDP** of **$19,100,** Puerto Rico remains much poorer than even the poorest US state. Unemployment hovered around 10% in 2007, over twice as high as the mainland. So while Puerto Ricans certainly have nothing to complain about in comparison to some countries in Latin America, it's not easy being the underdeveloped cousin of the US.

PEOPLE

DEMOGRAPHICS

Like most Latin Americans, Puerto Ricans are an ethnic mix of their Spanish, African, and Native American ancestors. Today, 80.5% of islanders identify themselves as white (of primarily Spanish origin), 8% as black, 0.4% as Native American, 0.2% as Asian, and the remaining 10.9% as mixed or other. However, almost everyone on the island has a dark complexion and darker hair, regardless of their self-classification. The island's African heritage is most prominent on the coast, especially in the town of Loíza, and people of Native American ancestry remain predominantly in the central mountains. Since Puerto Rico was too poor a country throughout much of its history to afford many African slaves, Puerto Rico's strong African cultural heritage stems more from free blacks than from slaves. Racial discrimination is rare in Puerto Rico.

Puerto Rico's population is most notable for its sheer size—the island is one of the most densely populated regions in the world. This population trend began in the early 19th century, when many Latin Americans immigrated to Puerto Rico in order to escape revolutions in their own countries. A high birth rate continued to push population numbers up until the mid 20th century. After the beginning of Operation Bootstrap, the birth rate began to decline, but the death rate also declined and life expectancy rose accordingly—keeping population numbers steady. Furthermore, as Puerto Rico became relatively prosper-

THE MOST BEAUTIFUL WOMEN IN THE WORLD. Do we have your attention yet? Like many Latin American countries, Puerto Rico hosts a plethora of beauty pageants, and the island prides itself on producing some of the most beautiful females in the world. Almost every major island festival elects some sort of queen or princess; the *crème de la crème* go on to represent Puerto Rico in the annual **Miss Universe** pageant, where the island has met with incredible success. Puerto Rico has had an unheard-of five wins throughout the pageant's history, the most in recent in 2006. Clearly, it's more than nature that makes Puerto Rico the *Isla Encantadora*.

ous, residents of neighboring islands Cuba and Hispaniola (especially the Dominican Republic) began immigrating in floods. The resulting population of around 4 million (as of the July 2007 estimate) on an island only three times as large as Rhode Island produces a staggering population density of 1127 people per square mile, higher than any of the 50 US states. Luckily, the annual growth rate has finally fallen to 0.393% and the population seems to be leveling off.

Operation Bootstrap encouraged Puerto Ricans to move to the cities, and today 71% of the population lives in urban areas, with almost one-third of the total population residing in the greater San Juan area. Currently, upwards of three million Puerto Ricans live in the US, at least one third of them in New York City (the so-called "Nuyoricans").

LANGUAGE

Spanish and English are both official languages of Puerto Rico, but the vast majority of islanders prefer to speak Spanish. In San Juan almost everyone speaks English, but it is polite for visitors who speak some Spanish to initiate conversations in that language; many Puerto Ricans will answer in English. English continues to be much less common in rural areas of the island, but because almost everyone in the tourist industry speaks English, non-Spanish speakers are not likely to have problems getting around.

The issue of language plays an important role in Puerto Rico's relationship with the US, since many Puerto Ricans oppose statehood because they do not want to sacrifice their Hispanic culture. In 1991, when statehood once again dominated the headlines, the Puerto Rican government abolished English as an official language in an attempt to prevent US cultural domination. The legislature revoked this policy two years later, but only after making a strong statement that Spanish is in Puerto Rico to stay.

RELIGION

Eighty-five percent of Puerto Ricans remain true to their Spanish roots and identify themselves as Roman Catholic, although most major religions are represented on the island. As a commonwealth of the United States, Puerto Rico maintains a strict separation of church and state. **Santería,** a blend of Catholicism and the religion of the Yoruba people who were brought to the Caribbean as slaves from Nigeria, continues to be important to the island's African community. *Santería* first emerged in the slavery era when Africans continued practicing their own religions but substituted the names of Catholic saints to appease their masters. Practitioners of *Santería* generally worship a hierarchy of saints and believe that it is possible to foretell the future.

FRUITS OF PARADISE

Puerto Rico is full of *batida* (smoothie) and *piragua* (shaved ice) stands that offer fruity refreshment to thirsty passersby. However, some popular Puerto Rican fruits may be unfamiliar to visitors from outside the Caribbean:

Acerola: Known to some in English as the West Indian cherry or haw fruit, the *acerola* is a soft, bright red fruit that tastes like a cross between an apple and a cherry. It is one of the more common fruit juices on the island.

Parcha: The *parcha*, or passion fruit, has a tart taste that mixes well with the sweeter elements of *batidas*. The fruit has a hard purple or yellow rind, with many black seeds inside.

Guanábana: In English, soursop. The Puerto Rican variety is the largest type. The fruit has a white, pulpy interior; the shape of a pear; and the skin of a lime. It can be identified by its acidic, fruity flavor with hints of nuts.

Guayaba: Guava, round with yellow skin and pink flesh, offers a sweet and slightly acidic kick when its juice is added to drinks. The many hard seeds make it difficult to eat the fruit itself.

Plátanos: Plantains look like large, rough bananas, but the similarities end there. Raw, green plantains, known as *verdes,* have a slightly bitter, crunchy taste. Deep-fried and mashed plantains, which can appear as *amarillos* (sweet variety) or *tostones* (dry variety) taste like a hearty bread.

CULTURE

FOOD

The wealth and diversity of restaurants in Puerto Rico, and especially San Juan, make it easy to visit the island without ever sampling regional cuisine. Don't make that mistake. Though similar to many other Latin American cuisines, Puerto Rican food (**comida criolla**) offers a unique blend of spices, textures, and tastes.

MAIN DISHES. The Puerto Rican day starts with **desayuno** (breakfast), a casual meal enjoyed before work frequently in a **cafetería.** For many locals, breakfast consists of a cup of hot coffee with milk and toast. Most restaurants also serve a larger American breakfast, including fried eggs, scrambled eggs with ham, bacon, oatmeal, pancakes, and, from Spain, *tortillas españolas* (Spanish omelets; a mix of eggs, potatoes, and onions). Unlike Americans, Puerto Ricans also enjoy a good sandwich for breakfast.

Sandwiches are some of the cheapest ways to fill up for **almuerzo** (lunch) as well. Puerto Rican sandwiches are typically served on *pan de agua*, a fresh, tasty, local version of French bread, and made with meat, cheese, lettuce, tomato, and mayonnaise or butter, then grilled in a press and served hot. Local favorites are the *cubano* and the *media noche*, two sandwiches made with roasted pork, *pepinillos*, ham, and swiss cheese. The local fast-food chain **El Mesón Sandwiches,** based in Aguadilla, makes terrific sandwiches and has a couple of vegetarian options.

Most Puerto Ricans head to a *cafetería* or an American fast-food restaurant for a quick lunch on the go. A traditional lunch includes a heaping pile of rice, either plain or served with pigeon peas, chickpeas, or red beans. Next is the meat; some common options include: *biftec encebollado* (strips of beef with onions), fried pork chops, fried chicken, chicken breast, breaded Spanish steak, and fried seafood. Finally, add either *tostones* (dry, fried plantains; good with salt or hot sauce) or *amarillos* (fried sweet plantains) and a small salad to complete the meal.

Cena (dinner) tends to be a more formal affair eaten at home with the family; smaller towns may not have any restaurants open late at night except fast food. You can't leave Puerto Rico without trying the famous *mofongo*, mashed plantain served with meat or fish inside. This traditional dish has been referred to as "the poor man's food" (despite the fact that it can be quite pricey), and one serving will leave you stuffed for days. **Soups** are another popular option—many are hearty enough to serve as a meal themselves. *Asopao* is a thick stew served with fish or chicken and occasionally pigeon peas. *Soncocho* is a salty, thinner fish soup. Travelers with adventurous palates may want to try less conventional options such as *sopón de garbanzos con patas de cerdo* (chickpea soup with pig feet).

Puerto Ricans love their **seafood**, though it's surprisingly expensive given that the nation is surrounded by water. The unofficial national fish is red snapper, served in most nice restaurants as a whole fish, head and all. On the coast you will find an abundance of seafood restaurants serving up shrimp, conch, octopus, trunk fish, crab, and, of course, lobster.

A few popular **spices** dominate Puerto Rican cuisine. The basic flavoring of most stews and soups is *sofrito*, olive oil seasoned with sweet chili peppers, onions, bell peppers, tomatoes, cilantro, oregano, and garlic. Meat dishes are typically marinated with the more simplified *adobo*, a mixture of vinegar, oil, black pepper, oregano, salt, and garlic. Many cooks also add a bit of *achiote*, a cooking oil made out of annatto seeds, to give the food a slight orange tint.

Vegetarians will have a hard time sampling local cuisine. Most beans are cooked with pork, many dishes are fried in lard, and almost everything comes with meat inside. There are **vegetarian cafeterías** in most big cities, but these typically only stay open for lunch. Puerto Rican restaurants can usually conjure up some type of vegetarian option, but be prepared for less-than-inspiring plain *mofongo* and frozen vegetable medleys.

SNACKS. Puerto Rico is not the place to travel if you want to lose weight, as it's hard to resist the delectable **fried snacks.** Roadside stands, food kiosks, and some restaurants sell *empanadillas*, fritters filled with meat, seafood, or cheese. For even more calories, try an *alcapuria*, fried plantains stuffed with beef or pork, or a *pinono*, a fried plantain wrapped around ground beef. To round out the fried family, *sorullitos de maíz* are tasty fried sticks of ground corn. Puerto Ricans go crazy for *pinchos*, hunks of meat barbecued on a stick like a kebab.

A couple of popular **frozen snacks** provide a great way to cool off during the day. Street vendors, mostly in big cities, sell *piraguas*, shaved ice with flavored syrup on top. Private individuals put up signs advertising the sale of *limbers*, frozen fruit juice. Puerto Ricans also enjoy **pastries**, and at any *repostería* you'll find *quesitos* (long pastries filled with white cheese) and *pan mallorca* (sweet bread).

DESSERTS. The combination of Puerto Rico's Latin heritage and its plethora of fresh fruits make for some delicious post-meal treats. The most common dessert is the popular *flan* (egg custard), served plain or with coconut or vanilla flavoring. Another dessert common throughout Latin America is *tres leches*, a sweet cake covered with condensed milk sauce. The **fruit** in Puerto Rico (see **Fruits of Paradise,** p. 64) is so tasty that it is often served for dessert; look for *guayaba con queso* (guava with cheese). Puerto Ricans also serve a variety of fruit-flavored *helado*, a smooth **ice cream** that resembles Italian *gelato*.

EATERIES. The cheapest place to dine is at one of the many **panaderías y reposterías** (bakery and pastry shops) found throughout the island. The local eateries generally have long hours (typically open daily 7am-9pm), but rarely have English menus, and many are so small that they don't have tables. Another cheap option is the ubiquitous *cafetería,* found even in Old San Juan. At some *cafeterías*—at least those open for lunch only—you order from the glass counter filled with steaming hot entrees. The *cafeterías* that are also open for dinner and breakfast are often informal sit-down restaurants with $5-6 lunch specials. Formal, sit-down restaurants are the most expensive option; even outside of San Juan it's hard to find an entree for less than $12. The Puerto Rican Tourism Company has recognized many of the best **comida criolla**

LIFE AND TIMES

YO HO HO AND A BOTTLE OF RUM

Rum is the drink of choice in Puerto Rico. The following beverages may tempt you to try a little of the local spirit:

Piña Colada. Supposedly invented on the island, it requires 1½ oz. white rum, 1 oz. coconut cream, 2 oz. pineapple juice, and ice. Blend well, then throw on a pineapple or cherry for garnish.

Coquito. Named after the island's tiny frogs, Puerto Rico's Christmas concoction makes an excellent drink year-round. For a full batch, mix 28 oz. coconut milk, 14 oz. condensed milk, 2 egg yolks, 2 cups of Bacardi rum, and blend well.

Puerto Rican Sunrise. This Puerto Rican version of the popular tequila sunrise is refreshingly easy to make. Mix equal parts of white rum with orange juice and grenadine, then stir. For a tropical twist, replace the orange juice with passion fruit juice.

Cuba Libre. The name may be Cuban, but this common drink is popular on the island of enchantment. Plus, it's one of the easiest mixed drinks to make—just mix rum and Coke, and add a lime. The quantities are up to your discretion.

Caribbean Seas. Hurricane season may bring dark and stormy waters, but this delicious drink is nothing but clear, blue waters. Start with 2 oz. rum and 3 oz. of Blue Caracao, 1 oz. sour mix, and a splash of Sprite and orange juice.

restaurants around the island as **mesones gastronómicos.** These fancy eateries are a great place to splurge on a quality Puerto Rican meal; check *¡Qué Pasa!* (p. 21) for a complete list.

RUM

AND (SOMETIMES) OTHER BEVERAGES. Rum is more than a drink in Puerto Rico; it's part of Puerto Rican identity. In the early 20th century, Puerto Rico's thriving sugar industry produced truckloads of rum. Though the sugar industry has since declined, the rum industry continues to thrive with sugarcane from the Dominican Republic. The three primary brands produced in Puerto Rico are **Bacardi, Don Q,** and **Palo Viejo.** Bacardi has been based in Puerto Rico since the 1959 Cuban Revolution and continues to be the world's best-selling rum (p. 141). However, Puerto Ricans prefer the older Don Q, which is still produced near **Ponce** at the Serallés Distillery. Rum connoisseurs declare that Palo Viejo, though not as popular, is the best Puerto Rican rum. The perennial bar favorite is the **Cuba libre,** commonly known as a rum and Coke. And, of course, Puerto Rico is the birthplace of the **piña colada,** a mix of rum, pineapple juice, and coconut juice. During the Christmas season, locals make **coquitos,** a mix of eggnog and rum named after the island's favorite frog. Over the last few years, new **alcohol taxes** have considerably raised the price of drinking, but that hasn't seemed to stop anyone.

But one can't survive on rum alone; sometimes Puerto Ricans drink **beer** as well. The locally produced **Medalla,** a light beer, is the cheapest and most authentic option. When it's too early for alcohol, many Puerto Ricans enjoy their **café con leche,** coffee served with lots of milk and sugar. Although coffee production has decreased greatly over the last 50 years, the towns of **Yauco** and **Maricao** are still known for their fine brews. Another popular beverage is **mavi,** a sweet, fermented drink made from the bark of a mavi tree and often served out of a large barrel.

CUSTOMS AND ETIQUETTE

Though many Puerto Ricans have spent time in the US, most retain a more Latin American sense of customs and etiquette. Puerto Ricans are generally very polite and friendly to travelers who treat them with similar respect. Most go out of their way to welcome foreigners.

GREETINGS. The common greetings in Puerto Rico are *buenos días* (good morning; used anytime before lunch), *buenas tardes* (good afternoon; before dinner), and *buenas noches* (good night; after dinner). It is polite to begin every conversation, in a personal or professional setting, with these phrases. Female friends often greet each other with a peck on the cheek or a quick hug. Sometimes men shake hands with women in a business situation, but the standard greeting between a man and a woman is a quick kiss on the cheek.

MEALTIME. Unless otherwise stated, Puerto Rican restaurants expect customers to come in and seat themselves. However, American chains in Puerto Rico (Chili's, Pizzeria Uno's, Denny's) generally ask that customers wait to be seated. Most waiters say **buen provecho** (enjoy your meal) when they deliver food. It is polite to say *buen provecho* to anyone already eating when you enter a restaurant that is not too crowded, especially smaller Puerto Rican establishments. Waitstaff expect a 15% tip for sit-down service (20% for good service in a city), but it is unnecessary to tip at most *panaderías*. Customers sitting down and eating at any restaurant (even a *panadería*) should pay after they eat, unless a sign says otherwise.

TIMING. Puerto Ricans, especially those outside San Juan have a much more laid-back sense of time than most Europeans and North Americans. Things get done when they get done. Restaurants, bars, and clubs in Puerto Rico **do not maintain strict closing hours.** Most will stay open as long as people are still around, even if this means staying open until 8am. On the flip side, if an establishment is empty, it will likely close early. Smaller establishments, even museums and stores, frequently change opening hours and will close if someone who's supposed to work happens to be sick or unavailable. Maintain some patience and a sense of humor, and you will appreciate Puerto Rican culture in its full authenticity.

CHURCHES. It is respectful to wear pants or a skirt and cover your shoulders when visiting Catholic churches in Puerto Rico. Church workers and worshippers also appreciate quiet voices.

THE ARTS

For a small island, Puerto Rico lays claim to a remarkably impressive tradition of art and culture. The **Instituto de Cultura Puertorriqueña** (www.icp.gobierno.pr), founded in 1955, has worked over the last 60 years to preserve Puerto Rico's cultural heritage for the public. This organization runs many of the island's museums. Check their online calendar for a list of upcoming events.

VISUAL ART

HISTORY. San Juan's new **Museo de Arte De Puerto Rico** (p. 128) is the island's manifestation of a rich tradition of visual art. Most Puerto Rican artists have been strongly influenced by the island, and their works tend to focus on the nature, history, and culture of Puerto Rico. The first prominent Puerto Rican artist, **José Campeche,** was born in 1751 in San Juan as the son of a freed slave. Despite the fact that he never left Puerto Rico to train in the European schools, Campeche became an internationally renowned artist. Some of his most important works include: *San Francisco, San Juan Bautista,* and *La Sacra Familia*. The next prominent Puerto Rican artist, **Francisco Oller,** studied in Paris and was deeply influenced by the 19th-century Impressionist movement, particularly the work of Paul Cézanne. Upon returning to Puerto Rico in 1853, Oller used these European styles to portray nationalist scenes of Puerto Rican lands and people. In addition to depicting Puerto Rico's flora and fauna, Oller also painted works of social commentaries about life on the island, including *El Velorio* (*The Wake;* 1893), a representation of a child's wake. Oller's hometown, Bayamón, maintains a museum devoted to the great painter (p. 148), and many of his works can be found in San Juan's Museo de Arte.

As Puerto Rico's economy began to flourish in the 1940s, so did its art scene. Around this time, the government began subsidizing **poster art**, graphic arts that dealt with social and political themes on the island. Later this material was used to produce announcements for cultural events and festivals. Prominent poster artist and painter **Lorenzo Homar** worked with fellow artists to found the **Centro de Arte Puertorriqueño** (Center for Puerto Rican Art), designed the symbol for the Institute of Puerto Rican Culture, and established and ran a graphic arts workshop at the Institute. Pennsylvania native **Jack Delano** was captivated by the spirit and poverty of the island when he visited Puerto Rico in 1941; since then, Delano has published several books of island photography.

TODAY. Though he was born in Brooklyn, **Rafael Tufiño Figueroa** moved to La Perla at an early age and is considered to be one of the island's most important contemporary artists. Tufiño used his background as inspiration to paint scenes of poverty in Puerto Rico. In one of his most famous works, *La Perla* (1951), Tufiño uses strong colors and lines to depict life in San Juan's most infamous slum. *Luquillense* artist **Tomás Batista** (1935) is one of the first Puerto Ricans to become famous for sculpture, primarily woodwork. Trained in New York and Spain, Batista has spent much of his artistic time creating busts of notable Puerto Ricans whom he had admired during his childhood, such as Eugenio de Hostos and Ramón Emeterio Betances. Batista has also created many of the statues adorning plazas in cities around the island, including Río Piedras, Ponce, and Luquillo.

ARTS AND CRAFTS

The sheer number of artisans at any island festival demonstrates that *artesanía* is alive and well in Puerto Rico. One common form of folk art is the **santo**, a small religious figure carved out of wood by a *santero*. The tradition of making *santos* began in the 16th century, when Spanish Catholic colonizers placed saints on their mantels to protect their homes from harm (see **Santos de Palos,** p. 72). *Santos* vary greatly: larger ones are placed in churches while smaller ones remain in the home. A high-quality *santo* is more complex yet still carved out of one piece of wood. *Santos* can be found at many tourist shops in Old San Juan as well as at almost any crafts fair.

Another popular Puerto Rican craft is the **vejigante mask,** a colorful mask with horns worn during **carnaval** celebrations. Some historians believe that *vejigante* mask-making originated in Spain, where the *vejigante* represents the Moors who fought with St. James. Others believe that it came from Africa with the slaves. Regardless, the art form now integrates both African and Spanish influences in a uniquely Puerto Rican tradition. There are two types of *vejigante* masks, each associated with a regional *carnaval* celebration. In **Ponce,** the masks are made out of **papier-mâché** and contain larger horns painted with bright colors, frequently red and black (the colors of Ponce) or yellow and red (the colors of the Spanish flag). In the small northern town of Loíza the masks are made out of **coconut shells** and have smaller horns, teeth made out of bamboo, and exaggerated features to frighten spirits. Both types of masks are worn with a coverall outfit featuring wide sleeves designed to look like wings. Several stores in Old San Juan and Ponce sell authentic *vejigante* masks, which start at around $25, but be prepared to shell out more for masks that are larger, have more horns, or are made by famous artists.

Finally, Puerto Ricans also excel in the art of **mundillo,** an elaborate kind of lace originally from Spain. Women spend hours and even days crocheting the intricate lace, which is then used to make baby clothes, doilies, hats, or other items. This tradition is found primarily in the northwestern town of **Moca** (p. 278), where visitors can find *mundillo* makers at work in their homes. You can also stop by the Museo de Arte in San Juan (p. 128) to see the world's largest piece of *mundillo*.

LITERATURE

Puerto Rico's literary tradition originated in the mid-19th century, when people began writing about social and political themes distinct to the island. The first noted Puerto Rican author, **Manuel Alonso Pacheco,** is best remembered for his work *El Jíbaro* (1849). This half-prose, half-poetry work discussed the life of rural peasants. **Alejandro Tapía y Rivera,** contemporary to Pacheco and namesake of Old San Juan's theater, was known primarily as a playwright but also composed the allegorical poem *The Satanic: Grandiose Epic Dedicated to the Prince of Darkness* (1874). However, the most internationally well-known author during this era was philosopher, teacher, and political activist **Eugenio María de Hostos,** who composed everything from social essays to children's stories. He spent his life traveling throughout Latin America working for reform and the independence of Puerto Rico and Cuba. During this time he wrote his famous book *La reseña historia de Puerto Rico* (*The Recent History of Puerto Rico;* 1873).

Puerto Rican literature shifted focus after the American occupation of the island. During the first few decades of the 20th century the so-called **Generation of '98** began writing about the juxtaposition of American influence and traditional Latin American life. Most of these writers, including **Cayetano Coll y Toste, José de Diego,** and **Luis Muñoz Rivera,** were better-known for their political work, but a few became renowned for their literary talents as well. In 1898 **Manuel Zeno-Gandia** penned Puerto Rico's first novel, *La charca* (The Pond), a story about the difficulty of life in the countryside.

The literary scene shifted after the Depression with the **Generation of the 30s.** The movement was ushered in by academic **Antonio S. Pedreira,** whose book *Insularism* (1934) looked at Puerto Rican values and culture under the influence of the US. Novelist **Enrique Laguerre** wrote on similar themes, focusing on the decline of Puerto Rico's agriculture. Around this time **Julia de Burgos** emerged as Puerto Rico's most famous female poet. After personally distributing her first works around the island and then moving to the US, de Burgos attained international acclaim for her English-language poem *Farewell from Welfare Island* (1953).

In the mid-20th century, Puerto Rican literature focused its critical lens on the lives of Puerto Ricans in New York. Foremost among this trend was Nuyorican **Pedro Juan Soto,** who authored *Spiks* (1956) and *Usmail* (1958). In the latter half of the 20th century, a number of Puerto Rican playwrights started turning the themes of identity into dramatic works. **René Marqués** gained notice for his play *La Carreta* (*The Oxcart;* 1970), which depicts a poor mountain family in Puerto Rico and their immigration to New York. Puerto Rico's most recent player in the international literary scene is **Esmeralda Santiago,** a Nuyorican who narrates her Puerto Rican childhood in *When I Was Puerto Rican* (1993).

MUSIC

From the gentle rhythm of salsa to the relentless beats of reggaeton, this tiny island plays a disproportionately large role in the international music scene.

SALSA

The history of salsa is an unwilling love story between Cuban beats, Puerto Rican rhythms, and New York streets. Both Cubans and Puerto Ricans would like to claim sole inventorship of this contagious music, but most can agree that the popular genre originated among Caribbean immigrant populations in New York in the 1950s and only came to be identified by the term *salsa* ("sauce," referring to music that literally spices things up) in the 1970s. Over the last 50 years, salsa has evolved into the most popular form of music in Puerto Rico.

WHAT STARTS AS MAMBO... Throughout the 1920s Puerto Ricans and Cubans immigrated en masse to New York, and they brought their music with them. In the 1940s, Latin music became increasingly popular and mambo developed as a combination of Cuban, Dominican, and Puerto Rican rhythms with American jazz and big band music thrown in. The undisputed king of this era was Puerto Rican **Tito Puente,** who founded an orchestra in New York. Other popular Puerto Rican artists of the 1940s included Tito Rodríguez, Charlie Palmieri, and Rafael Muñoz.

...SOON BECOMES SALSA. By the 1960s, New York was in love with the Caribbean-influenced music. Big bands used congas, *timbales,* bass, *güiro* (an openended wooden box with a wooden striker), bells, bongos, maracas, drums, a horn section, and several singers to create a new, rhythmic sound. As the music became increasingly popular, the word "salsa" surfaced. In 1962, Joe Cuba released a song claiming that you need "salsa" to dance; this is the first recognized mention of the word *salsa* in relation to music. After Carlos Santana released the disc *Oye Como Va* in 1969, Latin music swept across the mainland, and there was no turning back. In 1976 Billboard published a 24-page article on the salsa explosion, solidifying salsa's position as a recognized musical genre.

Although it has had its ups and downs in the US, salsa has been a consistent driving force in Puerto Rico's music scene. In 1962 El Gran Combo brought New York sounds of salsa to Puerto Rico and continued producing hits for the next 30 years. Gilberto Santa Rosa has been another consistently popular Puerto Rican salsa star. Despite the fact that the younger generation is turning to more contemporary music, such as rap and reggaeton, salsa continues to constitute a significant sector of Puerto Rican music. Current popular Puerto Rican salsa artists include Ismael Miranda, Tito Nieves, and Cheo Feliciano.

REGGAETON

Chances are, if you've heard of Puerto Rican music, then you've heard of reggaeton. In fact, even if you haven't heard of Puerto Rican music you've probably heard of reggaeton. This popular brand of music, a blend of Jamaican and Panamanian reggae, hip hop, bomba y plena, and dancehall music, came to maturity in garage recording studios throughout Puerto Rico during the 90s. This was the music of the post-salsa generation, often referred to as the underground, featuring explicit lyrics and topics ranging from drugs and violence to poverty, friendship, and sex. The music's overwhelming beat and its catchy melodies have catapulted it to worldwide acclaim, despite initial misgivings of more traditionally minded listeners. Popular artists include pioneering producers **Luny Tunes** as well as Puerto Ricans **Don Omar, Calle 13, Wisin y Yandel,** and the ubiquitous **Daddy Yankee.**

CLASSICAL

DANZA. For centuries, Puerto Rican musicians were influenced by Spanish classical music traditions. In the mid-19th century, they began incorporating Caribbean rhythms to create *danzas,* a uniquely Puerto Rican style of minuet or waltz with an Afro-Caribbean slant. *Danza* spread to urban areas throughout the late 19th century, becoming Puerto Rico's most popular form of music and one of the first genres of island music to be recognized internationally. Many *danzas* continue to be popular today, including the island's national anthem **La Borinqueña.**

THE 20TH CENTURY. Puerto Rico's music scene changed forever when Spaniard **Pablo Casals** immigrated to Puerto Rico, his mother's homeland, in 1956. The talented cellist, composer, and conductor founded the renowned **Casals Classical Music Festival** (p. 134) in 1957, then served as the first conductor of the **Puerto Rican Sym-**

phony Orchestra. The orchestra continues to perform 48 weeks per year, primarily in San Juan's Luis Ferré Centro de Bellas Artes (p. 133). In 1959, Casals recruited a prestigious faculty to teach at Puerto Rico's first music conservatory, which continues to produce talented musicians today. Other notable contemporary Puerto Rican composers include **Roberto Sierra, Ernesto Cordero,** and **Luis Manuel Alvarez.**

FOLK

Salsa may be better-known internationally, but the real heart of Puerto Rico's music scene lies in its folk legacy. First popularized in the countryside, the island's folk music borrows from **Spanish and Moorish traditions.** It centers on the **décima,** a 10-line rhyming verse with six to eight syllables per line. These stanzas can be either traditional songs or improvised, but both usually tell some kind of story about love, tragedy, or life lessons. The most common type of décima is the **seis,** a simple melody performed with one or two singers, a row of male dancers facing a row of female dancers, and a band consisting of a *cuatro* (a Puerto Rican guitar), a *güiro* (a percussion instrument made of a gourd), a *tiple* (another type of Puerto Rican guitar), and sometimes bongo drums, maracas, claves, and a bass.

BOMBA Y PLENA

Puerto Rico has two traditional forms of music that originate directly from the island's African population. **La Bomba** came from Africa in the late 17th century and became especially popular in the small, primarily Afro-Caribbean town of Loíza. In this complex song and dance, a group of people create a circle around three different drums. Everyone takes turns drumming and dancing in the center; a **caller,** or main singer, is echoed by the larger chorus as dancers take turns moving to the rhythm of the drums. In some regional variations only women or only men sing, but the basic idea remains the same. The best place to experience *bomba* music is at Loíza's carnival in late July (p. 146). **La Plena** originated in the southern sugarcane zones around Ponce in the early 20th century and served as a form of protest for peasants of all races. Referred to as a **periódico cantado** (a sung newspaper) the *plena* usually discusses, and sometimes satirizes, current events. In a *plena*, one primary caller sings and then a chorus responds, but unlike the *bomba*, the *plena* does not require dancing. The most important instrument for singing a *plena* is the *pandero*, a handheld drum that looks like a tambourine without the bello; other common instruments include *cuatros*, *güiros*, guitars, accordions, cowbells, and maracas. In the 21st century, the *plena* has emerged as a popular expression of Puerto Rican culture.

POP

When the **Latin Invasion** hit the United States in the late 1990s, most of the invaders came from Puerto Rico. Long popular throughout Latin America, Puerto Rican **Ricky Martin** hit the English-language market with his hit single *Livin' La Vida Loca* (1999). When Martin shook his bonbon at the 1999 Grammys, the world became transfixed, even though Martin had been performing since 1984 as a member of the boy band **Menudo,** Puerto Rico's version of the Backstreet Boys. Celebrity couple **Marc Anthony** and **Jennifer Lopez** are also of Puerto Rican descent and started their careers singing in Spanish. The local band **Algarete** has won many Puerto Rican hearts, although the four Boricuas have not yet made it in the international music scene.

FILM

The first Puerto Rican movie appeared in 1912 when **Rafael Colorado D'Assoy** produced *Un drama de Puerto Rico.* However, not much came of the island's film industry until the 1950s, when *Maruja* was the first film to be distributed in the US. Other important films of the era included *Una voz en la montaña* (1952),

LIFE AND TIMES

santos de palos

Traditional Art in the Context of Modern Culture

Sometime in the first two weeks of December, *santeros* (artisans who create the wooden saint figurines called *santos de palo*) congregate in the small mountain town of Orocovis to celebrate the historical practice of saint carving. Puerto Rico's tradition of saint carvings was inherited from Spain as part of the Catholic legacy. Originally, 16th-century Spanish clergy used polychrome sculptures and paintings to educate and convert. It is unclear when individuals began to make carvings, though some families, such as the Espadas, are known to have specialized in religious images during the 17th and 18th centuries. It was not until the 19th century that local carvers became firmly established.

Orocovis is home to one of the most talented and prolific carving lineages on the island, the Avilés family. There are at least three generations of carvers in the family, and the oldest living member, Don Ceferino Avilés, has been recognized by the Smithsonian as a master artisan. The family serves as the focal point of the festival, which brings together both established artisans and novices, as well as people coming to see and buy the carvings.

The carvings emphasize each saint's personal attributes. Such unique traits can include a miracle or important event related to the saint, the specific causes for which the saint is invoked, or even the instrument used to martyrize the saint. Thus, Saint Francis is accompanied by birds or small animals (he is the patron saint of animals), Saint Barbara holds a sword (she was decapitated by one), and Saint John the Baptist is accompanied by a lamb and water (referencing his baptism of Jesus).

Initially, these small carvings were placed on a shelf or small niche in the bedroom or living area of the home. They were sold by the carvers who traveled through the countryside peddling their wares and offering repair and paint services for saints in need. Because of the saints' power as inter-

mediaries, the carvings became objects of devotion and veneration. Thus, it was common for owners to have the saint repainted once a year before the saint's day, or as a way of showing gratitude when favors were conceded.

Today, the import of these figurines and the art of carving them continues to evolve. No longer just devotional, carvings provide a medium for social and political expression as well. Take, for instance, the numerous representations of saints supporting the cause of peace and freedom for Vieques. And while carving was once a male-dominated art, the emergence of women carvers has become a strong trend since the mid-1980s. In fact, there is a separate, all-female festival in the spring. Both women from established artisan families and newcomers have been able to establish their own style and interests.

Those who arrive at the festival early (around 7am) will mingle with very serious collectors, who come early to buy what they believe are the most valuable and unique pieces. In fact, collectors have been known to visit the

> ## "No longer just devotional, carvings provide a medium for social and political expression."

Avilés family the day before the festival, "by mistake," in order to get first pick of the master carvers' pieces. Both speculators and investors have inflated the prices of the increasingly popular carvings; it is now nearly impossible to find a $20 piece by one of the masters, as would have been possible several years ago. Even as the *santos de palo* become a financially viable market, however, they retain their cultural underpinnings. The carvings continue to serve as intermediaries of religion, art, society, and spirituality to their many devotees.

Camille Lizarribar has a PhD in Comparative Literature from Harvard University and a JD at Harvard Law. She has most recently returned to Puerto Rico to clerk for a Judge at the Federal District Court in San Juan.

A CLOSER LOOK

directed by Amilcar Tirado, and *Modesta* (1956), which won first prize at the Venice Film Festival. Unfortunately, the industry slowly died in the 60s and 70s as Puerto Rican filmmakers instead turned to joint productions in other countries.

Puerto Rico's film industry did a 180 in 1980 when **Jacobo Morales** wrote, directed, and starred in *Dios los cría (God Created Them)*. The movie, comprised of five stories that questioned contemporary Puerto Rican society, was well received by critics and fans alike. Morales's second major film, *Lo Que Le Pasó A Santiago (What Happened to Santiago)* did even better, winning the **1989 Academy Award** for Best Foreign Language Film. Morales is still considered to be Puerto Rico's greatest film director.

WEST SIDE CONTROVERSY. Ironically, the most famous Hollywood movie related to Puerto Rico had nothing to do with the island itself. The 1961 film *West Side Story* took Shakespeare's classic *Romeo and Juliet* and retold it in 1960s New York City, with a gang of second-generation white Americans, "the Jets," as the Montagues and a gang of Puerto Ricans, "the Sharks," as the Capulets. While the movie did bring international attention to the growing Puerto Rican diaspora in New York City, many Puerto Rican immigrants disliked the film. They complained that the movie confused Mexican and Puerto Rican culture; that it only portrayed poor Puerto Ricans and characterized them as lawless and prone to criminal activity; and that an American actress of European descent was cast as the Puerto Rican love interest (María), while the rougher Puerto Rican female character was portrayed by Puerto Rican native **Rita Moreno.** Despite the criticism, the film was an overwhelming success, winning **10 Academy Awards.** This classic continues to be one of the most widely viewed representations of Nuyoricans in American culture.

In the mid-1980s, director **Marcos Zurinaga's** first major movie, *La gran fiesta* (*The Great Party;* 1986), recounted the last days of San Juan's Casino, a great meeting spot of the rich and famous. Zurinaga directed two more major films, *Tango Bar* (1988) and *The Disappearance of García Lorca* (1997), a mysterious look into the final days of Spanish poet Federico García Lorca. Puerto Rico's most financially successful film of all time was **Luis Molina's** 1993 comedy *La guagua aérea (The Aerial Bus)*, which uses the pretext of a crowded flight to New York in the 1960s to explore the multitude of reasons that Puerto Ricans immigrate. Quite a few Puerto Ricans have left their marks on the American entertainment industry, including Nuyoricans **Jimmy Smits, Rita Moreno, Jennifer Lopez, Michael DeLorenzo,** and **Benicio del Toro.**

SPORTS AND RECREATION

DRY LAND SPORTS

BASEBALL. Forget soccer: Puerto Ricans shed their Latin American ties and choose baseball as the island's most popular sport. Every year from November to January, six regional teams (Santurce, Bayamón, Carolina, Caguas, Mayagüez, and Ponce) play five to six games per week in competition for the series title. In February, the winning team participates in the **Caribbean Series,** playing against the Dominican Republic, Venezuela, and Mexico. Most of the top Puerto Rican baseball players eventually head to the US to play in the major leagues. The result: this little island has had an enormous impact on American baseball. **Orlando Cepeda, Carlos Beltrán, Bernie Williams, Carlos Delgado,** or **Iván Rodríguez** are all Puerto Rican, along with over 200 other players in Major League Baseball history. The trend has become so strong that in the 1997 All-Star Game a Puerto Rican either scored or batted in every single run.

THE BIG SPLURGE

SNORKEL SAVINGS

Snorkeling is a fun and easy way to explore the underwater world, and with a little planning it can be done without taking a big hit to the wallet. Most dive shops rent snorkel gear for $15 per day. If you're staying for an extended period of time, it's worth buying a mask and snorkel: many dive shops have sales where sets are available for as little as $30. Below is a list of some of the best snorkel spots in the West, all free or costing only a few dollars to get to:

1. Playa Escaleras: Located in Rincón, this beach has brightly colored fish and coral just a few feet out. (See p. 288).

2. Guilligan's Island: Just off the coast of Guanica in the Southwest, this small mangrove island offers a chance to see coral as well as a variety of sea vegetation. San Jacinto's has hourly ferries to the island for $5. (See p. 230).

3. Isla Ratones: Only half a mile from the sea town of Joyuda, the small island draws people from all over Puerto Rico, offering a small stretch of beach and crystal-clear waters. $5 ferries run from the shore all day. Bring your own snorkel gear, as there are no dive shops around. (See p. 250).

4. Isla Gatas: La Parguera's main beach destination is a snorkeler's paradise when it's not too crowded. The island is just a short $5 boat ride away; plenty of boat companies by the docks can take you there. (See p. 234).

Puerto Rico's most famous baseball player of all time, hall-of-famer ▣**Roberto Clemente,** also had a long and illustrious career in the Major Leagues. During his 18 years with the Pittsburgh Pirates, Clemente led the team to two World Series and was the National League MVP in 1966, the World Series MVP in 1971, and the National League batting champion four times. Although Clemente was killed in a plane crash over 30 years ago while taking medical and food supplies to earthquake-stricken Nicaragua, Puerto Ricans still hold him in high esteem.

COCKFIGHTING. Though it's illegal in most of the US, cockfighting continues to be a popular tradition in Puerto Rico. Almost every city on the island has a cockfight arena, and fights are typically held every weekend, with as many as 40 to 50 games per day. Hordes of locals, primarily men, gather to watch and bet on the fight between two spur-wearing roosters. Though the tradition is primarily rural and private, San Juan does have one cockfight arena open to the public.

BOXING. Puerto Rico has produced some of the world's best professional boxers. In the 1930s, **Sixto Escobar** became the first Puerto Rican world boxing champion. Most recently **Felix "Tito" Trinidad** ruled the ring as the champion of welterweight and middle-weight boxing after he beat superstar Oscar de la Hoya in 1999. In 2000, **John "The Quietman" Ruíz,** raised in Massachusetts and Puerto Rico by Puerto Rican parents, became the first Latino heavyweight champion. **Miguel Santana** made boxing history in 2006 by becoming the first world champion to claim his title 18 years after winning it: judges reviewed his 1988 International Boxing Federation match with Greg Haugen, lost in an 11th-round technical decision, and decided to award Santana the title. Over the past 70 years Puerto Ricans have won six **Olympic medals** in boxing.

BASKETBALL. Puerto Rico also has an active basketball league, with 16 amateur and six professional teams. Internationally, the island has not fared so well since their gold medal at the 1991 PanAm games. However, several Boricuas have played for the National Basketball Association, including **Ramon Ramos, José Ortíz, Butch Lee, Carlos Arroyo,** and **Daniel Santiago.**

GOLF. Golf is the chosen sport of many tourists, and manicured green courses are spread across the island—most often with luxury resort complexes in tow. Both the ladies and senior Professional Golfer's Association tours end at one of Puerto Rico's magnificent golf courses. However, tourists don't have all the fun; 90% of the active members of the **Puerto Rico Golf Association** are Puerto Rican. Puerto Rican golfers have also made their name internationally: the

PGA Hall of Fame inducted Boricua **Juan "Chi Chi" Rodríguez** in 1992 after a long career. **Kitty Michaels** is a well-known female golfer.

WATER SPORTS

With over 700 mi. of coastline and year-round water temperatures of 74-80°F, Puerto Rico is a paradise for water sports lovers. From scuba diving to deep-sea fishing to surfing, Puerto Rico offers it all, with world-class conditions. Even beginners can dabble in the many activities listed below.

> **SEA WARNINGS.** Puerto Rico has its share of **fearsome sea creatures.** The ones you are most likely to encounter are **jellyfish, sea urchins,** and **sea lice** (tiny jellyfish). While encounters with them may be painful, most of these animals will do little permanent harm. When spending extensive amounts of time in the water (diving, surfing, windsurfing) it's best to wear spandex or a wet suit. There are **sharks** around Puerto Rico, but attacks are extremely rare. If you don't bother them, they most likely won't bother you.

SCUBA DIVING AND SNORKELING

Many people visit Puerto Rico exclusively for its superb diving and **snorkeling.** Numerous reefs surround the island, providing an arena in which to swim with hundreds of fish species. Puerto Rico's best snorkeling is on Culebra (p. 186), closely followed by Vieques (p. 170) and the small islands off Fajardo (p. 165), but there are many snorkeling spots around the island.

Scuba diving involves swimming underwater for longer periods of time with a tank of oxygen attached to your back. Today all divers must be certified by Professional Association of Diving Instructors **(PADI),** National Association of Underwater Instructors **(NAUI),** or Scuba Schools International **(SSI)** before they can dive alone. A certification course runs $150-600 and usually entails written work and up to four practice dives. Professional instructors can accompany non-certified divers on an introductory dive, called **Discover Scuba** or a **resort course.** This provides an excellent way to try diving before investing in a full course. It is possible to get certified in Puerto Rico, but this takes a significant portion of vacation time. Many travelers do the coursework at home and then get a **referral** to do the certification dives in Puerto Rico.

For information about the island's dive sites, see **In the Sea,** p. 2. Scuba diving requires a lot of equipment, and many shops have a hidden surcharge for **equipment rental.** Others do not rent equipment at all, so divers must purchase it. If you plan to do a lot of snorkeling or diving in Puerto Rico, it may be a worthwhile investment to buy your own gear; otherwise, it costs about $10-15 per day to rent snorkel and fins.

> **DIVING DISCERNINGLY.** Puerto Rico has over 40 certified dive shops that send expeditions to countless sights. In choosing a dive shop, it is important to consider several criteria. Divers prone to seasickness may prefer large boats that remain more stable in the water. The majority of dives are done from boats, but some shops also do shore dives, where divers simply walk into the water—a bit difficult with cumbersome equipment and strong shore currents, but typically less expensive. It is also a good idea to investigate how the trips are organized. Some shops take divers and snorkelers out together, which means that divers get most of the attention, leaving snorkelers to fend for themselves. Others have one divemaster for both certified and resort divers, which means that the experienced divers will have to go to a shallower site. Explore these possibilities before you head out on a trip, and you'll be most likely to get what you expect from the experience.

LIFE AND TIMES

SURFING

Puerto Rico ranks among the best surfing destinations in the world, and is certainly the best in the Caribbean. Ever since the **1968 World Championships** in **Rincón**, surfers from around the world, and particularly the US East Coast, have been descending upon the Isle of Enchantment to catch some world-class waves. Puerto Rico again saw some of the world's best competitive surfing in 2007, when Rincón hosted the International Surfing Association (ISA) World Masters Championship. Rincón continues to be the island's surfing paradise, with almost 20 breaks in a relatively small area; it is closely followed by Isabela's **Playa Jobos.** It is possible to surf almost anywhere along the north coast, but the southern Caribbean coast does not have many waves. The prime **surfing season** runs from November to mid-April, when a combination of low pressure systems and cold fronts creates excellent conditions. During the summer hurricane season, waves tend to be inconsistent but still surfable, especially on the east coast. For current live-cam images of surf on the island, check www.surfline.com. Private individuals in Luquillo, Dorado, Isabela, and Rincón teach lessons to surfers of all levels. Unlike many other surfing destinations, Puerto Rico has a fairly **local-dominated scene.** Visitors should respect the local hierarchy and be careful not to break into the line.

FISHING

Both the ocean and the many lakes and reserves of Puerto Rico provide ample entertainment for fishermen. **Deep-sea fishing** is popular, but expensive, with half-day boat charters starting at $150 per person or $400 per boat. Fishermen frequently return with mahi mahi, tuna, mackerel, sailfish, dorado, or blue marlin. Most standing water in Puerto Rico is manmade, but the DRNA fills these with a variety of fish, including tilapia, catfish, sunfish, and largemouth bass. Few charters supply equipment and almost nobody on the island rents supplies (except some deep-sea charters), so fishermen should bring their own poles. Fishing licenses can be obtained from the Puerto Rican Port Authority.

BOATING

The largest **recreational ports** are in Fajardo and Salinas, while San Juan, Mayagüez, and Ponce have the primary **commercial ports.** Many boats in the Fajardo area (p. 165) take small groups out for day-long expeditions to nearby islands. **Salinas** (p. 217) is the best place to go if you're looking for passage on a boat through the Caribbean. Several companies scattered throughout the island **rent sailboats,** but usually require that renters have some sailing experience. **Kayaking** is a popular activity on many of the island's freshwater reserves and in the bioluminescent bays in Fajardo and Vieques.

WINDSURFING

In recent years windsurfing has exploded in popularity in Puerto Rico. The island's largest windsurfing shop, **Velauno** (p. 131), rents equipment, teaches lessons, organizes events, and pretty much dominates the oceans around Punta las Marías in San Juan. Other popular windsurfing areas include La Parguera and Guánica. For more information and current wave reports, check www.windsurfingpr.com.

HOLIDAYS AND FESTIVALS

Puerto Ricans love a good party; there is some kind of festival or event somewhere on the island nearly every week. The island has three primary types of celebration—patron saint festivals, harvest festivals, and national holidays. Almost every town celebrates at least one **patron saint festival** (see list below) with singing, dancing, rides, religious processions, concerts, and banquets of regional food spread out over 10 days. Typically held in the town square, these festivals are based on Catholic saints, but some incorporate elements of African culture as well. **Harvest festivals** are celebrated with similar festivities to commemorate the end of the harvest season. Despite the fact that agriculture has become increasingly unimportant to Puerto

Rico's economy, many towns still host at least one harvest festival; see individual town write-ups. As for **national holidays,** Puerto Rico celebrates both US and Puerto Rican holidays. Because many of these holidays, such as Memorial Day and important birthdays, are held on Mondays, the island has a surplus of three-day weekends. Finally, Puerto Rico also has a smattering of festivities that do not fall into specific categories. San Juan (p. 133) hosts several festivals, from cultural events (San Juan CinemaFest and Heineken Jazz Festival) to events that are just an excuse to party (Gallery Nights, Festival de la Calle San Sebastián). The island also has three major festivals that incorporate *vejigante* masks. Though far from Rio, Ponce's *carnaval* festival is still a major event. Loíza's *carnaval*, held in late July (p. 146), incorporates more African traditions, while Hatillo's **mask festival** (p. 270) in late December is based on the island's Spanish heritage. One of the island's most unique festivals is Aibonito's spectacular **Flower Festival,** a modern-day variation on the traditional harvest festival (p. 296).

COMMONWEALTH HOLIDAYS

DATE	HOLIDAY	NAME IN SPANISH
January 1	New Year's Day	El Año Nuevo
January 6	Epiphany/Three Kings' Day	Día de Reyes
January 11	María de Hostos's birthday	Día del Natalicio de Eugenio Maria de Hostos
January 21, 2008/January 19, 2009	Martin Luther King Jr. Day	Día de Martin Luther King Jr.
February 18, 2008/February 16, 2009	President's Day	Día de los Presidentes
March 22	Emancipation Day	Día de Abolición de Esclavitud
March 2, 2008/April 10, 2009	Good Friday	Viernes Santo
April 16	José de Diego's birthday	Día de José de Diego
May 26, 2008/May 25, 2009	Memorial Day	Día de la Recordación
June 23	St. John the Baptist Day	Día de San Juan Bautista
July 4	US Independence Day	Día de la Independencia de los Estados Unidos
July 17	Luis Muñoz Riviera's birthday	Día del Natalicio de Luis Muñoz Riviera
July 25	Constitution Day	Día de la Constitución de Puerto Rico
July 27	José Celso Barbosa's birthday	Día del Natalicio de José Celso Barbosa
September 1, 2008/September 7, 2009	Labor Day	Día del Trabajo
October 13, 2008/October 12, 2009	Columbus Day	Día del Descubrimiento de América
November 11	Veterans Day	Día del Veterano
November 19	Discovery of Puerto Rico Day	Día del Descubrimiento de Puerto Rico
November 27, 2008/November 26, 2009	Thanksgiving	Día de Acción de Gracias
December 25	Christmas Day	Día de la Navidad

PATRON SAINT FESTIVALS

DATE	PATRON SAINT	TOWN
January 9	La Sagrada Familia	Corozal
February 2	La Virgen de la Candelaria	Coamo, Manatí, Mayagüez
February 3	San Blas	Coamo, Guayama
March 17	San Patricio	Loíza
March 19	San José	Ciales, Gurabo, Luquillo

DATE	PATRON SAINT	TOWN
March 31	San Benito	Patillas
April 29	San Pedro Martín	Guaynabo
May 1	Apóstol San Felipe	Arecibo
May 3	La Santa Cruz	Bayamón, Trujillo Alto
May 30	San Fernando	Carolina
June 13	San Antonio de Padua	Barranquitas, Ceiba, Dorado, Guayama, Isabela
June 24	San Juan Bautista	Maricao, Orocovis, San Juan
July 16	Virgen del Carmen	Arroyo, Barceloneta, Cataño, Hatillo, Morovis
July 25	Santiago Apóstol	Aibonito, Fajardo, Guánica, Loíza
July 31	San Germán	San Germán
August 30	Santa Rosa de Lima	Rincón
September 8	Nuestra Señora de la Monserrate	Jayuya, Moca, Salinas
September 29	San Miguel Arcangel	Cabo Rojo, Naranjito, Utuado
October 2	Los Angles Custodios	Yabucoa
October 7	Nuestra Señora del Rosario	Naguabo, Vega Baja
October 12	La Virgen del Pilar	Río Piedras
November 4	San Carlos Borromeo	Aguadilla
December 8	La Inmaculada Concepción de María	Humacao, Vieques
December 12	Nuestra Señora de la Guadalupe	Ponce
December 28	Día de los Inocentes	Hatillo, Morovis

ADDITIONAL RESOURCES

HISTORY

The Taínos: Rise and Decline of the People Who Greeted Columbus. Irvin Rouse (Yale University Press, 1993). The most informed and accessible history of Puerto Rico's first major civilization from their migration to the Caribbean to the decline of the civilization.

Puerto Rico: A Colonial Experiment. Raymond Carr (New York University Press, 1984). Though it can be difficult to find, this work by British historian Raymond Carr is one of the standard reads about Puerto Rico's complex relationship with the United States.

Puerto Rico: A Political and Cultural History, Antonio Morales Carrión (W.W. Norton and Company, Inc., 1983). A bit dry and overly academic, but one of the few comprehensive histories of Puerto Rico available in English.

SCIENCE AND NATURE

A Guide to the Birds of Puerto Rico and the Virgin Islands. Herbert Raffaele, Cindy House, and John Wiessinger (Princeton University Press, 1989). This is hands-down the best book for bird-watchers traveling to Puerto Rico.

Where Dwarfs Reign: A Tropical Rain Forest in Puerto Rico. Katherine Robinson (University of Puerto Rico Press, 1997). A thorough look at the historical, geological, biological, and mineral aspects of El Yunque.

CULTURE

Puerto Rico, Borinquén Querida. Roger A. Labrucherie (Imágenes Press, 2001). A photojournalist's account of the culture, history, and natural wonders of the island, highlighted with spectacular photos.

Stories from Puerto Rico/Historias de Puerto Rico. Robert L. Muckley and Adela Martínez-Santiago (Passport Books, 1999). Eighteen traditional Puerto Rican folk tales with short historical contextualizations. The book is part of the Bilingual Books series and all stories appear in both English and Spanish.

Puerto Rico Mío: Four Decades of Change. Jack Delano, Arturo Carrion, and Sidney Mintz (Smithsonian Institution Press, 1990). This widely-acclaimed work combines Delano's photographs from 1941, with photos of the same places in 1981 to illustrate the change, consistency, and beauty of island life.

Boricuas: Influential Puerto Rican Writings. Robert Santiago (Ballantine Books, 1995). With 50 short stories, plays, poems, and essays, this anthology provides a solid introduction to Puerto Rican writings of the 19th and 20th centuries, as well as a glimpse into the island's culture and history.

Clemente! Kal Wagenheim and Wilfrid Sheed (Olmstead Press, 2001). Using narrative and interviews, Wagenheim and Sheed detail the life and career of Puerto Rico's most famous baseball legend, Roberto Clemente.

FICTION

Juan Bobo Goes To Work: A Puerto Rican Folk Tale. Marisa Montes (Harper Collins Juvenile Books, 2000). This short children's book relates the misadventures of Juan Bobo, a Puerto Rican version of Foolish Jack. The protagonist, a popular Puerto Rican folk character, has his own statue in one of Condado's plazas.

When I Was Puerto Rican. Esmeralda Santiago (Vintage Books, 1994). Santiago recalls her childhood growing up in the Puerto Rican countryside and her move to Brooklyn at age 13. One of the most popular novels about Puerto Rican life.

The Rum Diary: A Novel. Hunter S. Thompson (Scribner Paperback Fiction, 1999). Though Thompson's novel falls far short of his dream to create the great Puerto Rican novel, it does provide an interesting glimpse of Condado in the 1950s. Plotless, but enjoyable.

LIFE AND TIMES

pisa y corre

Stop, Go: Public Transportation in Puerto Rico

As in the continental US, cities in Puerto Rico have given way to suburbs; as a result, people have become dependent on cars in their day-to-day lives. Today a great proportion of the island's land area is punctuated by streets and highways. At last count there were 2.2 million cars in Puerto Rico (about six for every ten residents)—three times the proportion of the US and many more times that of European countries.

Sprawl and lack of urban planning have made it almost impossible to design a public transportation system that competes with the car. But in a country where the average per capita income is about $12,500, not everybody can afford a car. That is why many low-income families, students, recent immigrants, and elderly persons keep alive a network of *pisa y corre* (roughly translated to "stop and go") public vans, also known as *carros públicos* (public cars) that move from town to town every day. For $3-20 a traveler can tour all of Puerto Rico and get a closer look at Puerto Rican culture along the way.

One great advantage of *pisa y corre* transportation is that the vans usually travel directly between town plazas. Because most museums, cultural centers, and stores, are centered around theses plazas, you will get right to the action. If you ask, people will tell you how to get from the van stop to any cultural spot or hotel in the area. If you are planning to go to a place between towns, talk to the van drivers and make sure the *pisa y corre* does drive past the area. To request a stop, tell the driver *"me deja aquí, por favor"* (leave me here, please) and you will be dropped off.

Pisa y corre vans are not intended for tourism, and because the presence of a foreigner provides diversion from the drag of the daily commute, fellow riders and the driver will usually share information about the cultural highlights of a town along with lessons and opinions about any subject imaginable, and a collection of life histories to fill many volumes. In other words, this is not the way to travel incognito. No matter how you look, people in small towns will know that you are new there, and at least somebody will want to know what you are doing. So, in a sense, *pisa y corre* transportation is a cultural experience.

The following is a possible museum trip using the *pisa y corre:*

On any given day (except Sunday) you can spend a morning in Río Piedras exploring the centennial campus of the University of Puerto Rico (p. 122), with its small but beautiful museum. Then walk to the plaza and take the *pisa y corre* to Caguas.

When you arrive in Caguas (p. 147) you will be able to visit museums about *trovadores*, tobacco, and others on subjects related to the history and people of the town. From there take the bus to Cayey.

In Cayey, visit the college's museum. The main gallery is dedicated to the painter Ramón Frade and his masterful representations of everyday people and landscapes in early 20th century Puerto Rico. Next, take the van to Guayama.

"In a sense, *pisa y corre* transportation is a cultural experience."

Right in Guayama you will find the Casa Cautiño Museum, a property co-managed by the Puerto Rican Institute of Culture and the Municipality of Guayama. It is an amazing example of late 19th-century architecture that houses a collection of furniture and decorative arts of the same period. From there, go on to Ponce, a good place to unwind and spend the night.

Those who travel by *pisa y corre* soon discover that asking people is the best way to get around and, if you are lucky, to find some unexpectedly beautiful places and experiences.

Adrián Cerezo is an education policy and non-formal education specialist currently directing the Community Based Education Center at Sacred Heart University in San Juan. He has a BA in clinical psychology from Sacred Heart University. In 1998 Cerezo received a Distinguished Alumni Award for his contributions to education.

A CLOSER LOOK

BEYOND TOURISM
A PHILOSOPHY FOR TRAVELERS

HIGHLIGHTS OF BEYOND TOURISM IN PUERTO RICO

RESEARCH sustainable forestry techniques at **Las Casas de la Selva** (p. 82).

BUILD homes for **low-income Puerto Ricans** in San Juan (p. 85).

SPEAK with locals in Spanish after studying at a **language school** in Puerto Rico (p. 86).

TEACH communities about **environmental preservation** (p. 84).

As a tourist, you are always a foreigner. While hostel-hopping and sightseeing can be great fun, you may want to consider going *beyond* tourism. Experiencing a foreign place through studying, volunteering, or working can help reduce that touristy stranger-in-a-strange-land feeling. Furthermore, travelers can make a positive impact on the natural and cultural environments they visit. With this Beyond Tourism chapter, *Let's Go* hopes to promote a better understanding of Puerto Rico and to provide suggestions for those who want to get more than a photo album out of their travels. The "Giving Back" sidebar features also highlight regional Beyond Tourism opportunities.

There are several options for those who seek to participate in Beyond Tourism activities. Opportunities for **volunteerism** abound with both local and international organizations. **Studying** in a new environment can be enlightening, whether through direct enrollment in a local university or in an independent research project. **Working** is a way to immerse yourself in local culture and finance your travels simultaneously. However, travelers who hope to work in Puerto Rico should be aware that because of the island's long-standing high unemployment rates, travelers who work may be taking much-needed jobs away from locals.

As a **volunteer** in Puerto Rico, you can participate in projects that range from helping to research sustainable hardwood foresting techniques in Dosque Estatal Carite to tutoring elementary students at risk of dropping out of school. Later in this chapter, we recommend organizations that can help you find the opportunities that best suit your interests, whether you're looking to get involved for a day or for a year.

Studying at a college or enrolling in a Spanish-language program are both popular options—most students immerse themselves in the Spanish language and Puerto Rican culture through a combination of classes and homestay with a Puerto Rican family. Many programs meet for around 20 hours per week, leaving students plenty of free time to enjoy the island.

VOLUNTEERING

Volunteering can be a powerful and fulfilling experience, especially when combined with the thrill of traveling in a new place. Puerto Rico's natural beauty makes the island a popular travel destination, but also an ecologically vulnerable one. As a result, many volunteer projects on the island aim to conserve Puerto Rico's forests, reefs, and beaches. In the last 50 years, a concentrated effort to preserve Puerto Rico's natural resources has emerged. Today, several of the island's endangered species, such as the Puerto Rican parrot and the leatherback sea turtle, are trying to make a comeback. Volunteers can do everything from guarding turtle eggs during breeding season on the beaches of Culebra to helping keep the island's coasts clean (p. 276). However, ecological work isn't the only volunteer opportunity in Puerto Rico. Inner-city volunteer programs address issues such as educational gaps, poverty, and housing shortages.

WHY PAY MONEY TO VOLUNTEER?

Many volunteers are surprised to learn that some organizations require large fees or "donations." While this may seem ridiculous at first glance, such fees often keep the organization afloat, in addition to covering airfare, room, board, and administrative expenses for the volunteers. (Other organizations must rely on private donations and government subsidies.) If you're concerned about how a program spends its fees, request an annual report or finance account. A reputable organization won't refuse to inform you of how volunteer money is spent. Pay-to-volunteer programs might be a good idea for young travelers who are looking for more support and structure (such as pre-arranged transportation and housing), or anyone who would rather not deal with the uncertainty implicit in creating a volunteer experience from scratch.

Opportunities to teach school children, advocate for social justice, and promote community education abound.

Most people who volunteer in Puerto Rico do so on a short-term basis, at organizations that make use of drop-in or once-a-week volunteers. Most short-term opportunities are in environmental conservation. The best way to find opportunities that match up with your interests and schedule may be to check with **VolunteerMatch** (☎ 415-241-6855; www.volunteermatch.org) or **www.idealist.org**, which list volunteer openings with various organizations in Puerto Rico. Current listings include working in disaster relief services and conducting field research on plant regeneration in Puerto Rico's rainforests. Another useful resource is the Puerto Rican NGO **Fondos Unidos** (☎ 787-728-8500; www.fondosunidos.com). This San Juan-based organization helps place volunteers all over the island and coordinates activities among over 150 nonprofit organizations, most of which are socially focused. The American government can also direct individuals toward volunteer opportunities at **www.volunteer.gov**, though many of these posts require long-term commitments.

Those looking for longer, more intensive volunteer opportunities usually choose to go through a parent organization that takes care of logistical details and often provides a group environment and support system—for a fee. There are two main types of organizations—religious and non-sectarian—although there are rarely restrictions on participation for either.

ENVIRONMENTAL CONSERVATION

By the mid-20th century, in the aftermath of the commonwealth's agricultural and industrial boom, just 1% of Puerto Rico's precious virgin rainforest still stood. Underwater habitats such as coral reefs and shoreline mangroves also suffered as a result of industrial pollution and unsustainable development. Over the last 30 years, grassroots movements and activists such as Alexis Massol González—who was awarded the 2002 Goldman Environmental prize, the equivalent of the Nobel Prize for environmentalists—have started to reverse this trend. Reforestation efforts have yielded encouraging results. The island now faces the challenge of promoting economic development while simultaneously preserving its unique natural habitats. Volunteers are able to spend time working in Puerto Rico's beautiful outdoor environments with the goal of preserving them for generations to come.

Las Casas de la Selva, Rte. 184 Km 17.6, (☎ 839-7318; www.eyeontherainforest.org), in **Reserva Forestal Carite** (p. 292), outside of Patillas, 00723. This 1000-acre project is dedicated to the idea that rainforest can be preserved even as some of its resources are used for profit. Owned by the nonprofit Tropic Ventures and monitored by the Department of Natural Resources, the organization welcomes groups and individual volunteers to stay a weekend or as long as several months to help with its projects, which range from planting trees to researching reforestation to building retaining walls. Rustic accommodations are available for a small, negotiable fee. Food is available at additional cost. For more information, see **Constructive Conservation, (**p. 294).

another side of paradise

Volunteering at a Public Library in San Juan

Puerto Rico is indeed an enchanted island, but *puertorriqueños* manage to pull themselves away from their beauti-

> ## "I was able to introduce the boy to a whole new world of information."

ful beaches and carry on normal lives beyond the coast. They go to school, debate local and international politics, and discuss news from around the world. However, although the number of TVs per household in Puerto Rico outnumbers people, computers and other forms of information technology are still privileged commodities. Many people rely on libraries and paper resources for information. Unfortunately, libraries are scarce. Though universities and private schools have growing collections, these are often intimidating and hard to access.

Some smaller community libraries, however, are beginning to offer other options. On Saturdays during high school, I worked the morning shift at the San Juan Community Library, a relatively small library that obtains most of its resources from book donations and philanthropic funding. Despite its diminutive size, San Juan Community Library has a diverse collection of novels, reference books, magazines, and children's books. When I worked there, it also had a copier, four computers with Internet access, and even a digitalized library catalog—not bad for a community library entirely run by volunteers! The best part was that anyone could become a member.

As a librarian, I did everything from cataloging and shelving books to maintaining databases and reordering supplies. The library held a children's reading hour on Saturdays, and I would read to the kids for about thirty minutes—or until they became distracted. I also helped to run the library's reading contests for schoolchildren, which challenged them to read a certain number of books in a set amount of time. Yet

my most fulfilling experiences came when I was able to help others use library resources. One particular incident still stands out in my mind: a teenage boy and his father from a nearby *barrio* came in search of information about dinosaurs for a school assignment. They didn't know where to begin. After I helped them perform various keyword searches and reference checks, we gathered enough information to complete the project, pictures and all. I distinctly remember how the boy's face lit up as we sorted out which information would be most valuable. The father's pride showed in his eyes as he stood back and watched his son energetically examine the pages in front of him. It was the most rewarding experience during my time as a volunteer because I was able to introduce the boy to a whole new world of information.

The library served as a haven for a regular group of book-loving patrons. One neighborhood boy would show up every Saturday asking if there had been any new additions to the library. Another little girl would come in regularly in search of the latest installments of *The Baby-sitters Club*. Unfortunately, the library is short-staffed and thus has limited hours. I would love to see the library expand its schedule and its size. If you find yourself on the island for an extended period of time, consider signing up to volunteer for a couple of hours a week, at this or other similar community libraries. The least you would gain would be a chance to meet the other volunteers; more likely, you would have the chance to open the world of books to someone who has yet to discover it.

For more information on how to help, contact Connie Estades, Executive Director of the San Juan Community Library (787-789-4600). Both English and Spanish speakers are welcome.

María Pilar Barreto is a native of Guaynabo. She has completed a BA in Latin American Studies at Harvard University and hopes to enter a career in diplomacy, or in any field where she can put her language skills to use.

Casa Pueblo, C. Rodulfo González 30, Adjuntas, 00601 (☎829-4842; www.casapueblo.org). Founded in 1980 to campaign against environmentally destructive mining (see In the **People's House**, p. 307), this local nonprofit runs projects in environmental education, research, and advocacy. Volunteers are accepted on a case-by-case basis and must provide their own accommodations and food.

Universidad de Puerto Rico Río Piedras Jardín Botánico, intersection of Hwy. 1 and Hwy. 3, Río Piedras, San Juan, 00917 (☎765-1845). Short-term volunteers work as tour guides, gardeners, or teachers. No housing offered.

Earthwatch Institute, 3 Clock Tower Place, Ste. 100, P.O. Box 75, Maynard, MA 01754, USA (☎800-776-0188; www.earthwatch.org). An international nonprofit organization that promotes the conservation of natural resources and cultural heritage around the world. Offers 1- to 2-week expeditions to Puerto Rico primarily dealing in flora and fauna preservation. Expeditions about $1000 per week. Membership $35 per year.

WILDLIFE CONSERVATION

Coupled with agricultural development and industrialization, deforestation has destroyed not only Puerto Rico's natural habitats but also the unique inhabitants of these environments, both on land and underwater. With the help of dedicated scientists, volunteers, and ecologically conscious travelers, Puerto Rico's rare and magnificently varied wildlife—from birds and turtles to the less animated coral—should flourish for years to come. Volunteering to help conserve Puerto Rican wildlife is an opportunity to work with some of the rarest animals in the world.

US Fish & Wildlife Service (☎800-344-9453; www.fws.gov) has 3 offices in Puerto Rico.

Cabo Rojo office, Rte. 301 Km 5.1 (☎851-7258, ext. 35). Participates in the **Student Temporary Employment Program,** which pays full-time students to spend 1 year working and studying on the reserve. Housing available.

Vieques office, Rte. 200 Km 0.4 (☎741-2138; http://southeast.fws.gov/vieques). Accepts volunteers on an individual basis but has no housing or structured program.

Culebra office, on Rte. 250 (☎742-0115; www.volunteer.gov). The best place to go if you want to work with turtles. Accepts individual volunteers and sometimes has housing available. Check website for information about projects around the island not associated with any particular office.

CORALations, P.O. Box 750, Culebra 00775 (☎556-6234; info@coralations.org). Focuses on coral reef preservation. Volunteers can assist with beach cleanup, underwater coral farm development, and water quality studies.

Vieques Conservation and Historical Trust, C. Flamboyán 138, Esperanza, Vieques 00765 (☎741-8850; www.vcht.com). Works to protect and preserve the natural resources of Vieques. Accepts volunteers on a case-by-case basis to help with various projects, including maintaining the marine tank, collecting animals from Vieques shores and coral reefs, feeding animals, staffing the gift shop, and occasionally fundraising.

YOUTH AND COMMUNITY

Poorer than any US state but wealthier than most Latin American countries, Puerto Rico is still feeling the growing pains of economic development. An unemployment rate of around 10%, low education levels, and a housing shortage of approximately 100,000 dwellings are among the island's biggest economic and social challenges. Volunteers can positively affect Puerto Rico's future by teaching in struggling schools, working as community educators, or constructing affordable housing.

Puerto Rico Center for Social Concerns, De Hostos 459, Hato Rey, San Juan 00918 (☎474-1912; www.prcsc.org). Recent college graduates can volunteer for 1-2 years in various capacities, including teaching English, working with the homeless, and constructing homes. Airfare, housing, and stipend provided.

Habitat for Humanity, 1357 Av. Ashford PMB 135, San Juan 00907 (☎368-9393; www.habitat.org). Builds houses around the world for low-income families. Puerto Rico does not have an established volunteer program, but the local chapter welcomes volunteers for a day or a year, and can help arrange projects for group trips or individuals. Room and board are not provided.

Americorps, 1201 New York Av. NW, Washington, D.C. 20525 (☎202-606-5000; www.americorps.org). Offers a variety of opportunities in Puerto Rico in education, conservation, and community-building for US citizens, nationals, or permanent legal residents ages 17+. Programs 10-12 months. Food and accommodations provided. Scholarships of $5000 for higher education available.

Museo del Niño, C. San Cristo 150, San Juan 00901 (☎722-3791; www.museodelninopr.org). Accepts university students as volunteers at various exhibits in 5hr. shifts Tu-Th. Applications must be made in person at the museum.

Vieques Humane Society, Rte. 200, Barrio Santa Maria, Vieques 00765 (☎741-0209; www.viequeshs.org). Educates communities about animal care and assists abandoned animals. Volunteers bathe, feed, and walk animals and sometimes assist in the clinic. Provides a shared room, bath, and kitchen in exchange for 20hr. per week of volunteering. Call at least a month in advance to check housing availability.

STUDYING

Study-abroad programs range from basic language and culture courses to college-level classes, often for credit. In order to choose a program that best fits your needs, research as much as you can before making your decision—determine costs and duration, as well as what kind of students participate in the program and what sort of accommodations are provided.

In programs that have large groups of students who speak the same language, there is a trade-off. You may feel more comfortable in the community, but you will not have the same opportunity to practice a foreign language or to befriend other international students. For accommodations, dorm life provides a better opportunity to mingle with fellow students, but there is less of a chance to experience the local scene. Living with a family offers the potential to build lifelong friendships with natives and to experience day-to-day life in more depth, but conditions can vary greatly from family to family.

VISA INFORMATION
Students enrolling in a program for less than 18hr. per week may be able to do so on a tourist visa. Students who wish to study more than that must apply for an **F, M,** or **J** visa. These can be obtained at the nearest US embassy or consulate and cost around $100. In order to obtain a visa, students must present a passport valid for more than 6 months, academic transcripts, standardized test scores, and proof of financial support. More information is available at www.travel.state.gov. **US citizens never need a visa to study in Puerto Rico.**

UNIVERSITIES

Most university-level study-abroad programs are conducted in Spanish, although many programs offer classes in English and beginner and lower-level language courses. Those relatively fluent in Spanish may find it cheaper to enroll directly in a university abroad, although getting college credit may be more difficult. You can search **www.studyabroad.com** for various semester-abroad programs that meet your criteria, including your desired location and focus of study. The following is a list of organizations that can help place students in university programs abroad, or that have their own branch in Puerto Rico.

AMERICAN PROGRAMS

Several institutions based in the United States offer summer- to year-long programs of study in Puerto Rico. These programs do not have citizenship restrictions, but often have academic requirements. Most programs arrange accommodations for students either in university housing or at a homestay.

National Astronomy and Ionosphere Center, 504 Spaces Sciences Building., Cornell University, Ithaca, NY 14853, USA (☎607-255-3735; www.naic.edu). Offers a 10 week research assistant summer program in Arecibo for 6-12 US citizens who are currently enrolled in an undergraduate program. Applications due early Feb. Housing and stipend provided. 1-2 positions available for graduate students enrolled at US schools. Graduate students need not be US citizens.

Two Worlds United Educational Foundation, 503 E. Jackson St., Ste. 250, Tampa, FL 33602, USA (☎888-696-8808; www.twoworldsunited.com). Offers programs of various lengths for Spanish-language studies in Puerto Rico. For ages 15-18.

PUERTO RICAN UNIVERSITIES

If you are not a US citizen, it may be more expensive to enroll directly in a Puerto Rican university than a foreign-sponsored one, since funding for some programs is restricted to US citizens. A US visa can be difficult to obtain for citizens of countries outside of Western Europe, Australia, and Canada. Most study-abroad programs are based in San Juan.

Universidad de Puerto Rico, P.O. Box 364984, San Juan 00936 (☎250-0000 ext. 3208 or 3202; www.upr.edu). The largest university system in Puerto Rico, with campuses in Aguadilla, Arecibo, Bayamón, Carolina, Cayey, Humacao, Mayagüez, Ponce, Río Piedras, and Utuado. The central Río Piedras campus alone has 23,000 students. Students must have at least an intermediate level of Spanish to enroll. Tuition for nonresident students $3192 per year. Some dormitories available.

InterAmerican University of Puerto Rico, C. Galileo Final, Urb. Jardines Metropolitanos, Río Piedras, San Juan; P.O. Box 363255, San Juan 00936 (☎766-1912; www.inter.edu). Campuses in Aguadilla, Arecibo, Barranquitas, Bayamón, Fajardo, Guayama, Ponce, San Germán, and San Juan. The original campus is in San Germán. With 38,000 students, this is the oldest and largest private university system in Puerto Rico. Most coursework is in Spanish, but the university offers a separate trimester program in English. Spanish immersion program available. Undergraduate tuition $140 per credit plus miscellaneous fees. Catalog available online in English. Many students live in dormitories on the San Germán campus.

Universidad del Sagrado Corazón, P.O. Box 12383, San Juan 00914 (☎728-1515; www.sagrado.edu), in the heart of Santurce. Known for its outstanding communications department, this university was established in 1880 and has a student population of 5000. Offers programs in humanities, communications, education, social sciences, business administration, and natural sciences. All classes are conducted in Spanish.

LANGUAGE SCHOOLS

Language schools can be independently run international or local organizations or divisions of foreign universities. They rarely offer college credit. They are a good alternative to university study if you desire a deeper focus on the language or a slightly less rigorous course load. These programs are also good for younger high school students who might not feel comfortable with older students in a university program. A listing of Spanish language programs can be found at www.studyspanish.com/schools/agencies_2.html. Some worthwhile programs include:

AmeriSpan, P.O. Box 58129, Philadelphia, PA 19102, USA (☎800-879-6640, outside of US 215-751-1100; www.amerispan.com). Offers language programs for all levels in San Juan for 1 week to 6 months. Price includes homestay with local family. Max. class size 6. Reserve at least 4 weeks in advance. Registration fee $100. 1 week $660, with meals $735; 4 weeks $2520/2820.

A2Z Languages, 5112 N. 40th St., Ste. 103, Phoenix, AZ 85018, USA (☎800-496-4596; www.a2zlanguages.com). Offers language programs for all levels in San Juan. Price includes homestay. Min. 1 week. Max. class size 6. 1 week $430, with 2 meals per day $500; 4 weeks $1580/1860. Private lessons available at an additional cost.

Instituto Interdisciplinario y Multicultural, Domingo Marrero Navarro Building, María Rivera Room, 3rd fl., College of General Studies. University of Puerto Rico, Río Piedras (☎764-0000; http://generales.upr.clu.edu/INIM/inim_english.htm). Programs in Spanish language and culture. Some offer college credit. Tuition from $600-2200 for 3-week courses. Meals, dorm housing, and transportation included.

Instituto Internacional Euskalduna, C. Navarro 56, Hato Rey (☎281-8013). Spanish immersion classes for speakers of all levels. Classes 20hr. per week plus weekly excursions and cultural activities. Max. class size 6. Courses start at $300 per week. Homestays $150 per week, with meals $225.

LanguagesAbroad (In North America ☎800-219-9924, elsewhere 416-925-2112; www.languagesabroad.com). Spanish-language programs for students of all levels in San Juan. Classes 20hr. per week year-round. Max. class size 6. Courses start at $680 per week. Homestay included.

Pan American Language Institute, PMB 295, P.O. Box 7891, Guaynabo (☎793-4995, toll-free 866-793-4995; www.panamericanlanguage.com). Offers individual Spanish lessons on a flexible schedule. Housing not provided. 60 lessons from $1680.

Language Immersion Institute, SCB 106, State University of New York at New Paltz, 1 Hawk Drive, New Paltz, NY 12561, USA (☎845-257-3500; www.newpaltz.edu/lii). 2-week summer language courses and some overseas courses in Spanish. Program fees are around $1000 for a 2-week course. Accommodations not included.

Spanish Abroad, Inc., 5112 N. 40th St., Ste. 203, Phoenix, AZ 85018, USA (US and Canada ☎888-722-7623, UK 800-028-7706, elsewhere 602-778-6791; www.spanishabroad.com). Spanish immersion programs at the Instituto Internacional Spanish Language School in San Juan. Class 20hr. per week plus outings. Max. class size 6. Courses start at $640 per week, with meals $710. Homestay included.

BEYOND TOURISM

WORKING

As with volunteering, work opportunities tend to fall into two categories. Some travelers want long-term jobs that allow them to integrate into a community, while others seek out short-term jobs to finance the next leg of their travels. Note that working abroad often requires a special work visa; see the box below for information about obtaining one.

VISA INFORMATION. Admission as a visitor to Puerto Rico does not include the right to work, which is authorized only by a work permit. US citizens can work in Puerto Rico without any type of work permit or visa. If you are not a US Citizen, you need a work permit or "green card" to work in Puerto Rico. Normally you must have a job offer before you can obtain the permit; your employer will fill out the appropriate forms enabling you to apply for a temporary work visa (for more details, see p. 11).

Travelers seeking both short-term or long-term work in Puerto Rico should be advised that because of the island's high unemployment rates they may be taking much-needed jobs away from locals. However, foreigners with multiple language skills may find luck in the island's highly developed tourist industry. Jobs range from working at a seaside restaurant to leading adventure tours. The island has a large American expat population (especially concentrated in Rincón, Vieques, and Culebra) that works largely in tourist-related fields; try looking in these areas as well as major cities like San Juan and Ponce for work.

FURTHER READING ON BEYOND TOURISM
Alternatives to the Peace Corps: A Guide of Global Volunteer Opportunities, by Paul Backhurst. Food First Books, 2005 (US$12).
The Back Door Guide to Short-Term Job Adventures: Internships, Summer Jobs, Seasonal Work, Volunteer Vacations, and Transitions Abroad, by Michael Landes. Ten Speed Press, 2005 (US$22).
Green Volunteers: The World Guide to Voluntary Work in Nature Conservation, ed. Fabio Ausenda. Universe, 2007 (US$15).
How to Get a Job in Europe, by Cheryl Matherly and Robert Sanborn. Planning Communications, 2003 (US$23).
How to Live Your Dream of Volunteering Overseas, by Joseph Collins, Stefano DeZerega, and Zahara Heckscher. Penguin Books, 2002 (US$20).
International Job Finder: Where the Jobs Are Worldwide, by Daniel Lauber and Kraig Rice. Planning Communications, 2002 (US$20).
Live and Work Abroad: A Guide for Modern Nomads, by Huw Francis and Michelyne Callan. Vacation-Work Publications, 2001 (US$16).
Overseas Summer Jobs 2002. Peterson's Guides and Vacation Work, 2002 (US$18).
Volunteer Vacations: Short-Term Adventures That Will Benefit You and Others, by Doug Cutchins, Anne Geissinger, and Bill McMillon. Chicago Review Press, 2006 (US$18).
Work Abroad: The Complete Guide to Finding a Job Overseas, by Clayton Hubbs. Transitions Abroad Publishing, 2002 (US$16).
Work Your Way Around the World, by Susan Griffith. Vacation-Work Publications, 2007 (US$22).

BEYOND TOURISM

SAN JUAN

This vibrant capital of the Caribbean defies classification: ritzy Isla Verde, historic Old San Juan, and working-class Santurce may as well be different worlds, though they sit less than seven miles apart. At 47.5 square miles in size, the city composes just 1.4% of the island's total land area, but houses an astounding 25% of its population. The diversity of San Juan's inhabitants—who range from multigenerational *sanjuaneros* to eager American expats and new Caribbean immigrants—is remarkable; yet, once in the city, many *sanjuaneros* have been known to go their entire lives without venturing outside the metropolitan area.

For centuries, San Juan has been the focus of attention in Puerto Rico. After Juan Ponce de León moved the island's capital from Caparra to San Juan in 1521, the Spanish constructed a giant wall around the city, regarding it as the only part of the island worth protecting. For 200 years, San Juan served as a military base, a legacy evident today in the city's profusion of fortresses. Old San Juan, the site of the old Spanish capital, continues to be perceived as the heart of the city. Overflowing with history, culture, and charm, the old city has enough museums, galleries, and restaurants to satisfy any traveler. It's true that at times the neighborhood can seem like just another cruise stop, with every business competing to impress the one-day visitors; however, a walk down the quiet streets of Calle Sol and Calle Luna proves that, notwithstanding, the old city continues to thrive.

Old San Juan's surrounding neighborhoods began developing in the 18th century, when economic reforms jump-started the city's growth. Working-class *sanjuaneros* migrated to Puerta de Tierra, while the white minority settled in suburban Santurce. In the early 20th century, the population of the city grew dramatically, producing a sprawling metropolitan area; in the 1950s, tourism hit the city. When the Cuban Revolution narrowed the choice of Caribbean travel destinations, Condado became the new hot spot. Today, Condado has become a center of tourism, Hato Rey has emerged as an international financial powerhouse, and Río Piedras is a hub for university students and vendors. These neighborhoods offer a taste of authentic Puerto Rican life and are San Juan's best places to rub elbows with locals, visit authentic markets, or check out city beaches.

HIGHLIGHTS OF SAN JUAN

STEP BACK IN TIME on the cobblestone streets of **Old San Juan** (p. 116).

PARTY with s*anjuaneros* at one of the city's multitude of **fiestas** (p. 133).

ADMIRE the impressive collections of art in Santurce's **Museo de Arte de Puerto Rico** (p. 128) and **Museo de Arte Contemporaneo** (p. 129).

LOUNGE on the **white sand beaches** of Condado (p. 92), Ocean Park (p. 93), and Isla Verde (p. 93).

MUNCH on tropical fruits and fresh *batidas* in Río Piedras's **Plaza del Mercado,** San Juan's largest food market (p. 122).

✈ INTERCITY TRANSPORTATION

Flights: Aeropuerto Internacional Luis Muñoz Marín, on the eastern side of San Juan in Isla Verde. Most major US airlines fly into San Juan (see **By Plane,** p. 24). Although more expensive than the bus, **taxis** are an affordable and very convenient way to travel to and from the

San Juan Overview

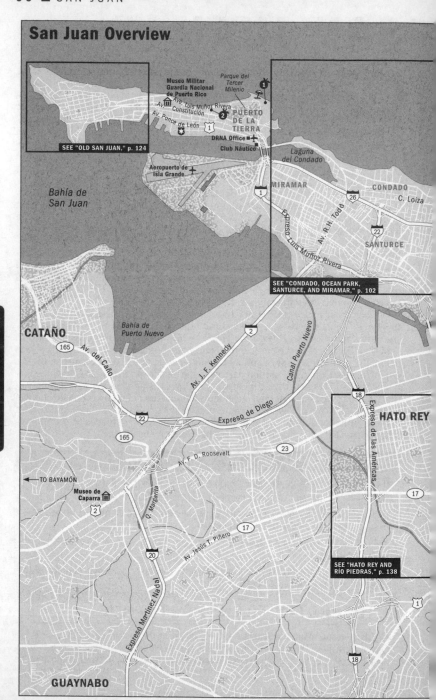

SEE "OLD SAN JUAN," p. 124

Museo Militar Guardia Nacional de Puerto Rico

Parque del Tercer Milenio

Ave. Luis Muñoz Rivera

Av. Constitución

Av. Ponce de León

PUERTO DE LA TIERRA

DRNA Office

Club Náutico

Laguna del Condado

Aeropuerto de Isla Grande

Bahía de San Juan

MIRAMAR

CONDADO

C. Loíza

Expreso Luis Muñoz Rivera

Av. R.H. Todd

SANTURCE

SEE "CONDADO, OCEAN PARK, SANTURCE, AND MIRAMAR," p. 102

Bahía de Puerto Nuevo

CATAÑO

Av. del Caño

Av. J. F. Kennedy

Canal Puerto Nuevo

Expreso de Diego

TO BAYAMÓN

Museo de Caparra

Av. F. D. Roosevelt

C. Margarita

Av. Jesús T. Piñero

HATO REY

Expreso de las Américas

SEE "HATO REY AND RÍO PIEDRAS," p. 138

Expreso Martínez Nadal

GUAYNABO

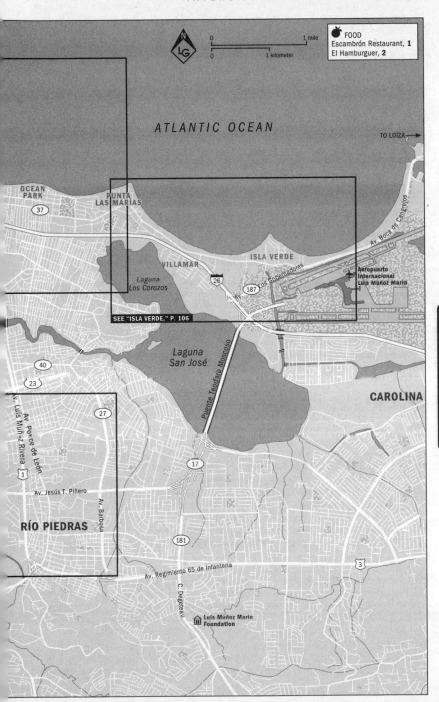

N
LG

0 |————————————————————| 1 mile
0 |————————————————————| 1 kilometer

FOOD
Escambrón Restaurant, **1**
El Hamburguer, **2**

ATLANTIC OCEAN

TO LOÍZA →

OCEAN
PARK
37

PUNTA
LAS MARIAS

Av. Boca de Cangrejos

VILLAMAR

ISLA VERDE

Laguna
Los Corozos

26

187

Los Gobernadores

Aeropuerto
Internacional
Luis Muñoz Marín

SEE "ISLA VERDE," P. 106

Laguna
San José

Puente Teofilo Moscoso

CAROLINA

40
23

27

Av. Ponce de León

Av. Luis Muñoz Rivera

17

1

Av. Jesús T. Piñero

Av. Barbosa

RÍO PIEDRAS

181

3

Av. Regimiento 65 de Infantería

C. Degetau

Luis Muñoz Marín
Foundation

SAN JUAN

airport. Go to a marked "Ground Transportation" booth outside the baggage claim, and an English-speaking official will provide a set fare and a taxi. The cheaper (and much longer) way is by **bus**. Take bus B40 or C45 from the 2nd level in front of terminal C, then sit back and relax: buses come about every 20-25min. and it's a 35min. ride to Isla Verde. From there, wait in front of the Isla Verde Mall for bus A5, which goes through Santurce and Puerta de la Tierra en route to Old San Juan. The trip takes about 45-60min. in total. To get to the airport, take bus A5 to Isla Verde and get off at the end of Av. Isla Verde, in front of the orange cockfight arena (40min. from Old San Juan). Then switch to bus B40 or C45 (5min.). The airport is a 5min. **drive** from Isla Verde, 12min. from Condado, and 15min. from Old San Juan. The **Puerto Rico Tourism Company** tourist information office is outside the lower level of terminal C. (☎791-1014. Open daily 9am-7pm.) **Aeropuerto de Isla Grande,** Av. Lindbergh Final, Isla Grande, Miramar, San Juan (☎729-8790; www.prpa.gobi-erno.pr), on the eastern edge of Puerta de la Tierra, hosts several smaller airlines flying primarily to Vieques, Culebra, and Santo Domingo. Taxis usually wait out front when flights come in; if they're not there, have the security guard call one. Open daily 6am-10pm.

Públicos: *Públicos* (shared vans) are Puerto Rico's only public form of intercity transportation. In San Juan, *públicos* congregate in **Río Piedras** and leave when full (approx. 6am-3pm, although a few may be available later). Drivers sit outside the vans waiting for passengers; just tell any driver your destination, and he'll point you in the right direction.

Terminal de Transportación Juan A. Palerm, at the intersection of C. Arzuaga and C. Vallejo, near the market, houses *públicos* headed east to: **Fajardo** (1hr., $3.50) via **Luquillo** (45min., $3); and **Loíza** (30min., $1.75).

Río Piedras's Plaza de Diego, 1 block south of Paseo de Diego sends shuttles to: **Bayamón** (30min., $3); **Caguas** (40min., $2.50); **Guaynabo** (30min., $0.75); **Humacao** (45min.-1hr., $2.50); **Ponce** (1½hr., $10) via **Salinas** (1hr., $10).

Línea Boricua, C. González 116 (☎765-1908), operates out of the Librería Norberto González parking lot. Walk downhill on C. González; the parking lot is on the right at the intersection with C. Jorge Romany. *Públicos* go to **San Sebastián** (1½-2hr., $12).

Línea Sultana, C. Esteban González 898 (☎767-5205 or 765-9377), at Av. Universidad, sends vans to **Mayagüez** (3½hr., every 2hr. 7:30am-5:30pm, $12).

Línea DonQ, C. Brumbaugh 102 (☎764-0540), sends *públicos* to **Ponce** (1½hr., 3-4 per day, $10).

 # ORIENTATION

San Juan is divided into numerous distinct neighborhoods, each with its own flavor. The neighborhoods normally frequented by visitors are described below.

> ❗ **NEIGHBORHOOD SAFETY.** Although San Juan is generally safe, visitors should avoid a few specific neighborhoods. **La Perla,** on the northern edge of Old San Juan between the cemetery and San Cristóbal, continues to be dangerous despite increased police surveillance. **Puerta de la Tierra** is fine during the day, but stay away from the residential streets in this area at night. In **Santurce, Calle Loíza** and the surrounding areas should be avoided after dark. The neighborhood around Río Piedras's **Plaza del Mercado** is also dangerous at night.

OLD SAN JUAN. Year-round, thousands of visitors disembark from cruise ships and find themselves on the romantic cobblestone streets of *Viejo San Juan*. Almost all of the capital's museums and sights are located in Old San Juan, and any visitor to the island should plan to spend at least a day or two here. The old city is easy to navigate on foot, and wandering through the narrow streets between brightly colored homes and storefronts is half the fun. As a general rule, streets that go downhill run south.

CONDADO. In the 1950s, tourists flocked to Condado, the hottest beach destination south of Miami. There are still a few guesthouses from that era, but the big resort chains have now taken up most of the beachfront property. **Avenida**

Ashford, a one-way street running westbound, parallel to the ocean, is the neighborhood's main drag and the place to find restaurants as well as practical services. The increasingly residential **Calle Magdalena** runs parallel to Ashford, but traffic goes in the opposite direction, eastbound.

MIRAMAR AND SANTURCE. Directly south of Condado and Ocean Park, Miramar and Santurce used to be the centers of San Juan's business community, but over the years the two neighborhoods have deteriorated. Today Miramar is more of a residential neighborhood with a few hotels, while Santurce continues to house many of the city's smaller businesses and government agencies. Santurce in particular has many vacant storefronts and construction sites that should be avoided at night. **Avenida Ponce de León,** the major street that connects the two areas, is home to most of the restaurants, hotels, and services. **Avenida Fernández Juncos** is the street's parallel counterpart, with traffic running in the other direction. **Avenida José de Diego** and **Calle Roberto H. Todd** connect Santurce to Condado. By night, many of the city's major discos open in Santurce; however, neither Av. Ponce de León nor C. Roberto H. Todd should be explored at night, especially on foot.

OCEAN PARK. Ocean Park proper is a gated, upscale residential community sitting on the ocean, between Condado to the west and Isla Verde to the east. Over the years, though, this title has come to include the surrounding streets as well. Cafes and some services line **Avenida McLeary** (an eastern continuation of Condado's Av. Ashford), but for groceries or the restaurant strip it's necessary to travel further west along Av. McLeary, toward Condado and Santurce. In recent years, this quiet neighborhood has gradually been overtaken by young Puerto Ricans and North Americans in search of the perfect wave. However, Ocean Park retains a laid-back, hometown atmosphere that the more touristy Condado and Isla Verde cannot match.

ISLA VERDE. Although technically it's within the city limits of Carolina, most people consider Isla Verde part of San Juan. Isla Verde is home to the best beaches in the city, which are bordered by the endless row of resorts and time-share condominiums that line the busy **Avenida Isla Verde.** The major roads that cut through the neighborhood can make Isla Verde a difficult area to navigate on foot. Many establishments in which they reside; instead, they are identified by the condo or building they reside in. If you get confused, ask a local; most have long since memorized the building names. Across the freeway lies tiny **Villamar. Punta Las Marías,** the small peninsula dividing Ocean Park from Isla Verde, is home to fantastic restaurants of all stripes. Many surfers have set up camp in this area, and it's a good place to find water sports equipment. In this chapter, establishments in Punta de las Marías are listed under the Isla Verde header.

HATO REY. This is San Juan's business district; almost all of San Juan's major banks call Hato Rey home, and each has its own skyscraper to prove it. **Avenida Ponce de León** and **Avenida Luis Muñoz Rivera (Highway 1),** the two major north-south thoroughfares, hold most of the skyscrapers, while smaller businesses radiate outward. Av. Franklin D. Roosevelt (not to be confused with Av. Eleanor Roosevelt), a busy street with lots of restaurants, connects Av. Ponce de León to Expreso de las Américas and to the big mall, Plaza las Américas. Hato Rey is difficult to navigate on foot, since many of the roads do not have sidewalks.

RÍO PIEDRAS. **Avenida Jesús Piñero (Route 17)** divides Hato Rey from Río Piedras, the most recent addition to San Juan. Río Piedras is the most Latin American part of the city, with a large produce and meat market, several *público* stations, Puerto Rico's largest university, and, on nearly every corner, tiny *cafeterías* that turn into bars at night. Most visitors spend their time around the university and the market. This area can be a bit confusing, so a map is helpful. Av. Ponce de León and Av. Luis Muñoz Rivera (Hwy. 1) continue south through Río Piedras and connect to east-west Hwy. 3.

▣ LOCAL TRANSPORTATION

Elevated Train: A commuter rail runs from Bayamón to Hato Rey (see **All Aboard,**). Tourists may be most interested in its stops in downtown Río Piedras and at the Universidad de Puerto Rico. Customer service ☎866-900-1284. $1.50; students, disabled, and ages 60-74 $0.75; 75+ free.

Buses: Metropolitan Bus Authority (☎250-6064; www.dtop.gov.pr/ama/rutas.htm), runs a comprehensive system throughout San Juan. Line A5 leaves from **Covadonga station** in Old San Juan, follows Av. Ponce de León through Miramar, turns left on Av. José de Domingo, continues along C. Loíza and Av. Isla Verde, and finally ends in Iturregui (last bus 8:45pm). A6 goes from Río Piedras to Carolina. Route B21 leaves from Old San Juan, crosses Puerta de Tierra, follows Av. Ashford through Condado, and continues south to Hato Rey and Plaza Las Américas shopping center (last bus M-Sa 9pm, Su 7:45pm). B29 leaves from Río Piedras, heads through the University of Puerto Rico, and ends up in Guaynabo. B40 and C45 both run from Isla Verde to the airport. Metrobús M1 leaves from Old San Juan and passes through Santurce and Hato Rey en route to Río Piedras (last bus 11:15pm). A map on the wall of the Covadonga station in Old San Juan provides a complete route list. There are **2 main bus stations:** one in Old San Juan, near Pier 4, and another in Río Piedras, 2 blocks north of Paseo de Diego. Metrobuses come every 10min., "A" routes come every 15min., "B" routes come every 20min., and "C" routes come every 30min., but only Metrobuses regularly run on schedule. All buses run less frequently on Su. Buses stop at green signs marked "Parada." When a bus passes, make sure the driver sees you or he may not stop. $0.75, students $0.60, ages 60-75 $0.35, 75+ free. Exact change required.

Taxis: Most licensed taxis in San Juan are called **taxis turísticos** and are identifiable by the yellow lighthouse logo on the side. Fixed rates include: airport to Isla Verde $10; airport to Condado, Miramar, or Convention Center $14; airport to Old San Juan and the cruiseship piers $19; within Old San Juan $7; Old San Juan to Condado or Miramar $12; Old San Juan to Isla Verde $19; Old San Juan to the Plaza las Americas Shopping Center $14. Outside tourist areas, all taxis should use a meter, or you should agree on a price before leaving. In **Old San Juan,** taxis gather around the Plaza de Armas, outside the El Convento and Sheraton hotels across from the piers, and behind the Teatro Tapia. Late at night, try the latter two options. In **Condado,** try one of the big hotels or just flag down a taxi along Av. Ashford. In **Santurce, Miramar, Ocean Park, Hato Rey,** and **Río Piedras,** taxis wait on the Plaza de Armas near the *públicos.* You can also call: AA American Taxi (☎982-3466), Cooperativa Major Taxi Cabs (☎723-2460), Metro-Taxi Cab (☎725-2870), or Rochdale Radio Taxi (☎721-1900).

NEIGHBORHOOD HOPPING. Even short taxi rides over the border between neighborhoods will be charged according to fixed prices. If you're close to a border in a safe area and have some time to spare, consider crossing neighborhoods on foot and then catching a cab to travel within the area.

Car rental: All major American car rental companies have booths in the Luis Muñoz Marín International Airport. Some of the less expensive companies are listed below. Unless otherwise stated, all price quotes are for compact cars with unlimited mileage.

AAA Car Rental (☎791-1465 or 791-2609), Av. Isla Verde 5910, Isla Verde. From $29-49 per day (cheaper on weekdays). $750 per month. 21+. Under-25 surcharge $10 per day. Open M-Sa 9am-6pm. AmEx/D/MC/V.

Hertz, in the terminal at the Luis Muñoz International Airport (☎791-0840), Carolina & downtown San Juan at Av. Ashford 1365, Condado (☎725-2027 or 800-654-3030; www.hertz.com). From $35 per day. 21+. Under-25 surcharge $27 per day. Open daily 7am-5pm. Old San Juan office located in the lobby of the Sheraton Hotel (☎721-5127). Open daily 7am-noon and 1pm-4pm. AmEx/D/MC/V.

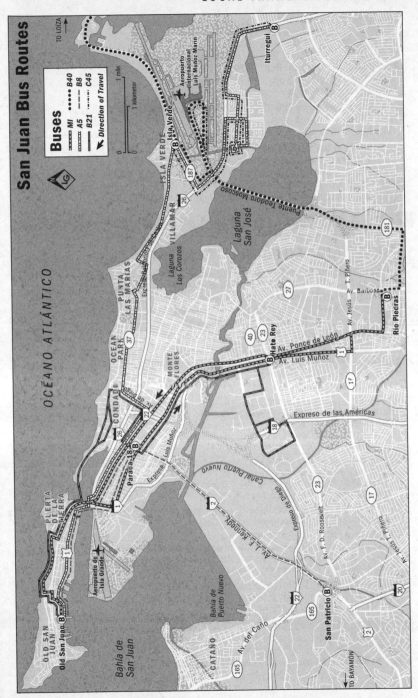

San Juan Bus Routes

Buses

- MI
- A5
- B21
- B40
- B8
- C45

➤ Direction of Travel

OCÉANO ATLÁNTICO

Bahía de San Juan

OLD SAN JUAN
Old San Juan Ⓑ
PUERTA DE LA TIERRA
Aeropuerto de Isla Grande

CONDADO
Parada 18 Ⓑ

ISLA VERDE
Isla Verde

PUNTA LAS MARÍAS
OCEAN PARK

VILLAMAR
Laguna Los Corozos

Aeropuerto Internacional Luis Muñoz Marín

Iturregui Ⓑ

TO LOÍZA

Puente Teodoro Moscoso

Laguna San José

181

MONTE FLORES

Hato Rey Ⓑ
Av. Ponce de León
Av. Luis Muñoz

Av. Jesús
Río Piedras Ⓑ
Av. Barbosa
Av. T. Piñero

Expreso de las Américas

Canal Puerto Nuevo

Bahía de Puerto Nuevo

CATAÑO
Av. del Caño

San Patricio Ⓑ

Av. J. E. Kennedy
Expreso de Diego
Av. F. D. Roosevelt
Av. Jesús T. Piñero

TO BAYAMÓN

Charlie Car Rental, Av. Isla Verde 150, Carolina and Av. Ashford 890, Condado (☎728-2418, toll-free 800-289-122; www.charliecars.com). In high season $32 per day, $230 per week; in low season about $24/164. Rates vary according to availability. 21+. Under-25 surcharge $10 per day. Open 24hr. AmEx/D/MC/V.

Bike Rental: Hot Dog Cycling, (☎791-0776) in the Plazoleta Isla Verde, Isla Verde, rents 21-speed bikes, $5 per hr.; $25 per day. 21+. Under 21 must have adult accompaniment. Open M-F 10am-5pm, Sa 10am-6pm. MC/V.

Ferries: AcuaExpreso (☎729-8714) sends a ferry from Pier 2 in Old San Juan to Cataño daily (10min., every 30min. 6am-9:40pm, $0.50) and Hato Rey (15min.̇, $0.75). Handicapped and ages 60-74 $0.25 to Cataño, $0.35 to Hato Rey. Ages 75+ free.

Trolleys: A **free trolley** *(trole)* passing all the major sites in Old San Juan departs regularly from the **Covadonga bus terminal** (daily 8am-10pm). Wait at any one of the marked trolley stops throughout the city (yellow signs that say "Parada" and have a picture of a trolley). The north route passes both forts and the museums along C. Norzagaray. The south route passes the Plaza de Armas and the piers.

🔢 PRACTICAL INFORMATION

TOURIST AND FINANCIAL SERVICES

Tourist Offices: The Puerto Rico Tourism Company's San Juan branch operates out of a yellow house called **La Casita,** at C. Comercio and Pl. de la Dársena, near Pier 3 (☎722-1709 or 721-2400, ext. 3902). Pick up a complimentary rum cocktail with your free copy of ¡Qué Pasa! magazine here. Free pamphlets and info. English spoken. Open M-W 9am-8pm, Th-F 8:30am-5pm, Sa-Su 9am-8pm. There is also a helpful municipal tourist office at C. Tetuán 250 (☎721-6363). Open M-Sa 8am-4pm.

Tours: Many big resort hotels, including the Sheraton in Old San Juan, open their tours to non-guests. Before booking, check to see if transportation and meals are included. For a list of island-wide adventure tour outfitters, many leaving from San Juan, see **Organized Adventure Trips,** p. 44.

Rich Sunshine Tours (☎647-4545 or 298-5100). Mr. Sunshine provides a wide spectrum of tours to the most popular destinations, including El Yunque (half-day $45, full day $60), El Yunque and Luquillo Beach ($65), Ponce ($65), Camuy Caves and Arecibo Observatory ($60), and Old San Juan and the Bacardi factory ($35). Also offers kayaking in Fajardo's bioluminescent bay ($70), snorkeling trips ($77), and horseback riding ($85). Open daily 8am-3pm. Calls 8am-11pm.

Atlantic San Juan Tours (☎644-9841; www.puertoricoexcursions.com). This smaller company offers fewer excursions than Rich Sunshine, at similar prices. To El Yunque (5½hr., $48); El Yunque and Luquillo Beach ($68); Old San Juan and the Bacardi factory ($48); and Camuy Caves and Arecibo Observatory ($82).

Countryside Tours (☎593-9014). Tours from San Juan to Bacardi rum distillery ($48), El Yunque rainforest ($48), Arecibo observatory and caves of Camuy ($90), from San Juan to Ponce ($90).

E & B Tours (☎318-1069 or 603-4067), an outfitter for the Hampton Inn in Isla Verde. Offers tours to: Old San Juan and the Bacardi Factory (includes 2 drinks, $45); El Yunque and Luquillo Beach (full day $60); Camuy Caves ($65 plus entrance); Ponce (full day $65). Prices do not include lunch or admission fees. Free pickup. Reservation required. Open 8am-5pm. MC/V.

Consulates: Canada, Av. Ponce de León 268, Ste. 802, Oficina 1350 (☎759-6629 or 250-0367), Hato Rey. Open M-F 9am-1pm. **UK,** Av. Chardón 350, Ste. 1236 (☎406-8777), Hato Rey. Open M-F 9am-5pm.

Camping Permits: Department of Natural and Environmental Resources (DRNA; ☎999-2200), in Río Piedras, next to the botanical garden on Av. Muñoz Rivera, Sector 5, Venezuela. Provides camping permits and reservations for 9 designated camping areas (see **Camping,**). $5 per person. Open M-F 7:30am-4pm.

Banks and Currency Exchange: Banco Popular cashes AmEx Travelers Cheques, exchanges currency, and gives MC/V **cash advances** (no commission). In Old San Juan, C. Tetuán 206 (☎725-2636). **ATM** out back, but avoid this poorly lit street by nightfall, as C. Tetuán and C. Tanca are known to be dangerous at night. Upstairs, visit a gallery with changing exhibits about Puerto Rican culture (Tu-Su). English and Spanish captions. Open M-F 8am-4pm, Sa 9am-noon. In **Condado**, Av. Ashford 1060 (☎725-4197). ATM and Internet for customers. Open M-F 8am-4pm. In **Santurce**, Ponce de León 701 (☎723-8078). ATM. Open M-F 8am-4pm. In **Isla Verde**, Av. Isla Verde with C. 6 de Palmar (☎726-5800). Open M-F 8am-6pm. In **Hato Rey** (☎725-5100), at Av. Ponce de León 526. ATM. Open M-F 8am-4pm.

Western Union: All **Pueblo** supermarkets have Western Union offices. Money sent to "San Juan" can be picked up at any location.

LOCAL SERVICES

English-Language Bookstores: Librería Cronopios, C. San José 255 (☎724-1815) at C. Tetuán. Open daily 9am-7pm. **Librería La Tertulia,** Av. Ponce de León 1002 (☎724-8200, www.tertulia.com) on the west side of Plaza Colón. Both stores sell a wide variety of Spanish and English novels and other media. Open daily 9am-8pm. MC/V.

Library: Biblioteca Carnegie, Av. Concepción 7 (☎722-4739 or 722-4753), Puerta de Tierra just east of Old San Juan, in the large pink building. A full library and free Internet on 25 computers (30min. max. per day if busy). Open June-July M-F 8am-5:30pm; Aug.-May M-Tu and Th 9am-8.30pm, F-sa 9am-5pm. **Biblioteca José M. Lázaro,** at the Universidad de Puerto Rico (p. 122), is also open to the public.

Publications: The San Juan Star, available at most newsstands, has been providing English-language news to the capital city for over 50 years ($0.45). The half-English, half-Spanish magazine ▨¡Qué Pasa! is available at every tourism desk and provides info on accommodations, food, and outdoor activities for the entire island. **Puerto Rico Wow (www.puertoricowow.com)** is a popular online source for locals and tourists alike, with daily news in English and Spanish. Includes festival and activity listings. The websites **www.lonitido.com** and **noctambulo.com** give the scoop on the hottest nightlife on the island but are both in Spanish. **El Nuevo Día** is San Juan's primary daily newspaper, distributed daily. Pick this up at any newsstand (Spanish only).

Ticket Agencies: Ticket Center (☎792-5000; www.ticketcenterpr.com), on the 3rd fl. of Plaza las Américas (p. 131), near the food court. Sells tickets for concerts and performances. Open M-W 9am-9pm, Th-Sa 9am-10pm, Su 11am-5:30pm. AmEx/MC/V. **Ticketpop** (☎294-0001; www.ticketpop.com) sells tickets for shows at the Centro de Bellas Artes (p. 133) and other venues. Pick up tickets at the store Casa de los Tapes, at select movie theaters, or have them mailed. Open M-Sa 9:30am-5:30pm.

Laundromats: La Lavandería, C. Sol 201 (☎721-1819), at C. Cruz. TV and magazines to entertain you while you wait. Wash 2 baskets for $2, $3 for small washer and $5 for large with full service; dry $0.25 per 5min. Change available. Open daily 8am-8pm. **Laundry Condado Cleaners,** C. Condado 63, will wash your clothes in 24hr. $2.50 per lb., $4 min. Open M-F 7am-7pm, Sa 8am-5pm. **Coin Laundry,** Av. McLeary 1950 (☎726-5955), Ocean Park. Wash $3, dry $0.25 per 5min. Open daily 6am-9pm.

Weather Conditions: ☎253-4586.

EMERGENCY AND COMMUNICATIONS

Emergency: ☎911. **Fire:** ☎722-1120.

Police: Tourist police (☎726-7020). English spoken. Open 24hr. **State Police** (☎977-8310), on Fernández Juncos, Puerta de la Tierra. Open 24hr. **Municipal Police** (☎724-5170), in the Covadonga bus station, on C. Harding, **Old San Juan.** Open 24hr. In **Isla**

WWWIRELESS. For those in need of a consistent Internet connection while in San Juan, consider taking a laptop on your trip. Many cafes allow customers to pick up their wireless signal "hotspots" free of charge. These establishments are much more widespread and convenient than Internet cafes with computers on location. **Cafe Berlin, Zesty Bites,** and **El Burén** outwardly offer their services (p. 107).

Verde, Av. Isla Verde 5980 (☎728-4770). Open 24hr. In **Río Piedras,** C. Georgetti 50 (☎765-6439 or 274-1612), on the plaza. Open 24hr.

Rape Crisis Line: ☎800-981-5721

Late-Night Pharmacies: Puerto Rico Drug Co., C. San Francisco 157 at C. Cruz (☎725-2202), on the Plaza de Armas, Old San Juan, has 1hr. photo developing. Open daily 7am-10pm. AmEx/D/MC/V. **Walgreens** has several locations around the city: in **Santurce,** Av. Ashford 1130 (☎725-1510). Open 24hr. In **Ocean Park,** C. Loíza 1963 (☎728-0599), at C. Santa Cecilia. Open 24hr. AmEx/D/MC/V. In **Isla Verde,** Av. Isla Verde 5948 (☎982-0392). Open 24hr. AmEx/D/MC/V. In **Río Piedras,** Av. Muñoz Rivera 999 (☎294-0506). Open M-Sa 7am-10pm, Su 8am-10pm. AmEx/D/MC/V.

Hospital: Ashford Presbyterian Community Hospital, Av. Ashford 1451 (☎721-2160), is the largest hospital in the tourist area. Ambulance service. Clinic open M-F 7am-6pm, Sa 8am-11am. Emergency room open 24hr. In an emergency, dial ☎911.

Internet Access: Internet is free at **Biblioteca Carnegie** (p. 97) in Puerto de Tierra, but the options below are more convenient if you are staying elsewhere in San Juan.

Ben & Jerry's (☎977-6882), at C. del Cristo and C. Sol, Old San Juan, has 2 computers. Hands down the hippest Ben & Jerry's ice cream around. Hosts live guitar performances and shows a weekly in-store movie night. $3 per 15min., $5 per 30min. 1 scoop of ice cream $2 in a cup, $3 in a cone. Open daily 10am-11pm. AmEx/D/MC/V.

Diner's Crew Lounge, C. Tetuán 311 (☎724-6276). This restaurant (see **Food,** p. 107) has the cheapest Internet in Old San Juan ($3 per 30min., $5 per hr.). Free local phone calls. Open daily 10am-10pm. AmEx/D/MC/V.

Internet Active (☎791-1916), Parking Covadonga building across from Pier 4 Connect with your laptop or use one of 8 new, fully equipped computers. 20min. $3, 40min. $5, 1hr. $7. Only open when cruise ship is docked at Pier 4 (look for white hotel on water).

CyberNet Café, Av. Ashford 1128 (☎724-4033), Condado. This techno-infused cafe also serves coffee ($1-2.50). $3 for 20min., $5 for 35min., $7 for 50min., $9 for 65min. Some computers have webcams. Fax service available. Open M-Sa 9am-11pm, Su 10am-11pm. AmEx/MC/V. **Isla Verde** location (☎728-4195), Av. Isla Verde between Pizza City and Walgreens. Open M-Sa 9am-11pm, Su 10:30am-10pm. AmEx/MC/V.

Postalnet, C. Loíza 1750 (☎726-5458), Santurce, near Ocean Park. $3.50 per 15min., $5 per 30min., $12 per hr. Open M-F 9am-6pm. AmEx/MC/V.

UPS Store, Av. Ponce de León 1507 (☎723-0613), Santurce. Internet $3.50 per 20min. min. $10 per hr. Open M-F 9am-5:45pm. AmEx/MC/V.

Post Offices: In **Old San Juan,** Paseo de Colón 100 (☎724-2098), between piers 3 and 4. Open M-F 8am-4pm, Sa 8am-noon. In **Condado,** C. Magdalena 1108 (☎723-8204). No General Delivery. Open M-F 8:30am-4pm, Sa 8:30am-noon. San Juan's largest post office is in **Hato Rey,** 585 Av. F.D. Roosevelt (☎622-1799). General Delivery open M-F 5:30am-6pm, Sa 6am-2pm. Lobby mailing area open M-F 6am-10pm, Sa 8am-4pm. Bring ID to pick up mail. All post offices: AmEx/D/MC/V.

Postal Codes: Old San Juan: 00901. **Puerta de Tierra:** 00902 or 00906. **Santurce:** 00907 or 00908. **C. Manuel Fernández Juncos:** 00909 or 00910. **Calle Loíza:** 00911 or 00914. **Hato Rey:** 00917 or 00919. **Río Piedras:** 00917 or 00919. P.O. Box postal codes vary.

♜ ACCOMMODATIONS

ACCOMMODATIONS BY PRICE

UNDER $40 (❶)	
Guest House (p. 100)	OSJ

$40-60 (❷)	
📷 The Caleta (p. 100)	OSJ
El Jibarito (p. 100)	OSJ
Hotel Metropol (p. 104)	SA
Hotel Olimpo Court (p. 104)	MI

$61-89(❸)	
Alelí by the Sea Guest House (p. 101)	CO
Atlantic Beach Hotel (p. 101)	CO
Borinquen Beach Inn (p. 105)	IV
Casa del Caribe (p. 101)	CO
📷 The Coqui Inn (p. 104)	IV
Coral by the Sea (p. 105)	IV
📷 Da House Hotel (p. 100)	OSJ
Hotel El Portal (p. 101)	CO
The Mango Inn (p. 105)	IV

$61-89(❸), CONTINUED	
📷 At Windchimes Inn (p. 101)	CO
Oceana Hostal Playero (p. 104)	OP
El Prado Inn & Villas (p. 104)	CO
Tres Palmas Guest House (p. 104)	IV
Villa Verde Inn (p. 105)	IV

$90-130 (❹)	
El Canario Hotels (p. 101)	CO
Hostería del Mar (p. 104)	OP
Hotel Milano (p. 100)	OSJ
Hotel La Playa (p. 105)	IV
📷 Hotel Villa del Sol (p. 104)	IV
Número Uno Guest House (p. 104)	OP

OVER $130(❺)	
The Gallery Inn (p. 100)	OSJ
SJ Suites (p. 100)	OSJ

CO Condado. **IV** Isla Verde. **MI** Miramar. **PT** Puerta de la Tierra. **OP** Ocean Park. **OSJ** Old San Juan. **OP** Ocean Park. **RP** Río Piedras. **SA** Santurce.

Accommodations in San Juan are quite expensive, with the exception of a few affordable guesthouses. In terms of memorable ambience, safety, and proximity to cultural attractions, Old San Juan can't be beat. Unfortunately, the closest beach is about a mile down the highway in Puerta de la Tierra. For fun in the sun, head to Condado, Ocean Park, or Isla Verde on San Juan's Atlantic Ocean strip. Condado is a very tourist-friendly beach area, with a selection of restaurants and a beautiful promenade, but it does not have the nicest beach in town. Most accommodations in Ocean Park are on residential streets that offer peace and quiet but little excitement. Isla Verde boasts the best beaches in the city, but accommodations generally offer less value and are sandwiched between huge resorts and condominiums. Furthermore, the entire neighborhood sits along a busy thoroughfare. Budget travelers who don't mind walking a few blocks to the beach may choose to stay in Santurce or Miramar, two neighborhoods inland from Condado where the accommodations offer much more bang for your buck, but they may feel unsafe at night. Remember that buses connect all neighborhoods and the longest commute (between Old San Juan and Isla Verde) takes less than an hour. Unless otherwise stated, all rooms below have private bathrooms. Most hotels have seasonal prices: "high season" (meaning higher prices) is generally November to May, and "low season" is generally June through October. However, many hotels have slight variations on these dates, which are noted wherever possible. Unless otherwise indicated, prices do not include the 9% Puerto Rico accommodations tax.

RENTAL AGENCIES

Several rental agencies offer short-term contracts specifically designed for travelers. Most of these are located in furnished condominiums along the beach, but make sure that you understand exactly what you are getting before you hand over your credit card number. Most have minimum stays of three days to one week, but some require monthly rentals.

SAN JUAN

ReMax (☎268-1241; www.remax-islaverde.com), on Av. Isla Verde, in the Marbella del Caribe strip mall, specializes in Isla Verde rentals. Website has photos. Utilities not included in monthly rates. Nov.-Apr. studios $1000-1100 per month; 1 bedroom $1900-2200; 2 bedrooms $2200-2500; 3 bedrooms $3000 and up. May-Oct. $900-1000/1400-1500/1800-1900/2800-3000. Weekly rates available. Open M-F 9am-6pm, Sa 9am-1pm. MC/V.

San Juan Vacations (☎726-0973 or toll-free 800-266-3639; www.sanjuanvacations.com), next to ReMax, Isla Verde. In the Marbella del Caribe strip mall. A smaller, but sometimes less expensive, selection of Isla Verde and Condado rentals. Prices vary widely from month to month depending on listings and area; quotes below are approximate. Studios $800-1400; 1 bedroom $1000-1600; 2 bedrooms $1400-2200. Open M-F 9am-6pm, Sa 8:30am-12:30pm. AmEx/MC/V.

OLD SAN JUAN

■ **Da House Hotel,** C. San Francisco 312 (☎977-1180 or 977-1182; www.dahousehotelpr.com), on the paseo Callejón de la Capilla, between C. San Francisco and C. Fortaleza. This fresh and modern hotel is housed in what was originally a convent for the 150-year-old San Francisco de Asís church and later a studio gallery for the National Center for the Arts. Original tiles line the floors and bold modern art stretches across the building's white walls. If you get especially attached to one of the pieces, fear not—the paintings are available for sale. Rooftop patio with hot tub and marvelous ocean views. High-season doubles $91-93. Low-season doubles $80-120. AmEx/MC/V. ❸

■ **The Caleta,** Caleta de las Monjas 11 (☎725-5347; www.thecaleta.com). Old San Juan's best deal for budget travelers, The Caleta's balcony suites overlook quiet cobblestone streets and the bay. Safe and central location. Modest but comfortable rooms have cable TV, phone, and kitchenette; some have A/C. Reception across the street at C. Clara Lair 151, M-F 10am-6pm, Sa-Su 11am-3pm. Check-out noon. 3 night min. stay. Low-season doubles and quads $50-120 per night, $210-700 per week. Long-term rentals throughout Old San Juan $450-800 per week, $475-750 per month. MC/V. ❷

The Gallery Inn, C. Norzagaray 204-206 (☎722-1808; www.thegalleryinn.com), on the north shore of Old San Juan. Ring the bell at the unmarked gate to enter a courtyard filled with plants, soothing waterfalls, original sculptures, and Paulina the talking parrot. Winding halls and wood stairwells lead to rooms with 4-post beds surrounded by antique books, art, and sculptures. The rooftop wine deck, at the highest point in Old San Juan, offers views that have to be seen to be believed. If you're going to splurge on 1 expensive hotel during your vacation, make it this one. Be sure to request a room with central A/C. Rooms $175-350. AmEx/MC/V. ❺

Hotel Milano, C. Fortaleza 307 (☎729-9050 or 877-729-9050; www.hotelmilanopr.com). Simple rooms come with all the amenities—cable TV, telephone, A/C, small fridge—but little of the city's charm. Steps from the upscale restaurant row. 4 rooms have Internet connections. Rooftop restaurant and terrace provide relative serenity over the loud, gray streets of the "centro." Breakfast included. Check-in 3pm. Check-out noon. Nov. 20-May singles $98-158; doubles $135 and up. June-Nov. 19 $87-104/115 and up. AmEx/MC/V. ❹

SJ Suites, C. Fortaleza 253 (☎725-1351; www.sjsuites.com), in between C. San Justo and C. Tanca. A safe hotel found just steps from the eclectic dining of Old San Juan's "SoFo" area. Dim lighting is outweighed by convenient location and cleanliness, though prices are steep for the value. Breakfast included. Reception daily 10am-9pm. Dec.-May $163-300, June-Nov. $136-212. MC/V. ❺

El Jibarito, C. Sol 280 (☎725-8375). The owners of this popular restaurant (see **Food,**) rent out a few bare bones guest rooms upstairs. Rooms are haphazardly furnished and can get hot, but are a good value with safe location, a double bed, small kitchenette, living area with futon, and private bathroom. Weekly stays only; about $350. Tax included. AmEx/D/MC/V. ❷

Guest House, C. Tanca 205 (☎722-5436). You get what you pay for at this inexpensive guesthouse. Larger rooms include both a queen and a twin bed, but stuffy smaller rooms seem like large closets; the top-floor room with balcony is most spacious. Call ahead, since the front gate is usually locked, and avoid wandering the unsafe C. Tanca at night. Common bathrooms in hallway. No English. $35 per night for solo travelers, $25 per person for pairs, and $20 per person with 6 people. Tax included. Cash only. ❶

CONDADO

▓ **At Windchimes Inn,** Av. McLeary 1750 (☎ 727-4153), at C. Taft. This restored Spanish villa has the amenities of a resort with none of the pretension. Wicker furniture and glass tables grace bright rooms, with fun, beach-themed bathrooms. Friendly staff. All rooms have cable TV. Small pool with a hot tub bench. Fully stocked outdoor bar and restaurant on the grounds. Free Wi-Fi in lobby. Parking $10 per night. Dec. 15-July $90-150; Aug.-Dec. 14 $60-95. AmEx/D/MC/V. ❸

El Canario Hotels (☎ 800-533-2649; www.canariohotels.com) has 3 locations in the Condado area. All have clean, bright rooms with cable TV, telephones, and A/C. Continental breakfast and newspaper included. Check-in 2pm. Check-out 11am. A $3 energy charge is added to all room prices. AmEx/D/MC/V. ❹

El Canario by the Sea, Av. Condado 4 (☎ 722-8640), is the only Canario located 10 steps from the beach. Rooms are similar to those of the other Canarios, with sparse decor and small bathrooms. Comfortable open-air back patio with growing book swap. Dec. 16-Apr. Singles $105; doubles $119-134. May-Dec. 15 $80/90-100.

El Canario Inn, Av. Ashford 1317 (☎ 722-3861). This self-dubbed B&B makes up for its plain rooms with its central location and charming yellow building. Dec. 16-Apr. 30 singles $105; doubles $119-134. May-Dec. 15 $80/90-100.

El Canario by the Lagoon, C. Clemenceau 4 (☎ 722-5058). 2 blocks from the ocean, across the main drag. The largest of the 3 locations, and the only one with an elevator, balconies, fridges, and free parking. Many rooms have views of the lagoon. Dec. 16-Apr. Singles $109-145; doubles $120-180. May-Dec. 15 $85/95.

Atlantic Beach Hotel, C. Vendig 1 (☎ 721-6900; www.atlanticbeachhotel.com). This hotel and its guesthouse counterpart, the Embassy Guest House, overlook the Atlantic Ocean on a popular stretch of beach with patio, bar and live music. Comfortable if not glamorous rooms have microwave, fridge, and coffeemaker. Pool and hot tub. Sundeck on penthouse floor. Complimentary beach towels and chairs. Continental breakfast. Coin laundry. High season oceanfront doubles M-W $129, Th-Su $149, non-oceanfront doubles M-W $115. Low-season oceanfront doubles M-W $89, Th-Su $115; non-oceanfront doubles M-W $79, Th-Su $95. Extra person $17. AmEx/MC/V. ❸

Alelí by the Sea Guest House, C. Sea View 1125 (☎ 725-5313; fax 721-4744). Although its exterior has been worn by the salty ocean air, bright rooms and an oceanfront patio make Alelí one of Condado's better deals. 1 room wheelchair-accessible. Cable TV and A/C. Common kitchen. Laundry $4. Free parking. Doubles Dec. 15-Apr. 15 $65-100; Apr. 16-Dec. 14 $55-90. Extra person $10. AmEx/D/MC/V. ❸

Casa del Caribe, C. Caribe 57 (☎ 722-7139, toll-free 888-722-7139; www.casadelcaribe.net). Enter through a white gate 4 buildings south of Av. Ashford on C. Caribe. The owners of At Windchimes Inn also manage this slightly cheaper option, which has more of a small-hostel feel than its sister hotel. Small book-swap corner under the open-air front desk, next to garden and waterfall. A/C, cable TV, and phone. 1½ blocks from the beach. Continental breakfast included. Parking $5. Doubles and quads Dec. 15-May 15 $75-125; May 16-Dec. 14 $55-65. Extra person $15. AmEx/D/MC/V. ❸

Hotel El Portal, Av. Condado 76 (☎ 721-8883; www.hotelelportal.com). Clean, standard rooms with A/C. The main drawback to this hotel is its location, about 3 blocks from the beach and less than 1 block from a highway overpass, an area that should be avoided after dark. The hotel compensates with a rooftop terrace that yields terrific views of the ocean. All rooms have fridge, phone, and cable TV. Continental breakfast included, High season doubles $170, low season $148, depending on availability. AmEx/MC/V. ❸

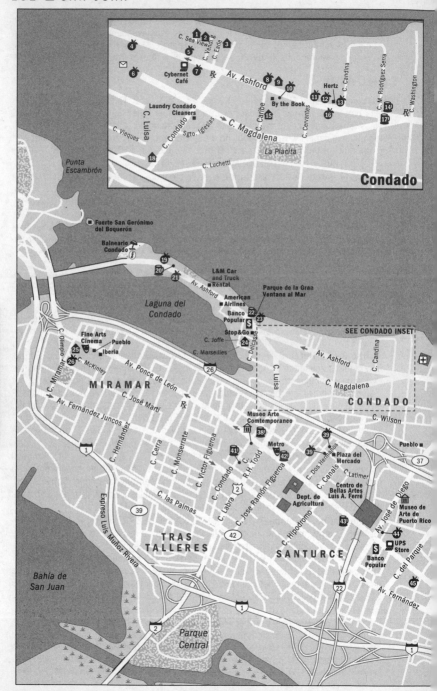

Condado

Punta Escambrón

Fuerte San Gerónimo del Boquerón

Balneario Condado

L&M Car and Truck Rental

Parque de la Gran Ventana al Mar

American Airlines

Banco Popular

Stop&Go

C. Joffe

C. Marseilles

Laguna del Condado

Fine Arts Cinema

Pueblo

Iberia

C. Olimpio

C. Miramar

C. McKinley

MIRAMAR

Av. Ponce de León

C. José Martí

Av. Fernández Juncos

Av. Ashford

C. Magdalena

CONDADO

C. Luisa

C. Candina

C. Wilson

Museo Arte Comtemporaneo

Metro

Plaza del Mercado

Pueblo

Centro de Bellas Artes Luis A. Ferré

C. Hernández

C. Cerra

C. Monserrate

C. Víctor Figueroa

C. Condado

C. R.H. Todd

C. Labra

C. José Ramón Figueroa

C. las Palmas

Dept. de Agricultura

C. Dos Hermanos

C. Canals

C. Latimer

Museo de Arte de Puerto Rico

UPS Store

Banco Popular

Av. José de Diego

C. del Parque

Av. Fernández

Expreso Luis Muñoz Rivera

TRAS TALLERES

SANTURCE

C. Hipodromo

Bahía de San Juan

Parque Central

SEE CONDADO INSET

SAN JUAN

Condado Inset:
C. Sea View
C. Velda
C. Earle
Av. Ashford
Cybernet Café
Rx
C. Luisa
C. Condado
Sgto. Iglesias
C. Vieques
Laundry Condado Cleaners
C. Caribe
C. Magdalena
By the Book
Hertz
C. Cervantes
C. Candina
C. M. Rodríguez Serra
Washington
Rx
La Placita
C. Luchetti

Condado, Ocean Park, Santurce, and Miramar

ACCOMMODATIONS
Alelí by the Sea Guest House, 1
At Windchimes Inn, 31
Atlantic Beach Hotel, 2
Casa del Caribe, 15
El Canario by the Lagoon, 24
El Canario by the Sea, 3
El Canario Inn, 9
Hostería del Mar, 29
Hotel El Portal, 18
Hotel Metropol, 46
Hotel Olimpo Court, 25
Numero Uno Guest House, 28
Oceana Hostal Playero, 32
Tres Palmas Guest House, 34

FOOD
Ajili-mójili, 21
Bla Bla Café, 44

Café del Ángel, 4
Cherry Blossom, 8
Cielito Lindo, 6
Colombo Café & Restaurant, 13
Compay Cheo, 39
Danny's International, 11
Di Parma Trattoria, 23
Dunbar's, 36
Kasalta Bakery, 37
Latin Star Restaurant, 7
Hacienda Don José, 19
La Patisserie de France, 27
Pinky's, 35
Piu Bello Gelato, 10
Pure and Natural Juice Bar, 5
Restaurant D'Arco, 26
Restaurant Godfather #2, 45
Sal y Pimienta, 39
Delirio, 30

Tijuana's Bar & Grill, 12
Via Appia's Deli, 16

NIGHTLIFE
Cups, 47
Krash, 42
Habana Club, 38
Junior's, 41
Kalí, 14
El Teatro, 43
La Terraza del Condado, 17
Sol de Luna Cafe, 22
Starz, 48
Waikiki, 20

OUTDOOR RENTAL ACTIVITY
Tres Palmas, 33

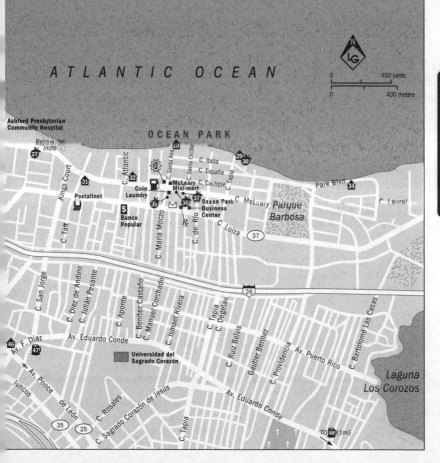

SAN JUAN

SANTURCE AND MIRAMAR

Hotel Olimpo Court, Av. Miramar 603 (☎724-0600), in Miramar. Once you get past the dorm-style hallways, Olimpio Court's very clean, white rooms with modern decor are more than satisfactory. All rooms have phone, cable TV, microwave, and A/C. Check-out noon. Singles $73; doubles $91; triples $111. AmEx/MC/V. ❷

Hotel Metropol, C. Saldania 1661 (☎725-0525), on the corner of Ponce de León, one block east of C. Bolívar, in Santurce. About a 10min. drive from the beach, this hotel does not cater to the whim of the tourist. Many rooms do not have TVs, the management speaks very little English, and it's not in the greatest of neighborhoods. But the rooms are large and clean, making the hotel a decent bargain. Long-term stays are the norm here: $200 per week, $680 per month. ❷

OCEAN PARK

Número Uno Guest House, C. Santa Ana 1 (☎726-5010; www.numero1guesthouse.com). Right on the beach—indeed, some of the restaurant's tables sit on the sand—this immaculate, white hotel has New Age-style rooms with cable TV, A/C, private baths, and free Internet. Common room with piano, books, and games; common balcony. Small pool. In an attractive main dining room and outdoor patio, Nuevo Latino food is served with gusto by Pamela's Restaurant. Check-in 3pm. Check-out 11am. Doubles Dec. 15-Apr. $135-275; May-July and Nov.-Dec. 15 $100-200; Aug.-Oct. $90-180. 15% service charge added to room price. AmEx/MC/V. ❹

Hostería del Mar, C. Tapia 1 (☎727-3302, toll-free 877-727-3302; www.hosteriadelmarpr.com). Brush by a serene waterfall to lounge in the small, dark-wood lobby, or enjoy ocean views from the patio of the adjacent Uvva restaurant. Standard A/C, phones, and cable TV. Doubles Nov. 15-May 15 $84-264; May 16-Nov. 14 $69-209. Extra person $25. Up to 2 children free. AmEx/D/MC/V. ❹

Tres Palmas Guest House, Park Blvd. 2212 (☎727-4617, toll-free 888-290-2076; www.trespalmasinn.com). Between Ocean Park to the west and Isla Verde to the east, Tres Palmas sits in a picturesque spot across the street from Punta Las Marías Beach. The view is especially good from the 2 rooftop hot tubs. Rooms are small, clean, and well decorated. Each has cable TV, a fridge, and a safe. Swimming pool. Sizable continental breakfast included. Doubles Dec. 16-Apr. $87-175; May-Dec. 15 $81-146. Extra person $15. AmEx/MC/V. ❸

El Prado Inn & Villas (☎391-1976, toll free 800-468-4521; www.elpradoinn.net). 11 apartments and villas around Ocean Park available for daily, weekly and monthly rentals. The lovely houses are 1-2 blocks from the beach, some with modern decor, others with original antiques. Equipped kitchens, TV, A/C, and linens. Housekeeping extra charge. 1-, 2-, or 3-bedroom suites $100-290 per night. MC/V. ❹

Oceana Hostal Playero, C. McLeary 1853 (☎728-8119). Attractive inner courtyard with small pool in main building. More worn, darker villas available apart from the hotel proper. 4-5min. from the beach. Doubles $85-$95. Villas from $130. MC/V. ❸

ISLA VERDE

🦑 **Hotel Villa del Sol,** C. Rosa 4 (☎791-2600 or 791-1600; www.villadelsolpr.com), on a quiet road off the main street just 2 blocks from the eastern end of the Isla Verde beach. This newly renovated, villa-style hotel is bright and charming, from the gorgeous pool to the suit of medieval armor in the lobby. Rooms are sparsely decorated, but quite large and very well kept. 2nd fl. terrace. All rooms have A/C, fridge, and cable TV. Free Wi-Fi in lobby and open cafe. Free parking. Doubles $98; quads $109-163. Tax included. AmEx/D/MC/V. ❹

🦑 **The Coqui Inn,** C. Mar Mediterraneo 14 and 36 (☎726-4330 or 726-8662; www.coqui-inn.com), next to Villa Verde Inn in Villamar. Across the highway from the beach; access from Isla Verde via bridge with stairs next to Banco Popular. Consists of 2 identical adjacent motel-style bungalows. Rooms with A/C, cable TV, fridge, safe, and phone; some with kitchenette. 2 computers free for guest use. Continental breakfast included. Check-in 3pm. Free Wi-Fi. Check-out noon. Value rooms M-F $89/99, Sa-Su $99; standard rooms $99/$109. Prices vary with season. Extra person $15. AmEx/D/MC/V. ❸

Hotel La Playa, C. Amapola 6 (☎791-1115 or 791-7298; www.hotellaplaya.com). Tucked away on a small peninsula, this family-run beach hotel offers clean rooms and a great location for surprisingly low prices. Steps from the beach. Basic TV and A/C. Attached lounge and restaurant. Check-in 2pm. Check-out noon. Dec. 14-Apr. 15 singles $90-105; doubles $100-115. Apr. 16-Dec. 13 $75-90/85-100. Extra person $15. AmEx/MC/V. ❹

Borinquen Beach Inn, Av. Isla Verde 5451 (☎728-8400; www.borinquenbeachinn.com). Borinquen is a surprising find, located among the big resorts along the beach. This and the large rooms make it a good value despite its spare facilities. Cable TV and A/C. Common kitchen. Check-in 2pm. Check-out noon. Free parking. Dec. 1-Apr. 15 and June 15-Labor Day singles $70-95; doubles $85-95. Apr. 16-June 14 and Labor Day-Nov. $56-76/68-76. Extra person $10. AmEx/D/MC/V. ❸

The Mango Inn, C. Mar Mediterraneo 46 (☎726-4230, toll-free 800-777-1946; www.themangoinn.com), in Villamar. From Villa Verde Inn continue straight and take your first right on C. Mar Mediterraneo. Parrots greet you in a small courtyard lobby. Rooms are clean and colorful, with basic A/C and cable TV. Across the freeway from Isla Verde and the beach, but low prices help to make up for this. Check-in 1pm. Check-out noon. Breakfast included. Free Wi-Fi in lobby. High season singles $55; doubles $65-70; triples $75. Low season $50/60-65/70. Extra person $15. AmEx/D/MC/V. ❷

Villa Verde Inn, C. Marginal 37 (☎727-9457 or 728-5912, toll-free 1-866-476-7327; www.villaverdeinn.net), in Villamar. From Av. Isla Verde, across the freeway bridge with stairs next to Banco Popular. Standard rooms come with fridge, A/C, cable TV, and phone. Some have a tiny balcony. A nice pool with a small hot tub. Friendly staff. Continental breakfast included. Check-in 3pm. Check-out noon. Dec. 15-Apr. 14 singles $64; doubles $74. Apr. 15-Dec. 14 $57/67. Extra person $10. Discounts for stays over 2 days. AmEx/D/MC/V. ❸

Coral by the Sea, C. Rosa 2 (☎791-6868; www.coralbythesea.com). The rich wood-paneled lobby gives way to dark hallways. Rooms with cable TV, phone, A/C, and tiny bathrooms. Free Wi-Fi. Check-in 1pm. Check-out noon. High-season doubles $76; triples $87; quads $98. Low-season $65/87/98. Tax included. AmEx/MC/V. ❸

WATERFRONT FACELIFT

One of the largest infrstructure projects in the history of Puerto Rico is currently underway in Puerta de Tierra, just east of Old San Juan. The San Juan Waterfront Project calls for a 10-year and 1.5-billion-dollar redevelopment of 100 acres on the north side of San Antonio Channel.

This ambitious vision, combining sophisticated coastal engineering and urban design, aims to construct a mega yacht marina and a new boulevard that will run parallel to Expressway Fernandez Juncos, in addition to parks, cafes, restaurants, condominiums, and small hotels. Scheduled to be completed in 2000, the marina will include 30,000 sq. ft. of commercial space for restaurants and retailers. The Puerto Rican Port authority explains that other Caribbean islands, including St. Maarten and St. Thomas, have built such facilities, and that the investment holds tremendous potential for economic growth.

All this development represents a major component of the Puerto Rican government initiative to promote tourism in San Juan, a long-term project fittingly entitled "Greatest City: Metropolis of the Carribbean." San Juan may well be a Caribbean metropolis, but only time will tell whether visitors will discover the more traditional Puerto Rico that lies, in many ways still untouched, just beyond the city.

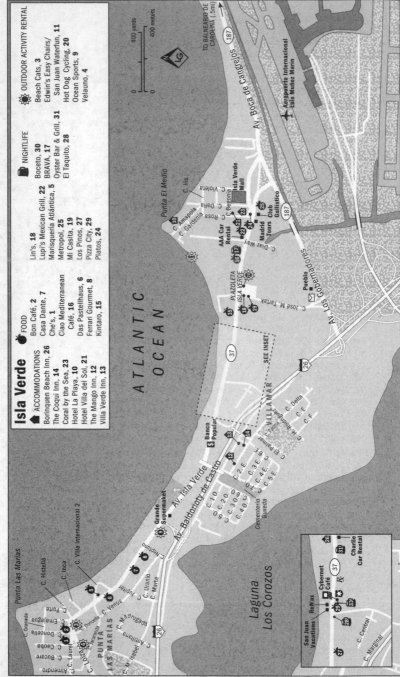

Isla Verde

▲ ACCOMMODATIONS
Borinquen Beach Inn, **26**
The Coqui Inn, **14**
Coral by the Sea, **23**
Hotel La Playa, **10**
Hotel Villa del Sol, **21**
The Mango Inn, **12**
Villa Verde Inn, **13**

🍴 FOOD
Bon Café, **2**
Casa Dante, **7**
Che's, **1**
Ciao Mediterranean Café, **16**
Das Pastellhaus, **6**
Ferrari Gourmet, **8**
Kintaro, **15**
Lin's, **18**
Lupi's Mexican Grill, **22**
Marisquería Atlántica, **5**
Metropol, **25**
Mi Casita, **19**
Los Pinos, **27**
Pizza City, **29**
Platos, **24**

🍸 NIGHTLIFE
Boceto, **30**
BRAVA, **17**
Oyster Bar & Grill, **31**
El Taquito, **28**

☀ OUTDOOR ACTIVITY RENTAL
Beach Cats, **3**
Edwin's Easy Chairs/
San Juan Waterfun, **11**
Hot Dog Cycling, **20**
Ocean Sports, **9**
Velauno, **4**

◘ FOOD

It's safe to assume that most restaurants have English menus, although some small *cafeterías* may cater exclusively to Spanish speakers.

FOOD BY TYPE

AMERICAN AND BURGERS

El Hamburguer (p. 110)	PT ❶
Dunbar's (p. 113)	OP ❹
El Patio de Sam (p. 110)	OSJ ❹

BAKERIES

Panadería España (p. 114)	IV ❶
Das Pastellhaus (p. 114)	IV ❷
Gelo's Bagel Bakery (p. 115)	IV ❷
Kasalta Bakery (p. 113)	OP ❷

CAFETERÍAS

Cafetería Janet Janez (p. 116)	RP ❷
Cafetería Mallorca (p. 108)	OSJ ❷
Los Pinos (p. 115)	IV ❷

CUBAN

Metropol (p. 115)	IV ❸

FRENCH

▩ Bistro Avant (p. 108)	OSJ ❶
La Patisserie de France (p. 112)	CO ❶

INDIAN, JAPANESE, AND CHINESE

Cherry Blossom (p. 112)	CO ❺
Dragonfly (p. 109)	OSJ ❹
Kintaro (p. 115)	IV ❸
Lin's (p. 115)	IV ❸
Tantra Restaurant and Bar (p. 108)	OSJ ❹

ITALIAN

Café El Burén (p. 110)	OSJ ❺
Di Parma Trattoria (p. 112)	CO ❸
Il Bacaro Venezia (p. 109)	OSJ ❸
Restaurant Godfather #2 (p. 112)	SA ❸

MEXICAN

Cielito Lindo (p. 112)	CO ❸
Hacienda Don José (p. 111)	CO ❸
Lupi's (p. 111) and (p. 114)	OSJ and IV ❸
Taquería Azteca (p. 116)	RP ❶

PIZZA

Danny's International (p. 112)	CO ❷
Ferrari Gourmet (p. 115)	IV ❷
Pizza City (p. 114)	IV ❶
Via Appia's Deli (p. 111)	CO ❸

PUERTO RICAN

Ajili-mójili (p. 111)	CO ❺
Barrachina (p. 110)	OSJ ❹
Café del Ángel (p. 111)	CO ❸
Café la Princesa (p. 108)	OSJ ❷
Casa Dante (p. 114)	IV ❸
El Jibarito (p. 109)	OSJ ❷
El Siglo XX Restaurant (p. 110)	OSJ ❸
La Bombonera (p. 109)	OSJ ❸
La Danza (p. 109)	OSJ ❸
Latin Star Restaurant (p. 112)	CO ❹
▩ Mi Casita (p. 113)	IV ❸
Platos (p. 114)	IV ❹
Plaza del Mercado (p. 112)	SA ❷
▩ Raíces Restaurant (p. 108)	OSJ ❹
Restaurant D'Arco (p. 113)	MI ❸

SANDWICHES AND CAFES

▩ Bla Bla Café (p. 112)	SA ❷
Bon Café (p. 114)	IV ❸
Ciao Mediterranean Café (p. 115)	IV ❹
Colombo Café and Restaurant (p. 111)	CO
❷Diner's Crew Lounge (p. 110)	OSJ ❸
El Mesón Sandwiches (p. 110)	OSJ ❶
▩ Guajanas Arte Cafe (p. 115)	RP ❷
Nadine's Café (p. 109)	OSJ ❺
Piu Bello Gelato (p. 111)	CO ❷
▩ Pinky's (p. 113)	OP ❷
Pure and Natural Juice Bar (p. 111)	CO ❶
St. Germain (p. 108)	OSJ ❷

SEAFOOD

Ostra Cosa (p. 109)	OSJ ❹
Escambrón Restaurant (p. 111)	PT ❺
▩ Marisquería Atlántica (p. 113)	IV ❺

SOUTH AMERICAN

Che's (p. 114)	IV ❹

VEGETARIAN

Cafe Berlin (p. 109)	OSJ ❹
Country Health Food (p. 115)	RP ❶
Uvva (p. 113)	OP ❺
Zesty Bites (p. 108)	OSJ ❶

CO Condado. **IV** Isla Verde. **MI** Miramar. **PT** Puerta de la Tierra. **OP** Ocean Park. **OSJ** Old San Juan. **OP** Ocean Park. **RP** Río Piedras. **SA** Santurce.

SAN JUAN

OLD SAN JUAN

Finding a good meal in Old San Juan is not difficult; it's finding an affordable meal that may prove problematic. Trendy restaurants along C. Recinto Sur and C. Fortaleza serve food from all over the world, with representatives hovering outside each establishment to compete for cruise passengers' dollars. Most restaurants near the docks theoretically close around midnight, but actually morph into hopping bars and stay open until the last customer leaves. The southern end of C. del Cristo, near the water, becomes a walkway with a series of outdoor restaurants serving traditional Puerto Rican food during the day (entrees $8-18). For a smaller or more wallet-friendly bite, cheaper food lies just off the beaten path at a number of *cafeterías*. During the day, several vendors set up around Plaza de la Dársena near the tourist office, selling coconut sweets and homemade tropical smoothies. Groceries are available at **Pueblo,** C. Cruz 201, on the Plaza de Armas. (☎725-4839. Open M-Sa 6am-midnight, Su 6am-6pm. AmEx/MC/V.)

■ **Raíces Restaurant,** C. Recinto Sur 315 (☎289-2121; www.restauranteraices.com), across from Doña Fela's parking lot. *Raíces,* meaning "roots," offers delicious gourmet renditions of the usual island specialties. The *mofongo* with steak (mashed plantains stuffed with chimichurri-style skirt steak) is the house special ($18). In case the food isn't enough to keep you entertained, waitresses serve in traditional Puerto Rican dress. Free Wi-Fi. Open M-W 11am-8pm, Th-Sa 11am-10pm, Su noon-8pm. MC/V. ❹

■ **Bistro Avant,** in a permanent booth in the Plaza de Armas, is a pleasant patio oasis amidst the bustle of San Juan's old city center. A local favorite for those in search of a quick meal. Sweet crepes such as Dulce de Leche and Choco Dream ($2-$3.50). When newspaper-wielding locals at the outside tables tell you to try the "Door to Hell," don't be offended—they're referring to a savory crepe with chicken in Asian hot sauce. Savory crepes $4-5.50. Pasta $3.50-7. Sandwiches $4.50-5.50. Soups and salads $3.50-4.50. Open M-F 6am-9pm, Sa-Su 9am-9pm. MC/V. ❶

Café la Princesa, Paseo la Princesa (☎724-2930). Take a stroll down the Paseo la Princesa promenade toward Old San Juan's western shore and find a shady table under palms on this quiet patio alongside the vine-covered old city wall. Island delights like the Fricasé de Ternera with rice and beans $6. Breakfast $1.50-3.50. Sandwiches, wraps, and burgers $3.50-4.25. Open M-W 7am-3pm, Th-F 7am-last customer, Sa-Su noon-last customer. D/MC/V. ❷

Cafetería Mallorca, C. San Francisco 300 (☎724-4607), on Plaza Salvador Brau. The 1930s live on at Mallorca, where waiters in black hats and bow ties serve standard *comida criolla* at tables or a diner-style bar. The largely local crowd is drawn by the tasty pastries ($1.10) in the front window, and entrees like the "Mallorca Especial," a sandwich filled with omelette and chicken salad ($7). Menu varies daily. Most entrees $7-10. Open daily 7am-7pm. D/MC/V. ❷

Zesty Bites, C. Tetuán 151, at the corner of C. San José (☎721-5436; www.zesty-bites.com). This is the only restaurant in Old San Juan specializing in whole, organic, and raw foods. Grab breakfast (muffin, granola, organic yogurt, or toast $1.50-3) or a sushi roll ($8) to go or enjoy sit-down service under shady mango trees overlooking the old city wall. Beware the noontime crowds—this place fills to the brim for lunch. Free Wi-Fi. Open M-F 7am-7pm, Sa-Su 9am-5pm. AmEx/MC/V. ❶

Tantra Restaurant and Bar, C. Fortaleza 356 (☎977-8141; www.tantrapr.net). Tantra presents an exoticized Indian atmosphere, complete with cushions on the floor and hookahs at the bar. The excellent food is Indo-Latino fusion, with numerous vegetarian offerings. The Tantra Mofongo ($12) with a "lust martini" ($7) should liven up any date, along with belly-dancing shows M 9:30-11pm. Open M-Th and Su noon-11pm, F-Sa noon-midnight. Bar open Tu-Sa until 2am. AmEx/D/MC/V. ❹

St. Germain, C. Sol 156 (☎725-5830), on the corner of C. Cruz. Relax in fresh white surroundings touched with tropical flowers and delicate antique decor at this European-style bistro and cafe. Creative gourmet sandwiches on wrap, baguette, or whole wheat come with salad; try the "Patrick" with avocado and hummus on 7-grain ($5.70). Open Tu-Sa 11:30am-3:30pm and Su 11am-3pm. MC/V. ❷

La Danza, C. Fortaleza 56 (☎723-1642; www.restaurantladanza.com), at C. del Cristo. Live music and great specials at this pleasant Puerto Rican restaurant. Paella for 2, with 2 glasses of wine, fried plantains, garlic bread, and coffee, is a bargain at $25. Alternatively, just sit outside and sip a Planter's Punch ($2). Most entrees $12-20. Open M-W and F-Su 11:30am-8pm. Kitchen closes at 7:30pm. AmEx/MC/V. ❸

El Jibarito, C. Sol 280 (☎725-8375; www.eljibaritopr.com). Since 1977, this casual diner in the residential cluster of northern Old San Juan has been equally popular with locals and tourists. Famous city-wide as one of the best places to find Puerto Rican food in the metropolitan area. Tasty and effortlessly authentic. Appetizers $1.50-4. Most entrees $6-10. Open daily 10am-9pm. AmEx/D/MC/V. ❷

Il Bacaro Venezia, C. Cruz 152 (☎977-5638), just north of the Plaza de Armas. Don't be deceived by the non-descript exterior of this local favorite. The classy, intimate setting is authentically Italian, from the owners to the waiters. Satisfy your sweet tooth with tiramisu ($5.50). Tapas $5-15. Pasta $9-13. Entrees $15-$22. M $5 tapas and $15 bottles of wine. Open Tu-Sa 11:30am-3pm and 6-10:30pm. MC/V. ❸

Dragonfly, C. Fortaleza 364 (☎977-3886; www.oofrestaurants.com), on the corner of C. Fortaleza and C. O'Donnell in the heart of trendy "SoFo." Latin-Asian fusion done right. Tourists and locals alike crowd into this combination cocktail lounge and sushi bar with dark red walls, embroidered pillows, and attentive waitstaff. Try the quesadilla spring rolls with Chinese sausage and lime sour cream ($12) or ask about the sushi special rolls ($11-18). The Asian chocolate cake is decadently delicious ($8). Dress code. Open M-W 6-11pm, Th-Sa 6pm-midnight. Kitchen closes 1hr. earlier. AmEx/MC/V. ❹

Nadine's Café, C. San Francisco 100 (☎724-0444), between C. del Cristo and C. San José. Pay homage to Marilyn Monroe at this hole-in-the-wall soda fountain plastered with posters of the diva herself. Mojitos ($7) and tropical shakes ($5 virgin, $6 with rum) pair well with quesadillas, tacos, and burritos ($3). Outdoor seating along a quiet cobblestone street. Very popular by day and especially during the early evening. Open daily 10am-10pm. D/MC/V. ❶

Cafe Berlin, C. San Francisco 407 (☎722-5205), facing Plaza Colón from the north side. This plaza-side cafe dishes up homemade bread, freshly squeezed juices, cocktails, and desserts. Famous for Sunday brunch ($15). Sandwiches $6-11, vegetarian versions with tofu and eggplant $5.50-9. Breakfast $1-10. Entrees $12-23. Free Wi-Fi. Open M-F 11am-10pm, Sa-Su 10am-10pm. AmEx/MC/V. ❹

La Bombonera, C. San Francisco 259 (☎722-0658). For over 100 years, this friendly soda fountain and restaurant has been serving the self-proclaimed "best coffee in town" ($1) to locals who line the long bar and many families who crowd into the red leather booths. Excellent *comida criolla* (most entrees $7-15) and a wide selection of pastries ($0.80) such as the Mmm...Mallorca (sweet bread roll with sugar icing), best heated with butter. Open daily 7:30am-8:30pm. D/MC/V. ❸

 CAFFEINATE ME. The best brands of Puerto Rican coffee beans are said to be Café Crema, Café Rico, Yaucono, and Rioja. These can be served *puya* or *negrito* (unsweetened), *negrito con azúcar* (black and sweetened with sugar), *cortado* (black with a touch of milk), or *con leche* (with milk).

Ostra Cosa, C. del Cristo 154 (☎722-3672), through the walkway to a beautiful open-air courtyard. At this sophisticated restaurant, all entrees (mostly seafood with some veggie and meat options) are rated on an aphrodisiac scale from one star (Oh!) to three stars (Ay Ay Ay!). The menu warns, "We are not responsible for increments in passion. Please direct your claims to your partner." Ay ay ay! Appetizers $8-11. Entrees $14-28. Open M-W and Su noon-10pm, F-Sa noon-11pm. AmEx/D/MC/V. ❹

El Siglo XX Restaurant, C. Fortaleza 355 (☎723-3321). A comfortable restaurant tucked among more formal options on Fortaleza Street. A friendly, local crowd lines the parlor bar stools and leans over handsome green checkered tablecloths to devour authentic *criollo* food: *amarillos* ($2.50), *tostones* ($2.50), rice with beans ($5), and sandwiches ($6-7). Meat and seafood entrees ($9-27) including shrimp *mofongo* ($19). Open M-Sa 8am-9pm, Su 8am-8pm. MC/V. ❸

El Mesón Sandwiches (☎721-5286), at C. San José and C. San Francisco. An exclusively *sanjuanero* crowd packs this Puerto Rican fast-food favorite at lunchtime for some of the quickest meals in the city. Only Spanish spoken, but the pictures of the sandwiches on the overhead menu will help you decide. Save on a combo meal (sandwich, fries, and a drink; $3-5), or choose from over 25 sandwiches ($4). Gigantic salads $4-5. Breakfast sandwiches $1.50-4. Open M-Sa 6am-10pm, Su 7am-10pm. AmEx/MC/V. ❶

Barrachina, C. Fortaleza 104 (☎721-5852; www.barrachina.com). A plaque outside this central restaurant announces that Don Ramón Portas Mingot crafted the first ever piña colada here in 1963. Terrace in the confines of the city center, complete with interior colonial patio and palms aglow. Choose from *mofongo* stuffed with chicken, seafood, or shrimp ($6-9) and entrees including Spanish paella or seafood stir-fry ($16-40). Lunch sandwiches $8-13. Open M-Tu, Th, Su 10am-10pm; W 10am-6pm; F-Sa 10am-11pm. AmEx/D/MC/V. ❹

Diner's Crew Lounge, C. Tetuán 311 (☎724-6276). Tucked away on a quiet side street, Diner's is more of a communication hub than a restaurant. Patrons sit alone and chat on the phone while eating (each table is equipped with a telephone, and local calls are free). Brick walls, tall ceilings, a fully stocked bar, and several Internet terminals make the lounge a pleasant place to work. Sandwiches $5. Puerto Rican entrees $9-17. Internet $3 per 30min., $5 per hr. Open daily 10am-10pm. AmEx/D/MC/V. ❸

El Patio de Sam, C. San Sebastián 102 (☎723-1149). Sam's wins praise for its convenient location, reasonable prices, and family-friendly atmosphere. Many a tourist has stopped here for a Sam's burger ($8-9) after visiting El Morro. The glass-covered dining area allows you to simultaneously enjoy the sun and the A/C. A somewhat popular bar on weekend nights. Puerto Rican entrees $10-20. Cocktails $4.50-6. Open M-Th and Su 11am-11pm, F-Sa 11am-midnight. AmEx/MC/V. ❷

El Burén, C. del Cristo 103 (☎977-5023; www.elburenpr.com). Like several other tourist-oriented restaurants, El Burén offers another variation on Latin-fusion cuisine, this time called *cocina creativa internacional*. The dimly lit restaurant features wood decor and modern art photographs, but little that could not be found elsewhere—and all this coolness comes at a price. Italian entrees $17-25. M-Tu $5 martinis. W-Th $3.50 mojitos. Free Wi-Fi. Open M 5:30pm-midnight, Tu-Su noon-midnight. AmEx/MC/V. ❺

Lupi's Mexican Grill & Sports Cantina, C. Recinto Sur 313 (☎722-1874). Autographed photos of athletes and conspicuous TVs give Lupi's the feel of an American sports bar. Sit on a cushioned, elevated seat against the wall to watch the game or crowd into a big booth and slurp "Island Famous Margaritas" ($7-15). However, the only things distinctly Mexican about this place are the appetizers (quesadillas, nachos, potato skins, and guacamole; $5.50-14) and the sombrero on the statue of Lupi outside. Salads, sandwiches, and burgers $7-13. Open M-Th 11am-10pm, F-Su 11am-2am. AmEx/MC/V. ❸

PUERTA DE TIERRA

El Hamburguer, Av. Muñoz Rivera 402 (☎721-4269). Good, cheap, fast, and popular with locals. This shack is conveniently located near the beach and dishes out small, thick burgers ($2-4), delicious thin fries ($1.60), and several varieties of tropically flavored cheesecake. Watch them grill dozens of burgers at a time, then add your choice of fixings. Open M-Th and Su 11:30am-12:30am, F-Sa noon-3:30am. ❶

FOOD ■ **111**

Escambrón Restaurant, Parque del 3er Milenio/Playa Escambrón (☎ 724-3344; www.escambron.com), on the western end of Escambrón Beach. Within easy walking distance of the beach, the Radisson, and the Hilton, Escambrón is a good option for beachfront dining. Taste the "Tipsy Lobster" (lobster flambéed with rum; $32) while looking out over its former home. Atmosphere somewhat austere on weekdays, but heats up with live music on weekends. Appetizers $4-8. Meat and poultry dishes $9-16. Seafood $13-32. ❺

CONDADO

Condado has restaurants that will satisfy almost every culinary craving. For those midnight munchies, **Stop & Go,** C. Magdalena 1102, a small convenience store, serves $3.50 sandwiches 24hr. a day (☎724-3106). For a more extensive selection of quick supplies, try **Pueblo,** Av. de Diego 114. (☎725-1095. Banco Popular branch inside. Open 24hr. AmEx/MC/V.)

Colombo Café & Restaurant, Av. Ashford 1357 (☎725-1212). This bright, centrally located shop on Ashford has been cooking, scooping, and delivering since 1988. In addition to frozen yogurt ($2.75), Colombo dishes up wraps and sandwiches ($7-8) as well as an assortment of dinner options, from burgers to gyros ($6-8). Free delivery to nearby hotels and houses. Open daily 8am-1am. MC/V. ❷

Via Appia's Deli, Av. Ashford 1350 (☎725-8711 or 722-4325). The walls are lined with liquor, but it's the pizza that draws crowds. Mediterranean tapas like grilled Italian sausages with garlic bread $4.50. Hot and cold sandwiches $6 8. Pies $7-18. Entrees $9-18. Homemade sangria $4. Happy hour Th 5-7pm. Open M-Th and Su 11am-11pm, F-Sa 11am-midnight. AmEx/MC/V. ❸

Café del Ángel, Av. Ashford 1106 (☎722-1245). This Caribbean-themed restaurant sticks to big, hearty portions of *comida criolla*. Seating on the patio or inside. Delicious hot bread with every meal. Island entrees $6-25. Stuffed *mofongo* $9-25. Open M and W-Su 11:30am-10pm. MC/V. ❸

Piu Bello Gelato, Av. Ashford 1302 (☎977-2121), on a raised platform of stores called "Plaza Sara." Yes, it's a chain, but this immaculate modern cafe draws in customers of all ages with its yummy *gelato* ($2.50-4) in creative flavors. A huge assortment of enticing pastries ($4-5) and cakes designed for chocoholics, such as Chocolate Madness and Blackout with brownies and Oreo ($4). Free Wi-Fi at tables overlooking Av. Ashford. Open M Th 8am 1am, F Sa 8am 3am. AmEx/D/MC/V. ❶

Ajili-mójili, Av. Ashford 1006 (☎725-9195). Widely acknowledged as one of the best options in the area for formal dining, Ajili-mójili serves up traditional Puerto Rican cuisine, with an emphasis on seafood. Huge windows with views of El Condado lagoon and candlelight after dark set the mood. No shorts or T-shirts. Lunches with drink and dessert $20. Dinner entrees $13-30. Open M-Th 11:45am-3pm and 6-10pm, F 11:45am-3pm and 6-11pm, Sa 6-11pm, Su 12:30-4pm and 6-10pm. AmEx/D/MC/V. ❺

Hacienda Don José, Av. Ashford 1025 (☎722-5880). This Mexican eatery is one of Condado's only oceanfront restaurants. A few tables lined against large, open, back windows yield views of the water, while a front patio looks out onto the street. Consider splurging on the Fajitas Hacienda Don José, filled with shrimp and lobster ($36 for 2 people). Breakfast $3.50-6. Puerto Rican and Mexican entrees $11-19. Margaritas $5. Pitcher of sangria $20. Open daily 7am-11pm. MC/V. ❸

Pure & Natural Juice Bar, Av. Ashford 1125 (☎725-6104). A modern juice spot with a classy, minimalist look blends nutrient-rich creations. Try the Honey, Peaches & Cream smoothie ($4.45) for something sweet or Leo's Power Shake (avocado slice, walnuts, banana, spirulina, bee pollen, and soymilk; $6) if you're not kidding around. Fruit juices $4-4.25, vegetable juices $3.50-4.50. Shakes with 2 fruits $4. M and Sa 11am-8pm, Tu-F 11am-10pm. MC/V. ❶

SAN JUAN

Di Parma Trattoria, Av. Ashford 1049 (☎721-7132; www.diparmatrattoria.com), in La Ventana al Mar park. This small Italian restaurant is one of the latest hot spots for 20- and 30-somethings to gather for food and drinks on a clear night. Classy patio overlooks the park and ocean. Choose from gourmet pizza ($8-14), pasta ($10-22), soup ($5.50), and salad ($12-15). Tango performances Su 6pm. Open daily 5pm-2am. ❸

La Patisserie de France, Av. Ashford 1504 (☎728-5508). This busy bakery, cafe, and restaurant is a popular lunch stop for Condado businesspeople and residents. A huge array of sandwiches and wraps ($7-9) and grill items ($12-17), as well as French bread and desserts ($1.50-3.75). Open daily 7am-9pm. AmEx/MC/V. ❷

Cielito Lindo, C. Magdalena 1108 (☎723-5597). Found on a quiet section of the street next to the post office, at the western junction of C. Magdalena and Av. Ashford. This classy eatery transports you to Mexico with bright walls and folkloric beats. The restaurant is small, but an annex opens on weekend nights. Tasty Mexican enchiladas, burritos, and quesadillas $10-18. 2 Tacos $5. More substantial entrees $18-21. Margaritas $6. Open daily 11am-10pm. AmEx/MC/V. ❸

Danny's International, Av. Ashford 1351 (☎724-0501). Outdoor and indoor seating. Dishes out a variety of international entrees ($4-13), but the real reason to come is to try 1 of the 52 varieties of pizza ($8.75-24). Most noteworthy is the *puertorriqueña*, a pizza topped with cheese, ground beef, and plantains. Make your own pizza $7.50 plus $1.75 per topping. Open M-Th 7am-1am, F-Sa 7am-2am. AmEx/D/MC/V. ❷

Latin Star Restaurant, Av. Ashford 1128 (☎724-8141; www.latinstarrestaurant.com). Serves Puerto Rican food and spaghetti around the clock. After a long night at the disco, nothing looks better than a big *mofongo* filled with chicken, beef or seafood ($10-29). Savor the A/C or chill on a large outdoor patio covered with sports pictures. Bar inside. Entrees $6-20. Specials $8-12. Open 24hr. AmEx/MC/V. ❹

Cherry Blossom, Av. Ashford 1309 (☎723-7300). This upscale Japanese steakhouse seats guests at large tables where enthusiastic chefs cook meals in front of them. Bar and lounge upstairs. Early-bird specials ($12-16) served 5:30-7pm. Dinner entrees $19-31. Open M-F 12:30pm-3pm and 5:30-11pm, Sa 5:30-11pm, Su noon-11pm. ❺

SANTURCE AND MIRAMAR

Groceries can be found in Miramar at **Pueblo,** Av. Ponce de León 670. (☎725-4479. Open M-Sa 6am-9pm, Su 11am-5pm. AmEx/MC/V.) Countless indistinguishable restaurants along Av. Ponce de León serve inexpensive *comida criolla*, barbecue, and sandwiches to office workers. A few stand-outs are listed below.

Bla Bla Café, Av. de Diego 353 (☎724-8321; www.blablacoffeehouse.com). The friendly staff at this art-filled cafe serves up wraps ($5-6) and burgers ($5-6), but the best deals are the daily specials ($6-9), which include a drink, salad, and dessert. Also serves delicious *batidas* ($2.50). Coffee $0.75-2.50. Breakfast $2-5. Open M-F 7:30am-3:30pm. AmEx/MC/V. ❷

Plaza del Mercado, 2 blocks north of Av. Ponce de León between C. Canals and C. Dos Hermanos. In the large yellow-and-brown building. A covered, well-organized **fruit and vegetable market** surrounded by clean restaurants serving *comida criolla* (entrees $6-11, seafood slightly more expensive; beer $1.25-2). Market open daily 6am-6pm. Most restaurants have a patio on the market square. One good option is **Compay Cheo,** C. Dos Hermanos 205 (☎724-2387). Open daily 11am-9pm. ❷

Cafe Restaurant Godfather #2, Av. Ponce de León Parada 23 (☎721-1556), in Santurce. A local, male crowd gathers at this restaurant, one of the oldest and most popular *comida criolla* joints in Santurce. The house specialty is seafood. Breakfast $1.50 and up. Menu ranges from seafood salad to *churrasco* beef ($4-13). Free delivery. Open 24hr. AmEx/MC/V. ❸

Restaurant D'Arco, C. Miramar 605 (☎ 724-7813), Miramar. This clean but unexceptional restaurant next to the Olimpo Hotel (p. 104) is a good place to get a Puerto Rican meal in Miramar. The sandwiches ($2-8), breakfasts ($1-3), and entree specials ($7-10) written on notecards at every table are the best deals. Plates come with traditional sides (rice with beans, fried plantains). Open M-Sa 7am-9pm. AmEx/MC/V. ❸

OCEAN PARK

A few good restaurants around Ocean Park cater to the beach crowd, but many only serve lunch. Dozens of *cafeterías* line C. Loíza, though it's not safe to wander here at night. So what's the budget traveler to do for dinner? One solution is to head to Isla Verde or Condado, where good restaurants abound. Another is to just stock up on chips and drinks at the **McLeary Mini-Mart** on the corner of C. McLeary and C. Santa Ana and wait until morning. (Open daily 8am-8pm. MC/V.)

▨ **Pinky's,** C. Maria Moczo 51 (☎ 727-3347), at C. McLeary. Where California meets San Juan, you get Pinky's, a bright pink urban surf shack famed for its creative sandwiches ($5-11) and cheap, big breakfasts ($2-6). The friendly staff will bring you a sandwich in the busy restaurant or deliver—even to the beach. Hungry beachgoers may enjoy the house specialty, the "Kite Surfer" ($7). Free delivery 9am-4pm. Limited free parking. Free Wi-Fi. Open M-Sa 7:30am-8:30pm, Su 7:30am-6:30pm. MC/V. ❷

Kasalta Bakery, C. McLeary 1966 (☎ 723-7340; www.kasalta.com), at the corner of Santa Cecilia. People have been known to come to Kasalta for lunch, but they never leave without dessert. This incredible bakery boasts a huge variety of sweets, from flan to chocolate-covered strawberries. All desserts $1.50. Sandwiches $4.50-7.25. Entrees $9-22. Open daily 5am-10pm. AmEx/D/MC/V. ❷

Dunbar's, C. McLeary 1956 (☎ 728-2920). Dark panels add to the English pub feel of this bar and eatery that has been serving the Ocean Park community for over 20 years. Offers a wide selection of American food, including Dunbar's famous potato skins ($6-10). By night, the restaurant becomes a lively pub. Entrees $10-24. Wraps and sandwiches $9-18. Happy hour daily 6-7pm. Sushi night (rolls $8-14) W 6pm-10:30pm. Open M-Th 11:30am-midnight, F 11:30am-1am, Sa 5pm-1am, Su 10am-midnight. AmEx/MC/V. ❹

Uvva, C. Tapia 1 (☎ 727-3302 or 727-0631), in the Hostería del Mar guesthouse (p. 104). Wood decor and a breezy beach patio make this Mediterranean-Puerto Rican fusion restaurant one of Ocean Park's best choices for an upscale night out. The house specialities are Vietnamese couscous and Latin parilla grilled meats. Vegetarian options. Sandwiches and lunch salads $12-16. Entrees $18-32. Grill menu $20-40. Open daily 8am-10pm. AmEx/D/MC/V. ❺

ISLA VERDE

Most of the restaurants listed below provide at least a few parking spaces as well as free or inexpensive delivery within the Isla Verde area. There is a **Pueblo Supermarket** in a large plaza on Av. Gobernadores near Embassy Suites. (☎ 791-3366. Open 24hr. AmEx/MC/V.)

▨ **Mi Casita** (☎ 791-1777), in La Plazoleta de Isla Verde. Dubs itself "the best local restaurant in town," and that may well be true, as it's filled with locals who will tell you this is the place to come for a real Puerto Rican meal. Steak and chicken entrees $8-15. *Mofongo* $10-19. Breakfast special $2.50. Open daily 7am-10:30pm. AmEx/MC/V. ❸

Marisquería Atlántica, C. Loíza 2475 (☎ 728-5444 or 728-5662; www.atlanticapr.com). Waiters dress as sailors and sea life adorns the walls in this San Juan favorite for fresh seafood. The elegant back room is a covered terrace with fountains and a pleasant bar with stools. *Ceviche* (marinated cold seafood salad; $9) and tapas ($7-9) partner well with a glass of wine ($4.50-7). Fresh catches can be bought from the adjoining seafood store and prepared at home. Entrees $18-41. Open M-Th noon-10pm, F-Sa noon-11pm. Store open M-Sa 9am-8pm, Su 10am-3pm. AmEx/MC/V. ⑤

Platos, C. Rosa 2 (☎453-2774 or 791-7474; www.platosrestaurant.com). A crisp, casual setting with designer editions of traditional Puerto Rican plates. *Vejigante* masks bring spice to conservative walls, and blue-lit full bar offers sleek seating below large-screen TV. Popular seafood and meat dishes include *mofongo* ($18-25) and paella ($45). Creative entrees ($14-38), such as risotto with mushrooms, pumpkin, fresh vegetables, or *el jibarito* ("the peasant") pork dish ($16). Open M-Tu 5pm-10pm, Th-Sa 5pm-10pm. AmEx/MC/V. ④

Bon Café, C. Doncella 2413 (☎728-7070; www.boncafe.net), on C. Laurel, an extension of Av. Isla Verde in Punta Las Marías at the west end of Isla Verde. By day and evening, this cafe, bar, and restaurant has a cozy, familiar feel. Wraps $7-9. Salads $7-13. Pasta and seafood entrees $12-35. At night, guests come for the full bar and often live music. Open Tu-Th 4pm-1am, F-Sa 4pm-2am, Su 4pm-midnight. MC/V. ❸

Das Pastellhaus, C. Loíza 2482 (☎728-7106 or 728-7107). At this bright and friendly German pastry house, glass cabinets tempt customers with puff pastries ($1.50-2.50), sweet pastries such as the "quesito with guava" ($2), and chocolate treats ($1.50-5.75). Sit-down menu includes breakfast eggs and omelets ($4-6), sandwiches ($5-10), and pasta ($11-16), but many loyal customers are captivated by the gourmet pizzas ($5.50-22), especially the unique "Special Cream Pizzas" with white sauce ($9.70-26). Open daily 7am-11pm. AmEx/D/MC/V. ❷

Casa Dante, Av. Isla Verde 39 (☎726-7310). Perhaps the most extensive selection of *mofongo* this side of Cuba: the crushed plantains are filled with creative stuffings from chicken soup to fajitas to turkey breast with mushroom sauce. Other options available for those who don't live on *mofongo* alone. Entrees $9-28. ½-jug of sangria $14. Cocktails $5-6. Delivery $3. Open M-Th 11:30am-11pm, F-Sa 11:30am-midnight, Su 11:30am-10:30pm. MC/V. ❸

Che's, C. Caoba 35 (☎726-7202 or 268-7507; www.chesrestaurant.com), in Punta Las Marías. Widely acknowledged as the best Argentinian restaurant in town. Blue-and-white checkered tablecloths, bright red chairs, and many families make you feel right at home—if home serves tasty Argentine *churrasco* skirt steak ($23). Meat entrees $18-30. Pasta $10-18. Wine $4.50. Sangria $5. Open M-Th and Su 11am-11pm, F-Sa 11am-midnight. AmEx/D/MC/V. ④

Lupi's Mexican Grill & Sports Cantina, Av. Isla Verde 6369 (☎253-1664). The Isla Verde version of this Old San Juan restaurant (p. 110) sports a larger space and a livelier evening crowd. The photo-plastered walls are devoted to Puerto Rican Yankees legend Eduardo "Ed" Figueroa, but with a daily 4am closing time, the kitchen and bar are devoted to you. Many customers sit outside on a wooden porch and sip a post-beach beer ($2.75-3.75). Entrees $9-22. Weekend crowds come for live rock and pop music F-Sa 11pm. Open daily 11am-4am or last customer. AmEx/MC/V. ❸

Panadería España (☎727-3860 or 727-4517), at C. Marginal and Av. Baldorioty de Castro, in Villamar. Cross the bridge heading to Villa Verde Inn from stairs at Banco Popular and walk 1 block west. This Spanish bakery is not very elaborate but is always packed, and the sandwiches are as popular as the desserts. Also functions as a deli, selling cold cuts and meat. Cakes, pies, cheesecakes, pastries, and other temptations $1-2. Delicious deli sandwiches $5-7. Open daily 6am-10pm. AmEx/MC/V. ❶

Pizza City (☎726-0356), at Av. Isla Verde and C. Diaz May. You won't miss this large pizza stand with outdoor barstool and patio seating. This large, informal, open-air pizzeria is a good place to satiate post-clubbing munchies. Pizza slices $2-7. Sandwiches $1.50-4.50. Puerto Rican and American bar food and fried entrees $2-10. Beer $1.75-2.75. Open 24hr. Cash only. ❶

Kintaro, Av. Isla Verde 5970 (☎726-3096), between Pizza City and CyberNet Café. An intimate setting with friendly staff serving sushi and other Japanese dishes and drinks into the wee hours. Steak and chicken teriyaki dishes ($15-21), noodles and fried rice ($2.50-16), maki ($5-14) and special design rolls ($12-19) comprise the menu. The chef's most unique item? "Sushi pizza," a concoction of tempura seafood with vegetables and other items on top ($12-14). Cocktails $7-10. Hot sake $7. Delivery available. Open M-Th 5pm-3am, F-Sa 5pm-4am, Su 5pm-3am. MC/V. ❸

Ferrari Gourmet, Av. Isla Verde 51 (☎982-3115; www.ferrarigourmet.com). This Argentine restaurant and gourmet pizzeria creates a warm atmosphere. The extensive menu includes "specially for you" pizzas created by loyal customers: the "Alberto," for example, delivers onion, mozzarella, blue cheese, oregano, and extra virgin olive oil. Small pizzas $6-11. Also sells sandwiches ($6-9) and meat entrees ($10-22). Pitcher of sangria $20. Free delivery (min. $15, 6-10pm). Open M-Th and Su 11:30am-10pm, F-Sa 11:30am-11pm. AmEx/MC/V. ❷

Lin's (☎791-6635), in La Plazoleta de Isla Verde. The creative, delicious food is what makes this Chinese restaurant worthwhile. Surprisingly classy for a strip mall complex. One interesting choice is "Butterfly Shrimp" (shrimp wrapped in bacon with special sauce; $14-16). Lunch specials $5-9. Chinese chicken and beef entrees $9-13. Open M-Th and Su 11am-10pm, F-Sa 11am-11pm. AmEx/MC/V. ❸

Metropol (☎791-5585 or 791-4046; www.metropolpr.com), on the eastern end of Av. Isla Verde, at the intersection with Av. Gobernadores. This slightly upscale restaurant offers an incredible array of Cuban food. Get the biggest bang for your buck by trying some of it all with the combo platter ($8-13). Or try the Cornish hen ($12), if you can ignore the fact that the restaurant is next to the cockfighting arena. Most specials $12-19. Seafood $14-36. Open daily 11:30am-11:30pm. AmEx/D/MC/V. ❸

Los Pinos (☎268-1259), on Av. Isla Verde between Banco Santander and 7-Eleven. The plastic-furnitured feel of a *cafetería* with slightly more expensive food. Popular bar with a TV and pool table where many locals like to camp out. Breakfast $1.50-3. Sandwiches $3-6. Entrees $6-15. *Mofongo* $9-16. Open 24hr. Cash only. ❷

Ciao Mediterranean Café, Av. Isla Verde 5961 (☎797-6100, ext. 280), in the InterContinental Hotel. Walk across the lobby, leave through the back door, and continue past the pool to the bar and restaurant on a beachside patio. This Mediterranean cafe offers budget travelers a taste of luxury without the cost of a ritzy hotel room. Personal pizzas $14-18. Sandwiches, salads, and wraps $8-14. Specialty drinks and frozen cocktails $8.50. Open daily 11am-11pm. AmEx/MC/V. ❹

Gelo's Bagel Bakery (☎791-2575), in La Plazoleta de Isla Verde. One of the few bagel stores on the island and surprisingly expensive. A clean, modern glass counter displays meats and other fixings to fill bagel sandwiches. Bagels $1.75-5. Bagel sandwiches $3.75-10. Open daily 6am-6pm. MC/V. ❷

RÍO PIEDRAS

Av. Universidad, leading up to the Universidad de Puerto Rico (UPR), has a number of small, cheap restaurants that cater to students. Real bargains await at the back of Plaza del Mercado, where countless *cafeterías* dish out local fare.

▨ Guajanas Arte Cafe, C. Amalia Marín 4 (☎766-0497), located at the southwest corner of UPR. Impressive student artwork lines the walls and complements brightly colored tables. Soothing, classy atmosphere. Puerto Rican lunch specials $5-8. *Batidas* $3.50. Free Wi-Fi. Open Aug.-May M-Sa 7am-5pm; June-July M-F 11am-2pm. MC/V. ❷

Country Health Food, C. Robles 53 (☎763-7056 or 767-8797), between the market and the University. This small cafe and health food store offers a break from greasy fare with 3 daily vegetarian entrees served *cafetería*-style. Huge combo platters with 2 sides and a salad $4-6. Delicious *batidas* $2. Open M-Sa 9am-3pm. AmEx/MC/V. ❶

Taquería Azteca, Av. Universidad 52 (☎763-0929 or 516-6638). This typical Mexican joint attracts UPR students out for a cheap lunch. Tasty Mexican staples, including guacamole and chips ($3.25), nachos ($4-7), burritos ($5-8), and quesadillas ($5-7). Open M-Sa 11am-8pm. MC/V. ❶

Cafetería Janet Janez, on C. Monseñor Torres, Río Piedras, but worn sign only reads, "Cafetería..." Dominican food south of the mercado and close to Hotel de Diego. Serves Dominican daily specials ($6.50) including *mangu* (mashed plantain) with rice and beans, *albondica* (breaded meat), and *químbonbo*, called *molondrón* in the Dominican Republic (a green, tube-shaped vegetable with small seeds, served alone or with meat). Open 8am; closing times vary. Cash only. ❷

SAN JUAN FOR POCKET CHANGE. San Juan is home to expensive resorts for the rich and famous; fortunately for the rest of us, the city can be enjoyed on just a few dollars a day. Check into the **Guest House** (p. 100) in Old San Juan before getting your dose of sun and sand at the city's **free public beaches** (p. 129). If you prefer the indoors, brush up on your history at **Museo Felisa Rincón Gautier** (p. 123) or **Museo de la Raíz Africana** (p. 126), both free. For some of San Juan's cheapest local eats, swing by **La Bombonera** or **Café Mallorca** (p. 108), two of the oldest restaurants in Old San Juan, or visit the **Plaza del Mercado** (p. 122) in Río Piedras. According to locals, this marketplace is renowned for the after-work party crowd it rouses on Friday evenings.

◎ SIGHTS

OLD SAN JUAN

CASTILLO DE SAN FELIPE DEL MORRO (EL MORRO FORT). Most of San Juan has changed considerably over the last 500 years. However, when you walk up to the walls of El Morro, you are transported back to a time when Puerto Rico was largely uninhabited and pirates still posed a threat to colonists. The awe-inspiring six-level fortress, named after the patron saint of Spain's King Philip II, draws over two million visitors per year and became a UNESCO World Heritage Site in 1983.

Construction on El Morro began in 1539, when the Spaniards realized that La Fortaleza was located too far inland to effectively prevent ships from entering the bay. El Morro originally consisted of one small tower, but as foreigners and pirates continued to besiege the island, the fortress expanded. El Morro's hour of glory came in 1625 when Dutch soldiers attacked the fort by land and by sea. Stationed inside El Morro, Spaniard Don Juan de Haro and his army refused to surrender. Rumor has it that even the released prisoners chose to stay and help fight. The defenders were aided by the low profile of the fortress, which gave cannons a minimal surface area to aim at. Finally, over a month after their arrival, the Dutch left, burning the rest of San Juan on their way. Encouraged by their success, the Spaniards continued renovating the fort, though it wasn't officially finished until 1786. In 1876 a lighthouse was added; it is now the oldest on the island and still in use. El Morro was put to the test once again in 1898 when the US Navy bombarded the fort for over two hours before taking it, leaving 100 men dead. Then, during both World Wars, the US Army (now working from inside the fort) used it as a lookout post to protect the island. Finally, in 1961, the military abandoned El Morro and donated it to the government. Today it is one of Puerto Rico's two US National Park protected areas (the other is **San Cristóbal,** down the road).

Visitors enter on the fourth floor, the Plaza Principal, which originally contained the prison, the chapel, and several cannon rooms. Today the prison room shows a 15min. video about the fort (shown in Spanish on the hour and 30min. past, in English 15min. and 45min. past), and several of the cannon rooms have become a museum with captions in English and Spanish. Look up and you will see three flags—the Puerto Rican flag, the US flag, and the old Spanish military flag, known as the Cross of Burgundy. The Artillery Ramp leads down to the Battery of Santa Bárbara on the second level, named after the patron saint of artillerymen, to whom the soldiers prayed for safety. *(C. Norzagaray 501. ☎ 729-6777; www.nps.gov/saju. Open daily June-Nov. 9am-5pm; Dec.-May 9am-6pm. $3, 15 and under free. Combination ticket with San Cristóbal $5.)*

■ **CASTILLO DE SAN CRISTÓBAL.** Frequently overlooked by tourists who visit El Morro and decide that one fort is enough, San Cristóbal is actually the larger of the two. After the Spaniards built El Morro to protect the bay, attacks by the British in 1598 and the Dutch in 1625 soon demonstrated that the city was still susceptible to assaults by land. Thus, in 1634 they began constructing San Cristóbal about half a mile down the road. The fort was not tested until 1797 when the British again tried, unsuccessfully, to take the city. Then, in 1898, Puerto Rico's involvement in the Spanish-American War was announced with a bang as a shot was fired from San Cristóbal. After the US won the war it took control of the fort, and in 1942 San Cristóbal was used as a WWII observation post.

Today, the fort is open to visitors, who are given a bilingual pamphlet for a self-guided tour. Although less area is open to the public than at El Morro, San Cristóbal offers some unique features, such as a fully decorated replica of troops' quarters (including three-cornered hats above every bed), a military fife and drum soundboard, and old uniforms on mannequins (check out the hot pink stockings on one Spaniard). Visitors can also walk through the tunnels to the old dungeon, where a group of Spanish galleons is skillfully drawn on the wall. Archaeologists believe them to be the work of a mutinous captain awaiting execution. Beyond these attractions, San Cristóbal does have the same basic structure as El Morro, including cannon openings, historical exhibits, and splendid views of the city. The same 15min. video is shown at both forts. *(C. Norzagaray 501. ☎ 729-6777; www.nps.gov/saju. Open daily June-Nov. 9am-5pm; Dec.-May 9am-6pm. $3, 15 and under free. Combination ticket with El Morro $5.)*

LA FORTALEZA. Reigning over the southwest corner of Old San Juan like a castle, La Fortaleza is the oldest governor's residence in the Western Hemisphere that is still used today. The Spanish originally began constructing the edifice in 1533 as a fort to protect San Juan, but after five years of work (and only one year shy of completion), they realized that the position of La Fortaleza would not allow them to see attackers entering the bay. Construction accordingly began on another fort, **El Morro** (above), and La Fortaleza became the official residence of the governor. Over the years, the Neoclassical building has housed 124 governors appointed by the Spanish crown, 20 appointed by the US government, and eight elected by the people of Puerto Rico. The governor lives on in the third floor of the mansion and works on the second. The flag out front waves only when the governor is on the island and flies at half-staff when he is away.

A free tour is the only way to see the mansion, but these are limited to the courtyard and never actually enter the house. If you lack time or interest, approach the building from C. Fortaleza for beautiful views of the facade. *(C. Fortaleza 1. Use the entrance at the west end of C. Fortaleza. ☎ 721-7000, ext. 2211, 2323, or 2358; www.fortaleza.gobierno.pr. Tours 9am-5pm; $3 per person, under 12 free. Tours last 30min. Visit the tour office, only steps from the palace gate, early in the day to join a tour group.)*

START: El Morro.
FINISH: Raíces.
DISTANCE: 1 mi.
DURATION: 4-5 hr.
BEST TIME TO GO: noon-1pm

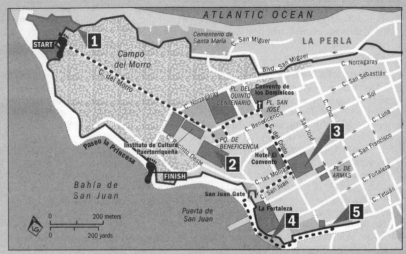

THE HISTORY OF OLD SAN JUAN

Puerto Rico's history is deeply rooted in the Spanish conquest of the island, which established its official language, dominant religion, and cultural traditions. Western Old San Juan can transport you back to the romance of an era when galleons and pirate vessels, rather than cruise ships, sailed into San Juan Port.

1. EL MORRO. Here you can spy the ocean through cannon embankments and understand how it must have felt to be stationed as a lookout for invading Dutch and English vessels. Through binoculars, you can see across the bay to El Cañuelo, the small fort in the town of Cataño that fought alongside El Morro. (See p. 116.)

2. MUSEO CASA BLANCA. The White House Museum was built in 1523 for the famous conquistador Juan Ponce de León, also the first Spanish governor of Puerto Rico. While Ponce de León himself never lived in the mansion, his family successor did for about 250 years. Today you may tour the old house, which contains a variety of artifacts. (See p. 123.)

3. CATEDRAL SAN JUAN BAUTISTA. Ponce de León is buried in this cathedral. In 1529, a few years after its construction, the cathedral also hosted the first ordination of a bishop in North America. Its ethereal beauty is augmented by the many lit candles throughout the church and the side chapels containing reliquaries and portraits of saints. (See p. 119.)

4. PASEO LA PRINCESA. As you pass through San Juan Gate, notice the thickness of the city walls, a point of defense in the colonial era. Turn left and walk toward Raíces, a statue that was sculpted by a Spaniard to commemorate the 500th anniversary of the conquistadors' arrival here. It celebrates Puerto Rico's cultural heritage, past and present, and provides a great vantage point for looking out over the ocean. (See p. 119.)

5. CAFÉ LA PRINCESA. At the foot of the vine-covered city walls, you will reach this palm tree-lined patio oasis under palms. Enjoy an afternoon drink in the shade of the gazebo or partake in a traditional Puerto Rican dinner under the stars before continuing west down the promenade toward the Bay of San Juan. (See p. 108)

PASEO LA PRINCESA. Extending from the San Juan Gate to the piers, this wide promenade lined with trees, benches, and flowers provides a nice place for an evening stroll or a morning run. Start your walk on the western edge of the old city at the **San Juan Gate,** the symbolic entrance to the city through which visitors in the 18th and 19th centuries passed on their way to the Catedral San Juan Bautista to give thanks for a safe voyage. After you pass through the gate, follow Paseo de la Princesa to the left, where the path continues between the water and **La Muralla,** the original walls fortifying the city that took the Spaniards almost 150 years to build. Take a look at the thickness of the wall (20 ft. in places) as you pass through the gate. As the path turns away from the sea, it approaches **Raíces,** a statue surrounded by a fountain. Possibly the most photographed sight in Old San Juan, the statue, sculpted in 1992 by Luis Antonio Sanguino, symbolizes Puerto Rico's cultural heritage. In front, a young man stands admiring the beauty around him, while in the back a young woman flanked by two dolphins welcomes visitors to the island. Images of a family and a *jíbaro* (traditional farmer) complete the sculpture. The ensuing broad promenade provides benches and a welcome respite from the sun. **La Princesa,** on the left, was constructed in 1837 as a prison. Today it is the central office of the Puerto Rico Tourism Company. Visitors may be more interested in the gallery inside that hosts a series of San Juan-themed temporary exhibits by local artists. There are no descriptions, but the front desk provides an information booklet in Spanish and English. *(Open M-F 8am-4:30pm.)* Continue past the enclosed botanical gardens on your left to reach Plaza la Princesa, a brick rotunda centered on **Al Inmigrante,** a sculpture by Prat Ventos.

CEMENTERIO DE SANTA MARÍA MAGDALENA DE PAZZIS. Nestled in the green hills of El Morro's historic grounds, this quiet plot of land yields some of the loveliest views in town. The cemetery hovers between the old town walls, La Perla neighborhood, and the Atlantic Ocean, which blows a light mist over the intricately carved, bright white headstones. Stroll along a central path at cemetery level, or visit El Morro point and the hills over the cemetery during early evening and see why lovers meet there to watch the sun set. Constructed in 1863, *el cementerio* has been the resting place for many of San Juan's most prominent citizens and is still in use today. Visitors should exercise caution in the surrounding areas, however; avoid the cemetery grounds and neighboring La Perla after dark. *(On the north side of the city between El Morro and Las Peñas. Walk down the street tunnel from C. Norzagaray. ☎ 723-3852. Open daily 8am-3pm.)*

CATEDRAL SAN JUAN BAUTISTA. Situated in the heart of the old city, the gorgeous San Juan Bautista is famous for more than housing the tomb of conquistador and former governor of Puerto Rico **Juan Ponce de León.** In 1529, the cathedral hosted the **first ordination of a bishop in North America,** while in 1984, it witnessed an event that it still celebrates: the visit of Pope John Paul II. The pope's visit is commemorated with displays of the actual vestments he used and in several larger-than-life pictures. Second in number only to those of Pope John Paul II, images of San Juan Bautista are found around the church—he appears in figurines on the outside facade, in the nave on the left-hand side of the interior, and in a stained glass window overlooking the main entrance. *(C. del Cristo 151-153. ☎/fax 722-0861; www.catedralsanjuan.com. Open M-Th 9am-noon and 1:30-4pm, F 9am-noon. Mass M-F 12:15pm, Sa 7pm, Su 9 and 11am. Free, but donations welcome.)*

PARQUE DE LAS PALOMAS AND CAPILLA DEL SANTO CRISTO. A pigeon phobiac's worst nightmare and many a child's greatest dream, Parque de las Palomas (Pigeon Park) is crawling with hundreds of these urban birds. Buy some bird food from the vendor in the corner ($0.50), and soon birds will be crawling all over you. If you don't like pigeons, consider skipping directly to the **Capilla del Santo**

Cristo, the tiny chapel next to the park. Legend has it that the silver altar inside, dedicated to the Holy Christ of Miracles, was constructed in honor of Baltazar Montañez, who barely survived a horse-racing accident in the 1750s. The altar is built entirely out of silver, and the women outside sell silver charms to leave as offerings. Come on Tuesdays when the gate is open to get a closer look. *(At the south end of C. del Cristo. Chapel open Tu 11am-4pm. Free.)*

EL TEATRO ALEJANDRO TAPIA Y RIVERA. One of the largest theaters in Puerto Rico, the Tapia serves as a monument of historical, architectural, and artistic interest. Governor Don Miguel de la Torre commissioned the building in 1824 as the first theater in San Juan, and the Tuscan-style Romantic edifice officially opened in 1836 as the Teatro Municipal (Municipal Theater). In 1937, the government renamed the theater after Alejandro Tapia y Rivera, one of Puerto Rico's most famous playwrights. The facade is beautiful, but it is the interior that really shines. The theater has 642 seats, but the third balcony and all of the booths are reserved for the governor and members of the municipal government—if they decide not to come, the seats remain empty. In order to see the inside, you'll have to buy a ticket for one of the weekend performances. For ticket information see **Entertainment,** (p. 133). *(On the south side of Plaza Colón. Tickets ☎ 721-0180 or 723-2079, administration 721-0169. Office hours vary by performance.)*

PLAZA DE ARMAS. On most days, Old San Juan's Plaza de Armas is just a large slab of concrete with a fountain, some benches, and a few kiosks. However, during holidays and special events (which tend to happen about once per week), the plaza fills with vendors hawking souvenirs, musicians playing traditional music, and hordes of festive people. The **Alcaldía** (Mayor's Office), on C. San Francisco on the plaza, is a Neoclassical building originally constructed in 1604 and restored in 1966-68 under the fashionable mayor Felisa Rincón. The mayor still works here, but visitors are free to visit the pleasant courtyard and **Sala San Juan Bautista,** which holds a small gallery of local artwork. A small tourist desk on the left-hand side of the lobby can answer questions. *(☎ 724-1875. Open M-Sa 9am-4:30pm.)*

PLAZAS. At the intersection of Caleta de las Monjas and C. Recinto Oeste, picturesque **Plazuela de la Rogativa** is a great place to snap a few photos and gaze out over the ocean. The statue in the middle of the plaza, La Rogativa, depicts the women and the bishop of San Juan tricking the English into believing that reinforcements are coming to protect the island, thus saving the city from the invaders. **Parque de Beneficencia** includes an impressive statue of Eugenio María de Hostos, "Citizen of America," behind the Museo de las Américas on Norazagaray. Otherwise, Beneficia is just a pleasant version of the standard mix of benches, lanterns, and concrete. **Plaza San José** seems to have a split personality. By day it's a typical plaza with a small outdoor dining area; at night it is transformed into a popular gathering place. Especially during festival nights, Puerto Ricans flock to San José to meet, greet, wine, and dine. A heavy police presence testifies to the exuberance of the crowds. Nearby, **Plaza del Quinto Centenario** was constructed in 1992 to commemorate the 500-year anniversary of Columbus's first voyage. The large totem pole in the middle, "Totem Telúrico," stands as a monument to the earth and the plenitude of America. The top level of the plaza supposedly represents the present while the lower level represents the past, and the stairs represent the connection between the two. The fountains in the ground intermittently spout water, causing delighted children to shriek with pleasure. Drivers may be more interested in the **parking lot** underneath the plaza. Back in lower San Juan, off C. San Francisco, **Plaza Salvador Brau** is the place to find pigeons, families, school groups, and old men playing cards. The focus of the plaza is a statue of its namesake, Salvador Brau (1842-1912), a noted journalist, historian, and politician. **Plaza Cristóbal Colón,** north of

Teatro Tapia between C. Fortaleza and C. San Francisco, plays host to a huge statue of Christopher Columbus, a five-tiered fountain, and several benches.

IGLESIA SAN JOSÉ. Built in 1523, Iglesia San José is the second oldest religious structure standing in the New World, and one of the earliest examples of Gothic architecture in the Americas. The church has been closed for repairs since 2005; it is unclear when it will reopen. *(On Plaza San José, at C. San Sebastián and C. del Cristo).*

PUERTA DE TIERRA

█ EL CAPITOLIO. San Juan's grandiose capitol building is the home of the legislative branch of the Puerto Rican government, with the Senate on the left (facing the building) and the House of Representatives on the right. Architect Rafael Carmoega designed the building in an Italian Renaissance Neoclassical style, modeled after the US Capitol in Washington, D.C., and it incorporates 22 different colors of marble. An interesting (and free!) tour shows off the entire building, including both the Senate and the House chambers. Even if one of the branches is in session, tours frequently enter the gallery and observe the proceedings. If you don't have time for a tour, it's worthwhile to enter the building and wander around. The main rotunda contains an original copy of Puerto Rico's constitution, a frieze (look at the top of the walls) depicting the history of the island from the Taínos to the time when Puerto Rico gained commonwealth status, four large mosaics (parts of which are covered in gold leaf), and the nine Greek Muses on the ceiling rotunda. The third floor provides a better view of the mosaics and the Muses. *(On Av. Muñoz Rivera, about ½ mi. from Old San Juan. ☎ 724-2030. Open M-F 9am-5pm, Sa-Su and holidays 9am-2pm. Free 45min. tours in English, Spanish, and French. Tour desk in the main rotunda, 1st fl..)*

CASA DE ESPAÑA. If you're in the area, Casa de España merits a stop for its beautiful Iberian architecture. Exquisite tiles cover the walls in the courtyard. The building was originally constructed in 1935 as a gentleman's club for the Spanish expat community, but today anyone may enter. Check the bulletin board at the building's entrance for current events such as dance classes, concerts, theater, gallery showings, and wine festivals. *(Av. Ponce de León 9, between Carnegie Library and the Capitol. Open daily 9am-5pm.)*

FUERTE SAN GERÓNIMO DEL BOQUERÓN. Hidden behind the Hilton, this small 15th-century fort looks like a miniature version of San Cristóbal and played a similar role in protecting San Juan from foreign attacks. The fort has been closed since 1995 and the entire area is still under construction, though it is still possible to view the fort from outside. *(☎ 721-0303. Enter the Hilton Caribe and follow signs to the San Cristóbal ballroom, then exit through the glass doors behind the ballroom.)*

HATO REY AND RÍO PIEDRAS

█ JARDÍN BOTÁNICO DE PUERTO RICO. Of San Juan's many attractive parks, the Botanical Garden in southern Río Piedras easily stands out as the best. The 175-acre gardens contain two small lakes, an orchid garden, a bamboo forest, an herbarium with over 36,000 plants, and countless scenic paths. The park has several gardens devoted to specific themes, including a "Monet Garden," which mimics the appearance of the French original. The Visitors Center provides a map of the premises, but it's equally enjoyable to just wander the well-marked paths and see what you stumble upon—it's easy to walk across the grounds in under an hour. The Visitors Center provides mainly Spanish-language tours to large groups, which individuals are welcome to join. The university also welcomes volunteers who are interested in working in the gardens. Call ahead for more information. *(Located directly south of the intersection of Hwy. 1 and 3. From San Juan, drive south on Av. Ponce de León to the end and follow signs. If you miss* the sign (which can be hard to see), make a U-turn and look for the sign heading north on Hwy. 1. To reach the Visitors Center, enter the park and veer uphill to the left just before the "Jardín Botánico" sign. If you are walking, exit downtown Río Piedras by heading south from the Plaza de Armas. From there, cross the bridge over the highway, turn left at the Texaco station, and walk 2 blocks. ☎ 758-9957 or 767-1710, ext. 4490. Gardens open daily 8am-5pm. Info center open M-F 7am-noon and 1-3pm. Inquire within about tours for groups up to 30. Admission free.)

■ PLAZA DEL MERCADO AND PASEO DE DIEGO. If the endless US chain stores have convinced you that Puerto Rico really is the 51st state, head to Río Piedras's Plaza del Mercado, the biggest market in San Juan, which offers a glimpse into daily life for many in Puerto Rico. This surprisingly well-organized air-conditioned building contains stalls hawking everything from herbal medicines to fresh vegetables to even fresher meat, along with an overwhelming variety of bananas and plantains. In the back food court, countless *cafeterías* serve up cheap *comida criolla* and fresh *batidas*. Near the entrance to the market is Paseo de Diego, a pedestrian street turned into an outdoor shopping mall. It features many American clothing chains and fast food restaurants alongside a few *cafeterías* and warehouse-type stores selling very inexpensive clothing. (Plaza del Mercado is located between C. José de Diego and C. Monseñor Torres. Open daily 6am-5pm. Paseo de Diego on C. José de Diego between Av. Ponce de León and C. William Jones. All stores close at 6pm, but the Paseo itself is open 24hr.)

UNIVERSIDAD DE PUERTO RICO. The largest university in Puerto Rico occupies a palm tree-filled campus in the heart of Río Piedras. Anyone who has wandered the streets of Río Piedras will appreciate the serenity of the grassy grounds, but the campus holds a number of interesting attractions in addition to its landscape. The **Museo de Historia, Antropología y Arte** (Museum of History, Anthropology, and Art) presents Puerto Rican art from the 18th century, indigenous artifacts, including some from the Taíno civilization, and a collection of Egyptian artifacts centered around burial and funerary customs including mummies, figurines, and amulets. Francisco Oller's expansive painting, "El Velorio," is perhaps the most famous in the art collection. (Enter the University's main entrance, go to the top of the circular driveway, and turn left. ☎ 763-3939 or 764-0000 ext. 5852. Open M-Tu and F 9am-4pm, W-Th 9am-8:30pm. Free.) Most of the university buildings are open to the public. The building directly opposite the main entrance on Av. Ponce de León has a colorful, intricately carved facade with a handsome seal dedicated to the American Republics for the Advancement of Learning. Continue along the same road to the **Centro Universitario** (Student Center), where students gather to eat and hang out. A food court in the basement serves several varieties of fast food. On the first floor, to the right, through the sliding glass door, the **Oficina de Organizaciones Estudiantiles** (Office of Student Organizations) provides information about concerts, movies, and cultural events on campus. Public restrooms and an ATM are also located on the first floor. (Campus at the intersection of Av. Ponce de León and C. Universidad. M: Universidad. Buses A3, A52, B4, B28, B29, C18, C31, and M1 pass in front. ☎ 764-1000.)

LUIS MUÑOZ MARÍN FOUNDATION. If one figure stands out in Puerto Rican history, it has to be Luis Muñoz Marín, the island's first elected governor and the founder of the Partido Popular Democrático (p. 62). It's not surprising, then, that there's an entire foundation dedicated to studying Muñoz Marín and preserving the great man's legacy. In addition to providing ample fodder for academics, the foundation also maintains the grounds and contents of the former governor's house and opens them to the public. Today visitors are welcome to explore; the house is closed, but anyone can peek through the windows at the furniture, decorations, and documents within. Muñoz Marín occupied the house with his second wife, Inés Muñoz Marín, from 1946-48 and 1964-80 (from 1948 to 1964 he lived in La Fortaleza). Two buildings out front hold Muñoz Marín's preserved office and a small gift shop. For true Muñoz Marín fanatics, this foundation also continually screens a 35min. video (in Spanish) about the man's life. *(Rte. 877 Km 0.4. From San Juan, take Hwy. 3 east, turn right onto Rte. 181, take the first left at the light, then a quick right; the house is on the left. ☎ 755-4506; www.munoz-marin.org. All info is in Spanish. Open M-F 8am-5pm. Tours M-F 10am, 2pm and Sa-Su 10:30am, 1pm, but call ahead. $3, under 12 $2, over 60 $1.)*

PARQUE LUIS MUÑOZ MARÍN. Situated on the border between Hato Rey and Río Piedras, Parque Luis Muñoz Marín offers an oasis of green amid the sea of concrete. This sizable park is a great place to take a bike ride on a weekend afternoon, but if you're looking for real greenery and lots of shade, head to the Jardín Botánico. In addition to the large grassy fields, the park has playground equipment, picnic tables, and concrete **bike paths.** *(Located south of Estadio Hiram Bithorn and west of Expreso las Américas. Enter on Av. Jesús Piñero. It is difficult to get to the park on foot—be prepared to walk along the edge of a busy 10-lane road. Bus B28 passes in front. ☎ 622-5200. Train $1.50. Parking $2. Open W-Su 8:30am-5pm. Free.)*

🏛 MUSEUMS

OLD SAN JUAN

Old San Juan is easily the cultural capital of Puerto Rico. In addition to the numerous museums listed below, many streets, especially C. del Cristo and C. San José, are teeming with local art galleries. Your best bet is simply to wander around and explore. Most museums close on Mondays.

▨ MUSEO FELISA RINCÓN DE GAUTIER. This small museum is dedicated to preserving the memory of an extraordinary woman who devoted her life to achieving recognition of the rights of Puerto Rican women and improving the lives of the poor. Felisa Rincón de Gautier (1897-1994), who never even finished high school, served as the mayor of San Juan from 1946 to 1968, becoming the first female mayor of a major city in the Western Hemisphere. She also began the Head Start program for pre-kindergarten learning, which has spread throughout the US. The museum celebrates Rincón's accomplishments by displaying many of her honors and medals, including 11 honorary degrees from Puerto Rican and American universities and keys to 113 cities from Manila, Philippines to Gary, Indiana. Rincón's personal life is portrayed through dresses, fans, and photos with countless foreign dignitaries, including Lyndon B. Johnson and Eleanor Roosevelt. *(Caleta de San Juan 51. ☎ 723 1897. Open M-F 9am-4pm. Free. Free tours in English and Spanish.)*

▨ MUSEO CASA BLANCA. This castle was originally constructed in 1521 as the home of the first Spanish governor of Puerto Rico, **Juan Ponce de León.** Unfortunately, a hurricane soon leveled the wooden edifice. Thus in 1523 the Spaniards reconstructed the house as the first building made of stone on the island. Ironically, Ponce de León never actually lived here (since he was off searching for the Fountain of Youth) but the house remained in his family's possession for the next 250 years. Casa Blanca also served as one of the few safe havens when invaders attacked the city, and in 1898 it became the home of the commander of the US Army in Puerto Rico. Today, the house has been redecorated in 16th-century style in honor of Ponce de León. The site's dynamic tour guide divulges the castle's secrets—learn why Ponce de León needed three keys for his chest, whom he called when he misplaced his stash of money, and why you are forbidden to descend to the basement. *(C. San Sebastián 1. From C. Norzagaray, turn down C. del Morro, pass Parque Beneficio, and enter the small gate on your right. Or, walk straight down C. San Sebastián toward the gate and veer left down the cobblestone path. ☎ 725-1454. Open Tu-Sa 8:30am-4:20pm. English and Spanish tours $3, under 12 and over 60 $2. Gardens free.)*

SAN JUAN

Old San Juan

🏠 **ACCOMMODATIONS**

The Caleta,	1	C3
Da' House Hotel,	2	D4
The Gallery Inn,	3	D3
Guest House,	4	D3
Hotel Milano,	5	E4
SJ Suites,	6	D4

🍎 **FOOD**

Barrachina,	7	D4
Bistro Avant,	8	D4
La Bombonera,	9	D3
El Burén,	10	C3
Cafe Berlin,	11	E3
Café La Princessa,	12	C5
Cafetería Mallorca,	13	E3
Casa España,	14	F3
La Danza,	15	C4
Diner's Crew Lounge,	16	E4
Dragonfly,	17	E3
Il Bacaro Venezia,	18	D4
El Jibarito,	19	D3
Lupi's Mexican Grill & Sports Cantina,	20	E4
El Mesón Sandwiches,	21	D4
Nadine's Cafe,	22	C4
Ostra Cosa,	23	C4
El Patio de Sam,	24	C3
El Quinqué Food Window,	25	C3
Raíces Restaurant,	26	E4
El Siglo XX,	27	E3
St. Germain,	28	D3
Tantra Restaurant and Bar,	29	C4
Zesty Bites,	30	D4

🏛 **MUSEUMS**

The Butterfly People,	31	D4
Casa de Don Ramón Power y Giralt,	32	D4
Casa de la Familia Puertorriqueña del Siglo XIX & Museo de Farmacia,	33	E3
Casa Don Q Puerto Rico,	34	E4
Escuela de Artes Plásticas,	35	B3
Museo Casa Blanca,	36	B3
Museo de Nuestra Raíz Africana,	37	C3
Museo de las Américas,	38	B3
Museo de San Juan,	39	C3
Museo del Niño,	40	C4
Museo Felisa Rincón de Gautier,	41	C4
Museo Pablo Casals,	42	C3

📷 **NIGHTLIFE**

Barú,	43	C3
El Batey,	44, 45	C3
Brick House,	46	E4
Cafe Hijos de Borinquen,	47	C3
Cafe San Sebastián,	48	D3
Krugger's,	49	C4
Lazer,	50	D4
Marmalade,	51	E3
The Noise,	52	D3
Nono's,	53	C3
Nuyorican Cafe,	27	E3
Oscar's Bar,	53	E4
Rumba,	54	C3
Señor Frog's,	55	E4

D　　　　E　　　　F

1

N
LG

200 yards
0
0
200 meters

2

OCEAN

C. Bajada Matadero

SAN JUAN NATIONAL
HISTORIC SITE
HEADQUARTERS

C. Norzagaray

Castillo
San Cristóbal

3

48

10

La Lavandería

C. San Sebastián

C. Sol

C. Tanca

19

C. del Cristo

C. O'Donnell

11

Av. Muñoz Rivera

3

Biblioteca
Carnegie

14　El Capitolio

28

C. San Justo

C. Luna

Iglesia de
San Francisco
PL.
SALVADOR
BRAU

C. Tetuán Infante

PL. DE
COLÓN

Avda. Costitución

25

C. Cruz

9

52　13

20

C. San Francisco

27

5

C. Capilla

51

33

27

17

33

Teatro Tapia
y Rivera

TAXI

Paseo de Covadonga

TAXI

46

18

Alcaldía

R

6

C. Fortaleza

C. Gambaro

Internet Active

Covadonga
Trolley & Bus
Terminal

A. Corretjer

PL. DE
ARMAS

2

Pueblo

16

53

C. Tetuán

C. Gen. Pershing

C. Nolasco Rubio

Paseo Gilberto Concepción de Gracia

4

TAXI

50

20　26

C. Recinto Sur

55

7

30

32

31

Municipal
Tourist
Office

C. Comercio

1

a del Libro

Cronopios
Books & Music

Old Post Office
and
Federal Building

34

C. la Marina

Puerto Rican Tourism Co.
Information Center

PL.
DÁRSENA

TAXI
AcuaExpreso

Pier 2

Pier 3

Pier 4

5

Bahía de
San Juan

Pier 1

Presidio Puntilla

6

La Puntilla

TO CATAÑO, HATO REY

SAN JUAN

MUSEO DE NUESTRA RAÍZ AFRICANA. Starting with a description of African tribes, the Museum of Our African Roots progresses through the history of blacks in the Caribbean with a series of photos and artifacts, including real handcuffs and collars. Upstairs the museum transcends the oppressive history of slavery to commemorate African contributions to Puerto Rican culture through displays of clothing, natural baskets, masks, drums and music. *(On the east side of Plaza San José, entrance right of the Museo Pablo Casals.* ☎ *724-4294. Spanish signs only, but one of the guides speaks English. Open Tu-Sa 8:30am-4:20pm. $2, under 12 and over 60 $1.)*

MUSEO DE LAS AMÉRICAS. Unlike most Old San Juan exhibits, this well-maintained museum extends beyond Puerto Rico and focuses on arts throughout the Americas in its three permanent exhibits. One of the museum's highlights is a permanent exhibit on folk arts and handicrafts in the Western Hemisphere, including tools, toys, masks, and religious artifacts. A second, smaller exhibit on the Western Hemisphere's African heritage has captions only in Spanish, but the handcuffs and photos speak for themselves. The third permanent exhibit, titled "The Indian in America," presents 22 ethnicities' survival of European colonization through life-size figurines, clothes, artifacts, and videos. The building itself is considered the best work of architecture constructed by the Spaniards in the 19th century and over the years has served as military barracks as well as a hospital. *(In Cuartel de Ballajá, off C. Norzagaray, in the large green-and-yellow building. Enter the large courtyard and take the elevator or any staircase to the 2nd fl.* ☎ *724-5052; www.museolasamericas.org. Open Tu-W and Sa-Su 10am-4pm, Th-F 9am-4pm. "El Indio en América" exhibit $2, all other exhibits free.)*

MUSEO DEL NIÑO. This carefully planned children's museum has been designed to simultaneously educate and entertain. Friendly, informative tour guides lead groups through the eclectic assortment of displays, ranging from a giant ear in the health room (teaching children how to clean their ears) to a replica of a Puerto Rican town center (educating about Puerto Rican heritage) to a fully intact front half of a car (to teach children about car safety and wearing a seat belt). More interactive rooms allow children to make crafts out of recycled materials and practice brushing and flossing a giant set of teeth. There is also a room for children ages one to three that includes a firehouse. The museum hosts special events on weekend afternoons; stop by for a three-month calendar. *(C. del Cristo 150.* ☎ *722-3791; www.museodelninopr.org. Open Tu-Th 9am-6pm, F 11am-6pm, Sa-Su 12:30-5pm. Under 14 $7, adults $5. Additional $1 to use arts and crafts room. AmEx/MC/V.)*

MUSEO DE SAN JUAN. There are few exhibits in this museum, but what is there is well done. The main room presents the history of San Juan in floor-to-ceiling exhibits and interactive computers. The display in the second room changes annually in July, always focusing on the island's capital. A recent exhibit explored the theme of security in the streets of San Juan. Information in English is available in a supplementary packet. *(C. Norzagaray 150.* ☎ *723-4317 or 724-1875. Open Tu-Su 9am-noon and 1pm-4pm. Free.)*

CASA DON Q PUERTO RICO. Although not quite as famous internationally as Bacardi, Don Q is the best-selling rum on the island. This small museum explains the history of the rum and shows actual Don Q rum in the process of being distilled. While the historical information is nicely displayed with photos and English and Spanish captions, the highlight of the museum is the ⊠**free sample** of a Don Q rum drink at the end. *(On C. la Marina, building 8A across from Pier 2.* ☎ *977-1721. Open Oct. 25-Apr. 30 M-W 11am-8pm, F-Su 9am-6pm; May 1-Oct. 24 M-F 9am-6pm. Free.)*

CASA DE LA FAMILIA PUERTORRIQUEÑA DEL SIGLO XIX AND MUSEO DE FARMACIA. This two-story museum recreates the life of a wealthy resident of 19th-century San Juan through two historical displays. Downstairs, the Pharmacy Museum contains a pharmacy counter (including such remedies as ricin and Spanish fly) and various other artifacts of early medicine, such as a model head with phrenological information. Upstairs, the Museum of the 19th-century Puerto Rican Family contains furniture from the 1870s. The chair with the hole in it served as the bathroom on nights when the outhouse was just too far away. Perhaps the most interesting object is the family portrait in the hall. Viewed from the front, it simply looks like a large family with many Caucasian children. Viewed from the side, however, a black child appears. According to the tour guide, this child was the product of the father's affair with a slave, and he wanted to include her in the family portrait. The museum merits a quick visit if you can understand the Spanish tour. *(C. Fortaleza 319. ☎ 977-2700. Open Tu-Sa 8:30am-noon and 1-4:20pm. Spanish tour included if staff is available. Few captions in Spanish, none in English. Free.)*

THE BUTTERFLY PEOPLE. Since 1970, the Butterfly People has been accumulating butterflies from Papua New Guinea and Brazil and artistically assembling them by color in beautiful floor-to-ceiling displays. *(C. Cruz 257. ☎ 723-2432; www.butterfly-people.com. Artwork made from butterflies $40-62. Open M-Sa 10am-6pm. Free.)*

GALERÍA NACIONAL (NATIONAL ART GALLERY OF PUERTO RICO). In early 2007, this national art gallery was launched in "El Convento de los Dominicos," a large convent and courtyard built in the 16th century. The National Collection of the Institute of Puerto Rican Culture is showcased in four crisp, bright rooms boasting about 175 beautiful paintings from the 19th century to the middle of the 20th. The audio/visual room offers a seven-minute bilingual video on the history of the convent, after which visitors can explore paintings ranging from art of Mexican and Spanish viceroyalty to 1950s interpretive works influenced by the hard life in Puerto Rican slums. Look out for the 20th-century *costumbrista* and popular imagery dedicated to the *jíbaro puertorriqueño* or Puerto Rican countryman, which contrast sharply with impressions of urban Puerto Rico circa 1950. *(Convento de los Dominicos, C. Norzagaray 98, between C. Norzagaray and Iglesia San José. ☎ 725 2670. Open Tu-Sa 9:30am-5pm and Sun 10:30am-6pm. Guides present to answer questions in both languages. $3, ages 6-12 $2, ages 5 and under free. Special discounts for seniors, students, and groups of 10 or more.)*

CASA DE DON RAMÓN POWER Y GIRALT. In the 18th century, this building sheltered Don Ramón Power y Giralt (1775-1813), an important Puerto Rican social reformer who served as Puerto Rico's representative to the Spanish courts. Today, this one-room museum has absolutely nothing to do with Don Ramón and instead contains the office and museum of the Conservation Trust of Puerto Rico, an organization dedicated to preserving the island's natural resources. Their permanent exhibition, Ojo Isla, uses a variety of media and interactive exhibits to explain Puerto Rico's current environmental situation. The live colony of honeybees and web-weaving spiders are behind glass, but you can try your hand at playing the *maraca* and the *güiro*, two traditional musical instruments of Puerto Rico. Captions are in Spanish. *(C. Tetuán 155. Yellow building on the corner of C. Cruz and Tetuán. ☎ 722-5834. Open M-F 9am-5pm. Free.)*

ESCUELA DE ARTES PLÁSTICAS. The large white building across from El Morro houses one of the largest fine arts schools in Puerto Rico. Originally constructed as a mental hospital in 1861, the building was used to shelter soldiers wounded in the 1863 war in the Dominican Republic before construction had even finished. In 1898, it became the US Army headquarters in San Juan until 1976, when it was converted into a school. Today visitors can wander in the tree-filled courtyard and watch students work or head back to the small gallery of excellent student art. A small food kiosk in the courtyard serves $2-4 sandwiches. *(On C. Norzagaray, across from El Morro. ☎ 725-8120. Open M-F 7:30am-4pm. Free.)*

MUSEO PABLO CASALS. Music lovers with some extra time in San Juan will appreciate this small but frequently updated museum devoted to Pablo Casals (1876-1973), world-famous cellist and humanist (p. 70). Casals was born in Spain but moved to his mother's homeland of Puerto Rico at an early age. Here he founded the annual Casals Music Festival (1959), the Puerto Rico Symphony Orchestra (1957), the Conservatory of Music (1960), and the Special String Program for Children (1960s). However, one step into the museum will remind you where Casals's musical interests began—with his cello bow. In 1971, Casals received the UN Peace Medal for his humanitarian and cultural achievements, and you will find this medal, his cello bow, and prized compositions in glass cases on the first floor. In the music room on the second floor, browse through biographical videotapes. *(C. San Sebastián 101. On the east side of Plaza San José. ☎ 723-9185. Open Tu-Sa 9:30am-4:30pm. English and Spanish. $1, under 12 or 60 and over $0.50.)*

PUERTA DE TIERRA

MUSEO MILITAR GUARDIA NACIONAL DE PUERTO RICO. Hidden amidst the government buildings on Puerta de Tierra, the Puerto Rico National Guard Museum presents a history of 20th-century American wars. Upstairs, a large room focuses on American participation in WWII. Another room highlights the participation of the Puerto Rican Air National Guard in the various wars. Most interesting are the airplane fuselage and the uniforms from different wars, including a WWII uniform for pregnant women. Portraits of heroic Puerto Rican soldiers and their stories line the walls. All captions are in English and Spanish. *(On C. General Esteves. From Old San Juan, walk down Av. Luis Muñoz Rivera; the museum is on your right about 5min. after the capitol building, in the National Guard Station. ☎ 289-1675. Open M-F 7am-3pm. Free.)*

SANTURCE

▨ MUSEO DE ARTE DE PUERTO RICO. It may be an exaggeration to say that Puerto Rico's largest art museum is comparable to the great European museums, but in terms of quality of displays, presentation, and facilities, it does not lag far behind. The 13,000 sq. ft. Museum of Art, which stages a comprehensive display of Puerto Rican art from pre-colonial times to the present, is a must-see for anyone interested in the island's culture. All exhibits are described in English and Spanish.

The third floor contains the bulk of the permanent collection, a chronological display of Puerto Rican art. The North Wing starts with a display of pre-colonial and colonial art from throughout Latin America, then later becomes exclusively Puerto Rican. A large section is devoted to **José Campeche** and another to the still-lifes of **Francisco Oller,** one of the first major artists to focus explicitly on Puerto Rican images. The South Wing moves into 20th-century art and introduces a few different types of media. The exhibits explain the Puerto Rican poster of the mid-20th century and display several works by **Rafael Tufiño** and poster art pioneer **Lorenzo Homar.** The fourth floor houses a display of Puerto Rican art post-1970, including photography, ceramics, installation art, and works in a variety of other media that are arranged thematically rather than chronologically. The most interesting room is filled with leaf-covered barber's chairs, TVs playing Puerto Rican images, hubcaps on the walls, and a pool table in the center. Another gallery, entitled "None of the Above," discusses Puerto Rico's 1998 referendum on its political status, in which a majority of the respondents selected "none of the above" (a vote for the status quo in Puerto Rico's political relationship to the US), rejecting statehood, independence, and a new version of commonwealth status. This exhibit emphasizes the island's unique culture through film, sculpture, and modern art.

Behind the museum, a five-acre **sculpture garden** houses countless sculptures, beautiful flora, and a large screen for special events. The first-floor **education center** provides child and adult classes on subjects from yoga to art and holds a rotating exhibit of local student work. The center also accepts volunteers to work at the museum. The second-floor **Galería activARTE** is a children's gallery that contains computer programs, games for visitors to create their own artwork, and child-friendly introductions to various media. Finally, the museum's **400-seat Raúl Juliá Theater** hosts regular events, including orchestra concerts, dance performances, and plays. The theater curtain is created out of the world's largest piece of **mundillo** lace; see the museum's website for more information on special events. (Av. de Diego 299. Buses A5 and B21 have stops here. ☎977-6277, ext. 2215 or 2230; www.mapr.org. Open Tu and Th-Sa 10am-5pm, W 10am-8pm, Su 11am-6pm. Inquire about tours Tu-Su. Students $6, under 12 and ages 60-74 $3, over 75 free. Entrance free W after 2pm.)

MUSEO DE ARTE CONTEMPORANEO. Devoted to cultural, artistic, and political aspects of Puerto Rico, four crisp, remodeled rooms display works by artists from Puerto Rico, the greater Caribbean, and Latin America in a permanent collection and periodic special exhibitions. An expansive inner courtyard provides space and open air for eye-catching displays and educational children's activities. The museum also holds a computer lab and art conservation lab. (Rafael M. Labra historical building on the southeast corner of Av. Ponce de León and R.H Todd in Santurce. ☎977-4030; www.museocontemporaneopr.com. Open Tu-Sa 10am-4:30pm, Su noon-4pm. Free.)

◪ BEACHES

As a general rule, the beaches get better as you go farther east. Few beaches in the San Juan area have amenities or public bathrooms. **Do not swim near Old San Juan**—although small sandy beaches do appear during low tide, the bay is quite polluted.

PUERTA DE TIERRA

Encompassing Parque Escobar, Estadio Sixto Escobar, and Balneario Escambrón, the extensive **Parque del Tercer Milenio** boasts the closest beach to Old San Juan—several swimming areas with calm, shallow water inside a manmade reef. Some easy **snorkeling** can be done in the reef that surrounds the swimming area, especially in the morning before the crowds arrive. The eastern beaches tend to be nicer than the western beaches, which progressively have less and less sand area. Parque del Tercer Milenio has many amenities, including restrooms, snack bars, trash cans, and signs identifying the current water quality. The park also includes several picnic tables, an area for barbecuing, a well-lit walkway, a bit of grass, a playground, and a large parking lot. (At the western end of Puerta de Tierra, near Av. Muñoz Rivera. Parking $3. Pier 9 wheelchair-accessible.)

CONDADO

Almost every street running north—south in Condado ends at the beach, which is fairly empty on weekdays and crowded on weekends. While this is far from being the nicest strip of beach on the island, it is clean and the location is unbeatable. The official public beach, **Balneario Playa de Condado,** is relatively small and is located at the far western edge of Condado near the bridge to Puerta de la Tierra. A line of rocks protects the bay here, creating a lagoon of shallow, wave-free water, a contrast to the crashing waves outside the swimming area. The beach also has lifeguards (daily 8:30am-5pm) and outdoor showers. Be forewarned—there are few public bathrooms in the area, and many restaurants along Av. Ashford let only customers use their facilities.

OCEAN PARK

Condado may have the reputation, but the clean, calm Ocean Park beach strip can deliver. The shores of this posh suburb boast nicer sand, less trash, and better waves for swimming. However, Ocean Park's beaches have few amenities and may often be filled with teenagers playing loud reggaeton.

ISLA VERDE

Isla Verde has the best beaches in San Juan. Narrow, barely marked paths between condominiums along Av. Isla Verde lead to the beach. The eastern side of Isla Verde has long, beautiful beaches that are most easily reached by turning toward the water at the Isla Verde Mall, then taking C. Dalia to C. Amapola to the end. Near the San Juan Hotel on the beach, **Edwin's Easy Chairs** rents for $3 a day. The far eastern end of the beach, in front of the airport and the Ritz Carlton, is farther away from the amenities and shops but consequently has fewer people, smoother sand, and a more picturesque landscape.

 THE GREAT ESCAPE. If too many sunburnt backsides are obstructing the view from your beach chair, escape to the virgin white sands and healthy palms of Piñones. Hop on San Juan city bus B40 in front of the cockfight arena on the east end of Isla Verde for a 15-25min. ride east. The food kiosks, breezy promenade and nearly deserted beach inlets merit an afternoon in Piñones.

BALNEARIO DE CAROLINA

The best public beach in the San Juan metropolitan area lies beyond Isla Verde in the city of Carolina. On weekends, this enormous *balneario* is packed with Puerto Ricans enjoying the long stretch of white sand and crashing waves. Come on a weekday, and the beach is one of the least crowded in the area. Facilities include covered benches, a playground, bathrooms, fire pits, vendors, trash cans, and lifeguards. (☎791-2410. Rte. 187, past the Ritz Carlton about 1 mi. past Isla Verde. Cars $3, vans $4. Open May-Aug. 15 daily 8am-6pm; Aug. 15-Apr. Tu-Su 8am-5pm.)

🏖 OUTDOOR ACTIVITIES

WATER SPORTS

DIVING AND SNORKELING

Ocean Sports, Av. Isla Verde 77 (☎723-8513 or 268-2329; www.osdivers.com), in Isla Verde, specializes in advanced diving but also offers water-sports equipment rental and lessons. Snorkeling gear rental $30 per 24hr. Boogie boards $35 per 2hr. Half-day diving trips in San Juan $75-95; full-day trips to the Fajardo area with equipment and transportation $145; half-day shore dives $65-75. Once a month leads trips to more exotic dive sites, such as Isla Mona, La Parguera, or St. Thomas (2-tank dive $100-150, equipment $25; min. 10 people). 4-day NAUI/SSI certification course $375 with materials. Ocean Sports also offers rebreather dives, Nitrox and advanced Nitrox dives, and Normoxic Trimix diver training. Open M-F 10am-7pm, Sa 9am-6pm. AmEx/D/MC/V.

La Casa del Buzo, Av. Jesús Piñero 293 (☎758-2710; www.lacasadelbuzo.com), in Río Piedras. Possibly the cheapest PADI certification courses in San Juan. 3-week course includes evening classroom instruction twice a week and 3 weekend dives ($210 per person). Open M-Sa 9am-6pm. AmEx/MC/V.

Scuba Dogs, C. Buen Samaritano #D.13, Gardenville (☎783-6377 or 399-5755; www.scubadogs.net), in Guaynabo. Has a big pool for SCUBA training ($250). Also offers excursions every weekend to dive sites around the island. These trips vary from 1 to 3 days and cost $75-150. In Sept., the company organizes a huge beach cleanup in which anyone can participate. Call ahead. MC/V.

SURFING, SAILING, AND WINDSURFING

Reefs lining the coast of San Juan create several good surfing spots, and any surfboard rental company listed below can provide the full scoop. Many people surf off Parque del Tercer Milenio, in Puerta de Tierra, but local surf shops recommend that beginners head to Pine Grove, near the Ritz Carlton in Isla Verde.

Tres Palmas, C. McLeary 1911 (☎ 728-3377), in Ocean Park, rents longboards ($40 per 24hr.), fun boards ($35), and shortboards ($30). Open M-Tu 10am-6pm, Th-Sa 10am-7pm, Su 11am-5pm. AmEx/D/MC/V.

Beach Cats, C. Loíza 2434 (☎ 727-0883), Punta Las Marías, runs catamaran sailing lessons ($100 per hr., including all equipment). It also sells kayaks, windsurfers, Hobie Cats, sunfish, kite surfing equipment, and surfboards. Also repairs surfboards. Open M-Sa 10am-6pm. AmEx/MC/V.

Velauno, C. Loíza 2430 (☎ 728-8716), Punta Las Marías, rents surfboards ($25 for the first day, $15 each additional day; $120 per week) and windsurfers ($75 per day). They also teach classes in surfing ($50 per hr.), windsurfing ($50 per hr., $150 for a 4hr. beginning class), and kite surfing ($225 per 3hr. class). Open M-Th 10am-7pm, F-Sa 11am-7pm. MC/V.

FISHING

Mike Benítez Sport Fishing, Av. Fernández Juncos 480 (☎ 723-2292 or 724-6265; www.mikebenitezfishingpr.com), in Miramar. In the Club Náutico. Sends a 45 ft. boat with A/C on daily deep-sea fishing trips. Half-day (4hr.) $197 per person, min. 2 people. Private charter for up to 6 people, $746 per person for 6hr. Oct.-Apr., fish for dorado, aahu, and yellow-fin tuna; May-Sept., it's blue marlin season. Shellfish and marlin must be tagged and released. Equipment provided. Open daily 7:30am-6pm. AmEx/MC/V.

DRY LAND ADVENTURES

Aventuras Tierra Adentro, Av. Jesus Piñero 268-A (☎ 766-0470; www.adventurespr.com), Río Piedras. Specializes in rappelling and zipline in the Río Camuy caves (p. 268). Experienced guides lead full-day trips to Ángeles Cave, and canyoning trips to El Yunque. No experience necessary—all expeditions begin with a short lesson. $160 per person includes transportation, equipment, and classes. Open Th-F 10am-6pm, Sa 10am-4pm. AmEx/MC/V.

🔲 ENTERTAINMENT

CASINOS

Gambling is a popular activity in San Juan, but unless you stick to the five-cent slot machines, it can quickly eat up your budget. Almost all the large chain hotels have sizable casinos. For a night of betting, hit up the glamorous row in **Isla Verde**—the Wyndham El San Juan, the InterContinental, the Embassy Suites, and the Ritz Carlton. On Av. Ashford in **Condado**, the Radisson Ambassador Plaza, the Diamond Palace Hotel, and the San Juan Marriott provide places to bet. Old San Juan's only place to gamble is the **Sheraton Old San Juan,** by the piers. The general dress code at casinos prohibits jeans and T-shirts; the legal gambling age is 18.

CINEMA

Most movie theaters are located away from the primary tourist districts. To see showtimes and buy tickets online, check out www.caribbeancinemas.com. **Metro,** Av. Ponce de León 1255, in Santurce, screens three American films. (☎ 721-5903. $5.50, under 10 and seniors $3.50.) **Plaza las Américas,** Av. F. D. Roosevelt (see **Shopping,** p. 134) has two large movie theaters. On the third floor, **Plaza Theaters** is the cheaper of the two. (☎ 758-3929. 9 movies with Spanish subtitles. $5.50, children and seniors $3.50. MC/V.) One floor down, **Caribbean Cinemas** has a slightly larger selection. (☎ 767-4775. 13 movies with Spanish subtitles. $6, ages 2-10 $3.50, seniors $4.) The **Fine Arts Cinema,** Av. Ponce de León 654, in Miramar, shows three American films in English, sometimes with Spanish subtitles. (☎ 721-4288. $5.50, children $3.50, over 60 $4. W women $3.50.)

PARTICIPATORY SPORTS

San Juan's premier outdoor sports area, **Parque Central,** has exceptional sports facilities. The large well-manicured park holds 20 tennis courts, four racquetball courts, a playground, several large fields, a well-lit stadium, a series of jogging paths, a track, a cafeteria, public restrooms, and telephones. Covered benches provide a shady place for parents to sit while their children play. Parque Central is open to the public, but it is almost impossible to reach without a car. It can also be quite busy on evenings and weekends when San Juan families head out after work, so if you want to play tennis during these peak hours, it's best to stop by in the morning and reserve a court (in person; telephone reservations not accepted). The tennis shop sometimes offers free tennis lessons for beginners—all you need to bring is a new set of tennis balls. Call ahead for more information. The park is located in Santurce. Drive south on C. Roberto H. Todd until it turns into a highway, then look for signs. Or, from Puerta de la Tierra take Hwy. 1 south to the Parque Central exit. (☎ 722-1646. Parking $1. Tennis courts $3 per hr., after 6pm $4. Racquetball courts $8 per hr. Open M-F 6am-9pm, Sa 6am-7pm, Su 6am-5pm.)

Parque Barbosa, next to Ocean Park, also offers a plethora of athletic facilities. Named after notable politician José Celso Barbosa (1857-1921), the park includes three basketball courts (one of which is covered), half- and full-length soccer fields, a track, a baseball field, and three tennis courts. Unfortunately, the tennis courts are really the only part of the park that is well maintained. A 24hr. police station is on the premises. (Directly east of Ocean Park, next to the ocean. Police ☎ 726-7020. Free parking. Track lights on all night.)

There are a few good areas for **running** in San Juan, if you can bear the heat. **Paseo de la Princesa,** along the western edge of Old San Juan (p. 119) hosts several joggers at dawn and dusk when it is a bit cooler. A nice track passes through **Parque del Tercer Milenio** in Puerta de la Tierra (p. 129).

SPECTATOR SPORTS

BASEBALL. Puerto Rico has an active professional baseball league, and most of the action takes place in San Juan. From the end of October until the beginning of January, the Santurce Cangrejeros and the San Juan Senadores play about three times per week at **Estadio Hiram Bithorn.** Tickets and schedules are available at the stadium box office on game days. (At the southwest corner of F.D. Roosevelt Boulevard and Route 18, across from Plaza las Américas. Enter from Av. F.D. Roosevelt. Box office open from 9am on the day of the game. Most games 8pm, Su 4pm. $5-7, children $2.50. MC/V.)

BASKETBALL. From April to June, professional basketball descends on Puerto Rico. The Santurce Cangrejeros play most of their home games at the Coliseo de Puerto Rico. (Tickets are available at www.ticketpop.com.)

COCKFIGHTS. The **Club Gallístico,** Av. Isla Verde 6600, at the intersection of Av. Isla Verde and Av. Los Gobernadores in Isla Verde, is the only **cockfighting arena** in Puerto Rico open to tourists. While Gallístico is a tourist attraction, it is also a working arena, and the crowd is largely local. Betting is a rather informal affair; only those in the first three rows can easily place bets, and they bet by yelling out "azul" or "blanco" (the color on their desired cock's ankle) and then a number of dollars. Bets are mentally recorded by a few men working the gambling operation, but these men are not officially labeled. After the fight, bettors pay up or get paid. If you would like to bet, it is best to make friends with someone in the first three rows and have him bet for you. Each fight lasts 15min. or until one of the roosters is knocked down; one session can include up to 40 fights. Waitresses serve beer, ice cream, and (interestingly enough) fried chicken. Come on Saturday for a rambunctious experience. Women are welcome, but will be something of a curiosity. (☎791-6005. Ringside seats $12, men general admission $10, women free. Fights Tu 4pm, Sa 2:30pm, sometimes Th 2:30pm. Buy tickets at the door. Office open M-F 8:30am-3pm.)

THEATER AND MUSIC

San Juan's premier fine arts center, the **Centro de Bellas Artes Luis A. Ferré** in Santurce, built in 1981, hosts a variety of different performances, from dance shows to symphony orchestra concerts to theater to stand-up comedy. The center has four theaters: the **Antonio Paoli** seats 2000 people, the **René Márques** seats 760, the **Carlos Mavrichal** seats 210, and the **Sylvia Rexach** seats 200. Twice a month the Puerto Rican symphony orchestra performs here, and in January the center hosts the **Casals Festival** (see **Festivals,** p. 133). For tickets, check **Ticketpop** online (see **Ticket Agencies,** p. 97) or visit the box office. Often, you can simply show up at the box office on the night of the show and buy tickets. (On Av. Ponce de León, west of the intersection with C. de Diego. ☎620-4444; www.cba.gobierno.pr. Wheelchair-accessible. MC/V.)

Teatro Tapia (p. 120), on Plaza Colón in Old San Juan, has theater performances or musicals every weekend. Shows rotate every two to three weeks, and most are in Spanish. (☎721-0180 or 723-2079. Shows F-Su $25-30. Ticket office hours vary. MC/V.) The small **Corralón de San Juan,** C. San José 109, in Old San Juan, occasionally hosts student performances, but the schedule is erratic.

Many of the biggest acts touring the US also make a stop at San Juan's **Coliseo Roberto Clemente.** Over the last few years, the 10,000-seat theater has seen concerts by Jennifer Lopez and reggaeton superstar Vico C; special events such as the Miss Universe Pageant, National Salsa Day, and Disney on Ice; and sporting events from basketball to volleyball. To buy tickets or find information about coming events, check **Ticket Center** (see **Ticket Agencies,** p. 97), in Plaza las Américas or online. (Located in Hato Rey, south of Av. F.D. Roosevelt, west of Expreso las Américas. ☎754-7422. Parking $1, during events $2.)

※ FESTIVALS

San Juan hosts more festivals—and more outlandish celebrations—than any other city on the island. Most are held in Old San Juan, and the hordes of visitors can create horrendous traffic jams; if you go, take the bus or park in one of the several parking garages on the eastern edge of town. Some of the largest events are listed below. For more information about any festival, or exact dates, contact the Puerto Rico Tourism Company (see **Tourist Offices,** p. 96).

LELOLAI FESTIVAL. This series of weekly cultural performances was designed by the Puerto Rico Tourism Company to highlight Puerto Rico's multicultural heritage. The ongoing festival offers salsa lessons, tropical music, and rumba performances. Some of the events are free, but others require the "Puerto Rico is Fun" card, available for purchase at over 50 island hotels. Check online listings for performance times and locations around San Juan. *(4 nights per week. Primarily in San Juan, but shows held throughout the island. ☎721-2400, ext. 2215; www.gotopuertorico.com.)*

MARTES NOCHE DE GALERÍA. On the first Tuesday of every month, galleries across Old San Juan keep their doors open into the night, presenting new exhibitions and hosting special events. However, many young people skip the galleries and head straight to C. San Sebastián, which becomes an enormous street party lasting until the wee hours of the morning. This has caused many galleries to avoid participating altogether. Nevertheless, the party prevails: the Plaza de Armas, C. del Cristo, and Plaza San José on C. San Sebastián tend to be the centers of activity. *(1st Tu of the month year-round. Old San Juan.)*

FESTIVAL DE LA CALLE SAN SEBASTIÁN. By day, this is one of the biggest *artesanía* festivals on the island, and hundreds of artisans exhibit their wares in the Cuartel de la Ballajá (the same building as the Museo de las Américas). As night falls, the government shuts down C. San Sebastián for an incredible party attended by thousands of drunken revelers. *(The week of Jan. 20, though the party gets going on the weekend. Old San Juan.)*

LA NOCHE DE SAN JUAN BAUTISTA. Wishing for luck in the coming year, hundreds of *sanjuaneros* fall backward into the ocean seven times at the stroke of midnight. In addition to offering traditional art, music, and food, this festival dedicated to San Juan Bautista has evolved into a massive, island-wide beach party complete with bonfires, drums, marshmallow roasting, and fireworks. *(Sa preceding June 24th. Puerta de Tierra, Condado, Ocean Park, Isla Verde, and throughout the island.)*

HEINEKEN JAZZ FESTIVAL. This is Puerto Rico's largest jazz festival, drawing acts such as Manhattan Transfer and Eddie Palmieri. The event focuses on Latin jazz, but musicians from all over the world come to play under Caribbean skies. *(Apr.-June Th-Su 8-10pm. Anfiteatro Tito Puente in Parque Luis Muñoz Marín, San Juan. www.prheineken-jazz.com. 1-day tickets $23, 4-day tickets $65; available from Ticketpop, p. 97.)*

LA FERIA DE ARTESANÍA. Vendors selling everything from soap to handmade *guiros* pack Old San Juan's Paseo la Princesa in one of the island's largest craft fairs. Orchestras, folkloric dancers, and big-name salsa acts like El Gran Combo de Puerto Rico put on free shows on the western end of the Paseo and in the Plaza de la Dársena. *(1st weekend in June 7-10pm. Paseo la Princesa, Old San Juan. ☎ 721-2400.)*

CASALS FESTIVAL. Created by Spanish composer **Pablo Casals** (p. 70), this two-week festival consists of a series of classical music performances by the Puerto Rican Symphony Orchestra and visiting musicians. Posters from past Casals Festivals are on display in the Casals Museum in Old San Juan. *(Dates vary widely, but the festival is always held in the spring. In the Centro de Bellas Artes Luis A. Ferré (p. 133), Santurce. ☎ 723-9185; www.festcasalspr.gobierno.pr.)*

PUERTO RICO SALSA CONGRESS. This annual salsa exhibition and convention features dancers from around the world and classes for visitors of every skill level. *(Last weekend in July. ☎ 470-8888.)*

CINEMAFEST DE PUERTO RICO. This internationally renowned film festival draws producers, directors, and actors from around the world. Films relating to the Caribbean may compete for prizes. Over 100 short and feature-length films are shown. *(Held over 1 week in Nov. Screenings at various locations around the island, but primarily in San Juan. ☎ 723-5015; www.sanjuancinemafest.com.)*

BACARDI FERIA DE ARTESANÍA. The Bacardi Corporation hosts yet another enormous artisans festival. Every December, over 100,000 people venture out to Cataño to check out local arts and crafts, dance to live salsa and merengue, and, of course, sample their favorite rum. The drinks aren't free, but all proceeds go to charity. *(1st 2 weekends in Dec. Bacardi Factory (p. 141), Cataño.)*

⌐ SHOPPING

Paseo de Diego, in Río Piedras (p. 122), is a pedestrian boulevard lined with clothing stores and fast-food restaurants. The clothing stores run the gamut from American chains like Foot Locker to bargain-basement wholesalers. **Old San Juan** is a great place to shop for hokey Puerto Rican souvenirs, designer clothing, local artwork, and expensive jewelry: meander through the narrow cobblestone streets and see what catches your eye. C. Fortaleza has an abundance of souvenir and clothing shops, while stores on C. San Francisco are almost all high-end jewelry shops. A designer store outlet strip (with staples like Coach and Ralph Lauren) sits on C. Del Cristo. C. San José and C. del Cristo are the best places to find original (and expensive) Puerto Rican modern art.

More generic shopping awaits in Hato Rey, at **Plaza las Américas,** the largest shopping mall in the Caribbean. This three-story extravaganza has over 300 stores, two movie theaters, a food court, a ticket center, a fountain, a multi-story Old Navy, and everything else you could want in a mall. (Av. F.D. Roosevelt 525, in Hato Rey. Take Expreso Las Américas to the Av. F. D. Roosevelt exit. The B21 bus route goes around the mall. ☎767-5202. Open M-Sa 9am-9pm, Su 11am-5pm.)

NIGHTLIFE

Check out Lo Nítido at www.lonitido.com in Spanish or Puerto Rico Wow at www.puertoricowow.com in both Spanish and English for more information on the latest nightlife happenings (see **Publications,** p. 97).

> **! NIGHTCLUB SECURITY.** Many San Juan nightclubs have tighter security than the airport. To save time and hassles, do not bring pocket knives, pens, or any potentially hazardous object when you go out, and prepare to be frisked.

OLD SAN JUAN

In terms of bars and restaurants, Old San Juan has the trendiest nightlife in the capital, though it is mostly bar-based. **Calle San Sebastián** and **Calle Fortaleza** are consistently the hubs of activity. On weekend nights, **Paseo de la Princesa** is crowded with vendors and young couples. A popular spot to end the night on weekends is **Pink Skirt,** C. Fortaleza 301.

🏮 **Nuyorican Café,** C. San Francisco 312 (☎977-1276 or 366-5074), with entrance from the walkway Callejón Capilla between C. San Francisco and C. Fortaleza. "El Nuyorican" is the mainspring for contemporary music (salsa, jazz, rock, Latin fusion), theater, film, and art in Old San Juan, bringing diverse types together nightly through an appreciation for urban culture. F-Sa salsa is an experience. "Nuyo pizzas" $5-7. Open daily 8pm-last customer. Kitchen open until 1am. MC/V.

🏮 **Rumba,** C. San Sebastián 130 (☎725-4407). The Latin club you've always been looking for. Rumba packs in a crowd of all ages, races, and nationalities to dance the night away. Sip a drink up front or push your way to the back where live bands play charanga, salsa, and rumba (F-Sa 11pm). Beer $3 and up. Mixed drinks from $5. Open Tu-Su 8pm-3am. AmEx/MC/V.

Café Hijos de Borinquen, C. San José 51 (☎723-8126), at C. San Sebastián. Crowds of tipsy Puerto Ricans pack this bar, the oldest standing on C. San Sebastián, on weekends. Push your way in, grab a beer ($2-3.50), and just try to make conversation over the shouts and the loud Latin dance music. Although it looks like a bar, it functions as a dance club for local teenagers. Mixed drinks $3.50-6. Live music F-Sa 10pm-2am. Happy hour daily 10pm-1am. Open Th-Sa 8pm-last customer. MC/V.

El Batey, C del Cristo 101. "Go out to the *batey,*" Puerto Rican mothers tell their children when they want them to play in the yard. El Batey is essentially a nighttime playground. College-aged locals sit at the bar playing *generala,* their version of Yahtzee, while others are drawn to the back pool tables. Graffiti covers the walls, and patrons hang their business cards from the light fixtures. Beer $2.75-4. Mixed drinks $3-6. Cash only.

Marmalade, Fortaleza 317 (☎724-3969; www.marmaladepr.com). A Space Age restaurant and wine bar that's well worth the splurge. The mod decor is set by white curtains, bright low stools, and bubble-like lamps, which recently earned this SoFo destination a spot on Conde Nast Traveller's Hot List. Try the Kiwi Libre (white rum and fresh lime) or Spanish Saffron vanilla bean martini (about $8.50). M-W and Su 5-10pm the bar hosts a "bottomless glass of wine" party, with over 35 wines to choose from ($25). Appetizers $13-23. Entrees $24-29. Open M-Th 6pm-midnight and F-Sa 6pm-4am. AmEx/MC/V.

Barú, C. San Sebastián 150 (☎977-7107; www.barupr.com). The place to go on C. San Sebastián for a more mature night out. On weeknights and before 10pm, an older crowd sips mojitos under softly glowing lights. Later in the night and on weekends, 20-somethings make Barú one of C. San Sebastián's hot spots. Wine $7 and up. Mixed drinks $4-12. Sangria pitchers from $20. Caribbean tapas 4 for $12 and up. Dress to impress; no jeans. Open M-Sa 6pm-1am, Su 5pm-1am. AmEx/D/MC/V.

Brick House Bar and Grill, C. Tetuán 359 (☎559-5022), in Plaza Somohano, adjacent to the Teatro Tapia. Locals and vacationers alike can't get enough of this grillhouse-cum-nightspot. The self-proclaimed home of "Gringo-Rican Cuisine" offers up mahi-mahi tacos ($12) and famous wings and ribs ($16 per platter). Live jazz M 7-11pm. "Keggers" W 7pm-last customer. Cruise ship karaoke F 10pm-2am. Happy hour M-Sa 3-7pm. Open M-F 4pm-last customer, and Sa-Su 10am-last customer.

Krugger, C. San José 52 (☎723-2475), ½ block south of C. San Sebastián; enter under the sign and turn left through the green doors. Everybody needs a karaoke fix from time to time, and Krugger has it. Bar food and inexpensive dinner plates $6-12. Beer $1-3. Mixed drinks $1-5. Free daytime delivery. Open M and W-F 10am-3pm and 5pm-midnight, Tu 10am-3pm, Sa 5pm-midnight, Su 11am-noon and 5pm-midnight. D/MC/V.

Nono's, C. San Sebastián 109 (☎725-7819), at C. Fortaleza, is a good place to drink. And drink. And drink. A relatively sedate macho crowd settles down at the bar with a drink in hand, buys cigars out of the vending machine ($3-13), and whiles the night away as the breeze comes through the open doors. Beer $4-5. Mixed drinks $4-8. Open daily noon-4am. AmEx/MC/V.

Lazer, C. Cruz 251 (☎725-7581; www.clublazer.com), at C. Cruz and C. Fortaleza. The many levels, hidden corners, and smoke machines combine to make Lazer one hot nighttime destination for (very) young *sanjuaneros,* who get down on the 2 big dance floors to hip hop and techno or chill out on the palm-filled rooftop terrace. Mixed drinks $5-7. F reggaeton; cover $15, wine free for women. Sa *melaza* with guest DJs and hard Reggaeton; no cover for women before midnight. Other nights cover $5-10. Open Th-Su 10pm-last customer.

Señor Frog's, Paseo Portuario, C. Comercio (☎977-4142, ext. 46), behind the Sheraton Hotel. Every night is a party at this flashy Mexican chain where drinks are sold in "yard" (really about 1½ ft.) bottles. Señor Frog arrived in San Juan in early 2003 and instantly became the hottest venue in town for tennis-skirt-clad cruise passengers and vacationers who heed the restaurant's sign: "If the music is too loud... You're too old." This hasn't stopped the 30-something men who make up a decent part of the crowd before midnight. Beer $3-3.50. Mixed drinks $6. Yards $7.50-20. Good live rock and pop nightly at 9pm. Open daily 10am-1am or last customer. AmEx/D/MC/V.

Cafe San Sebastián, C. San Sebastián 153 (☎725-3998), at Plaza del Mercado. A laid-back crowd heads to San Sebastián to relax on wicker furniture and enjoy the breeze coming through the large open doors while listening to good salsa music. San Juan's best chill-out bar. Beer $2-3.50. Mixed drinks $3-6.50. Claims to be open Tu-Su 8pm-3:30am, but will open late or close early if there are no patrons.

Oscar's Bar, C. Recinto Sur 321 (☎724-7255), across from Doña Fela parking lot. Past the giant fish in the tank at the entrance is a cavernous bar filled with red Budweiser lamps. With 4 pool tables, mirrors on the walls, and countless TVs, this hole in the wall doesn't seem to fit in with its trendy, touristy neighbors, but some might find that its simple quality makes it a good place to relax with friends and a beer ($3.50). Open daily noon-last customer. AmEx/MC/V.

¡QUÉ CHEVERE! Here's a look at what spots are hottest on which nights:
Monday: Café Seda (guest hip-hop DJ every M); Brick House (live jazz M nights 7-11pm and "wing-ding happy hour" M-Sa 3-7pm.)
Tuesday: Dunbar's (70s and 80s rock and roll and Brazilian music. Wings, pool, darts, and Happy hour daily 5-7pm.)
Wednesday: Krash (clubbing); Zabó, Condado (Happy hour 4-7pm); La Terraza del Condado, Condado ("2.99" house drink only $0.99).
Thursday: Rumba (Th Salsa).
Friday: Santurce's Mercado from 5pm onward (post-work party over beers), El Batey and Café Hijos de Borinquen (for a more laid-back F).
Saturday: Nuyorican Café (Sa salsa); BRAVA (Isla Verde's classiest club); Marmalade/Dragonfly; Starz; Lazer (Sa is Melaza night: hard reggaeton).
Sunday: Pink Skirt (after-hours techno 1-4am); Señor Frog's.

CONDADO

Condado has a relatively mellow nightlife scene, primarily limited to a few low-key bars. Most of the local crowd heads to the open-air restaurant patios—**Via Appia's** is lively every night of the week. Tourists generally stick to the hotel nightclubs and casinos, of which many line Av. Ashford.

La Terraza del Condado (☎ 723-2770), a large concrete gazebo at the eastern intersection of Av. Ashford and C. Magdalena. Teens and 20-something locals sip beer ($2.25) and margaritas ($5.50) in this plant-filled bar and dance the night away to reggaeton. The "299" house drink (an exotic concoction of liquors and tropical juices) costs $2.99 and only $0.99 every W night. AmEx/D/MC/V.

Kalí, Av. Ashford 1407 (☎ 721-5104). Popular with night owls of all ages, this trendy lounge is named for the Hindu god of destruction. Sweep aside the gauzy curtain to find dark maroon walls, candlelit nooks, and huge black leather couches. Tapas $8-14: black bean hummus $8, tuna and salmon *ceviche* $14. Mixed drinks $5-7. Open Tu-3a 8pm-last customer. Kitchen closes 3am. AmEx/D/MC/V.

Waikiki, Av. Ashford 1025 (☎ 977-2267). A large crowd of Condado's young professionals fill up this upscale bar and restaurant every night of the week, sipping wine (bottles $21-30) on the retro oceanfront patio or in the wine-cellarish interior. Those who stay out too late can come back for breakfast ($2-5). Open daily 7am-last customer. MC/V.

Sol de Luna Café, La Ventana al Mar park (☎ 721-7132), on Av. Ashford. Come early to stake out a metal table and stools under blue lights at this oyster and drink bar on an outdoor terrace in "The Window to the Sea" park. One of the newest nightspots for 20- and 30-somethings along the chic strip of Condado neighborhood. 6 oysters $10, 6 clams $12. Marlin on skewer $4.50. Burger $10. Mixed drinks $7-8. Open daily 5pm-2am.

SANTURCE

Santurce is home to San Juan's most outlandish and popular discos. However, with its many empty storefronts and construction sites, it is very dangerous at night. Travelers still looking to party in Santurce should plan in advance for transportation and never venture out alone. The popular **Habana Club,** C. Condado 303, is a salsa mecca. Enter from C. Todd next to Stargate, across the street from Burger King. (☎ 722-1919. Live salsa F-Sa. Age restrictions and cover may apply.) On Fridays after 5pm in the **Plaza del Mercado** (p. 112), young *puertorriqueños* ride into the plaza on their motorcycles, business people join them from their offices, and the place becomes completely packed. Locals hang out on the patios of the small restaurants and mingle in the streets, while salsa blares from every direction. Another club in the area is **El Teatro,** C. Ponce de León 1420, with daily dancing, DJ, and pop music (☎ 722-1132).

SAN JUAN

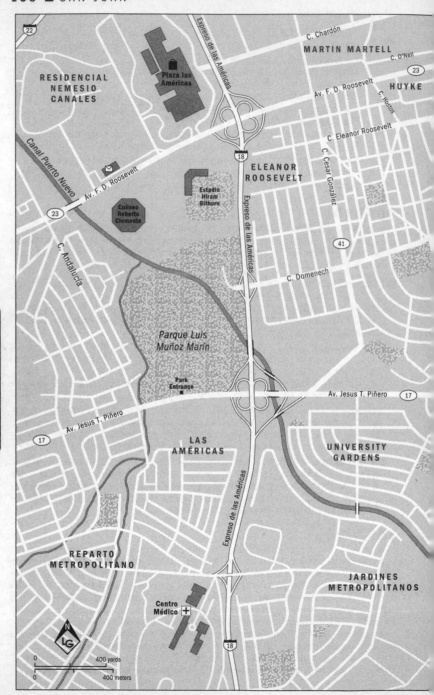

SAN JUAN

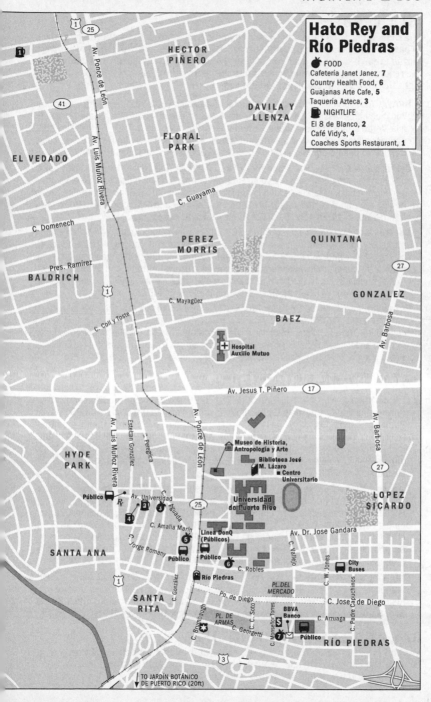

Hato Rey and Río Piedras

🍅 FOOD
Cafetería Janet Janez, **7**
Country Health Food, **6**
Guajanas Arte Cafe, **5**
Taquería Azteca, **3**

🍸 NIGHTLIFE
El 8 de Blanco, **2**
Café Vidy's, **4**
Coaches Sports Restaurant, **1**

SAN JUAN

HECTOR PIÑERO

DAVILA Y LLENZA

FLORAL PARK

EL VEDADO

Av. Ponce de León

Av. Luis Muñoz Rivera

C. Domenech

Pres. Ramirez

BALDRICH

C. Guayama

PEREZ MORRIS

QUINTANA

C. Mayagüez

GONZALEZ

C. Coll y Toste

BAEZ

Av. Barbosa

✚ Hospital Auxilio Mutuo

Av. Jesus T. Piñero

HYDE PARK

Av. Luis Muñoz Rivera

Esteban González

C. Peregrina

Av. Ponce de León

Museo de Historia, Antropología y Arte

Biblioteca José M. Lázaro

Centro Universitario

Av. Barbosa

LOPEZ SICARDO

Público 🚌 R

Av. Universidad

Aguada

Universidad de Puerto Rico

SANTA ANA

C. Jorge Romany

C. Amalia Marín

Linea DonQ (Públicos)

Público

Público

Av. Dr. Jose Gandara

C. Vallejo

City Buses

C. W. Jones

C. Robles

Río Piedras

PL. DEL MERCADO

Po. de Diego

C. Jose de Diego

C. González

C. Brumbaugh

SANTA RITA

PL. DE ARMAS

C. C. Soto

C. Georgetti

C. Monseñor Torres

BBVA Banco

$

✉

Público

C. Arzuaga

C. Padre Capuchinos

RÍO PIEDRAS

TO JARDÍN BOTÁNICO DE PUERTO RICO (20ft)

ISLA VERDE

The rich and famous (and wannabe rich and famous) flock to Isla Verde after dark to party in the casinos, bars and clubs of San Juan's resort strip. Dress to impress in this area: T-shirts, sandals, and other beachwear are generally not allowed in the resort nightspots. Some restaurants and bars double as more relaxed, casual nightlife options and are listed under **Food**, p. 107.

BRAVA, Av. Isla Verde in El San Juan Hotel and Casino (602-8222; www.bravapr.com). You'll be hard-pressed to find anything as chic or as current as BRAVA, located in one of Isla Verde's most lavish hotels. 2 remodeled floors house 2 DJs: 1 plays hip hop, house, and reggaeton, and the other electronica and progressive house. The club hosts over 1000 people on busy nights. Cover $13-20. Open Th-Sa 10pm-4am. AmEx/MC/V.

Oyster Bar & Grill, Av. Isla Verde 6000 (☎726-2161). This New Orleans-themed bar is one hot place to party, with the younger crowd grinding to pop music on the dance floor and kicking back at tables hidden in nooks and crannies. Mixed drinks $5 and up. Open bar Th 7-11pm $10. 15-oyster bucket $14. Karaoke and live rock. 21+. Open M-Tu 11am-2am, W 11am-4am, F-Sa 11am-5am. Kitchen closes 3am. MC/V.

Boceto, Av. Isla Verde, Local 2480 (☎268-2627; www.galeriaboceto.com). Part Cuban art gallery, part techno dance bar, this chic new restaurant and nightspot is tough to classify. Enter and you'll feel as though you've stepped into a bourgeois salon, complete with ornamental wallpaper and chandeliers. Lounge at the mood-lit bar or groove to electronica beats in the back room, where the walls are laden with Cuban oil paintings. Happy hour W-F 5-9pm. Open Tu-Su 6pm-midnight. MC/V.

El Taquito, Av. Isla Verde 5940 (☎726-5050), across from Pizza City. This new but cheap bar and restaurant allows you to sip margaritas ($5; half-gallon $20) or their fruit frappe concoctions ($4.50) while watching TV and chowing down on Tex-Mex staples like tacos ($1.50) and quesadillas ($5-7). If you stay out too late, don't worry: they serve big breakfast wraps, too ($2.50-5.25). Beer starts at $1. Open 24hr. AmEx/MC/V.

HATO REY AND RÍO PIEDRAS

El 8 de Blanco, Av. Universidad 102 (☎751-5208; www.elochodeblanco.com), at Av. Universidad and C. Consuelo Carbo, in Río Piedras. Located 2 blocks from UPR, El 8 de Blanco is happening every day with all-day Happy hours ($1 beer), funky graffittied walls, loud music, video games, pool tables, a dominoes, table and an upstairs restaurant (combos $4-6). The place fills up early every night of the week. Beer $1-3. Mixed drinks $3-4. Live salsa and merengue F 6pm. 18+. Open M-Sa 2pm-4am, Su 5pm-last customer. AmEx/MC/V.

Coaches Sport Restaurant, Av. F.D. Roosevelt 137 (☎758-3598; www.coachespr.com), in Hato Rey. Huge American-style sports bar with pool tables, many TVs, and large bar. Football helmets on the wall keep track of the week's NFL matchups. Packed on big game nights. Weekday lunch specials start at $5. Entrees $6-16. Beer $3-3.50. Mixed drinks $5-7. W-Th 7pm-midnight beers $2.50, F mojitos $6. Live Spanish rock W-Sa when there's not a big game on. Happy hour W-Sa; themes vary, so check website. Open M-F 11:30am-2am, Sa 8pm-4am, Su 5pm-last customer. AmEx/D/MC/V.

Café Vidy's, Av. Universidad 104 (☎767-3062), in Río Piedras. You can hang out with the locals and drink a Medalla on the street-side patio at just about any time of day. Also a popular *cafetería* serving Puerto Rican food. Sandwiches and entrees $2-10. Beer $1-4. Karaoke W 9pm. Happy hour daily 9-11pm. Open daily 10am-1am. MC/V.

GAY AND LESBIAN NIGHTLIFE

For the latest information on gay nightlife and events, check out *Puerto Rico Breeze*, the capital's gay and lesbian newspaper, available at stores in Condado's gay district and for free in some hotels and restaurants.

Krash, Av. Ponce de León 1257 (☎722-1131; www.krashklubpr.com), in Santurce, plays house, tribal, retro, and reggaeton with some hip hop thrown in. The new management here takes over one of the oldest names in San Juan gay nightlife. Weekly special events listed on site. Open W-Sa 10pm-last customer.

Starz, Av. de Diego (☎721-8645; www.starzclub.com), at the corner of Av. Ponce de León 1257, in Santurce. A hopping disco with weekly specials ranging from theme nights to strip shows. Open Tu and Sa-Su 11pm-last customer.

🛂 DAYTRIPS FROM SAN JUAN

CATAÑO

From Pier 2 in Old San Juan, take the AquaExpreso ferry (10min., every 30min. 6am-10pm; $0.50) to Cataño. To get to the Bacardi factory, walk outside, turn right, and walk to the large green parking garage where públicos wait inside ($2 per person for 4 or more people or $6 alone). If driving, take Rte. 165 from San Juan and turn right after the John Deere factory; if you see the huge Bacardi sign, you've gone too far.

Rum's the word on most visitors' minds as they head across the bay to Cataño, home of the **Bacardi Rum Factory.** Although Bacardi originated in Cuba and now has factories in Mexico and the Bahamas, the Cataño factory is the world's largest producer of Bacardi rum and one of the largest companies on the island. All of this combines to make the Bacardi Factory one hot attraction for families, couples, and those looking for a free drink.

Around San Juan

Tours, which last 45min., are offered every 15min., alternating between English and Spanish. Upon arrival, visitors receive **two free drink tickets.** Many *sanjuaneros* have been known to come for the free drinks and then leave before the tour. However, Bacardi fanatics may find that the tour provides an interesting explanation of the rum-making process and the company's history. The tour begins with a tram ride to the new Visitors Center, where guests watch an amusing film—suspiciously like a long Bacardi commercial—telling the story of "the king of rums and the rum of kings." Next, audio tours allow visitors to explore a re-created antique distillery room (ca. 1900) and another room devoted to the Bacardi family. Guests are also given the chance to smell the various Bacardi products at different stages in the fermentation process. Then, visitors are taken to a high-tech room playing hot Bacardi commercials. Here they are allowed to dance and tape 10-second video clips to email home. Finally, another tram passes the working distillery and bottling plant before heading back to the start of the tour and the requisite Bacardi store. (☎788-1500. Open M-Sa 9am-4:30pm, Su 10am-3:45pm. Free.)

Few visitors make it past the Bacardi factory, but Cataño has more to it than rum. Just down the road, Isla de Cabras used to be an island with its own leper colony, but has long since morphed into a grassy peninsula with picnic tables and some superb views of Old San Juan. And unlike the bustling capital, Isla de Cabras is quite peaceful, making it an ideal spot for a picnic. The island also houses El Cañuelo, a Spanish fort built in the 1500s to create crossfire with El Morro. The fort looks like a miniature version of El Morro, and no one is allowed to enter, so there's not much more than what can be seen through binoculars from atop El Morro. Unfortunately, public transportation to Isla de Cabras is difficult. A taxi from the Bacardi factory costs at least $6 each way, so the island is only worth a visit if you have a car. From Rte. 165, drive past the Bacardi factory, turn right on Rte. 870, and continue to the end. (Open daily 8:30am-5:30pm. $2 per car.)

CERRO GORDO

Take a público out of Río Piedras to Vega Baja ($3), where very occasional públicos traveling to Cerro Gordo from Vega Baja will let you off at the beach ($2). On weekdays, during daylight hours, you may be able to catch a passing público back to Vega Baja from the beach. By car from Hwy. 22, take Exit 31 onto Rte. 690 and go north all the way to the beach. From the west, take Rte. 688 or 689 to Rte. 690, which ends at the beach.

The beaches of San Juan simply cannot compare to those found around the rest of the island. **Balneario Cerro Gordo** has a lot to offer travelers who are looking for a short, convenient excursion to sublime sands. The Puerto Rican government has invested $3.4 million into remodeling this **public beach,** creating first-rate facilities in an already first-rate environment. The *balneario* currently boasts tiny waves of crystal-clear water, a palm-tree-lined beach, and views of the picturesque village of Cerro Gordo. The beach and the town make an ideal daytrip from San Juan. (☎883-2730. Lifeguards, picnic tables, food stands, and public showers. Parking cars $3, vans $4. Open daily 8:30am-6pm.) If you work up an appetite lounging on the beach, try some of the cheapest eats in the area at the various beach kiosks, which serve fried food and ice cream. If you decide to extend your daytrip a little, Cerro Gordo has a nice **campground ❶** in the woodsy area up the hill on the eastern edge of the beach. Some sites have ocean views, but there is little privacy. Guards control access, but it's still wise to keep valuables out of sight. Call the beach for reservations, especially from June to August. ($13 per person.)

PIÑONES

San Juan city bus B40 travels from the Isla Verde bus stop, in front of the Cockfight Arena, along Av. Boca de Cangrejos to the eastern edge of Piñones. By car from Isla Verde, take Rte. 187 through the forest. By far the best way to experience Piñones is by bicycle. Bike path open daily 6am-6pm.

Although physically separated by less than 1 mi., wild and rugged Piñones State Forest and ritzy Isla Verde could not be more different. Where Isla Verde has upscale "authentic" Puerto Rican restaurants, Piñones has stands with open flames frying African-influenced Puerto Rican foods. Isla Verde's population of wealthy Puerto Ricans and expats contrasts with Piñones' relatively poor community. Piñones is the locals' pick for a stroll or bike ride on the beachside promenade, a swim at more remote beaches east of the city center, and a bite to eat or a sunset drink at numerous oceanfront kiosks. Travelers who want to experience a more traditional Puerto Rico but don't have time to stray far from San Juan should head straight for this area.

Coming from San Juan along Rte. 187 visitors will first pass **Boca de Cangrejos,** a small peninsula filled with restaurants and food shacks, or "kioskos." An offshore reef makes this a bad area to swim, but a great place to stop for a snack. Keep going—it's not until around Km 9 that you will find the nearly deserted **beaches** with pristine sand and rows of palm trees. Drivers can pull off on any one of the sandy roads leading to the ocean and relax. Piñones is also a popular **surfing** spot; surf shops in Isla Verde and Ocean Park can point out the best breaks.

Lying on the beach is nice, but the best way to experience Piñones is by riding along the ⊠**Paseo Piñones bike path.** A combination of paved trails and wooden bridges, the path weaves through the forest, providing incomparable views of the flora, the small communities of houses, and the beach. A fabulous daytrip from San Juan can be spent riding along the path, swimming for an hour or two at a deserted beach, and then stopping for a snack at a food kiosk on the way home. It is possible to rent a bicycle at any shop in the city (see **Bike Rental,**), and then ride along the road to the reach the path. To avoid riding down busy streets in the urban section, rent a bike at **El Pulpo Loco,** located on the water behind Soleil in the second cluster of restaurants, right on the bike path. (☎791-8382. Bikes $5 per hr., $20 per day. Open daily 10am-6pm. AmEx/ MC/V.) Farther inland, the forest also encompasses **Laguna de Piñones** and **Laguna la Torrecilla.** These two lakes are quite swampy and can emit a powerful smell, but it is possible to kayak on them. To reach the lake, drive to Km 9 and turn right at the sign pointing toward Bosque Estatal de Piñones. Continue all the way down the road to the parking lot and the kayak launch.

Piñones is filled with dozens of kiosks small food shacks. The best and the cheapest option is to grab some fried chicken, an *empanada* or a *batida* from one of these vendors ($1-4) and head to the beach. Those looking for more refined dining options can usually find one in each of the restaurant clusters. In addition to renting bikes, **El Pulpo Loco** ❸ (see above) doubles as a clean restaurant with palm-covered picnic tables and tasty Puerto Rican seafood. Specialties include octopus, but the menu also offers less adventurous options such as beef and chicken. (☎791-8382. Entrees $9-17. Open M-Th and Su 10am-11pm, F-Sa 10am-2am. AmEx/MC/V.) **The Reef Bar and Grill** ❸, in the first inlet of restaurants directly after the bridge coming from San Juan, has the best view in Piñones, with crystal clear water breaking on the reef in the foreground and the San Juan skyline in the distance toward the west. The menu includes seafood entrees as well as chicken and beef. (☎791-1374. Sandwiches and burgers $5-7. Entrees $7-13. Beer $2.75-3. Mixed drinks $4-6. Open M-Th 10am-midnight, F-Sa 10am-3am, Su 10am-3am. Kitchen opens at 11am. MC/V.) Piñones also has an impressive **nightlife scene.** Many restaurants, including both of the above, double as bars, but the most widely advertised hot spot is **Soleil.** Located in front of El Pulpo Loco in the second inlet, the two-story restaurant draws the larger crowds from San Juan. One of the most modern-looking bars in the park, it boasts a gorgeous ocean view from the patio (☎253-1033; www.soleilbeachclub.com. House specialty mixed drinks $5.50-6. Appetizers $7-9. Open M-Th and Su 11am-11pm, F-Sa 11am-1am. AmEx/D/MC/V.)

TIME: 5-7hr.

DISTANCE: 50mi.

BEST TIME TO GO: Dec.-Mar., or when no rain is expected.

CENTRAL MOUNTAINS SCENIC DRIVE

Countless visitors come to San Juan, lie on the beach for a week, and never discover the treasures of inland Puerto Rico. For those who want to experience just a little bit more but don't have time to venture very far inland, this scenic drive offers a glimpse of Puerto Rico's incredible natural and cultural diversity. From the towering office buildings of Hato Rey to the towering peaks of the Cordillera Central, from the traditional devotion of Trujillo Alto to the traditional roadside snacks of Piñones, this roadtrip highlights the island's variety in a great one-day excursion from Puerto Rico's capital.

Travelers should take note that the times given are highly variable estimates, dependent on traffic and weather conditions. The trip travels along narrow, winding mountain roads, which become perilous after dark. Make sure to leave early and allow plenty of time for your trip. From San Juan, take Hwy. 1 south through the business district of Hato Rey. After passing through the city, take Hwy. 3 heading east toward Carolina. This is far from the most picturesque part of the journey, but it also provides a closer look at San Juan's problems with urban sprawl and traffic congestion. Stay on Hwy. 3 for about 1 mi., then turn right and head south on Rte. 181, a pleasant tree-lined street that leads to the suburb of Trujillo Alto.

1. LA GRUTA DE LOURDES. After passing the intersection with Rte. 850, take the next exit to the right and head up the hill on the middle street; then turn right at the sign for La Gruta de Lourdes. This small place of worship was created in 1925 as a replica of the sanctuary in Lourdes, France where, it is said, three girls saw the apparition of the Virgin Mary in 1858. Continue to the top of the hill to visit a 12-pew chapel with a small but beautiful altar. A path out back passes a large church and several beautiful statues depicting various biblical scenes. The lush grounds that surround the church make a nice escape from the road. (Church open daily 7am-10pm.) After taking a look around, continue on Rte. 181, bearing right at the intersection; shortly thereafter, the highway turns into a small road without lane lines. You will cross **Río Grande de Loíza**, one of the largest rivers in Puerto Rico, before turning onto Rte. 851.

2. EMBALSE RÍO GRANDE DE LOÍZA. Tiny Rte. 851 continues to ascend through the mountains, providing excellent views before it eventually descends into more tropical vegetation. When you reach a small village, turn onto Rte. 941 for panoramic views of the 422-hectare **Lago Loíza**, which was constructed by the government in 1954 to provide water for the metropolitan area. It is difficult to actually reach the lake, as most side roads lead to private, gated residences. The village of **Jaguas** has a couple of small mini-markets if you need to make a stop. Here, you've finally escaped the traffic of San Juan, and soon the surroundings flatten out and the road passes through idyllic arches of trees and vegetation. Continue past the end of the lake.

3. GURABO. Rte. 941 leads straight into the village of Gurabo. Gurabo is known as the city of the stairs, and it's easy to see why—streets leading toward the mountain all end in steep steps heading up the hill. Hike all the way up for a great view of the city and the surrounding valley. There's not much else to Gurabo, but the newly remodeled Plaza de Recreo is a pleasant place to sit and relax. The **Departamento de Arte y Cultura**, on C. Santiago, across from the church, supposedly has a small gallery of local artwork on the second floor, but hours of operation are sporadic. (☎ 737-8416. Theoretically open M-F 8am-4pm.) If you're starving, or looking for a dirt-cheap meal, there are a few inexpensive *comida criolla* and pizza joints along C. Santiago. If you're looking for a more sophisticated meal, hop back in the car and drive east toward Juncos.

4. EL TENEDOR. To leave Gurabo, head east on C. Anuz Rivera, which perpendicular to C. Santiago next to the plaza. Turn right at the stoplight, then hop on Hwy. 30 east. Those in a hurry can skip to ❺. Otherwise, take the second exit at **Juncos Centro,** and follow the road toward the building with the tall brick chimney, **El Tenedor ❸.** Formerly a rum distillery, the stately edifice now holds one of the best restaurants on the island, where well-dressed waiters

bring every customer glasses full of water, buttered bread, and steak or seafood entrees. *Sanjuaneros* have been known to drive all the way out here for a meal. The entrees are a bit heavy for lunch, but after such a long drive you deserve a hearty 8 oz. steak, and at only $10, it's quite a deal. (C. Emelia Príncipe 1. ☎ 734-6573. Entrees $9-19. Open M-Th and Su 11am-9pm, F-Sa 11am-10pm. AmEx/MC/V.) To leave El Tenedor, go to the intersection with Hwy. 30 and take Rte. 952, then turn right on Rte. 185.

5. FINAL DESCENT. To continue the scenic route, head north on the small, winding Rte. 185, which leads through more mountains, villages, and grassy fields. (If you want the more direct route home, take Hwy. 30 west to Hwy. 52, which will lead right back to San Juan.) After about 15 mi., head east on Hwy. 3 for about 1 mi., then exit onto Rte. 188 north. Now you're back at a lower elevation, where the vegetation is wilder and more tropical. If you're up for another stop, Rte. 951 leads to the small town of **Loíza,** with its historical church and fascinating African culture (p. 146). Otherwise, continue on Rte. 188 and take a left onto Rte. 187 west.

6. PIÑONES. Rte. 187 leads through the incredible wilderness of Piñones State Forest (p. 142). Here, the scenery along the Atlantic Coast is as stunning as the mountain regions you just left, but in a more stereotypically Caribbean way. If your stomach has any room left, grab a snack at one of the many roadside kiosks and eat while watching waves crash over the reefs. Or, if it's still before sunset, stop at one of the deserted beaches for a quick swim. Then it's back onto Rte. 187, which will take you straight back to San Juan.

FESTIVAL DE SANTIAGO APÓSTOL, OR THE CARNAVAL DE LOÍZA

Nowhere on the island is Puerto Rico's rich African heritage more evident than in the small northeastern town of Loíza during its annual *carnaval* festival. Celebrated every year over five days at the end of July, this lively party combines the island's Catholic and African traditions through a religious ceremony, parades, food, and intricate costumes. After dark the entire town settles down to participate in the interactive *bomba* song and dance (p. 71). The *carnaval* festival originated in 15th-century Spain, as the Spaniards reenacted the defeat of the Moors, and it has remained faithful to its roots. In Loíza, participants dress up either as finely dressed *caballeros* (Spanish gentleman) or brightly colored *vejigantes* (representations of the Spanish Moors). Though they are supposedly the villains, *vejigantes* have become renowned for their beautiful masks (see **Arts and Crafts**, p. 68). The distinct Loíza-style masks are made out of painted coconut shells with several thin, protruding horns. In recent years, the Loíza *carnaval* has attracted an increasing number of tourists; still, it remains a local and authentic festival, with many *puertorriqueño* participants.

For more information and exact dates contact the San Juan office of tourism ☎ 722-1709.)

LOÍZA

Públicos go from Río Piedras (p. 92) to Loíza (30-75min., M-Sa 5am-3pm, $1.75). From the público terminal in Loíza face the grassy area, turn left, and walk 3 blocks to the plaza. By car, take Rte. 187 east through the Piñones Forest. After you cross the large bridge over Río Grande de Loíza, follow signs into the town center.

The small town of Loíza has a culture that reflects Puerto Rico's African heritage more than anywhere else on the island, but unfortunately its tourism infrastructure is undeveloped. Nonetheless, all faults disappear during the last week in July, when the town's annual *carnaval* festival is celebrated. During the rest of the year, it is a sleepy town with a few small attractions, but local artisans' studios make Loíza a worthwhile stop on your way to El Yunque and Fajardo. Three miles south of town at Rte. 187 Km 6.6, the **Estudio de Arte Samuel Lind** is one of the best working art galleries in the San Juan metro area. The studio, gallery, and home of Loíza's premier artist houses a collection of colorful geometric paintings and big bronze sculptures, both finished and in-progress. Lind's work of over thirty years is largely inspired by the natural beauty he sees in the people and traditions of Loíza. His media vary from painting to silk screening, sculpture, and some lithography. Small reproductions are sold for as little as $25 and $50, but plastic sculptures go for $100-300 and original paintings and bronze sculptures can run $700-100,000. However, Lind welcomes people who just come to look, as he is eager to teach about the town's African culture. Drive toward Río Grande and look for the small sign pointing to the studio, then turn left onto the small road; it's the third house on the left. Or take a *público* to Río Grande and ask to be let off at the studio. (☎ 876-1494. Open Tu-Su 9:30am-5:30pm, when Lind is home. AmEx/MC/V.) Across the street, at Rte. 187 Km 6.6, **Artesanía Castor Ayala** displays *vejigante* masks crafted by Raúl Ayala, a second-generation Loíza mask artist. The masks ($20-400) are all for sale, from the small, ornamental ones to the head-sized masks used in festivals. (☎ 886-1654. Open daily 11am-6pm.) Loíza's only other sight is **La Iglesia de San Patricio**, the large yellow-orange church on the plaza. Registered as a National Historic Sight, the attractive church is unfortunately closed most of the time. But the plaza itself is a shady and relaxing stop, with a fountain and a large tile mosaic focusing on the town's African heritage. **Yawa's Café ❶**, C. Espíritu Santo 20, on the plaza, is a *cafetería*-style restaurant, and one of the few places to eat in the town center. Hamburgers ($2), sandwiches ($1.50-3), and breakfast combos ($1-2.50) are the standard fare. (☎ 886-6084. Open M-F 7am-1pm.)

CAGUAS

Públicos make the trip from Río Piedras to Caguas (35min., $2.50). From Caguas públicos travel to Cayey (30min., $1.25), Gurabo (20min., $0.70), and Río Piedras (35min., $2.50). If driving, take Hwy. 1 south out of San Juan, then exit onto Hwy. 52 (toll $0.70) and follow the signs to Caguas Centro (30-45min.).

Although few foreign visitors make it to Caguas, the city makes a great daytrip from San Juan. Caguas has opened five small but informative ▨**museums** highlighting various aspects of island culture. Although all exhibits are in Spanish, many tour guides speak English and are more than happy to show you around. (All museums open Tu-Sa 8am-4pm. Free). **Casa del Trovador,** C. Tapia 18 (☎744-8833, ext. 1843), is devoted to Puerto Rico's traditional island musicians, the **trovadores.** Found primarily in the central mountains, these musicians sing a popular rhythm called the *décima.* The museum explains the *trovador* through photos, musical instruments, and a full costume, while *trovador* music plays in the background. The special exhibit on female *trovadores* is particularly interesting. The **Museo del Tabaco,** C. Betances 87 (☎744-2960), contains artifacts and several display boards about the history of tobacco and its importance in Caguas, a major tobacco producer in the 19th century. Today the city's tobacco farms are gone, but the art of cigar-making lives on in the second half of the museum, where several elderly *cagüeños* spend four hours each day making cigars by hand. Many were employed in the tobacco industry in their younger years; working in the museum allows them to preserve their *artesanía* while earning some extra cash. Visitors can watch them work from behind glass and even buy the finished products afterward (25 cigars $4). At the corner of C. Ruiz Belvis and C. Padial, the **Museo de Arte de Caguas** (☎744-8833) upholds Puerto Rico's tradition of impressive art collections with an exhibit of primarily local work. Visitors will recognize the scene in Alejandro de Jesús's "Jugadores de Dominó" as a familiar sight in any San Juan street. Make sure you don't miss the huge mural hidden behind the side wall.

Continue down C. Ruiz Belvis to reach the **Centro Musical Criollo José Ignacio Quintón** (☎744-4110 or 744-4075), at the corner of C. Intendente Ramírez. The bright yellow First Baptist Church of Caguas was converted into a museum in 1995, and it now features displays showing how traditional Puerto Rican instruments are made and the history of various musical styles on the island. The museum becomes more engaging when local groups perform inside; call ahead or ask at the tourist office for more information. Finally, head half a block down C. Intendente Ramírez to **Casa Rosada Abelardo Díaz Alfaro,** C. Intendente Ramírez 12 (☎286-7640), former home of **Carlos Manuel "Charlie" Rodríguez,** a native *cagüeño* who was beatified by the Pope and continues to be Puerto Rico's highest-ranking Catholic. The first floor is a reconstruction of an early 20th-century home, but the second floor is devoted exclusively to Rodríguez, with an explanation of his life, pictures of his beatification, and a bone held in a reliquary. There is also an altar in the museum that many Puerto Ricans visit to pray for Rodríguez's intercession. For more information, stop by **Oficina de Turismo,** on Pl. Palmer next to the Alcaldía. (☎744-8833, ext. 2906. Open M-Sa 8am-noon and 1-4pm.)

Caguas

TO ❷ (100yd)

🍴 FOOD
Kam Ying, 1
Marcelo Restaurant, 2
RexCream, 7

🏛 MUSEUMS
Casa del Trovador, 3
Casa Rosada Abelardo Díaz Alfaro, 4
Centro Musical Criollo José Ignacio Quintón, 6
Museo de Arte de Caguas, 5
Museo del Tabaco, 8

0   100 yards
0   100 meters

While upper-end restaurants are located outside of the city center, budget travelers can find several good, affordable eateries within walking distance. **Kam Ying ❶**, C. Acosta 22, serves Chinese fast food with a Puerto Rican twist. Everything comes with french fries and most patrons order fried chicken. (☎743-3838. Huge entrees with shrimp, rice, and french fries $4-7. Open daily 10:30am-11pm. MC/V.) Travelers with a sweet tooth should not miss a trip to the popular **Rex-Cream ❶**, just off the Plaza on C. Ruis Belvis 47, the local kids' pick for fruity and sweet ice cream. Most flavors are Caribbean fruits, like *parcha* (passion fruit), but Oreo, pistachio, and peanut butter are also served, among over 25 flavors. (☎746-9222. Ice cream $2. Open daily 9am-10pm.) For Puerto Rican fare, try **Marcelo Restaurant ❸**, at the corner of Av. Mercado and Highway 1. (☎743-8801. Daily house specials $9-16. Open daily 11am-10pm.)

BAYAMÓN

The new Urban Train travels from Hato Rey and Río Piedras to Bayamón ($1.50). If driving from San Juan, take Rte. 2 (J.F.K. Expressway) all the way into Bayamón. When you see the immense City Hall hanging over the center of the road, turn right and park in a garage near the central plaza or in the ample on-street parking.

The dense population and many shopping malls of Bayamón just don't match up with most tourists' dreams of tropical paradise. However, one sight that does captivate visitors (mostly Puerto Rican schoolchildren) is the **Luis A. Ferré Parque de las Ciencias** (Science Park). This educational theme park contains over 10 museums, a trolley, a planetarium, a 500-seat amphitheater, a panoramic elevator, a zoo, a mock town square, and an artificial lake with paddle boats. Though definitely geared toward a pre-adolescent audience, the museums are interesting for visitors of all ages. The **Museo de Transportación** contains a collection of historical cars, including a 1907 Ford Model N and a Batmobile. The somewhat politically incorrect **Museo de Ciencias Naturales** commemorates the safaris of Puerto Rican Ventura Barnés and holds about 100 stuffed heads of African animals, from zebras to warthogs. Rifles, stools made from elephant feet, and tables held up by ivory tusks are also on display. The **Museo de Reproducciones Artísticas** contains reproductions of famous artwork from around the world, as well as some original work by lesser-known artists. The central **Anfiteatro Tito Rodríguez** frequently has shows that teach children, interestingly, through reggaeton songs. With the largest concentration of museums outside of Old San Juan, Parque de las Ciencias, on Rte. 167, about half a mile from central Bayamón, merits a visit. The highway is a difficult place to walk; instead, drive or take a taxi from in front of the *público* station. The park is mark by the US spaceships towering over the entrance. (☎740-6878. Open W-F 9am-4pm, Sa-Su 10am-6pm. Ticket sales stop 1½hr. before closing time. Parking $1. $5, ages 2-12 $3, ages 65-74 $2.50, 75 and over free.)

Although Bayamón is largely residential, the government has restored a historical downtown area and opened three interesting museums near the plaza behind the mayor's office. The ▨**Museo Francisco Oller** has a slightly misleading name, as it only holds five works by Oller, who was born in Bayamón. Nonetheless it houses a respectable collection of artwork by artists and sculptors such as Tomás Batista and Juan Santos. The many sculptures, made of everything from jade to lava rock, are well preserved and depict various subjects including fish and famous Puerto Ricans. Upstairs, the museum crams a substantial body of incredible work by contemporary Puerto Rican artists into a relatively small space. The helpful guides are eager to talk about the art and answer questions. (C. Degetau 15, at C. Maseo. ☎787-0620. Open M-F 8:30am-4pm. Free.) Next door, the **Museo Archivo Bayamón** is neatly divided into two sections. The first floor details the history of the city and its astounding growth through pictures,

Otel.com

Are you aiming for a budget vacation**?**

city models, and maps. The second floor is devoted to plaques, newspaper clippings, and other memorabilia from Bayamón's former mayor, Ramón Luis Rivera, who governed the city for 24 years before his son's election in 2000. Rivera's suit from his first inauguration sits at his desk, arranged as if he were still working. (C. Degetau 14. ☎780-0673. If the door is locked at either the Museo Archivo or the Museo Oller, go to the other one and ask them to open it. Open M-F 8am-4pm. Free.) The most unique of the museums is undoubtedly the two-story, excessively pink **Museo de Muñecas** (Doll Museum), C. Degetau 45, which contains an incredible collection of international dolls—including African, Chinese, and Russian nesting varieties—displayed in several fully decorated bedrooms. (☎787-895-1517. Open M-F 8:30am-4pm. Free.)

The rustic wooden sign at **Nino's Café** ❷ beckons passersby to come enjoy steaming plates of *comida criolla*. At night, the cafe turns into a hopping bar filled with couches, pool tables, cheap drinks (piña coladas $2.50), and live music. (On Rte. 167. From C. Degetau, walk uphill past the plaza, turn left on C. Dr. Veves, and continue down to Rte. 167. Turn right and walk for 5min. Nino's is just after the Universidad Metropolitano on the left. ☎740-5324. *Criollo* lunch combo $5. Entrees $7-17. F salsa classes 6-7pm, $5. Open M-Th 6am-11pm, F-Sa 6am-2am, Su 1pm-10pm.)

NORTHEAST

Northeast Puerto Rico has several extraordinary natural attractions within a relatively small area, making it easy for visitors to take a daytrip from San Juan to explore the island's great outdoors. This area encompasses the lush rainforest of the central east and the turquoise Atlantic waters of the north. Playa Luquillo and Balneario Seven Seas are beautiful palm-tree-lined crescents of sand, good for both swimming and sunbathing. La Cordillera, an archipelago off Fajardo, looks like a series of desert oases in the midst of the deep blue Caribbean. At night, Fajardo's bay glows with natural luminescence. However, the highlight of the northeast lies inland. The tropical rainforest of El Yunque, the largest protected area on the island, inspires pride in residents and awe in visitors. You can "see" El Yunque in one day, and even summit El Yunque mountain in about 2hr., but camping offers visitors the opportunity for more quality time in the forest. The only downside to visiting this region is the heavy traffic on Hwy. 3 from San Juan, but, with that behind you, prepare to be astounded by unparalleled natural beauty.

HIGHLIGHTS OF NORTHEAST PUERTO RICO

DISCOVER the 24 mi. of hiking trails, 2 waterfalls, and countless mountain peaks of the only tropical forest in the US, **El Yunque** (p. 150).

SNORKEL, DIVE, SWIM, OR TAN on an excursion to La Cordillera, the archipelago of islands off **Fajardo** (p. 165).

MONKEY-WATCH from the deck of a boat near the infamous **Cayo Santiago** (p. 169).

EL YUNQUE

Occupying over 28,000 acres of land, the Caribbean National Forest, referred to as "El Yunque," is one of the island's greatest treasures. El Yunque is the only tropical rainforest in the US Forest Service, and the largest protected land area in Puerto Rico. With four different types of forest, over 200 native species of trees, 50 species of native orchids, several varieties of mammals, and countless insects, El Yunque is one of the best places to experience and examine the natural landscape of Puerto Rico. The narrow Rte. 191 cuts through the forest, providing access to the park for the over one million annual visitors. On busy afternoons, it can seem like a good portion of them are right behind you on the path. Longer, more difficult trails offer more seclusion and often better views.

◗ TRANSPORTATION

Because there is no public transportation to El Yunque, most visitors come either with a tour group or by car. **Renting a car** is the best option, as it's cheapest and allows you to hike the trails at your own pace. It usually takes a little over an hour to drive the 25 mi. from San Juan to the park. From San Juan, take Hwy. 26 east to Hwy. 3. About 4 mi. past Río Grande, turn right on the small Rte. 191 and follow signs up the hill. Alternatively, from Isla Verde take Rte. 187 east through Piñones until it intersects Hwy. 3. This route takes about 10min. longer, but offers scenic ocean views. Although the park is easily navigable without a guide, those who can't rent a car may want to book a **tour** from San Juan (p. 96).

EL YUNQUE AT A GLANCE

AREA: 28,000 acres.

CLIMATE: Tropical. Rainy season begins in June and picks up in mid-July, continuing until November. However, showers occur year-round.

HIGHLIGHTS: Hiking over 24 mi. of trails, swimming in pristine waterfalls.

FEATURES: Tropical forest, diverse flora, 2 waterfalls (La Mina & Coca), Yokahú Tower.

HOURS: Park open daily 7:30am-6pm.

GATEWAYS: Fajardo (p. 160), Rio Blanco (SW of Fajardo), Luquillo (p. 157), and San Juan (p. 89).

CAMPING: Free along all trails and roads except for those within the central area marked on park map as no camping zones. A permit from the park office is required (see below).

FEES: Entrance to El Portal Visitors Cente $3; ages 15 and under or over 65 $1.50; education groups free. Entrance to the park free.

ORIENTATION AND PRACTICAL INFORMATION

Although El Yunque occupies almost 25% of the land area of northeast Puerto Rico, most tourist activities occur around **Route 191,** which leads past the tourist centers and the trailheads.

Visitors Center: El Portal Visitors Center, Rte. 191 Km 4.0 (☎888-1880; www.southernregion.fs.fed.us/caribbean), is the first stop for most visitors. The well-maintained center offers a 12min. movie (in Spanish on the hour and half-hour, in English on the quarter-hour), gift shop, snack bar (smoothies $4, sandwiches and wraps $5), and small museum with interactive exhibits. The friendly staff distributes brochures with rudimentary maps and lots of information. Bathrooms, pay phones, and snack machines. Entrance $3, ages 5-12 and seniors $1.50, under 4 free. Open daily 9am-5pm.

Palo Colorado Information Center, Rte. 101 Km 11.0, has a souvenir shop, the same maps as El Portal, and a park ranger who can answer questions. Entrance free. Park tours (see below) also leave from here. Open daily 9am-5pm.

Maps: Campers and serious hikers should purchase the National Geographic map available at both Visitors Centers; day visitors should be able to navigate with the Visitors Center brochure and the map in this book.

Hours: The gate at Coca Falls is open daily during official park hours, 7:30am-6pm.

Supplies: All visitors should bring comfortable clothes, insect repellent, bottled water, food, a swimsuit, and sturdy walking shoes. Many visitors prefer getting wet to sweating in a raincoat if it rains, but you might want a light jacket if you would rather stay dry.

Tours: Many companies in **San Juan** offer excursions to El Yunque (p. 150). A National Forest Service ranger leads 1hr. English/Spanish tours from the Palo Colorado Information Center along the Caimitillo and Baño de Oro trails (every hr. 10:30am-2:30pm; $5, children under 12 and seniors $3). Tours are first-come, first-served.

WARNINGS. The National Park Service warns that all visitors should watch out for **flash floods,** especially during the rainy season. If it starts to rain heavily, head away from streams, to higher ground, or toward the road. Visitors should also be aware of the threat of **mongoose attacks.** Mongeese look like light-colored skunks, and most mongeese who approach humans are infected with **rabies**—avoid contact at all costs.

NORTHEAST

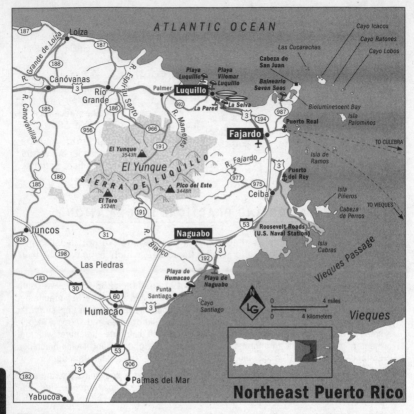

ATLANTIC OCEAN

Northeast Puerto Rico

CAMPING

To **camp ❶** in El Yunque you must get a **free permit,** available in the park. From Monday to Friday, permits can be arranged before 4pm at the **Catalina Service Center,** Rte. 191 Km 4.3, directly after El Portal Visitors Center. (☎888-1880. Open M-F 8am-4:30pm.) On weekends and holidays, permits can be found at the **Palo Colorado Information Center** (p. 151). Permits can be used within the dates specified by camper. Park rangers also hand out a map designating permissible camping areas. There are no facilities in the park, so campers should plan to take out everything that they bring in (including trash). There are no hotels along the northern section of Rte. 191, but upscale options await near **Naguabo** (p. 167) and on the western edge of the park, near Río Grande. **Fajardo** (p. 160), with its large selection of hotels, is only a 15min. drive away.

FOOD

There are no food stands along the hiking paths, so many families come with picnics. **Covered picnic tables** at Caimitillo, Palo Colorado, and Quebrada Grande have running water and grills. Palo Colorado, at the head of La Mina trail, is the most popular area, and fills up with families and parties every day around lunchtime.

For those who don't want to cook their own food, there are several options inside the park. **El Bosque Encantado ❶**, Rte. 191 Km 7.2, has a small seating area with cliff's edge view; also serves up whole coconuts sliced into drinkable sections ($2), *batidas* ($4), freshly fried *empanadas* ($1-3), and "pincho" shish kebabs. (Open daily 9am-6pm.) Just down the road, **La Muralla ❶**, Rte. 191 Km 7.3, serves similar fare, minus the coconuts and view. (Tacos $1.50, piña coladas $4. Open daily 9am-6pm.) For slightly healthier fare, try **Yuqulyú Delights ❶**, Rte. 191 Km 11.2. (Smoothies $4. Sandwiches and wraps $4.50. Open daily 9am-5pm.)

🞇 SIGHTS

Heading up Rte. 191, the first major sight is **Coca Falls**, Km 8.1. There is not much more to see than the view of the waterfall from the road. **Yokahú Tower** appears on the left at Km 8. Built in the 1930s, the tower provides spectacular views of the mountains of El Yunque, Luquillo, and far-off Fajardo. **La Mina Falls,** accessible via a 25-35min. walk along Big Tree Trail or La Mina Trail, is undoubtedly the most popular destination in El Yunque. On weekend afternoons it can seem like every family in San Juan (and every tour group of North Americans) has journeyed out to the falls to picnic on the rocks and swim in the small lagoon. The sight merits its popularity, but if you come early in the morning, you may have the place to yourself. In any case, bring a swimsuit and join in the merriment.

🞇 HIKING

TRAILS	DURATION (ONE-WAY)	DIFFICULTY	LENGTH	ALTITUDE
El Yunque	2hr.	Moderate-Difficult	2½ mi.	2067-3445 ft.
La Coca	1hr.	Moderate-Difficult	1¾ mi.	820-1476 ft.
Big Tree	35min.	Moderate	¾ mi.	1667-1833 ft.
La Miña	25min.	Easy-Moderate	¾ mi.	1040-2102 ft.
Baño de Oro	20min.	Moderate	¼ mi.	2132-2362 ft.
Los Picachos	5min.	Moderate	¼ mi.	2952-3051 ft.
Mt. Britton Spur	10min.	Easy	¼ mi.	2788-2952 ft.
Mt. Britton	40min.	Moderate	½ mi.	2493-3087 ft.
National Recreation Trail	7hr.	Difficult	6¼ mi.	2533-3578 ft.

EL YUNQUE. This aptly named path travels from Rte. 191 all the way to the peak of El Yunque mountain, offering a challenging trek that can be completed in an afternoon. The path passes over countless tiny waterfalls and through several cloud forests on the way up. This route is much less traveled than any of the shorter trails, and it is unlikely that you will encounter any other hikers until you reach the summit. Several turn-offs (Mt. Britton Spur, Los Picachos) allow hikers to choose an alternative ending along the way. When you reach the road at the end of the trail, turn left and go past the many satellites dishes, all the way up to the El Yunque tower for the best views. On a clear day you can see all the way out to St. Thomas, and even if it's foggy, the haze shrouding the surrounding mountains looks mysterious and beautiful.

LA COCA. The first trail on the way up Rte. 191 is the ideal path for exploring the forest in blissful solitude and seeing a secluded waterfalls. The path descends from the trailhead, making the uphill return trip extremely challenging. This is one of the more rugged hikes, with dirt trails and small streams that you must cross without the aid of a bridge. The steep inclines get quite muddy, so do not try this hike in the rain.

El Yunque (Caribbean National Forest)

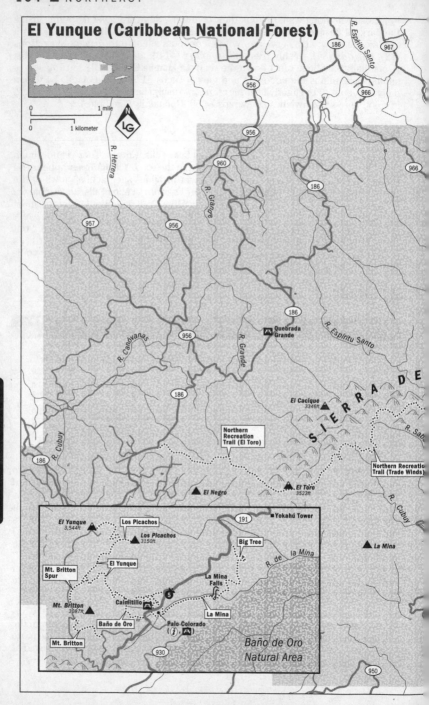

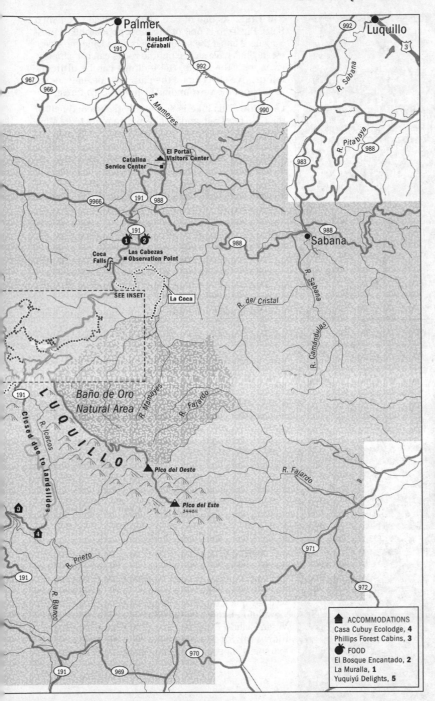

Palmer
Hacienda
Cárabalí
191
992
967
966
992
R.° Mameyes
990
El Portal
Visitors Center
Catalina
Service Center
191
988
9966
191
988
191
988
1 2
Coca
Falls
Las Cabezas
Observation Point
988
988
Sabana
SEE INSET
La Coca
R. del Cristal
R. Camándulas
R. Sabana
R. Pitahaya
988
983
R. Sabana
992
Luquillo
3
Baño de Oro
Natural Area
R. Mameyes
R. Fajardo
L U Q U I L L O
191
Closed due to landslides
R. Joacos
Pico del Oeste
R. Fajardo
Pico del Este
3445ft
0
4
R. Prieto
191
R. Blanco
191
969
970
971
972

NORTHEAST

ACCOMMODATIONS
Casa Cubuy Ecolodge, 4
Phillips Forest Cabins, 3

FOOD
El Bosque Encantado, 2
La Muralla, 1
Yuquiyú Delights, 5

GIVING BACK

THE REAL EL YUNQUE

Every day, hundreds of visitors drive their cars or ride tour buses up the winding roads of the Caribbean National Forest of El Yunque, where they parade down glistening flagstone paths to La Coca and La Mina falls, climb to the heights of Mt. Britton Tower, and take snapshots from the satellite dishes on El Yunque summit. For many, this is the extent of interaction with the U.S. National Forest System's only rain forest.

However, if you're interested in enhancing your experience in the forest and contributing to the longevity of the ecosystem and the quality of public trails, you might consider volunteering with the USDA Forest Service. Volunteers answer visitors' questions about the forest and its Visitors Centers. They help to rebuild and maintain trails and picnic areas, assist with land surveys, restore the forest after landslide damage, and train to become volunteer guide assistants. Sometimes, short-term volunteers may be asked to join forest research conservation programs led by visiting and local experts.

Volunteers save the Forest Service management thousands of dollars that can be better invested in preserving the forest, while making the most of their own, unique El Yunque experience.

For applications and more information, check out www.fs.fed.us/r8/caribbean/volunteering/index.shtml.

BIG TREE. As one of two hikes that lead to La Mina Falls, Big Tree is one of the most popular hikes in El Yunque. Almost the entire path is paved and the steepest inclines have stairs, but the rocks can get slippery. Even with the stairs, the inclines can be difficult. Informative signs along the path provide educational facts about the surrounding lush *tabonuco* forest.

LA MINA. This hike is essentially the second half of the Big Tree Trail, and an alternative route to La Mina Falls. La Mina receives slightly larger crowds than Big Tree and is completely paved; it runs alongside Río de la Mina, allowing hikers to take a quick dip on the way down. La Mina is slightly easier than Big Tree. It is possible to walk down one trail and up the other, but you will have to walk 1.5km along Rte. 191 to return.

BAÑO DE ORO. This short trail across from Palo Colorado is one of the park's hidden treasures. Baño de Oro is easy enough to be accessible to most visitors, but retains the naturalism of the longer trails and is much less crowded than La Mina or Big Tree. It also makes a good warm-up for those ascending El Yunque. Be aware that you may have to cross small streams without a bridge if there has been rain recently.

LOS PICACHOS. A small turn-off about 30min. from the peak of El Yunque, Los Picachos provides an alternate ending for hikers who would like to turn back, or a stopover for those who want to see views unobstructed by the electronic equipment that mars the peak of El Yunque. The short, rocky trail ends in 59 steep steps, which make for a tough finale.

MT. BRITTON SPUR. Mt. Britton Spur is an easy pebble path connecting El Yunque to Mt. Britton. To make a full loop, head up El Yunque (perhaps via Baño de Oro), cross over on Mt. Britton Spur, then head down Mt. Britton. At the end you will have to walk a mile or so down the road to get back to your car. Mt. Britton has a steep incline that can get very slippery, so it is easier to ascend El Yunque, then descend Mt. Britton, rather than vice versa. If you're coming off Mt. Britton Spur, walk downhill on the road to reach Mt. Britton (walking uphill will get you to the Mt. Britton Tower lookout point).

MT. BRITTON. Rugged hikers may be disappointed that the entire Mt. Britton trail is paved and ends with a short walk along the road. However, the trail is shorter than El Yunque and offers great views of the forest as well as a quick route to another observation tower with views of Fajardo, Luquillo, San Juan, and the Spanish Virgin Islands. For this reason, Mt. Britton is quite popular with foreign tourists. The steep path gets extremely slippery when wet—proceed with caution.

NATIONAL RECREATION TRAIL. Consisting of El Toro Trail and Trade Winds, the National Recreation Trail, the longest trail in El Yunque, follows the mountain peaks from Rte. 191 to Rte. 186. The highlight of the path is the summit of El Toro, the tallest mountain in El Yunque. Along the way, the path passes through all four types of forest present in the park: *tabonuco, palo colorado,* palm, and dwarf. Only experienced hikers should attempt this hike, as they must battle mud, overgrown plants, steep hills, and isolation.

LUQUILLO

Many visitors to Luquillo never see the town: they come for the beach, spend a day lounging in the sun, then return to San Juan. In comparison to San Juan, Luquillo Beach is undoubtedly paradise; it is lined with palm trees, has ample amenities, and during weekdays in the winter offers the solitude that visitors to Isla Verde can only dream about. Don't be misled—Luquillo does not have the best beach on the island, just the best developed swimming beach close to San Juan. Those with only a short time on the island may find this small town to be the perfect escape.

▐ TRANSPORTATION. Públicos traveling between San Juan and Fajardo will let passengers off at **Luquillo** (45min., $3). To get back, sit on a bench on Hwy. 3 beneath the pedestrian bridge that connects Luquillo and Brisas del Mar, and flag down a passing *público*. If you choose this option, remember that *públicos* primarily run M-Sa 6:30am-5pm. Driving from San Juan (45min.-1¼hr., depending on traffic), head down Hwy. 3 and get off at Rte. 193, when signs point to Luquillo. If you want to travel between the main beach and the center of town, a car is very helpful—walking along the beach is not possible without doing some wading, and your other choice is to walk along Rte. 193.

▐▐ ORIENTATION AND PRACTICAL INFORMATION. Most of the city is located along **Route 193,** which becomes **Calle Fernández García** as it passes by the main plaza. The parallel street C. 14 de Julio holds most of the city government buildings, including the post office, police station, and town hall. La Pared beach is directly in front of the town square, and is distinguished by its white wall and big waves. La Pared is almost deserted most of the time. To the west of it is Vilomar Luquillo, which becomes very popular for a predominantly Puerto Rican crowd on weekends. To reach Playa Luquillo from town, take Rte. 193 to its western end.

Banco Popular, on Hwy. 193, is just off the highway at the main entrance to the town. (☎889-2610. **ATM.** Open M-F 8am-4pm, Sa 9am-noon.) **Amigo,** on Hwy. 2 in Brisas del Mar, a large grocery chain, also offers Moneygram, a money transfer service (☎889-1919. ATM inside. Open M-Sa 7am-10pm, Su 11am-5pm. AmEx/MC/V.) **La Selva,** C. Fernández Garcia 250, two blocks off the plaza away from the beach, rents **surf** and **snorkel** equipment to travelers. (☎889-6205. Surfing lessons $25 per hr. Open M-Sa 9am-5pm, Su 9am-3pm. AmEx/MC/V.) The **police station,** C. 14 de Julio 158, is visible from the plaza, next to the Alcaldía. (☎889-2020 or 889-5500. Open 24hr.) The **post office,** C. 14 de Julio 160, is next to the police station. (☎889-3170. Open M-F 8am-4:30pm, Sa 8am-noon.) **Postal Code:** 00773.

PARKING IN PUERTO RICO. A thick yellow line on the edge of the curb means parking is prohibited. In actuality, almost all locals park anywhere. However, if you'd rather not pay a fine, it's best to heed the yellow markings—police are beginning to crack down on parking violations.

⌐⌐ ACCOMMODATIONS AND FOOD. Considering its popularity, Luquillo has surprisingly few accommodations options. Unless you are looking for a long-term stay or wish to camp, you should consider finding accommodations in Fajardo or San Juan and commuting to the beach. Those looking for rentals should consult the rental agencies listed in San Juan, all of which have many listings in various price ranges (❸ to ❺) for Luquillo. **Luquillo Sunrise Beach Inn ❹**, on Ocean Blvd. A2, just northeast of the Plaza J.T. Piñero in town is virtually the only option for a beach-front short-term stay in Luquillo. Across the street from the eastern end of La Pared beach at Costa Azul, all 14 rooms offer ocean views and beach access at a fair price. (☎409-2929 or 889-1713; www.luquillosunrise.com.Wi-Fi in king deluxe, common terrace, and conference room. Doubles $95-125. AmEx/MC/V.) **Camping** at **Balneario La Monserrate ❶** is usually like attending a big, family-oriented party. The beach has a large grass camping area with concrete picnic tables, gazebos, and grills scattered throughout. (☎889-5871. Call ahead. $13, with electricity $17.)

Most of the food in Luquillo comes straight from the sea and can be found at the famous *kioskos*, **food kiosks** that line Hwy. 3 at the western edge of Playa Luquillo. Over 60 kiosks, ranging from full restaurants to grill stands, serve traditional food (full lunches $3-5) and fried *empanadillas* stuffed with just about anything ($1-2). Hours vary with the size of the crowd, but when the beach is open, chances are that a few food kiosks will be also. In town, ▨**Erik's Gyros & Deli ❶**, C. Fernández García 352, is three blocks south of the plaza on the eastern end of town. Erik's provides delicious deli sandwiches and Greek specialties like Baklava for $3.49. (☎889-0615. Gyros $4-4.50. Sandwiches $0.75-8. Eggs, ham and toast $2.50. Open W-Sa 7am-5pm. MC/V.) For an American bar-style meal, try **The Brass Cactus ❸**, on Rte. 193 just west of Playa Azul. With US license plates lining the walls, fake cacti on the bar, a big TV tuned to ESPN, and sizzling steaks, the Brass Cactus provides visitors from the States with a little taste of home. (☎889-5735; www.thebrasscactus.com. Wi-Fi. Burgers $7-9. Big steaks $18-25. M-F daily meal specials. Happy hour M-F 5-7pm. Open bar Sa 10pm-midnight $10. Open M-Th and Su 11am-midnight, F-Sa 11am-1am. Kitchen closes 1hr. earlier. MC/V.) The simple but mainstay **La Exquisita Bakery ❶**, Av. Jesús Piñero 1, on the plaza, serves up big sandwiches and a small selection of pastries. (☎633-5554. Breakfast $3-4. Sandwiches $1.50-4. Pastries $0.50-1.50. Open M-Tu 6am-7pm, W-Su 6am-9pm. MC/V.)

Luquillo

▲ ACCOMMODATIONS
Luquillo Sunrise
Beach Inn, 4
✦ FOOD
Erik's Gyros & Deli, 8
King Seafood, 3
La Exquisita Bakery, 5
Sandy's Seafood, 7
William's Pizza, 6
▮NIGHTLIFE
The Brass Cactus, 1
El Flamboyán, 2

⌐🏖 BEACHES AND OUTDOOR ACTIVITIES. The crescent-shaped **Playa Luquillo,** or more properly **Balneario La Monserrate,** is the city's primary attraction and one of the most beautiful public beaches on the island. As a public *balneario*, Playa Luquillo has lifeguards, picnic tables, souvenir shops, bathrooms, showers, food kiosks, and lawn chair ($4 per day) and umbrella ($8 per day) rental.

It is also one of the most popular beaches on the island, and on weekends in the summer it can become packed with Puerto Ricans. Still, anyone who comes to Luquillo prepared to deal with the crowds should enjoy this picturesque setting. To reach the beach, take Rte. 193 (off Hwy. 3) all the way to the west. (☎889-5871. Parking $2, minivans $3. Open daily 8:30am-5:30pm.)

Playa Luquillo is also home to the remarkable ⬛**Mar Sin Barreras** (Sea Without Barriers), **the island's only wheelchair-accessible beach** (☎889-4329). The idea originated when 14-year-old Rosimar Hernández wrote a letter to then-governor Pedro Rosselló, pointing out that people in wheelchairs, including herself, could not enjoy the natural attractions of Puerto Rico. Today Hernández's dream has become a reality. Mar Sin Barreras has incredible facilities—including a ramp to the water, a clubhouse, and showers—all specifically designed to help handicapped people and elderly citizens enjoy the water. Bathrooms and change-rooms only for use by the handicapped and elderly.

East of Balneario la Monserrate, but not contiguous with it, **Playa Azul** is a cleaner beach with better sand, slightly larger waves, and usually much smaller crowds. However, it is not officially a public beach and thus lacks the facilities of Monserrate. If you don't mind that this beach does not have public bathrooms, the palm-lined strip and promenade of Playa Vilomar and La Pared to the east may be the best option. Luquillo is also a popular destination for **surfers** and snorkelers. The next beach to the east, **La Pared,** in front of the central plaza, has good waves and a sandy bottom ideal for beginners. The surfing extends for about 2 mi. to the east and just gets better. Farther to the east, try **La Selva,** another surfers' favorite with both sand and reef bottom. Or, just walk along the beach until you find a break that suits your fancy.

Just outside of town, **Hacienda Carabalí** offers **horseback rides** on Paso Fino horses over the foothills of El Yunque along the Río Mameyes. From Luquillo take Hwy. 3 west about 5min. past the *kioskos*, turn left on Rte. 992, take the first right up the hill, and go through the second gate. (☎889-5820. 1hr. rides need no reservation; $30, ages 3-12 $20. 2hr. rides must be reserved in advance; daily 10am, 12:30, 2:30pm; $60/40. Am/Ex/MC/V.)

TURTLE PATROL. Every two weeks, on the sands of La Selva beach, you might catch sight of large tracks in the sand that look like tractor treads. These are actually marks left behind by sea turtles emerging from the ocean to lay their eggs. La Selva is one of the most important turtle nesting grounds in the Caribbean: the large waves in the area help the giant creatures out of the water, and because of the minimal light pollution, new hatchlings find their way into the water without the potentially fatal distraction of artificial light sources. If you're willing to pry yourself out of bed before sunrise, you can join the **Sierra Club of Puerto Rico** in witnessing baby hatchlings as they crawl over the sand to ride the surf into the ocean (☎727-2283).

⬛▦ **SIGHTS AND FESTIVALS.** The attractive **Centro de Arte y Cultura** (Center for Art and Culture), Hwy. 3 Km 38.4, is located across Hwy. 3, just east of the beach. The complex has great facilities, with an exhibition hall, a 550-seat theater, and an open-air amphitheater. Open M-F 8am-4:30pm. Free. Performances usually around $20-25, children $8-10.)

In addition to the Luquillo's patron saint festival (held on the week preceding Mar. 19), the city also celebrates an annual **Festival de Platos Típicos,** or the Festival of Traditional Foods, the last weekend in November. The festival brings music, *artesanía,* and feasts of delicious coconut-flavored Puerto Rican food to the Plaza de Recreo.

NORTHEAST

■ **NIGHTLIFE.** Luquillo's nightlife scene is small and bar-oriented. Most expats and visitors down a couple of beers at **The Brass Cactus** (see **Food,** p. 158). Down the street **El Flamboyán,** on highway 193 at the corner of C. A, hosts a friendly and local crowd, who come for the open air, pool tables, cheap beer (Medalla $1.25-1.50), and funky tile-covered cement picnic tables. (☎889-2928. Happy hour Sa 10pm-1am. Open M-Th and Su 8am-midnight, F-Sa 8am-2am.) The bars at the food kiosks also attract a number of locals in the evening.

FAJARDO

Most travelers simply zip through Fajardo on their way to Vieques and Culebra and never see the real city. But Fajardo and its surrounding area deserve a closer look. In the hills above sits Las Croabas, a fishing village and informal port where fishermen wait to shuttle visitors to small islands nearby. To the north, the Las Cabezas de San Juan nature reserve offers visitors a tour of the region's ecosystems and a glimpse of a restored 19th-century lighthouse. Additionally, the reserve's Laguna Grande bay is one of the few places in the world to see the incredible phenomenon of bioluminescence. Closer to the city, between Hwy. 987 and Fajardo Bay, sits Villa Marina, a busy port full of seafood restaurants and yachtsmen ready to take you on a snorkeling excursion. Even the congested downtown area is full of excellent Puerto Rican *cafeterías*, and its beautiful, newly-renovated town square and mayor's office may be a sign of better things to come.

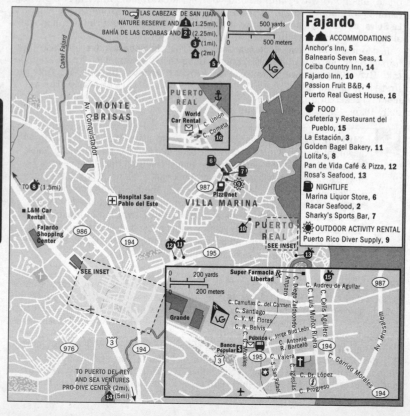

Fajardo

▲▲ ACCOMMODATIONS
Anchor's Inn, 5
Balneario Seven Seas, 1
Ceiba Country Inn, 14
Fajardo Inn, 10
Passion Fruit B&B, 4
Puerto Real Guest House, 16

🍴 FOOD
Cafetería y Restaurant del Pueblo, 15
La Estación, 3
Golden Bagel Bakery, 11
Lolita's, 8
Pan de Vida Café & Pizza, 12
Rosa's Seafood, 13

■ NIGHTLIFE
Marina Liquor Store, 6
Racar Seafood, 2
Sharky's Sports Bar, 7

OUTDOOR ACTIVITY RENTAL
Puerto Rico Diver Supply, 9

⎚ TRANSPORTATION

It is almost impossible to get around Fajardo without a car. Getting to one sight should be no problem, but visiting multiple destinations on public transportation will be frustrating and time-consuming.

Flights: Fajardo's tiny airport (☎863-1011) sends even tinier planes to Culebra, San Juan, St. Croix, St. Thomas, and Vieques. Most airlines sell tickets by phone or at the airport. Reserve in advance or the flight may not leave. To reach the airport, take the main entrance to central Fajardo, then follow signs. Parking $9.10 per 24hr.

Air Flamenco (☎801-8256) flies to **Culebra** (7am, noon, 5:45pm; $30, round-trip $60). MC/V.

Isla Nena (☎877-812-5144) flies to **Culebra** (15min.; 1-2 per day; $30, round-trip $60) and **Vieques** (10min.; on demand only; $25, round-trip $50). Open daily 8am-5pm. MC/V.

Vieques Air Link (☎1-888-901-9247) sends flights on demand 6am-6pm. To: **Culebra** (30min.; 3 per day; $28, round-trip $54), **St. Croix** (45min.; 2 per day; $83, round-trip $163), and **Vieques** (15min.; 8 per day; $23, round-trip $42). AmEx/MC/V.

Ferries: The **Puerto Rican Port Authority** (☎863-0705 or 863-4560) runs ferries from Puerto Real to the Spanish Virgin Islands. To get to Puerto Real from central Fajardo take C. Celis Aguilera (parallel to C. Muñoz Rivera) away from the plaza, then turn right on Rte. 195 (1 mi.). To avoid the traffic downtown, from Hwy. 3 take the 2nd Fajardo exit onto Av. Conquistador, then turn right onto Rte. 194, then turn left on Rte. 195. Long-term **parking** $5 per day. *Públicos* from Fajardo go to the port ($1) and are usually waiting when a boat comes in. **Travel With Padin taxi service** takes passengers from the San Juan airport to the ferry terminal ($60 for 2 people, $65 for 4 people). Call for reservations (☎644-3091).

Passenger ferries go to **Culebra** (1½hrs.; daily 9am, 3, 7pm; $2.25, ages 3-11 and 60-74 $1, over 75 free) and **Vieques** (1½hrs.; M-F 9:30am, 1, 4:30, 8pm; Sa-Su 9am, 3, 6pm; $2, ages 3-11 and 60-74 $1, over 74 free). **Cargo ferries** take a few cars to **Culebra** (M-Tu and Th 4am and 4:30pm; W and F 4, 9:30am, 4pm; $27) and **Vieques** (M-F 4, 9:30am, 4pm; $26). Reservations are required for cars and should be made at least 3 weeks in advance. For passenger ferries, show up at least 1hr. in advance. When possible, buy round-trip tickets. Office open M-F 7:30am-11:30am and 12:30pm-4pm. Reservations office open M-F 8-11am and 1-3pm.

Públicos: *Públicos* are based out of the **Terminal de Transportación Pública Fajardo,** on C. Valera between Banco Popular and the Plaza de Armas. To: **Ceiba** (10min., $1); **Humacao** (45min., $2.45); **Las Croabas** (5min., $1); **Luquillo** (15min., $0.75-1); **San Juan** (1hr., $3.50). If you take a *público* from San Juan to the ferry terminal, ask the driver to go all the way to the port. If you go to the terminal early in the day and ask around, you can find one heading to any major sight. They can also be flagged down on Rte. 194 or 195.

Taxis: *Públicos* are the only vehicles that function as taxis in Fajardo.

> **WHAT'S IN A NAME.** Once you've met a *público* driver, a good rule of thumb is to write down his or her name and contact information for future rides. This should help you plan for returning from more remote sites, and alleviate some stresses of the public transportation process.

Car Rental: L&M Car Rental, Hwy. 3 Km 43.7 (☎860-6868), just south of plaza with movie theatres. Compact cars $40 per day. Insurance $16. 25+. Open M-F 8am-5pm, Sa-Su 9am-2pm in El Conquistador Hotel. AmEx/D/MC/V. Another recommended local company is **World Car Rental,** C. Unión 466 (☎860-4808 or 863-9696), entrance on C. Cometa, about a 7min. walk from the ferry terminal. Compact cars $38 per day. Insurance $12. 21+. Open daily 7:30am-7pm. AmEx/MC/V.

✦⑦ ORIENTATION AND PRACTICAL INFORMATION

Fajardo is difficult to navigate without a car. **Highway 3** runs north to Luquillo and west to San Juan. Fajardo is best described as having four parts: a bustling port and marina, a small town center, city sprawl along the highway, and a more peaceful fishermen's port and beach in Las Croabas to the north. All of these are located to the east, between the highway and the sea. The first exit off Hwy. 3 goes to **Route 194**, which travels parallel to Hwy. 3 and passes the center before intersecting Hwy. 3 again. The second major exit leads to Av. Conquistador, which goes to the Wyndham hotel. The third and most prominent exit deposits visitors on **Route 195**, which passes the plaza then continues to the **ferry dock. Route 987** originates from Rte. 195, passes **Villa Marina** (a major port with a shopping center), intersects Av. Conquistador, and leads to the beach, the nature reserve, and Las Croabas.

Banks: Banco Popular (☎863-0101), on C. Garrido Morales at the corner with C. Valero. **ATM.** Open M-F 8am-4pm, Sa 9am-noon.

Laundromat: Wash n' Post, C. 2 #100, Local 4 (☎863-1995), in the Santa Isidra Shopping Center in Villa Marina. Wash $2, dry $0.25 per 4min. Change available. Wash-and-fold service $0.85 per lb., min. $7. Fax 1st page $2, additional pages $1. Also **Western Union** and FedEx. Open M-Sa 8am-8pm, Su 11am-5pm. AmEx/MC/V.

Police: ☎863-2020 or 863-2430. Across from the *público* station. Open 24hr.

Pharmacy: Super Farmacia Libertad, C. Muñoz Rivera 206 (☎863-0810). Open M-Sa 8am-8pm, Su 11am-5pm.

Hospital: Hospital San Pablo del Este (☎863-0505), on Rte. 194 just off Av. Conquistador. The largest hospital in eastern Puerto Rico. 24hr. emergency room.

Internet Access: Pizz@net (☎860-4230), in Villa Marina. Internet $3 per 30min., $5 per hr. Lunch combo with huge personal pizza and soda $5. **ATM.** Pool table and arcade games. M-Th 11am-10pm, F-Sa 11am-11pm. MC/V.

Post Office: Large regional headquarters **Correo Principal,** C. Garrido Morales 113 (☎655-8779), next to Banco Popular. Open M-F 10am-7pm, Sa 8am-4pm. In **Puerto Real,** C. Unión 477 (☎863-1827). General Delivery available. Open M-F 8am-4:30pm, Sa 8am-noon. **Postal Code:** In Central Fajardo: 00738. In Puerto Real: 00740.

🏠📷 ACCOMMODATIONS AND CAMPING

Fajardo's claim to fame as a tourist destination may be its attractive accommodations. The city is home to several guesthouses and inns that offer clean, comfortable, amenity-filled rooms for a fraction of what you'd pay in a more touristy town.

▨ **Passion Fruit Bed & Breakfast,** Route 987 (☎801-0106 or toll-free 800-670-3196; fax 801-1633; www.passionfruitbb.com), in Las Croabas between El Conquistador hotel and Las Croabas waterfront. Every morning, Gladys welcomes her guests like a member of the family with too-good-to-be-true breakfasts on the sunny pool terrace. Bright, clean rooms with queen beds, tropical plants, cable TV, and A/C. Each is named for a prominent Fajardeño. Gorgeous, clean swimming pool, poolside gazebo and bar, 2nd fl. lobby, balcony, and Wi-Fi. Doubles $85; quads $130. AmEx/MC/V. ❸

▨ **Ceiba Country Inn,** Rte. 977 Km 1.2 (☎885-0471; prinn@juno.com), 5 mi. from Fajardo in Ceiba. When you exit Hwy. 53, turn right toward the mountains (not left toward Ceiba). On a clear day you can see St. Thomas from this quiet mountain lodge. The outdoor patio is a tranquil place to enjoy breakfast, and the indoor seating area and cocktail lounge offers TV and board games. Large, sparkling-clean rooms include phone, A/C, and fridge, as well as wicker furniture and large showers. Continental breakfast included. Singles $75, doubles $85. Extra person $10. AmEx/D/MC/V. ❸

Fajardo Inn, Parcelas Beltrán 52 (☎860-6000; www.fajardoinn.com), off Rte. 195; look for signs pointing uphill to the Inn. With a big, white building, grand palm-lined entrance road, and manicured grounds, the Fajardo Inn looks like an expensive resort—with prices that rival those at guesthouses. All rooms with A/C and cable TV; some with kitchenette and hot tub. 2 restaurants and a bar. Puerto Rican families flock to the massive waterpark with wave pool, slide, hot tub, swim-up snack bar, mini-golf, and playground. Fitness center ($5); tennis and basketball courts. Internet ($5.35 per 30min, free Wi-Fi.) and coin laundry available. Doubles $118-135; triples $156; 6-person $189; suites $156-354. Extra person $10. AmEx/MC/V. ❹

Puerto Real Guest House, C. Cometa 476 (☎863-0018 or 617-8755). Homey is an understatement for this small guesthouse—the lobby is actually someone's living room. Amazing amenities for the price: A/C, cable TV, and small fridge. Call ahead, as owner is often away during the day when guest rooms are in use. Doubles $50; quads $60. Tax included. Cash only. ❷

Anchor's Inn, Rte. 987 Km 2.6 (☎863-7200; frenchman@libertypr.net). A French couple manages this small guesthouse adjacent to their nautical seafood restaurant by the same name. Rooms are worn, with antique furniture, but they supply cable TV and A/C at reasonable prices. Doubles $62; quads $73; 6-person room $97. Tax included. AmEx/MC/V. ❸

Balneario Seven Seas (☎863-8180), off Rte. 987 (see **Beaches,** p. 165), has an RV park and a large field for tents. The beach and the tent area are close together, so be prepared for neighboring beachgoers during the day. $10 per tent. ❶

🍴 FOOD

The city center is filled with countless small *cafeterías* where you can find filling Puerto Rican lunches for under $5, though most close mid-afternoon. Further afield, the waterfront in Las Croabas is a great choice for weekend nights, when locals eat out and most restaurants turn into lively bars. For groceries, try **Grande** on Hwy. 3, just east of the intersection with Rte. 195. (☎863-3420. Open M-Sa 6am-10pm, Su 11am-5pm. AmEx/MC/V.)

La Estación: Una Parilla New Yorican, Hwy. 987 Km 3.5 (☎863-4481), in La Croabas. This brainchild of a former Brooklyn restaurant manager and a Manhattan chef offers the best food and ambience for miles, not to mention the best prices. Patrons sit out on a cottage-like cedar terrace with tiki lamps, wicker rocking chairs and elegant patio furniture. Specials include

GO BANANAS

On every menu in every street corner *cafetería* in Puerto Rico, you will almost certainly find *mofongo*, one of the island's food staples. This hearty starch is made by crushing *tostones* (friend plantains), garlic, olive oil, and *chicarrones* (pork rind) or bacon into a thick, mashed-potato consistency.

To craft the dish yourself, you will need:

3 green plantains
1 tbsp. crushed garlic
1 tbsp. olive oil
0.5 lb. *chicarrón* or crumbled, cooked bacon
Vegetable oil for frying.

Peel the plantains and cut them into one-inch slices. Fry the slices in hot vegetable oil for 15min., then allow to cool slightly. Now comes the fun part: combine the garlic, olive oil, some of the pork, and some of the plantain slices, and mash away! You can use a mortar and pestle, or, if you're in a pinch, a spoon and bowl. Work in small portions.

Once the mixture is pureed, mold the batter-like substance into three large balls and serve with fried pork and onions, or beef tips, or chicken or shrimp; as a side dish or as a main course—with anything, really. The *mofongo* will acquire the flavor of its partner sauces, and nothing is more traditionally Puerto Rican than a melange of *mofongo* stuffings.

charcoal grilled meat and seafood as well as Big Apple favorites gone Puerto Rican, like Nathan's NY Hot Dog wrapped in bacon and avocado ($3). Whole grilled fish or *churrasco* steak $13. Open M and Th-F 5pm-11pm, Sa-Su 3pm-2am. Bar open 1hr. later than kitchen on weekdays. MC/V. ❸

Rosa's Seafood, C. Tablazo 536 (☎863-0213 or 627-4077). Heading into Puerto Real on C. Unión (Rte. 195), take a right at the last turn-off before the archway; it's at the end of the street, on the right. Widely acknowledged as the best seafood restaurant in Puerto Real and one of the 10 best on the island. Enjoy fresh seafood—including conch and octopus ($18) and lobster ($26)—on white tablecloths in this big, orange house. Green salad $1.25. Johnnycake $0.40. Seafood entrees $16-26. Small selection of non-seafood entrees $8.50-19. Open M-Tu and Th-Su 11am-10pm. AmEx/MC/V. ❹

Pan de Vida Café & Pizza, C. Unión 1 (863-2437). A small bakery with mod white chairs specializing in delicious wheat bread sandwiches ($2.50-4.25) and pizzas ($3.25-4). Also sells simple breakfast items ($1-2), calzones ($4-6), and a small selection of fresh and tasty wheat bread pastries ($1). Open daily 5am-10pm. MC/V; min. $10. ❶

Cafetería y Restaurant del Pueblo, C. Unión 60 (☎860-2212). One the nicest *cafeterías* in Fajardo and one of the only ones that stays open into the early evening. Puerto Rican entrees ($5-15) are huge and delicious. Green-and-white tile tables and wicker chairs add a touch of class. Breakfast, which curiously includes cheeseburgers, $3-5. Sandwiches $2-7. Open M-F 6am-5pm, Sa 6am-3pm. MC/V. ❷

Lolita's, Hwy. 3 Km 41.3 (☎889-0250 or 889-5770), is technically in Luquillo, but it's closer to Fajardo and a welcome change from standard seafood fare. The popular Mexican restaurant serves up all the favorites, from tacos to enchiladas to fajitas. Sit at breezy, tiled booths alongside open windows, or enjoy more formal seating in the main room. Lolita's is packed at all times, but wait staff are well prepared with microphones and earpieces. Tacos $1.75 with any meat or soy. Most burritos $3-4. Entrees $7-20. Margaritas $6. Open M-Th and Su 11am-10pm; F-Sa 11am-midnight. AmEx/MC/V. ❸

Golden Bagel Bistro & Café, C. Unión 171 (☎860-8987), is a little out of place in Fajardo. Even the food seems more east coast US than east coast Puerto Rico, with a variety of sandwiches on bagels, croissants, and wraps ($3.50-8), and big American breakfasts ($2.50-5). But don't worry—you can still get your entrees ($6-8) served with rice and beans. The cheerful, modern interior is a lovely place to enjoy a casual lunch. Soups and salads $3.25-6.50. Open M-F 6am-6pm, Sa-Su 6am-8:30pm. ❶

◎ SIGHTS

LAS CABEZAS DE SAN JUAN NATURE RESERVE. This 316-acre nature reserve is by far the most interesting land attraction in Fajardo. The reserve contains **seven different ecological zones**—coral reef, Thalassia bed, sandy beach, rocky beach, mangrove forest, lagoon, and dry forest—in addition to over 40 species of fish, more than 100 species of birds, and several species of mammals. Most visitors will at the very least see tiny fiddler crab and huge iguanas. Although Hurricanes Hugo (1989) and George (1998) destroyed over 80% of the reserve, it has recovered quickly and seems to be thriving again.

The privately run Conservation Trust of Puerto Rico maintains the reserve and offers 2hr. guided tours through all seven ecosystems, including an informative tram ride through the dry forest, a 30min. stroll along a boardwalk over the mangroves, a stop at a rocky point overlooking the ocean, and a visit to the small lighthouse museum. The **lighthouse**, which has been in continuous operation since 1882 but was relegated to the Conservation Trust in 2007, affords views of La Cordillera, Culebra, Vieques and St. Thomas. The only other way to see the reserve is to take a **kayak trip** through Laguna Grande, the bioluminescent bay that occupies over 100 acres of the park. The Conservation Trust does not offer kayak tours, but it is possible to arrange your own rental (see **Kayaking,** p. 167). Night tours of wildlife and the lighthouse, featuring a 30min. presentation on bioluminescence, are offered Thursday to Saturday; inquire about times and prices. *(Off Rte. 987 just past Seven Seas beach (p. 165). M-F ☎ 722-5882, ext. 240, Sa-Su ☎ 860-2560; www.fideicomiso.org. Reservations required–call at least a week in advance. Tours 2½hr., Tu-Su Spanish 9:30, 10, 10:30am, 2pm; English 2pm. $7, under 11 $4. AmEx/MC/V; min. $25)*

BAHÍA DE LAS CROABAS. Despite its proximity to commercialized Fajardo, Las Croabas retains the feel of a small fishing village. Here local fishermen still head out every morning to catch the sea creatures that take center stage in the restaurants along Rte. 987. All of the action takes place in the morning, but in the afternoon the boardwalk becomes a serene place to walk. If you come early (before 6am), it may be possible to negotiate with one of the fishermen for an inexpensive trip to the small, raw islands of Icacas, Palomino and Palominito. *(At the end of Rte. 987. Públicos from central Fajardo take 10min. and cost $0.65-0.75.)*

🟫 BEACHES

On a sunny day, Fajardo's public beach, **Balneario Seven Seas,** Rte. 987 Km 5, glistens as one of the best on the mainland; the water really does look like it has seven different colors. However, when the camping area is full on weekends or holidays, the beach may fill with litter. There is good **snorkeling** on the far right side. While this is a nice beach, much more stunning stretches of sand are a $2 ferry ride away on Vieques or Culebra. (☎ 863-8180. Trash cans and several shelters. Lifeguards daily 9am-5pm. Parking $3. Open 24hr.)

🔲 WATER SPORTS

Most visitors to Fajardo head straight toward the sea and La Cordillera, a series of smaller outlying islands that extend from the eastern tip of Puerto Rico to the Spanish Virgin Islands. The most popular among these are Cayo Icacos, Cayo Lobos and Isla Palominos, although the latter is owned by the Wyndham Resort and theoretically closed to visitors. These beautiful tropical islands and their surrounding coral reefs provide opportunities for snorkeling, diving, fishing, swimming, or just relaxing. Charters usually have their own favorite spots and they will take you wherever the weather looks good and the crowds are relatively small. (See **"Land no!"** p. 166.)

BOATING

Fajardo has two enormous marinas, Villa Marina and Puerto del Rey (about 2 mi. apart). Many of the boats anchored here offer charter expeditions to La Cordillera with snorkeling, swimming, and sunbathing. Some boats are listed below; check a recent issue of *¡Qué Pasa!* (p. 49) for the most current offerings. Most boat owners operate out of their sailboat homes—call in advance to make a reservation.

Caribbean School of Aquatics (☎ 383-5700). Captain Greg Korwek offers snorkeling trips on the *Fun Cat* (includes all equipment, lunch, and transportation from San Juan; $89, without transportation $69) and diving trips on the Island Safari (includes 2 dives, equipment, and picnic lunch; $125 with and $179 without certification). The mast of the boat reads "Sail-Dive-Party," and that's exactly what you'll do. AmEx/D/MC/V.

LAND NO!

For those tired of the crowds that swamp Puerto Rico's land-based nature reserves, or of the mad weekend rush to catch ferries to Vieques and Culebra, perhaps the time has come to graduate to a more remote alternative: the Cordillera Natural Reserve. This small string of cays, located 1½ mi. northeast of Fajardo, includes Isla Palominos, Isla Palomonitos, Cayo Icacos, Cayo Diablo, Cayo Lobos, Cayo Ratones, and Cayo la Banquilla, as well as immense rock formations like Las Cucarachas. The small islands host numerous species of marine life, birds, and iguanas, but the real pull to this area is the surrouding turquoise water, perfect for open-sea snorkeling. Swimmable reefs are inhabited by schools of bright fish, sea fans, elkhorn coral, and sometimes even rays. Perhaps most refreshing, the only other people around will likely be those sharing a boat with you.

The only way to reach La Cordillera is to board a boat in Fajardo. It is possible to negotiate with a fisherman to shuttle you there in his motorboat; many line the docks in Las Croabas and offer competitive prices. Another alternative is to shell out $59-85 for a sailboat or catamaran charter to the island; trips typically run 10am-3:30pm and include snorkel equipment, lunch, and beverages. Two recommended companies are **Erin Go Bragh** and **Salty Dog** (see p. 166).

Erin Go Bragh (☎860-4401; www.egbc.net), Puerto del Rey Marina, dock #1204. Guests have been known to return to the hospitality of Captain Bill and his wife Ingrid, a knowledgeable earth scientist, aboard their 50 ft. sailboat. Trips to 2 islands on La Cordillera include gourmet barbecue lunch, homemade snacks, open bar, fishing poles, and snorkel gear. 6 person max. Trips (10am-5pm) $85 per person, 2-person min. Sunset cruises (5-7pm) $75, 4-person min. Dinner cruises (5-9pm) $85, 4-person min. Also offers overnight charters to Vieques and Culebra; call for info. AmEx/MC/V.

Getaway (☎860-7327), a 32 ft. catamaran in Villa Marina. Trips (10am-3:30pm) include soda, lunch, and a piña colada; $60 cash, $65 with credit card. Sunset cruise $45. MC/V.

Traveler (☎863-2821), a 50 ft. catamaran (with a waterslide) operating out of Villa Marina. Trips (10am-3:30pm) include snorkeling equipment, lunch, and an all-you-can-eat salad bar. $59 cash, $65 with credit card; ages 5-12 $45. MC/V.

Salty Dog (☎717-6378 or 717-7259; www.saltydreams.com), in Villa Marina. Sails to Cayo Icacos or Palomino Island. Trips include lunch, drinks, snorkel equipment and "Pain killers," their rum punch and cocktail creation. $59 per person. AmEx/D/MC/V.

Ventajero 4 (☎645-9129; www.sailpuertorico.com). 52 ft. sloop at Puerto del Rey dock #1267, holds up to 6 people. Trips (10am-5pm) include beer, snorkeling equipment, and a full Puerto Rican lunch. Up to 6 guests; $550 per trip. MC/V.

DIVING

Puerto Rico Diver Supply, A-E6 Santa Isidra III (☎863-4300; www.prdiversupply.com), in front of Villa Marina Shopping Center, sends their 36 ft. boat on regular expeditions to La Cordillera (2-tank dive $85, 1-tank dive $55, snorkeling $69). Discover Scuba 1-tank dive $95. Snorkeling trip $55. Also rents snorkeling and diving equipment. Open daily 8am-5pm. AmEx/D/MC/V.

Sea Ventures Dive Centers (☎863-3483 or 800-739-3483; www.divepuertorico.com), at Puerto del Rey. Sends out 2-tank dives every morning ($89, with gear $99), but the location changes daily due to weather and visibility conditions. Discover Scuba package $150. Transportation from San Juan round-trip $25 per person. 4-day PADI certification course $450. Trips every morning; visit the office early to arrange dives in person. Open daily 7:45am-1pm, later if an afternoon dive is scheduled. AmEx/MC/V.

KAYAKING

The Fajardo area is home to one of Puerto Rico's three amazing **bioluminescent bays.** All tours are done through private companies. One reliable outfitter is Yókahu Kayak (☎ 604-7375 or 863-5374; www.yokahukayaks.com), which offers 2 hr. tours for $35 per person. (Open M-Sa 8am-5pm. MC/V.)

🎵 🌺 NIGHTLIFE AND FESTIVALS

Despite its size, Fajardo has no real nightlife scene. A few restaurants along Rte. 987 double as bars and stay open late on weekend nights. **Racar Seafood,** Rte. 987 Km 6.7, next to Las Croabas, has live music from 7pm to midnight on Saturday nights. (Beer $1.50-2. Open M-F and Su 8am-around 9:30pm, Sa 8am-midnight). For a more lively scene, head to the active **Marina Liquor Store,** in Villa Marina Shopping Center. A motley collection of yachters and Puerto Rican men gather at this liquor/convenience/cigar store to sit at outdoor tables and drink their purchases. Come on Friday or Saturday night for live Latin music 10pm-2am. (☎ 860-8112. Beer from $1. Mixed drinks $4-5. Open W-Th 8am-midnight, F-Sa 8am-2am. MC/V.) **Sharky's Sports Bar,** next to the liquor store, looks like a standard sports lounge from the outside. But don't be deceived: with a long full bar and a dance floor, this is the place to take salsa lessons on Thursday, sing karaoke on Friday, listen to live rock with a young crowd on Saturday, and slow dance to Bohemian traditional music with a more mature clientele on Sunday. (☎ 860-8112 or 309-6007. Beer $2-3. Mixed drinks $3-5. Open W-Th 6pm-midnight, F-Sa 6pm-2am. MC/V.)

Every Presidents' Day weekend (mid-Feb.), from Friday to Monday, Puerto del Rey hosts the Caribbean's largest in-water **boat exhibition,** with local music and an incredible display of boats and boat merchandise. (For more information, call ☎ 860-1000, ext. 4214. Tickets $10 per person.)

NAGUABO

Life goes by a little bit slower in Naguabo. South of tourist-oriented Fajardo, residents sit on their porches watching the traffic go by. The small town itself has no real attractions, but the vistas from Playa Naguabo, trips to Monkey Island, and several attractive accommodations nearby make it a good place to relax.

🚌 ℹ TRANSPORTATION AND PRACTICAL INFORMATION

Naguabo is located just off Hwy. 53, along Rte. 31. From Rte. 31, turn down **C. Garzot,** at the **Econo** supermarket, to reach the town plaza. C. Muñoz Rivera runs perpendicular to C. Garzot along the plaza; C. Goyco is on the other side of the plaza, running parallel to C. Garzot. **Públicos** leave from Terminal de Carros Públicos Salvador Clara Cotto, next to the plaza across C. Garzot, for: Fajardo (20min., $1.65); Humacao (20min., $1.40); and Playa Naguabo (15min., $0.70). **Banco Popular,** C. Garzot 19, at the corner with C. Muñoz Rivera, has an **ATM** in front. (☎ 874-2880. Open M-F 8am-4pm.) **Econo,** on Rte. 31 at the corner with C. Garzot, sells groceries. (☎ 874-0170. Open M-Th 7am-9pm, F-Sa 6am-10pm, Su 11am-5pm. MC/V.) To reach the **police station** from Rte. 31, head down C. Garzot, turn right on C. Muñoz Rivera, and continue three blocks. (☎ 874-2020. Open 24hr.) The **hospital,** Centro de Salud Familiar, Rte. 31 Km 4, next to the court, has a 24hr. emergency room. (☎ 874-2837, emergency room ☎ 874-3152.) The **post office,** Rte. 31 #100, lies across from the Econo. (☎ 874-3115. Open M-F 8am-4:30pm, Sa 8am-noon.) **Postal Code:** 00718.

▌▐ ACCOMMODATIONS AND FOOD

For many, ▓**Casa Cubuy Ecolodge** ❹ is the only reason to venture out to Naguabo. From Naguabo, go west on Rte. 31, then turn right on Rte. 191, and head all the way up, almost to the end of the road, for about 20min. This perfectly positioned B&B perches on the edge of Rte. 191, 1500 ft. above sea level, and is the only accommodation inside the El Yunque forest. With a small library, forest trails surrounding the property, and spectacular views of the lush rainforest valley below from every room, the tranquil lodge is the ideal spot to get away from it all. Delicious breakfasts are served family-style and include large plates of fruit, oatmeal and cereal, and hot dishes. Expansive rooms are tastefully decorated with wooden furniture and comfortable mattresses. It's worth it to pay for one of the rooms with an entire window wall and a private balcony overlooking the forest. (☎874-6221; www.casacubuy.com. No phones or TVs. Dinner $18.50, $12 children 12 and under. $7 sack lunches. Doubles $100; with balcony $115. Extra person $25. AmEx/MC/V.) **Phillips Forest Cabins** ❶, Rte. 191 Km 24.2, located just up the road from Casa Cubuy, provides the opportunity to get up close and personal with El Yunque rainforest. Despite its name, the property has just one operating cabin; about a quarter mile off the road, deep in the forest, with cold water and a double bed. A two-bedroom house sleeps between six and ten people, and is slightly more refined with two full beds and hot water. Four campsites provide cheap and rustic accommodations. (☎874-2138; www.rainforestsafari.com. Turn left off Rte. 191 about 15min. up the road, immediately before El Bambú restaurant. Cabin $35. Extra person $10. House $35 per double room. Extra person $15. Campsites $15.)

The best restaurants serve fresh seafood in Playa Naguabo or Punta Santiago. Within city limits, busy and centrally located **Joe's Pizza Place** ❶, C. Muñoz Rivera, on the plaza, offers big slices of mouth-watering pizza, even for breakfast. (☎874-1519. Large pizza $10-17. Calzones $3.50-6. Open daily 8am-midnight. Cash only.)

▌ DAYTRIPS FROM NAGUABO

PLAYA NAGUABO

A público runs from Naguabo to the beach ($0.70). Públicos between Humacao ($1.40) and Fajardo ($1.65) also stop at Playa Naguabo. By car from Hwy. 53, take Exit 18 onto Rte. 31. Turn left, then go south on Hwy. 3 toward Humacao to Playa Naguabo (Km 66).

The serene bay at Playa Naguabo provides a terrific escape. Technically called **Playa Húcares,** this bay doesn't have a beach; nevertheless, an attractive boardwalk overlooks the light blue water, Cayo Santiago, and, in the distance, Vieques. At the southern end of the bay sit two large pink turn-of-the-century houses, both on the list of National Historic Sights. One has been kept up and is now the most attractive residence in the area. The other, **El Castillo Villa del Mar,** was built at the same time, but it has fallen into such a state of disrepair that it now looks like the set of a horror movie. Playa Naguabo has several restaurants with a good view and equally good food. The $4.50 lunch special at **Bar-Restaurante Vinny** ❶, at the northern end of the beach, is an excellent deal with rice, beans, beverage, and either pork chops or chicken. Add a side of *amarillos* for just $0.25. For countless locals, Vinny's is the destination for a fresh catch; visit his garage to the left of the restaurant, where fish fresh out of the sea are sold between 1:30 and 2pm. (☎874-7664 or 874-2428. Frozen seafood $5-15. Beer $1.25-2. Open daily 8am-10pm. MC/V.) If you're looking for something without plastic tables, the air-conditioned **Restaurante Griselle Seafood ❸**, where Hwy. 3 hits the boardwalk on Playa Húcares, serves live lobsters right out of the tank for $22 per lb. (☎874-1533. Entrees $7-25. Open M-Tu, Th, Su 11am-8pm; F-Sa 11am-midnight. D/MC/V.)

CAYO SANTIAGO

The island is only accessible via private tour by boat. Contact Frank "Palo" López (see below).

A tiny island uninhabited by humans is certainly not unique in Puerto Rico. But one inhabited solely by their primate cousins is a rarity, and it's precisely this that makes Cayo Santiago one of the most unusual attractions in the Northeast. In 1938, the University of Puerto Rico and Columbia University in New York City teamed up to create a new research area: they took 500 Indian rhesus monkeys, isolated them on 38-acre Cayo Santiago, and **Monkey Island** was born. The monkeys thrived in their new environment, and today over 1200 primates frolic on the tropical shores. Only scientists and researchers are allowed on the island, but visitors can take a boat close to the island and watch the monkeys from afar. A 1944 boat wreck just off the shore and a small reef on the other side of the island make this a great place for snorkeling. Amiable Captain Frank López leads 2-2½hr. excursions from Playa Naguabo to Monkey Island on his boat, **La Paseadora.** For only $35 per person, Lopez offers the opportunity to fish, kayak, snorkel, and swim in the waters surrounding the island. Come with expectations of friendly faces, lively music, and personal attention, and you'll have a great time. (You can look for López's boat at the northern end of Playa Naguabo on Sa-Su, but calling ahead is advisable. ☎850-7881 or 316-0441. 6 person max. Trips any day with reservation. Limited equipment provided. Cash only.)

NORTHEAST

VIEQUES

The first thing that comes to mind when one thinks of Vieques is the US Navy base on the island, which was protested vocally by locals. As of May 2003, however, the Navy left Vieques, leaving *viequenses* with the prize that they had long been fighting for: their beautiful island. Once again, the only sounds heard on the island are the chirps of *coquís* and the crows of roosters—a marked contrast to the recent past, when it was common to hear bombs falling less than 10 mi. away. But even Vieques's tumultuous history is not as remarkable as the island's natural beauty. Often referred to as *La Isla Nena* (the little girl island), Vieques is covered with lush tropical forests and surrounded by crystalline seas that rival any in the Caribbean. The entire island feels a bit untamed—palm trees are scattered amidst gnarled jungle vegetation, bumpy dirt roads crisscross the land, and herds of wild horses wander through the forest as though they owned it. On the south coast, the island has two bioluminescent bays that are among the best in the world.

With fewer than 10,000 residents, Vieques is just large enough to contain two small settlements. Isabel II (Isabel Segunda), the largest city, feels like any small Puerto Rican town, complete with a plaza, a busy main strip, and, when the ferry arrives, a bit of traffic congestion. The ferry terminal, the fort, most local services, and several of the best restaurants are located in Isabel II. Esperanza, on the south side of the island, is more tourist-oriented and has a large population of US expats. This primarily residential neighborhood becomes increasingly commercialized as you head toward the water. The street running parallel to the sea, called Calle Flamboyán, the Malecón, or simply "the strip," is almost completely lined with guesthouses, restaurants, gift shops, tour operators, and English speakers.

With the Navy gone, the island must figure out how to deal with high unemployment rates, a budding tourism industry, and the allocation of hundreds of acres of valuable land. Locals have set up nonprofit organizations to tackle these issues and to protect the island for future generations. But *viequenses* know that even if the island's future is a bit unsure, in many respects, they live in a paradise.

HIGHLIGHTS OF VIEQUES

MAKE WATER GLOW in the world's most vibrant **bioluminescent bay** (p. 183).

LOUNGE on the white sands of **Sun Bay** (p. 182).

LEARN ABOUT Vieques's fascinating history, including the controversial US Navy presence, at **Fortín de Conde de Marisol** (p. 180).

⊏ INTER-ISLAND TRANSPORTATION

Flights: Aeropuerto Antonio Rivera Rodríguez (☎741-8358 or 741-0415), on Rte. 200, may be the most attractive airport in Puerto Rico. The following airlines sell tickets over the phone or at their airport desks. Reserve at least 24hr. in advance, and even farther ahead during high season and holidays. A *público* waiting on Rte. 200 when flights come in will take visitors anywhere on the island (see **Públicos,** p. 173). Open 24hr.

Air Sunshine (☎741-7900, toll-free 888-879-8900; www.airsunshine.com) flies to **San Juan International** (25min.; 4 per day; $80, round-trip $160). Open M-F 8am-6pm, Sa-Su 10am-5pm. AmEx/MC/V.

Isla Nena (☎741-1505, toll-free 877-812-5144) Offers 4-12 flights per day to **Culebra** (10min.; $35, round-trip $70), **Fajardo** (10min.; $25, round-trip $50), and **San Juan International** (35min.; $92, round-trip $172). Open daily 8am-5pm. MC/V.

M&N Aviation (☎741-3911, toll-free 877-622-5566) flies to: **San Juan Isla Grande** (18min.; daily 7pm; $64, round-trip $118) and **San Juan International** (20min.; daily 7pm; $86, round-trip $161). Open daily 8am-7pm. AmEx/MC/V.

Vieques Air Link (☎in airport 741-8211, in office 741-8331 or 741-0470, toll-free 888-901-9247) flies to: **Fajardo** (10min.; on demand; $23, round-trip $42); **San Juan International** (30min.; 3 per day; $85, round-trip $167); **San Juan Isla Grande** (30min.; 3-4 per day; $48, round-trip $92); **St. Croix, USVI** (30min.; 2 per day; $70, round-trip $145). AmEx/MC/V. Or stop by their **reservations office,** C. Antonio M. Mellado 358. Open M-Sa 8am-noon, 1pm-5:30pm. Airport Office open daily 6am-6:30pm.

Ferries: Puerto Rican Port Authority (☎1-800-981-2005, in Fajardo 863-0705, 863-0852, or 860-2005) operates ferries between Vieques and Fajardo. In addition to the routes below, a ferry runs between Vieques and Culebra (W only; leaves Vieques 7:30am and 2:30pm, returns from Culebra 9am and 3:30pm; round-trip $4). No reservations are accepted for passengers, so show up at least 1hr. in advance. Reservations are required to take a car onboard and should be made several months in advance to snag one of the few spots (by phone M-F 8am-11am, 1pm-3pm). Ticket window open daily 7:30am-11:30am, 12:30-4pm. MC/V.

FERRIES	FAJARDO-VIEQUES	VIEQUES-FAJARDO	PRICE
PASSENGER	M-F 9:30am, 1, 4:30, 8pm; Sa-Su 9am, 3, 6pm	M-F 6:30am, 11am, 3, 6pm; Sa-Su 6:30am, 1, 4:30pm	$2
CARGO	M-F 4am, 9:30am, 4:30pm	M-F 6am, 1, 6pm	$15; round-trip $26.50

◢ ORIENTATION

Lying 13 mi. east of the mainland and measuring 21 mi. by 3 mi., Vieques looks like a miniature, elongated version of Puerto Rico. Almost the entire eastern half and the westernmost quarter of the island's former US Navy lands are controlled by the US Fish and Wildlife Service. Most of the region is open to the public as a natural reserve, although certain areas containing unexploded bombs or other hazardous materials remain closed (these areas are clearly marked and cordoned off). Most people arrive in Isabel II, the island's largest town and home of the ferry dock. The dock is also the home base for *públicos*, which congregate there by the dozen when a ferry is scheduled to arrive. If you are driving your own car and wish to leave Isabel II, take a right at the ferry dock, then take a left on C. Benítez Guzmán, then a right just past the plaza to reach Rte. 200 and leave town. The fastest route between Isabel II and Esperanza is Rte. 997; however, for a much more scenic route, drive west on Rte. 200, then south along Rte. 995, one of the most beautiful roads on the island. Turning right on Rte. 201 and left onto Rte. 996 will lead you straight into Esperanza. Driving eastward on Rte. 996, the ocean will come into view on your right. The road runs alongside the water as you approach the Malecón boardwalk and what expats call **"the strip,"** home to the town's restaurants and hotels.

WARNING. Vieques has its share of petty crime. Lock your hotel room and **never bring valuables to the beach.** Thieves have been known to break into cars parked behind the beach or grab cell phones, purses, or wallets from the beach while owners are in the water. Sun Bay has been especially vulnerable to these crimes.

To avoid break-ins, car rental agencies recommend leaving your car unlocked and your windows rolled down (with no valuables inside) while you are at the beach.

VIEQUES

Vieques

ACCOMMODATIONS
Abreeze, 3
Balneario Sun Bay, 10
Cabañas Playa Grande, 4
Casa La Lanchita, 1
The Crow's Nest, 2
La Finca Caribe, 5
Great Escape B&B Inn, 7
Hacienda Tamarindo, 8
Hix Island House, 6
OUTDOOR ACTIVITY RENTAL
Island Adventures, 9

⊫ LOCAL TRANSPORTATION

Unless you plan to stick exclusively to one of the towns, it is very time-consuming and almost impossible to get around Vieques without a car. *Públicos* run between Isabel II and Esperanza but rarely head to any beaches except Sun Bay, and there may be as long as a 1hr. wait, even if you call ahead.

Públicos: Shared vans travel the island, usually circulating between the airport, the **ferry terminal** in Isabel II, and **the strip** in Esperanza. If you flag down a *público*, it will usually take you anywhere on the island. Passengers traveling alone may have to pay the fare of 3 passengers. When ferries arrive, all of the operating *públicos* will be at the dock, and about 30min. later most will end up on the strip in Esperanza; plan your schedule accordingly. Transport anywhere on the major roads should cost about $3 per person; transport to the beaches on former Navy lands runs $5 or more; extra luggage costs $0.50 per item. Keep in mind, especially if you want to go to the more remote beaches, that *públicos* may not be around to pick you up, so have some numbers handy and be prepared to wait. *Público* drivers include: **Ana** (☎ 741-2318, cell 313-0599), **Ángel** (☎ 741-1370, cell 484-7896), **Eric** (☎ 741-0448), **Fernando** (cell ☎ 605-4100), **Henry** (☎ 741-8621, cell 380-1866), **Ismael** (☎ 741-0095), **Jorge** (☎ 741-2116), **Nito & Abby** (☎ 741-4469), and **Pepe Car Service** (☎ 741-3392).

Car Rental: Several small companies rent Jeeps and SUVs, but there are no major chains. Make reservations far in advance during high season (Dec.-May) as it's not uncommon for every car on the island to be booked. Even during low season, call a few days ahead. Most of the former Navy roads are unpaved, extremely bumpy, and rife with water-filled potholes; these should not be attempted without 4WD. Even the island's paved roads can be challenging, as many are only 1 lane wide but have traffic going in both directions. There are two **gas stations** around Rte. 200 Km 1.5.

Island Car Rental, Rte. 201 Km 1.1 (☎ 741-1666). SUVs $55-70 per day; minivans $70. Insurance $12 per day. $5 per day discount for 7 or more days. Driver's license required. 25+. Open daily 8am noon and 1 5pm. AmEx/MC/V.

Martineau Car Rental, Rte. 200 Km 3.4 (☎ 741-0087 or 636-7071; www.martineaucarrental.com), across from the Wyndham resort. Jeeps $65-75 per day. Insurance $20 per day. Under-25 surcharge $5 per day. Pickup and dropoff available. Credit card required. Open daily 8am-6pm. AmEx/MC/V.

Maritza's Car Rental, Rte. 201 Km 1 (☎ 741-0078). Rents Jeeps for $45-65 per day. Insurance $12 per day. 25+. Dropoff service. Open daily 8am 6pm. AmEx/MC/V.

Acevedo's Car Rental, Rte. 201 Km 0.4 (☎ 741-4380), in the Cabañas Playa Grande complex. Rents 3 types of Jeeps ($45-60) and SUVs ($55-65). 26+. Dropoff service. Open M-Sa 9:30am-6pm, Su 10am-noon. AmEx/MC/V.

Acacia Car Rental (☎ 741-1856). The owners of Acacia Apartments also rent 4 Jeeps (in winter $65 per day, in summer $55). 3 days min. Driver's license required. 25+. Rentals come with an orientation. Pickup and dropoff service. MC/V.

Bike Rental: La Dulce Vida (☎ 970-222-1007, www.bikevieques.com), rents 15- to 27-speed mountain bikes ($25 per day including helmet, lock, and delivery). The owner leads ½-day bike tours around the western end of the island ($75 per person including bike, gear, snacks and water; min. 2 people, max. 4). New 2-day bike/kayak/snorkel tours $75-120 per person. Reservations required. MC/V.

🛈 PRACTICAL INFORMATION

Unless otherwise stated, all services are located in Isabel II.

Tourist Office: Puerto Rico Tourism Company, C. Carlos LeBrun 449 (☎ 741-0800), on the corner of the plaza in Casa Alcaldía. Helpful staff offers maps, magazines, and

ISLAND INFO. Several publications and websites provide information about Vieques in English. Take a look at the following: **www.enchanted-isle.com.** Almost every tourist service on the island has a link on this comprehensive site. Resident expat Judy writes *What's Happenin'!*, which lists many island events, including unscheduled closings of establishments and special nights at bars and restaurants. **www.vieques-events.com.** On the first of every month this helpful newsletter appears on the web with a calendar of current events, articles about recent happenings, and a small classifieds section. Almost every tourist-related business on the island carries a hard copy. **www.elenas-vieques.com.** A longtime expat and owner of Blue Heron Kayak, Elena has compiled a personal website with information about Vieques.

brochures. Open daily 8am-4:30pm. Island tourism websites external to the government-endorsed tourism office include www.viequesvisitor.com, www.vieques-island.com and www.isla-vieques.com.

Bank: Banco Popular, C. Muñoz Rivera 115 (☎741-2071). **ATM.** Open M-F 8am-3pm.

Laundromat: Familia Ríos, C. Benítez Castaño 1 (☎374-6823), across from Al's Mar Azul bar. Washers $3-5, dryers $1 per 10min. Detergent included. Wash-and-fold $2 per lb.; available by 4pm if in by 10am. Change unnecessary; uses declining-balance cards. Open M and Th-Sa 10am-7pm. Cash only.

Police: Rte. 200 Km 0.2 (☎741-2020 or 741-2121), at Rte. 997. Open 24hr.

Pharmacy: Isla Nena Pharmacy (☎741-1906), on C. Muñoz Rivera. Open M-Sa 8am-6pm. AmEx/MC/V.

Hospital: Centro de Salud Familiar, Rte. 997 Km 0.4 (☎741-0392, emergency room 741-2151). Next to the fire station. Clinic open M-F 7am-3pm. Emergency room open 24hr.

Internet Access: Museo de Esperanza, C. Flamboyán 138 (☎741-8850), Esperanza, allows travelers to use their own computers ($3 per 30min.). Open Tu-Su 11am-4pm.

Post Office: C. Muñoz Rivera 97 (☎741-3891). General Delivery available. Open M-F 8am-4:30pm, Sa 8am-noon. **Postal Code:** 00765.

ISLAND TIME. All hours and prices in Vieques are subject to change. Hours change with the season, and owners (and *público* drivers) frequently close down shop in the middle of the day for lunch. Even restaurant service is slow: where could you possibly be going in a hurry? To avoid frustration, make plans with a grain of salt and retain a sense of flexibility.

ACCOMMODATIONS AND CAMPING

Vieques has excellent accommodations for travelers of all budgets. If you want to be in the middle of local action, stay in Isabel II; if you want to join the expat crowd and be close to the beaches, try Esperanza. If you just want to get away from it all, try one of the accommodations in the middle of the island, but you will need a car. Many hotels do not allow children; generally, the more expensive an accommodation is, the less likely it is to allow children.

REALTORS

The realtors below, along with several others, offer short-term vacation rentals around the island. Prices are for weekly rentals and are taxed at the rate of 7%.

Rainbow Realty, C. Flamboyán 278 (☎/fax 741-4312; www.enchanted-isle.com/rainbow), in Esperanza near La Tienda Verde. Most rentals have washer and dryer, some have pool and A/C. Min. stay 1 week. Nov. 15-May 15 $650-4000; May 15-Nov. 15 $450-3000. Open in winter M-Sa 10am-5pm, Su 10am-2pm; in summer M-Sa 10am-4pm, Su 10am-2pm. MC/V with 5% surcharge; personal checks preferred.

Crow's Nest Realty, Rte. 201 Km 1.6 (☎741-0033 or 1-888-484-7837; www.crowsnestvieques.com). Min. stay 1 week. Rentals $800-3,500. AmEx/MC/V.

Connections Real Estate, C. Muñoz Rivera 117 (☎741-0023 or 741-0366; www.viequesrealtor.com), in Isabel II. Houses vary. Min. stay 1 week in high season, 3 nights during low season. 50% deposit. $1300-2500 per week. Open Nov.-May M-F 10am-5pm, Sa-Su by appointment; June-Oct. W-Th 10am-5pm, F-Su by appointment. Credit card deposit required. MC/V.

ISABEL II

■ **Casa de Amistad,** C. Casa Benítez Castaño 27 (☎741-3758; www.casadeamistad.com), in the heart of Isabel II. Helpful and enthusiastic owners have created an affordable, attractive guesthouse. 7 artistically decorated rooms with A/C and wicker furniture. Rooftop deck. Tiny pool. Common area with TV. Kitchen and dining room. Snorkel equipment ($10), Internet ($3 per 30min.), and bar. Free use of coolers and beach towels. Doubles $80; quads $80-90. MC/V. ❸

■ **Casa La Lanchita,** North Shore Rd. 374 (☎741-8449 or 774-4717, www.viequeslalanchita.com), north on Plinio Peterson from the ferry docks to North Shore Rd. running northeast. This impressive and sparkling white mansion juts out over the Bravos de Boston coast, offering

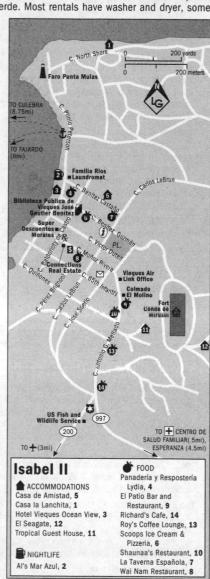

Isabel II

🏠 ACCOMMODATIONS
Casa de Amistad, **5**
Casa la Lanchita, **1**
Hotel Vieques Ocean View, **3**
El Seagate, **12**
Tropical Guest House, **11**

🌙 NIGHTLIFE
Al's Mar Azul, **2**

🍎 FOOD
Panadería y Repostería Lydia, **4**
El Patio Bar and Restaurant, **9**
Richard's Cafe, **14**
Roy's Coffee Lounge, **13**
Scoops Ice Cream & Pizzeria, **6**
Shaunaa's Restaurant, **10**
La Taverna Española, **7**
Wai Nam Restaurant, **8**

VIEQUES

backyard beach and snorkeling access. Rooms of resort quality still have a personal, beach cottage feel. All suites face the ocean and have balcony, fully equipped kitchen, A/C, and cable TV. Books, chairs, and towels to borrow. Doubles $95-140. Extra person $10. Min. stay 4 nights in high season. MC/V. ❹

Hotel Vieques Ocean View, C. Plinio Peterson 571 (☎741-3696). Conveniently located in town. Standard budget hotel—except for the balconies and pool that look out over the ocean. All rooms have A/C and TV; most have fridge. Aug. 15-May 15 doubles $78; quads $118; 6-person rooms $144; 8-person rooms $172. May 16-Aug. 14 $59/99/131/144. ❸

El Seagate (☎741-4661), on the hill above the fort. With the fort's entrance at your back, take the left fork and continue to bear left up the hill; the house will be on your right. The grounds look overgrown in some areas, but rooms are well decorated and have all of the amenities you could need at prices that are too good to be true. All rooms have ceiling fan; some have a full kitchen or balcony. Pets welcome. Large book exchange. Pool. Free Wi-Fi. Doubles $65-90; quads $85. AmEx/MC/V. ❸

Tropical Guest House, C. Apolonia Gittings 41 (☎741-2449; www.viequestropical-guesthouse.com). Leaving Isabel II on Rte. 200, take the first left after El Patio restaurant, then take the left fork and then the right fork; the guesthouse is on your left. Away from town, but with simple, bright rooms and a friendly staff. All rooms have private bath, A/C and TV. Singles and doubles $60; triples $65; 4- to 6-person suites with kitchen $85-105. Tax included. MC/V. ❷

 THE NUMBER GAME. When a store owner or island resident gives you their telephone number and it's only 4 digits long, don't despair: because all Vieques numbers begin with "741" and all of Culebra's with "742," islanders have long grown accustomed to memorizing only the last four digits of friends' phone numbers.

ESPERANZA

Winds Guest House, C. Flamboyán 107 (☎741-8666; www.enchanted-isle.com/tradewinds). Cozy guesthouse and great beachfront location on the Malecón make this a good value. Colorful rooms with bright, Caribbean-themed wall murals. Some rooms share an ocean-view patio. All rooms have fridges, reading lights, and ceiling fans. Free use of beach towels. Check-out 11am. Check-in 2pm. Singles $60-70; doubles $70-80. Extra person $15. AmEx/MC/V. ❷

Bananas Guest House, C. Flamboyán 142 (☎741-8700; www.bananasguesthouse.com). An elegant wood cabin with accommodations above a lively restaurant and bar, just across the street from the beach. Friendly backpacker atmosphere. 7 rooms all have private bath and mini-fridge. Check-in 1pm. Check-out 11am. Open Nov.-May; call ahead. Doubles $65, with A/C and screened porch $80-$90. Extra person $15. MC/V. ❸

Pablo's Guest House, C. Piños 217 (☎741-8917). The cheapest option on the island, but a 7-10min. walk from the fun of the strip. Incredibly clean rooms are located on the 2nd fl. of Pablo's home. 4 identical rooms each contain a full and a twin bed. All rooms include A/C, hot water, and fridge. Triples $70 1st night, $60 thereafter. Cash only. ❷

Ted's Guest House, C. Húcar 103 (☎741-2225; www.vieques-island.com/rentals/ted), big coral-and-blue house ½ block from the strip. Though they are located on the 2nd fl. of the owner's home, these 3 clean apartments look professional. All come with a full kitchen, A/C, TV, and a kitchen table. Common balcony. Min. stay 2 nights. Doubles $80; 2-bedroom quads $125; per week $525/800. Cash only. ❸

Amapola Guest House, C. Flamboyán 144 (☎741-1382; www.amapolainn.com). Enter through the corridor between Bananas and Bilí, on the strip. Amapola can best

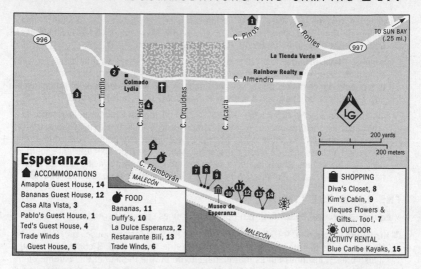

Esperanza

▲ ACCOMMODATIONS
Amapola Guest House, **14**
Bananas Guest House, **12**
Casa Alta Vista, **3**
Pablo's Guest House, **1**
Ted's Guest House, **4**
Trade Winds
Guest House, **5**

🍎 FOOD
Bananas, **11**
Duffy's, **10**
La Dulce Esperanza, **2**
Restaurante Bilí, **13**
Trade Winds, **6**

🏛 SHOPPING
Diva's Closet, **8**
Kim's Cabin, **9**
Vieques Flowers &
Gifts... Too!, **7**
☀ OUTDOOR
ACTIVITY RENTAL
Blue Caribe Kayaks, **15**

be described as colorful, from the bold orange exterior to the colorful bedspreads and decorative details in each room. Excellent location. All rooms have A/C. Free morning coffee. Suites come with a well-equipped kitchen and sleep 4-6 people. Doubles $75-95; quads $125. AmEx/MC/V. ❸

Casa Alta Vista, C. Flamboyán 297 (☎ 741-3296; www.casaaltavista.net), above a small grocery store in a large white and terra-cotta house just west of Esperanza's strip. Casa Alta Vista is a great deal for groups, with rooms fitting up to 5 people. Ocean views from a rooftop patio and hammocks on common balcony. All rooms have A/C and fridge. Doubles $75; quads $85; quints $95. AmEx/MC/V. ❸

AROUND VIEQUES

La Finca Caribe, Rte. 995 Km 2.2 (☎ 741-0495; www.lafinca.com). If you enjoyed summer camp as a kid, try this rustic but clean and colorful hotel on a farm in the center of Vieques. The owners strive for tranquillity and simplicity; rooms share bathrooms and guests use private outdoor solar-heated showers. All rooms have a loft bed. Friendly conversation ensues in the common kitchen, lounge, and patio. Pool. Book exchange. Doubles mid-Nov. to mid-May $85; mid-May to mid-Nov. $65. 2 large cabins sleep 1-4 $1050/795 and 1-3 $735/550 per week. AmEx/MC/V with 4% surcharge. ❸

Abreeze, Rte. 997 Km 1.6 (☎ 741-1856; www.abreezeapartments.com). The owners of Acacia Car Rental rent out 2 apartments in their beautiful yellow house. With 3½ acres of land on the top of a hill with nearly panoramic views, this house feels like a Caribbean country estate. Rooms include kitchen, living room, private terrace, and free Internet. All guests can use pool, grill, beach towels and chairs, coolers, washer, and dryer. Min. stay 1 week. 2-person studio Nov.-May $1150 per week; June-Oct. $850. 4-person apartment $1350/1050. MC/V. ❹

The Crow's Nest, Rte. 201 Km 1 (☎ 741-0033 or 741-0993, toll free 1-888-843-7837; www.crowsnestvieques.com). On 5 acres of lush grounds just off busy Rte. 201, this hotel looks like an expensive resort from the outside, with a pool, poolside restaurant, and newly painted yellow-and-blue exterior. Inside, the rooms are very large but aging a bit. A/C, satellite TV, phone, and balcony. Complimentary coolers, umbrellas, beach chairs, boogie boards, and towels. Most with full kitchen. Continental breakfast

VIEQUES

included. Use the free Wi-Fi or pay for Internet access on 1 computer ($4 per 20min). Reception 8am-7pm. Doubles Nov. 16-Apr. $136; May-Dec. 19 $104. Extra person $17. No pets or children under 12. Tax included. AmEx/MC/V. ❺

Cabañas Playa Grande, Rte. 201 Km 1 (☎741-4380). Playa Grande provides well-equipped, clean apartments with A/C, TV, and fully stocked kitchen. All rooms sleep up to 5 people, which makes this a very good deal, though the grounds are less than inspiring. 1 - to 2-person apartments $80, 4- to 5-person $100. AmEx/MC/V. ❸

Balneario Sun Bay (☎741-8198), on Rte. 997, ¼ mi. east of Esperanza, is essentially a large field next to the beach. Nothing compares with falling asleep to the sound of waves crashing on the shore 20 ft. from your tent. Relatively popular; crowded during holidays. Facilities include trash cans, picnic tables, fire pits, concrete grills, surprisingly nice bathrooms, showers, and a water fountain. The only downside is that the area has virtually no shade. Parking $2 if you enter Tu-Su 8:30am-6pm. $10 per tent. ❶

THE SKY'S THE LIMIT

Vieques has several beautiful high-end guesthouses spread throughout the island.

🏠 **Hix Island House,** Rte. 995 Km 1.2 (☎741-2302; www.hixislandhouse.com). Hix Island House may be the most unique accommodation in Puerto Rico. 3 concrete buildings house breezy, luxurious suites that manage to be private in spite of the extreme open-concept design—some rooms have only 3 walls! Elegant and funky geometric structures include fully stocked kitchen with complimentary breakfast, homemade bread, semi-outdoor shower, and private terrace. Concrete pool fits ingeniously into the landscape. Free Wi-Fi. Doubles Nov. 20-Apr. 30 $235-295, min. stay 3 nights.; May 1-Nov. 19 $185-245, min. stay 2 nights. No children under 13. AmEx/MC/V. ❺

Hacienda Tamarindo, Rte. 996 Km 4.5 (☎741-8525; fax 741-3215; www.haciendatamarindo.com). Picture-perfect views and beautiful rooms make this one of Vieques's best small accommodations. Each room is adorned with themed murals and trinkets. Common library and lounge. Big pool. A/C and ceiling fans. American breakfast included. Reception 8am-6pm. Check-out 8:30-11am. Nov. 16-May 4 singles $165-215; doubles $175-285; 4-person apartment with kitchen $325. May 5-Nov. 15 $125-175/135-225/$275. Extra person $35. 10% service charge. No children under 8. AmEx/D/MC/V. ❺

Great Escape Bed & Breakfast Inn (☎741-2927; www.enchanted-isle.com/greatescape), on Rte. 201 between Rte. 995 and Rte. 996. Follow signs to the side road, then drive up it and turn right onto the dirt road after the pink concrete fence. Located on 3.8 acres of land in farm country, the Great Escape offers fresh air, tranquility, and great mountain views. The 10 rooms are nice, with high ceilings, fans, wrought-iron beds and private balconies. Pool. Continental breakfast included. Reserve well in advance. July-Oct. doubles $125; Nov.-July $115. Apartments $200-400. Extra person $25. Tax included. MC/V. ❹

🍴 FOOD

Keep your ATM card handy; with the food prices on Vieques as high as they are, you may be making frequent withdrawals. Several American expats have opened delicious but expensive restaurants. However, it is easy to find high-quality, filling eats for less money at one of the *comida criolla* joints in Isabel II. Groceries can be found at **Super Descuentos Morales,** Rte. 200 Km 1.3 (☎741-6701. Open M-Sa 6:30am-7pm, Su 6:30am-noon. MC/V.) and **Colmado El Molino,** C. Antonio G. Mellado 342 (☎741-0015. Open M-Sa 7am-11pm, Su 10am-11pm. AmEx/MC/V.) in Isabel II. In Esperanza, try **La Tienda Verde**, C. Robles 273, Rte. 996 (☎741-8711. Open daily 9am-9pm. MC/V.) or the centrally located **Colmado Lydia** on C. Almendro in Esperanza. (☎741-8678. Open M-Sa 7:30am-6pm, Su 7:30am-noon. MC/V.)

ISABEL II

■ **Shaunaa's Restaurant** (☎741-1434), on C. Antonio Mellado. Vieques's best *cafetería*. Extremely popular with locals throughout the week; crowded, so it'll be tough to find a seat inside. A budget traveler's dream. Huge lunch platters with a choice of meat, rice, plantains, and beans $6. Open M-F 10:30am-2pm. MC/V. ❶

■ **Scoops Ice Cream & Pizzeria**, C. Benítez Guzmán 53 (☎741-5555). Vieques's only ice cream parlor offers a tasty variety of flavors (1 scoop $3, 2 scoops $4.50). However, Scoops is possibly more famous among locals for its hot food: brick-oven pizza (big slice $2, full pizza $25-27) and hot gourmet sandwiches ($5-6). Down the short driveway on the left, club music spices up simple picnic table seating. Open daily 11am-11pm. MC/V. ❶

Panadería y Repostería Lydia (☎741-8679), at C. Plinio Peterson and Benítez Guzmán. No seating area inside, but there are 2 plastic tables out front. A great bargain. Simple sandwiches on delicious, freshly baked bread ($1.50-$2.50). Huge pastries $0.50-1, including the Puerto Rican pineapple-and-cheese danish. 1lb. fresh bread $1.25. Pastries served M-F. Open M-F 5am-2pm, Sa 5am-noon. Cash only. ❶

Roy's Coffee Lounge (☎741-0685), on C. Antonio G. Mellado, in the pink building. Bright paintings, masks, shells and funky lights adorn this cafe. Out back, wicker chairs and tables invite customers to lounge with Roy's iced coffee ($4.50) or a bagel ($1.75), or to borrow a book from the lounge's collection. Free Wi-Fi 1hr. max. Basic brews $1.75-4. Frozen coffee or fruit drinks $4.50. Sandwiches and wraps $5.50. Pastries $1.75-3.50. Open M-F 8am-2pm, Sa-Su 8am-noon. MC/V. ❶

El Patio Bar and Restaurant, C. Antonio G. Mellado 340 #01 (☎741-6381). At El Patio, you'll find a small, bright terrace and cheery yellow room with a daily-changing menu. Seafood, chicken, and meat entrees $6-16. Beer $1-2. Mixed drinks $2-3. Open M-F 6:30am-5pm, Sa 8am-4pm. AmEx/MC/V. ❷

La Taverna Española (☎741-1175), at the corner of C. Carlos LeBrun and C. Benítez Castaño. The decor is bland and the food overpriced at this Spanish restaurant, but the reason to come is the delicious sangria (glass $3, pitcher $12). Entrees $15-25. Open M-Sa 5-10pm. MC/V. ❹

Richard's Cafe (☎741-5242), on C. Antonio G. Mellado, at the intersection of Rte. 997 and Rte. 200. Popular with families. Standard Puerto Rican cuisine ($7-30) such as *pastelillo* turnovers ($3-9) and big burgers ($6-7). *Mofongo* $14-19. Open daily 11am-11pm. AmEx/MC/V. ❸

Wai Nam Seafood Restaurant, C. Plinio Peterson 571 (☎741-0622). Like any good Puerto Rico town, Isabel II must have the requisite Chinese/seafood/fried chicken restaurant, where all the entrees are served with french fries. However, this may be the only one with a great sea view. Chinese entrees $3-11. Open M-Th and Su 10am-9pm, F-Sa 10am-10pm. MC/V. ❷

ESPERANZA

■ **Duffy's**, C. Flamboyán 140 (☎741-7600). Johnny Cash and the Beatles greet guests from posters on the wall in this cool, open-air restaurant with bar island. All day long, locals and tourists eat large burgers ($10), sandwiches such as the Big Daddy Duffy piled high with salami and other meats ($12) and seafood salads ($13). Cool off with a Medalla ($2), margarita, or *parcharita* ($6). Open Tu-Su 11am-11pm. Bar open until midnight. MC/V. ❸

VIEQUES

PAZ PARA VIEQUES?

As far back as most *viequenses* can remember, islanders have clashed with the US government over the US Navy presence on the island. And even though the bombing range that formerly occupied two thirds of the island was closed in 2003, the controversy over land use continues.

The US began expropriating land on Vieques for naval training in the 1940s, and by 1949, the Navy controlled 72% of the island. In the early 1960s, US President John F. Kennedy proposed taking over the rest of Vieques and moving all of its residents to the mainland, but repercussions from the Cuban Revolution thwarted this plan. As early as 1964, locals spoke out against the Navy's plans for expansion, but the Navy argued that Vieques's combination of jungle and ocean environments made it an invaluable training site.

Protests continued throughout the 1980s, but in 1999 Vieques erupted. On April 19, two live bombs accidentally hit an observation post, killing resident patrol guard David Sanes Rodríguez. Vieques made international news as hundreds of Puerto Ricans camped out on Navy land, preventing military exercises from taking place. Between 1999 and 2003, over 1500 individuals were arrested on charges of civil disobedience in relation to the naval presence. Finally, the US Navy left the

Bananas, C. Flamboyán 142 (☎741-8700), at the guesthouse of the same name. A lively bar with TV attracts the crowds. ½ lb. burgers, sandwiches, and salads ($6-10) are a good deal. Beer $2. Frozen drinks $6-7. Occasional live music. M after 5pm Medalla $1. Restaurant open daily 11am-9:30pm. Bar open M-Th and Su until 1am, F-Sa until 2am. MC/V. ❷

La Dulce Esperanza (☎741-0085), on C. Almendro. Located just off the strip, but feels worlds away. One of the few affordable yet appetizing restaurants in Esperanza. Serves breakfast subs (6 in. $2-3; 12 in. $4-5.50), dinner pizza (slice $2-2.75; full pizza $11-15), calzones ($7-9), and pastries ($1) all day long. Take your food to go and catch a baseball game down the street. Open daily 7-11am and 5-9pm. Cash only. ❶

Trade Winds, C. Flamboyán 107 (☎741-8666). Soft music plays while you sit in a big wooden chair, gaze out over the water, and dine on some of the best food on the strip. Resort-type food with an island twist: chicken, bacon, and veggie wrap with passion fruit sauce $8.50. Breakfast $4.50-7. Lunch $6-14. Dinner $13-28. Open M and W-Su 8am-2pm and 6-9:30pm, Tu 6-9:30pm. AmEx/MC/V. ❸

Restaurante Bilí, C. Flamboyán 144 (☎741-1382). The friendly staff at Bilí invite passersby to lounge in bright orange chairs while enjoying upscale Puerto Rican cuisine in an airy sitting area. Delicacies include the mahi mahi with black bean papaya chutney ($20). Appetizers $8-12. Entrees $18-39. Open daily 10am-10pm. AmEx/MC/V. ❸

◎ SIGHTS

Unlike Culebra, Vieques does have a fair share of cultural sights. It's worth an afternoon of missed beach time to check out the island's major museums.

FUERTE DE CONDE DE MIRASOL. Vieques's most impressive sight was constructed between 1845 and 1855 as the last Spanish fort in the New World. Over the years it housed militia and served as a prison—most inmates were Puerto Rican separatists—and later as a United States seismographic station. In 1989 the Puerto Rican Institute of Culture restored the fort and installed a museum inside. The majority of the museum is devoted to standard displays of pre-Hispanic archaeological artifacts, histories of various European groups on Vieques, and tools used by early *viequenses*. In addition, the museum hosts exhibits of local and visiting artists, many of which focus on the US Navy presence. The criticism of the US often voiced in the Fuerte exhibitions is complicated by the fact that the US government partially funds the museum. The fort merits a visit for both its architecture and its well-thought-out displays. Although almost all of the signs are in Spanish only, bilingual tour guides are happy to show visitors around. *(Rte. 989 Km 0.5. Follow signs to the Fuerte neighborhood.* ☎ *741-1717; www.icp.gobierno.pr. Open W-Su 8:30am-4:20pm. $3, ages 12 and under and over 60 free.)*

FARO PUNTA MULAS. From the ferry, the view of the Punta Mulas lighthouse crowning the hill is quite stunning. From the lighthouse itself, it is no less so: the 360-degree views—the ocean on one side and mountains on the other, and Culebra in the distance—are about as good as it gets. The lighthouse was built by the Spaniards in 1895-96, but was partially destroyed when the Americans attacked; it was finally restored in 1992. *(On Calle A, uphill from the ferry dock. Closed for tours indefinitely.)*

MUSEO DE ESPERANZA. The Vieques Conservation and Historical Trust has established a small museum in Esperanza to display artifacts and educate the public about their work. The front area focuses primarily on Taíno artifacts recovered from the island (600BC-AD1492), artifacts from the era of Spanish conquest, and histories of the production and export of tobacco and coffee. Unfortunately, the exhibits are displayed in old, dark cases. A popular draw to the museum is the small **aquarium** in the back. The Trust collects animals from the waters surrounding Vieques then displays them in tanks for a few weeks before returning them to the sea and catching new ones. The workers sometimes even let visitors hold and touch the creatures. Previous displays have included starfish, sea urchins, lobsters, and frog fish, which are camouflaged to look like sponges. *(C. Flamboyán 138, Esperanza.* ☎ *741-8850 or 741-2844; www.vcht.com. Also has Internet for $3 per 30min. and a book exchange. Open Tu-Su 11am-4pm. Free.)*

📷 SHOPPING

Vieques does not share Culebra's wealth of yuppie boutiques, but there are a few good places to get some local art or a classy souvenir.

> **Diva's Closet,** C. Flamboyán 134 (☎741-7595; divasclosetpr@aol.com). This colorful boutique caters mostly to a hipster under-30 crowd. Mostly women's clothing, but some men's items. Also carries bathing suits, flip-flops, beach jewelry, and lotions. Open daily 10am-5pm. AmEx/MC/V.

western half of the island and turned the land over to the US Fish and Wildlife Service. But *viequenses* were not satisfied, and protests continued. On May 1, 2003, the Navy was forced to leave Vieques. A huge celebration ensued, but the problems were far from being resolved.

Viequenses are still not able to use and enjoy much of their land. About half of the 8,000 acres on the west end of Vieques is open to the public, and only about 10% of the 15,000 acres formerly controlled by the Navy on the eastern end of the island is accessible.

The rest of the land is still closed off due to the possibility that unexploded ordinance (UXO) is still buried there. The slogan, *"Paz Para Vieques"* (Peace for Vieques) is still visible on yard signs and bumper stickers. Among the populace, there is a bitter divide over what should be done with the former Navy land. Some want US government agencies to leave and turn over the land to the Puerto Rican government for preservation. Others argue that if the commonwealth government owns the land, it will not be as well preserved as if the federal government were in control. Still others believe that the land should be privatized for commercial development. The controversy surrounding the US government's presence on Vieques is largely a reflection of the eternal Puerto Rican question: how should this "Free Associated State" relate to the larger US?

Vieques Flowers & Gifts...Too!, C. Flamboyán 134 (☎ 741-4197), Esperanza. Manages to stuff a full flower shop and an array of locally made handicrafts into its small space. A great destination for Vieques souvenirs. Open daily 10am-4pm. AmEx/MC/V.

Kim's Cabin, C. Flamboyán 136 (☎ 741-3145), Esperanza. Sells men's and women's clothing mostly for older adults, as well as local art and high-quality jewelry. Open daily 9am-5pm. MC/V.

◪ BEACHES

Spectacular beaches ring the island of Vieques. The southern coast tends to be slightly more appealing than the north, but really, who's complaining? Major spots are listed below, but the best strategy is to take a map of the dirt roads and just start driving. Make sure you rent a truck or an SUV, as many roads are bumpy and require four-wheel drive. On the former Navy lands, especially on the eastern half of the island, just about any dirt road will take you to your own tiny private beach, so even if you make a wrong turn, you should still end up somewhere special.

BALNEARIO SUN BAY. At Vieques's only public beach, medium-sized waves of crystal clear water hit an enormous crescent of white sand lined with palm trees. On weekday mornings, you can have this sumptuous stretch of sand to yourself, although it is Vieques's most popular beach on weekends and holidays. Snorkelers may want to head to Navío, as the water is clearer there. Like most public *balnearios*, Sun Bay has picnic tables, fire pits, a huge parking area, a drinking fountain, trash cans, lifeguards, bathrooms, and a camping area. *(On Rte. 997, ¼ mi. east of Esperanza. ☎ 741-8198. Parking $2; minivans $3. Fee covers Balneario Sun Bay, Playa Media Luna, and Playa Navío. Open Tu-Su 8:30am-5pm; the gates are always open, but during these hours you have to pay to park and lifeguards patrol the beach.)*

PLAYA MEDIA LUNA. Located directly east of Sun Bay, Half Moon Beach is part of the *balneario* complex, but it is physically separated and feels worlds away. This quiet bay has soft waves and perfectly turquoise water that stays about waist deep for over 40 ft. out, making it a popular place for kids to play. The only facilities are trash cans and a couple of covered picnic tables. *(Enter the Sun Bay complex, then drive east on the dirt road for about ½ mi. 4WD required.)*

█ PLAYA NAVÍO. The third member of the Sun Bay *balneario* complex, Navío feels more secluded than its western neighbors. This small bay is less protected by cliffs and thus waves pound directly against the shore, creating large waves that are great for boogie boarders but dangerous for small children. Due to the its rough access roads, Navío is usually nearly deserted and feels like a private beach. This is the Sun Bay complex's best **snorkeling site,** due to the depth and clarity of the water. *(Continue ½ mi. past Playa Media Luna on the bumpy dirt road. 4WD required.)*

█ GREEN BEACH. Green Beach actually consists of a series of small, disconnected sandy areas running south from Punta Arenas. The gentle waves lap against the palm-lined beach, making for enjoyable swimming and picturesque sunsets. Mainland Puerto Rico is visible in the distance. The shallow-water reef at the south end of Green Beach is also home to some of the **best snorkeling** in Vieques. The trek through jungle-like forest to get out to the beach is half the fun. *(Take Rte. 200 west into the old Navy base, then continue onto the dirt road. Veer right at the fork, and cross 2 bridges. The road forms a T at the end—go left for snorkeling and right for Punta Arenas. Facilities include trash cans and 1 covered picnic table. 4WD required.)*

RED, BLUE, AND GARCÍA BEACHES. These three popular, incredibly beautiful beaches can be accessed on the former Navy lands. Red Beach, also known as "Playa Caracas," has the island's second-best **snorkeling**, which can be found by swimming out to the small island about 100 yd. offshore, on the right-hand side of the beach. Red Beach is very family friendly, offering gazebos, picnic tables, and portable toilets. All three have perfect white sands and bright blue waters, although Blue Beach, known in Spanish as "Bahía de la Chiva," is by far the largest and has some gazebos. *(Take Rte. 997 to the Camp García gate, then follow the dirt road east. 4WD is required for Blue and García Beaches, and is strongly recommended for Red Beach.)*

GRINGO BEACH. Located on the island's north shore between the airport and the Wyndham Martineau Bay resort, this aptly-named narrow stretch of sand provides a place to rest in the sun and take in the sea breeze and view, if you don't mind the sound of nearby traffic. Although it is nowhere near being the best beach on the island, the reason to visit is its accessibility—it is one of the few that can be reached via a paved road. *(Rte. 200 Km 3.8. Park on the side of the road.)*

PLAYA GRANDE. For a bit more privacy, head to Playa Grande. This long, narrow beach has coarse sand and no facilities, but offers a unique landscape, with several small inlets dotted with large boulders. This is the place to sit on a rock, watch the tide roll in, and let your mind drift. The water has big waves and gets deep quickly, making swimming difficult. *(Drive west on Rte. 996 past Esperanza to Rte. 201, continue to the end of the road, and turn left. Park in the circle of pavement.)*

🏔 OUTDOOR ACTIVITIES

BIOLUMINESCENT BAY

Nowhere on Puerto Rico does the water shine like it does in **Bahía Mosquito.** This large bay on the south coast of Vieques is the most impressive example of dinoflagellitic bioluminescence anywhere in the world. When you jump in the bay, it looks like you are radioactive; when you float, it looks as though you have thousands of glowing sprinkles all over your body. Local organizations and the U.S Department of Fish and Wildlife are working to preserve the bay's magic by reducing

THE BIG SPLURGE

SWIMMING IN STARDUST

It looks like naturally occurring radioactivity, a fluorescent blue-green glow around one's body. To some, it looks like underwater fire. Others say it shimmers like fairy dust. The visual effects of swimming in Vieques's bioluminescent bay may be difficult to describe, but for many travelers, this experience is the main reason for visiting the island of Vieques. Of the three bioluminescent bays in Puerto Rico, Mosquito Bay is the least polluted, and as such has the strongest and most beautiful glow.

The bioluminescence is caused by microscopic marine plankton called dinoflagellates; there are an estimated 720,000 organisms per gallon of bay water. The plankton are supported by the mangrove trees surrounding the bay. These deposit large quantites of B-12, a major dinoflagellate nutrient, in the water. When the dinoflagellates sense a predator (or in this case, a human body) in the water, they light up to warn their companions of the danger. As result, swimmers moving through the water look as though they are leaving a trail of glowing fire behind them.

Several companies operate bioluminescent bay tours in Vieques. **Abe's Snorkeling and Bio Bay Tours** *and* **Blue Caribe Kayak** *are known to the be the best for kayak adventures. All tours close with a 30min swim and cost $30 for a 2hr. trip.*

A SIGNATURE AMPHIBIAN

Throughout the Puerto Rican outdoors, you are likely to hear the sound of a singsong "ko-kee" daily from dusk to dawn, resonating from the bulging throats of male frogs across the island. This is the mating call of the Coquí, a type of frog that is native to Puerto Rico and has come to be a widely recognized cultural symbol.

The song begins every day at dusk, continuing through the night and increasing in volume with rainfall. The first syllable, "co," reaches 1160 Hz and serves to scare off nearby males. The second syllable, "quí," reaches 2090 Hz and is an invitation to females to breed. You will likely hear this sound most vividly from June through November, as mating season is concentrated during the wet season.

Puertorriqueños use the name Coquí in reference to more than 16 species of this small frog. The amphibians range greatly in size and color, from 15-80mm and green to yellow, and are sometimes multicolored or striped. Also of note, the Coquí frog cannot swim, and therefore is not born as a tadpole. Instead, fertilized eggs develop inside the female; once deposited, they must be kept dry for 17-26 days. The male watches over the eggs, and protects the babies once they have hatched. What gallant gentlemen this land has raised!

artificial light pollution and educating locals about the bay's value, but Mosquito Bay continues to be threatened. **Barracuda Bay,** the next inlet to the east, is also bioluminescent, but most tours don't head out that far. The Department has issued a restriction on trips to the **Bio Bay,** stating that only official tour groups can swim in the bay; this limits traffic to a handful of tours every evening. It is a good idea to call ahead to reserve spaces in the tour of your choice, as the companies below can become swamped during high season.

Abe's (☎741-2134 or 436-2686; www.abessnorkeling.com). Abe has received glowing reviews for his 2hr. Night BioBay kayaking tour ($30). Also available are daytime tours to Cayo Afuera (adults $45, children under 12 $18) and Mosquito Pier (adults $30, children under 12 $15) for snorkeling. Open daily 8am-8pm. Cash only.

Island Adventures, Rte. 996 Km 4.5 (☎741-0720; www.biobay.com), at corner of driveway for Hacienda Tamarindo. Run by the Bio Bay Conservation Group, Island Adventures leads 1½-2hr. tours through the bio bay. First, groups listen to an informative talk, then they take a bus to the bay for the electric boat tour and swimming. Trips almost every night, except during a full moon. Call ahead for reservations. Adults $32, under 12 $16. Tax included. MC/V.

Blue Caribe Kayaks, C. Flamboyán 149 (☎741-2522), in Esperanza. Offers 2hr. kayak tours of the bioluminescent bay, with a chance to swim ($30). Also leads and 2½hr. kayaking and snorkeling trips around Cayo Afuera ($35). Single kayak rental $10 per hr., $55 per day; double kayaks $15 per day. Also rents bikes ($5 per hr., $13 per day), fishing poles ($12 per day) and boogie boards ($5 per day). Open daily 9am-5pm. MC/V.

Aqua Frenzy Kayaks (☎741-0913) rents double kayaks ($15 for the 1st hr., $10 per hr. thereafter; $45 per day). Allows renters to take the kayaks overnight, and provides information about kayaking in the bio bay. Also offers bio bay tours ($30 per person) and 3hr. snorkeling tours ($45 per person). Kayak drop-off available. MC/V.

BOATING

The specialty at **Marauder Sailing Charters** is a full-day sail on a 34 ft. yacht, with swimming and snorkeling in reefs only accessible by boat, and a BBQ lunch with open bar (☎435-4858. $100 per person. Open 10am-3pm. Cash only.)

DIVING AND SNORKELING

Like Culebra and Fajardo, the area around Vieques is flush with good, relatively shallow diving opportunities. However, the island does not have a scuba shop, so you can only dive here with a charter from the mainland. Vieques also has some great snorkeling, but the best areas are accessible only by boat. The best place to snorkel from land is **Green Beach** (p. 182), followed closely by **Red Beach's Mosquito Pier** (p. 183). At Red Beach, good snorkeling can be found under the pier and the four pylons júst off to the side. In **Esperanza,** the small dock in front of Playa Esperanza attracts a few fish. **Cayo Afuera,** the island in front of the strip, has good reefs, but it's quite a swim.

HORSEBACK RIDING

Penny Miller's daughter at **El Seagate** (p. 176) leads horseback rides through the mountains, the beach, and Isabel II. (☎741-4661 or 667-2805. Reservations requested. 2hr. ride $65 per person, group rates available. MC/V.)

🗼 🌺 NIGHTLIFE AND FESTIVALS

Vieques may be a major tourist area, but its nightlife scene is laid-back and oriented toward an older crowd. The island of Vieques celebrates two annual festivals. The weekend after Easter, the Institute of Puerto Rican Culture hosts a **cultural festival** at the fort with local artwork and music (☎741-1717). Vieques's **festivales patronales** are celebrated during the third weekend in July in the Sun Bay area. Contact the tourist office (☎741-0800) for exact dates.

Al's Mar Azul, C. Plinio Peterson 577 (☎741-3400), in Isabel II. Some tourists and all the local characters stop by daily to shoot pool and hang out on the wooden patio overlooking the water. Dare to try the Coquí hot sauce ("sweat factor 10") and don't miss the annual **Spam Cook-Off,** held in May. This one-of-a-kind celebration features competitions for best entree, appetizer, and sculpture, and at the end everyone eats the winning entries. Pool tables. Beer $1.50-3.25. Mixed drinks $3-7. Sa karaoke 10pm-1am. 18+ after 9pm and to use pool tables. Happy hour daily 5-7pm. Open M, W-Th, Su 11am-1am, F-Sa 11am-2:30am. MC/V.

Restaurante Bilí, C. Flamboyán 144 (☎741-1382), located along the Malecón or "the strip" in Esperanza. The specialty martini ($8) are the reason to come. Beer $2-3. Frozen drinks $5-6. Open M and W-Su 11am-5pm and 6-11pm. AmEx/MC/V.

CULEBRA

If you came to Puerto Rico in search of a picture-perfect beach, look no further than Culebra. The island easily has the most beautiful beaches in Puerto Rico, and thanks to its crystalline water, it is also home to several superb snorkeling spots. What makes this prime tourist destination unique is the small-town charm it has retained. With just over 2000 inhabitants, this is an island where neighbors stop to chat with each other and the ferry arrival is the big event of the day. Because nearly everyone is employed in the tourist industry, Culebrans are friendly to travelers: from helping change a flat tire to reminding you to wear sunscreen, they go out of their way to make sure you enjoy their island. Tiny Culebra has few cultural attractions, and the dry vegetation is more like that of the Virgin Islands than tropical eastern Puerto Rico, but the beaches alone are reason enough to visit.

Culebra has not always been such a haven of tranquility. In 1901, two years after winning the Spanish-American war, the US government established military bases on Culebra, forcing residents to resettle in the area now known as Dewey. In 1975, after years of using the island as a bombing range, the military moved all exercises to Vieques, but Americans continued to flock to Culebra. The island now houses a significant expat population, composed mostly of Americans who came on vacation and never left. During holidays such as Christmas and *Semana Santa*, the island's population can increase by as much as 15,000, as Puerto Ricans head east on their own vacations. In recent years, some locals have complained that a younger generation more interested in rowdy beach antics than peace and quiet has discovered Culebra. But for the majority of the year—and anywhere outside of the road between the ferry landing and Playa Flamenco—Culebra continues at the slow pace to which it is accustomed, where nobody has anything to do but go to the beach.

HIGHLIGHTS OF CULEBRA

ESCAPE THE CROWDS with an adventurous hike down to the wild waves at isolated **Playa Resaca** (p. 196).

JOIN THE CROWDS at stunning **Playa Flamenco** (p. 194).

DIVE IN at one of Puerto Rico's best snorkeling sites, **Playa Carlos Rosario** (p. 195).

TAKE A RIDE to the cays of **Isla Peña** or **Culebrita,** with their pristine beaches and prime snorkeling (p. 195).

INTER-ISLAND TRANSPORTATION

Flights: Aeropuerto Benjamín Rivera Noriega (☎ 742-0022), 21 mi. north of town at the intersection of Rte. 250 and Rte. 251. A 15min. walk or a $2 taxi ride. All of the airlines flying out of Culebra use tiny 6- to 8-seat planes and leave on demand. For reservations call or stop by the airport at least 1-2 days in advance. During major holidays reserve a few weeks in advance. Open daily 6am-6pm.

Air Flamenco (☎ 742-1040, reservations 724-6464) flies to **Fajardo** (15min.; 4-5 per day; $30, round-trip $60) and **San Juan Isla Grande** (30min.; 4 per day; $55, round-trip $110). Open daily 6am-6pm. AmEx/MC/V.

Isla Nena (☎ 742-0972 or 863-4447) flies to **Fajardo** (15min.; 1-2 per day; $30, round-trip $60) and **San Juan International** (35min.; 4 per day; $92, round-trip $172). Open daily 6am-6pm. MC/V.

CULEBRA

Vieques Air Link (☎742-0254, reservations 888-901-9247) flies to **Fajardo** (15min.; 3 per day; $28, round-trip $54) and **San Juan Isla Grande** (30min.; 2 per day; $54, round-trip $98). Open M-Sa 6am-6pm. AmEx/MC/V.

Ferries: The **Puerto Rican Port Authority** (☎742-3161 or 800-981-2005) runs ferries between Culebra and Fajardo. In addition to the routes below, a passenger ferry goes between Culebra and Vieques (W only; leaves Vieques 7:30am and 2:30pm, returns from Culebra 9am and 3:30pm; round-trip $4). There is an additional charge for beach equipment, including tents ($2) and sleeping bags ($1). Reservations are required for cars, but are not accepted for passengers. Car reservations should be made at least 3 weeks in advance to secure one of the few spots. Passengers should arrive 1hr. in advance. Reservation office open daily 8-11am and 1-3pm. Ticket window open daily 7:30-11:30am, 12:30-4pm. MC/V.

FERRIES	FAJARDO-CULEBRA	CULEBRA-FAJARDO	PRICE
PASSENGER	M-Su 9am, 3, 7pm	M-Su 6:30am, 1, 5pm	$2.25
CARGO	M, Tu, Th 4am and 4pm W and F 4, 9:30am, 4pm	M, Tu, Th 7am and 6pm W and F 7am, 1, 6pm	$15; round-trip $27

◾ ORIENTATION

Culebra lies 17 mi. east of the port of Fajardo on the east coast of Puerto Rico and 12 mi. west of St. Thomas in the Virgin Islands. Measuring 7 mi. in length and 3 mi. in width, the island is tiny, and seems even smaller because almost all its attractions are concentrated on the eastern side. The ferry arrives at the only town, **Dewey,** which is located on the southwest corner. From Dewey, **Route 251** heads north past the airport to Playa Flamenco. **Route 250** goes east, past Fish and Wildlife and the turn-offs for Playa Resaca and Brava, before finally ending up at Playa Zoni. The only other real road, **Calle Fulladoza,** heads south from town along Ensenada Honda to Punta Soldado. When people refer to Dewey's "main road" or "calle principal," they are usually talking about **Calle Pedro Márquez,** which originates at the ferry terminal and continues through town. **Calle Escudero** connects the airport with Dewey and is home to several accommodations and restaurants.

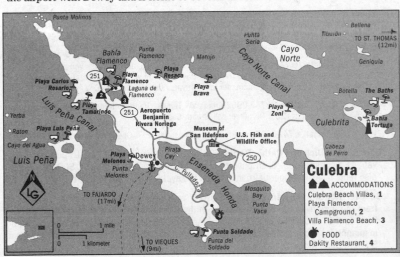

Culebra

▲▲ ACCOMMODATIONS
Culebra Beach Villas, 1
Playa Flamenco
Campground, 2
Villa Flamenco Beach, 3

● FOOD
Dakity Restaurant, 4

▣ LOCAL TRANSPORTATION

Culebra's diminutive size makes it very easy to get around. Travelers staying in Dewey or Playa Flamenco can get by using only public transportation, but will be relatively stranded after dark. Those who want to explore the island and get to a beach other than Flamenco or Carlos Rosario should rent a Jeep. Don't bring a rental car to Culebra, as transporting cars over the ferry is difficult and the island terrain is tough on most vehicles without four-wheel drive; instead, rent one when you arrive. Driving a scooter can be fun in the greater Dewey area, but a Jeep or SUV is necessary to brave the potholes on roads leading to beaches beyond Playa Flamenco. In theory, biking seems like a good option, but the combination of hilly roads and the hot afternoon sun can tire even the most athletic travelers.

CAR TROUBLE. Culebra police are extraordinarily vigilant about parking violations. Do not park in front of a fire hydrant, along a yellow curb, in a handicapped area, in a public vehicle spot, or along any curve in the road. Also, many streets are one-way or only allow parking on one side of the street, but are not marked as such.

Públicos: Carros públicos, or shared taxi vans, run from the ferry terminal past the airport to **Playa Flamenco,** stopping at **Culebra Beach Villa.** Any trip between these points should cost $2-3. For an additional fee, vans will go almost anywhere on the island. During the day it is easy to hail down a *público* along Rte. 251. At night, or from a different location, try one of these: **Kiko's Transportation Services** (☎514-0453), **Willy's Taxi** (☎742-3537), **Rubén Taxi** (☎405-1209), **José** (☎363-2183), or **Luis** (☎223-3428).

Car Rental: Several companies rent Jeeps and other off-road vehicles, but during major holidays you should reserve at least 1 month in advance. Most companies require drivers to be at least 25, but some do not rigidly enforce this requirement. The age and condition of vehicles varies greatly; the condition of the car should be reflected in the rental price. Almost all companies offer airport and ferry pickup service and weekly discounts.

Carlos Jeep Rental (☎742-3514 or 613-7049, at airport 742-1111; www.carlosjeeprental.com), on Rte. 250 at Vacation Property Realty. One of Culebra's more professional operations. $60 per day. Insurance $6 per day. Also rents infant car seats ($5 per day). Discount for weekly rentals $5 per day. 25+. Pickup and dropoff available. Open M-Th and Su 7am-6:30pm, F-Sa 7am-9pm. AmEx/MC/V.

Jerry's Jeep Rental (☎742-0587), on Rte. 251 across from the airport. When you pick up the Jeep, Jerry explains a map of Culebra. $45-50 per day. Discount with weekly rental $5 per day. 25+. Open daily 8am-5pm; arrangements for later arrivals possible. AmEx/MC/V.

Dick and Cathie Rentals (☎742-0062), rents VW Things. Standard transmission only. No pickup service. $45 per day. 25+. No office; call ahead. Cash only.

Willy's Jeep Rental (☎742-3537), on Rte. 250. $45 per day. 25+. Open daily 8am-5pm. AmEx/MC/V.

Bike Rental: Dick and Cathie Rentals (☎742-0062), delivers bikes. $15 per day. Reservations recommended. Cash only. **Club Seabourne** (☎742-3169 or 1-800-981-4435), also rents bikes ($15 per day), in addition to kayaks and beach furniture. MC/V.

Scooter Rental: JM Rentals (☎742-0521; www.scooterspr.com), on Rte. 251 across from the airport, in the same office as Thrifty Car Rental. 150cc scooters $10 per hr., 9am-5pm $25, $45 per day; 2 helmets included. 7th day free. Liability coverage $6; no insurance for scooter. Ages 21+. Pickup and dropoff service. Open M-Sa 8:30am-6pm, Su 9am-5pm. AmEx/D/MC/V.

⁊ PRACTICAL INFORMATION

Tourist Office: The **municipal tourist office** is a small desk on the semi-outdoor patio of the big building that you see immediately when you get off the ferry. Has standard Puerto Rico tourism booklets. Open M-F 8am-4:30pm, but frequently unattended. Culebra also has several very good tourism websites: www.culebra-island.com, www.islaculebra.com, and www.culebra.org.

Bank: Banco Popular (☎ 742-3572), across from the ferry terminal at the corner of C. Pedro Márquez, is the only bank on the island. **ATM.** Open M-F 8:30am-3:30pm.

Publications: The Culebra Calendar (www.theculebracalendaronline.com), an invaluable monthly island publication, lists local events, advertisements, a tide table, a ferry schedule, classified ads, letters to the editors, and articles on current Culebra issues.

Laundry: There are no laundromats on Culebra, but **Dick and Cathie Rentals** (☎ 742-0062) provides wash, dry, and fold service ($1.25 per lb.). Call ahead. Cash only.

Police: ☎ 742-3501. On C. Fulladoza, about ¼ mi. past Dinghy Dock. Open 24hr.

Pharmacy: Culebra has no real pharmacies. The **hospital** (below) has a pharmacy with prescription drugs only. **Superette Mayra** (see **Food,** p. 192) has a decent selection of over-the-counter remedies, such as Dramamine, for the ferry ride. Bring your own tampons, contact lens supplies, condoms, and any other hard-to-find supplies.

Medical Services: Hospital de Culebra (hospital and ambulance service ☎ 742-3511 or 742-0001) at the end of C. William Font, in the building marked "recetas" (prescriptions) at the top of the hill. Small health clinic. Small pharmacy open M-F 8am-4pm. Emergency room 24hr. Clinic open M-F 8am-4pm.

Internet Access: eXcétera, (☎ 742-0844; fax 742-0826), on C. Escudero between Culebra Gift Shop and the corner with C. Pedro Márquez, offers Internet ($5 per 15min., $15 per hr.), **fax service,** a long-distance telephone station, **Western Union,** and a 24hr. **ATM.** Open M-F 9am-5pm, Sa 9am-1pm. D/MC/V.

Post Office: C. Pedro Márquez 26 (☎ 742-3862). General Delivery available. Open M-F 8am-4:30pm, Sa 8am-noon. **Postal Code:** 00775.

⋔ ⋔ ACCOMMODATIONS AND CAMPING

Culebra may host a plethora of visitors, but most of its accommodations are either lackluster or severely overpriced. An attractive room here will cost at least $90 per night, and summer offers little relief from high prices. Most accommodations offer discounts for stays over a week or during low season (Aug.-Oct.). Add a 7% realty tax to quotes.

REALTORS

The following realtors rent properties equipped with linens, towels, and a kitchen. Check out the houses online, then call for rates and availability.

▧ **Vacation Planners** (☎ 742-3112, toll-free 866-285-3272; www.allvacationreservations.com), across from the ferry under Hotel Kokomo. Most properties have A/C, and some have TVs. Free pickup. $40-500 per night. 15% discount for week-long stays. Open daily 9am-1pm, 4-6pm, and 7:30-9pm. MC/V.

Culebra Island Realty (☎ 742-0052; www.culebraislandrealty.com), at the intersection of C. Romero and Escudero. Rents a wide range of homes and assists in car rental. Free pickup. Min. stay 1 week. 2- to 8-person homes $900-4500 per week. 50% deposit required. Business conducted primarily over the phone; leave a message. Checks only.

LIKE A BIRD

You could take the ferry from Fajardo to Vieques or Culebra for a meager $2. But shelling out for a 10min. plane ride between island and mainland is well worth the $20 splurge. Instead of spending an hour rocking back and forth on a boat, you can fly over the most beautiful part of the Caribbean, looking down on the dozens of tiny cays and perfect turquoise water. Planes fly low enough that you can clearly see the landscape below, down to the individual trees on tiny islands.

The ride is spectacular from any seat, but the secret to the best flight is to request the copilot's seat. The companies that run these 6- to 10-passenger planes sometimes allow one person to sit up front, next to the pilot. This vantage point opens up a breathtaking 270-degree view for lucky passengers, who are encouraged to take pictures as they fly.

Flights head out to the offshore islands on **Vieques Air Link** (☎888-901-9247) and **Isla Nena** (☎877-812-5144). One-way tickets run $20-30 and should be reserved ahead of time, although single passengers can often find last-minute spots, even during holiday weekends. Keep in mind that since the planes are quite small, passengers are routinely asked to state their weight upon boarding and are limited to 25 lb. of luggage. Enjoy the ride!

DEWEY

Villa Boheme, C. Fulladoza 368 (☎742-3508 or 370-4949; www.villaboheme.com), has bright, beautiful grounds, several cheery orange buildings, and a common patio area with elegant patio furniture and several hammocks, all right on Ensenada Honda Bay. Rooms are very colorful, with a fun aquatic theme. Fully equipped communal kitchen with cable TV and outdoor BBQ area. Rooms for 4 or more people have fridge or kitchen. Check-in noon. Check-out 10:30am. Min. stay 2 nights on weekends; 3 nights on holiday weekends. Doubles $95; quads $130-135; 6-person rooms $135. AmEx/MC/V. ●

Villa Fulladoza (☎742-3576 or 742-3828), on C. Fulladoza. A combination of low prices and large rooms makes this waterside guesthouse a good deal. Sparkling, brightly colored rooms come with a kitchen, fan, balcony, and ocean view. Spacious common patio filled with mango trees. Private dock. Book exchange. Check-in 2:30pm. Check-out 10am. $10 surcharge for 1-night stay. Doubles $65-80; $420-525 per week. Extra child (in larger rooms only) $10. MC/V. ●

Mamacita's, C. Castelar 64-66 (☎742-0090; www.mamacitaspr.com). Feels like a fun European hostel painted in tropical Caribbean colors. Restaurant below by the same name, though with different ownership, is a popular place at all hours of the day. All rooms come with microwave, fridge, A/C, TV, and DVD player. Check-in 2pm. Check-out 11am. Nov.-June doubles $103; 2-person suites with kitchen $114; 4-person suites $149, with kitchen $179. Prices lower Sept.-Oct. Extra person $15. MC/V. ●

Palmetto Guest House, C. Manuel Vásquez 128 (☎742-0257; www.palmettoculebra.com), in a residential neighborhood a 10min. walk from town. Only 1 block from the airport, 5 newly remodeled rooms come with fridge and A/C. Common kitchen, living room, TV, and DVD collection. Call ahead. Free pickup and dropoff. $20 surcharge for 1-night stay. Doubles Nov. 23-Apr. 30 $95 and $115; May 1-Sept. 3 $90/$110; Sept. 5-Nov. 22 $85/$105. MC/V. ●

Casita Linda (☎742-0360 or 403-5292; www.culebra-sanjuan.com), in the brightly colored house on the right after you cross the bridge. This small 3-room guesthouse was clearly a labor of love. The friendly owners have hand-decorated every room with flowers and unique furniture. All rooms have a full kitchen, a balcony or patio with canal views, a TV, and VCR with videos. No reception office; call ahead. Quad $100; 6-person suite $150; 8-person house $250. Tax included. MC/V. ●

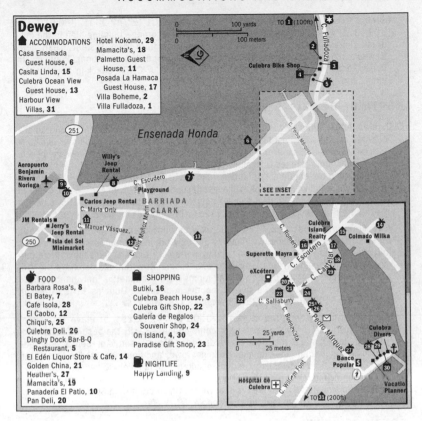

Dewey

▲ ACCOMMODATIONS

Casa Ensenada
  Guest House, **6**
Casita Linda, **15**
Culebra Ocean View
  Guest House, **13**
Harbour View
  Villas, **31**

Hotel Kokomo, **29**
Mamacita's, **18**
Palmetto Guest
  House, **11**
Posada La Hamaca
  Guest House, **17**
Villa Boheme, **2**
Villa Fulladoza, **1**

Ensenada Honda

■ FOOD

Barbara Rosa's, **8**
El Batey, **7**
Cafe Isola, **28**
El Caobo, **12**
Chiqui's, **25**
Culebra Deli, **26**
Dinghy Dock Bar-B-Q
  Restaurant, **5**
El Edén Liquor Store & Cafe, **14**
Golden China, **21**
Heather's, **27**
Mamacita's, **19**
Panadería El Patio, **10**
Pan Deli, **20**

🛍 SHOPPING

Butiki, **16**
Culebra Beach House, **3**
Culebra Gift Shop, **22**
Galería de Regalos
  Souvenir Shop, **24**
On Island, **4, 30**
Paradise Gift Shop, **23**

🍹 NIGHTLIFE

Happy Landing, **9**

Posada La Hamaca Guest House, C. Castalar 68 (☎742-3516 or 435-0028; www.posada.com). Small guesthouse rooms are standard, with a recent paint touch-up. A/C and ceiling fans. Book exchange. Snorkel gear $10 per 24hr. Free use of beach towels. Check-in 2pm. Check-out 10am. Doubles $92-97; quads $112-146; 8-person room $190. Extra person $11. Tax included. MC/V. ❹

Hotel Kokomo (☎742-3112 or 866-285-3272; www.allvacationreservations.com), across from the ferry dock. The great location and clean rooms with A/C make this hotel a good value, though some rooms crave new paint and blinds. Suites on the top floor are huge and have great ocean views and full kitchens. Office is in Vacation Planners (p. 189). Check-out 11am. Doubles $43, with bath $65; triples $76-87; 4- to 6-person apartments with kitchen $125-150. MC/V. ❷

Harbour View Villas (☎742-3855 or 742-3171; www.culebrahotel.com), 1½ mi. west of town en route to Playa Melones. Look for the "Bienvenidos" sign and the 3 rustic A-frame houses on the hill. Quiet location with great views, but far from beaches. 1- and 2-bedroom suites have A/C in the bedroom and some sort of kitchen and hot water. Villas are houses with kitchens, but no A/C. No office. Free pickup and dropoff. Suites: doubles in winter $125, in summer $100-125; quads $175/150. Villas: doubles $175/125-150; quads $225/175. Extra person $25/20. Cash only. ❹

Culebra Ocean View Guest House, C. María Ortíz 201 (☎742-2601, 360-9807, or 309-4301; www.culebra-ocean-view.com), a simple orange building high in the hills above Dewey. About a 20min. walk or 5min. drive from town. Distant ocean view. New furnishings spruce up otherwise standard budget accommodations. Popular with Puerto Rican vacationers. Common balcony. Fridge, A/C, TV. Check-in 1pm. Check-out 11am. Doubles $84-99; quads $134. MC/V. ❸

NORTH OF DEWEY

■ **Culebra Beach Villas** (☎754-6236 or 767-7575; www.culebrabeachrental.com), on the dirt road off Rte. 251, just before Playa Flamenco. This is the only hotel and villa complex on the beautiful sands of Playa Flamenco. A 3-story wooden hotel faces the beach, and several boldly painted bungalows hide in back. This is the place to be at Playa Flamenco, with a bar out front and barbecues in the back. All rooms are clean and include A/C, TV, and a full kitchen. Book exchange. Reception 10am-1pm and 2-7pm. Check-in 3pm. Check-out 11am. In main building doubles $125, 4-person room $195, 6-person $215 or 225, 8-person $300. In villas $125/175/300. Tax included. MC/V. ❹

Villa Flamenco Beach (☎742-0023; www.culebra-island.com). Villa Flamenco Beach, next to Culebra Beach Villas, is the only other accommodation that boasts direct access to Playa Flamenco. With only 6 rooms, Flamenco feels much more personal than its neighbor. Neat and functional rooms. Airy front studios have big windows, balconies, and an ocean view. All rooms have kitchenettes; only doubles have A/C. Communal grill. Reserve several months in advance. Doubles $140; 4-person apartments $190, 6-person $250, 8-person $328. MC/V. ❺

Playa Flamenco Campground (☎742-0700 or 742-3525), at Playa Flamenco. Located just 20 ft. from the beach, this campground is easily the best in Puerto Rico. Unfortunately, it's also the most crowded; during high season (Apr.-Sept.), hundreds of people squeeze into the big field. It can get rowdy and liquor-oriented in Area C, but Areas A and E tend to be quieter and more suitable for families. Toilets, outdoor showers, a bike rack, trash cans, and picnic tables. Reservations recommended during high season. Cancellations up to 5 days in advance. Office open 6am-6pm. Check-in 8am. Check-out 4pm. $20 per tent; up to 6 people. MC/V. ❶

SOUTH OF DEWEY

Quiet C. Fulladoza receives little traffic, and the accommodations on the hill offer tranquility and beautiful bay views. Unfortunately, there are no sandy beaches and it's quite a walk to town; if you're staying here, it's a good idea to rent a car.

■ **Bahía Marina Condo-Resort,** Punta Soldado Road Km 2.4 (742-0535 or 1-866-285-3272; www.bahiamarina.net), on a secluded inlet with gorgeous view of greenery and sparkling water. Very reasonable group prices, beautiful views, and endless amenities give this new resort strong appeal. 2 pools, wading pool and hot tub. 1-bedroom and 2-bathroom suites with fully equipped kitchen, ocean view balcony or patio. All rooms have A/C, cable TV, and free Wi-Fi. Wheelchair-accessible. Doubles weekdays $139, weekends $179; quad $179/205. MC/V. ❺

☕ FOOD

Food in Culebra tends to be expensive. Luckily, many accommodations offer kitchen facilities; it's more affordable to cook at home. **Superette Mayra,** C. Escudero 118, is Culebra's largest grocery store and has a good selection of over-the-counter pharmaceuticals. (☎742-3888. Open M-Sa 9am-1:30pm, 3:30-6:30pm. MC/V.) **Colmado Milka,** C. Escudero, Barrio Sardinas 2, across the bridge and to the right, is Culebra's second-largest grocery store and has a small butcher shop and fresh fruits and vegetables. (☎742-2253. Open M-Sa 7am-7pm, Su 7am-1pm. MC/V.) To reach **Isla del Sol Minimarket,** located on a side street off Rte. 251, turn left immediately after Jerry's Jeep Rental and follow the signs. The market has a small selection of groceries and fresh hot bread. (☎742-0886. Open M-Sa 7am-7pm, Su 8am-5pm. MC/V.)

DEWEY

■ **Mamacita's,** C. Castelar 66 (☎742-0322). Hands-down the most popular dinner destination and nightspot in Dewey, Mamacita's is located just around the corner from the ferry dock's main street. Covered patio seating right on the channel, under the guest house by the same name. Breakfasts include sandwiches ($3-5) and omelets ($5-7), and lunches feature burgers and fajitas ($7-9). However, the main draw is the relatively upscale dining that offers large, delicious daily seafood specials ($15-19). The patio bar rouses dancers with live conga drums on Sa nights from 9pm on. Open daily 8am-3pm and 6-9pm. MC/V. ❸

■ **Dinghy Dock Bar-B-Q Restaurant** (☎742-0233), on C. Fulladoza. Dinghies actually dock beside your table as you enjoy tasty Puerto Rican, American, and Mexican food at this relaxed and colorful local favorite. Big breakfasts $5-10. Sandwiches, grill items, and Mexican entrees $5-25. Seafood dinners $14-30. Open daily 8am-2:30pm and 6:30-9:30pm. Bar open daily 8am-midnight. MC/V. ❸

El Edén Liquor Store and Deli Cafe (☎742-0509). Turn left on the gravel drive just beyond Colmado Milka and follow the signs. This sit-down cafe with gourmet breads and sandwiches is concealed in a very simple, unassuming building removed from the road. Construct your own sandwich ($6.50-7) by choosing from various meats, breads, cheeses, and toppings, or devour a large plate of homemade lasagna (vegetarian $9.50, meat $12). All sandwiches are on fresh homemade bread, and scrumptious desserts are also homemade ($2.50-4.50). Also a deli and liquor store. Open M-Sa 7am-7pm, Su 7am-2pm. MC/V. ❷

Heather's (☎742-3175), on C. Pedro Márquez. It's difficult to walk past Heather's in the evening; if the smell doesn't draw you in, the rowdy crowd will. Indulge in an extra big pizza ($10 medium is really a large; toppings $1.50-2) or go for a sandwich ($7) or pasta ($8) instead. Maybe even join the locals for a beer ($1.75-3). Open M and Th-Su 6-10pm; may stay open later F-Sa. Kitchen closes 9:30pm. Cash only. ❷

Barbara Rosa's, C. Escudero 189 (☎742-0773). Chef Barbara Rosa's restaurant has the perfect budget dining formula: a relaxed vibe, counter service (no tip), and BYOB. The wooden cabin with patio is removed from the highway and serves up simple but delicious entrees such as vegetarian spaghetti ($7), shark nuggets ($9) and calamari in red wine sauce ($13). Gets buggy at night. Lunch entrees $6-12. Dinner $7-16. Open Nov.-Apr. Tu-Sa 11:30am-9:30pm; May-Oct. M and Th-Su 5-9:30pm. Cash only. ❸

Pan Deli, C. Pedro Márquez 17 (☎742-0296). Centrally located on Dewey's main street, this bakery sells fresh food at very affordable prices. A new local favorite for delicious breakfasts including traditional *mallorca* sweet buns, pancakes, eggs, ham and toast ($1.25-4), sandwiches ($3-6), and salads ($3-5). Lattes $1. Open M-Sa 5:30am-5pm, Su 6:30am-5pm. AmEx/MC/V. ❶

Chiqui's, C. Pedro Márquez 30 near the post office. The only store in Dewey devoted to iced delights. 1-topping sundaes are ludicrously cheap ($1.35). *Batidas* and "Black Cow" milkshakes $3.75. Also serves *piraguas* (flavored shaved ice; $1), nachos ($2), and packaged snacks. Open daily approximately 11am-10pm. Cash only. ❶

El Batey, Rte. 250 Km 1.1 (☎742-3828), ½ mi. north of town, next to Parque de Pelota. Choose between a dim, aquatic-themed wood interior and a patio with harbor view from across the road. Casino games, music and pool tables give this popular local bar a relaxed feel. Appetizers $5-5.50. Meaty sandwiches $5.50-7.50. Burgers $6-6.50. Dinner $9-17. Open daily 11am-11pm. Cash only. ❸

Dakity Restaurant (☎ 742-0535). Drive south on C. Fulladoza; near the end, turn left up the steep hill. One of the nicer places on the island but has a surprisingly relaxed, cottage-like atmosphere in a wooden loft above the Shipwreck Bar & Grill. Incredible views of the entire island. Wi-Fi at bar patio. Lunch $10-12. Seafood $17-26. Steak, pork, and chicken entrees $16-19. Open daily 12:30-3pm and 6:30-9:30pm. MC/V. ❹

Panadería El Patio (☎ 742-0374), at the end of the airport runway. A typical Puerto Rican sandwich counter in a convenience store. The restaurant has an outdoor seating area, but the sandwiches ($3-4) taste even better as a beach picnic. Serves sandwiches until 11:30am. Shop open daily 5:30am-7pm. Cash only. ❶

El Caobo (☎ 742-0505 and 409-0872), on C. Luis Muñoz Marín in the residential neighborhood adjacent to the airport. Rustic charm, complete with handwritten menu and big plates of genuine Puerto Rican food; however, more expensive than the casual atmosphere might suggest. Entrees $9-20. Open M-Sa 4-10pm. Cash only. ❸

Golden China (☎ 742-0060), C. Pedro Márquez 16. A large seating area where patrons enjoy inexpensive Chinese food with *mofongo*. Also serves seafood ($7-8) and meat ($5-8) entrees, *mofongo* ($7.50), and ice cream ($1.50). Open daily 11am-10pm. Cash only. ❷

◢ BEACHES

The water around the island is a translucent aqua that looks unmistakably Caribbean and invites swimmers to float in the sun for hours. While popular Playa Flamenco is amazing, it is worthwhile to venture out to other, less populated beaches, especially if you have access to a car, preferably one with four-wheel drive. Regardless of where you travel, don't search for palm-tree-lined beaches. Culebra has a very dry landscape and there are only a few scattered palms; shade-lovers should grab a spot early.

BEACHES	ACCESSIBILITY FROM DEWEY	CROWDS	ACTIVITIES	FACILITIES
Flamenco	8min. drive	Large	Swimming, snorkeling, boogie boarding	Bathrooms, picnic tables, trash cans, outdoor showers, grills, lifeguards
Carlos Rosario	25min. walk from Flamenco	Medium	Swimming, snorkeling	None
Culebrita	25min. boat ride	Small-Med.	Swimming, snorkeling, turtle-watching	None
Luis Peña	15min. boat ride	Small-Med.	Swimming, snorkeling,	None
Zoni	15min. drive	Small-Med.	Swimming, boogie boarding	None
Brava	15min. drive plus 20min. hike	Small	Boogie boarding, tutle-watching	None
Resaca	15min. drive plus 30min. hike	Small	Boogie boarding, turtle watching	None
Punta Soldado	15min. drive	Small-Med.	Snorkeling	None
Melones	15min. walk	Medium	Swimming	Trash cans

▧ **PLAYA FLAMENCO.** In comparison to this exquisite beach, every *balneario* on mainland Puerto Rico looks like a dirty swimming pool. Numerous media outlets, including the Travel Channel, have listed Flamenco among the best beaches in the world—with good reason. Playa Flamenco is Culebra's largest, most popular, and most accessible beach. It is also the only beach on the island with facilities, including lifeguards (on duty 9am-5:30pm), bathrooms, showers, picnic tables, a campground, and a selection of kiosks offering typical beach fare. Because of these amenities, and because Flamenco looks like it was created to be on a postcard, the beach can get crowded, especially on holidays when thousands of Puerto Ricans descend from the mainland. Luckily Flamenco is huge and there's more than enough room for everyone. Near the parking lot, there is a tourist information kiosk (open daily 10am-2pm) that distributes copious amounts of literature. (☎ 742-0700. *Drive north on Rte. 251 until the road ends. A público from Dewey costs $2-3. Públicos line up at a special stand in the parking lot, so it should not be difficult to catch one going back to Dewey. Tourist office at entrance to parking.)*

 SWIM WITH THE FISHES. Many locals claim that Flamenco Beach offers more than picture-perfect sands to the adventure-hungry explorer: For good **snorkeling,** swim out from the right end of the beach to visit a gorgeous reef nicknamed "Shark's Teeth," or kick out from the waters at the brightly painted old army tanks on the left end to see a wide variety of tropical fishes.

■ **PLAYA CARLOS ROSARIO.** Culebra's premier snorkeling beach requires a bit of effort to reach, and therefore tends to have far smaller crowds than Flamenco. The crescent-shaped beach has coral on the right and boulders on the left, a sandy passageway in the center, and the clearest ocean water you've ever seen. Enter the water in the middle, then swim about 15-30 ft. in either direction to find amazing schools of blue tang, sergeant majors, and the occasional barracuda. Don't forget to bring water and a snack, as Carlos Rosario has no facilities. *(From the back left corner gate of the Playa Flamenco parking lot, walk 25min. on the dirt path over the hill. Carlos Rosario is the second beach; Playa Tamarindo, a popular kayakers' gateway to Luis Peña, is the first.)*

■ **CULEBRITA.** If you're looking for a deserted island, and Culebra doesn't quite do the trick, continue east to the tiny island of Culebrita. With adequate hiking, gorgeous beaches, and a lighthouse, Culebra's little sister easily merits a day of exploration. Most water taxis drop passengers at the pier on the west side of the island. This beach has great **snorkeling,** best done in the numerous tide pools and in the coral reefs that surround much of the island. Continue along the marked trail for 10min. to reach **Bahía Tortuga,** the biggest and best beach on Culebrita. Few people make it out here during the week, so it's not uncommon to share the brilliant waters only with the other people on your boat. Culebrita is a protected wildlife refuge and popular turtle breeding ground. From the pier, a different trail leads 15-20min. uphill to the lighthouse. This relic of the Spanish occupation was condemned in 2003, but conservation groups are working to have it restored. The peninsula on northeast Culebrita known as **The Baths** also has some great snorkeling, although the water can sometimes be a bit rough as it crashes against the rocks. Culebrita is worth the transportation costs, but avoid the little island on weekends and holidays, when it turns into a zoo of private boats. *(From Dewey, water taxis, p. 198, take 25min. to reach Culebrita and cost $40. No facilities.)*

■ **LUIS PEÑA.** For yet another quasi-deserted Caribbean beach with white sand, blue water, and lots of fish, head out to Luis Peña, a short water taxi ride from Dewey. On weekdays, the long, narrow beaches surrounding the island are almost always empty and the water is as calm as a lake. The snorkeling is superb all the way around the little island, especially in the channel facing Culebra. The best beach is Luis Peña beach, located on the north side of the island. Like Culebrita, Luis Peña is a designated wildlife refuge, and there are several marked nature walks on the island. *(15min. from Dewey or a short kayak ride from Playa Tamarindo. Tanamá, p. 198, charges $35. No facilities.)*

■ **PLAYA ZONI.** Not many people make it out to the eastern side of the island, but those who do will be rewarded with acres of undeveloped land at Culebra's second-most-popular swimming beach, Playa Zoni. It seems impossible, but the water here tends to be an even more impressive aquamarine than the water at Flamenco. The waves are a bit bigger, too, making for some excellent boogie boarding. There are no facilities, and crowds are generally rather small. The long, narrow, sandy beach is lined with palm trees and affords views of numerous tiny cays, the Culebrita lighthouse and, in the distance, St. Thomas. *(Take Rte. 250 all the way east to the end: At fork after Hacienda de los Sueños, bear right on narrow, steep road. No signs for beach. Continue straight to the small parking lot.)*

PLAYA BRAVA AND PLAYA RESACA. It's just you and the turtles at these two bays on Culebra's northern coast. Visitors rarely make the long, hot trek out to these secluded beaches, but those who do will be rewarded with long stretches of beautiful tan sand and azure water. Both Brava and Resaca have strong waves that create conditions bad for swimming but decent for surfing and boogie boarding. There are reefs on both sides of Resaca's bay, but the water is generally much too rough to snorkel. From March to August, leatherback turtles lay their eggs on Resaca and Brava, as you will see from the numerous marked turtle nesting sites; never stay at these beaches after dark and if you see tracks during the day, try not to disturb them. *(To reach Playa Brava drive east on Rte. 250, past the cemetery on the left, continue uphill and turn left on the road just after the red-roofed, stone house engraved with "1905." Park at the end of the pavement, then follow the dirt road for 20min. Turn right at the fork. To reach Playa Resaca, drive east on Rte. 250 and turn left on the road directly after the airport. Drive to the top, stopping at the landing just before the radio tower. Follow the narrow trail through the brush and mangroves for 30min. until you reach the beach. Call Fish and Wildlife ☎ 742-0115 before attempting the difficult hike; if it hasn't been marked recently, you may get lost.)*

PUNTA SOLDADO. Located on the southern tip of Culebra, the coral beach at Punta Soldado has excellent snorkeling; the best site is on the left-hand side of the beach, but reefs line the entire shore. Many adventurers also enjoy night diving here. However, if you just want to lie on the sand, it's best that you go elsewhere, as the beach is covered with rocks and coral. *(Drive all the way down C. Fulladoza, and down the dirt road until the end.)*

PLAYA MELONES. Melones's claim to fame is that it is the most easily accessible beach from Dewey. The rocky, coral-laden location on the Luis Peña Channel makes for decent snorkeling, but the water is not as clear as it is on Carlos Rosario. There are few shady areas and no facilities, so come prepared with lots of sunblock. The best snorkeling is on the right side of the beach. Swim all the way north, past the peninsula, and you'll end up at Playa Tamarindo, another good snorkeling beach and the kayakers' gateway to Luis Peña. *(From town, walk uphill past the tourist office, veer left, and continue walking for 15min. Melones is the second beach at the end of the road.)*

👁 🌼 SIGHTS AND FESTIVALS

Apart from the condemned lighthouse on Culebrita, Culebra does not have many sights. However, the Culebra Foundation has been working to preserve the island's history by renovating abandoned buildings and promoting island culture. The first fruit of this project is the **Museum of San Ildefonso,** Rte. 250 Km 4, just behind the DRNA office. Located in a 1905 US Navy magazine, the museum contains historical pictures and some pre-Taíno artifacts. The Foundation plans to add an art museum and more historical markers. (In the building with the "1905" sign, next to the water. Open daily M-F 8am-noon and 1-3pm, Sa-Su on request. Free.) Culebra does not celebrate *fiestas patronales*, but Dewey hosts a large **artisans festival** every year over a weekend in late July. For information contact the tourist office (☎ 742-3116, ext. 441 or 442).

🔟 OUTDOOR ACTIVITIES

Ocean Safari Kayaks (☎ 379-1973), rents single kayaks for $30 per day (until 5:30pm) and tandem kayaks for $60, including a free lesson; $75 for 3 people. Most people go from Playa Tamarindo to Luis Peña. Free pickup and delivery.

Club Seabourne (☎ 742-3169 or 800-981-4435; www.clubseabourne.com), on State Road No. 252, rents beach equipment at steep prices. Tandem kayaks ($20 per hr., $30 per 3hr., $40 per day). Snorkel and mask $13 for adults, $11 for children. Also rents beach chairs and umbrellas ($5 each). MC/V.

DIVING AND SNORKELING
Over 50 attractive dive sights surround Culebra and its cays. Conditions here are very similar to those in Fajardo, with visibility around 30-60 ft. and plenty of shallow dives for beginners, making this a great place to get certified. Many beaches around Culebra have amazing snorkeling (see **Beaches,** p. 194).

Culebra Divers, C. Pedro Márquez 4 (☎ 742-0803; www.culebradivers.com), across from the ferry terminal, has two 26 ft. boats that make dive trips in the morning (1-tank dive $60, 2-tank dive $85, equipment rental $15) and 3hr. snorkel trips in the afternoon ($45, children ages 6-12 $30; min. 2 people). 1-tank night dive $70. 1-dive first-time instruction package $95. 3hr. week-long NAUI Scuba Diver certification $575. All trips include beverages. Snorkel rental $13 for 1st day, $10 for each additional day. During high season reserve up to 1 month in advance. High season open daily 9am-noon and 2-5.30pm, low season call for hours. MC/V.

HIKING
While most of Culebra's land is privately held, the US Fish & Wildlife Service protects over 1500 acres of the island, including all of the off-shore cays (except Cayo Norte), the majority of the Flamenco Peninsula, a large section of land around Playa Resaca, and all of the wetlands and mangroves. The trail down to Playa Resaca (see p. 196) is more than just a beach path; this intense 30min. hike descends Culebra's tallest hill. You must crawl over boulders and claw your way through a mangrove grove before reaching the beach. The trail to Playa Brava is also quite an adventure, although it is somewhat less strenuous. Another path leads across Culebrita from the boat landing to Bahía Tortuga. The friendly staff at the US Fish and Wildlife Service is happy to answer questions about hikes, beaches, or the turtle-watching program. (Drive east on Rte. 250 and look for the sign just after the cemetery. ☎ 742-0115; www.fws.gov. Open M-F 7am-4:30pm.)

SURFING
Culebra's surf can't compete with the mainland's northern coast, but if you have your own board there are a few waves to be found. It's best to hit the beach from May to July, the beginning of hurricane season, when heavier winds create larger waves. Locals recommend **Brava, Resaca, Carlos Rosario, Punta Soldado,** and **Zoni** as some of the best surfing beaches. Almost all of the beaches along the northern coast occasionally have big waves that are great for boogie boarding.

CULEBRA

WATER TAXIS

Small motor boats take visitors on daytrips primarily to Luis Peña and Culebrita, but also to other parts of Culebra. All certified boat captains charge $35 round-trip to Luis Peña and $45 to Culebrita. Trips do not leave every day; call ahead.

Tanamá (☎501-0011). Culebra's only glass-bottom boat. Tanamá does a 2-3hr. harbor cruise ($40), a ½ mi. cruise over the reefs ($25), a 3-4 hr. snorkeling trip ($50; equipment not included), and other trips upon request. Also sails to Culebrita ($55) and Luis Peña ($35). Typically leaves from Dinghy Dock. Cash only.

Culebra Water Taxi (☎360-9807). 1hr. tour of the bay $20. Full-day trip (10am-3:30pm) to Dakity with BBQ lunch $59. Also drops off at Culebrita ($45) and Luis Peña ($35). MC/V.

🛍 SHOPPING

Over the past few years Culebra has experienced an influx of little shops full of assorted gifts and gadgets.

Butiki (☎708-935-2542 or 708-267-7284; www.butikiculebra.com), on C. Romero, next to Superette Mayra. Colorful handicrafts and local art, jewelry, high-quality clothing and excellent photography, paintings, and prints made by the owner. Also a wide selection of women's islandwear. Open M and Th-Su 9am-1pm and 3-6pm.

On Island, C. Pedro Márquez 4 (☎742-0439), at the ferry landing; 2nd location at C. Fulladoza 372 (☎742-0704). The typical mix of tchotchkes and jewelry at the C. Pedro Márquez location, but higher quality islandwear, linens, and artwork at the store on Calle Fulladoza. Oceanfront store open daily 10am-1:30pm and 3-5:30pm. Fulladoza store open daily 11am-7pm. MC/V.

Paradise Gift Shop, C. Sallisburry 110 (☎742-3569), has an excellent selection of locally made items, from artwork to clothing. Open M-Tu and Th-Su 9am-6pm. MC/V.

Culebra Gift Shop (☎742-0566), on C. Escudero near the corner with C. Sallisburry, sells the usual mix of clothes, Culebra-themed knick-knacks, and local art. The biggest souvenir shop on the island sets itself apart with general store products including meats, fish fillets, and ice cream. Open daily 9am-6pm. AmEx/D/MC/V.

Galería de Regalos Souvenir Shop (☎742-2294), on C. Pedro Márquez, has a small room with Culebra T-shirts, some women's clothing and men's beachwear, and a larger room full of souvenirs. The only souvenir shop on the main road, so it's often packed. Open M-F 9:30am-5pm and Sa-Su 9am-5:30pm. AmEx/MC/V.

Culebra Beach House, C. Fulladoza 372 (☎742-0602). Sells island-themed houseware, beach gear, and toys. Rents beach chairs, umbrellas, and coolers ($6 per day, $5 for multiple days, $30 per week). Open M and Th-Su 9:30am-5:30pm. MC/V.

🎵 NIGHTLIFE

Don't come to Culebra specifically for its nightlife. On weeknights the loudest sound is the song of crickets, and even on weekends, most of the more popular bars double as restaurants during the day and are shut down by 11pm. During summer weekends and holidays, the biggest party may be at Flamenco's campground.

■ **Mamacita's,** C. Castelar 64-66 (☎742-0090). On weekend nights Mamacita's is hugely popular with foreigners and young locals. The trendy tropical bar is straight out of a travel brochure. Come on F when a DJ mixes from 8:30pm-11pm and Sa when conga drummers shake the place up (9-11pm). House mixed drinks include the Iguana Colada ($6). Beer $2.50-3. 18+. Happy hour daily 3-6pm. Open M-Th and Su 8am-10pm, F-Sa 8am-11pm. MC/V.

El Batey, Rte. 250 Km 1.1 (☎ 742-3828). A 5min. walk from town, next to Parque de Pelota, this is the only place on the island to bust a move—or stay out past 11pm. This local favorite dominates the nightlife scene with a large dance floor and cheap beer. But don't expect glamour and glitz; the walls are decorated with giant fake fish. Beer $1.50-2. Mixed drinks from $3. Open daily 11am-11pm. Club open F-Sa 10pm-2am. Cash only.

El Patio (☎ 724-0374), at the end of the airport runway next to small parking lot. Panadería El Patio opens bar at night and hosts Karaoke nightly from 8pm-1:30am. A popular post-dinner destination for locals and the crowd of tourists that befriends them. Beer $1.75-2.25. Mixed drinks from $3.50. Cash only.

Heather's (☎ 742-3175), on C. Pedro Márquez. A long bar dominates the front of this popular pizzeria (p. 193). Join the locals and watch TV with a bottle of Medalla or chat with the friendly bartenders. Beer $1.50-3. Mixed drinks $3-7. Open M, Th, Su 6-10pm; F-Sa 6-11pm. Cash only.

Happy Landing, at the end of the airport strip. When even El Batey gets too touristy, there's always Happy Landing, Culebra's own dive. Local men gather here all day long. Just about the one place on Culebra you'll hear only Spanish. Jukebox, electronic slot machines, and 2 pool tables. Beer $2-3. Mixed drinks $3-4. Open daily 8am-midnight. Cash only.

SOUTHEAST

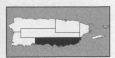

In southeast Puerto Rico, the mountains abruptly give way to miles of flat land that reach all the way to the ocean; this was once sugar country, and years of crops transformed the landscape from dry forest to empty plains. After sugar stopped being profitable, the region turned to manufacturing, building the horde of factories that lines Rte. 3. Though this is officially the Caribbean, beaches are generally better on the northern, Atlantic coast. West of Patillas, palm-tree-lined beaches with tiny waves make for postcard-perfect sunsets, but are not great for swimming or sunning—the exceptions are found along Rte. 901. For a really good beach, you'll have to take a trip to Isla Caja de Muertos, off Ponce, or travel farther west. Ponce is the undisputed capital—and star—of southern Puerto Rico. Its 19th-century architecture, rich history, and myriad museums make a trip over the mountains worthwhile. However, apart from this "Pearl of the South," southeast Puerto Rico does not have much to attract tourists looking for a prescribed Caribbean vacation. But, maybe that's just the reason to come. On this coast, you can escape the congestion of San Juan in the tree-lined thoroughfares of Naguabo, soak in the hot springs of Coamo, and visit turn-of-the-century sugar mansions outside Ponce.

HIGHLIGHTS OF SOUTHEAST PUERTO RICO

TRY OUT TURN-OF-THE-CENTURY LIFE at the spectacular museums, houses, and sights in dignified **Ponce** (p. 201).

BECOME A BEACH BUM at any one of the many idyllic accommodations along **Route 901** (p. 221).

WASH AWAY YOUR WORRIES in the hot springs of **Coamo** (p. 216).

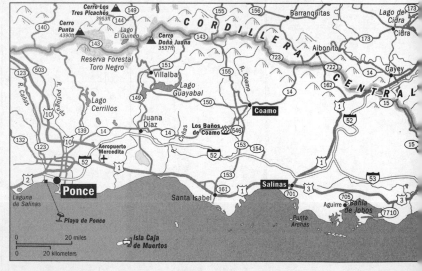

PONCE

Elegant, proud, and steeped in tradition, Ponce is one of the most attractive cities in Puerto Rico. In many ways the city still lives in the 19th century: ornate buildings line the streets, and locals seem to have a sense of hospitality from a different era. Ponce first found fame in 1511, when the city's namesake, Juan Ponce de León, finally defeated the Taínos there. Far from the Spanish government in San Juan, the city thrived as a port for contraband goods. But in the early 1700s, *ponceños* transferred their resources into more legitimate business ventures and the city became an exporter of tobacco, coffee, and rum. By the mid-19th century, Ponce had the largest concentration of sugar cane on the island. When sugar diminished in importance, the city began producing other goods, including metals and textiles. Throughout their early history, *ponceños* remained fiercely independent—when the Americans took over in 1898, Ponce still had its own currency.

The city hit its peak at the turn of the century and by 1950, Ponce was in need of revitalization. Most of the big factories created by Operation Bootstrap (see **Let the Good Times Roll,** p. 58) landed in the north, while Ponce continued to subsist on cement and textiles—not exactly quick money-makers. Fortunately, the government's second goal within the Operation was to provide substantial government investment in tourism. Since the 1950s, Ponce has gradually become a cultural center: this is Old San Juan minus the tourist kitsch, plus a couple of suburban comforts. The municipal government and the Institute of Culture maintain several good museums, and nearby Hacienda Buena Vista and Tibes Indigenous Ceremonial Park are among the most interesting historical sites on the island. However, the heart of the city continues to be its charming plaza; standing on a balcony overlooking the busy city center can give you an overwhelming sense that you've traveled back to Ponce's glory days.

✈ INTERCITY TRANSPORTATION

Flights: Aeropuerto Mercedita (☎848-2822), 4 mi. east of town. From the plaza take Rte. 1 (C. Cristina) east to Rte. 5506. Hwy. 52 also passes by the airport. A taxi from the city center runs $12-15 during the day and up to $20 midnight-6am. Only 1 airline

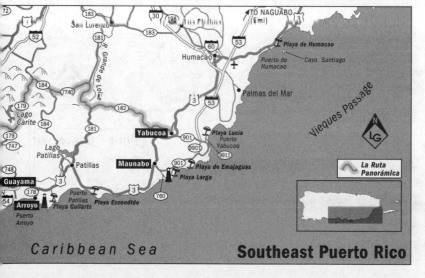

Southeast Puerto Rico

flies out of Ponce: **Cape Air** (☎844-2020 or 253-1121) goes to Aeropuerto Luis Muñoz Marín in **San Juan** (25min.; 3 per day; $100, round-trip $160). Open daily 6am-7pm.

Públicos: Ponce's *público* terminal is 3 blocks north of the plaza at C. Unión and C. Vives. More popular routes run approximately 6am-5pm. *Públicos* head to: **Adjuntas** (45min., $2); **Centro Ceremonial Indígena Tibes** (15min., $6); **Coamo** (30min., $2.50); **Guayama** (1hr., $5); **Mayagüez** (1hr., $6); **Playa Ponce** (5min., $1.10); **Salinas** (45min., $3); **San Germán** (45min., $5); **Utuado** (1½hr., $5); **Yauco** (25min., $2.75). 2 companies go to Río Piedras, **San Juan** (45min.-2hr., $15), including **Línea Don Q** (☎842-1222 or 764-0540) and **Línea Universitaria** (☎844-6010, 844-6010, or 765-1634). If given advanced notice, these companies can pick you up or drop you off at the San Juan airport in Carolina.

Car Rental: Several car rental companies operate out of the airport. All prices are for the smallest compact cars available. Some of the cheapest are listed below.

Dollar Rent-A-Car, Rte. 2 Ponce Bypass (☎843-6970 or 843-6940), between Wendy's and Baskin Robbins. $30 per day, with insurance $47-89. 21+. Under-25 surcharge $10 per day. Open M-Sa 4am-5pm. AmEx/D/MC/V.

Payless Car Rental, Av. Hostos 1124 (☎842-9393), on Rte. 10 between Av. las Américas and Rte. 2. $40 per day, with insurance $46. 21+. Under-25 surcharge $5 per day. Open M-F 7:30am-6pm, Sa 8am-5pm. AmEx/D/MC/V.

Thrifty (☎290-2525), in the airport. $35 per day, with insurance $50. 21+. Under-25 surcharge $7 per day. Open daily 4am-5pm. AmEx/D/MC/V.

ORIENTATION

Don't be intimidated by Ponce's size; the city is rather easy to navigate once you get your bearings. The vast majority of sights cluster around the compact city center and **Plaza las Delicias,** making it feasible to get around on foot or by public transportation. Rte. 1, 10, and 14 lead toward the city center. Just south of the center, **Route 163 (Avenida las Américas)** is a large tree-lined street that is also a convenient landmark. **Highway 2,** also referred to as the **Ponce Bypass,** originates just east of the city, skirts around the edges, and continues toward the western half of the island. Hwy. 52 avoids the center entirely and deposits travelers on Rte. 2, west of the city. Rte. 12 connects the city center to the **port** area, the boardwalk, and the beach. *Ponceños* do their shopping at the malls along Rte. 1 and Rte. 2.

LOCAL TRANSPORTATION

Taxis: Ponce Taxi (☎840-0088 or 842-3370), on C. Méndez Vigo, just south of C. Villa. Open daily 6am-midnight. **Coop Taxi del Sur,** C. Concordia 8130 (☎848-8248 or 848-8249), has cabs at its office and at the intersection of C. Estrella and C. Salud. Open daily 4am-midnight. **Victory Taxi** waits on C. Vives at the intersection with C. Atocha. Open daily 6am-6pm. Most taxis charge $1 plus $0.10 for each third of a mile; min. $3.

Trolleys and Trains: The city of Ponce operates a **tourist trolley** that takes visitors from the plaza to various sites around the city. The route takes about 1½hr., depending on demand and traffic. The route includes the Pancho Coímbre Museum, the Plaza Juan Ponce de León, Pantheon Nacional Román Baldorioty de Castro, Museum of Arts of Ponce, Museum of Puerto Rican Music, Museum of History of Ponce, and the Plaza las Delicias. $2, over 60 $1, under 2 free. Another option, the **Train of Ponce,** departs in front of City Hall from 10am to 4pm on the hour. $2.

Parking: A free municipal lot is located under Parque Dora Colón Clavell. The entrance is on C. Concordia between C. Jobos and C. Ferrocarril; the exit is on C. Marina. Another is found in the "José Dapena Lugo" building in the Paseo Miguel Apou.

PRACTICAL INFORMATION

Tourist Offices: The **municipal tourist office** (☎284-3338 or 284-4141, ext. 2245; www.visitponce.com), is located in the red and black Museo Parque de Bombas in the central Plaza las Delicias on C. Cristina, across from the entrance to Hotel Meliá. The booth is manned by a very friendly, English-speaking team that distributes maps and brochures and answers questions. A **tourist information computer terminal** allows users to select sights and museums from its menu to learn about their history and hours (in Spanish and English). The Tourist Transportation Center, which manages the tourist trolleys, trains, and walking tours is also located here. Open daily 8am-5:15pm.

Tours: Walking tours leave the Museo Parque de Bombas at 9:30, 10:30am, and from 1-4pm on the hour. Tours last 1hr. and stop at 34 sites along the way. $2. Additional information for these services is available in the municipal tourist office.

Camping Permits: DRNA (☎844-4660 or 999-2200, ext. 5158), on the 2nd fl. of the building across from Pier 5, near the turn-off to La Guancha. Look for the only multi-story building, called the Ponce Nautic Center. Provides camping permits ($4, children 10 and under $2). Open M-F 7:30am-midnight, 1-4pm.

Banks: Numerous banks line Plaza las Delicias. **Banco Popular,** C. Marina 9205 (☎843-8000), has an **ATM** on Paseo Arias to the left of the bank. Open M-F 8am-4pm.

Publications: *La Perla del Sur,* Ponce's largest newspaper, comes out every W and can be found at the tourist office in Museo Parque de Bombas or online at www.periodicolaperla.com. Free.

Police: State police, Av. Hostos 1242 (☎284-4040). **Municipal police,** at Rte. 10 and Av. las Américas (☎848-7090). Open 24hr.

Pharmacy: Walgreens, Rte. 2 Km 225 (☎812-5978), west of Ponce, just past the intersection with Rte. 2R. Open 24hr. AmEx/D/MC/V.

Hospital: Hospital Dr. Pila (☎848-5600, emergency room ext. 3127 or 3124), on Av. las Américas, across from the police station. Emergency room open 24hr.

Internet Access: Free Wi-Fi throughout Plaza las Delicias. **Archivo Municipal,** C. Marina 9215 (☎843-1422), on Pl. Las Delicias next to Banco Santander, has free Internet access. No games or chat rooms. Open M-F Aug. 8-May 8am-4:30pm; and June-July 8am-8pm.

Post Office: C. Atocha 93 (☎842-2997). General Delivery. Open M-F 7:30am-4:30pm, Sa 7:30am-noon. **Postal Code:** 00717.

ACCOMMODATIONS

The only reason to pass up the convenient location and cheap rates of the plaza hotels, which are nicely positioned for sightseeing, is to take advantage of the El Tuque recreation complex.

■ **Casa del Sol,** C. Unión 97 (☎812-2995; www.thecasadelsol.com). Budget travelers as well as those who simply enjoy the intimate guesthouse experience will surely jump to stay at the surprisingly inexpensive Casa del Sol, conveniently located just 1½ blocks from the Plaza las Delicias. This converted traditional house exudes character, from its lush, sunny back patio to its black iron chandeliers and intricately tiled walls. 9 double rooms with A/C and satellite TV are uniquely decorated with a touch of modern class that brings current style to old architecture. Small breakfast included. Free Wi-Fi. Full bar with complimentary discount for guests. Doubles $65. MC/V. ❸

■ **Hotel Bélgica,** C. Villa 122C (☎/fax 844-3255; www.hotelbelgica.com), is an amazing deal just off the plaza. Founded in 1872 and featuring tall ceilings, high green doors, and balcony access in rooms with charming views of the historic district, this hotel brings Ponce's old-world charm (and prices) to today's travelers. Bright rooms have A/C, TV, and modern bathrooms. Continental breakfast served on sunny small balcony. Check-out noon. Doubles $65-75; quads $75. MC/V. ❸

■ **Fox Delicias Hotel,** C. Isabel 6963 (☎290-5050; www.foxdeliciashotel.com), on the plaza. With an incredible location, a beautiful mosaic facade, an in-house restaurant, room service, valet parking, and even a beauty salon, the Fox Delicias has all the trappings of a fine resort at reasonable rates. Rooms, while somewhat dimly lit, are large and immaculate, with hardwood furniture, A/C, and cable TV. Free Wi-Fi in lobby. Check-in 3pm. Check-out noon. Doubles $69-105; quads $115-124. Extra person $20; children under 10 $10. AmEx/MC/V. ❸

Hotel Meliá, C. Cristina 75 (☎842-0260 or 800-448-8355; fax 841-3602; www.hotelmeliapr.com). Like most of Ponce, Hotel Meliá has a keen sense of its own history—it opened in 1915 and is still under family management, even sporting its own coat of arms. Beautiful high-ceilinged lobby and 2nd-fl. outdoor hallways overlooking the Plaza las Delicias. Rooms have cable TV with HBO, A/C, and telephone. Free Internet in business center. Continental breakfast on rooftop patio included. Singles $95; doubles $105-130. AmEx/MC/V. ❹

Hotel El Tuque, Ponce Bypass 3330 (☎290-2000; www.eltuque.com), at Rte. 2 Km 220.1. This racecar-themed, chain-style hotel is part of the El Tuque entertainment complex (see **Sights,** p. 208). During the winter this is a relatively peaceful retreat away from the city, but in summer the place fills up with families headed to the water park. Cable TV, A/C, free broadband Internet connection, and telephone. Large, clean rooms. Lively courtyard with pool, hammock pavilion, and poolside restaurant. Continental breakfast included. Check-in 3pm. Check-out noon. Doubles May-Aug. $99; $65 M-Th, and Su $65, F-Sa $85. Extra person $10; ages 3-12 $5. AmEx/MC/V. ❹

Ocean View Hotel, Rte. 2 Km 218.7 (☎844-9207), is far from downtown, but inexpensive and right on the ocean. The rooms, though a bit small and dim, are surprisingly full of amenities: A/C and cable TV. Most rooms have stove and sink and those rooms in back have ocean views. Tiny pool and small access area to ocean. Singles, doubles and triples $60. MC/V. ❷

◘ FOOD

Groceries and basic supplies can be found at **Pueblo,** Rte. 2 Ponce Bypass, in Plaza del Caribe. (☎840-4095. Western Union. Open M-Sa 6am-midnight, Su 11am-5pm. Cash only.)

▧ **El Bohío,** Rte. 2R #627 (☎844-7825), near the intersection with C. Villa. *Comida criolla* goes gourmet at this excellent restaurant. Laid-back, local atmosphere. The "Pechuga Bohío" is a favorite: baked chicken stuffed with ham, cheese, and red bell peppers in mushroom sauce. Every good meal can be topped off with a homemade flan ($2.75) made with tropical flavors such as guava and coconut. Entrees $6-27. Open M-F 11:30am-9pm, Sa-Su noon-10pm. AmEx/D/MC/V. ❸

▧ **La Guarina Bakery,** (☎840-7601), at C. Muñoz Rivera and Hwy. 2 Ponce Bypass. Come for breakfast ($2-2.75), stay for lunch (sandwiches $2.25-5) or stay out all night! This citywide favorite is just about the only eatery open at all hours in Ponce. La Guarina's bravest customers try the namesake sandwich, piled high with lettuce, tomato, and any meat from the kitchen—ham, chicken, pastrami, turkey, beer, shrimp, or octopus ("La Guarina"; $7.50). Coffee $0.45. Delicious pastries $0.50-1.50. Open 24hr. MC/V. ❶

Pizza's Heaven, C. Concordia 8023 (☎844-0448; fax 844-3836). Slightly off the beaten track, this casual restaurant and steak house was founded in 1958 and today is one of the best Italian eateries in town. Tasty, cheesy personal pizzas $4-5.50. Vegetarian lasagna $9. Entrees $9-19. Open Tu-Th and Su 11am-10pm, F-Sa 11am-11pm. AmEx/MC/V. ❸

Rincón Argentino, C. Salud 69 (☎840-3768 or 409-7818), on the corner of C. Isabel. Where the locals go for a romantic night out. Diners choose between the intimate interior and the softly lit, relaxed outdoor patio. Carefully prepared meat, seafood, and pasta options are delicious, and the artistically presented desserts are well worth the splurge. Entrees $11-40. Wine $5. Open M W and Su noon-10pm, Th noon-11pm, F-Sa noon-midnight. MC/V. ❸

Café Paris, C. Isabel (☎840-1010), on the plaza, is remarkably hip considering that it's half of a jewelry store. Indulge in a rich chocolate drink ($1-3) or fruity house cocktail ($3-6) on the 2nd-story balcony, which overlooks the plaza. The best gourmet coffee in town $1-5. Sandwiches $4-6. Lunch special with sandwich, drink, and soup $5.25. The small cafe turns into a cozy post-night out destination until 3am on F and Sa. Open M-Th 7am-6pm, F 7am-6pm and 9pm-3am, Sa 8am-6pm and 9pm-3am. Cash only. ❶

Classic Delights, C. Comercio 3 (☎259-0558), at the corner of C. Marina. Hungry *ponceños* flock to this large bakery just off the plaza, where walls are lined with paintings by local artists, display cabinets are filled with sugar-free specialties, and Wi-Fi is free. Regular sweets $0.50-1.50. Sugar-free flan $1.25-1.50. Salads $1.50-4. Pizza with drink and cookie combo $4.49. Open daily 6am-7pm. AmEx/MC/V. ❶

King's Cream, C. Marina 9322 (☎843-8520). Stocked with Puerto Rican flavors like *tamarindo* and *parcha*, whipped through a mixer and served up soft. Refreshingly low prices. Ice cream $1.10-1.60. *Batidas* $2. Open daily 9am-11:40pm. Cash only. ❶

Tompy's (☎840-1965), at C. Isabel and C. Mayor, looks like a standard Puerto Rican *cafetería*, but its meaty sandwiches, convenient location, and late hours set it apart. Breakfast $1-3. Sandwiches $1-8.50. Open M-Tu 7am-4pm, W-Sa 7am-11:30pm. MC/V. ❶

Pito's Seafood Café & Restaurant, Hwy. 2 Km 218.7 (☎841-4977; www.pitosseafoodrestaurant.com). Large patio over the sea and seafood with a Puerto Rican twist. Cigar room with extensive menu. Entrees $13-32. Delicious house martinis $7. Piano bar on balcony overlooking the rich blue water F-Su. Open M-Th and Su 11am-11pm, F-Sa 11am-midnight. AmEx/MC/V. ❹

El Sabor, C. Isabel 6963 (☎290-5050), in the Fox Delicias Hotel. A cafetería in the atrium of the spectacular Fox Delicias Hotel (see **Accommodations,** above). Serves great daily lunch specials, including a Puerto Rican entree, 2 sides, and a drink ($4.50). Open M-F 11am-2pm. AmEx/MC/V. ❶

Naturismo Health Food, Av. las Américas 223D (☎284-1300), in a health-food store. The menu at this vegetarian restaurant with a large, pleasant dining room changes daily but usually includes rice, beans, *tostones*, and vegetables. Menu revolves around protein alternatives such as soy and beans, but also serves some white meat such as chicken. Lunch $5.50. Drinks $1.50-2. Open M-F 10am-2pm. AmEx/MC/V. ❶

Restaurante El Ancla, Av. Hostos 805 (☎840-2450 or 840-2454), at the end of the street overlooking the water, 3-5min. by car from La Guancha boardwalk and the Ponce Hilton. This *mesón gastronómico* is a convenient choice for a sit-down meal after spending a Sa or Su at La Guancha boardwalk. Features a nautical theme, subtle sea-inspired artwork and a long menu of seafood options. Entrees $14-30. Extensive wine list; wine sold by the bottle. Live traditional Bohemian music Su 2-6pm. Open Tu-Th and Su 11am-9pm, F-Sa 11am-11pm. AmEx/D/MC/V. ❹

◐ SIGHTS

▨ **PLAZAS LAS DELICIAS.** With an enormous fountain, a stately church, and one of the funkiest museums in Puerto Rico, Ponce's legendary central plaza provides hours of entertainment. The first stop is the **Parque de Bombas,** the bright red-and-black structure on the northern side of the plaza. Featured on dozens of postcards, calendars, and tourist brochures, this unique museum serves as the unofficial symbol of Ponce and a monument to the city's long history. Three years after a fire nearly destroyed the city in 1820, Ponce officials created Puerto Rico's first firefighter corps, and in 1883 the fire department moved to an Arabic Pavilion on the main plaza. Fast-forward over 100 years and the city government transformed the same building into a monument to honor the many fire officials who have protected the city from countless disasters. Today the small museum contains old fire equipment, a timeline of firefighting, and portraits of famous firefighters. The highlight is the old fire engine, whose bell you can ring and siren you can sound. *(☎284-3338. Open daily 9am-6pm. Free.)* You can't miss the enormous **Catedral de Nuestra Señora de Guadalupe,** behind the Parque de Bombas. The largest cathedral in Ponce was built in 1836 on the site of the city's first church, which was constructed in 1670. There aren't many surprises inside, but the stained-glass windows and golden altar are striking. This is a functioning Catholic church, so do not enter unless you are appropriately attired. *(☎842-0134. Open M-F 6am-1pm, Sa-Su 6am-12:30pm and 3-8pm.)* Across the street, at C. Unión and C. Reina, the exquisite **Casa Armstrong Poventud** was

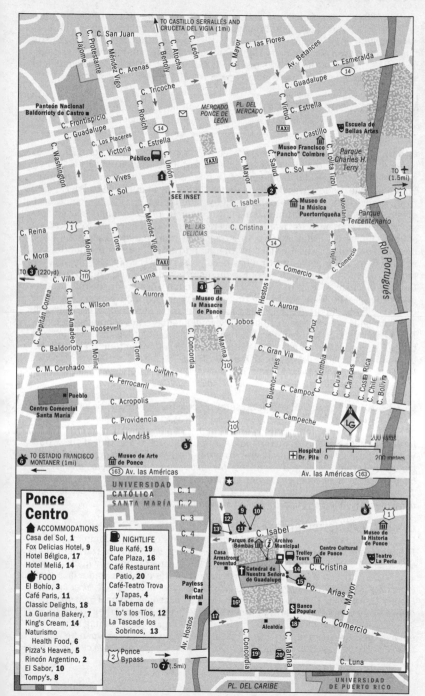

built in 1899 as a residence and most recently housed the offices of the Institute of Puerto Rican Culture. The house is currently under construction and may eventually become another museum. On the southern border of the plaza sits the beautiful **Casa Alcaldía** (City Hall). Built in 1490, the building was once a jail, as well as the site of the island's last lynchings. Today, it does not have much to spark interest except a pretty facade. *(☎ 284-4141. Open M-F 8am-4:30pm.)*

GET YOURSELF CONNECTED. If you have a laptop with you, take advantage of the free Wi-Fi available throughout the outdoor Plaza las Delicias.

CASTILLO SERRALLÉS. It may have been over a century since Puerto Rico was ruled by a monarch, but the island has its own royalty. One such dynasty is the Serrallés family, the original producers of Don Q rum, and their house reigns over Ponce like the castle it was designed to be. The family immigrated to Puerto Rico from Spain in the mid-18th century and by 1890 their Hacienda Mercedita produced over 4000 acres of rum-making sugar cane. In 1930 the family started construction on a Spanish Revival house overlooking Ponce; intended to serve as a summer home, the elaborate structure took over four years to complete. This is one of the most beautiful homes on the island that is open to the public, and almost all of the original furniture has been preserved. The only way to visit the interior is with a 1¼hr. guided tour, which starts with a 15min. film, continues through the many elegant rooms, and passes through a display on the rum production process. The highlight of the tour is the formal dining room and its hand-carved ceilings, imported from France and Italy in three kinds of wood and crystal. The tour ends at a gift shop selling the Serrallés family's many brands, including Don Q and Captain Morgan rum. The large, manicured gardens are also open to the public, providing an excellent place to wander after the tour. *(El Vigil 17. Just downhill from the Cruceta del Vigía, p. 209. ☎ 259-1774 or 259-1775. Open Tu-Su 9:30am-5pm. Free English and Spanish tours. $6, ages 3-15 or over 60 $3. Combo ticket with Cruceta la Vigía $9; ages 3-15, over 60, and students with ID $4. AmEx/D/MC/V.)*

LA GUANCHA. Ponce makes good use of its coastal location with La Guancha, an elaborate boardwalk strip lined with food *kioskos*. By day this is a pleasant, quiet place to walk, but come weekend nights the boardwalk overlooking the harbor is packed. Thousands of *ponceños* of all ages come out of the woodwork on Sundays to look out at the yachts in port while enjoying a cool drink, traditional fried foods, and *mofongo*. *(Av. Santiago de los Caballeros off Hwy. 12. From the plaza head south on Av. Hostos, turn left on Rte. 2, then turn right onto Rte. 12 and follow the signs. Kiosk hours vary, although at least a couple are usually open during the day and everything is open on weekend nights.)*

COMPLEJO TURÍSTICO RECREATIVO EL TUQUE. There's no better place in Puerto Rico to relive your childhood than El Tuque Recreation Complex at Hotel El Tuque (see **Accommodations,** page. p. 205), 4 mi. west of Ponce. The highlight is the **Speed & Splash Water Park,** open during the summer months, which has several water slides, a wave pool, a splash area for little children, and a lazy river. *(Open May-July W-Su 10am-6pm; Aug. Sa-Su 10am-6pm. $14, under 12 $11. Inner tubes $5. Lockers $3. AmEx/MC/V.)* In the same complex, the **Ponce International Speedway Park** offers a ¼ mi. drag strip, 1½ mi. raceway, and ½ mi. go-cart track, open to any group that wants to race; call ahead for information about upcoming races. Racers use their own cars on the drag strip and raceway, but go-carts can be rented. *(Hwy. 2 Ponce By-Pass 3330, Km 220.1. ☎ 290-2000; www.eltuque.com. Open mid-Jan. to Nov.*

M drag race, Th and sometimes Sa full circuit on raceway.
Race entry M $5, Th $10 for "Money Hunter" winner takes all.
Go-carts $5 for 8 circuits. Children under 8 free. Cash only.)

CRUCETA DEL VIGIA. This popular monument can
be seen towering overhead from every point in the
city. The original Vigia cross was built on this spot
(233 ft. above sea level) in 1801 to mark the spot
where guards sat to watch ships entering the harbor. If the ship was an enemy to the Spanish crown,
they would alert the authorities; if it was an ally,
they would alert local traders to come fetch their
goods. The current cross was built in 1984 to honor
these faithful guards. A glass elevator leads to the
observation tower, which has the best views in the
city and an interactive directory in English and
Spanish pointing out the dozens of visible land-
marks. *(On Vigia Hill. From the plaza drive down C. Cristina,
turn left on C. Salud, turn left on C. Guadalupe, and turn right
on C. Bertoly, which leads all the way up the hill. ☎ 259-3816.
Open mid-May to July daily 9:30am-5pm; Aug. to mid-May Tu-
Su 9:30am-5pm. Ticket $4. Combo ticket with Castillo Ser-
rallés $9; ages 3-15, over 60, and students with ID $4.)*

TEATRO LA PERLA. Designed in 1941 in imitation of
the original 1864 theater that was destroyed in an
earthquake, La Perla has a large balcony and 1047
velvet seats. The beautiful Neoclassical building is
regularly open to the public, and the lobby has a
small museum commemorating past shows. By far
the best way to experience the theater, though, is by
attending one of the many musical and theatrical performances. *(Corner of C. Mayor and C. Cristina. ☎ 843-4322,
box office 843-4080. Theater open M-F 8am-noon and 1-
4.30pm, box office open M &a 10am-4pm. Performances late
Aug. to early July F-Su. Play tickets $20-25. Ballet tickets $45-
100. Student and senior discounts available occasionally.)*

PANTEÓN NACIONAL ROMÁN BALDORIOTY DE CASTRO.
In 1843 the city of Ponce constructed a Catholic
cemetery at what was then the edge of the city. For
over 70 years Ponce's most prominent citizens
were buried here, including members of the Serraillés family and Román Baldorioty de Castro, an
instrumental figure in the emancipation of Puerto
Rico's slaves (see **Castillo Serraillés,** above). The
cemetery closed in 1918 for public health reasons
and has been severely vandalized over the years,
but in 1991 the government reopened the area,
began renovations, and even buried famous tenor
Antonio Paoli and former governor **Roberto Sánchez
Vilella** here. The graves of the famous people are

THE LOCAL STORY

DANCEOFF!

You haven't truly experienced traditional Puerto Rico until you've
watched—and danced—the
bomba y plena. In this interactive
combination of music and dance,
a "caller" shouts a repeating chorus that is echoed responsively
by a band playing strong, rhythmic drum beats. Once the music
is loud enough and the beat
begins to speed up, the dance
floor is open to the audience,
and the challenge is on.

Any dancer may participate.
Female dancers are traditionally
garbed in a flowing skirt that is
tossed and spun in time with the
music. Once a woman steps onto
the floor and bows to the band,
the danceoff begins. In the beginning, the dancer simply follows the
music. Once she gets into rhythm,
however, she starts to move
quickly and precisely, challenging
the band to follow her every move.
The band responds accordingly,
keeping a close eye on her movements; they hit hard downbeats in
time with every shake of the hips
and pause each time the dancer
comes to an abrupt halt.

In this fashion, control of the
dance moves back and forth
between the band and the
dancer. All the while, the caller
and surrounding crowd continue
to participate vocally. In the end,
there are no judges and no winners and losers, just an amazing
experience for all to enjoy.

beautifully wrought in marble, but the older graves are still in disrepair. *(At C. Simón de la Torre and C. Frontispicio. ☎841-8347. 1½-2hr. tour. Open W-Su 8:30am-5pm. Free.)*

MARKETS. Ponce has two traditional markets within walking distance of the plaza. The **Plaza del Mercado,** in a 1970s-style building, has stands for everything you'd expect to see in a Puerto Rican market, including *cafeterías,* lottery stands, salted fish, and thousands of plantains. *(Between C. Victoria and Paseo Atocha. Open M-Sa 6am-6pm. Arrive early for freshest produce.)* Next door, the smaller **Mercado Juan Ponce de León** has a more eclectic collection of kiosks, where you can get your sewing done, watch a cobbler at work, buy hand-rolled cigars, or sample a tasty *batida.* In both markets about half of the storefronts are empty. *(Between C. León, C. Mayor, C. Estrella, and C. Guadalupe. Most kiosks open M-Sa 9am-3pm.)*

🏛 MUSEUMS

■**MUSEO DE ARTE DE PONCE.** While San Juan's new art museum consists primarily of Latin American and Puerto Rican works, the Ponce museum focuses almost exclusively on European art and has been called the premier European art museum in the Caribbean. The two-story building includes rooms of the Spanish School, the Dutch School, the British School, and several Italian schools. Some of the more famous artists include El Greco, Peter Paul Rubens, Charles Le Brun, and Edward Coely Burne-Jones. Of course, the museum also has a room dedicated to Latin American artists, including Francisco Oller, José Campeche, and Tomás Batista, as well as temporary exhibitions of modern work. A small sculpture courtyard with a reflecting pool provides a pleasant place to sit. From the outside, the building, designed by Edward Durell Stone, a student of Frank Lloyd Wright, looks unexceptional; however, the interior is exquisitely designed to display art, with unusual window and lighting schemes. All captions are in Spanish and English. *(Av. las Américas 2325. ☎848-0505 or 840-1510; www.museoarteponce.org. Open daily 10am-5pm. $5, children under 12 $2.50, students with ID $1.25, clergy or handicapped free.)*

MUSEO DE LA HISTORIA DE PONCE. It is only appropriate that a city with so much local pride should also have a museum dedicated exclusively to its history. The Ponce History Museum is housed in three adjacent buildings—Casa Salazar, Zapater, and Casa Ernesto Ramos Antonini—each with its own unique architecture. The museum presents a combination of historical documents, artifacts, furniture, textiles, descriptive signs, and hundreds of photos to describe every aspect of the city, with separate rooms dedicated to subjects such as health, education, ecology, and geology. The most unique exhibit has to be the photo montage of the "personajes," or local celebrities of Plaza las Delicias; the display depicts people of all social strati, from former governors to street dwellers and local celebrities like "Juana la loca" (Juana the madwoman). All captions are in Spanish, but employees may offer English tours on request, which can be very helpful in navigating the materials. *(C. Isabel 47, 51 and 53, at C. Mayor. ☎844-7071; museodelahistoriade-ponce@yahoo.com. Open Tu-Su and holidays 9am-4:30pm.)*

MUSEO DE LA MÚSICA PUERTORRIQUEÑA. The Institute of Culture has filled this museum with musical instruments and artwork that tell the story of Puerto Rican music, from instruments used by the Taínos to salsa. Two rooms focus on *bomba y plena* (see **Music,** p. 69), the latter of which is said to have originated in Ponce and continues to play an important role in the city's culture. Exhibits include many types of guitars, from an 18th-century *bordonúa* to a Hawaiian steel guitar from the 1930s. Tours are excellent, and guides may even let you play some of the instruments. All captions are in Spanish but guides speak English. *(C. Isabel, at C. Salud, in a large beige mansion. ☎848-7016 or 840-9239; www.icp.gobierno.pr. Open W-Su 8:30am-4:30pm. Free English and Spanish tours. Free.)*

MUSEO FRANCISCO "PANCHO" COIMBRE. Named after one of Ponce's all-time greatest baseball players, this one-room museum honors *ponceño* athletes in all sports. There are a few interesting pieces of memorabilia, including a uniform from Ponce's short-lived women's baseball team and a baseball bat that was the only object to survive the house fire that killed Coimbre. Ask for a tour; the endless rows of photos have little meaning without one. *(On C. Lolita Tizol, near C. Castillo. ☎843-6553. Open Tu-Su 9am-5:30pm. Free.)*

MUSEO DE LA MASACRE DE PONCE. In 1937, 19 Puerto Rican Nationalist demonstrators were killed by police forces in Ponce. For a long time afterwards the government denied any responsibility and schools did not teach students about the controversial event. In an effort to remedy this situation, the Puerto Rican Cultural Institute opened a small museum to promote awareness of the tragedy and prevent something similar from happening again. The museum contains informative timelines and posters, but few actual artifacts. The most interesting are the 1930s-era government cards listing laborers who were suspected to be dangerously revolutionary. Although most captions are in Spanish, there are a few English translations, and the English-speaking guides are happy to answer questions. *(C. Marina at C. Aurora. ☎844-9722; masacredeponce@hotmail.com. Open W-Su 8am-11am. Free English- and Spanish-language tours. Museum free.)*

CENTRO CULTURAL DE PONCE. This dark pink Neoclassical building was built in 1870, and the owner was the first to have a phone connection to his office in Ponce Playa. Ponce's first museum of art was established here in 1959, but it was closed when the current building was constructed. Now the Institute of Culture sometimes hosts temporary art exhibits. Although they vary in form and medium, the exhibits usually explore the theme of blending European and American cultures. *(C. Cristina 70. ☎844-2540.)*

🎵 ENTERTAINMENT

BEACHES

Beaches are not Ponce's strong point, but the city has created one acceptable beach area in the La Guancha area just east of the boardwalk. The imported sand barely covers a concrete surface and the water doesn't get much more than two feet deep, but *ponceños* fill the beach on hot weekend days. Bathrooms, playground equipment, parking, a beach volleyball court, and fried food in kiosks appease the masses. Lifeguards on duty 9:30am-6pm. For a better beach, catch the boat to **Isla Caja de Muertos** (p. 214).

CINEMA

Caribbean Cinemas has two locations in Ponce. The first, in **Ponce Towne Center,** Rte. 2 Km 24.3, (☎843-2601), behind the Big K-mart, has 10 theaters. The **Plaza del Caribe Mall** location (☎844-6704), at the intersection of Rte. 2 and Rte. 123, has six. Both play Hollywood films. ($5.50, under 9 or over 60 $3.50. W women $3.50.)

CONCERTS

Founded in 1883 as the Firefighter's Corps Band, the **Municipal Band of Ponce** has been entertaining locals for well over a century. Today the group sounds like a

THE LOCAL STORY

PONCE'S FAT TUESDAY

Ponce's biggest shebang is its elaborate *carnaval*, one last party in the days prior to the sacrifices of Lent. The celebration combines Puerto Rico's Spanish, African, and Taíno heritages. Masqueraders (referred to as *vejigantes*) dress up in brightly colored costumes and ornate masks hand-carved from wood or coconut shells. They represent the "good" characters, who are supposed to scare away the evil ones by dancing to *bomba y plena* folk songs. The primary character is **King Momo**, a local who dresses up in an enormous doll costume. Throughout the week, people try to guess the identity of the *Rey Momo;* the winner receives a monetary reward. While it's no Rio de Janeiro, Ponce's *carnaval* offers a whole week of festive fun. Unless otherwise stated, all events take place in the plaza at 7:30pm.

Day 1 (W): Masquerade Dance. Everyone shows off their costumes.

Day 2 (Th): Entrance of King Momo: Celebrated with a parade.

Day 3 (F): Crowning of the Infant Queen. Parade again.

Day 4 (Sa): Crowning of the Queen. Another parade.

Day 5 (Su): Grand Carnaval. A massive parade. Starts at 1pm.

Day 6 (M): Carnaval Grand Dance. A big party with live music.

Day 7 (Tu): Burial of the Sardine: This mock funeral represents the sacrifice that is to come with Lent.

professional symphony orchestra and performs lively classical music every Sunday in the Plaza las Delicias, across from the Alcaldía (8pm). Every so often, outdoor concerts are also held in the Concha Acústica, an outdoor stage behind the statue of a chained slave at the intersection of Calle Marina and Calle Mayor. Contact the tourism office for concert announcements (☎ 284-3338).

FESTIVALS

Ponce's big shebang is undoubtedly *carnaval* (see **Ponce's Fat Tuesday**, p. 212). However, the following festivals have also been known to bring out the crowds. The city's **patron saint festival,** "Las Mañanitas," for the Virgin de la Guadalupe, is held on December 12 in Ponce Centro, in the Plaza las Delicias. At midnight a procession moves down Calle Isabel into the Catedral de Nuestra Señora de Guadalupe, led by marchers holding high a replica of the Virgin of Guadalupe, with *mariachis* and dozens of revelers on their trail. The *mariachis* play on until breakfast at 7am, when Ponce closes the celebration with a feast in the Casa Alcaldía or City Hall. During a three-day weekend in March, the city hosts a **Feria Artesanal.** Over 100 artists set up booths on the south side of the plaza for this enormous artisan festival with music, typical food and seemingly endless parties. The tourist office staff recommends that visitors contact them in March for exact dates (☎ 284-3338).

SHOPPING

Ponce's best shopping awaits on the pedestrian **Paseo Atocha,** just north of Plaza las Delicias. This market fills three blocks just off the central plaza, and its presence can't be missed: vendors hawk over microphones with the attitude of auctioneers, and reggaeton blasts from the storefronts of Puerto Rican discount stores. This busy shopping experience is most active on weekdays. For a more conservative shopping experience, try **Plaza del Caribe,** the largest mall in the Ponce area. Here you can stock up on products from American favorites like the Gap, Sears, Puma, American Eagle, and Foot Locker. There is also a large, intricately carved carousel and a food court. (At the intersection of Rte. 2 and Rte. 123. ☎ 259-8989; www.plazadelcaribepr.com. Open M-Sa 9am-9pm, Su 11am-5pm.)

SPORTS

The **Leones de Ponce** (Ponce Lions), Ponce's professional baseball team, play from November to January at **Estadio Francisco Montaner,** near the intersection of Av. las Américas and Rte. 2. Games are held Tuesday through Sunday. Purchase tickets at the stadium box office. (☎ 848-0050. $10, children and seniors $5.)

THEATER

La Perla (see **Sights,** p. 209), is the city's primary venue for theater. Ponce's **Escuela de Bellas Artes,** on C. Lolita Tizol at C. Castillo, holds occasional student ballet and theater performances. Contact the school or check La Perla del Sur for info. (☎848-9156. Most performances F during the school year. Admission $5.)

🖭 NIGHTLIFE

Ponce is home to a variety of nightlife hot spots, including clubs blasting reggaeton, quiet corner bars, and a popular boardwalk filled with night owls of all ages. The best place to enjoy a drink, live music, and even livelier Puerto Rican company is ⏷**La Guancha,** the seaside boardwalk south of town. Mixed drinks run $2.50-6, beer $1-2. Sandwiches, pizza, and *empanadillas* are also served. Gamblers can head to one of the city's two **casinos,** the **Ponce Hilton,** just off Rte. 124 (see **La Bohemia,** below; open daily 8am-4am), or the **Holiday Inn,** which is open 24hr., Ponce Bypass 3315 (☎259-8300), about 2 mi. west of town down Hwy. 2.

PLAZA LAS DELICIAS

Blue Kafé, C. Luna 70, at C. Concordia (☎284-3774). Arguably the most popular bar on C. Luna, the destination street for bar-hopping in downtown Ponce. Blue Kafé is where Ponce's young and beautiful go for a night out. The exuberant crowd spills into the street, and big signs on the walls list nightly drink specials, including $2 Bacardi all day Tu and F. Serves Puerto Rican lunch plate ($5.50) M-F 11am-3pm. Cover for performances $5-10. Open M and W-Su 11am-3am, Tu 11am-1am. MC/V.

Café-Teatro Trova y Tapas, C. Marina 40 (☎848-5506 or 939-642-9604; www.trovaytapas.com). Young professionals fill this classy new wood-paneled cafe, bar, and live music venue every night of the week. Patrons chat over delicious "picadera" tapas to share ($8-50). The "flairtender" bartenders throw shots on fire every W 9-11pm, when cosmopolitans are free. Special events are delivered most Th, and live 80s rock makes the shiny wood floor buzz every F-Sa 10pm-3am. Cover for special events $5-10. Beer $2.50-5. Mixed drinks $3-6. Open Tu 5pm-1am, W-Sa 5pm-3am. MC/V.

Café Restaurant Patio, C. Luna 35 (☎848-3178), at C. Marina. Located in the center of the action on the hip (and loud) C. Luna, this cafe by day and bar by night keeps things relaxed with a family-friendly environment and chill vibe. A 25-and-up crowd takes advantage of killer Happy hour 10pm-1am. Specials change by the day, including Th Heineken $3; F Coors $2; and Sa Medalla $1.50, Bacardi $2, and Dewar's $3.50. 18+ after 10pm. Open M 7:30am-3pm, Tu 7:30am-1am, W-Sa 7:30am-3am. MC/V.

Bar Code, Corner of C. Luna and C. Marina (432-3313). A large club-style black room is decked out with multiple TVs and electronic games. A young crowd fills Bar Code to the brim until it has spilled onto the entirety of C. Luna on weekend nights. Tu Coronita Special $1; F-Sa 11pm-2am Happy hour Bud Select $1.75. Beer from $2.25. Mixed Drinks from $3.25. 18+. Open Tu-Sa 9pm-3am. MC/V.

La Taberna de to's los Tíos & La Tasca de los Sobrinos (☎844-3344; www.lastiaspr.com), in La Casa de los Tías Restaurante at C. Unión at the corner of C. Reina. Connected to the upscale corner restaurant is a softly lit bar frequented by an artsy crowd. Deep blue walls, wood paneling, small cocktail tables, and plenty of dancing space. Highlights are Salsa every F 9pm-2am and poetry readings twice a month. Upstairs, teens and young adults step to the DJ's Spanish rock, reggae, samba, and batucada beats, escape to the balcony for fresh air, and return to belt out karaoke. Hours vary; call ahead. Open M-Sa noon-10pm or 2am, Su noon-6pm. MC/V.

A PIRATE'S TALE

With a name like **Isla Caja de Muertos** (Coffin Island), it is not surprising that this small piece of land is tied to a book's worth of legends. Over the years, the island has served as a hideout for several pirates, including notables such as Sir Frances Drake and the local menace Roberto Cofresí. Originally from the Cabo Rojo area, Cofresí supposedly traveled the southern shores on a 60 ft. schooner, burning Spanish ships and stealing their treasures. Although some historians claim that Cofresí was a sort of Puerto Rican Robin Hood, sharing his plunder with the poor, legend has it that he divided his treasure in two and buried half on the north side of Coffin Island and the other half in a cave to the south. In 1954, after one of these caves collapsed, excavators discovered a human skeleton inside, still chained to the wall.

Of course, eager visitors have searched for the treasure, but with no success. Then again, many locals have stories about cousins or friends who mysteriously disappeared during an expedition to Caja de Muertos. Maybe they got a little bit too close to the pile of gold? No one knows for sure, but an aura of mystery continues to shroud the island today. As for the name, well, that's no mystery at all. An 18th-century French writer called the island "Coffre A'morr" (Coffin Island), because from a distance the island looks a little like a large coffin.

For information on how to plan your own getaway to the mysterious Isla Caja de Muertos, see (p. 214).

Cafe Plaza, C. Unión 3 (☎812-3873), on the plaza, is popular with locals and tourists who enjoy the convenient location. A nice spot for post-dinner drinks and conversation. Nightly karaoke every night and a DJ spinning every F-Sa. Beer $2-3. Mixed drinks $4-5. Open Tu-Sa 6pm-3am. MC/V.

OUTSIDE THE PLAZA

La Bohemia (☎259-7676, ext. 5121), in the Ponce Hilton. Take Rte. 12 toward La Guancha, then turn left after the Texaco station and drive about 1½ mi. down the road. A slightly older crowd hits up this retreat on weekend nights. It's two-thirds classy, with candlelit tables and a live salsa, *merengue*, or *bachata* band, and one-third sporty, with a big-screen TV showing athletic events. Dance floor for when the salsa party gets going. Don Q drinks $3 daily 7-9pm. Beers $5-6. Mixed drinks $7-9. Live music F-Sa 10:30pm-4am. 18+. Open daily 1:30pm-3:30am. AmEx/MC/V.

▶ DAYTRIPS FROM PONCE

ISLA CAJA DE MUERTOS

Island Ventures (☎842-8546 or 608-3082) offer trips out to Isla Caja de Muertos. Boat trips depart from La Guancha F-Su 8am-3:30pm and cost $17 per person. The only other means of accessing the island is to ask fishermen around the docks for a ride.

Isla Caja de Muertos (Coffin Island), a 500-acre island with subtropical dry forest surrounded by a few nice beaches, provides one of those relaxing escapes that you imagine before traveling to the Caribbean. The secret behind Caja de Muertos's magic is the limited means of transportation; in an attempt to minimize human influence and protect the island's animal population, the DRNA mandates that only private boats carrying fewer than 150 people can visit the island. Therefore, from May to December hawksbill turtles are able to lay their eggs on the eastern side of the island without human interference. Moreover, nobody is allowed on the southern tip of the island, which serves as a protected bird sanctuary.

Caja de Muertos's main attractions are the quiet beaches, small strips of sand that stay relatively empty, and gentle, clear waters that make for excellent **snorkeling. Scuba divers** can explore a 40 ft. wall just offshore, and on a good day the visibility can be as extensive as 100 ft. Back on land, the DRNA maintains bathrooms and covered picnic tables. Caja de Muertos is large enough that it also offers activities beyond the beach. An easy 30min. **hike** leads through the shrubs and cacti and up the hill to a 19th-century **lighthouse.** Because the US Coast Guard operates the lighthouse today, visitors cannot enter, but they can enjoy the astounding view from the top. A small cave on the island has **Taíno petroglyphs** inside, but there is no trail. The resident DRNA employee sometimes offers guided tours.

HACIENDA BUENA VISTA

No public transportation goes to Buena Vista. It may be possible to have a público head-ing to Adjuntas drop you off, but getting a ride back will be almost impossible. If driving, head west on Av. las Américas (Rte. 163) past the Museo de Arte, then turn right on Rte. 2R. Then turn left onto Rte. 123 and continue until Km 16.8 (30min.).

This restored fruit, corn flour, and coffee plantation has one of the best-preserved farm houses on the island and one of Ponce's must-see attractions. Back in 1821 Salvador de Vives arrived in Ponce and began looking for land to buy. Unfortu-nately, he couldn't afford the prime real estate by the sea, which was used to grow sugar cane, so instead in 1833 he purchased 482 acres in the mountains just north of the city. Initially the land was used as a fruit farm, and it later became a corn flour factory; however, by 1872, when the third generation of the Vives family took over, the plantation was used almost exclusively to grow Arabica coffee. The fre-quent changes in production mean that a variety of equipment can still be found on the grounds. Most interesting is the 1121 ft. canal system that the Vives family used to extract water from Río Canas, power the machinery, and return the water to the river without polluting or damaging the ecosystem. The farm remained in use until the 1950s when it was abandoned by the family and divided among local farmers.

Since 1984, the site has been managed by the Conservation Trust of Puerto Rico, a private organization that strives to preserve the island's natural resources while educating the public. The only way to visit the plantation is through a 1½hr. guided tour that includes a beautiful walk along the canals through the subtropical forest, a visit to the restored and refurnished house, and fascinating demonstrations of the plantation's still-functioning machinery. In October, the hacienda has a cele-bration of coffee called *actividad del café*, which includes a tasting of coffee grown-on site; call for more information. (Rte. 123 Km 16.8. ☎722-5882, weekends 284-7020; www.fideicomiso.org. **Reservations required.** Call at least one week in advance. Tours F-Su Spanish 8:30, 10:30am, 1:30, 3:30pm; English by request only 1:30pm. $7, ages 5-11 or over 65 $4, under 4 free. MC/V.)

CENTRO CEREMONIAL INDÍGENA TIBES

Públicos to Tibes leave from the main station on C. Unión (15min., $6). From central Ponce, drive down C. Cristina, turn left on C. Salud, then turn left on C. Guadalupe and right on C. Mayor, which turns into Rte. 503. Alternatively, drive north on Hwy. 10, then exit at the Tibes sign onto Rte. 503. Rte. 503 Km 2.8. ☎840-2255 or 840-5685; www.ponce.inter.edu/ tibes/tibes.html. Open Tu-Su 9am-4pm. Visits with guided tours only; free English and Spanish tours every hr., usually on the hr. $3, ages 5-12 or over 60 $2, under 6 free.

Tibes is the largest known indigenous center on the island. Technically this is not a Taíno site, as it was constructed between AD 600 and 1200, during the reign of the pre-Taínos and Igneris, but many of the customs were continued; Tibes is accordingly the best place on the island to learn about the area's indige-nous peoples. The sight was uncovered in 1975 when Hurricane Eloise flooded the banks of the Río Portugués, unearthing several Taíno artifacts. The city expropriated the land and upon excavation unearthed 12 structures, including seven *batey* courts, lots of pottery, and 187 sets of human remains (see **Taíno Terms,** p. 216). The presence of multiple structures leads archaeologists to believe that this was one of the largest ceremonial sites in the Caribbean.

TAÍNO TERMS

Today, the only traces of the Taínos, who lived in Puerto Rico from AD 600 to 1600, are stone walls, ancient tools, and mysterious drawings, but this group of people once ruled the entire island. When you visit archaeological sites dedicated to the Taínos and try to decipher the broken stones and remaining petroglyphs, the following terms may help you understand the artifacts you see.

Batey: A traditional Taíno ball game that was used as both a sport and a religious ritual. Two teams of between 10 and 30 men tried to keep a 3-5 lb. ball made of tree fiber in the air; the first team to drop the ball lost. The rectangular court used for the game is also called a *batey.*

Bohío: A circular hut made of straw and wood that served as home for Taínos. *Caciques* (chiefs) lived in rectangular huts.

Borikén: This word roughly translates as "land of the lords." Puerto Ricans still refer to their island by the Spanish variant: *Borinquén.*

Caguana: A woman traditionally associated with fertility.

Cemís: Stone icons shaped like a cone, with bulbs on either side of the base; these served as Taíno objects of worship. The shape combines elements of the mountains and of male and female reproductive organs in an expression of the earth's fertility.

The small museum introduces visitors to the various aspects of the Taíno and pre-Taíno cultures, displaying most of the pottery found on the site. A 25min. film illustrates many aspects of indigenous life, from warfare to recreation. Finally, during the 1hr. tour, guides lead visitors through the subtropical forest, explaining the indigenous peoples' uses of each type of tree. The tour then heads past a replica of a Taíno village, and finally to several *batey* courts. The site does not boast an overwhelming number of artifacts, but as a whole the complex provides a thorough introduction to Puerto Rico's indigenous culture. Some years, the Centro hosts celebrations in April and November, when actors don indigenous dress and recreate Taíno ceremonies; call ahead for more information.

COAMO

Públicos between Ponce and Coamo will drop passengers off at the intersection of Rte. 546 and Rte. 153, 1 mi. from the baths ($2.50). They may go all the way to the end if arranged in advance ($5). From Ponce, take Hwy. 52 east to Exit 76, then drive north on Rte. 153 to Rte. 546. The baths are at the end. ☎825-1150. Offices open M-F 9am-5pm.

Puerto Rico has plenty of opportunities to de-stress, but few compare to the hot springs just outside of Coamo. With temperatures reaching 109°F, the baths are like all-natural, communal jacuzzis—without the bubbles. These are reportedly the oldest thermal baths in the New World, discovered in 1571; legend says that this was the fountain of youth sought by Ponce de León, Puerto Rico's first Spanish governor. As early as 1847, a hotel at the baths allowed rich Puerto Ricans to access the soothing waters. Today, two public baths just behind the hotel are free to the public. These look like Old World baths, with small brick- and concrete-lined pools and little waterfalls. Park at the end of Rte. 546, then walk past the gate and down the dirt path. If the lure of the hot springs tempts you to extend your daytrip to an overnight stay, Hotel **Baños de Coamo ❸,** at the end of Rte. 546, offers a more modern take on the baths, with a swimming pool fed by hot springs. The attractive *parador* looks and feels like a ski lodge plopped down in the middle of a tropical forest. Rooms are large and wood-paneled, and have cable TV, phone, and A/C. (☎825-2186 or 825-2239; fax 825-4739. Pool, restaurant, game room, and souvenir shop. Check-in 3pm. Check-out 1pm. Singles $87; doubles $91. Extra person $10; 2 children under 12 free. Tax included. AmEx/D/MC/V.)

SALINAS

On the surface, Salinas looks like any other city in southern central Puerto Rico, with congested streets and a town square surrounded by *cafeterías*. But just south of town is Playa Salinas, one of the island's largest ports and the best place for wandering island-hoppers to find passage on vessels traveling throughout the western hemisphere. The activity centers around Marina de Salinas & Posada El Náutico, a hotel complex with a bulletin board that travelers use to coordinate carpools. Playa Salinas also offers scrumptious seafood, some boating opportunities, and a funky international charm rarely found in small Puerto Rican towns.

TRANSPORTATION. Two of Puerto Rico's major thoroughfares, Rte. 1 and Rte. 3, meet in downtown Salinas. From San Juan take Hwy. 52 south to the final intersection with Rte. 1; this road becomes **Calle Muñoz Rivera**. **Públicos** travel to Guayama (30min., $1.55) and Playa Salinas (5min., $0.45). To reach the plaza from the *público* station, turn left onto C. Amadeo and walk one block.

ORIENTATION AND PRACTICAL INFORMATION. The convergence of **Route 1** and **Route 3** is Salinas's main street; off the central plaza, Rte. 1 is called C. Amadeo, and to the east, Rte. 3 becomes C. Barbosa. C. Muñoz Rivera runs perpendicular to this street along the plaza. To reach **Playa Salinas,** drive west on **Route 1,** then turn south on **Route 701,** which follows the bay. All of the services are located near the town center, about 1 mi. north of Playa Salinas. **Banco Popular,** C. Muñoz Rivera 1, on the plaza, has two **ATMs.** (☎824-3075. Open M-F 8am-4pm.) **Grande** supermarket, on Rte. 7701 across from the post office, has a **MoneyGram** service. (☎824-1400. Open M-Sa 7am-8pm, Su 11am-5pm. AmEx/MC/V.) The **police station,** C. Muñoz Rivera 500, is a quarter mile north of the plaza. (☎824-2020. Open 24hr.) **Sur Med Medical Center,** C. Colón Pacheco 8, lies east of town off Rte. 3, behind the Esso Station. (☎824-1100 or 824-1199. 24hr. emergency room. Open 24hr.) It also has a well-stocked **pharmacy** inside (Open M-Sa 8am-10:30pm, Su 9am-10:30pm.) The **post office,** Rte. 7701 #100, off Rte. 701 near the intersection with Rte. 1, has General Delivery. (☎824-2485. Open M-F 8am-4:30pm, Sa 8am-noon.) **Postal Code:** 00751.

ACCOMMODATIONS AND FOOD. Marina de Salinas Posada El Náutico ❸, C. Chapin G8, on Rte. 701, past the seafood restaurants, is both an upscale yachters' marina and the best hotel in Salinas. Colorful rooms with nautical paintings have A/C, cable TV, wicker furniture, and nice showers. Spacious suites come with a full kitchenette. The hotel also has laundry facilities, a restaurant, a book exchange, a small pool, a waterfront snack bar, and a playground area. (☎824-5973 or 824-3185; www.marinadesalinas.com. Check-in 2pm. Check-out 1pm. Doubles $77; quads $88-99; suites $110-150. Extra person $15; children under 11 free. AmEx/D/MC/V.)

Food options tend to clump together in Salinas. C. Muñoz Rivera and C. Amadeo, near the plaza, have several inexpensive *comida criolla* lunch options. The seafood restaurants near Playa Salinas, along Rte. 701, are somewhat more expensive, but offer fresh surf 'n' turf on patios overlooking the water. Few come close to **El Balcón del Capitán ❸,** C. A 54, on Rte. 701. The restaurant's balcony provides seating directly over the water, with incomparable views and a cool sea breeze. El Balcón specializes in seafood flavored with the local favorite, *mojo isleño,* a tomato-based sauce. (☎824-6210. Entrees $7-27. House tropical drink $5. Open M-Th 11am-10pm, F-Sa 11am-10:30pm, Su 11am-9:30pm. AmEx/MC/V.)

⛵ OUTDOOR ACTIVITIES. The many off-shore islands provide ample opportunity for nautical exploration. **Marina de Salinas & Posada El Náutico** rents **kayaks** ($15 per hr., $40 per day) and **waterbikes** ($15 per hr., $60 per day). Or, forget the kayaks and bikes and hop on **La Paseadora**, a fun-filled, music-blasting boat that takes groups on tours of the bay ($3, children $2) or drops people off at a nearby island ($5, children $3). The boat leaves every weekend; for more info contact Ity Jiménez (☎824-2649) or wait on the dock next to El Balcón del Capitán (see **Food**, above) in the morning. Playa Salinas's only swimming area is at **Polita's Beach**, Rte. 701 Km 2.1. There is no sand, but a lively kiosk and bar offers jet ski rental ($5 per hr.) and parking for $3. (☎824-4184. Open Sa-Su and holidays 9am-dusk.)

GUAYAMA

At the turn of the 20th century, Guayama was the center of Puerto Rico's sugar industry; today, it is a busy business hub congested with traffic. Nevertheless, several attractions await those visitors who dare venture off Highway 53. With an historic square that hearkens back to the sugar cane glory days, Guayama is also close to several natural attractions, from beaches to a butterfly sanctuary.

⎘ TRANSPORTATION

Rte. 3 leads directly into downtown Guayama. **Públicos** leave from the station at the corner of C. Ashford and C. Enrique González for: Patillas (30min., $0.90) via Arroyo (10min., $0.60); Ponce (45min., $4.35); San Juan (1½hr., $7) via Caguas (45min., $7); and Salinas (30min., $1.55). Most *públicos* leave in the morning or early afternoon. From the público station exit onto C. Ashford, turn left, walk two blocks, and turn left again to reach the plaza.

⭐🛈 ORIENTATION AND PRACTICAL INFORMATION

The commercial area of Guayama is near the intersection of Rte. 3 and Hwy. 54. **Route 3** runs southwest from Hwy. 54 to Jobos, and Rte. 7710 breaks off to Jobos Bay and the *barrio* Pozuelo, which is known for its seafood. Route 3 also heads northeast toward the **plaza**. The tall church steeple on the plaza is visible from a distance and serves as a useful landmark. Coming from the east, Rte. 3 becomes **Calle Ashford**, a major thoroughfare that runs parallel to C. Santiago Palmer, which passes the plaza. Drive past the church, then turn left on C. Vicente Pales, then left again on C. Martínez, going around the plaza, to stay on Rte. 3. C. Derkes forms the southern border of the plaza. **Plaza Guayama Mall,** Rte. 3 Km 135.2, east of town, has many shops and services, including a six-screen movie theater.

Banks: Banco Popular (☎866-0288), in front of Plaza Guayama Mall, has an **ATM.** Open M-F 8am-4pm, Sa 8am-3pm, Su 11am-3pm.

Camping Permits: The **DRNA office,** Rte. 3 Km 144.5 (☎864-8903 or 999-2200 ext. 5120, 5158 in San Juan; fax 864-1147), west of town, issues camping permits ($4). Allow 3-4 days for processing. Open M-F 8am-noon and 1-4pm.

Police: ☎866-2020. Located on Av. José Torre 240, behind the hospital. Open 24hr.

Hospital: Hospital Episcopal Cristo Redentor, Hwy. 54 Km 2.7 (☎864-4300). Clinic open M-F 8am-5pm. Emergency room open 24hr.

Post Office: C. Ashford 151 (☎864-1150), several blocks east of the plaza, next to the Autoridad de Energía Electrica. General Delivery available. Open M-F 7:30am-4:30pm, Sa 7:30am-noon. **Postal Code:** 00784.

ACCOMMODATIONS

Hotel Brandemar (☎864-5124), at the end of Rte. 748. From Guayama drive east on Hwy. 54 to Km 5.7, then turn right on Rte. 748 until you reach the parking lot at the end; reception is inside the restaurant. Located in a quiet neighborhood near a small, picturesque beach, this affordable hotel has everything travelers need, including clean rooms with new bedspreads, private bath, TV, A/C, and a huge swimming pool. Rooms equipped with insect repellent. Doubles $68-85; quad with kitchenette $190. Tax included. AmEx/D/MC/V. ❸

Molino Inn Hotel, Hwy. 54 Km 2.1 (☎866-1515; www.molinoinn.net), is the only hotel within city limits. Clean, chain-hotel-style rooms outfitted with wicker furniture include A/C, phone, cable TV, and a balcony overlooking the courtyard and the large, narrow pool. As the hotel is located on a busy highway, it's worth asking for a room in the back. Check-in 3pm. Check-out noon. Doubles Nov. 15-Feb. 14 and May 15-Aug. 14 M-Th and Su $92, F-Sa and holidays $97. Feb. 15-May 14 and Aug. 15-Nov. 14 $87/ 92. Extra person $10. Tax included. AmEx/MC/V. ❸

FOOD

Fine dining is sparse in Guayama; however, several restaurants in the *barrio* of **Pozuelo,** off Rte. 3 at the end of Rte. 7710, west of town serve fresh seafood near the water. The city center is filled with *panaderías* serving up hearty sandwiches. Stock up on basic supplies at **Pueblo Xtra,** next to Plaza Guayama Mall. (☎866-1225. Open M-Sa 6am-midnight, Su 11am-5pm. AmEx/MC/V.)

La Casa de Los Pastelillos, Rte. 7710 Km 4 (☎864-5171), in Pozuelo. Serves dozens of different types of *pastelillos* (fried dough; $3-6), filled with everything from pizza to shark. The highlight of this creative restaurant is the laid-back atmosphere; chow down on the large deck or lie in a hammock right on the beach. Happy hour Th 5:30pm-7:30pm; beer $2. Open M-W 10:30am-6pm, Th 10:30am-10pm, F-Sa 10am-11pm. MC/V. ❶

Supreme Bakery (☎866-0175 or 864-7501), at C. Derkes and C. Hostos. This *panadería* deserves its popularity; it dishes out loaded baked potatoes ($3-5) and even bigger grilled sandwiches ($3-9) to the local crowds. Great baked goods $0.60-3. Breakfast $3-4. Open daily 6am-9:30pm. Takeout until 9:50pm. AmEx/MC/V. ❶

SIGHTS

MUSEUMS. The cultural tour of Guayama begins on the plaza at **Museo Casa Cautiño.** Built in 1887 by a *guayamés* architect, this magnificent house has been restored to its former glory and decorated with much of the original artwork and furniture, including magnificent chandeliers and sculptures. A 40min. tour provides insight into the life of Guayama's wealthy sugar producing families. *(C. Vicente Pales 1, at the corner of C. Palmer on the plaza. Recommended that groups reserve tour. ☎864-9083 or 864-0600, ext. 3001. Open Tu-Sa 9am-4:30pm, Su 10:30am-4pm. Free.)* Housed in a Classical 1927 Superior Tribunal building, Guayama's **Centro de Bellas Artes** displays a variety of paintings, sculptures, and prints by professional Puerto Rican artists and incredibly talented art students. One room holds Taíno artifacts, but all the explanatory signs are in Spanish. *(Rte. 3 Km 138, heading northeast toward plaza from Hwy. 53. ☎864-7765. Open Tu-Su 9am-4:30pm. Free.)* The quirky **Pabellón de la Fama Deporte Guayamés** (Pavilion of Guayaman Sports Fame) details local sports accomplishments through photos, newspaper clippings, and memorabilia. A good number of track stars are represented, and who knew that a *guayamés* had played for the Yankees? *(C. Ashford 22, at C. Derkes. ☎866-0676. Open M-F 8am-noon and 1-4:30pm.)*

RESERVA NATURAL MARIPOSARIO LAS LIMAS. The first butterfly sanctuary in Puerto Rico hides high in the hills, about 5 mi. north of Guayama. Created by an environmentally minded Puerto Rican couple, the 198-acre, semi-tropical reserve has received support from several government facilities, including the DRNA, but still retains the personal feel of a private enterprise. A 1¼hr. guided walk leads visitors from a small museum filled with hundreds of butterfly specimens, past ponds filled with shrimp, turtles, and fish, and into the woods, where guides point out the various species of plants and animals. Of course, there is time for a stop at the small butterfly cage, and a cafeteria and gift shop await at the end. *(From Guayama take Rte. 15 north to Rte. 179. After about 2 mi., turn onto Rte. 747 and make a right at Km 0.7 where signs lead to the forest. ☎864-6037 or 864-5133. Open only by reservation; Th-Su 10am-3pm preferred. Mostly Spanish, but guides speak some English. Mandatory tour $5. Cash only.)*

ARROYO

When the sugar boom came to an end and Guayama developed as an industrial town, little Arroyo lagged behind. The result is a much smaller, and much more charming, oceanside town where the main attraction is walking down the boardwalk and watching the boats dock. Nonetheless, the city also has several worthwhile cultural attractions. Arroyo's **Tren del Sur,** Rte. 3 Km 130.9, rekindles the atmosphere of the sugar era on a 1hr. ride through sugar fields and past plantation ruins. However, the train is currently under renovation until further notice. Consult the **tourist office,** in the same parking lot as Tren del Sur, for updates (☎271-1574). Arroyo's colorful and beautifully carved old customs house has been converted into the **Museo de la Antigua Aduana,** C. Morse 65, which was under construction at the time of publication. (South of the plaza. ☎839-8096. Open daily 9am-noon and 1pm-4pm.) The charming **malecón** or **boardwalk** at the end of C. Morse is lined with palm trees on one side and seafood restaurants on the other; you can find locals strolling here in the evenings and on weekends. The most popular part of Arroyo is not the town itself, but rather **Centro Vacacional Punta Guilarte,** the most popular swimming beach between Yabucoa and Guánica. This enormous government-run vacation center doesn't have too much sand, but makes up for that with scattered palm trees, lush vegetation, and incredible sunsets. Here, families picnic in the grass and children play in the shallow water. Facilities include outdoor showers, bathrooms, trash cans, picnic tables, and lifeguards during daylight hours. A few kiosks sell *empanadillas* and beer.

The accommodations options at this large complex fit any budget. An enormous grassy camping area called **Balneario Punta Guilarte ❶** at the far eastern edge of the complex has trash cans and a bathroom. The tiny cement **cabañas ❸** provide a roof and two cramped bedrooms that hold up to six people. The rooms are less than comfortable, but *cabaña* guests also have access to the large, clean pool, as well as **beach volleyball courts.** For a more relaxed sleeping experience, head straight to the **villas ❹,** which are similar to the *cabañas* but have been newly renovated and include A/C and hot water. (Rte. 3 Km 128.4 to 129.6, east of Arroyo. The western entrance leads to the villas; the eastern entrance leads to the *cabañas*, the camping area, the public beach, and the office. ☎839-3565 or 839-3565; www.parquesnacionalespr.com. Office open daily 8am-4:30pm. Entrance to complex $3 per car. Camping $10 per tent. *Cabañas* $66; villas $109. Tax included. AmEx/D/MC/V.) Arroyo's best restaurants line the boardwalk, where guests enjoy seafood on patios overlooking the water. For a cheap option, **Panadería and Repostería La Familia ❶,** on C. Morse, two blocks south of the

SOUTHEAST

plaza, serves pizza (slices $1.25-1.75), sandwiches ($1.25-4.50), a daily lunch special ($4), and of course, pastries. (☎271-5162. Open daily 6:30am-9pm. MC/V.)

Públicos between Patillas and Guayama stop in Arroyo along C. Morse; flag down a van and ask which direction it's going (15min., $0.50). If you're going to Centro Vacacional Guilarte, ask the driver to drop you off at the intersection, then walk 1 mi. down to the beach. It's about a 2 mi. walk back into town.

ROUTE 901

Following the southeast corner of the island through the heart of sugar country, Rte. 901 is the tail end of Puerto Rico's Ruta Panorámica. Here, it seems that the crest of every hill opens on yet another gorgeous ocean vista. The road's ideal location has invited the building of attractive accommodations and appetizing seafood restaurants. Foreigners and Puerto Ricans alike make the trek out onto this corner of the island to relax on hammocks, bake in the sun, or just watch the waves. Yabucoa, at the northern end of the road, serves as the starting point for the scenic Ruta Panorámica (p. 290).

▐ TRANSPORTATION. From San Juan take Hwy. 52 south to Caguas, get on Rte. 1 temporarily to catch the exit for Hwy. 30 east, then exit onto Hwy. 53 south. At the end of Hwy. 53 turn right to reach Yabucoa or turn left for Rte. 901. Rte. 901 is easiest to navigate by car; however, **públicos** do go from Yabucoa to **Humacao** (20min., $1.20) and **Maunabo** (20-25min., $1). From Yabucoa's *público* station, walk uphill and turn right on C. Cristóbal Colón to reach the plaza and the taxi stand. **Taxis** travel to **Playa Lucía** ($6), **Maunabo** ($15), and everywhere in between. (☎266-4047. Open 6am-6pm.) If you do plan to reach a hotel by public transportation, either bring your own food or head to an all-inclusive—the mountain roads are not suited to walking and food establishments are scattered.

▐▐ ORIENTATION AND PRACTICAL INFORMATION. Rte. 901 follows the southeast coast of the island between Yabucoa and Maunabo, however, the scenic route continues south past Maunabo along Rte. 3 all the way to Patillas. If you get lost, follow the numerous signs to the *parador*. Coming into Yabucoa, when you reach the concrete island, turn right onto **Calle Cristóbal Colón** (also called Rte. 9010) to reach the plaza, or continue straight onto Rte. 182 (also called C. Catalina Morales) for most government buildings and the beginning of the Ruta Panorámica. All of the services listed below are in Yabucoa. **Banco Popular,** on Rte. 9914 1 mi. south of town, has one walk-up and several drive-thru **ATMs.** (☎266-2600. Open M-F 8am-4pm, Sa 9am-noon.) **Yabucoa Municipal Library,** on C. Catalina Morales, past the post office, houses the city's small **Casa de la Cultura** and its collection of Yabucoan artifacts that range from pre-Taíno ceramics of 250 BC to dishes made of squash shells from the 1940s. (☎893-5520 or 893-3385. Open when school is in session M-Th 8am-7pm, F 8am-4:30pm; in summer M-F 8am-4:30pm.) **60 Minute Cleaners,** C. Cristóbal Colón 67, has washers ($1.25) and dryers ($0.50). (☎893-2855. Open M-Sa 6:30am-4pm.) The **police station,** C. Catalina Morales 102 (☎893-2020), is open 24hr. **Farmacia Feliciano** is next to Supermercado del Este. (☎893-6709. Open M-F 7:30am-9pm, Sa 8am-9pm. AmEx/D/MC/V.) Yabucoa's **hospital** is across from the supermarket. (☎893-7480. 24hr. emergency room.) **PostNet,** on Rte. 901, about half a mile south of town, across from the stadium, has **Internet** access. (☎893-0520. $5 per hr. Also has UPS and FedEx service. Open M-F 8:30am-1:30pm and 2-5pm.) The **post office** is at C. Catalina Morales 100. (☎893-2135. No General Delivery. Open M-F 7:30am-4:30pm, Sa 8am-noon.) **Postal Code:** 00767.

KIOSKOS 101

Open-air restaurants and snack shacks called *kioskos* sustain beachgoers across Puerto Rico. Here is a guide to the fried flavors of *comida criolla*:

Alcapurrias: Mashed banana and *yautia* (taro root) dough, filled with meat and fried.

Amarillos: Ripe yellow plantains sliced lengthwise and fried.

Asopao: Hearty gumbo made with chicken and fish.

Bacalao: Salty, dried whole codfish.

Bacalaito: Deep-fried codfish fritter.

Chicarrones: Crispy, dark, fried pork rinds.

Chuletas: Large, juicy, grilled or fried pork chops.

Empanadillas: Baked turnovers filled with seafood, beef, or cheese; also known as *empanadas.*

Jueyes: Battered and fried land crab.

Lechón asado: Roasted or barbecued pig eaten with *aji-li-mojili* sauce, which combines garlic with sweet seeded chili peppers.

Mofongo: Fried green plantains, mashed with garlic and topped with chicken, beef, or seafood.

Pastelillos: Deep-fried meat and cheese turnover.

Pinchos: Barbecued shish kabobs made from chicken, pork, and fresh fish.

Tostones: Flattened, fried plantains that are yellow and crispy, and slightly more dense than french fries.

⌐ ACCOMMODATIONS. The inviting accommodations along this scenic route are one of the region's major draws. Like the region itself, most are relatively quiet and the management will frown upon groups of drunk teenagers. **Playa Emajaguas Guest House ❷,** Rte. 901 Km 12.5, is a family-owned budget accommodation that combines a great location overlooking the beach with excellent prices. 1½ mi. north of Maunabo, this two-story guest house comes with a tennis court, pool, picnic tables, hammocks and a path down to Playa Emajaguas (see **Beaches,** below). The downside is that it is a bit messy and beginning to show its age. (☎861-6023. TV, A/C, and fridge. In summer small rooms $60; apartments with stove $80. Rest of the year $50/70. Cash only.) A parrot on an open stand greets guests in the lobby of **Parador Palmas de Lucía ❹,** at Rte. 901 and Rte. 9911, about 5 mi. southeast of Yabucoa. As one of the island's premier *paradores*, this peach-colored hotel encloses a courtyard and pool area. Large, carpeted rooms are clean and tasteful, and the hotel is just steps away from the fun Playa Lucía. (☎893-4423; www.palmasdelucia.com. Volleyball and basketball courts. Cable TV, A/C, and phone. 4-person double $90. Extra person $17. Also offers all-inclusive packages. Tax included. AmEx/MC/V.) The **Caribe Playa Beach Resort ❺,** Rte. 3 Km 112.1, south of Maunabo in Patillas, exudes a boutique-hotel professionalism; this is the romantic getaway of the Rte. 901 coast. All guest room doors open only ten steps from the beach, and the striking location is enhanced by lush tropical plants, numerous hammocks and beach chairs, a barbecue, beachside pool, and a hot tub. All suites contain 2 queen beds, a fridge, cable TV, phone, shared balcony, and of course, an ocean view. (☎839-6339 or 839-7719; www.caribeplaya.com. Restaurant on covered patio on the water. All rooms $134 per night. Tax included. AmEx/MC/V.)

◖ FOOD. Supermercado del Este, on Rte. 901, just south of Yabucoa in the plaza labeled "La Reina," has groceries. (☎893-7557. Open M-Sa 7am-7pm, Su 11am-5pm. MC/V.) Several restaurants along Rte. 901 are upscale eateries offering spectacular views and equally amazing seafood entrees. Many more are cheap kiosks hawking *pinchos* to beachgoers. Rarely is a lookout point combined with both a kiosk and a popular bar, but **Baloncito Cielo** has done it, at arguably the most breathtaking spot on Rte. 901. Perched on a wooden patio overlooking gorgeous palms, rolling hills, rustic *cabañas* and the ocean horizon, people from across the region snag afternoon seats under umbrellas and then stay late. (☎893-5492. Km 8.8. Fried *pastilillos*, *jueyes*, and *empanadas* $2.25. Daiquiris and piña coladas $3.50. Bottled beer $2.25-2.50. Open Th-Sa 11am-10pm, Su 11am-8pm. Cash.) If you decide to stay in Yabucoa, **Doredmar Restaurant ❸**, on Rte. 3 just south of the intersection with Rte. 901, is one of the few standouts. A small back patio lit with lanterns and surrounded by lush forest is a great location to enjoy fresh steak and seafood. (☎893-3837. Meat entrees $7-18. Seafood $11-23. Open M-Th 11am-8:30pm, F-Sa 11am-10pm, Su 11am-7pm. AmEx/MC/V.) The well-marked **Los Bohíos Restaurant ❹**, off Rte. 760 on Playa Maunabo, provides a refreshing change from the dozens of roadside kiosks; it offers seafood and *mofongo* in a large dining room with one wall knocked out to provide a full beach view. Bohíos keeps it classy—you may not want to come straight from the beach. (☎861-2545. Seafood entrees $12-22. *Mofongo* $11-22. Open W-Th 11am-3pm, F-Su 11am-7:30pm. AmEx/MC/V.)

🏖🔆 **BEACHES AND SIGHTS.** Rte. 901 is lined with beaches, but many are rocky and have minimal shore area. Just below the guesthouse of the same name, palm-lined **Playa de Emajaguas** has an unusually wide stretch of smooth sand, few rocks, medium-sized waves, and remarkably small crowds. Although, there are no facilities, this is still one of the best sites for lounging and swimming in the clearest waters along Rte. 901. Another attractive beach is **Playa Lucía**, located just past Parador Palmas de Lucía (see **Accommodations**, above). The long beach lined with palm trees is often filled with guests from the *parador*. A few food kiosks open when the beach is crowded.

The only sight in this area is located on a beach; the lighthouse called **Faro Punta Tuna**, just outside of Maunabo, is visible from both Playa Maunabo and Playa Larga. Built by the Spanish in the late 1800s, the lighthouse is now open to the public. (Open W-Su 9am-4pm.) For the best views, head down to the secluded **Playa Larga**. Coming south on Rte. 9011, turn toward the ocean on Rte. 7760, and look out for hotel Villas del Faro; turn left onto the dirt driveway across the street. Park your car in the dirt clearing here and walk down the path through brush to the beach. Alternatively, pass Villa del Faro on Rte. 7760 and take the first left going downhill at the mailboxes. You will have to find somewhere on Rte. 7760 to park your car, as the street that leads to the beach does not allow parking. When you get to the closed gate, walk down the short path to the beach. The sand sometimes accumulates seaweed, but it is a small price to pay for this beach's rare solitude.

Traveling southwest on Rte. 760, the next beach area is **Playa Maunabo**, which is frequented by families looking to lounge and play on the sand. Its big waves are not safe for children because of the current, but they are good for boogie boarding. Minimal facilities include grills. To reach the beach, follow signs to Restaurant Los Bohíos on a road that veers south off Rte. 760. A widespread favorite for beachgoers from Maunabo and Patillas is **Playa Escondida**, more commonly known as **Bajo de Patillas**. To reach this preferred swimming beach with public bathrooms and open showers, continue west on Hwy. 3 about ten minutes past Caribe Playa Beach Resort; at Villa Liquor Store turn left down the dirt road, which will take you straight to the water's edge.

SOUTHWEST

Forget those images of lush palm-tree-lined beaches; here, the landscape is dramatic and dry, and the coastline alternates between striking cliffs, stretches of uninterrupted sand, and rocky ports. Inland lies the cactus forest of Bosque Estatal de Guánica, and, just offshore, hundreds of mangrove-filled islands invite exploration. Southwest Puerto Rico feels so different from San Juan that the Spaniards gave the region its own capital in 1514. Nowadays, college towns attract young people while the beaches draw families and partygoers from around the island. The fruits of the sea make up the majority of the southwest's extensive culinary offerings, enticing visitors and Puerto Ricans alike. Summer weekends can be very crowded, but during the week and particularly in the low season, travelers can have a dramatic cliff-top or a quiet beach all to themselves. Casual hiking, kayaking, diving, and snorkeling in some of the island's best state forests and protected waters attract active visitors, but the greatest natural wonders are found on protected Isla Mona, nearly 50 mi. offshore. Cultural offerings are not lacking either. The region's long colonial history has resulted in architecture that rivals anything in Old San Juan, while legends of pirates, nuns, smugglers, and town fathers speak to 500 years of contested ownership.

HIGHLIGHTS OF SOUTHWEST PUERTO RICO

REVEL in the many delights of **Guánica's** superb dry forest (below).

GET IN TOUCH WITH YOUR WILD SIDE on **Isla Mona,** land of enormous iguanas, gorgeous beaches and the best diving in Puerto Rico (p. 246).

ESCAPE TO THE END OF THE EARTH at the **Cabo Rojo Lighthouse,** where breathtaking cliffs produce some of the most dramatic scenery in Puerto Rico (p. 241).

SAVOR the seafood and other culinary delights of small-town **Joyuda** (p. 250).

BOSQUE ESTATAL DE GUÁNICA

The mountain forests of the north may get 15 ft. of rain per year, but the dry forest of Bosque Estatal de Guánica gets an average of only 35 in. The forest contains such a unique diversity of plant and animal life, including the largest variety of birds on the island, that it was named a United Nations Biosphere Reserve in 1981. This is Puerto Rico's paradise for outdoor pursuits, as it has some of the best hiking and water sports on the island. With over 20 mi. of trails, two islands just offshore, and cactus-covered cliffs that give way to the gently lapping waves of Caribbean beaches, it's not unusual to see visitors lacing up their hiking boots, taking a kayak off the roof rack, unpacking snorkeling gear, or just wandering off with a picnic.

TRANSPORTATION AND PRACTICAL INFORMATION

From Hwy. 2, turn south onto Rte. 116. The first important left is Rte. 334, which leads to the forest info center. The next left, onto Rte. 333, leads to most of the beaches, the accommodations, and the ferry dock. At the next intersection, Rte. 116R becomes **Calle 25 de Julio** and leads to Guánica's center. C. 25 de Julio passes the plaza and veers left before intersecting with Rte. 333. C. 39 de Marzo intersects C. 25 de Julio just past the plaza. Inquire at the Alcaldía about

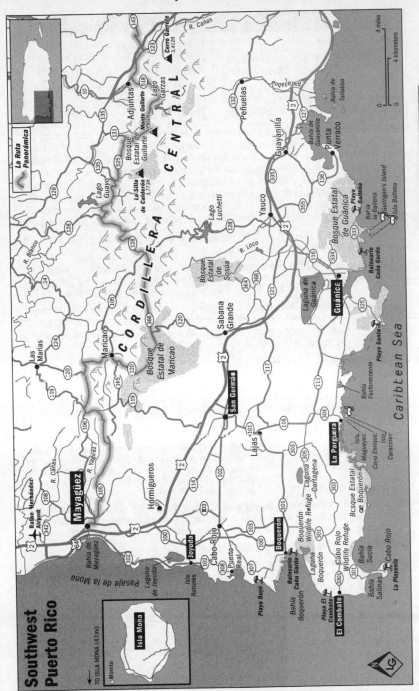

SOUTHWEST

Southwest
Puerto Rico

La Ruta
Panorámica

Isla Mona

TO ISLA MONA (47mi)

Monito

Caribbean Sea

Pasaje de la Mona

CORDILLERA CENTRAL

Cerro Garrote
3,412ft

R. Cañas

R. Cañas

Monte Guilarte
3,950ft

La Silla
de Calderón
3,773ft

Lago
Gázas

Lago
Guilarte

Adjuntas

Bosque
Estatal de
Guilarte

Peñuelas

Guayanilla

Punta
Verraco

Bahía de
Tallaboa

Bahía de
Guayanilla

Playa
Ballena

Bahía
la Ballena

Guilligan's Island

Isla Ballena

Yauco

Lago
Luchetti

R. Loco

Bosque
Estatal
de Sosia

Bosque Estatal
de Guánica

Balneario
Caña Gorda

Guánica

Laguna de
Guánica

Playa Santa

Bahía
Fosforescente

Lago
Guayo

R. Blanco

R. Cañas

Las
Marías

Maricao

Bosque
Estatal de
Maricao

Sabana
Grande

San Germán

Lajas

La Parguera

Isla
Magüeye

Cayo Enrique

Isla
Caracoles

Rafae Hernández
Airport

Mayagüez

Hormigueros

R. Yagüez

Bahía de
Mayagüez

Laguna
de Joyuda

Isla
Ratones

Joyuda

Cabo Rojo

Puerto
Real

Boquerón

Balneario
Caña Garda

Laguna
Boquerón

Bahía
Boquerón

Playa Buyé

El Combate

Playa El
Combate

Bosque Estatal
de Boquerón

Laguna
Cartagena

Boquerón
Wildlife Refuge

Cabo Rojo
Wildlife Refuge

Bahía
Sucia

Bahía
Salinas

La Playuela

Cabo Rojo

Caribbean Sea

N

4 miles

4 kilometers

AT A GLANCE

AREA: 9876 acres.

CLIMATE: Hot and dry. Average temperature 79°F. Little variation. Average yearly rainfall 35 in.

HIGHLIGHTS: Hiking through dramatic landscapes, water sports, birdwatching.

FEATURES: Rare dry limestone scrub, incredible Caribbean coastline.

GATEWAYS: Guánica, Ponce (p. 201).

CAMPING: Unfortunately, there is no camping in or near Guánica.

FEES: None.

schedules for **públicos** and the **free trolley** that goes around the city during the week. It leaves from the Alcaldía on C. 25 de Julio on the plaza at various times. Bosque Estatal de Guánica is divided into two sections. The larger eastern half contains the hiking trails, the two most popular beaches, and the two offshore islands, Isla Ballena and Guilligan's Island. The western section is smaller and doesn't have any trails but surrounds Playa Santa. In between, the small town of Guánica is a good place to stock up on supplies, but none of the streets have signs, making it difficult to get around or find visitor information.

Bank: Banco Santander, C. S.S. Rodríguez 63 (☎821-2700 or 821-2283), off C. 25 de Julio. **ATM.** Open M-F 8:30am-4pm.

Visitors Center: The **DRNA info center** (☎821-5706), at the end of Rte. 334, about 3.3 mi. from Rte. 116, provides extensive info about the trails (in English and Spanish). Open daily 8:30am-4:30pm. The DRNA parking area and most trails are open daily 8:30am-4:30pm.

Supplies: Sunscreen and water are the most important items you will need in Guánica; many paths don't have shade and there are no water sources. Bring at least 35 oz. of water per person per hr. of hiking. Wear comfortable walking shoes, which will serve you much better than flip-flops or sandals.

Equipment Rental:

Dive Copamarina, in Copamarina Beach Resort (see **Scuba Diving,** p. 229), rents tennis rackets ($5 per hr., $9 per 2hr.), kayaks (singles $12 per hr., $20 per 2hr.; doubles $20/35), snorkel gear ($10 per 3hr., $15 per 6hr.), water tricycles ($15 per hr.), Barracuda paddle boats ($20 per hr.) and Hobie Cats ($40 per hr., $70 per 2hr.).

Pino's Boats and Water Fun (☎821-6864 or 484-8083), a trailer on the beach at Playa Santa, rents jet skis ($45 per 30min.), kayaks (singles $12 per hr., doubles $20), paddleboats (2-person $12 per hr., 4-person $20), umbrellas ($8 per day), and lounge chairs ($6 per day). The owner also offers 40min. motorboat ecotours through the mangroves with narration of the ecological features along the way ($6 per person), 20min. banana boat rides ($7 per person), and jet ski tours of the mangroves ($45). Open Sa-Su and most weekdays; hours depend on crowds, but usually 11am-5pm. MC/V.

Museo de Arte e Historia de Guánica, on C. 25 de Julio in the Old Alcaldía on the corner of the plaza. The Old Alcaldía has been magnificently renovated, giving travelers the chance to learn about the town and the surrounding area. $1, students $0.50.

Police: C. 13 de Marzo 51 (☎821-2020). Open 24hr.

Pharmacy: Farmacia Quesada, at the corner of C. 25 de Julio and C. 13 de Marzo, near the post office, has a basic selection of medicines. Open M-F 8am-6pm, Sa 8am-5pm. AmEx/MC/V.

Hospital: (☎821-1481). From Rte. 116, drive down C. 25 de Julio and turn right after the plaza, turn right at the end of the street, then take the first left. The small 1-story building has a 24hr. emergency room.

Post Office: C. 13 de Marzo 39 (☎821-2645). No General Delivery. Open M-F 8am-4:15pm, Sa 8am-noon. **Postal Code:** 00653.

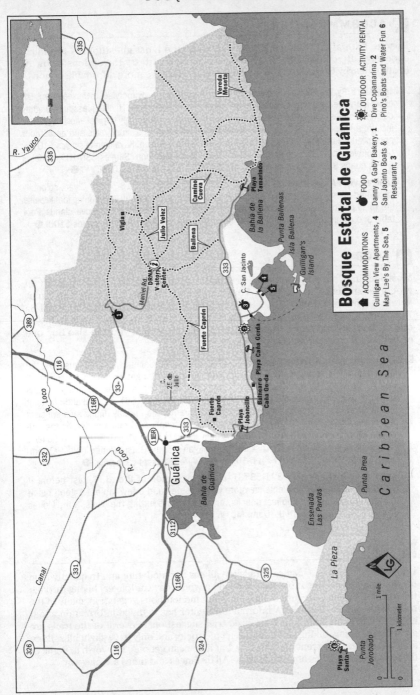

Bosque Estatal de Guánica

▲ ACCOMMODATIONS
Guilligan View Apartments, **4**
Mary Lee's By The Sea, **5**

● FOOD
Danny & Gaby Bakery, **1**
San Jacinto Boats & Restaurant, **3**

☀ OUTDOOR ACTIVITY RENTAL
Dive Copamarina, **2**
Pino's Boats and Water Fun **6**

ACCOMMODATIONS

Bosque Estatal de Guánica has no camping, and most guesthouses are fairly expensive. If you don't want to splurge on a big resort, try the options below or head to nearby Guayanilla and La Parguera, which have more affordable options.

■ **Mary Lee's By The Sea,** C. San Jacinto 25 (☎821-3600; www.maryleesbythesea.com). US expat Mary Lee has put great care into the decoration of each room. Haitian grass rugs, brightly colored curtains, and lots of seaside knick-knacks create a charmingly tropical effect. All rooms include a kitchenette, A/C, and access to a deck with a BBQ. 2 small piers and an outdoor patio overlook the water. Trips to Guilligan's Island $6 per person. Kayak rental singles $10 per hr., doubles $15. Laundry free. Check-in 3pm. Check-out noon. Singles $80-100; doubles $120; quads $130-140; 6-person rooms $140-250. Extra person $10. MC/V. ❸

Guilligan View Apartments, C. San Jacinto 27 (☎821-4901 or 316-7488). Clean, colorfully decorated rooms, all with full kitchens. Busy during the summer when vacationing families use the small pier to go swimming and jet-skiing. Offers a nice view of the mangrove islands. Pool table and common yard in back. Kayak rental $35 per day. Doubles $75; quads $100. ❸

FOOD

Most lodgings have full kitchens, so the best budget option is to stock up on groceries and cook for yourself. You can pick up food at the Econo supermarket, at the intersection of Rte. 116 and Rte. 116R. (☎821-2789. ATM. Open M-Sa 7am-8pm, Su 11am-5pm. AmEx/D/MC/V.) If you never learned to cook, hit up one of the fast-food places right off Rte. 116 near the city; you can also find one or two small *cafeterías* near the plaza.

■ **San Jacinto Boats & Restaurant** (☎821-4941), on C. San Jacinto. Turn right just past the Copamarina Resort and look for the large parking lot on the right. This bayside restaurant wears many hats: by day it sells ferry tickets ($5), rents snorkel gear ($15) and kayaks ($10 per hr.), and serves inexpensive *comida criolla* lunches ($6); on weekend nights, it opens up as one of Guánica's best seafood restaurants. The midday dining area consists of a few outdoor picnic tables, but the nighttime atmosphere is much better, as the intimate interior resembles a ship's hull. Also delivers lunches to Islas Guilligan and Ballena ($5). Dinner entrees $18-23. Last trip to Guilligan's 5pm. Outside open daily 9:30am-6pm; inside restaurant open F-Sa 6-10pm. MC/V; ferry tickets cash only. ❹

Danny & Gaby Bakery (☎821-5373), on the right side of Rte. 334, just before it heads uphill. A small convenience store with pastries and a few tables. A good place to stock up on picnic supplies, snacks, or water before hitting the trails. Sandwiches $1.25-3. Open daily 6am-9:30pm. MC/V. ❶

HIKING

Unlike most reserves, Guánica's trails are all easy or moderate and frequently loop between sights, making it pleasant to spend a whole day (or longer) hiking through the forest. However, because of the somewhat monotonous vegetation, many of the trails look similar. The DRNA Information Center has detailed information about each trail and can provide personalized trail suggestions. Several of the trails are great for mountain biking since they aren't too rocky and only have slight hills; there aren't any places that rent bikes nearby, but if you can get one, it's worth it. Some of the more popular hikes are listed below. All distances and times are one-way.

🏖VEREDA MESETA. *(3.5km, 45min. Easy.)* Meseta is the only trail in Guánica that borders the ocean. The path departs from the Playa Tamarindo parking lot, then continues west along the coastline, and heads all the way to the eastern edge of the forest. The view remains consistently incredible. At the beginning there are several good beaches just off the path, but farther east sand gives way to steep oceanside cliffs. Well-suited to mountain biking, Meseta also offers an up-close view of the coastal dry forest and a chance to see several sea birds, including frigate birds and white tropic birds. After the hike, you can head for a refreshing swim at Playa Tamarindo.

🏖CAMINO BALLENA. *(2km, 30min. Easy.)* This gravel trail is one of the easiest and best paths in Guánica. Not only does it pass through some of the wildest desert scenery, but it also conveniently leads from the information center down to Rte. 333 at Bahía La Ballena. Along the way, you'll pass Guayacán Centenario, a 700-year-old tree that rises proudly above the lowland vegetation. The marked, northern trailhead is next to the DRNA Visitors Center, to the left as you walk away from the parking lot. The southern trailhead is not marked but is easily identifiable by the large green gate on Rte. 333.

CAMINO JULIO VELEZ/CAMINO LOS GRANADOS. *(2.5km, 1hr. for full loop. Easy.)* This circular route leaves from the information center and provides a nice introduction to the forest. Reserve workers recommend this path because it is well marked, relatively short, and a great place to see many of the forest's birds; over 40 bird species have been identified in this area. A detour at the eastern edge of the circle leads to La Vigía, the highest hill in the forest, which offers incredible views of its surroundings. The loop ends at Rte. 334, just a short walk back to the parking lot.

FUERTE CAPRÓN. *(5.5km, 1½hr. Moderate.)* One of the forest's longer trails, the gravel road follows a ridgeline and leads southwest from the info center toward a small fort. Don't expect to see El Morro—this is a tiny observation tower built by the Civilian Conservation Corps in the 1930s on the site of a former Spanish fort. The path does not pass through particularly dramatic vegetation, but it does have great views of the city of Guánica and the bay. The trail undulates up and down small hills and has three small turn-offs (from east to west: Hoya Hunda, Picua, and El Ver). The trail ends at Rte. 333 Km 3.2 at Playa Jaboncillo. Coming from the south, park in the small turn-off at Km 3.2 and take the narrow path that heads toward the old water tower. If you don't want to leave your car on the road, park in the Visitors Center and head down the trail, but be ready for an uphill return trip.

CAMINO CUEVA. *(1.5km, 20min. Easy.)* This unmarked path leads uphill from the Playa Tamarindo swimming area parking lot to the intersection with Camino Llúberas. Here you can find 3m-tall prickly pear cacti as well as several brightly colored butterflies. There is also a large cave that contains petroglyphs and two species of bats; to visit it, you must obtain permission from the DRNA and be accompanied by a guide. The trail is clear, but lacks adequate signage. To enter from the south, step over the short wire gate next to the green gate at the parking lot entrance, then continue uphill. When you reach Camino Llúberas, you can turn around or veer to the left and eventually you'll reach Camino Julio Velez, adding another 2.5km (40min.) to your hike.

◤ BEACHES

Guánica's coastline alternates between steep cliffs and sandy beaches, and the water ranges from large, rough waves to tiny, shallow pools. There are several nice public beaches, but the most rewarding experience may be to explore until you find your own quiet stretch of sand. **Dive Copamarina,** in the Copamarina Beach Resort, Rte. 333 Km 6.5, offers two-tank dives to The Wall. (☎821-0505, ext. 729, toll-free 800-981-4676; www.copamarina.com. 2-tank dive $85, equipment $10. 3-day certification course $450; advance registration required. Discover Scuba package $150. Open daily 9am-5pm. AmEx/MC/V.)

▧ PLAYA JOBONCILLO. For true privacy, head down the steep rocky dirt road to this beautiful blue bay surrounded by rocky cliffs on either side. A covered picnic table and fire pit reveal that others enjoy this beach, but on weekdays it provides an oasis of picturesque solitude. *(Rte. 333 Km 3.1. 4WD is helpful but not necessary. Walk down the road a bit to see if your car can handle the conditions.)*

THE ISLANDS. If you've ever wanted to visit **Guilligan's Island,** here's your chance. A 10min. motorboat ride takes you to the tiny mangrove-covered island, where a few small beaches hide amid trees. There's not much sand, so arrive by 11am on weekends to get a spot. The water here is shallow and clear, making for nice **snorkeling.** Guilligan's Island has an outhouse, a DRNA office, and covered picnic tables. Nearby **Isla Ballena** is a different story. Ballena is less crowded and has a long sandy isthmus good for lounging, but no facilities. *(Ferries travel from Restaurant San Jacinto (see **Food,** p. 228) to Guilligan's Island and Isla Ballena. Tu-F every hr., Sa-Su every 30min. 9am-5pm; $5 round-trip. Open Tu-Su 9am-5pm.)*

PLAYA SANTA. To reach Playa Santa from Guánica, follow Rte. 116 west, turn off onto Rte. 3112, turn south onto Rte. 325, continue to the end, turn left at the T, and take the first right to the parking area. Playa Santa is at the doorstep of a *centro vacacional* for state employees; it is open to the public and offers good swimming but no facilities. **Ancla Flotante,** at the parking lot, plays music all day and draws a beach crowd with its *empanada* stand and $1 Corona Happy hour. (Bathrooms for customers only.) Around the corner you can also grab a drink or shoot some pool at **Brisas de Santa Plaza.** Both are open as long as there are people on the beach. If lying on the beach makes you restless, stop by **Pino's Boats and Water Fun,** which rents a variety of water equipment (see **Equipment Rental,** p. 226).

BALNEARIO CAÑA GORDA. Situated right next door to the Copamarina Beach Resort, this long, white sand beach lined with dry forest trees has some excellent sunning areas.Caña Gorda has all the amenities of a *balneario,* including lifeguards, showers, bathrooms, chair rental ($5 per day with ID), covered picnic tables, a cafe, and a mini-market. *(Rte. 333 Km 6. ☎821-5676. Parking cars $3, vans $4. Open daily Sept.-May 8am-5pm; June-Aug. 7am-6pm.)*

BAHÍA LA BALLENA/PLAYA TAMARINDO. Driving along Rte. 333, you'll find cars and people sprawled all along Bahía la Ballena. The road ends at Playa Tamarindo, a long patch of sand with ample space for sunbathing and water deep enough for swimming. However, the only facilities are trash cans, and the area can get relatively crowded. Head along the Vereda Meseta trail (p. 229) to find a more secluded spot. *(At the end of Rte. 333, about 2 mi. past Copamarina Resort.)*

LA PARGUERA

Puerto Ricans know that this small town makes an excellent destination for a long-weekend getaway. Just offshore, several mangrove islands and calm, shallow water create a paradise for boaters as well as a main research spot for marine biologists. Most foreigners come to La Parguera to see the phosphorescent bay, frequently touted as the best in Puerto Rico. Don't be confused—this is not La Parguera's principal attraction; although it is the cheapest place to be dazzled by glowing water, both Fajardo and Vieques have better bioluminescent bays. Farther out to sea, The Wall, a 20 mi. long coral reef cliff, attracts serious scuba divers from around the island. On weekends and holidays, the small neighborhood takes on the feel of a seaside carnival, with crowds of people wandering the streets munching on *pinchos* and *empanadas.*

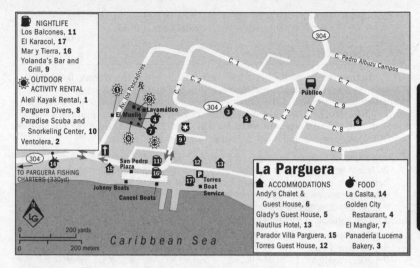

NIGHTLIFE
Los Balcones, 11
El Karacol, 17
Mar y Tierra, 16
Yolanda's Bar and
  Grill, 9

OUTDOOR
  ACTIVITY RENTAL
Alelí Kayak Rental, 1
Parguera Divers, 8
Paradise Scuba and
  Snorkeling Center, 10
Ventolera, 2

La Parguera

ACCOMMODATIONS
Andy's Chalet &
  Guest House, 6
Glady's Guest House, 5
Nautilus Hotel, 13
Parador Villa Parguera, 15
Torres Guest House, 12

FOOD
La Casita, 14
Golden City
  Restaurant, 4
El Manglar, 7
Panadería Lucerna
  Bakery, 3

SOUTHWEST

TRANSPORTATION AND PRACTICAL INFORMATION

Coming from the east, drive west on Hwy. 2, turn toward Guánica on Rte. 116, and continue west to the intersection with Rte. 304, which leads south into town. From the west, take Rte. 2 to Rte. 100, then turn left on Rte. 101. Continue on Rte. 303, then Rte. 305, and finally take a right onto Rte. 116; this leads to Rte. 304, which in turn leads to La Parguera. Many of the streets in the tiny town of La Parguera do not have names. Luckily, almost nothing is more than a short walk away from the central wharf area. Rte. 304 leads straight into town and becomes the main thoroughfare. After the church, turn right on Av. los Pescadores to find the **Centro Commercial El Muelle,** a small shopping center filled with many traveler-friendly amenities. A block east away from the plaza is a large parking lot where you can leave your car and walk around town.

Públicos: Shared vans pick up travelers from the brightly painted bench just north of town on Rte. 304 and take them to **Lajas** ($1), but this service is very sporadic. From Lajas, *públicos* continue to **San Germán.**

ATMs: La Parguera has no banks, but there are ATMs in the Centroahorras supermarket (p. 232), at Parador Villa Parguera (p. 232), and in front of Panadería Lucerna Bakery (p. 233).

Equipment Rental: Ventoera (☎808-0396 or 505-4541), in El Muelle, rents 12-17 ft. sailboats ($125 per day) and kayaks (singles $10 per hr., $45 per day; doubles $15/ $55). Also offers lessons in kitesurfing ($55 per hr.), sailing ($35 per hr.; 12hr. over 2 days to complete course), and windsurfing (8hr. course $275). All equipment included. Open in summer M 9am-8pm, Tu-Sa 9am-8pm, Su 9am-5pm; fall-spring Tu-Sa 9am-8pm, Su 9am-5pm. AmEx/MC/V.

English-Language Books: A free book exchange in the corner of El Muelle next to the Ventolera has a large selection of English-language books.

Laundromat: Lavamático (☎899-4844), on the left side of El Muelle. Wash $1.50, dry $1. No detergent. Change available in the supermarket. Open M-Sa 7am-8:45pm, Su 7am-7:45pm.

Police: On Rte. 304, across from Guacataco (☎899-2250 or 899-2020). Open 24hr.

Pharmacy: Farmacia San Pedro (☎899-8719), in El Muelle. Open M-Sa 7am-9pm, Su 7am-8pm. AmEx/MC/V.

Post Office: The small postal service in El Muelle (☎899-6075) has General Delivery. Open M-F 7:30am-4pm, Sa 7:30am-noon. **Postal Code:** 00667.

▌ ACCOMMODATIONS

La Parguera offers a pick of relatively affordable accommodations, from quasi-ocean-side resorts to rustic guesthouses. If possible, reserve a room a few weeks ahead, especially during the summer when places fill up quickly. The bigger hotels offer weekend packages and may have a two-night minimum on weekends during the summer; guesthouses are more flexible. During the week, the town is less crowded and most accommodations are cheaper.

▨ **Andy's Chalet & Guest House,** C. 8 #133 (☎899-0000). Entering the town from Rte. 304, turn left on C. 7, then right on C. 8. This 3-story residential guesthouse offers the best price in the region for standard rooms with TV and A/C. Common 2nd fl. patio with microwave and fridge. Rooftop area with small pool. Breakfast included. Limited parking. No 24hr. reception. Call ahead for reservations. Doubles $55; triples $65; quads $71; 2-room apartments with kitchen $80-95. Tax included. AmEx/MC/V. ❷

Nautilus Hotel (☎899-4565 or 899-4004; www.nautilushotelpr.com), near the boat parking lot. Rooms with TV and A/C are just as nice as those at the *paradores*, at a fraction of the price. Private balconies look out on the parking lot. Pool and hot tub. Reception in the gift shop 3 doors down. Mid-June to mid-Sept. doubles $88; quads $109. Mid-Sept. to mid-June doubles M-Th $66, F-Sa $76; quads $98. Tax included. AmEx/MC/V. ❸

Parador Villa Parguera (☎899-7777; www.villaparguera.net). On Rte. 304 across from the church. The exceptional ocean-side setting makes it a popular wedding location. Beautiful poolside grass patio and courtyard waterfall with white-washed deck and pier. Pristine rooms. A/C, phone, TV, and private balcony. Restaurant offering breakfast and dinner and Sa night dance show. Parking. Check-in 3pm. Check-out noon. Doubles Su-Th $97-107, Sa with dinner and dance show $187. AmEx/D/MC/V. ❹

Glady's Guest House, C. 2 #42B (☎899-4678), near the intersection with Rte. 304 near Lucerna's bakery. Above the owner's house, exudes professionalism and maintains tidy rooms just steps from the town center. A/C and TV. Doubles $60; triples $65; 4-person apartment $75. Tax included. AmEx/MC/V. ❷

Torres Guest House, on Rte. 304 (☎899-5476 or 899-4281), across from the boat parking lot, next to Nautilus Hotel. Conveniently located near the town center and nightlife. This small guesthouse offers 6 simple rooms, all with 2 queen beds, A/C, and small TVs. Check-in 2pm. Check-out noon. Rooms $95. Tax included. Cash only. ❹

◖ FOOD

La Parguera is the place to come for seafood, but also offers visitors the choice of American, Chinese, and Mexican cuisine. Wander along the waterfront and you'll find several small *cafeterías, empanada* stands, ice cream stands, and even a kebab stand, perfect for grabbing refreshments or a cheap bite. The **Centroahorras** supermarket in El Muelle carries a full stock of groceries. (☎899-6065. Open M-Sa 7am-10pm, Su 7am-8pm. AmEx/MC/V.)

▨ **El Manglar** (☎899-4742), in El Muelle. With a large outdoor patio and Bob Marley playing, this is where locals and tourists come for a good meal and good music (see **Nightlife,** p. 239). Serving an "international" menu, Manglar offers typical fried Puerto Rican food, as well as burgers, pizza, and several linguine and alfredo pasta dishes. All-you-can-eat *comida criolla* lunch buffet ($6; daily 11am-2pm) and weekend breakfast buffet ($7). Open M-Th and Su 11am-10pm, F-Sa 11am-1pm. MC/V. ❷

La Casita (☎899-1681), on Rte. 304 at the western edge of town. This big family-friendly restaurant fills up on weekend nights with Puerto Ricans who know that they don't have to go to a 5-star restaurant to get the freshest seafood in town. House wine $5.50. Entrees $10-25. Seafood *monfongo* $18-25. Open July daily 11am-10pm; Aug.-June Tu-Sa 11am-10pm, Su 11am-9pm. AmEx/MC/V. ❹

Panadería Lucerna Bakery (☎899-7637), at the intersection of Rte. 304 and C. 2. This tiny bakery is a good place to go for a hearty island breakfast or simply to grab sandwiches or *comida criolla* for lunch. If it's not on the menu, just ask nicely and the friendly staff will whip up just about anything. Everything under $5. Open M-Th 7am-9pm, F-Sa 7am-10pm, Su 7am-7pm. MC/V; min. $5. ❶

Golden City Restaurant (☎899-5644), in El Muelle, has the ambience of a strip mall eatery, but it's hard to argue with standard Chinese-American favorites in large portions at affordable prices. Combos $4-6. Open M-W 11am-10pm, Th and Su 11am-10:30pm, F-Sa 11am-11pm. Cash only. ❶

🐾 OUTDOOR ACTIVITIES

La Parguera is one of the most popular boating destinations in Puerto Rico; during school vacations, the area becomes packed. Boating companies offer motorboat rentals as well as tours of the mangrove channels, nearby mangrove islands and the bioluminescent bay at night. The calm waters of this area provide excellent opportunities for beginners to try a hand at windsurfing, kitesurfing, sailing, or kayaking (see **Equipment rental,** p. 231). Dense mangrove forests lining the coast mean that there is not much sandy beach, but plenty of marine life exists for snorkelers and divers; the huge offshore reefs are home to fascinating sea creatures.

BOATING

Most Puerto Rican boaters head to **the mangrove canals** *(los canales manglares)* just west of the main docks, where they anchor their boats and jump into the shallow water. On busy days, the wharf is full of fishermen and families heading to the islands. To get away from the hubbub, it's possible to hire a boat and visit the relatively isolated and very pretty **Cayo Enrique.** Farther south, **Isla Mata Gatas** is the most distant island accessible by small motorboat, and supposedly the best area for **snorkeling.** The small island has a dock, bathrooms, picnic tables, and trash cans, but as a result it is quite over-visited; you might be happier parking your boat offshore and exploring the shallow waters. (Open June-Sept. Tu-Su 9am-5pm; Oct.-May Th-Su 9am-5pm. If M is a holiday, open M and closed Tu. $1.) **Caracoles Tierra** has a bit of land in the middle where people have been known to **camp,** but none of the boating services or kayak rentals provide dropoff and pickup service or allow overnight rental. On the way out to any of the islands, you'll pass **Isla Magueyes,** an island managed by the University of Puerto Rico Marine Sciences Department. You have to get special permission from the Mayagüez campus to visit, but if you take one of the smaller boat tours, the guide may hop out and open the gate so that the huge iguanas (used for research) can come out on the dock.

 THE REAL DEAL. La Parguera's bioluminescent bay is the attraction that draws most of the town's visitors, but pollution has damaged the dinoflagellate population, taking some of the sparkle out of the water. For the same price, any of the boat companies on the dock should be willing to take a small motorboat (6-8 people) away from the bay to surrounding canals—and brighter waters. Just make sure your group is large enough to fill the boat.

The **Bahía Fosforescente** (Phosphorescent Bay) is the attraction that draws most visitors to the water off La Parguera. This all-natural water light show is produced by bioluminescent dinoflagellates, which light up like small sparks in the water when stirred. The nighttime trip to the bay takes about 20min. each way, and the best time to go is on a cloudy night or when there is no moon at all. While most companies only stay for 5-10min., smaller boats allow more flexibility and sometimes a chance to swim in the bay. The best option might be to find enough people to charter a small (6- to 8-person) boat and ask the boatman to take you to a bioluminescent spot away from the main bay, which is crowded and not necessarily any better than some of the closer mangrove canals. **Paradise Scuba & Snorkeling Center** offers a sunset snorkeling trip in the bay.

Theoretically, most of the boat companies at La Parguera's main dock are open every day. On busy weekends in the summer, this may be true, but on slower weekdays it may be difficult to find anyone at all; ask around at any of the shops on the dock, and someone should be able to track down a boatman. At least one company opens every night for trips to the phosphorescent bay from 7:30pm until people stop arriving. All companies operate from the wharf and charge $5-6 per person for the 1hr. trip, but there are slight variations in the service. Trips only leave if and when enough customers arrive.

Cancel Boats (☎ 899-5891 or 899-5494). By far the biggest operation in town. The 150-passenger glass-bottom *Cristal Fondo III* takes daytrips through the mangrove channels to see Isla Mata Gata and the coral reefs (Sa 2:30pm, Su 2 and 5pm) and night trips to the phosphorescent bay for only $6 per person (Sept. to late Dec. and early Jan. to Mar. Sa-Su 7:30pm; Mar.-Sept. and late Dec. to early Jan. daily 7:30pm). Smaller motorboats lead private tours throughout the day ($25 for 1-5 people or $5 per person for up to 10 people). MC/V.

Johnny Boats (☎ 299-2212). The only company that lets you swim in the phosphorescent bay. Daytime tours of the mangroves in small motorboats are $5 per person with at least 5 people. $5 trip to Isla Gata and $6 night trip to the phosphorescent bay. Motorboat rental for licensed boaters or those over 35 ($25 for the 1st hr., $20 for the 2nd hr.). Cash only.

Alelí Kayak Rental (☎ 899-6086 or 390-6086), across the street from El Muelle. The retired Coast Guard captain rents kayaks (singles $10 per hr., $30 per ½-day, $50 per day; doubles $15/40/60) and leads 2-4hr. guided ecotours through the mangrove channels ($50 per person, min. 4 people). Open daily 10am-5pm. Call ahead, as owner also occasionally operates a chartered catamaran tour ($700 per day) and the shop may not be open during posted hours.

Torres Boat Service (☎ 396-2089). Rents small motor boats ($25 per hr. for 4 people, min. 2hr.) and offers 40min. guided tours of the bay on a larger boat ($5 per person). Also runs frequent trips to Isla Gatas for $5. Open June-Aug. daily 9am-6pm and 7:30pm-last customer; Sept.-May Sa-Su 9am-6pm and 7:30pm-last customer.

DIVING AND SNORKELING

SNORKELING ON A BUDGET. Renting snorkel gear can cost $10-$20 dollars a day. Keep an eye out at dive shops for summer sales, and you might be able to buy a snorkel and mask for as low as $30. This investment will more than pay itself back, given the West's numerous snorkeling opportunities.

Many of the dive operators in San Juan actually head to La Parguera when they want to do some serious diving—that's how good it is here. The big attraction is **The Wall** (*La Pared*), a 20 mi. coral reef cliff that starts at 60 ft. and drops down to over 150 ft. Visibility tends to be 40-80 ft. and divers have reported seeing sea turtles, manatees, and even dolphins. But beware; The Wall is 6 mi. offshore in open sea, and the voyage tends to be rough. Even those who don't normally get seasick may consider taking anti-nausea medication. Snorkelers can hire a boat (see **Boating**, p. 233) or guide to take them out to one of the nearby, fertile mangrove islands for shallow-water snorkeling.

Paradise Scuba & Snorkeling Center (☎899-7611; paradisescubapr@yahoo.com), next to Hostal Casa Blanca. Although all trips have a min. number of people required, during the summer it is easy for 1 or 2 people to jump into an existing group. Opportunities include: daytime snorkeling trips to 3 areas (3hr., 10am, $35); a sunset snorkeling trip that includes a swim in the phosphorescent bay, dinner cooked by the owner's wife, and all the beer you can drink (4hr., 4pm, $50); a 2-tank dive to The Wall ($70, with equipment rental $80); a 1-tank night dive ($60); and a Discover Scuba package with 1 pool lesson and 2 open-water dives ($125). Private PADI certification course $350, 3-week group course $200 per person. Snorkeling trips include all equipment and a snack. Also rents kayaks (singles $10 per hr., doubles $15 per hr.). Open daily 9am-9pm. 7% tax for all prices. AmEx/MC/V.

Parguera Divers (☎899-4171; www.pargueradivers.com). The main office is in el Muelle; a stand in the Parador Posada Porlamar parking lot is open upon return from dives. Daily trips to The Wall on a 30 ft. Island Hopper. 2-tank dive $70, equipment rental $15; wet suit not included. 1-tank night dive $45, equipment $10. 4-day PADI & NAUI open-water certification courses $350, plus $50 for books. 3hr. snorkeling trips $30. Open M-Th and Su 10am-5pm, F-Sa 9am-6pm. MC/V.

West Divers (☎899-3223), on Rte. 304, next to the police station. Offers 3hr. snorkeling trips ($35, min. 3 people) as well as 2-tank dives out to The Wall ($80). Also has a variety of certification courses ($200-300). Rents equipment, but check availability. Open daily 9am-6pm. MC/V.

FLYING

Experiencing the southwestern corner of the island and the Caribbean's clear, shallow waters from the air provides a new perspective on the coastal environment. Several local aircraft owners give aerial tours of the coastline. Call Micky Rivera, who is a certificated pilot, for more information. (☎448-7629. $70 per 30min., $120 per hr.) The private airfield is halfway between Boquerón and La Parguera.

NIGHTLIFE

La Parguera knows how to party. On summer weekends and holidays, the many bars along the main street are packed until 1am, when local law requires them to shut down. On Saturday nights, the restaurant at **Parador Villa Parguera** (p. 232) hosts an elaborate live music and dance comedy show that attracts a fair number of older visitors ($35 includes dinner and show).

El Karacol (☎899-5582), in front of the docks. For over 30 years, this classy bar and *cafetería* serves up the house specialty, Coño Sangría ($4.50) alongside Spanish and Puerto Rican cooking ($5-15) for the hungry dockside crowds. Arcade room with a Mrs. Pacman/Galaga machine. Open June-Aug. M-Th and Su 11am-11pm, F-Sa 11am-1am; Sept.-May M-Th and Su 11am-11pm, F-Sa 11am-midnight. MC/V.

El Manglar (☎899-4742), in El Muelle. With its large patio and full schedule of live music, this is the place to mix it up with locals while enjoying live *bomba y plena*. Since it's a few blocks away from the wharf, you can avoid the large tourist crowds and enjoy some table space as you kick back and relax. Don't get too comfy in your seat, though—the music will have you dancing in no time. Beer $2-3. Mixed drinks $4. Open M-Th and Su until 10, F-Sa until 1pm. Kitchen closes at 10pm. MC/V.

Yolanda's Bar and Grill, Rte. 304 across from the police station. This little wooden cabin draws a regular crowd during the evening for grilled entrees ($5-13) and later in the night for cheap drinks. Sa night karaoke fills up the patio, with people sitting on the railings and spilling into the street. Beer $2-3. Mixed drinks $4. Open M-Th and Su 7pm-11pm, F-Sa 7pm-1am. Cash only.

Los Balcones (☎899-2145), across from the plaza. Attracts a college crowd, especially on certain Sa nights when live music packs the place. Pool tables ($0.50) and the dance floor draw a loyal crowd. Beer $2-2.50. F-Sa live Spanish rock 10pm. 18+. Happy hour Sa 7pm-midnight. Open June-Aug. M-W 5pm-midnight, F-Sa 5pm-1am; Sept.-May M-W and F-Sa 5pm-midnight. MC/V.

Mar y Tierra (☎899-4627), on Rte. 304. Young male Puerto Ricans practice their game at the 4 pool tables ($0.50) at this popular sports bar. In the back, the *cafetería* attracts an entirely different crowd—families who enjoy hot *empanadillas* with their beer ($1-2.25). Piña colada $4. Open June-Aug. M-Th 5pm-midnight, F-Sa 6pm-1am; Sept.-May M-Th 5pm-midnight, F-Sa 6pm-midnight. MC/V.

SAN GERMÁN

As one of the oldest settlements on the island and home to the island's oldest chapel, San Germán is steeped in Puerto Rican history. The delicate architecture of many homes reflects the city's cultural heritage, while the presence of the Universidad Interamericana gives San Germán a college-town feel outside of the historic center. Travelers come here for a break from the beach and an opportunity to absorb the culture of what was once the western capital of the island. Though nightlife and accommodations are limited, San Germán is a great place to spend a day exploring the streets, soaking up history and culture.

🖿 ⁊ TRANSPORTATION AND PRACTICAL INFORMATION

From Hwy. 2 exit onto Rte. 122, then turn right onto C. Luna. Coming from Boquerón, La Parguera, or anywhere southwest of the city, follow Rte. 101 all the way into the old center of town. San Germán's busy main street used to be called **Calle Luna**, but the government recently changed the name to Av. Universidad Interamericana. Like most *sangermeños*, *Let's Go* still refers to the street as C.

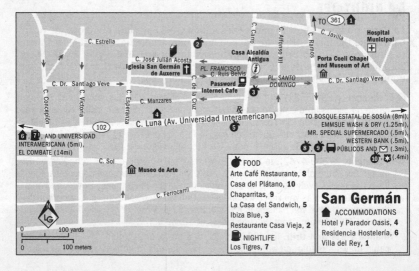

Luna. The two plazas sit a couple of blocks north of C. Luna. Many services are available around the western end of C. Luna, where the university is located, or near its eastern end, where Rte. 122 leads to a shopping plaza and Hwy. 2.

Públicos: The *público* station is near the intersection of C. Luna and Rte. 122; turn right and walk up C. Luna to reach the historical center. *Públicos* connect San Germán to: **Cabo Rojo** (20min., $1.75); **Lajas** (20min., $1); **Mayagüez** (35min., $3.50); **Sabana Grande** (15min., $1.30).

Tourist Office: Oficina de Turismo (☎892-3790) is located on the 2nd fl. of the Casa Alcaldía Antigua facing Pl. Franciso. The friendly staff provides a detailed walking map of the city and also gives free tours for groups of up to 10 people. Call 2 days in advance to set up a tour. Open daily 8am-4pm.

Bank: Western Bank, C. Luna 170 (☎892-1207). Exchanges traveler's checks, but not foreign currency. Drive-thru ATM. Open M-F 7:30am-5pm, Sa 8:30-11:30am.

Laundromat: Emmsue Wash & Dry, Rte. 102 Km 34 (☎892-5252), behind Panadería La Marqueta, 1½ mi. east of town. Regular wash $1.75, double load $3.75; dry $0.25 per 4min. No change available. Open daily 5am-9pm.

Police: On C. Casto Perez (☎892-2020), behind the *público* terminal. Open 24hr.

Pharmacy: Walgreens (☎892-1170), at the corner of C. Luna and C. Carro. Open M-F 8am-7pm, Sa 8am-6pm. AmEx/D/MC/V.

Hospital: Hospital Municipal, C. Javilla 8 (☎892-5300), just behind the Porta Coeli chapel. 24hr. emergency room.

Internet Access: Biblioteca Pública, C. Acosta 11 (☎892-6820), on Pl. Francisco Quiñones. Free Internet access; 1hr. limit. Open June-July M-F 8am-6pm, Sa 8am-1pm and 2-4:30pm; Aug.-May M-Th 8am-8:30pm, F 8am-6pm, Sa 8am-1pm and 2-4:30pm. **Password,** C. Ruiz Belvis 9 (☎892-7947), at C. Carro, charges $3 per 30min., $5 per hr. Open M-F 8am-5pm, Sa 9am-2pm. MC/V.

Post Office: C. Luna 101 (☎002-1313), near the intersection with Rte. 122. No General Delivery. Open M-F 7:30am-3:50pm, Sa 8am-noon. **Postal Code:** 00683.

▐ ACCOMMODATIONS

San Germán's accommodations are relatively budget friendly, but don't come looking for first-class rooms, as options are limited.

Residencia Hostelería (☎264-1912, ext. 7300 or 7301, at night 7302). Continue on C. Luna to the university's 2nd entrance, then enter the blue building to the left of the track field. The university rents several clean single-sex dorm rooms with a small living room in the front, a bedroom in the back, and 2 dorm-style showers in the middle. Busy during the school year but mostly empty during the summer. Alcohol and drugs strictly prohibited. Reserve in advance M-F 8am-noon and 1-5pm. With TV, A/C, and sheets singles $49; doubles $59; triples $65; quads $75. Larger rooms available. $450 and up for a semester. Tax included. AmEx/MC/V if you check in M-F 8am-5pm. ❷

Hotel y Parador Oasis, C. Luna 72 (☎892-1175). All the amenities are here—pool, cable TV, A/C, and parking. Prime location makes this a good base for exploring downtown. Rooms are clean but the decor might make you feel like you're spending the night at grandma's. Breakfast $4. Check-out noon. Singles $79; doubles $89. Extra person $10. Tax included. MC/V. ❸

Villa del Rey, Rte. 361 Km 0.8 (☎642-2627 or 264-2542), just across Hwy. 2 from town. Bright, tile-floored rooms. Modern amenities, but without the historic charm of traditional *paradores*. Cafeteria (lunch buffet $6) and pool. TV, A/C, and fridge on request. Office open 9am-11pm. Doubles $93; quads $126. MC/V. ❹

C. Luna (Av. Universidad Interamericana)
← TO 5 (.5 mi.)

HISTORIC HOUSES OF SAN GERMÁN

Although the city is full of interesting old buildings, the following are well worth viewing.

1. Casa Jaime Acosta y Forés **(1918),** C. Dr. Veve 70, grabs your attention with its bright yellow, Art Nouveau exterior.

2. Casa de los Ponce de León o Lola Rodriguez de Tió **(1870),** C. Dr. Veve 13, once served as the holiday home for famous poet and political activist Rodriguez de Tió.

3. Casa de Los Kindy **(19th century),** C. Dr. Veve 64, stands out with polychrome stained-glass windows.

4. Casa Morales **(1915),** was built in Victorian style and remains one of the city's best-maintained houses.

5. Museo de Arte **(19th century)** (p. 239), is the only historic house in town that allows visitors inside. Continue south on C. Ramos, west on C. Luna, and south on C. Esperanza.

⦿ FOOD

For groceries, stop by **Mr. Special Supermercado,** Rte. 102 Km 32.9, past the intersection with Rte. 122. (☎892-1098. Also has a **Western Union.** Open daily M-Sa 6:30am-9pm, Su 11am-5pm. AmEx/MC/V.)

🍴 **Casa del Plátano,** C. Oriente 174 (☎892-2633), across from the *público* station. Uses island-grown bananas with sandwich toppings to create banana sandwiches ($4). That's right, no bread. The most popular cafeteria in town; expect a large crowd and a long line during lunch. Open M-Sa 6:30am-8pm. Cash only. ❶

Chaparritas, C. Luna 171 (☎892-1078). Successfully combines classy decor, quality food, and affordable prices. This brightly colored restaurant serves a variety of meat-heavy Mexican entrees ($11-15) which are so elegantly presented that you'll want to take a moment to admire your food before digging in. Beer $3. Open W-Th 11:30am-3pm and 6-9pm, F 11:30am-3pm and 6-10pm, Sa 6-10pm. MC/V. ❸

Ibiza Blue, C. Carro 13 (☎458-8933), at C. Dr. Veve. At the intersection of both plazas, Ibiza draws people from all over town, offering hearty breakfast, pastries, sandwiches, and hot *comida criolla.* Sit at the clean indoor tables or grab your food and enjoy the daily bustle in Plaza Santo Domingo. MC/V. ❷

Restaurante Casa Vieja (☎264-3954), on the corner of C. de la Cruz and C. Estrella. In a yellow traditional Spanish building, the 1st fl. is full of old antiques as the restaurant spills out from the ground floor into a shady courtyard. This is where the business class comes to wine and dine. Like the local artwork on the walls, the menu is constantly changing, but in general it sticks to Caribbean-Spanish fusion. Entrees $15-23. Open W-Th 5-10pm, F noon-11pm, Sa 5-11pm. Bar open W-Th 5pm-midnight, F noon-2am, Sa 5pm-2am. ❹

Arte Café Restaurante, C. Luna 179 (☎892-6727). Cafe during the morning and restaurant at night, Arte serves coffee and breakfast ($2-3), sandwiches for lunch ($2-4), and *comida criolla,* seafood, and pasta entrees for dinner ($8-11). Come in and enjoy the A/C or get delivery during lunch (11am-1pm). Open M-Tu 7am-6pm, W-Th 7am-10pm, Sa 8am-10pm. Cash only. ❶

La Casa del Sandwich, C. Luna, across from Walgreens. This small *cafetería* serves up hot and cold sandwiches all day as locals come in for a quick bite or a cold beer. The menu runs from the simple ham and cheese to more elaborate breakfast sandwiches, *cubanos,* and chicken and tuna, all for less than $4. Behind the counter is the front-page picture of Puerto Rico's smashing victory over the US men's basketball team in the 2004 Olympics; some local customers claim the triumph as Puerto Rico's proudest moment. Open daily 9am-11pm. Cash only. ❶

◉ SIGHTS

Apart from the two exceptional churches, most of San Germán's "sights" are actually private residences with exquisite architecture. Many are close to the main plazas— **Plaza Francisco Quiñones,** a quiet tree-lined area overshadowed by the enormous modern church, and **Plazuela Santo Domingo,** a slightly more active plaza just to the east. The most informative way to sightsee is to arrange a free tour through the tourist office (p. 237); if the office is closed, you can just wander the picturesque streets. Some of the more historically significant houses are described below.

PORTA COELI CHAPEL AND MUSEUM OF RELIGIOUS ART. This orange structure on the southern edge of Plazuela Santo Domingo, known as "The Gate to Heaven," is the oldest chapel in Puerto Rico, and the second-oldest religious building (only Iglesia San José in Old San Juan is older). The building was constructed in 1609 as a convent, but over time it slowly deteriorated, and by 1866 only the chapel remained. Finally, in 1949, the Puerto Rican Institute of Culture took control of the Porta Coeli and restored it to a recognizable shape, though only the columns, walls, and stairwell from the original remained. The chapel is no longer used for services, but it now houses a small museum of religious art. This collection of paintings and large *santos* are worth the visit; entering the chapel is one of the best ways to get in touch with San Germán's extensive history. *(At C. Ramos and C. Dr. Veve. ☎892-5845. Open W-Su 8:30am-noon and 1-4:30pm. $3. ages 6-11 and over 60 $2.)*

IGLESIA SAN GERMÁN DE AUXERRE. Church fathers spared no expense in building the impressive Neoclassical Iglesia San Germán. The original wooden church was built in 1737 and reconstructed in the Neoclassical style in 1842. The church closes for most of the day, but it's worthwhile to stop by just before mass in order to see the elegant interior, with its tall ceilings, side altars, numerous chandeliers, and colorful stained-glass windows. Dress nicely, as this is an operational church. *(☎892-1027. Office on C. José Julian Acosta open M-F 8-11am and 1-3pm, Sa 8-11am. Mass M-Sa 7am and 7.30pm, Su 7.30, 8.30, 10am, 7.30pm.)*

MUSEO DE ARTE Y CASA DE ESTUDIO ALFREDO RAMÍREZ DE ARELLANO Y ROSELL. On the way back from a walking tour through San Germán's historic district, you may want to stop by this turn-of the-century home that now holds a small art and history museum. The collection contains oils with both Catholic and Taíno subjects. An upstairs room recreates a 19th-century parlor, while another contains indigenous relics and artwork. *(C. Esperanza 7. ☎892-8870. Open W-Su 10am-noon and 1-3pm. Free; donations accepted.)*

UNIVERSIDAD INTERAMERICANA. You can't miss the presence of the Interamerican University in San Germán. Founded in 1912 as the Instituto Politécnico de San Germán, this is now the largest private university in Puerto Rico. The attractive campus on the western edge of town, off C. Luna, is a pleasant place to wander and absorb the hustle of student activity. The campus grounds include the only round chapel in Puerto Rico.

◖ NIGHTLIFE

Considering the size of the university, San Germán has a remarkably tame nightlife scene, as most students head to Mayagüez or La Parguera for their nights out; during the summer don't expect much nightlife at all. ◖**Los Tigres,** C. Luna 6, at the main university entrance, is the student hangout. College kids shoot pool in the wooden house or chill on the porch with a beer, taking advantage of daily Happy hour specials. This is the place to bond with the younger crowd. *(☎264-5504. Th live music. Happy hour daily 8pm-midnight; beer $1-1.50. Open Sept.-May M-W 11am-1am, Th-Sa 11am-2am; June-Aug. M-W 4pm-1am, Th-Sa 4pm-2am. MC/V.)*

BOSQUE ESTATAL DE SOSÚA

Just 40min. east of San Germán, the 3341-acre Bosque Estatal de Sosúa provides an excellent taste of the Puerto Rican countryside and a refreshing return to nature for anyone overwhelmed by city life. Sitting on the border between the mountainous rainforests and the coastal dry forests, Sosúa is the only state forest with both dry and humid forests, which contributes to a diversity of over 150 tree species. Peaceful and impressive, this forest has several trails for hiking and one for mountain biking.

Sosúa is one of the island's more isolated forest reserves, and unlike most of the forests along the Ruta Panorámica, it is not bisected by a thoroughfare. Instead, visitors must drive east on Rte. 102 through Sabana Grande, then follow Rte. 368 past Rte. 365 to Km 2.1, where they'll turn left at the DRNA sign and climb up the small road for about 3.5 mi. to reach the forest center. The DRNA office is located at the end of the road in a valley next to a large and attractive picnic area. (☎487-4890. Open M-F 7am-3:30pm, Sa-Su 9am-5pm.) There are many covered **picnic tables** (although some don't have benches), fire pits, bathrooms, and even a snack machine. Two **hiking trails** leave from the same trailhead, "Vereda al Río," located between the DRNA office and the visitors' center. Walk down and cross the little creek and climb back up the bank where the trail splits into two. Heading uphill into mountainous country means a short, steep climb; when the trail levels out, hikers are rewarded with great views of the forest. The other path follows the Río Loco and is overgrown with plants but is still navigable. Both trails are at least 2 mi. long. More compelling is the rigorous **mountain bike trail,** which narrows to a single track on its 3-mile loop. You must bring your own bike, but rangers can provide you with a hand-drawn map of the trail.

The DRNA has built a camping site with **rustic cabins** ❶ that contain a set of wooden bunks with thin mattresses. The cabin area has water spigots, a brick grill but no electricity, and pit toilets. Make sure to bring a flashlight and toilet paper. Tents are not allowed in the cabin area. Cabins by permit only; call the permit office in San Juan a few days in advance. (☎999-2200, ext. 5156 or 5158. Check in noon-3pm. Check-out noon.)

EL COMBATE

If you're one for long walks on the beach, then you've come to the right place. El Combate's beach is one of the longest on the island; its white sand extends for miles in either direction. During weekdays this tiny *barrio* feels like a ghost town, but during holidays and summer vacations it fills up with Puerto Ricans. There's not much to do here except lie on the beach and drink beer, but that's exactly what most people come for.

Almost every house in town becomes some sort of vacation rental, and countless signs advertise rooms for rent. However, snagging this sort of rental can be difficult because few owners live near their properties or answer their phones. For more traditional accommodations, try **Combate Beach Hotel** ❹, Rte. 3301 Km 2.7, a real hotel with clean, spacious rooms with TV, fridge, and A/C. The hotel's biggest assets are the pool and direct beach access. Locals place the hotel's seafood restaurant among the best in town. If the rooms are all booked, ask about the owner's guest house in town. (☎/fax 254-2358. June-Aug. doubles $100; quads $120. Sept.-May $85/100. Discounts for long stays. MC/V.) On the northern edge of town, directly across C. 1 from the beach, friendly **Apartamentos Kenny** ❹ is El Combate's best value for groups. The small, one-bedroom apartments manage to accommodate a double bed, a set of bunk beds, a satellite TV, a kitchen area with stove and fridge, a small kitchen table, bedroom A/C, and up to six people—although two must sleep on a small fold-out couch. Some rooms are smaller and come without

DISTANCE: 10 mi.

DURATION: 2-5hr.

WHEN TO GO: Year-round. The beach is more crowded June-Aug.

CABO ROJO SCENIC DRIVE

The landscape of the southwest corner couldn't be more different from the rain forests of El Yunque on the east coast; a short drive brings you through rolling drylands, down through the salt flats, and then to the staggering cliffs at the tip of Punta Jagüey. The Cabo Rojo lighthouse and its surroundings are the highlight of this roadtrip, but if you have a bit more time, meander down Rte. 301, through the flat plains and dry vegetation, to take in the region's fascinating topography.

If you're intrigued by the landscape and want to see more, once you double back on Rte. 301, take an hour-long detour east on Rte. 303, which winds through rolling desertlands with gorgeous coastal views. Rte. 303 is 14km long, and will hit Rte. 305; this leads you to Rte. 116, which you can take north to Lajas and San German.

1. CABO ROJO SALT FLATS AND INTERPRETATIVE CENTER. The landscape becomes progressively flatter as you continue south to Puerto Rico's largest salt production facilities. The scenery alone is impressive, but this area is also the Caribbean's most important meeting point for migratory shore birds, with 40,000 birds of over 125 different species stopping here. The newly built **Centro Interpretativo** is a small museum that explains the ecological importance of the salt flats and gives information on the various plants and wildlife found within the refuge. If the great views from the new 3-story observation tower (Km 11.1) don't get you interested in learning more, the friendly staff will. (Open W-Sa 8:30am-4:30pm, Su and holidays 9:30am-5:30pm.)

2. CABO ROJO LIGHTHOUSE. From the salt flats, continue south on Rte. 301 all the way to the end, after it becomes a bumpy dirt road; the Cabo Rojo Lighthouse will eventually be visible. The parking areas are about 1 mi. past the Bahía Salinas Hotel. Park at either metal gate and continue on foot uphill to this Neoclassical structure, built by the Spanish in 1881. Inside you'll find several rooms with wooden chairs, each with a different edition of the *Odyssey*. A projector overhead highlights the text on the walls as an audio system (in English and Spanish) tells the epic story of long voyages spent out at sea. (Open W-Su 9am-3pm.) Finally, standing on a limestone cliff 200 ft. over the crystal waters of the Caribbean crashing below is one of the most amazing experiences to be had in Puerto Rico.

3. PLAYUELA. Anyone who explores the lighthouse area will eventually stumble upon La Playuela, the beautiful beach just east of the point. Continue on foot on the dirt road left of the path to the lighthouse to reach it. The clear, turquoise water hits the white sand in a gentle, shallow arc, making it arguably the most picturesque and serene beach on the whole island. There are no facilities, but the remote location also means that there are fewer people than you will find at other beaches.

4. PARADOR BAHÍA SALINAS BEACH HOTEL. If you're ready to splurge on seafood, stop at **Agua al Cuello Restaurant ❹**, Rte. 301 Km 11.5. This *mesón gastronómico* scores big points for its elegant wooden balcony over the calm water. (☎254-1212. Sa live music. Entrees $15-30. Open Th-Su noon-9pm. AmEx/MC/V.) The tropical, award-winning **Parador Bahía Salinas ❹** is one of the island's premier *paradores*, with two pools, an oceanside location, and a mineral water jacuzzi. (☎254-1212; www.bahiasalinas.com. Continental breakfast included. Check-in 3pm. Check-out noon. Doubles $150. Extra person $20; 2 children under 12 free. Max 4 people per room. AmEx/MC/V.)

bunks. (☎254-0002 or 509-8833. Check-in 4pm. Check-out 3pm. Rooms Easter-Labor Day $105; Labor Day-Easter $90. Cash only.) Although **Annie's Place ❸**, offers six guest rooms right on the beach with A/C, cable TV, and kitchenettes ($85-110), it shines as El Combate's best seafood █**restaurant ❸**. Auspiciously located at the turn in the road at the end of Rte. 3301, this is the place to sit over the ocean enjoying *mofongo* filled with fresh seafood ($14), and watch the sunset. In the evening, the front half of the restaurant comes to life as a bar and *empanadilla* stand. (☎254-2553. Beer $1.50-2. *Empanadas* $1.75. Entrees $7-23. Open M-Th 10:30am-9pm, F-Sa 10:30am-1am, Su 10:30am-9pm. MC/V.)

El Combate sits at the end of Rte. 3301. Turn left at the Combate Hotel sign to reach the beach parking lot and the better, southern half of the beach. Or continue straight on Rte. 3301 to enter town, which extends north on four parallel streets: C. 1 is closest to the water, C. 2 is the next inland, and so on. *Públicos* occasionally journey out from Cabo Rojo, but service is sporadic.

BOQUERÓN

Situated on a large bay, Boquerón has plenty of great seafood as well as an attractive public beach. Clear, shallow water laps on the long *balneario* of white sand lined by a grassy park with palm trees and a picnicking area. By day, the quiet beach attracts families; by night, the tiny two-road town comes alive, closing down its streets to traffic so that people can roam freely. Boquerón is geared more toward Puerto Ricans on summer vacation than foreigners; and although the entire town feels prepackaged for tourist consumption, if you don't mind the family crowds, Boquerón is a great place to grab some tasty eats and just sit back and relax.

▊ ▊ TRANSPORTATION AND PRACTICAL INFORMATION

Coming from the east (Ponce, San Germán, Lajas, and La Parguera), take Rte. 101 west straight into town. From Mayagüez and San Juan, take Hwy. 2 to Rte. 100, which travels south and intersects with Rte. 101 just outside of Boquerón. The main street, **Route 101,** becomes Calle Muñoz Rivera as it enters town, then turns north along the coast and changes its name again, this time to Calle José de Diego. **Route 307** splits off from Rte. 101 just as you enter town and becomes Calle Estación, which heads north toward Joyuda. Boquerón is tiny, and if you want to find most practical necessities you'll have to head into Cabo Rojo or Mayagüez, but basic food and accommodations are available.

Públicos: Shared vans go from Boquerón to **Cabo Rojo** (10min., M-F and some Sa, $1.75). From Cabo Rojo, *públicos* go on to **Mayagüez** (15-20min., $2).

ATM: Boquerón has an ATM located at Calda's Food Warehouse, on the left as you enter town from the intersection of Rte. 100 and Rte. 101; another is on Rte. 101, just east of the intersection with Rte. 100, under the Plaza Boquerón sign next to Church's Chicken. Nearby Cabo Rojo has several banks.

Equipment Rental: Boquerón Kayak Rental, C. de Diego 15 (☎255-1849), rents single kayaks ($10 per hr., $40 per day), double kayaks ($15/65), 5-person pedal boats ($15 for the first 2 people, $5 for each additional person), and surfbikes (a combination surfboard and bike; $15 per hr.). They also give 15min. banana boat rides ($5 per person). Call in advance. Open in summer daily 10am-5pm; Labor Day-Easter F-Sa 10am-6pm. Cash only.

Laundromat: Adamaris Apartments, on C. de Diego. Wash $1, dry $0.25 per 7min. Open daily 7am-7pm.

Police: Located in the Centro Vacacional, past the reception office (☎851-1122). Open 24hr.

Internet Access: Boquerón Travel Agency, C. Muñoz Rivera 60 (☎851-4751; fax 254-2144) offers fax service and 1 computer with Internet access. $3 per 30min., $6 per hr. Open M-F 9am-5pm, Sa 9am-noon.

Post Office: Rte. 101 Km 18.3 (☎851-3848). Open M-F 7am-4:15pm, Sa 7am-2:15pm. **Postal Code:** 00622.

ACCOMMODATIONS

Boquerón does not lack accommodations, but many of the rooms are actually one- to two-bedroom apartments designed to be affordable for large groups (see **Vacation Rentals**, p. 38). Prices go up considerably during the summer, which generally begins during *Semana Santa* (the week of Easter) and ends on Labor Day, in the beginning of September. Among the condos and villas there are a few hotels.

Boquerón

⚑ ACCOMMODATIONS
Boquerón Beach Hotel, **14**
Centro Vacacional
 de Boquerón, **16**
Hotel Tropical Inn, **15**
Parador Boquemar, **6**
Velero Beach Hotel, **12**
Wildflowers, **11**

🍴 FOOD
The Fish Net, **8**
Galloway's, **3**
Pika-Pika, **13**
Pizzeria Lyken, **2**
Roberto's Villa Playera, **10**
La Sandwicheria, **5**

☀ OUTDOOR ACTIVITY RENTAL
Boquerón Kayak Rental, **4**

🌙 NIGHTLIFE
Rincón del Olvido, **1**
El Schamar, **7**
Sunset Sunrise, **9**

■ **Centro Vacacional de Boquerón** (☎851-1900). Coming into town on Rte. 101, turn left at the sign for the beach and continue to the end. The office is down the road past both giant parking lots. This enormous vacation complex, run by the CPN, is remarkably well maintained; *cabañas* have ideal beachfront locations, making it a popular spot for families during the summer. If you go for a *villa*, request one of the newer units at the south end of the beach. Check-in 4pm. Check-out 1pm. Reserve a week in advance, longer if in the summer. *Cabañas* without A/C $66; larger villas with A/C $109. 6 people max. Tax included. AmEx/MC/V. ●

Boquerón Beach Hotel (☎851-7110; www.boqueronbeachhotel.com), at the turn-off to the beach. One of Boquerón's more professional accommodations and a 10min. walk from the beach. An inviting blend of old Spanish tile floors, French wrought-iron work, and modern rooms. All rooms have TV, A/C, and fridge; some have balconies. Large pool area with grill and bar. Continental breakfast included. Parking. Check-in 1pm. Check-out noon. Doubles $80 on weekdays, $104 on weekends; quads $90/175. Tax included. MC/V. ❹

Parador Boquemar (☎851-2158; www.boquemar.com), just off C. de Diego. You can't miss this blue-and-white building rising above town, located near the happening nightlife. Lacks the elegance of other *paradores*, but modern rooms come with phone, A/C, and a small TV. Pool area. Check-in 4pm. Check-out noon. Full deposit required upon reservation. Doubles $91-102; quads $113-118. Extra person $20; 2 children under 12 free. AmEx/MC/V. ❸

Wildflowers, C. Muñoz Rivera 13 (☎851-1793 or 851-8874). This Victorian house exudes charm. Rooms have been carefully decorated with dark wood furniture and coordinated linens, but also include practical benefits like TV, A/C, and fridge. All rooms fit 4 people: smaller rooms have 1 full bed and 1 bunk bed; larger rooms have 2 beds, though one may be a fold-out sofa. Parking. Check-in 1pm. Check-out noon. Reserve ahead. June-Aug. small rooms $109; large rooms $135. Sept.-May $87/98. Tax included. MC/V. ❹

SWIMMING WITH SAN JUAN

The eve of the festival of Puerto Rico's Patron Saint, San Juan Bautista, is an eventful night across the island. At the stroke of midnight, Puerto Ricans walk backward toward the ocean. The agile can also choose to backflip toward the sea, but the correct number of flips is disputed: is it 12 for the months of the year, or seven for good luck? However you get to the water, it is generally agreed that you must fall in backward three times. The waters are thought to be blessed with special powers on this night, and immersion in them is supposed to bring good luck for the next year.

The ladies on Puerto Rico's west coast have teamed up with San Juan Bautista not just for good luck, but for a glimpse into their futures. Some women swirl water and egg white in a glass, which, according to tradition, will show a woman the face of her future husband. Because a pretty face isn't everything, thorough women will also tuck three beans under their pillows. One is peeled, one is half-peeled, and the other is left unpeeled. The bean the woman pulls out from under her pillow in the morning reveals her husband-to-be's financial status: a peeled bean means a poor man, half-peeled suggests a man of·moderate means, and an intact bean means she's hit the jackpot.

(The Festival de San Juan Bautista is celebrated June 24th each year.)

Velero Beach Hotel, Rte. 307 Km 9.3 (☎255-1000; www.velerobeachhotel.com). Clean, large rooms with A/C, cable TV, and VCR. Balcony on request. Limited parking. Check-out noon. Summer doubles $100; quads $195. Winter $65/85. AmEx/MC/V. ❹

Hotel Tropical Inn, Rte. 101 Km 18.7 (☎851-0284), across from the road to the beach. One of the smallest but cheapest places in town. Only a few rooms, all with TV and A/C. A sign in the office may direct you across the street to the owner's cafeteria **Rice & Beans** for check-in or check-out; it's also a great place for a cheap, filling breakfast. May to mid-Sept. doubles $65; quads $95. Mid-Sept. to Apr. $55/80. AmEx/MC/V. ❸

🍴 FOOD

Boquerón is the only place in Puerto Rico where you'll find multiple vendors, often in front of **El Schamar,** selling fresh oysters (*ostiones;* about $6 per dozen) and clams (*almejas;* about $8 per dozen). Visitors can stop by a cart, peel apart the shells, and dump hot sauce onto the succulent centers. If you're not a fan of seafood, grab breakfast ($2-3) or a filling sandwich ($3-4) at **La Sandwicheria,** on C. de Diego, across from Boquerón Kayak Rental. (Open daily 8am-2pm. Cash only.) For a limited selection of groceries, stop by **Super Colmado Rodriguez,** C. Muñoz Rivera 46. (☎851-2100. Open M-Sa 6am-6:30pm, Su 6am-noon. MC/V; min. $10.) While the cheapest option is cobbling together a meal from the various stands along C. de Diego, the restaurants below provide quality food for the hungry.

The Fish Net and **Roberto's Villa Playera** (☎254-3163), both on C. de Diego. Roberto had such success with his first seafood restaurant that he opened another one right across the street. These 2 restaurants share the undisputed title of best seafood in town; they both have nautical decor, although only Villa Playera has a view of the canal out back. Seafood entrees ($16-25) include shrimp, lobster, and crab in a variety of creative dishes. Fish Net open W-Su 9am-11pm. Villa Playera open M-Tu and F-Su 11am-8pm. AmEx/D/MC/V. ❸

Pika-Pika Mexican Grill, C. Estación 224 (☎851-2440), is slightly on the expensive side, but its delicious entrees and hearty servings are well worth it. If the name intrigues you, try the house special Pika-Pika, chicken or steak (or both) with grilled onions and bacon, covered in melted Monterey cheese, and served with refried beans, rice, and tortillas ($14). Save room for dessert because you don't want to miss the incredible *tres leches* cake ($4) or the chocolate lava cake ($5). Margaritas $5.50. Entrees $13-24. Open W-Th 5-10pm, F-Sa noon-11pm, Su noon-10pm. AmEx/MC/V. ❹

Galloway's (☎254-3302), next to Club Náutico. Americans, this is your home away from home. Galloway's caters to the foreign crowd with an English menu, US TV, rows of US license plates, and creative T-shirts lining the ceiling. The oceanfront dining room sits out on the water next to the mangroves and is a great place to watch the sunset. Lunch specials from $4. *Comida criolla* with a few American faves $6-26. Open M-Tu, Th, Su 2pm-midnight; F-Sa noon-1am. AmEx/MC/V; min. $25. ❸

Pizzeria Lyken (☎851-6335), on C. de Diego. Offers an alternative to Boquerón's endless seafood selection, but never fear—they also serve a full spread of seafood entrees, as well as seafood pizza ($24). Windchimes liven up the outdoor seating area, where the walls are lined with pictures of satisfied customers. If you like your meal, ask to have your picture taken. Entrees $10-20. Pizza slices $1.50-1.75. Small pizza $10-12, large $13-15. Open Th-Sa 11am-10pm. Bar open until midnight. AmEx/MC/V. ❸

OUTDOOR ACTIVITIES

The 4773-acre **Bosque Estatal de Boquerón,** Rte. 101 Km 1.1, encompasses the mangroves west of La Parguera (p. 233), the salt flats in Cabo Rojo (p. 241), the Boquerón Wildlife Refuge near the intersection of Rte. 101 and 301, and Joyuda's Isla Ratones (p. 257). It also protects over 120 species of birds, including the endangered Mariquita. Unfortunately, the DRNA now limits guests to a boardwalk outside the office; keep an eye out for the fiddler crabs crawling in the shallow waters beneath it, but don't expect to see much else. (☎851-4795. Open daily 7:30am-4pm.) The forest's main office, just past Club Náutico, provides information about the park and can tell you whether any new hiking trails have opened up. (☎851-7260. Open M-F 7:30am-3:30pm.)

BEACHES AND WATER SPORTS

The **public balneario,** Rte. 101 Km 18.8, is the only show in town, but it is stunning with its turquoise waters and its long white crescent of sandy beach. Like most beaches run by the Compañía de Parques Nacionales, it includes picnic tables, showers, bathrooms, a cafeteria, and lifeguards. The beach attracts crowds, but there is plenty of sand to go around and a multitude of palm trees to provide shade. (Open daily June-July 8am-6pm; Aug.-May 8am-5pm. Parking $3, vans $4. Showers $1, children $0.50.) If the lack of waves gets you down, try a $15 banana boat ride (see **Boquerón Kayak Rental,** p. 242). **Mona Aquatics,** C. de Diego 59, next to the Club Náutico, has a 42 ft. boat. The PADI- and YMCA-certified owner leads diving expeditions (2-tank dive $65; 1-tank night dive $40), but does not rent equipment. (☎851-2185; www.monaaquatics.com. MC/V.)

NIGHTLIFE

Boquerón draws large crowds on weekend nights. The plaza in front of El Shamar closes down to traffic after 6pm and people gather around tables to play dominoes, beers in hand. Students and younger adults gather farther north, near the Club Náutico. The entire town turns into a street party, and as people walk in and out of bars, it's almost impossible to miss the hot spots.

It is illegal to drink from a bottle on the streets in Boquerón, so get a plastic cup or a can from any bar before heading outdoors.

El Schamar, C. de Diego 1 (☎851-0542). With tasty *empanadillas,* a plaza overlooking the ocean, and a location right in the center of town, this bar has a lot going for it. Add a pool table ($0.50), $1 Medalla beers, and $1.50 Coors, and it's no wonder that it's perpetually busy. Beer $1-2. Mixed drinks $2-6. Open daily 11am-midnight. Cash only.

Sunset Sunrise, C. Barbosa 65 (☎255-1478), on the main square. This little hole in the wall, dimly lit by a few neon signs, is a popular gathering spot for an older crowd that grabs a drink and then sits on the tables out front playing dominoes. Beer $1-2. Mixed drinks $2-4. Open M-Th and Su 10am-midnight, F-Sa 10am-1am.

Sweet & Sour, in the main square, across from Sunset Sunrise (☎851-5205). This large pool hall has 7 tables and draws a big crowd with its bumping music and $1 Medalla beers. Throw your quarters on a table to call next game or head out into the street to watch the ongoing games of dominoes. Beer $1-2. Mixed drinks $3-6. Open daily noon-midnight. Cash only.

Galloway's (☎254-3302), on C. de Diego (see **Food,** p. 244). The countdown to St. Patrick's Day hangs on a wall at this popular American-Irish pub. The bar provides a relatively quiet place to relax and make some new friends, with a fantastic view of the sunset over the water. Parking. Beer $2.50. Mixed drinks $3.75-5. Appetizers $3-7. Open M-Tu, Th, Su noon-midnight; F-Sa noon-1am. AmEx/MC/V.

ISLA MONA

Cynics who claim that Puerto Rico is too developed for adventure have clearly never heard of Isla Mona. Touted as "the Galápagos of the Caribbean," Isla Mona offers one of the best excursions into the Caribbean's untamed wilderness. At just over 13,500 acres, the island is twice as large as Culebra but remains completely uninhabited except for a few researchers. Nature still reigns on this protected reserve, as enormous iguanas, thousands of hermit crabs, and non-native goats and pigs roam the island. Visitors arriving by sea may be surprised by the flatness of the island, which looks like a large pancake sitting on the water. Closer still, it becomes apparent that the edge of the island is actually composed of cavernous limestone cliffs. Strips of bright white sand emerge along the water, which shines an incredible clear blue. While most people stay near the beaches or venture inland on short hikes, a trip to Mona could include exploring the extensive cave network, hiking through the dry scrub forest, diving and snorkeling at the flourishing reefs, or simply lounging on the exquisite beaches. In addition to adventure, Mona offers almost absolute tranquility. The only sounds are the waves crashing on the beach and the quiet rustling of hermit crabs. Most charters head to the island for three or four days; this taste of Mona is just enough time for adventurous visitors to get hooked and begin planning the next trip.

AT A GLANCE

AREA: 13,590 acres.

CLIMATE: Semi-arid subtropical. Average year-round temperature 79°F.

HIGHLIGHTS: Climbing through caves, diving in 120 ft. visibility, swimming through aquamarine water, hiking with endemic animals.

FEATURES: Wildlife, caves, Taíno petroglyphs, spectacular beaches, coral reefs, the ruins of a lighthouse.

GATEWAYS: Boquerón (p. 242), Joyuda (p. 250), Rincón (p. 279), San Juan (p. 89).

CAMPING: Permitted at Playa Sardinera and Playa Pájaro with a DRNA permit. ($10 per person, 3 day max. Special permit required to stay longer.)

FEES: Boat passage alone costs $135-400. Most charters charge more for food, equipment, tour services, and snorkeling or diving.

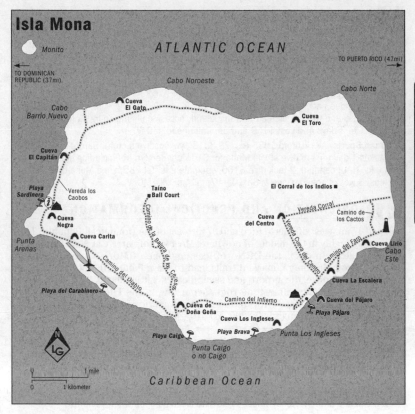

Isla Mona

TRANSPORTATION

It takes a bit of tenacity to reach Isla Mona. The small airstrip is currently closed, so anyone who doesn't have a private boat will have to find passage on a Puerto Rican charter. If you have a group of at least six people (or a lot of money) the easiest option is to arrange a trip with one of the operators below. However, the ordinary traveler will have to join a pre-existing group that is still accepting additional passengers; this requires a lot of advance notice and flexible travel dates. Dive shops travel to Mona most regularly, though they don't always land on the island, in order to avoid DRNA permit hassles. Individuals or small groups attempting to go to Mona should call the charter below to inquire about expeditions planned during the time period when they're interested in going. If that is unsuccessful, try calling the various dive shops based away from the west coast. All prices listed below are round-trip.

Tourmarine Adventures, Rte. 102 Km 14.1 (☎375-2625; tourmarine@yahoo.com), Joyuda (p. 257), sends charters to Isla Mona. Headed by Captain Elick Hernández, who has a 34 ft. boat. 10 person min. 1-day passage $135 per person. AmEx/MC/V.

A ROUGH JOURNEY. Getting to Mona requires taking a relatively small boat 50 mi. across open seas; if you have ever been **seasick,** or are worried about seasickness, it's wise to plan ahead. Some boat captains recommend that potentially queasy travelers take Dramamine® the night before the boat ride. For a more natural cure, ginger tea has been known to ease seasickness.

Scuba Dogs, C. 5 #D-4, Prado Alto (☎ 783-6377 or 399-5755; scuba-dogs@yunque.net), Guaynabo. Has a big pool for scuba training. Also offers excursions every weekend to dive sites around the island, occasionally including Mona. Trips vary from 1 to 3 days and cost $150 and up. Call ahead. MC/V.

Ocean Sports, Av. Ashford 1035 (☎ 723-8513; www.osdivers.com), San Juan (p. 130). Makes 1-day trips to dive at Isla Mona for $105 per person, not including equipment or tanks. NAUI certified. 2-tank dive $100, equipment rental $35. For a Mona dive, call at least 3 weeks ahead. Open M-Sa 10am-7pm. AmEx/D/MC/V.

ORIENTATION AND PRACTICAL INFORMATION

Located 47 mi. west of Puerto Rico and 37 mi. east of the Dominican Republic, Isla Mona sits roughly in the middle of nowhere. Most visitors arrive at **Playa Sardinera,** home of the main dock, the DRNA offices, and one of Mona's most beautiful beaches. From Sardinera, marked trails lead to **Playa Pájaro** (the other camping area), the lighthouse, the airport, and several caves. Little **Monito,** 3 mi. northwest of Mona, is a 160-acre limestone rock; according to the DRNA, it is officially closed. To get up-to-date information on the conditions of the island, call the DRNA office in San Juan (☎ 999-2200, ext. 5156).

WHEN TO GO. The DRNA prohibits camping on weekdays during goat- and pig-hunting season (Dec.-Apr. M-Th). During school vacations Puerto Ricans with private boats significantly decrease the serenity of Mona.

Visitors Center: The DRNA office next to Playa Sardinera is often open during the day, but call one of the regional offices to be sure it will be open when you arrive.

Maps: Theoretically, the DRNA provides a map of hiking trails, but it frequently runs out of copies. However, it's also possible to get maps at the DRNA office in Mayagüez.

Supplies: There are absolutely no supplies on Mona. You must bring everything that you might want on the island, including food, drinking water, and toilet paper. In addition to the typical supplies, don't forget a basic first-aid kit, mosquito repellent, long pants, sneakers if you plan to do any hiking, trash bags (to take your trash out when you leave), and a flashlight. There are no camp fires allowed, so bring a camping stove, matches, and plenty of fuel.

CAMPING AND FOOD

If you're looking for the Ritz, head back to San Juan. On Mona, the only option is to camp at the two official beachfront camping areas. **Playa Sardinera ❶,** on the west coast, is the larger of the two and has two rustic cold-water showers and two flush toilets. For more seclusion, head to **Playa Pájaro ❶,** on the southeast coast. This beautiful beach has a dock and room for 30 campers but no facilities. Visitors looking for isolation and the "real" Mona tend to head here.

Isla Mona also has no food apart from fresh fish (bring your own pole) and **no potable water** (consult with tour operators about how much you should bring). Many tour groups provide food and a cook, but otherwise, travelers must be entirely self-sufficient. Furthermore, the DRNA does not allow open-flame fires.

ALCOHOL. Alcoholic drinks are not permitted on Isla Mona due to the risk of death from dehydration and inebriation.

🏞 OUTDOOR ACTIVITIES

It's best to decide what activities you're interested in before heading to Mona in order to procure the necessary supplies. Obviously, divers should invest in a dive trip, but everyone should bring snorkeling equipment. Visitors planning to explore the caves need a good flashlight, and those seeking further adventures should look for a tour group with a knowledgeable guide. The DRNA office in Mayagüez (p. 254) can help to arrange a tour with the biologists living on the island.

BEACHES
Isla Mona has over 5 mi. of beautiful beaches, and the most popular activity may be lounging oceanside. **Playa Sardinera** is a long white beach with relatively calm water protected by an offshore reef. The pine trees lining the sand drop some needles, and there are occasionally bothersome sand flies, but these two small inconveniences do not tarnish Sardinera's beauty. This is also the only beach with facilities, including bathrooms, picnic tables, and showers. The other camping area, **Playa Pájaro,** looks similar but has more palm trees, rocks, and seaweed. Although these are the two most frequented beaches, all of the sand on Mona is a bright white color that far outshines the mainland beaches, and, yes, the water maintains the same incredible blue color all the way around the island. Other beaches include **Playa Carabinero,** along the airport's shoreline, **Playa Caigo,** past the airport near the southernmost tip of the island, and **Playa Brava,** past the airport on the way to the lighthouse, before Punta Los Ingleses.

DIVING AND SNORKELING
Isla Mona has the best diving in Puerto Rico, with visibility regularly reaching 150-180 ft. Reefs nearly surround the island, and many organisms grow underwater on the island's steep cliffs, creating almost limitless dive opportunities. Because the island is undeveloped and has no erosion damage, the reefs around Isla Mona are remarkably healthy and house species that are hard to find on the main island. Advanced divers head to one of Mona's most spectacular sights, a sea wall surrounding the island that starts at 50-60 ft., descends to 150 ft., then plunges to the seafloor. Due to potentially strong currents and profound depths, divers should choose their sites carefully according to experience level and dive conditions.

CAVE EXPLORATION
Mona has over 150 acres of limestone caves that vary greatly in terms of size (heights range 3-30 ft.) and accessibility. Only experienced spelunkers should attempt to navigate the caves without a guide. DRNA employees occasionally accompany interested visitors to various caves, but don't count on this. Some tour groups and boat captains also lead visitors through the caves; check before departing to see if your trip includes any cave exploration. **Cueva Negra** and **Cueva Carita,** near Playa Sardinera, are some of the most easily accessible caves. There are more spectacular caves on the southeastern shore, near Playa Pájaro, but these can be difficult to find. Visitors with a guide should not miss **Cueva del Agua,** which includes a crawl through a tiny passage to reach a pitch-black pool of water.

HIKING
Over 10 trails wind through Isla Mona, but not all are regularly maintained. The most frequented path is a dirt access road traveling south from Playa Sardinera to:

Cueva Negra (33 ft., 2min.); Cueva Carita (½ mi., 15min.); the airport (¾ mi., 20min.); Playa Carabinero (2 mi., 40min.); Playa Caigo (3½ mi., 1½ hr.); Playa Pájaro (6mi., 3hr.); and the lighthouse (8mi., 4hr.). Another trail, known as the Bajura de los Ceresos, branches off from the access road near Playa Caigo and heads north to the Taíno ball court. On the east coast, the Vereda Cueva del Centro leads from the lighthouse trail to the Cueva del Centro. Before undertaking any hikes, check in with the DRNA to ensure that the trails are still open and let the organization know of your plans. Remember that water is not available on the island and you may require much more water than usual when hiking in the heat.

> **TROUBLE IN PARADISE.** The flat terrain makes it very easy to get lost when hiking on Isla Mona, and every couple of years visitors die from dehydration after losing their way on the featureless plateau. Also watch out for deep limestone holes and plants with sharp spines. Wear long pants and don't touch anything that you cannot identify.

▒ FLORA AND FAUNA

Isla Mona's wildlife is fascinating. The small island is home to 700 species of animals, 58 of which are endemic to the island and 75 of which have never been found on the Puerto Rican mainland. By far the most famous is the **Mona Iguana**, a gargantuan 4 ft. reptile found nowhere else in the world. These stunning creatures frequently emerge from their burrowed nests to observe new campers. Visitors will also be greeted by piles of crawling **hermit crabs,** crustaceans that migrate to the sea during early August to breed. The only amphibian on Mona is the unique **Mona coquí,** which has a song slightly different from its Puerto Rican relative. Unlike the mainland, Mona also has a significant number of creepy-crawlies. Watch out for the 52 species of spiders and the three species of scorpions. Fortunately, the 3 ft. **Isla Mona boa,** yet another endemic species, generally only comes out at night and is not harmful to humans. This curious creature is one of the only snakes that gives birth to developed offspring and does not lay eggs. **Birdwatchers** will enjoy looking for the 100 species of birds found on Mona. Only two, the yellow-shouldered blackbird and the ground dove, are native to the island. The **goats** and **pigs** that were left behind after earlier attempts to farm the island roam freely as wild animals. Every year, the two animals are hunted from December to April, Monday through Thursday, closing the island to camping. There are over 270 species of **fish** around Mona, including silky sharks, nurse sharks, barracudas, flying fish, and moray eels. Dolphins and humpback whales populate the waters as well. From May to October the endangered **hawksbill turtle** nests on the shores of Mona. The **loggerhead sea turtle** also swims in Mona waters; if you see a turtle, leave it alone, since human interference is one significant cause of the species's decline.

Mona's flora cannot match the diversity of its fauna, but the island does contain four endemic plant species. The vegetation is a combination of eastern Hispaniola's and southwestern Puerto Rico's, and most of the island consists of **dry plateau forest** filled with white cedar, cactus, and poisonwood. Most of the coastal forest consists of princewood and oysterwood, with a few acres of mangroves.

JOYUDA

This 3 mi. strip of coastal road contains more seafood restaurants than any other place in Puerto Rico, and *mayagüezanos* regularly drive down to sample the fresh delicacies and watch the sunset. The town has few beaches, but **Isla Ratones,** about half a mile offshore, has a small sandy beach. A ferry runs out to the island from Rte. 102 Km 13.7, next to Island View Restaurant. (☎851-7708. $5 round-trip.

Open Tu-Su 9am-5pm.) If you're going to Ratones for the day, you can grab groceries at **Conchitas** supermarket, which offers a basic selection of food and beverages. (Rte. 102 Km 14.1. ATM and bakery. Open M-Sa 7am-7pm.) For a much longer trip out to sea, check in with **Tourmarine Adventures**, Rte. 102 Km 14.1. Captain Elick Hernández charters his 34 ft. boat for the 3hr. trip to Isla Mona ($135 per person; min. 10 people) or for more local sightseeing. He is very flexible, but you must either have a group or pay for the entire boat. Common trips include all-day snorkeling at Desecheo Island ($75, snacks and gear included, group of 10), a 5-6hr. whale-watching trip in the Mona Passage (Feb.-Mar.; $65 per person), or local 2hr. snorkeling trips ($35 plus $10 for equipment). Call ahead to see if you can join another group. (☎375-2625; www.tourmarinepr.com. Cash only.)

Considering the area's limited attractions, the plethora of hotels in Joyuda is rather extraordinary. Several small hotels and guesthouses are tucked between larger, pricier offerings. Little **Hotel Costa de Oro Inn ❸**, Rte. 102 Km 14.7, is a modern building with a friendly guesthouse feel and immaculate rooms that live up to the standards of a much larger hotel. A pool fills the courtyard. A small cafeteria also serves food costing $4-12. (☎851-5010. A/C and cable TV. Check-in 2pm. Check-out noon. June-Aug. doubles $70; quads $95. Sept.-May $55/70. Extra person $15. MC/V.) Beyond the rows of modern, commercial hotels sits **Tony's Restaurant and Hotel ❹**, Rte. 102 Km 10.9. The bright blue rooms surround a parking lot, with a pool in the back. (☎851-2500; fax 851-6349. TV, A/C; quads have fridges. Doubles $90; quads $110.) Portraits of Tony's musician friends hang on the walls of the upscale **restaurant ❹**. (Entrees $15-25.) If you're looking to stay right on the beach, try **Parador Joyuda Beach**, Rte. 102 Km 11.7, which has a small beach area and a volleyball net. Rooms have A/C and cable TV, and a restaurant with breakfast buffet sits right on the water. (☎851-5650. Doubles $105; quads $125. AmEx/MC/V.)

Choosing a restaurant in Joyuda is like picking a bar in San Juan; there are just too many good options. Most of the seafood is fresh, and almost all restaurants serve crab, mahi-mahi, red snapper, lobster, shrimp, conch, trunk fish, and octopus. The only real variety is in location and atmosphere. **Mao's Seafood House ❹**, Rte. 102 Km 13.8, is one of the friendlier places along this stretch of road, owned and operated by a lifelong Joyuda resident. All the standard seafood dishes and a casual atmosphere combine with a view of Isla Ratones for a pleasant dining experience. (☎255-1801. Appetizers $3-8. Entrees $13-20. Open Tu-Su 11:30am-11pm.) The Puerto

THE MONA PASSAGE

The uninhabited nature of Isla Mona and its proximity to the mainland have long made it an access point for those who would sneak into Puerto Rico. During colonial times, the island was a boon to smugglers, pirates, and foreign governments intent on hounding Spanish settlements on Puerto Rico's west coast. It is even rumored that the infamous Captain Kidd hid out on the island briefly and stashed treasure there in 1699. Today, Mona's location approximately halfway between the Dominican Republic and the Puerto Rican mainland has made it a lightning rod for an invasion of a different sort. As many as 2000 illegal immigrants from the Dominican Republic and as far away as Cuba are caught each year by the US Coast Guard attempting to cross the Mona Channel. The seas in this area are made dangerous by the presence of the undersea Puerto Rican Trench, the second deepest in the world. The trench produces strong waves and rough sailing on the ocean's surface, making for a difficult crossing that often lasts four days. Many immigrants leave the Dominican Republic in rickety handmade boats called *yolas*, and it is unknown how many never complete their journey. However, the prospect of a backdoor entry into Puerto Rico and the US and a chance to experience prosperity seen nowhere else in the Caribbean, continues to attract hopeful immigrants.

Rican Tourism Company selected **Tino's Restaurant ❹**, Rte. 102 Km 13.6, as their Joyuda *mesón gastronómico*. Although it does not look out over the water, Tino's offers a touch of class and specialty seafood-filled *mofongo* $12-16 (☎851-2976. Entrees $8-26. Open W-Su 11am-10pm. AmEx/MC/V.)

MAYAGÜEZ

The self-proclaimed capital of the west coast has few attractions but ample spirit. With over 100,000 inhabitants, Mayagüez is one of the island's major metropolitan areas, yet only in the last few years has it begun to develop a tourist infrastructure. Mayagüez's deep port is currently used primarily for industrial purposes, but has cruise ship stops planned in the next few years. Like Ponce, the city has some beautiful turn-of-the-century houses, though many have fallen into a state of disrepair. Although Mayagüez is less of a tourist destination than a stopover on a tour of the west coast, the active university district's bars do provide ample entertainment for an evening visit, and the city is home to the island's only zoo. Construction in preparation for the Juegos Centroamericanos y del Caribe in 2010 indicates that Mayagüez does have potential to become a more attractive tourist destination.

▛ TRANSPORTATION

Flights: Aeropuerto Eugenio María de Hostos (☎832-3390), 4 mi. north of town. Take a right onto Rte. 342 off Hwy. 2; after 1 mi. on Rte. 342, turn left at the airport sign. The one airline, **Cape Air** (☎834-2870) sends flights to **San Juan** (1 per day, one-way $114). A taxi from Mayagüez costs about $7 (plus luggage. see **Taxis,** p. 252).

Públicos: The *público* terminal is located at the end of C. Pablo Maiz, near Parque de los Proceros. Call ahead and they'll pick you up from your hotel. *Públicos* head to: **Aguadilla** (30-40min., $3); **Añasco** (10-15min., $2); **Cabo Rojo** (15-20min., $2); **Ponce** (1½ $5-6); **Rincón** (20min., $2). **Linea Sultana** (☎832-1041 or 832-2502) sends vans to San Juan (3-3½hr.; 5, 7, 9, 11am, 1, 3, 5pm; $12).

Ferries: Ferries del Caribe (☎832-4800 or 832-4905, www.ferriesdelcaribe.com), north of town. From Hwy. 2 turn left at Km 152.2 on Rte. 102 and follow it until it ends. At the split, stay right on Rte. 3341 and the ferry will shortly appear on your left. A taxi costs about $6. An enormous 1000-passenger ferry travels between **Santo Domingo, Dominican Republic** (12hr.; M, W, F 8pm) and Puerto Rico (Tu, Th, Sa 8pm). Prices vary depending on cabin size: general one-way ticket (no cabin) $182, round-trip $189; suites (shared 4-person rooms) round-trip $193 per person; single cabins round-trip $289; double cabins round-trip $213 per person. The boat has airplane-style seats for those who do not purchase a bed. To purchase a one-way ticket you must have an airplane ticket or some other proof of departure from the Dominican Republic. Cars round-trip $200; vans, minivans, and pickups $230; motorcycles $130; bikes $20. You must reserve at least 1 day in advance or pay a $10 fee. If bringing a car, you must arrive 6 hours before departure. The ferry terminal does not have parking. Arrive 2hr. early. Terminal office open M, W, F 8am-8pm; Tu, Th, Sa 8am-5pm; Su noon-4pm. AmEx/MC/V.

Cars: The car rental companies below operate out of the airport. All prices are for the smallest compact cars available. Rates rise during Christmas, Easter, and summer.

Avis (☎833-7070). $44 per day. 25+. Open daily 7am-9:30pm. AmEx/D/MC/V.

Budget (☎832-4570). $44 per day, with insurance $53. 21+. Under 25 surcharge $10 per day. Open daily 8am 9pm. AmEx/D/MC/V.

Thrifty (☎834-1590). $52 per day. 21+. Under 25 surcharge $10 per day. Open daily 8am-noon and 1-5pm. AmEx/D/MC/V.

Taxis: White Taxi Cab, C. de Diego 18 (☎832-1154), at C. Peral. Open daily 6:30am-midnight. City Taxi (☎265-1992) leaves from the *público* station. Open daily 6:30am-11pm. Western Taxi (☎832-0562), at C. del Río, up from C. Antonini. Open daily 6am-midnight.

SOUTHWEST

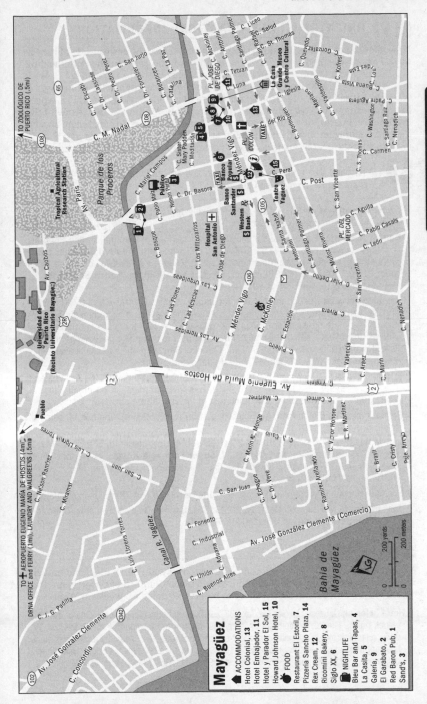

Mayagüez

▲ ACCOMMODATIONS
Hotel Colonial, 13
Hotel Embajador, 11
Hotel y Parador El Sol, 15
Howard Johnson Hotel, 10

◆ FOOD
Restaurant El Estoril, 7
Pizzeria Sancho Plaza, 14
Rex Cream, 12
Ricomini Bakery, 8
Siglo XX, 6

◼ NIGHTLIFE
Bleu Bar and Tapas, 4
La Casita, 5
Galería, 9
El Garabato, 2
Red Baron Pub, 1
Sand's, 3

✈ 🛈 ORIENTATION AND PRACTICAL INFORMATION

Mayagüez has a relatively small, walkable city center on the eastern side of Hwy 2. **Calle Post,** also called Hwy. 2R, is the main road and runs north-south, leading north from Plaza Colón to the university area. The main cross streets are C. Mendez Vigo and C. McKinley, both one-way. To reach the city center from Hwy. 2, take Rte. 2R and cross the canal by turning right at the small bridge (this is where Rte. 2R becomes C. Post), or exit Hwy. 2 toward C. McKinley. This is one of the few cities in Puerto Rico where most hotels and restaurants do congregate around the plaza. **Mayagüez Town Center,** located at the intersection of C. Post and Hwy. 2, just north of the center, holds some convenient services and a food court.

> ❗ After dark, stick to the well-lit streets on and around Plaza Colón, or the university area at the northern end of C. Post.

Tours: AdvenTours (☎831-6447) offers walking tours of downtown Mayagüez (3hr., M-Tu, $22). min. 2 people. Cash only.

Banks: There are several banks in Mayaguez and ATMs are plentiful. **Banco Popular,** C. Méndez Vigo 9 (☎832-0475). ATM. Open M-F 8am-4pm. **Western Bank** has buildings all over Mayagüez; the main office is on C. Méndez Vigo halfway down the block from C. Post. Open M-F 7:30am-6pm, Sa 8:30am-12:30pm. **Banco Santander,** C. Méndez Vigo 5, is open M-F 8:30am-4pm.

Camping Permits: The Departamento de Recursos Naturales (DRNA; ☎833-3700 or 833-4703), north on Hwy. 2. Turn right at the Alturas de Mayaguez sign immediately after Rte. 104, before the split for C. Marginal. Take the first left; the office is at the end of Alturas de Mayagüez shopping center. Issues permits to camp ($4 per person) and visit Isla Mona ($10 per person), but you must call the San Juan office to check availability and make a reservation. Open M-F 7:30am-noon and 1-4pm.

Internet Access: C. McKinley 14, **The Biblioteca Municipal,** between the Alcaldía and the Teatro Yaguez (☎834-8585, ext. 440), has free Internet, but no email allowed. Open during the summer M-F 8am-4pm, rest of the year 8am-6pm.

Police: Policía de Puerto Rico, Av. Corazones 1059 (☎832-9699), about 2 mi. south of town. Turn left at Denny's. Open 24hr.

Pharmacies: Walgreens, Av. Hostos 2097 (☎805-4005), just north of town at Hwy. 2 Km 152.7, is open 24hr. AmEx/D/MC/V. **Super Farmacia Hostos,** corner of C. Post and C. Méndez Vigo, has a good selection of basic medicines. Open M-F 7:30am-4:30pm, Sa 7:30am-2pm.

Hospital: Hospital San Antonio, C. Post 18 Norte (☎834-0056). 24hr. emergency room.

Post Office: C. McKinley 60 Oeste (☎265-3133). General Delivery available. Open M-F 7am-5pm, Sa 7:30am-1pm. Postal Code: 00680.

🛏 ACCOMMODATIONS

Mayagüez is one of the most affordable places to stay in Puerto Rico, and though rooms tend to be small, you will still live and sleep comfortably. Hotels are frequently filled almost to capacity, so try to reserve at least two weeks in advance.

Hotel Colonial, C. Iglesia 14 Sur (☎/fax 833-2150, www.hotelcolonial.com). One of the best values on the island. The colonial building has most of the traditional amenities—A/C, TV, parking—and throws in tall ceilings and 24hr. reception. With clean and cozy rooms, this place is a real bargain. Continental breakfast 7-10:30am included. Parking. Check-in 1pm. Check-out noon. Singles $39; doubles $59; triples $89; quads $99. Extra person $10. MC/V. ❶

Western Bay Mayagüez, C. Santiago Palmer 9 Este (☎834-0303). This 5-story building is one of Mayagüez's tallest, and has all the formality of a big-city hotel, including a conference room and a small pool tucked into the courtyard. The rooms are a little snug but still manage to fit in phone, A/C, cable TV, and a small fridge. Clean and well-maintained. Restaurant. Continental breakfast included. Limited parking. Singles $70; doubles $85; extra person $10. AmEx/MC/V. ❸

Hotel Embajador, C. Antonini 111 (☎833-3340), brings a cosmopolitan feel to Mayagüez with its modern art and slick nightclub, El Chapas. Rooms feature futuristic artwork as well as cable TV and A/C. Singles $60; doubles $80. AmEx/D/MC/V. ❷

Howard Johnson, C. Méndez Vigo 70 Este (☎832-9191). This HoJo is the nicest hotel downtown. Tropical bedspreads brighten clean, airy rooms with glistening bathrooms. Ideally located right behind the church. Cable TV, A/C, phone, and small swimming pool. Continental breakfast included. Parking $4 per night. Check-in 3pm. Check-out noon. 1 queen bed $96; 2 full beds $107; 2 queen beds $118. Tax included. MC/V. ❹

🛒 FOOD

Mayagüez has a number of attractive dining options around the plaza, and fast food abounds in the malls surrounding town, but for authentic *boriquen* food, try one of the *cafeterías*. Quick supplies are available at **Pueblo** on the 1st floor of the Mayagüez town center. (☎833-1444. Open M-Sa 6am-midnight, Su 11am-5pm. AmEx/MC/V) or **Todo a Peso, y Algo Mas,** across from the library (Open M-Sa 8:30sm-5:30pm. AmEx/D/MC/V.)

🍴 **Ricomini Bakery/Brazo Gitano,** C. Méndez Vigo 101 (☎833-1444), takes the cake (and the flan, and the *quesito*, and the *arroz con dulce*) for the best bakery/cafe/eatery in town. This clean, airy cafe swarms with activity during lunch hour, when it seems like everyone in Mayagüez stops by. Delicious food, efficient service, immaculate setting. Pastries $0.30-1.50. Breakfast $2.50-3. Sandwiches $4-6. Open daily 6am-midnight. Hot *comida criolla* $4.50 per lb. AmEx/MC/V. ❶

Restaurant Siglo XX, C. Peral 9 Norte (☎265-2094). A popular *cafetería*-style diner, with hot sandwiches ($3-6) and heavier fare available. Speedy service and upstairs seating with dark wood furniture. Entrees $8-13. Open M-Sa 6am-8:30pm. ❷

Restaurant El Estoril, C. Méndez Vigo 100 Este (☎834-2288). The owners claim this is "The Best in the West," and they're not far off. First-rate Portuguese food in a first-class setting, with fountains, porcelain plates decorating the walls, and a huge wine rack. Lunch buffet $10. Seafood, meat, and chicken entrees $17-30. Open June-July Tu-F 11:30-10pm, Sa 5-10pm; Aug.-May M-F 11am-10:30pm, Sa 5-11pm. AmEx/MC/V. ❹

Rex Cream, C. McKinley 17 (☎832-2121). The best way to beat the humidity is to enjoy some ice cream ($1.50-3) from Rex's. This ice cream stand is so popular that there are 2 locations around the corner from each other, one on C. McKinley and one on C. Mendez Vigo. Open M-Th 10am-10pm, F-Sa 10am-11pm, Su 11am-11pm. MC/V. ❶

Restaurante Vegetariano La Familia, C. de Diego 151 Este (☎833-7571). Clean, spacious, and super friendly, not to mention one of the few vegetarian options in Puerto Rico. A full buffet serves a variety of vegetarian entrees, usually including *veggie empanadas*, several kinds of rice, a tofu dish, and fresh salad. Mix and match your favorites. $6 meal. Open M-F 11am-3pm. Cash only. ❶

Pizzeria Sancho Panza, C. McKinley 87 (☎833-0215). A bit of a trek from the town center, this Italian pizzeria offers a range of delicious pizzas ($1.50 per slice, $7-14 for pies), calzones ($3-5), and salads ($7-12). Enjoy sit-down service in the clean, air-conditioned shop, or grab takeout. Open M-Th 11am-8pm, Sa 11am-9pm. AmEx/MC/V.

IN RECENT NEWS

LET THE GAMES BEGIN

Mayagüez recently earned the honor of hosting the **Juegos Deportivos Centroamericanos y del Caribe de 2010** (Games of Central America and the Caribbean 2010). Although they are still a long way off, the games are already changing the face and character of the city.

Mayagüez has budgeted $68 million for construction to prepare for the event, including new sports facilities and an improved tourist infrastructure. The city is reinventing itself as the symbolic port of entry for west-coast Puerto Rico. The port itself is being renovated and brought up to the code of international cruise line standards in an effort to attract some of the bustling cruise traffic away from Old San Juan to this sleepy coast. Although the sporting events of the Games will be held along the entire west coast, Mayagüez will serve as the center of festivities. In preparation, the town plaza is under construction, as is the **Teatro Yagüez** downtown.

Today, all the changes in in Mayagüez have greatly strengthened the town's tourist industry, transforming it into a bustling city with a lively nightlife scene. As the Games approach, the city continues to prepare for large crowds and strives to do residents and their fellow *puertorriqueños* proud.

☞ SIGHTS

ZOOLÓGICO DE PUERTO RICO. If you're still lamenting the fact that Puerto Rico is not home to any large mammals, you may enjoy a visit to Puerto Rico's largest zoo. Managed by the Compañía de Parques Nacionales, the zoo contains a selection of animals including monkeys, zebras, lions, camels, caimans, and hippopotami. The newly developed *aves* section displays birds from all over the world. Visitors can enter the *aviario*, a giant fenced-in cage where parrots and other birds fly around. *(Take Rte. 108 north past the university, then turn right at the sign for the zoo. Don't attempt to walk, as the road is narrow and cars drive fast. Taxis about $4. ☎834-8110. Open W-Su 8:30am-4pm. Parking $3, vans $4. $6, ages 11-17 and 60-74 $4, ages 5-10 $2, under 5 and over 74 free. MC/V.)*

TROPICAL AGRICULTURE RESEARCH STATION. Ecologists and botanists may drool over this 127-acre agricultural center where the US Department of Agriculture conducts research on over 2000 plant species suited to the South Atlantic. For less scientifically inclined visitors, the station provides a wonderful place to walk and the chance to encounter a wide range of tropical fauna. A self-guided tour leads past more than 70 labeled plant species native to the island and only takes 30min. to an hour. *(Between Rte. 108 and Rte. 2R. Coming from Rte. 2R, make a left turn directly after the gate to the university. ☎831-3435. Open M-F 7am-noon and 1-4pm. Free.)*

RECINTO UNIVERSITARIO MAYAGÜEZ (RUM). Any university with the acronym RUM has to be something interesting, and Mayagüez's branch of the University of Puerto Rico does not disappoint. NASA and other government agencies have been known to recruit engineering students from this primarily science-focused division of UPR. The attractive, palm-filled campus is among the more picturesque in Puerto Rico. Enter the gate across from Mayagüez Town Center and follow the broad Av. Palmeras to reach the main university plaza, the general library, and the student center. *(North of the city at the intersection of C. Post and Hwy. 2.)*

TEATRO YAGUEZ. Mayagüez has one of the most attractive public theaters in Puerto Rico. In 1976, the municipal government bought a historic church and converted it into the city's grandiose theater, complete with enormous chandeliers and two balconies. Unfortunately, restoration keeps it under wraps: the 900-seat theater has been undergoing renovation since 2003 and should be ready in 2009. *(Behind the Alcaldía between C. McKinley and C. Antonini.)*

NIGHTLIFE

University students dominate Mayagüez's nightlife, which heats up Wednesdays and Thursdays, then dies down over the weekend when everyone heads to the beach. If drinking with college kids is not your cup of tea, **Sand's** and **Galeria** have more of a young professional feel, and several malls on Rte. 2 have movie theaters.

El Garabato, C. Post 102 Norte (☎834-2524). A university pub with open windows and wooden stools where students gather throughout the day and night to grab a beer, play dominos, and chat. Daily Happy hour specials with various $1 beers. Regular beer $2-3 and mixed drinks $3. Open M-Sa 3pm-1:30am. AmEx/MC/V.

Red Baron Pub, C. Post 102 Norte (☎805-1580), upstairs from El Garabato. Once they've gotten good and toasted downstairs, RUM students head up to this steamy pub to dance the night away. Beer $1-2. Particularly popular during Tu karaoke. A live DJ plays reggaeton, rock, and hip-hop W-Sa. Occasional live Spanish rock. Open Tu-Sa 6pm-last customer. Cash only.

La Casita, C. de Diego 65 (☎805-1505). True to its name, located in a little house. Reggae, rock, and reggaeton give the cheerful 20-something crowd something to nod their heads to while drinking at the bar and watching the Yankees. Beer $2.25-2.50. Mixed drinks $3-5. Cover bands Th-Sa 11pm. $1 Medalla Happy hour W-Th. Open M-F 5pm-1:30am, Sa-Su 8pm-1:30am. MC/V.

Bleu Bar and Tapas, C. de Diego 63 (☎831-1446). One of the largest dance floors in town, lit, of course, in blue. The polished metal doors and trimmings make it feel industrial and hip—so hip that the 2nd fl. is VIP-only, and a dress code of no shorts or flip-flops is strictly enforced. Beer $2.50. Mixed drinks $4. Tapas $3-8. W DJ. Live music Th-Sa. Cover Sa $4. Open W-F 6pm-1:30am, Sa 8pm-1:30am.

Galeria, adjoining the elegant El Estoril, has a changing display of local artwork. Warm yellow walls produce an intimate feel at this art-gallery-turned-dance-party which caters to an older, more sophisticated crowd. Mixed drinks $3-6. F live rock or jazz. No cover. Open W-Sa 10pm-last customer.

Sand's, C. Peral 36 (☎831-5587). Packed with *mayagüezanos* young enough to enjoy Fnight karaoke but old enough to afford the pricey drinks. Dance floor with mirrors and flashing colored lights. Appetizers $6-20. Beer $2.75-3.25. Mixed drinks $3.75-6. 21+. Cover W 7-11pm $10, includes limited open bar. Open M-Tu and Su 11am-11pm, W 11am-1am, Th 11am-2am, F-Sa 11am-3am. AmEx/MC/V.

Mayagüez Beer Garden and Sports Bar, entrance on C. Mendez Vigo. If you're looking for the party overlooking the plaza, climb up 2 flights of stairs to reach this converted rooftop pool hall. A younger crowd fills the many balconies while enjoying pool, cheap beer, loud music, and dancing. A large stage and plenty of floor space makes this bar one of the only big concert venues in the city. Sa live music. Pool $0.75. Beer $2-3. Open W-Sa 7pm-3am. Cash only.

SOUTHWEST

NORTHWEST

West of San Juan, the terrain becomes more rugged, the locals more laid-back, and somewhere between the volcanic surfing beaches of the north coast and the dramatic *mogotes* of the inland mountains, you realize that you have arrived in western Puerto Rico. The Atlantic Ocean pounds the coast with the heaviest waves on the island, creating ideal surfing territory, while the limestone cliffs and sinkholes, a topography known as karst, create a rugged, otherworldly atmosphere.

Most travelers leave San Juan and head east, but the wilder country of the northwest has attractions to rival any others. Just south of Arecibo, the Camuy Caves and Arecibo Observatory (containing the world's largest radio telescope) are two of the most impressive sights on the island and make an excellent daytrip from San Juan. Farther west, Isabela and Rincón have some of the best surfing in the Caribbean, but even non-surfers will be enamored with the beautiful terrain, the friendly atmosphere, and the comfortable accommodations. However, strong waves make beautiful beaches less than ideal for swimming, and the region is also one of the most developed on the island, meaning that overpopulation, huge factories, and heavy traffic may mar an otherwise pleasant journey. City centers on the north coast—Manatí, Arecibo, and Aguadilla—provide the basic necessities but can mainly be thought of as bases for exploring the surrounding sights.

Hwy. 22 skirts most of the heavy traffic and deposits travelers in Arecibo within an hour and a half. However, the adventurous can explore the region more extensively by bypassing the main highways and taking small, one-lane roads along the northern coast or through inland karst country; this is the best way to experience all of the beautiful views the northwest has to offer.

HIGHLIGHTS OF NORTHWEST PUERTO RICO

HANG TEN OR JUST HANG OUT in **Rincón,** Puerto Rico's favorite expat haunt and home of some of the world's best surfing and nightlife (p. 279).

TRAVEL TO ANOTHER PLANET by exploring the underground world at the **Camuy Caves** (p. 268) or the **Arecibo Observatory** (p. 267).

GET UP CLOSE AND PERSONAL with karst country by hiking in **Bosque Estatal de Guajataca** (p. 277) or mountain biking in **Bosque Estatal de Cambalache** (p. 261).

START THE WEEKEND EARLY at **Jobos's relaxed surfer beaches** with the young Puerto Rican crowd and bass-bumpin' reggaeton (p. 271).

MANATÍ

A practical town sprawled along Hwy. 2, Manatí serves as a convenient roadside source of necessities, but isn't really a destination in its own right. Fast-food joints and big-box retailers have taken over the town itself. Despite the commercialization along Hwy. 2, rugged surfing beaches, state parks, and lakes full of caimans within a short distance of Manatí provide incentive to venture out to this area.

▐▄ TRANSPORTATION. Manatí centers on Hwy. 2, but it is much faster to travel via Hwy. 22—despite the intermittent tolls ($0.75)—then exit onto Rte. 149 and turn right at the intersection with Hwy. 2. *Públicos* traveling between Parada 18 in Santurce and Arecibo will stop in Manatí, or anywhere along Hwy.

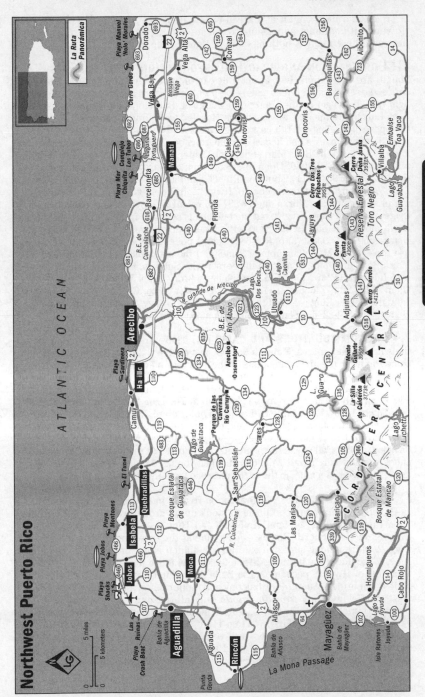

Northwest Puerto Rico

ATLANTIC OCEAN

NORTHWEST

2. To catch a *público*, sit at a green bench along Hwy. 2 and flag one down. However, it is almost impossible to reach most sights via public transportation, and there really is nothing to do in Manatí proper.

⚡🔊 ORIENTATION AND PRACTICAL INFORMATION. Most businesses in Manatí are located on Hwy. 2, but they can only be reached using the one-way *calles marginales* (service roads)—be prepared to turn around at the following light in order to get on the appropriate marginal. Barceloneta lies to the west and Vega Baja lies to the east. Most sights are located to the north, between Hwy. 2 and the ocean. Traveling west to east along the ocean, Rte. 685, Rte. 686, and Rte. 692 provide superb views and access to numerous beaches. **Banco Popular,** at Hwy. 2 and C. Vendig in the Bella Maria Shopping Center, just before Rte. 685 on the right, has an **ATM.** (☎854-2030. Open M-F 8am-4pm, Sa 9am-1pm.) The **police station** (☎854-2020 or 854-2011), south on Rte. 668 and a block up on the right, is open 24hr. **Walgreens,** at the intersection of Hwy. 2 and Rte. 149, in Manatí Plaza, parcels out pharmaceuticals 24hr. a day. (☎884-0545. AmEx/D/MC/V.) The **Manatí Medical Center** is visible from Hwy. 2, but the building is set back from the road one block north along Rte. 668. (☎623-3700. 24hr. emergency room.) The **Manatí Municipal Library,** on Rte. 669 just off of Rte. 668 near the police station, allows 1hr. of **Internet** use free. (Open M-Th 9am-5pm, F 9am-3pm.) **The net pl@ce,** in Manatí next to the Maria Bella Shopping Center on the corner with Subway, is a small cafe with reliable Internet. ($2 for 15min., $3 for 30min., $4 for 45min., $5 for 1 hr. ☎854-4320. Open M-F 11am-7pm, Sa-Su 11am-5pm.) The **post office,** C. Eliot Velez 29, across from the Burger King west of Rte. 668, set back from Hwy. 2, does not have General Delivery. (☎854-2296. Open M-F 6am-5:30pm, Sa 6am-3pm.) **Postal Code:** 00674.

🔊🔊 ACCOMMODATIONS AND CAMPING. There are not many accommodations in the Manatí area. **Motel La Roca ❷,** just off Hwy. 2 near Barceloneta, rents some rooms by the night and others by the hour (see **A Room Without a View,** p. 270). Rooms come with TV, A/C, and music dials on the walls. Not all have windows. (From Hwy. 2, turn south on Rte. 663. ☎881-0483. 1 double bed $50; 2 double beds $60. Cash only.) The best option is to camp at **🔊Bosque Estatal de Cambalache ❶** (see **Sights,** below). The large La Rosa area holds up to 30 people and has covered picnic tables, trash cans, showers, and toilets (when the water is turned on). You must have a DRNA permit ($4 per person) and a reservation to camp here (see **Camping,** p. 40). Call ahead to ensure that the gate is left open for your arrival and check to make sure that it will be open when you need to leave. The camp area is about a quarter of a mile up the rocky dirt road from the recreation area.

🔊🔊 FOOD AND SHOPPING. Grande, on Hwy. 2 in the same shopping center as Banco Popular, is a good place to stock up on groceries. (☎884-7273. Open M-Sa 7am-9pm, Su 11am-5pm. AmEx/MC/V.) They also have **Moneygram** money transfer service. Puerto Ricans usually dine at the fast-food restaurants lining Hwy. 2. More unique sit-down eateries are hidden along the marginal roads of Hwy. 2, including the hopping **🔊Wine Gallery and Diego Restaurant ❹,** C. B3 Marginal, off of Hwy. 2, past the Maria Bella Shopping Center and after the white pedestrian bridge. An outdoor balcony and indoor bar attract chatty young professionals, who enjoy *comida criolla* and international dishes. (☎884-0109. Beer $2. Lunch $7-12. Entrees $14-30. Wine bottles from $20. Sa live music F karaoke. Open Tu 11am-8pm, W 11am-11pm, Th-Sa 11am-2am.) If storm clouds are keeping you off the beaches, or if you just like shopping, head to the **Prime Outlets,** at the intersection of Hwy. 2 and Rte. 140 (Exit 55 off Hwy. 22), to search for deals at stores like Ralph Lauren, Puma, and Liz Claiborne.

⑤ SIGHTS. **Bosque Estatal de Cambalache** provides a welcome retreat from the development along Hwy. 2. At slightly under 1000 acres, this humid, subtropical forest is large enough to provide a full day of activity but small enough to be manageable. For visitors staying in San Juan, this is a convenient day-long introduction to karst country. Over 4 mi. of well-marked, beginner-friendly hiking trails wind through the forest, including an interpretive trail with signs and a **mountain biking path.** Unfortunately, San Juan (p. 96) is the closest place to rent bikes. The picnic area contains covered tables, a brick grill, and playground equipment. From Hwy. 22, take the exit immediately after the Arecibo tollbooth, then go north on Rte. 683. Turn right on Rte. 682 and look for the large sign on the right. To get to the forest **office,** take a right as soon as you enter the premises, directly before the welcome sign. (☎ 881-1004. Open M-F 8am-4:30pm.)

> **STOP BUGGING ME.** Pesky mosquitoes are rampant in the tropical forests, so consider using insect repellent on your hike. It is helpful to apply repellent not only on your skin but also on your clothes and tent in order to enjoy the outdoors bite-free.

To reach **Laguna Tortuguero,** classified by the Department of Natural Resources as the only natural lake in Puerto Rico, take Exit 41 from Hwy. 22, turn right on Hwy. 2, then left on Rte. 687, and look for the second big sign on the left. Tortuguero's other claim to fame is its reptile population—the lake is full of **caiman,** which are similar to crocodiles. In the mid-1970s, many Puerto Ricans began purchasing the South American animals as pets; however, they soon discovered that caimans are cranky little critters that rapidly outgrow fish tanks, so they ditched the animals in the lake. Unfortunately, the introduction of a new species disrupted the existing ecosystem. The DRNA attempted an eradication program in the early 1980s, with little success. Now both humans and reptiles have accepted a peaceful coexistence: the caimans only come out at night, so most visitors remain blissfully oblivious to their presence. The curious can obtain a permit from the office in Manatí to visit after nightfall and attempt to see one of the animals. During the day, the peaceful lake is a great place to fish, kayak, or just sit and enjoy the scenery. Walk down the dirt road at the end of the parking lot and look for a path on the left; a short climb leads to great views of the lake and the ocean. Covered tables and bathrooms are available. The Manatí DRNA office (☎ 884-2587) is open W-F 8am-4pm and Sa-Su 6am-6pm.

North of Manatí, **Reserva Natural Hacienda la Esperanza** has the potential to be a regional attraction. This 19th-century sugarcane plantation occupies over 2200 acres with six different ecosystems, from mangroves to coral reefs, much of it preserved as it was 100 years ago. The Conservation Trust of Puerto Rico has big plans to renovate the house and expects to open the area to the public in 2008. For now, the area offers solitude and a nice view along the beach. From Manatí, head north on Rte. 685, then turn left on Rte. 616, continue past the town, and pass through the empty fields until you see the reserve sign on the left. To reach the **beach** at Punta Manatí, continue on the road through a tiny neighborhood to the Fideicomiso gate (open weekends and holidays to vehicles, always open to foot traffic) and continue on the dirt road through the dense mangroves. There are several turnoffs where you can park and enjoy a picnic lunch in the shade of the mangroves or lay out on the sandy beach.

⑥ BEACHES. The rugged beaches lining the northwest coast rival those of Piñones in terms of solitude, surfing potential, and sheer beauty. The best way to find your own private spot is to drive along the oceanside highway and pull off on

TIME: 3-4hr.

DISTANCE: 55 mi.

BEST TIME TO GO: Dec.-June, or when it's not raining.

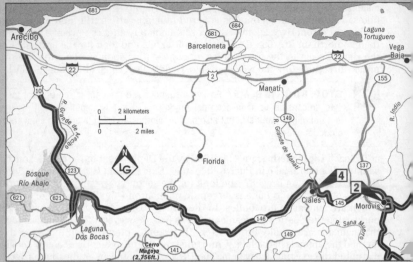

The drive to Arecibo's principal sights, the observatory and the nearby Camuy Caves, leads past the steep limestone sinkholes and looming *mogotes* of karst country (p. 268). However, the fastest route from San Juan entails a substantial drive along a series of freeways that cut through the beautiful countryside. For a more leisurely and scenic route, try the following series of back roads that twists and turns through the spectacular landscape of northern Puerto Rico, from verdant farmlands to the heart of karst country. The drive is more interesting than most of the man-made sights along the way, but these serve as nice breaks during the long trip. Because the route runs parallel to Hwy. 2 and Hwy. 22, it is easy to head back north at any time and zip on to Arecibo.

The drive begins just past Manatí. From San Juan, take Hwy. 22 west, then take Exit 22 north onto Rte. 165. Turn onto Hwy. 2 and drive west to take Rte. 142 toward Corozal. When Rte. 142 ends, go right on Rte. 159. Then turn right (west) on Rte. 818 and continue past the residential neighborhood to Km 2.5.

1. CENTRO HISTÓRICO TURÍSTICO DEL CIBUCO (HISTORICAL TOURIST CENTER). Nestled in the middle of a valley with steep karst cliffs and wide vistas, this tourist center offers a sampling of various Puerto Rican cultural attractions on the grounds of an old sugar plantation. The guided visit begins at the plantation's old home, **Casa Museo Aurora.** The next stop is the small **Museo de la Caña de Azucar** (Museum of Sugar Cane), which explains the history of sugar cane in Spanish. Tours then skip backwards 500 years as visitors hop on a tram to see **Taíno petroglyphs.** Next is a small mock sugar mill where travelers can sample the sickeningly sweet sugar milk., while the last stop is the **Artificial Lake.** There, visitors can borrow a paddle boat or just stand at the edge and watch the turtles swim below. The complex is designed for groups, and visits require a guided tour. However, when it's not busy, guides are happy to accommodate individual visitors. (Rte. 818 Km 2.5. ☎859-8079 or 859-0213. Open Th-Su and most holidays 9am-5pm. Free.) In mid-July the center hosts an **artisans festival.** If you plan to visit during October, don't miss Corozal's **Festival del Plátano,** which features artisans, music, and lots of plantain-based foods in the city plaza. After leaving the complex, turn left and backtrack on Rte. 818 to Rte. 159, then head west toward Morovis.

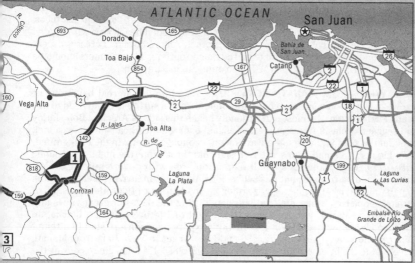

2. MOROVIS. Upon reaching Morovis, turn left onto Rte. 137, then turn right at Rte. 155, which leads right into town. Despite the fact that Morovis serves as the production center for much of Puerto Rico's *artesanía* (artesanal work), including traditional musical instruments such as *cuatros* and *tiples*, there is almost no tourist infrastructure. The **Alcaldía** public relations office on the plaza provides a list of contact information and specialties of current artisans. Open M-F 9am-4:30pm.

3. CASA BAVARIA. The Dutch may have been turned back at the walls of Old San Juan, but the Germans seem to have left their mark on the island at this charming Bavarian beer garden. The drive up to **Casa Bavaria** ❸ is stunning; as you enter Morovis, turn left onto Rte. 137, then left again onto Rte. 155, and continue for about 20min. to Km 38.3. Around Km 41, look left to see a waterfall cascading down the mountain across the valley. At the Casa, join bikers and tourists at long wooden tables for a breathtaking view of the valley below; the perfect location to enjoy *schnitzel*, Bratwurst, and Lowenbräu. During the third weekend of October, Casa Bavaria springs to life with its own Puerto Rican version of **Oktoberfest.** (Rte. 155 Km 38.3. ☎862-7818. www.casabavaria.com. Puerto Rican and German entrees $8-16. German beer after 3pm $2.50. Sa live jazz *criollo* music. Open Th and Su noon-8pm, F-Sa noon-10pm. Bar open until 2am. MC/V.) Take Rte. 155 back to Rte. 137, then turn right onto Rte. 137, then right again onto Rte. 155 (avoiding town). Don't be confused when you hit Rte. 137 again; go straight and then turn left onto Rte. 145, which leads to Ciales. As you approach Ciales, take a left onto Rte. 149 to reach the center of town.

4. CIALES. From Morovis it's a straight shot to Hwy. 22 and a speedy return to Arecibo. However, if you're looking for a break, try Ciales, which offers beautiful views and a miniscule coffee museum. (At C. Santiago Palmer and C. Hernández Usera, on Rte. 149, 1 block past the plaza. ☎871-3439. Open by appointment. $2, university students $1.50, secondary students $1, under 12 free.) From Ciales, continue west on Rte. 146 to reach **Lago Dos Bocas** (p. 269). Watch out for the several sharp turns in the road, as they aren't particularly well marked. From Dos Bocas it's a quick 20min. drive down to Hwy. 2 and the town of Arecibo.

any dirt road. Unfortunately, the coast is rocky in places, creating superb vistas but not the best swimming conditions. The westernmost beach in the Manatí area, **Playa Mar Chiquita**, at the end of Rte. 648, is also one of the most popular—several beachgoers can usually be found watching the waves crash over a small rock isthmus. The rocks provide a small protected swimming area great for children. If you head to the right side of the rocks, you'll find a longer stretch of beach with some small waves, slightly rocky in places. From Hwy. 2, take Rte. 685 north to Rte. 648, which ends at the beach. (No facilities.) Surfers recommend **Complejo Los Tubos**, just down the hill on Rte. 686, which has a more developed beach area with a gated parking lot, covered picnic tables, and bathrooms. An offshore reef creates decent surfing conditions for intermediate and advanced surfers, but swimmers should be aware of the rip current. (Open W-F 8am-4pm, Sa-Su 9am-5pm.)

⚑ DAYTRIP FROM MANATÍ: VEGA BAJA. Vega Baja is the real beginning of the west. Here, you can leave your cares behind, grab a surfboard, and head to **Balneario Puerto Nuevo**, the most party-friendly beach this side of Arecibo. Bob Marley and reggaeton blasts from car stereos as laid-back Puerto Ricans of all ages kick back on the sand and watch the waves with a couple of beers. In the background, food kiosks and small bars serve refreshments throughout the night. As a public *balneario*, Vega Baja has a small recreation area with covered picnic tables, showers, and bathrooms, but it is set back from the ocean, leaving plenty of room to party after dark. Despite signs warning against strong riptides, the sea is full of **surfers, snorkelers, swimmers,** and **jet-skiers** during the day. For great views and even better surfing, continue east to the end of Rte 692 to reach **Cibuco,** an advanced, shallow break over a reef. Only experienced surfers should attempt this. (At the intersection of Rte. 686 and 692. To get to Vega Baja from Manatí, drive east to the intersection of Rte. 686 and 692. ☎855-4744. Lifeguards during the day. Several open lots for parking, but do not leave valuables in your car. Recreation area open M-F 8am-5pm, Sa-Su 8am-6pm.)

ARECIBO

Although the town itself offers little to attract visitors, the impressive sights just outside of Arecibo make it the hidden treasure of Puerto Rico's travel destinations. The star attractions are the Arecibo Observatory, which contains the world's largest single radio telescope, and the Camuy Caves, incredible formations created by the world's third-largest underground river. Traveling to these two parks also means a trip through the stunning karst country of the north coast; the views may inspire you to spend more time exploring nearby lakes and natural reserves. To avoid the traffic and endless chain stores on Hwy. 2, consider taking the **Karst Country Scenic Drive** (p. 262) to reach Arecibo's backcountry treasures.

▐ TRANSPORTATION

Driving to Arecibo is the only way to see the sights without battling irregular *públicos* and spending extensive amounts of time in the city. From San Juan, take Hwy. 22 west, exit onto Rte. 129, and go north to reach the town and the lighthouse or south to reach the other attractions. From the **Terminal Sur,** *públicos* go to Manatí (1hr., $2.50), San Juan (2-3hr., $7-10), and Utuado (30min., $2.50). However, most vans leave before 8am. The **Terminal Norte** sends *públicos* to Camuy (10-25min., $1.25), Hatillo (15-25min., $1.25), and Quebradillas (30-45min., $2.50). To reach the observatory or caves, negotiate with a *público* driver to see if he will drop you off and come pick you up later. Even better, head down C. José de Diego

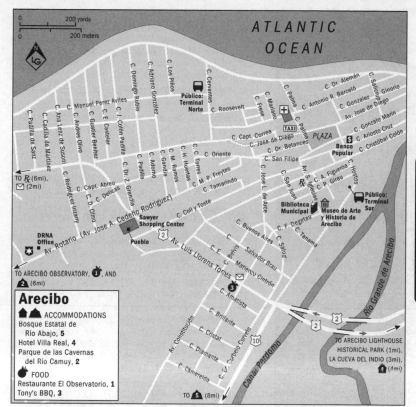

Arecibo

▲▲ ACCOMMODATIONS
Bosque Estatal de
Río Abajo, **5**
Hotel Villa Real, **4**
Parque de las Cavernas
del Río Camuy, **2**

🍴 FOOD
Restaurante El Observatorio, **1**
Tony's BBQ, **3**

to **Arecibo Taxi Cab,** on the plaza, where taxis can take you to the observatory ($15) or the Camuy Caves ($20) and pick you up later. (☎ 878-2020. Open daily 4am-9pm.) Another option is **Diego Taxi Cab** (☎ 878-1050).

✈ ℹ ORIENTATION AND PRACTICAL INFORMATION

Arecibo's city center sits between Hwy. 2 and the Atlantic Ocean. To reach the central plaza and city center, turn left where Rte. 10 goes to the right. The major sights lie about 30min. south of Arecibo proper, just off Rte. 129. Av. Rotario holds most of the government offices and connects Hwy. 2 to Rte. 129. It is entirely possible for a physically fit person to explore the city of Arecibo on foot.

Bank: Banco Popular, Av. Gonzalez Marín 67 (☎ 878-8500), on the plaza. **ATM.** Open M-F 8am-4pm. Numerous other banks line Hwy. 2.

Camping Permits: The **DRNA** office (☎ 878-9048) is in Centro Govermental Building A, behind the police headquarters on Av. Rotario. Reserve 2 weeks in advance. Open M-F 7:30am-noon and 1-4pm.

Library and Internet Access: Arecibo Public Library, 210 Av. Santiago Iglesias (☎ 878-1178 or 817-1005). Located in the green Casa Pizá, built in 1913. Free Internet access 1 hr. Open M-Th 8am-6:30pm, F 8am-4:30pm.

THE LOCAL STORY

KARST CRAZY

The first thing that most visitors to Puerto Rico's north coast notice are the bizarre formations in the countryside, which look like something out of a modernist painting. A geological formation, known as karst, produces steeply eroded cliff sides, sinkholes, underground rivers, and *mogotes*—dramatic hills that form around holes where underground caverns have collapsed. Karst is a kind of limestone that forms when carbon-dioxide-carrying water (which is mildly acidic) slowly dissolves the stone, carving out eye-catching rock formations.

The word "karst" comes from a region in the former Yugoslavia that contains such formations, but it also describes several regions around the world, including Puerto Rico's north coast, Vieques, Isla Mona, and Cabo Rojo. The area traversed by the Karst Country Scenic Drive (p. 262) is so important as a watershed that the US Congress recently passed a bill authorizing the purchase of land to protect Puerto Rican water supplies and this unique environment.

Many of the attractions in this region exist thanks to the karstic geology. The Arecibo Observatory (p. 267) is nestled in a natural sinkhole, and erosion produced the enormous Camuy Cave system (p. 268). Explorers can see karst up-close on a tour (p. 304) through the caverns of the Tanamá River.

Police: Av. Hostos 300 (☎878-2020). Open 24hr.

Pharmacy: Farmacia del Pueblo, Av. Santiago Iglesias (☎878-2450), in Arecibo, near the library. Open M-Sa 7am-6pm. MC/V. **Walgreens,** Hwy. 2 Km 81.8 (☎880-0290), across from Plaza del Norte mall, in Hatillo. Open 24hr. AmEx/D/MC/V.

Hospital: Hospital Metropolitano Dr. Susoni (☎650-1830), on the plaza, has a 24hr. emergency room.

Post Office: There are 2 branches in Arecibo, both on Hwy. 2. The main branch is at Km 80.6, across from the Plaza del Atlántico shopping center, on the side of the hill. Open M-F 10am-7pm, Sa 8am-4pm. AmEx/MC/V. The smaller branch is at Km 75.8, before the bridge over the canal (☎878-1246). No General Delivery. Open M-F 8am-4pm, Sa 8am-noon. **Postal Code:** 00612.

ACCOMMODATIONS AND CAMPING

Arecibo has very few accommodations. There are some camping options to the south; if you're looking for an actual hotel, try Hatillo (p. 270) or Utuado (p. 304).

Hotel Villa Real, Hwy. 2 Km 67.2 (☎881-4134 or 881-8277; fax 881-1992), about 4 mi. east of Arecibo. Designed for businessmen on the go, this roadside hotel has all the necessities but few perks. Clean rooms with linoleum floors, A/C, refrigerator, phone, and TV. Pool. Coin laundry. Key deposit $25. Check-in 3pm. Check-out noon. 1 queen bed $66; 2 queen beds $77; suites $87-98. AmEx/MC/V. ❸

Parque de las Cavernas del Río Camuy (☎898-3100), 30 min. south of Arecibo (p. 268). The CPN allows visitors to camp at this tourist attraction (see below). Campers pitch their tents in the picnic area, but the site does have bathrooms, showers, and a 24hr. guard. Bring your own food—there aren't many options nearby. Reservations required. $5 per person. AmEx/MC/V. ❶

Bosque Estatal de Río Abajo, on Rte. 621. From Hwy. 2 take Hwy. 10 south, then turn right onto Rte. 6612, which soon intersects Rte. 621. A beautiful creekside camping area in the middle of karst country. Includes trash cans, water spigots, bathrooms, rustic showers, fire pits, and picnic tables. 1 marked trail. Office open M-F 7am-noon and 1-3:30pm, Sa-Su 8:30am-12:30pm and 1:30-5:30pm. Must have a permit ($4) and a DRNA reservation (p. 265). ❶

FOOD

When asked to recommend a good restaurant, most *arecibeños* generally appear stumped and eventually start mentioning the chain restaurants in Plaza del Norte, on Hwy. 2 in Hatillo. There are establishments near every attraction, but nothing outstanding. You will find a more authentic option in the cheap roadside *panaderías* (bakeries) offering sandwiches and supplies for making your own meals. Groceries can be found at **Pueblo,** in the shopping center at Hwy. 2 and Av. Rotario, which also has a **Western Union.** (☎878-1975. Open M-Sa 6am-midnight, Su 11am-5pm. AmEx/D/MC/V.)

Tony's BBQ, Hwy. 2 Km 75.8 (☎881-2871), across from the post office, is very popular. Although Tony's seems like just another fast food joint in Arecibo, its lunches are exceptionally filling. Combos of chicken, steak, and pork, along with a variety of side dishes, $5-6. Open daily 9:30am-10pm. Cash only. ❶

Restaurante El Observatorio, Rte. 625 Km 1.1 (☎880-3813), just outside the observatory. Clearly geared toward passing tourists, with a souvenir shop and pictures of the observatory on the walls. Standard seafood and *comida criolla.* Seating inside or on the back patio with a limited view of karst country. Good, quick service. Medalla $2.50. Entrees $8-17. Open W-Su 11am-5pm. AmEx/MC/V. ❸

🔘 SIGHTS

■ **OBSERVATORIO DE ARECIBO.** Known as "El Radar" to Puerto Ricans, the Arecibo Observatory is the largest single radio telescope in the world, and has the unique capability to both send and receive signals from a similar sender up to 1500 light years away. The observatory was built in the late 1960s about 6 mi. south of Arecibo because the site fits two specific requirements: it is close to the equator, thereby providing observers with access to most of the sky, and the karstic geography provides a natural sinkhole for the enormous reflector. Since then, the observatory has served as a workstation for scientists from around the world, including 1993 Nobel Prize winners Joseph Taylor and Russell Hulse. The observatory has also served as the site of several less scientific projects, including the filming of four movies (*Contact, GoldenEye, Survivor,* and *Dream Team*) and an episode of *The X-Files.* The observatory is run by Cornell University's National Atmosphere and Ionosphere Center.

Visits begin at the two-story **museum,** where all exhibits are explained in English and Spanish. The lower level has several interactive displays designed to introduce curious visitors to astronomy. Upstairs, signs describe the different projects undertaken at the observatory. An infrequent 20min. movie explains how the telescope operates. Finally, head

FROM THE ROAD

BASEBALL, A COMMON LANGUAGE

Traveling solo for extended periods of time can be demanding. Even when the fun and adventures seem endless, there comes a point when all you want is to be surrounded by familiar people and things that give you a sense of comfort. For me, working my way through a different language and culture, that feeling of comfort would come through a regular game of baseball.

It was the third game of the semifinals of the Northern Conference. The town of Camuy was facing Aguada, playing under lights in the newly built Camuy Stadium. The stands were packed, and the fans of each town rallied behind their own makeshift bands, competing to see who could be loudest. I had been invited by Ana Amador, a Camuy native, whom I had met earlier that day. She insisted that I attend the game with her and her family.

While I ate my peanuts and hot dog, Ana translated baseball terminology from Spanish into English. *El lanzador* was the pitcher, and *el receptor* was the catcher. I couldn't understand most of what the announcer said, but I knew to cheer at a *pochado* (strikeout) and go wild for a *cuadrangular* (home run). I cheered for the home team as they went on to a 7-2 victory, and as I watched that game of baseball, I had never felt more at ease.

-Paul Hamm

out to the viewing platform and see the main attraction: the telescope itself. Not nearly as white or solid as it appears in the movies, the dish, 1000 ft. in diameter, is actually made out of tens of thousands of perforated aluminum quadrangles that collect the grayish grime of their jungle surroundings. Hanging 450 ft. above the reflector, the receiver (resembling an enormous golf ball) houses 11 different instruments for collecting data from the dish; intrepid astronomers and technicians can sometimes be seen walking the long catwalk out to it. The sight is especially impressive when the entire platform rotates. *(From Arecibo, take Rte. 129 south, turn left on Rte. 134, continue east on Rte. 635, and finally turn right onto Rte. 625. You can take a público from Terminal del Norte in Arecibo headed to the barrio of Esperanza, but there will be a surcharge. Or take a $15 taxi from Arecibo. ☎878-2612; www.naic.edu. Open W-Su 9am-4pm. $5, ages 5-12 and 65+ $3, under 5 free. AmEx/D/MC/V.)*

LA CUEVA DEL INDIO (INDIAN'S CAVE). This attraction is less a cave and more a wild limestone cavern that the ocean has carved out over the years. Leave your car in the dirt parking area in front of the owner's house, then climb out over the moon-like landscape to the rock steps on the left that lead down into the cave. The petroglyphs on the wall were supposedly created by the Taínos over 500 years ago, though on the whole the crashing ocean may prove more impressive. Wear good shoes and watch your step, since holes in the limestone open to the ocean over 20 ft. below. Farther down the cliffs to the right are Big Arch and Little Arch, formed where the ocean cut into the cliffs and left the impressive formations. Don't stand too close to the edge, since the wind can be very strong, and the drop is steep. The owners of the parking lot can sometimes be prevailed upon to give an unofficial tour with the history of the cave in return for a tip. *(2 mi. past the lighthouse on Rte. 681, turn left at the red "Aceso a la Cueva" on the left, just past the Esso station. Parking $2. Admission $0.50.)*

KARST COUNTRY CRUISING. The best way to experience the karst country of the Northwest is to drive along the back roads that wind through the countryside. Many of these roads have sharp curves and steep hills. Remember to shift to a lower gear when going down hill in order to save your brakes.

PARQUE DE LAS CAVERNAS DEL RÍO CAMUY. The Camuy Cave Park is one of Puerto Rico's most extraordinary and accessible natural attractions. For millions of years, the Río Camuy has been slowly eroding away the soft karstic limestone to create the third-largest cave system in the world. In 1958 scientists discovered this unique phenomenon, and the site opened to the public in the 1980s. Today Puerto Rico's National Parks Company operates 250 acres of the incredible terrain as a tourist attraction. Visitors can walk on a paved path through one of the enormous caves amidst slowly dripping water and hundreds of sleeping bats. Most people come to Camuy in the morning, then continue to the observatory in the afternoon. Consequently, the park is often quite crowded before noon; arrive right when the park opens or in the early afternoon to avoid a long wait for the tour. Tours are conducted in either English or Spanish.

The tour starts with a 20min. film that covers a brief history of the park. Afterward, tour groups of up to 30 people board trolleys that lead to the main attraction, **Cueva Clara.** At 170 ft. in height, Clara awes even big-cave veterans. Groups follow a winding path through the artistically lit cave past a series of stalactites and stalagmites (which grow at a rate of 1 in. every 100 years), as mist rises eerily around them. At the Palma Sinkhole, visitors can look down at the river rushing past 150 ft. below. Groups then head to **Tres Pueblos Sinkhole,** an enormous 400 ft. hole located at the intersection of Lares, Camuy, and Hatillo. The last stop, **Spiral Sinkhole,** is the park's most recent addition. A 205-step wooden staircase leads to a platform looking into a huge ravine. [...] ley for a stop at the cafeteria, the gift shop, and the [...] can take up to two hours, but after it's over you'll w[...]

Most visitors will be satisfied with a tour through [...] turous may try a guided expedition into the caves. [...] Utuado, leads intense hiking/tubing trips into the ca[...] ling (p. 304). In San Juan, **Aventuras Tierra Adentro** [...] trips (p. 131). *(Rte. 129 Km 18.9. 20min. from Arecibo.* ☎ [...] *8am-3:30pm. Parking $3. $12, ages 4-12 $7, ages 60+ and* [...]

ARECIBO LIGHTHOUSE HISTORICAL PARK. Areci[...] one of the few in Puerto Rico that has been develope[...] The historical park around the lighthouse has the feel of a theme park, with mod els of a Taíno village, Christopher Columbus's three ships, a pirate vessel, and a slave hut complete with recorded African music. The entire assortment is just as tacky as it sounds, but two wooden platforms afford great ocean views that almost compensate for the kitsch. The lighthouse has a small nautical museum with assorted maritime artifacts but no explanations. You can climb up the stairs, but be aware that the US Coast Guard still uses the top of the lighthouse. *(Take Hwy. 2 to Rte. 681, then turn left on Rte. 655. Well marked by brown signs.* ☎ *880-7250. Open M-F 9am-6pm, Sa-Su 10am-7pm. Parking $2. $9, children and seniors $7. MC/V.)*

MUSEO DE ARTE E HISTORIA DE ARECIBO. "A town that doesn't know its own history and doesn't preserve it is a town destined to die," says this museum's curator, Cynthia Velázquez. Located in the center of Arecibo, the recently opened museum is an effort to keep Arecibo alive by combining its history with a rotating art exhibition that showcases work from various Latino artists. One section is dedicated to local artists. *(203 Av. Santiago Iglesias, across from the library, next to the Público Terminal Sur.* ☎ *879-4403. Open M-F 9am-3:30pm. Free.)*

◼ BEACHES AND WATER SPORTS

Arecibo's most popular **beach** for both surfers and swimmers is **Poza del Obispo,** just east of the lighthouse. On the western edge of the beach, a small protected inlet provides a good place to swim. Surfers head east, where the surf gets progressively more impressive. Unfortunately, the beach offers neither shade nor facilities. (From Hwy. 2 turn north on Rte. 681 and continue past the lighthouse.) If you continue down Rte. 681, several turn-offs mark additional popular surf breaks. To reach the public Balneario Morillo, follow directions to the Arecibo Lighthouse (see **Sights,** p. 267); the beach is on the left, across from the parking lot.

LAGO DOS BOCAS

After a long day of driving around Arecibo, visitors may welcome the tranquility of Lago Dos Bocas. Surrounded by steep limestone cliffs and lush mountain vegetation, this calm lake in the hills of karst country offers opportunities for several activities. Dos Bocas is a popular fishing lake, but no fishing equipment rental is available. Perhaps the most relaxing way to explore is by riding the **free government ferry** that makes a trip around the lake every hour. The ferry picks up and drops off residents at their homes along the lake, but visitors can always ride along and enjoy the scenery. Depending on the number of stops, the loop can take 20-40min. (☎ 879-1838. Ferries leave M-F 6:30, 8:30, 10, 11am, noon, 3, 5pm; Sa-Su every hour 6:30am-3pm. Office open daily 7am-3pm.)

At **Rancho Marina Restaurant ❸,** wooden platforms over the water provide a picturesque setting from which to enjoy delicious *comida criolla*. Accommodations are also in development, with renovations on several *cabañas* expected to be com-

pleted in summer 2009. (Ask the ferry to drop you off here. Also accessible by car from Rte. 146 Km 7.6, but you must have four-wheel drive and call for directions. ☎894-8034; www.ranchomarina.com. Entrees $10-15. *Cabaña* prices not established at press time; call ahead. Open Sa-Su and holidays 10am-6pm. AmEx/MC/V.) To get to Lago Dos Bocas, drive south on Rte. 10, then turn left at the sign and take Rte. 621 east to Rte. 123 south. You can't miss the dock at Km 67.1.

HATILLO

Founded in 1823 when Puerto Rico was still a Spanish colony, Hatillo has since become the island's dairy capital, producing one-third of all milk consumed in Puerto Rico. Indeed, the town has a ratio of 1 cow for every 1.3 people. Dairy industry aside, however, Hatillo's renowned mask festival and attractive beaches make the town worth visiting. Also, because of its cheap accommodations, Hatillo is a convenient base from which to explore the sights around Arecibo.

The annual ⬛**Festival de las Máscaras** (Mask Festival), held on December 28, is the island's third-largest mask exhibition. Inspired by a traditional festival in the Canary Islands, this popular celebration includes parades, music, and colorful costumes, as participants dress up to reenact the Biblical tale of King Herod. When it is not hosting large festivals, Hatillo is a quiet town with two attractive beaches. **Playa Sardinera,** Hwy. 2 Km 84.6, at Centro Vacacional Luis Muñoz Marín, is one of the best north coast beaches for young children. Several large boulders shelter a calm, shallow wading area perfect for youngsters. Older visitors can head past the boulders where big waves pound the beach, though the entire area is a bit rocky. Just west, in the actual town of Hatillo, wild **Playa Marina** makes an ideal destination for sunbathing or long beach walks. **Camuy** also offers a nice stretch of beach, accessible from Rte. 485. There is a good surf break, **El Peñon de las Amadores,** right before the rock with a giant cross. (To reach Playa Sardinera, from Hwy. 2 turn north onto Rte. 119 and continue to downtown Hatillo. Turn north again at Rte. 130. To reach Camuy take Hwy. 2 to Rte. 119 and then go west into the city. Pass the church in the plaza on the right-hand side and continue on to Rte. 485 for a short distance. Once past the houses, turn right into the sandy parking area.)

Centro Vacacional Luis Muñoz Marín ❸, Hwy. 2 Km 84.6, marked by a sign for Punta Maracayo Resort, offers a bit more entertainment than typical government-run beach *cabañas*. The complex sits in front of Playa Sardinera and contains two pools and a water slide. Clean six-person *cabañas* have yellow walls, A/C, cable TV, full kitchens, and balconies. Don't forget to request an ocean view—it's the same price. The grassy **camping/RV area ❷** offers water spigots, indoor bathrooms, and cold-water showers. (☎820-0274; fax 544-0225. Cafeteria and picnic tables. Office open daily 8am-5pm, except holidays. Non-guest entrance $3, with water slide $5. Check-in 3pm. Check-out 2pm. Camping $50 per tent for a 3-day weekend; $70 for a 4-day holiday weekend; $20 per additional night. 6-person cabins with A/C $250/290/60; 6-person cabins without A/C $220/255/40. Tax included. MC/V.) There are basic amenities at **Parador El Buen Cafe ❹**, Hwy. 2 Km 84, across from Sam's Club, just west of Arecibo. The roadside *parador* has big, clean rooms with cable TV, fridge, A/C, and phone. The friendly staff adds a touch of life to the business-like hotel. (☎898-3484; fax 898-1000; www.elbuencafe.com. Restaurant. Pool. Check-in 3pm. Check-out noon. Doubles $95-110. Extra person $15. AmEx/MC/V.)For quick eats head to **Cafetería El Buen Cafe ❸**. Locals flock to the large diner for inexpensive Puerto Rican breakfasts and lunches. (☎898-3495. Breakfast $2.75-5. Sandwiches $1.75-5. Entrees $7-15. Open daily 5:30am-10pm. AmEx/MC/V.)

The town has **Internet access** at the **Biblioteca Electronica Pedro Lopez**, which has several computers and allows one hour of free Internet use. (On the right side of Rte. 119 as you enter the town from the west. Open M-F 7am-4pm.)

NORTHWEST CORNER

This remote corner of the island includes the northern part of Aguadilla, the Jobos area, and the city of Isabela. Though the region remains relatively undiscovered, it is fully equipped for an ocean getaway. When the surf is poor in Rincón, surfers in the know head to the Jobos coastal area, where northern winds reliably kick up big waves year-round. Even non-surfers will be impressed by sight of lonely cliffs overgrown with tropical vegetation at Las Ruinas and fierce Atlantic waves pounding the crescent beaches of Playa Monetes and Playa Shacks. Rte. 446 between Isabela and Jobos winds through miles of uninterrupted natural landscape—a real change from the malls and factories that typify the north coast, and a great place to bike or explore on foot. Though the beach is the main draw here, inland adventures ranging from horseback riding to golfing also await. Jobos boasts cheap accommodations and makes a convenient base from which to reach the practical necessities of Isabela, the attractions of Ramey, and the transportation hub of Aguadilla. Outside of Jobos, establishments are sprawled along the highways between Isabela and Aguadilla, making travel by car the only way to go.

⌐ TRANSPORTATION

Flights: Aeropuerto Rafael Hernández, on the former Ramey Air Force Base north of town on Rte. 107, is the only direct link from the US to the west coast of Puerto Rico. **Continental Airlines** (☎800-525-0280) flies direct from Newark, US (4hr., daily 9:25am, round-trip $250-350). **JetBlue** has direct service from JFK Airport, New York City, US (4 hr., twice daily, round-trip $250).

Públicos: The *público* hubs in the area are Aguadilla and Isabela. The terminal in Aguadilla offers service to: **Isabela** (25-30min., $1.75); **Mayagüez** (30-45min., $3); **Moca** (15min., $1.25); **Ramey Base** (30min., $1.30). **Choferes Unidos** (☎891-5653 or 630-5725) travels from Aguadilla to San Juan (2-3hr.; 7 per day 4am-noon; $10, with reservation $15). Public transportation from Isabela offers more limited destinations. *Públicos* to **Aguadilla** leave from Av. Augustín Ramos Calero at the intersection of Rte. 113 and Rte. 112; those to the **Jobos area** leave from the small concrete pavilion 2 blocks east of the plaza, across from Econo supermarket (15min., $0.60).

Car rental: Numerous agencies operate out of the airport; the most affordable are generally **Budget** (☎890-1110; $30-43 per day, insurance $15; ages 21-22 surcharge $10 per day, ages 23-24 surcharge $6; open daily 4am-6pm; AmEx/D/MC/V) and **L&M** (☎890-3010; $33-46 per day; insurance $13-20; 23-24 surcharge $5 per day; open daily 8am-5pm; AmEx/D/MC/V).

✦ ⚡ ORIENTATION AND PRACTICAL INFORMATION

Almost all of the area's tourist activity takes place along the coast. Although distinct beaches have their own names, most locals refer to the entire north coastal stretch as **Jobos.** The majority of hotels and restaurants are located at the intersection of Rte. 466 and Rte. 4466, near Playa Jobos proper. Once you get to Playa Jobos, it's easy to walk to and from beaches, restaurants, and most accommodations. The services most convenient to this area are located in Isabela, 5mi. west of Jobos. Ramey is the area between Aguadilla and Jobos. Rte. 107 leads north from Hwy. 2 towards the Ramey Base and Rte. 110 heads away from it. Both stretches include gas stations, small restaurants, and a few hotels. Bosque Estatal de Guajataca, also part of Isabela's jurisdiction, lies another 7 mi. inland, south of Hwy. 2, on Rte. 446. Coming from the east on Hwy. 2, turn north at Rte. 112 to reach Isabela. To go straight to Jobos, continue through town onto Rte. 466, which leads to the beach. To head toward Aguadilla, take Rte. 466 west until it turns into Rte. 4466. Then take Rte. 110 south to Rte. 107, which connects to **Route 111,** Aguadilla's main road. Aguadilla's city center is located on a strip of land between Hwy. 2 and the ocean. All accommodations and sights lie north of the center.

Tourist Office: Puerto Rican Tourism Company, in the Ramey airport (☎890-3315) provides *¡Que Pasa!* and information about the area. Open M-Sa 8am-4:30pm.

Bank: Banco Santander, C. Barbosa 19 (☎872-2050), on the plaza in Isabela, has an **ATM.** Open M-F 8:30am-4pm.

Equipment Rental: Hang Loose Surf Shop, Rte. 4466 Km 1.1 (☎872-2490) near Isabela, rents surf and boogie boards ($25 per day, $650 deposit for surfboard), sells gear, and offers lessons ($50 for 1½hr., including board, no deposit). Minor ding repairs possible. Open Tu-Sa 10am-5pm, Su 10am-3pm. AmEx/MC/V. **Pelicano Surfboards and Surf Shop,** Rte. 4466 Km 1.2 (☎872-7311) near Isabela (across from the yellow Seaside Court apartments), carries a similar selection and rents boards for $20-25 a day. Open M-F 10am-5pm. MC/V.

Police: Av. Hernández Ortiz 3201 (☎872-2020 or 872-3001), in Isabela. From the plaza, go south on Rte. 112, take the first left, and continue for about ¼ mi. Open 24hr.

Pharmacy: Super Farmacia Rebecca, C. Barbosa 51 (☎872-2410), in Isabela; facing the Catholic church, head down the right-hand street off the corner of the plaza. Open M-Sa 8am-9pm, Su 9am-9pm. AmEx/D/MC/V.

Hospital: Centro Isabelino de Medicina Avanzada (☎830-2705 or 830-2747), 1½ mi. south of Isabela on Rte. 112. Clinic open M-F 7am-3pm. Emergency room open 24hr.

Internet Access: Cocina Creativa, Rte. 110 Km 9.2 (☎890-1861), between the Best Gas and SuperCoop. This surf-shop-turned-coffeehouse lives up to its name with a varied menu of sandwiches and salads. Enjoy the laid-back atmosphere and the free Wi-Fi as you check your email or look up the local surf conditions. Regular Internet $5 per 30min. and $9 per hr. Open daily 9am-5pm. MC/V.

Post Office: C. Jesus Piñero 5 (☎872-2284), in Isabela, behind the *público* station. No General Delivery. Open M-F 8am-4:30pm, Sa 8am-noon. **Postal Code:** 00662 near Isabela and 00603 near Aguadilla.

ACCOMMODATIONS

The most unique and budget-friendly accommodations are situated in the Jobos area. Nearer to Aguadilla, more upscale options await.

NEAR JOBOS

Ocean Front Hotel, Rte. 4466 Km 0.1 (☎872-0444; www.oceanfrontpr.com). If you're going to spend a little more on accommodations, this is the place to do it. Bright ocean-view rooms with TV, A/C, and private balconies make staying here worth the splurge. Enjoy the hotel restaurant or walk down the road to one of the nearby bars. The back porch is great for watching sunsets. Check-out noon. Doubles M-Th and Su $85 ($75 if 1 person), F-Sa $100, holidays $125. Extra person $20. AmEx/MC/V. ❸

La Torre Guest House, Rte. 466 Km 7.2 (☎872-7439 or 473-1573), ¼ mi. from the beach near the intersection of Rte. 4466 and Rte. 466. This friendly guesthouse is located on the 1st fl. of the owner's home. Popular surfer hangout. Standard rooms are clean and include TV and A/C. Busy during summer, so reserve ahead. Doubles $55, with kitchen (no dishes) $65; quads $80-90. Prices rise on weekends. Cash only. ❷

Pelican Reef Apartments (☎872-6518 or 895-0876; www.pelicanreefapartments.com), at the intersection of Rte. 466 and Rte. 4466, is actually a small apartment complex with a few nightly rentals. The concrete hotel-style building was not built with aesthetics in mind, but it does overlook the ocean and has clean, comfortable rooms with TV, A/C, stove, and fridge. Call ahead to check availability. Doubles $95-145. Extra person $20. Weekly rates available. Cash only. ❹

Costa Dorada Beach Resort, (☎872-7255, US toll-free 877-975-0101; www.costadoradabeach.com), on Rte. 466 right before the uphill turn to Isabela. Standard beach resort. 3-story buildings surround a grassy courtyard filled with palm trees, a bar, tennis courts, and a big pool. Rooms include telephone, TV, fridge, and courtyard balcony. Beach access across the street. Doubles $122; villas with kitchen $195. Extra person $20. AmEx/D/MC/V. ❹

RAMEY AREA

Ramey Guest House, Loop 102 #16-17 (☎890-4208 or 431-2939; www.rameyguesthouse.com). From Rte. 107, stay straight at the turn for the airport, then make the first left after the BQN Pro Shop. Go straight through 2 stop signs and loop around to the house at the end of the street. 4 full houses provide all the conveniences of home, from a laundromat to a coffee maker. A/C and TV. 2-bedroom house $75; 3-bedroom $99-139; 4-bedroom $159. MC/V. ❸

La Cima Hotel, Rte. 110 Km 9.2 (☎890-2016; www.lacima.com), just past the airport, offers standard double hotel rooms equipped with A/C, cable TV, fridge, and Wi-Fi. Halfway between Jobos and Aguadilla, it's a convenient access point for most of the northwest. 2 restaurants, pool, and parking. Doubles $95. MC/V. ❹

NEAR AGUADILLA

Hotel Villa Forín (☎882-8341 or toll-free 877-723-6746), north on Rte. 107, Km 2.1 just past the intersection of Rte. 458. Maintains the aura of a professional hotel, but with reasonable prices. All rooms have A/C and cable television; some have cooking facilities. Small pool. Check-in 2pm. Check-out noon. High season doubles $80; quads $90. Low season doubles $64; quads $70. AmEx/MC/V. ❸

Hotel Cielo Mar, Av. Montemar 84 (☎882-5959; fax 882-5577; www.cielomar.com), sits high up on a hill overlooking the ocean. From Rte. 107 take Rte. 111, turn right onto Av. Montemar, and then follow signs. Almost every room boasts views of the water

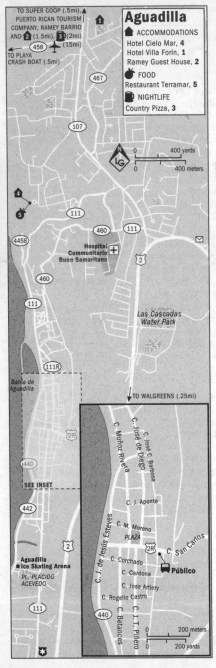

Aguadilla

🏠 ACCOMMODATIONS
Hotel Cielo Mar, **4**
Hotel Villa Forín, **1**
Ramey Guest House, **2**

🍴 FOOD
Restaurant Terramar, **5**

🍸 NIGHTLIFE
Country Pizza, **3**

TO SUPER COOP (.5mi),
PUERTO RICAN TOURISM
COMPANY, RAMEY BARRIO
AND **2** (1.5mi), **3** (2mi)
458   (15mi)
TO PLAYA
CRASH BOAT (.5mi)

467

107

400 yards
400 meters

4
5

111

460   111

4458

Hospital
Communitario
Buen Samaritano

460

111

Las Cascadas
Water Park

111R

Bahía de
Aguadilla

↓ TO WALGREENS (.25mi)

2R

C. Muñoz Rivera

C. José de Diego

C. José C. Barbosa

440

SEE INSET

442

C. J. Aponte

C. M. Moreno
PLAZA

2R   C. San Carlos

C. Corchado

Público

C. J. de Jesús Esteves

Aguadilla
Ice Skating Arena

PL. PLÁCIDO
ACEVEDO

C. Cardona

C. Jose Artieri

C. Rogelio Castro

111

440   C. J. T. Piñero

C. Betances

200 meters
200 yards

and the spectacular sunset from a private balcony. Rooms with plenty of space, A/C, TV, VCR, and phone. Pool. All-inclusive packages available. Check-in 3pm. Check-out noon. Doubles $90; quads $105. Extra person $15; up to 2 children free; ocean-view rooms extra. Also home to **Restaurant Terramar,** with a patio overlooking the ocean. Entrees $15-30. Open M-Th and Su 7am-10pm, F-Sa 7am-midnight. AmEx/MC/V. ❸

🍴 FOOD

Inexpensive *cafeterías* and fast food abound on the highways in the city centers of this corner of Puerto Rico. Some of the more unique eateries, which can be found in the Jobos area, are listed here. For quick supplies head to **Econo** in Isabela, a few blocks west of the plaza (☎872-4033. Open M-Sa 6:30am-9:30pm, Su 11am-5pm. AmEx/MC/V.) or **SuperCoop** at Rte. 107 Km 3 (☎882-1425. Open M-Sa 7am-9pm, Su 11am-5pm. MC/V.)

Ocean Front Restaurant, Rte. 4466 Km 0.1 (☎872-3339), in the hotel of the same name, is Jobos's premier seafood restaurant. Over 15 years this restaurant has perfected its recipe for the best salmon on this side of the island. Classy interior dining room decorated with tiny lights and lush plants. Relaxed outdoor patio offers a great view of the sunset. Occasional live guitar music. Wine $6. Entrees $16-22. Open W-Th and Su 11:30am-10pm, F-Sa 11:30am-midnight. AmEx/MC/V. ❸

Happy Belly's (☎872-6566), on Rte. 466, just east of Rte. 4466, is your stereotypical ocean-front tourist bar. The wooden patio overlooking the water is a perfect place to enjoy shrimp *mofongo* ($15) with a lively crowd. If you need a big meal, try any of the aptly named Belly Buster entrees. Sandwiches $6-7. Entrees $10-19. Open M-Tu 11am-10:30pm, W-Su 11am-2am. AmEx/MC/V. ❸

Sonia Rican Restaurant (☎872-0808), on Rte. 466, at the Playa Jobos parking lot, benefits greatly from its beachfront location. Essentially just a very long bar, Sonia Rican serves up affordable seafood and well-prepared Puerto Rican cuisine. Sit inside for great views of the surf. After dark a quiet crowd comes to enjoy drinks at the bar. Beer $1.50-2. Entrees $6-26. Open W-Su 11am-2am, M-Tu 11am-9pm. Kitchen closes 9pm. AmEx/MC/V. ❸

Restaurante Sonido del Mar, Rte. 466 Km 5.6 (☎872-5766), along Playa Jobos. Serves seafood entrees ($7-16) and beer ($3) and has pool tables; shoot a game while you wait for your food. The back patio fills with a lively crowd as the sun goes down. Open Tu-Th and Su 11am-10pm, F-Sa 11am-2am. Kitchen closes 10pm. ❸

Three Brothers Restaurant, Hwy. 2 Km 110.8 (☎830-1883), 1 mi. east of Rte. 112, serves hot *comida criolla,* sandwiches ($4-6), salads ($5-7), and their delicious *mofongo* ($7). Come early for breakfast or late for dinner to enjoy sit-down service or takeout. Open daily 7am-10pm. MC/V. ❶

🌀 BEACHES AND SURFING

LAS RUÍNAS. Named for the ruins of several Air Force buildings, Las Ruínas provides a relatively quiet and scenic white sand beach. The first turn-off leads to a parking lot alongside the edge of a dramatic cliff. Continue along the bumpy dirt road to find remains of the old Spanish lighthouse built in 1886 and destroyed by an earthquake and tsunami in 1918. Along this stretch you'll find big waves popular with surfers and beautiful vistas popular with young couples. *(Drive north on Rte. 107 into Base Ramey, turn left on the unmarked road with white posts that goes through the golf course. Proceed slowly and watch for golf carts and continue to the end. No facilities.)*

PLAYA JOBOS BAY. Second only to Rincón, this is the island's surfing mecca and the site of the 1989 World Surfing Championships. Waves almost always pound the coast, especially when there is a north shore wind. Even Rincón's surfing crowd comes here in the summer when the waves are weak elsewhere. On the eastern edge of the beach, in front of the parking area, a protected bay provides a calm, shallow area for swimmers. Because of its popularity with surfers and sunbathers, the eastern edge of Playa Jobos can get crowded and filled with trash at times. *(At the intersection of Rte. 4466 and Rte. 466; the parking area is just past this intersection.)*

EAST OF JOBOS. The road to the east of the popular Jobos Bay is a largely undeveloped green jewel of a coastline. Surfers use these beaches to avoid crowded Jobos when the waves are up. First is the sandy, close-breaking surf break known as **Golondrinas,** which attracts intermediate surfers. Past that is **Middles,** a more advanced break requiring an entry over rocks, which is one of the shallower breaks in the area. Last is the grimly named **Sal Si Puedes** (Get Out If You Can), which provides a rare leviathan break across rocky reefs.

PLAYA SHACKS. This bay looks similar to Jobos, but has a few more rocks and no parking area, and thus remains significantly less crowded. Shacks is known as the best **snorkeling and diving area** near Isabela. For the best snorkeling, swim out 20 yd. to the second major reef. The consistent waves make Shacks one of the best wind and kite surfing beaches on the island. Even without all the diversions, Shacks provides a nice place to lie on the beach. *(Coming from Rte. 4466, turn right at the Villa Montanas sign before the intersection with Rte. 110. Follow signs to Tropical Trail Rides, but don't go over the little bridge. Park just past the bridge and continue to the end of the road on foot. No facilities.)*

A DAY AT THE BEACH

Puerto Rico may be known as the "Isla Encantadora" (the enchanting isle), but it has a less-than-enchanting problem with litter. Public beaches are often marred by heaps of garbage, sometimes just feet from garbage cans provided by coastal authorities. Playa Jobos and Playa Mar Chiquita stand out as particularly trash-covered. Snorkelers here may excitedly spy a glint of light from the bottom of a colorful reef, only to be disappointed when they find a crushed beer can. Sunbathers must choose their sand carefully to avoid the waste of their fellow beach-goers.

After a holiday weekend, dozens of DRNA clean-up crews hit the beaches to pick up the trash. If you're looking for a way to help keep Puerto Rico beautiful, volunteering with the DRNA clean-up effort may be the perfect way to pitch in and log some hours at the beach. The crews are generally made up of a DRNA employee leading a volunteer student group, making it easy for solo travelers to join in with little advance notice. This is a great opportunity to get to know Puerto Rico's beaches and the people who maintain them for the enjoyment of travelers and locals alike.

Call one of the region DRNA offices in Aguadilla (☎ 882-5893), Arecibo (☎ 878-9048), Mayagüez (☎ 833-3700), or Ponce (☎ 723-1373) to join other volunteers in the effort to combat litter.

PLAYA CRASH BOAT. This Aguadillan beach is known for its excellent swimming; old concrete piers provide a place to jump into the water. Unfortunately, local crowds can get quite large, especially on weekends during the summer. The beach has two overhead showers and bathrooms, but only the most desperate would consider using them. Shaded picnic tables make a great lunch spot. *(From Hwy. 2 turn west onto Rte. 107, then follow Rte. 458 to the left-hand turn-off for the beach. Parking $3 until 5:30pm.)*

PLAYA MONTONES. This small, calm beach occasionally produces big surfing waves in the winter, but is usually relatively deserted. There are no facilities, but there is a long bay and lots of sand, making it a great spot to lay out and catch some rays. The water is deep, but gets shallower as you head east. *(Drive east on Rte. 466, then turn left just before Villas Monte del Mar and continue to the end of the road. Access the beach through the walkway between the concrete walls.)*

🔯 WATER SPORTS AND OUTDOOR ACTIVITIES

Playa Shacks is the area's best **snorkeling** beach and one of the few places on the island where **shore diving** is feasible and worthwhile. **La Cueva Submarina,** Rte. 466 just south of the intersection with Rte. 4466, in the Jobos area, has a friendly and professional staff that lead two shore dives every day (9:30am and 1:30pm; 1-tank dive $45 including equipment; extra tank $20). They also offer Nitrox dives ($65), guided snorkeling trips ($25), Discover Scuba packages ($55), and 3-day open-water certification courses ($250, including equipment). Rental snorkel gear costs $15 per day. Cave dives are arranged upon request for advanced divers only. (☎ 872-1390; fax 830-7177; www.lacuevasubmarina.com. Open daily 8am-5pm. AmEx/MC/V.) **Aquatica Adventures,** Rte. 110 Km 10, just before the Esso station slightly back from the road, is a full-service dive shop that offers shore dives in Isabel and Aguadilla ($60; private certification courses for $325, less for groups), bike tours (around $50 for 2-3hr.), surf lessons, and guided snorkeling tours. (☎ 890-6071; aquatica@caribe.net. Open M-Sa 9am-5:30pm, Su 9am-3pm. AmEx/MC/V.)

This area also features several unusual (and affordable) options for adventures on land. The popular **Las Cascadas Water Park,** Hwy. 2 Km 126.5, just before Rte. 107, is built into a hillside near Aguadilla and contains several waterslides and a large wave pool. (☎ 819-1030. Open late Mar. to May Sa-Su 10am-5pm; June-Sept. daily 10am-5pm. Slides close 4pm. $16, ages 4-12 $14, ages 55-74 $8, under 3 and over 75 free. Parking $2. MC/V.) Eighteen-hole **Punta Borinquen**

Golf Club, between the airport and the sea, boasts palm trees, distant ocean views, and reasonable prices. (Enter the former Ramey Base on Rte. 107 and turn left at the golf club entrance. ☎890-2987. Green fees M-F $20, Sa-Su and holidays $22; golf cart $34, required on weekends. Club rental $15. Open M-F 7am-dusk, Sa-Su 6:30am-dusk. AmEx/MC/V.) **Tropical Trail Rides,** Rte. 4466 Km 1.8, can be reached by taking the driveway for the Villa Montañas off Rte. 4466 just before Rte. 110. This American-run operation leads 2hr. rides along beautiful Jobos coastline, through the almond forests, and then back along the cliff caves. (☎872-9256; www.tropicaltrailrides.com. Rides leave daily at 9am and 4pm. $40 per person. Reservations required. Open daily 7:30am-6:30pm. AmEx/D/MC/V.)

◾ NIGHTLIFE

Most locals head to the beach for their evening fun, but a variety of exciting options await visitors who are interested in a livelier night out.

Happy Belly's Sports Bar & Grill (☎872-6566), on Rte. 466, just east of Rte. 4466 near Jobos. As the night goes on, this popular restaurant morphs into a relaxed beach bar with mellow music to match the laid-back local crowd. Balcony over the beach. Beer $3. Mixed drinks $5-6. Live DJ W and F-Sa. No cover. Open daily 11am-midnight. AmEx/MC/V.

Mi Casita Tropical (☎872-5510), next door to Happy Belly's. On busy nights young travelers chill on the ocean-front balcony. On slow nights, a local crowd congregates around the bar. Beer $2.50. Mixed drinks $2.50-5. Karaoke W. No cover. Open W-Su noon-2am. AmEx/MC/V.

Aguadilla Ice Skating Arena, Rte. 442 Km 4.2 (☎819-5555), south of Aguadilla. Popular with young locals. Indoor rink offers dance music and a light show in the evenings. Couples night W has 2-for-1 tickets. Student night Th, half-price with ID. Sessions start at 10am and begin every 1½ hr. Before 7pm $10 per hr., 7-11pm $13 per hr., including skates. $1 lockers available. Open daily 9:30am-11pm. Cash only.

Country Pizza, Bar Y Salon Billar, Rte. 110, across from La Cima Hotel. With a large dance floor, pool tables, and some of the island's best pizza, Country Pizza draws a big weekend crowd, especially for F karaoke. Locals fill the parking lot to show off their hot rides, while cheap drinks and good music keep the dance floor busy. Beer $2-3. Mixed drinks $4-5. Open for food M-Sa 10am-9pm, bar open Th-Sa 7pm-2am. MC/V.

◾ DAYTRIPS FROM THE JOBOS AREA

BOSQUE ESTATAL DE GUAJATACA

No public transportation goes to the Bosque de Guajataca. To reach Guajataca from Hwy. 2 drive east to Rte. 446, then follow Rte. 446 south all the way into the forest.

As if having some of the island's most beautiful shoreline weren't enough, the municipality of Isabela also contains the 2300 acres of Bosque Estatal de Guajataca, one of the island's prime examples of karst country. Despite its diminutive size, this subtropical forest is one of the more clearly organized reserves on the island, with a cave, several picnic areas, and an abundance of **well-marked trails.** Unlike almost all other trails in Puerto Rico, these narrow dirt paths were originally constructed as trails (not access roads) and they have not yet been paved over, providing one of the best hiking experiences on the island. First stop by the **Visitors Center,** 5 mi. down Rte. 446 in the middle of the forest, where rangers distribute maps and info about which trails are open. Note that this is the only place to fill up on water. (☎872-1045. Open daily 8am-5pm.) The most popular trail, with good reason, is the 1½ mi. **interpretive trail** (*Veredera Interpretiva*), which starts at the Visitors Center and loops past 14 marked points of interest, including an observation tower. **Trail #1** (2.55km) starts on the interpretive trail, then breaks off to lead to ▨**Cueva del Viento,** where wooden stairs lead down into a dark cave filled with stalactites and stalagmites. Bring a flashlight to explore the 180 ft. cave, and make sure the rangers know you're inside. The DRNA maintains several small **pic-nic areas** along Rte. 446 near the Visitors Center. The first has a bathroom, but continue south for more serene and spacious eating areas.

▨LAGO DE GUAJATACA

No public transportation goes to Lago de Guajataca. From Hwy. 2 drive east to Rte. 446, then follow Rte. 446 south to Rte. 457. Take Rte. 457 to Rte. 119.

The 3.6 sq. mi. Lago de Guajataca has some of Puerto Rico's best fishing. Located in the heart of karst country, but less than 30min. from Hwy. 2, Guajataca is also a pleasant place to experience Puerto Rico's serene countryside. The best destination for daytrippers is the **DRNA Visitors Center,** Rte. 119 Km 22. This office lends out a few fishing poles (bring your own bait; they recommend corn kernels) and provides full bathrooms with shower, as well as a grassy picnic area with several tables and a special wash table on which to clean fish. (☎896-7640. Open Tu-Su 6am-6pm.) During holidays the area gets crowded, but on weekdays it is the perfect place to relax with a fishing pole while enjoying the refreshing lake breeze. Swimming is prohibited, but kayaking is allowed. ▨**Luna y Sol Kayak Rentals** rents kayaks and offers hour, half-day, and full-day tours of the lake for all ages and abilities, as well as an advanced trip up the river which feeds the lake. The knowledgeable guides can point out different species of birds and turtles. (☎280-5555, www.kayakscuba.com, Rte. 455 Km 2.7. Trips range from $10-70 depending on length and ability. Cash only.)

If the serenity of the lake seduces you, check out ▨**Nino's Camping ①,** Rte. 119 Km 22.1, with a lakeside camping area, three small cabins, and a clean pool. The rocky tent area includes water spigots, a few outlets, and a bathroom with cold-water shower. If it's too warm to sleep in your tent, there is also a hammock available. Ask Nino and he'll kindly let you borrow a fishing pole *(un cano)*. The cabins look like *centro vacacional cabañas,* with linoleum floors and rooms stuffed with lots of beds. All cabins have a balcony with a hammock, a full kitchen, a TV, and fans, but only one has A/C. Bring your own sheets and utensils. No guard, but Nino's family lives on the premises. (☎896-9016 or 349-5074. $25 per tent per night. 4- to 7-person cabin M-Th and Su $75, 3-day weekend $200, 4-day weekend $250. 12 person *cabaña* with A/C $350 for the weekend, $80 per night. Cash only.)

MOCA

Públicos make the short trip from Aguadilla to Moca (15min., $1.25). From Aguadilla, continue south on Rte. 111 past Hwy. 2, and follow the road as it turns east. Turn right just before the pedestrian bridge to reach the town center.

The small town of Moca is the island's center for the production of *mundillo,* an intricate type of lace originally imported from Spain and now famous in Puerto Rico. Many *mocanos,* especially women, spend hours hand-weaving the fine lace that adorns shirts, towels, and, most frequently, beautiful baby clothes. *Mundillo* is considered to be one of Puerto Rico's premier handicrafts (see **Arts,** p. 67). A walk through town proves the importance of the art, as several houses advertise *mundillo* that women weave and sell in the comfort of their own living rooms. To read the history of the town's relationship with *mundillo* and to see framed copies of newspaper articles about local *mocanos,* visit the **Museo de Mundillo,** C. Barbosa 237. Facing the church on the plaza, take the first right-hand street and the museum appears on the left. At the museum, local artisans spend several days a week teaching their art to the next generation and are always willing to talk to visitors about their work. (☎877-3815. Open W-Su 9am-5pm.) Local Augusto Hernández has written a several-hundred-page book called *Historia y Desarrollo del Mundillo Mocano* (History and Development of Moca Mundillo; $17) that is sometimes available at the museum. **Artesanía Leonides,** C. Blanco E. Chico 185, the only real *mundillo* store in town, sells a variety of products, but focuses primarily on elaborate baby dresses. (☎877-4092. Open M-Sa 10am-6pm, Su 10am-5:30pm. MC/V.) The best time to visit Moca is during the annual three-day **Festival de Mundillo,** when the town's artisans gather on the main plaza to display and sell their wares. The festival takes place in December and May.

RINCÓN

Most surfers already know about Rincón; the city leapt into the spotlight as the host of the 1968 World Surfing Championships. Waves here can get as high as 25 ft., and at least 15 breaks lie within close proximity to town, making this the best surfing area in Puerto Rico and the Caribbean. But Rincón is a lot more than a big wave. This beautiful area remains largely undeveloped, with a series of tiny roads winding through tropical forests down to pristine beaches that justify the many stickers dubbing Rte. 413 "The Road to Happiness." Travelers who want a real taste of Puerto Rican culture may be disappointed, since the English language and American culture predominate, but a robust US expat community welcomes visitors with open arms. Life in Rincón is essentially one relaxed party, and even non-surfers find it easy to join right in. First-rate diving, snorkeling, and whale-watching conditions ensure that there is no lack of activities, even in the summer when the waves are flat. Whether you're looking to just lie on the beach or to get your fill of the outdoors, spending a few days here is definitely worth your while.

TRANSPORTATION AND PRACTICAL INFORMATION

Even veteran travelers may initially find themselves a bit lost in Rincón. Take Hwy. 2 to Rte. 115, which eventually leads through the town of Rincón. There are no taxis in Rincón, but the town center is walkable. With only about 10 streets, the town itself is reasonably straightforward, but most of the action takes place in the surrounding hills. From the town center, continue north on Rte. 115 to the intersection with **Route 413,** which follows the coastline. After about half a mile you'll reach a turn-off to the Black Eagle Marina, marked by a huge sign for Taíno Divers. Another half a mile down the road, a sign points left to **"the lighthouse road,"** which leads to the lighthouse and to Maria's Beach. North of the lighthouse, you are officially in **Puntas.** Five steep roads lead downhill to the beach, but only three intersect with Rte. 413. The westernmost road, at Km 3.3 near Puntas Bakery, passes the dead-end Nuclear Vista Rd. and leads to the flat road lining the beaches, known as **Beach Road.** The next road to the east is **Vista Linda Road.** The next road connecting Rte. 413 to Beach Rd. doesn't have a name, but runs past the Rincón Surf and Board shop to Casa Isleña. The easternmost road is **Alfonso Arzmendi Road.** The **Estella** neighborhood, about 14 numbered streets south of town near the intersection with Rte. 429, houses several condos on Playa Corcéga.

Públicos: Very few *públicos* come to Rincón from other cities, but you can occasionally find transport from the terminal to Aguadilla (20min., $2) and Mayagüez (20min., $1.75). More frequent *públicos* follow Rte. 413 to Puntas (15min., $0.50). Most long-distance *públicos* leave by 7am.

Car Rental: Angelo's Car Rental, Rte. 115 Km 12.3 (☎823-3438 or 306-6771), in the Vista Mar Plaza. Rents cars and picks up customers from guesthouses and the Aguadilla and Mayagüez airports. 25+. Cash rentals $40 for the first day, $35 each additional day; $500 deposit. Credit card rentals $43/38. Open F 8am-noon and 1-4pm. MC/V.

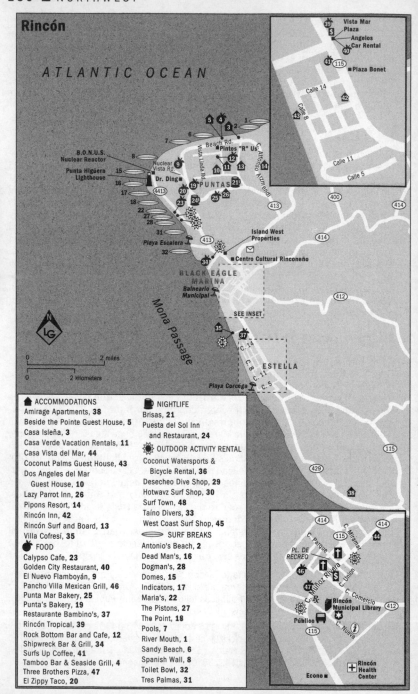

Rincón

ATLANTIC OCEAN

NORTHWEST

B.O.N.U.S. Nuclear Reactor
Punta Higüera Lighthouse
Nuclear Vista Rd.
Dr. Ding
Beach Rd.
Pintos "R" Us
PUNTAS
Vista Linda Rd.
C. Alfonso Armendi
Playa Escalera
Island West Properties
Centro Cultural Rinconeño
BLACK EAGLE MARINA
Balneario Municipal
SEE INSET
Mona Passage
ESTELLA
Playa Corcega

Vista Mar Plaza
Angelos Car Rental
Plaza Bonet
Calle 14
Calle 8
Calle 11
Calle 5

Calle 14
Calle 8
Calle 13

400   413   414   412   414   115   429

C. 14   C. 8   C. 11   C. 5

0 ___ 2 miles
0 ___ 2 kilometers

ACCOMMODATIONS
Amirage Apartments, **38**
Beside the Pointe Guest House, **5**
Casa Isleña, **3**
Casa Verde Vacation Rentals, **11**
Casa Vista del Mar, **44**
Coconut Palms Guest House, **43**
Dos Angeles del Mar
  Guest House, **10**
Lazy Parrot Inn, **26**
Pipons Resort, **14**
Rincón Inn, **42**
Rincón Surf and Board, **13**
Villa Cofresí, **35**

FOOD
Calypso Cafe, **23**
Golden City Restaurant, **40**
El Nuevo Flamboyán, **9**
Pancho Villa Mexican Grill, **46**
Punta Mar Bakery, **25**
Punta's Bakery, **19**
Restaurante Bambino's, **37**
Rincón Tropical, **39**
Rock Bottom Bar and Cafe, **12**
Shipwreck Bar & Grill, **34**
Surfs Up Coffee, **41**
Tamboo Bar & Seaside Grill, **4**
Three Brothers Pizza, **47**
El Zippy Taco, **20**

NIGHTLIFE
Brisas, **21**
Puesta del Sol Inn
  and Restaurant, **24**

OUTDOOR ACTIVITY RENTAL
Coconut Watersports &
  Bicycle Rental, **36**
Desecheo Dive Shop, **29**
Hotwavz Surf Shop, **30**
Surf Town, **48**
Taíno Divers, **33**
West Coast Surf Shop, **45**

SURF BREAKS
Antonio's Beach, **2**
Dead Man's, **16**
Dogman's, **28**
Domes, **15**
Indicators, **17**
Maria's, **22**
The Pistons, **27**
The Point, **18**
Pools, **7**
River Mouth, **1**
Sandy Beach, **6**
Spanish Wall, **8**
Toilet Bowl, **32**
Tres Palmas, **31**

PL. DE RECREO
C. Parque
C. Miramar
C. Union
C. Comercio
Rincón Municipal Library
Muñoz Rivera
Público
C. Nueva
Econo
Rincón Health Center
414   115   414   412   115   44

Tourist Office: Rincón Municipal Tourist Office (☎823-5024), at the end of C. Nueva, behind the police station. The English-speaking staff can answer questions and provides a tourist map that lists all the area businesses. Open M-F 8am-4:30pm.

Bank: Western Bank, C. Muñoz Rivera 18, (☎823-1280), in the plaza. **ATM.** Open M-F 7:30am-5pm, Sa 8:30-11:30am.

Equipment Rental: Coconut Watersports (☎309-9328 or 823-2450), at Parador Villa Cofresí (p. 283), rents kayaks (singles $10 per hr.; doubles $15), inflatable tubes ($5 per day), boogie boards ($10 per day), beach umbrellas ($5 per day), and snorkel gear ($10 per day). Open Sa-Su during daylight hours, M-F by phone only.

Publications: The free bilingual community newspaper, *El Coquí of Rincón*, offers an inside look into local events. It is also a handy guide to local restaurants, bars, hotels, and other businesses. Published monthly; pick up a copy at most major businesses.

Laundromat: In the Plaza Bonet shopping center, across the street from Bambino's. Wash $1.50, dry $0.25 per 5min. Open daily 8am-7pm.

Police: At the end of C. Nueva (☎823-2020 or 823-2021), in town. Open 24hr. A 2nd station is at the intersection of Rte. 115 and 414.

Pharmacy: Farmacia del Pueblo, C. Muñoz Rivera 33 (☎823-2540), has a relatively large selection. Open M-Sa 8am-9pm, Su 10am-6pm. AmEx/D/MC/V.

Medical Services: Rincón Health Center, Rte. 115 Km 13.6, (☎823-0909), across from the Econo. Open 24hr. Not to be confused with the day clinic by the same name downtown.

Internet Access: Rincón Public Library (☎823-9075), on C. Nueva, has computers with free, medium-speed Internet access. 1hr. limit. Open M-F 8am-5:30pm and 6:30-9pm. The laid-back **Rincón Inn,** on Rte. 115, 2 blocks from Bambino's, has 2 computers for Internet use. $3 per 30min., $5 per hr. Open daily 10am-7pm. Across the street in the Rincón Shopping Center, **Taíno International Cafe** has free Wi-Fi and an impressive selection of coffees and cappuccinos ($2-3). Open M-Sa 8am-9pm. AmEx/MC/V. **Surfs Up Coffee Shop,** also on Rte. 115, down from Bambino's, is a small coffee shop with free Wi-Fi and friendly surfers.

Post Office: Rte. 115 #100 (☎823-2625), has General Delivery M-F until 3pm. Open M-F 8am-4:30pm, Sa 8am-noon. **Postal Code:** 00677.

ACCOMMODATIONS

Outside of San Juan, Rincón has the best selection of accommodations on the island. Several American-run guesthouses cater to both surfers and vacationers. If you want to jump into the surfer scene, hang out with Americans all day, and drink lots of beer, head to Puntas. For more Puerto Rican accommodations, try the area south of town, where a few nice hotels hide in quiet residential neighborhoods.

PUNTAS

Rincón Surf and Board (☎823-0610; www.surfandboard.com). Take Rte. 413 out of downtown toward Puntas and take the 2nd intersection, marked by a white tractor tire wedged in the ground. Bear right at the next intersection and the guesthouse will appear on the right. A 20min. walk from the beach. With inexpensive dorm rooms and an on-site surf school (p. 285), it's no wonder that this guesthouse has become Rincón's prime surfer hangout. The building sits on stilts 70 ft. above a jungle canopy, creating a unique tropical atmosphere. Attractive private rooms have handmade mosaics, balconies, cable TV, and a private library. Dorms have fans and a common room with cable TV. The only downsides are the voracious mosquitoes and the neighborhood's frequent but short power outages. A small pool with waterfall sits beneath the shady bar. Private rooms include continental breakfast in the winter. Breakfast $3. Quiet time starts at 10pm. 4-

bed dorms $20; doubles $60; 2-person suites with kitchen $90. Extra person $10. In winter 3-bedroom house $185; in summer $145. $5-10 discount Apr. to mid-Nov. Discount for repeat visits. 50% deposit, must cancel 2 weeks prior for full refund. MC/V. ❶

Dos Angeles del Mar Guest House (☎431-6057; www.dosangelesdelmar.com), up the street from Casa Verde. This 3-story house glows with an aesthetic charm unavailable at most other guesthouses in the area. 5 spotless rooms with microwave, fridge, TV, A/C, wicker beds, daily maid service, and ocean views offer peace and quiet. The friendly owners offer a small continental breakfast and have also installed a backyard pool with a poolside, wheelchair-accessible room. Doubles $100-120; quads $130-150. Discount for longer stays. MC/V. ❹

Casa Verde Vacation Rentals (☎605-5351), on Beach Rd. This green hotel has become one of the most hopping surfer hangouts, primarily due to its ideal location (1min. from Sandy Beach) and its well-stocked bar. Recently renovated suites all include kitchen, A/C, and TV. Doubles $89; 2-bedroom apartment $129; 3-bedroom house $200. MC/V. ❸

Lazy Parrot Inn, Rte. 413 Km 4.1 (☎823-5654; www.lazyparrot.com), uphill from the beach and conveniently next door to Punta Mar Bakery. This bright guesthouse is filled with parrots, both live and painted. Elegant rooms with TV, A/C, and fridge have stunning views overlooking the forest heights of Puntas. Sunny restaurant area offers continental breakfast (included), lunch (11am-3pm), and dinner (5:30-10pm). Pool. Doubles $110-140; panoramic view triples $125-155. Extra person $15; 12 and under free. 50% deposit. AmEx/D/MC/V. ❹

Beside the Pointe Guest House (☎/fax 823-8550; www.besidethepointe.com), on Beach Rd. This guesthouse boasts a great location right on Sandy Beach in the center of the nightlife area and is connected to the popular **Tamboo Bar** (p. 283). 8 brightly painted rooms with mural-covered walls have cable TV, fridge, and A/C. Dec. 15-Apr. 15 doubles $90-150; quads $120; 2- to 6-person apartments with kitchen $135-180. Apr. 16-Dec. 14 $70-120/100/110-165. 50% deposit. MC/V. ❹

Casa Isleña, Rte. 413 interior Km 4.8 (☎823-1525; www.casa-islena.com), on Beach Rd. Gorgeous 9-room *hacienda* right on the beach. Spacious rooms with Mexican tiles offer incomparable ocean views. All rooms have A/C and cable TV; most have fridges, and 2 have balconies. Big patio, direct beach access, and restaurant (p. 284). Reception 9am-5pm. Doubles $115-165. Extra person $15. AmEx/MC/V. ❹

Pipons Resort (☎823-7154; www.piponsresort.com), on Bummer Hill, ¼ mi. from the beach. 6 spacious luxury apartments in a huge white house overlooking Antonio's Beach. Every room has a private balcony, ocean view, A/C, kitchen, and cable TV. 5th and 6th guests per room sleep on couches. Doubles $105; quads $125-165. MC/V. ❹

SOUTH OF TOWN

Amirage Apartments, Rte. 429 Km 4 (☎/fax 823-6454; www.proceanfront.com), slightly down a driveway, is the spot to find tranquility. An expat couple has constructed their dream home here in a beautiful white villa overlooking the water, and happily they've opted to share it. 3 rooms with tasteful murals feel just like home, down to the bathrobe waiting in the closet. Courtyard contains a lush garden and a hot tub. All rooms have cable TV, A/C, kitchen, and balcony with terrific sunset views. Free kayak and snorkel equipment. The one fault is the rocky beach, but it's a short kayak trip to sandier stretches. 2- to 3-person suites $135; 5-person suites $180. Cash only. ❹

Rincon Inn, Rte. 115 Km 11.6 (☎823-7070, www.rinconinn.com). Offering the cheapest accommodations in Rincon, this place is a great deal. Rooms with queen-size bed, A/C, and cable TV are available, as well as several dorm rooms connected to a big living area, full kitchen, and wrap-around balcony that is full of surfers during the winter. Linens and towels included. Free Internet in the main office. Pool and parking in rear. Reception M-Sa 10am-7pm, Su noon-5pm. Dorm rooms $25; private rooms $55. MC/V. ❶

Villa Cofresí Hotel, Rte. 115 Km 12 (☎823-2450; www.villacofresi.com). This hotel, named after the famous Puerto Rican pirate Roberto Cofresí, is located right on the water. Big pool area, bar, and 4 pool tables are right on the beach and are enormously popular with large family groups, who get discounts. Cable TV, A/C, and fridge. Check-in 3pm. Check-out noon. High season doubles $125-135; 2-bedroom apartments $160. Low season $115/140. Extra person $15. 2 children under 12 free. AmEx/D/MC/V. ❹

Coconut Palms Guest House, C. 8 #2734 (☎823-0147; www.coconutpalmsinn.com). Turn onto C. 14 before Cantina Pepon, then go to the end and turn left on C. 8. Right on Playa Córcega. A low-key beach villa in a quiet residential neighborhood, conveniently blocks away from the restaurants on Rte. 115. Natural courtyard garden with birds and a hot tub. Board games, used-book library, kitchenette, and cable TV. Studios $100; apartments $125-150. Extra person $15. Higher rates in winter. 50% deposit, only redeemable in credit towards a future stay. MC/V. ❹

Casa Vista del Mar (☎/fax 823-6437; www.casavistadelmar.net), at the top of the steep hill on the road that goes past Rincón Shopping Plaza. This newly built villa offers peace and quiet in cozy studios with queen beds, kitchenettes, A/C, cable TV, and balconies with views of Rincón. Enjoy fresh mangos off the trees in the front driveway. Free laundry. Rooms $90 or $110 per night for stays of 7 nights or longer. MC/V. ❹

Island West Properties, Rte. 413 Km 0.7 (☎823-2323; www.island-west.com.), has a friendly and knowledgeable staff that rents condos, beach houses, and villas throughout Rincón for $150-550. A handyman is on call if any problems arise. 3-night min. 50% deposit required, 100% if within 30 days of renting. Open M-F 9am-3pm. MC/V. ❹

◪ FOOD

Rincón offers a smorgasbord of dining options designed to satiate the healthy surfer appetite. Most of the food options are heavily American-influenced, and almost all Puntas restaurants have a vegetarian option. For groceries, try **Econo** supermarket, Rte. 115 Km 13.2, south of town. (☎823-2470. Open M-Sa 7am-9pm, Su 11am-5pm. AmEx/MC/V.)

THE SURF BREAK (PUNTAS, LIGHTHOUSE AREA, THE MARINA)

Shipwreck Bar and Grill (☎823-0578), at Black Eagle Marina. When you tire of burgers, sandwiches, and beach grub, head to Shipwreck for a satisfying gourmet meal. Its marina location means top-notch seafood, with daily catch specials and creative entrees. If you like the turf better than the surf, grilled steak and chicken options are available as well. Entrees $12-27. Happy hour 3-6pm; $2 rum punch and Medalla. Open Oct.-May noon-midnight; June-Aug. Th-Su noon-10pm. AmEx/MC/V. ❹

El Nuevo Flamboyán (☎307-6905), down the road from the intersection of Rte. 413, just up the hill from Beach Rd. This simple eatery offers candlelit dinner in a small house hanging over a cliff in prime sunset-viewing position. Brush up on your Puerto Rican history with the patriotic posters on the wall. Entrees, mostly *comida criolla*, $10-17. Open daily 5-9pm. Bar open later in winter. Cash only. ❸

Tamboo Bar & Seaside Grill (☎823-8550), at Beside the Pointe Guest House (p. 282). In addition to being a popular bar, Tamboo serves a variety of grill items, including fish, burgers, chicken, and wraps, on a big patio. Right on Sandy Beach with a volleyball net, this makes for a good lunch spot. Sandwiches $7-10. Entrees $9-18. Open M-Th and Su noon-midnight, F-Sa noon-2am. MC/V. ❷

Rock Bottom Bar and Cafe (☎605-5351), next door to Casa Verde, sits on an upstairs deck with retired surfboards from locals mounted on the beams and roof. Restaurant serves burgers and other American food ($4-12) daily from 11am-9pm. ❷

Punta Mar Bakery, Rte. 413 Km 4.1 (☎823-2455), next to Lazy Parrot Inn. This standard *panadería* is one of the cheapest eateries in Puntas. Grab a quick breakfast ($2) or sandwich ($2-3) on the go. Very limited indoor and outdoor seating. Also sells some toiletries and groceries. No written menu. Open daily 6am-10pm. AmEx/MC/V. ❶

Punta's Bakery (☎823-6240), Rte. 413 at the intersection with Beach Rd. Not to be confused with Punta Mar Bakery, this small *panadería* in Puntas is where surfers and locals come for quick, cheap food. Indoor counter or outdoor patio seating. Breakfast $2-3, hot cafeteria lunch $4-6. Pastries and limited groceries also available. Open M-Tu 6am-8:30pm, W-Sa 6am-9pm, Su 6:30am-7pm. Cash only. ❶

Casa Isleña (p. 282), on Beach Rd., dishes up a more sophisticated menu than nearby establishments. Enjoy an elegant lunch of walnut pineapple chicken salad ($9). Lunch $7-15. Dinner $9-18. Open Th-Su 11am-9pm. AmEx/MC/V. ❷

Calypso Cafe (☎823-1626), on the road to the lighthouse, stands out for its prime location overlooking María's Beach. Use the outdoor patio to watch either the sunset or the surfers below. Popular lunch spot for surfers. Caribbean grilled seafood and beach food $5-15. Open in winter 11am-2am; summer noon-last customer. MC/V. ❷

THE REAL WORLD (TOWN, SOUTH OF TOWN)

Pancho Villa Mexican Grill (☎823-8226; www.pancovillapr.com), in the plaza in town, left of the church. Serving up hot Mexican favorites such as fajitas, enchiladas, and *empañadas*, this restaurant's large portions and fully stocked bar would satisfy even the toughest group of revolutionaries. Entrees $8-15. Delicious wings $0.25 on F. Live Mexican music Th 7-10pm. Open Tu-Sa 5-10pm. MC/V. ❷

Rincón Tropical, Rte. 115 Km 12.4 (☎823-2017), south of town, after the Berrios furniture store. Forgo the American-run places in Puntas and try out a more authentically Puerto Rican Rincón. Reasonably priced seafood and *comida criolla* at a clean outdoor restaurant. Lunch special M-F $6. Entrees $8-22. Open daily 11am-9pm. MC/V. ❸

Restaurante Bambino's, Rte. 115 Km 12 (☎823-3744), 2 blocks down from Econo. A friendly Italian restaurant with well-priced sit-down meals. Italian and *comida criolla* entrees $11-19. Also a nice selection of wines; bottles from $20. Lunch buffet M-F $7. Open M-Th and Su 11am-10pm, F-Sa 11am-11pm. AmEx/MC/V. ❸

Golden City Restaurant, Rte. 115 in Vista Mar Plaza (☎823-5829). Good, cheap Chinese food. The generic City serves all the basic dishes ($3.50-6.50) and *comida criolla* ($4.75). Entrees $4-7.25. Open Tu-Su 11am-10pm. Cash only. ❶

The Brothers Pizza, C. Muñoz Rivera (☎210-1615), in the plaza. Offers breakfast, hot pizza, and sandwiches. Different lunch combos along with A/C and a lively staff make it a great place to grab a cheap, filling lunch. Open M-Sa 9am-6pm. Cash only. ❶

El Zippy Taco, Rte. 413 up on the hill, before the intersection with Beach Rd. Zippy is a small taco stand where surfers and locals alike come to grab some delicious tacos, kicked up a notch by the special hot sauce. Chicken or pork tacos $1.65, fish tacos $2.50, and the hearty Zippy Changa $5. Open daily 10am-10pm. Cash only. ❶

◎ SIGHTS

Nobody comes to Rincón for its sights, but there are a couple of attractions.

PUNTA HIGÜERA LIGHTHOUSE. Rincón's lighthouse is both newer and less dramatic than others on the island. The original 1892 lighthouse was destroyed in 1918 and rebuilt in 1921, then again in 1922. A fire severely damaged the structure in the 1930s, but, undeterred, officials rebuilt the lighthouse in 1993 to commemorate the 500th anniversary of Columbus's landing on the island. You cannot enter the lighthouse, but the manicured park is a popular and pleasant place to walk and watch the surfers below as well as enjoy the sunset. Sometimes a Puerto Rican couple offers horse-and-carriage rides around the lighthouse and over to María's Beach, a particularly romantic trip at sunset. *(At the end of the lighthouse road.)*

B.O.N.U.S. NUCLEAR REACTOR. This large green dome just past the lighthouse can be seen from Rte. 413 was built in 1964 as the first nuclear energy plant in Latin America, but it quickly closed later that year. There have been plans to turn the plant into a nuclear museum. *(Just past the lighthouse.)*

MIRADOR DE AÑASCO. A yellow concrete tower located just where the land rises toward Rincón offers a stunning southerly view over the water. *(Rte. 115, 1.2 miles before the intersection with Rte. 402. Open daily 6am-7pm. Free.)*

RIDING THE WAVES

Rincón is not only the premier surfing spot in the Caribbean, but also one of the top surfing destinations in the world. Below is a list of the area's various surfing spots and services; however, this is just a brief summary of a rapidly changing industry. Conditions change daily, surfing instructors come and go, and prime surfing weather may surface unexpectedly. To get the scoop, head to Surf Town to ask the knowledgeable staff, or just mix it up with the surf crowd during Happy hour at **Calypso Cafe** (p. 289).

SURF SHOPS AND LESSONS

▨ **Surf Town,** C. Muñoz Rivera 40 (☎823-2515), in town, sells surfboards ($450+) and surf gear. The shop doesn't offer rentals, but a friendly staff answers questions about the area and will sketch a map for newcomers. Can recommend local surf instructors for lessons. Open M-Sa 9am-6pm, Su 10am-4pm. AmEx/MC/V.

Rincón Surf and Board (p. 281), is the only surf school in town. Full-day lessons for all levels (9am-4pm $89, 2 days $169, 3 days $239, 5 days $369) include transportation and equipment, but bring a towel, plenty of sunscreen, and money for lunch. All instructors are CPR-certified and have years of experience. The shop also rents surfboards ($20 per day), boogie boards ($13 per day), snorkel gear ($12 per day), kayaks ($35 per day) and beach supplies. Discounts for hotel guests. 7% tax not included. 50% deposit required for lessons, and you must cancel 2 weeks prior for full refund. MC/V.

A CLEANER RINCÓN

Travelers to Puerto Rico will be blown away by its beautiful beaches and breathtaking scenery, though they may be surprised at the sight of beaches and roadways covered with trash and debris. In 2005, the mayor of Rincón decided he wanted not only to clean up the town and its beaches, but also to make the area a more colorful and vibrant place for people to enjoy.

With the help of a local resident known to all as "Nanny," the group *Rincón Brilla* was formed. Since then, its projects have helped brighten up the popular surfing town. Organized clean-ups and signs advising everyone to clean up trash and recycle remind citizens and visitors that they must take an active stand to keep Rincón's beauty intact.

Rincón Brilla's biggest project to date was the renovation of the town dump, an effort that involved turning the massive landfill into a flourishing garden complex composed of four greenhouses, a honey bee program, and a craft shop where local artisans sell their goods. The greenhouses provide all the trees planted along Rincón's roadways, and also offer trees to the public for free. Since its creation, the group has grown significantly, gaining several full- and part-time employees. With this growth, it will garner new energy and support to continue working toward its goal of making Rincón the brightest and cleanest town in Puerto Rico.

West Coast Surf Shop, C. Muñoz Rivera 2E (☎823-3935; www.westcoastsurf.com), in the plaza across from the Catholic church. Rents surfboards ($25 per 24hr.) during the winter. Arranges surfing lessons ($35-50 per hr. per student, depending on the instructor) and sells a wide selection of surf gear and clothing. Open M-Sa 9am-6pm, Su 10am-5pm. AmEx/MC/V.

Hotwavz Surf Shop (☎823-3942), on the lighthouse road below Calypso (p. 284), rents surf and boogie boards ($8 for the 1st hr., $2 per additional hr.; $15 per day; $20 per 24hr.). Provides info about surfing lessons and sells original T-shirts and accessories. Open daily noon-6pm. MC/V.

Desecheo Dive Shop (☎823-2672 or 823-0390), on the lighthouse road. A small surf shop that rents surfboards ($25 per day), boogie boards ($15), and snorkeling equipment ($10 per ½ day, $15 per day). Conveniently located right by Maria's Beach. Open daily 9am-7pm. AmEx/MC/V.

SURFBOARD REPAIRS

Dr. Ding (☎823-6082), on Nuclear Vista Rd., repairs boards and makes new ones. Open in winter daily 11am-5pm; call ahead for an appointment.

Ocean Tribe (☎242-7985 or 242-7978), upstairs from Brisas on Rte. 413 and the road to Rincón Surf and Board, repairs and makes boards. Open in winter Tu-Su 11am-3pm.

SURF BEACHES

The principal surfing beaches in Rincón are listed below from south to north. Remember that winter and summer conditions differ dramatically. For instance, the best snorkeling spot in the calmer summer months is The Stairs, which is right next to the strongest surf break in the winter, Tres Palmas. Call one of the surf shops to get the latest conditions or just hop in your car and judge for yourself.

Tres Palmas. The best surfing spot in the Caribbean. Waves sometimes up to 25 ft. during winter and beyond break about ¾ mi. out, drawing big-name surfers and accompanying film crews. Experienced surfers only.

Toilet Bowl. With a strong undertow and lots of washout, the surf at this corner of Dogman's will pull you under—as a toilet bowl would.

Dogman's. A shallow beach with fast, well-formed waves. Better for more advanced surfers. A local favorite.

María's. A popular break right underneath Calypso Cafe (p. 284). The waves break relatively close to the shore here, so you won't have to paddle out much. Attracts the biggest crowds, but not very beginner-friendly. **The Point** is the beginning of María's toward the right and is only distinguished from it when the surf is low. When María's is big, a wave can run from here through Dogman's. **The Pistons** is a portion of María's named after the shipwreck's engine pistons that remain lodged in the water. The prominent pistons can be dangerous if you get caught up in them. Experienced surfers only.

Indicators. Located under the lighthouse, this break is rocky and shallow, has stinging sea urchins, and only attracts locals.

Dead Man's. No, it's not folklore: this beach was actually named after the dead bodies that have washed up here. This is an advanced break right against a perilous cliff.

Domes. One of the most popular and consistent breaks in the Rincón area. Can get extremely crowded, since it is beginner-friendly. Located in front of the nuclear reactor.

Spanish Wall. A shallow break that requires walking from the Domes parking lot along an old wall. Popular with local bodyboarders.

Pools. At the turn in Rte. 413, marked by Pools Guest House. Right-hand waves break quickly across this shallow, uncrowded spot, but don't ride the wave for too long or you'll hit the big rocks on the right.

Antonio's Beach (a.k.a Parking Lots). Located in front of the parking lot at Casa Isleña. Best surfed in the morning. Beginner-friendly.

River Mouth. The most difficult to access of the Rincón breaks. Only gets big during the winter. 2 sandy breaks formed by the sand bars at a river's mouth. Requires walking east along the shore from Antonio's Beach.

Sandy Beach. Come early in the morning to beat the crowds. A sandy bottom and consistent waves make this a good place for beginners and boogie boarders.

🛶 OUTDOOR ACTIVITIES

BEACHES

In spite of the ample coastline, many of the beaches near Rincón are too rough or inaccessible for swimming during the winter. However, a few patches of white sand and calmer waters invite more tame recreation. A couple of miles south of town, **Playa Córcega** has the best swimming beaches near Rincón and remains refreshingly empty. Drive south on Rte. 429 to the area around Km 1, then turn west at the blue whale sign between two condos, park near the condos, and walk between buildings to the beach. The *balneario municipal* (public beach) has both gentle Caribbean waves and larger Atlantic waves. Half of the beach has almost eroded away, but the other half is still a nice place for swimming. Facilities include trash cans, a playground, parking, a few outdoor showers, and bathrooms that occasionally work (bring your own toilet paper). To reach the beach, take the road marked *balneario* that splits to the right just south of town, past Surf Town surf shop (p. 285). During the summer months when the swells are down, head to **Sandy Beach** in the Puntas area for some great swimming and good boogie boarding. Be careful of riptides when the water is rough. On Beach Rd. just down from Casa Islena, there is a big parking area but no facilities.

FISHING

Captain José Alfonso of **Makaira Fishing Charters** leads fishing charters on his 34 ft. boat (half-day $525, full day $800). He also charters whale-watching and sunset cruises upon request. (☎823-4391 or 299-7374; www.makairafishing-charters.com. Price includes refreshments, gear, and tackle for up to 6 people. 50% deposit required for reservations. MC/V.)

HORSEBACK RIDING

It is illegal to ride horses on beaches in Rincón. However, **Pintos "R" Us,** next to Casa Verde (p. 282), leads rides along the Domes trail through fields and woods during the day (2hr., $40) and beach rides (2hr., $50) after dark. The owner can also lead rides to your bar or restaurant of choice. (☎361-3639 or 516-7090. Cash or traveler's checks.)

SNORKELING AND DIVING

Some of Puerto Rico's best diving and snorkeling waits just 14 mi. from Rincón around rocky, deserted **Isla Desecheo.** With thriving reefs, visibility consistently over 100 ft., and ample fish species, this ranks among the best diving spots in Puerto Rico. The DRNA prohibits visitors from camping on the island, but

DESECHEO DIPPING

One thing you're certain to notice when checking out the surf or enjoying the beaches in Rincón is the small island of Isla Desecheo peeking over the horizon just 12 mi. away. Desecheo may look tiny relative to its larger siblings—Isla Mona, to the south, seems continent-sized by comparison—but Desecheo is well worth a visit. The waters surrounding the island offer some of the best snorkeling and dive sites in the Caribbean.

Desecheo is an offical nature reserve protected by the Puerto Rican government, which has forbidden fishing anywhere within a half mile of the island's shores. As a result, Desecheo's crystal-clear waters are teeming with brightly colored organisms, among them angelfish, trigger fish, sea turtles, coral, and sting rays. On a clear day, visibility ranges from 60 to 100 ft..

In Rincón, head to **Taíno Divers** (see p. 279) to book a reservation for one of the daily snorkeling ($75) or diving ($109) trips. It's a bumpy 45min. ride out, but once at the island, enjoy snorkeling at two different sites. Candyland, named for its bright colors and coral formations, is the first. Cuevas, the second, more sheltered site, has long channels and tunnels of corals with connecting caves. The island offers more than any shore dive could, and its proximity to the mainland makes it cheaper and more accessible than a trip to Isla Mona.

Rincón's superb dive shop takes visitors out to dive and snorkel near the shore. If you don't want to head out on a boat, **Playa Escalera** is the best snorkeling beach in Rincón and offers a perfect place for beginners to check out coral formations and colorful fish. The best spot is about 60 ft. out in front of the set of concrete stairs; it can be accessed via a dirt road from Rte. 413 labeled "Playa Escalera" on a whale-shaped sign, between the marina and lighthouse road. **Taíno Divers,** Rte. 413 Km 1, in Black Eagle Marina, sends a 34 ft. boat to Desecheo almost daily (2-tank dive $109, snorkeling $75). Shorter, less frequent trips go to reefs around Rincón (2-tank dive $75, snorkeling $35). (☎823-6429; www.tainodivers.com. Lunch included. Scuba equipment rental $25. 2hr. whale-watching and sunset cruises, 6 person min., $35. 1-tank Discover Scuba package $125. 5-day open-water certification $425, plus $50 for books. Open daily 10am-6pm. MC/V.

WHALE WATCHING

As if there weren't already enough to do, Rincón also has a prime location to watch the humpback whales migrate through the deep waters of the Mona passage every winter. From January to April, it is quite common to see the massive creatures spurting water or even breaching. The lighthouse park is a prime observation area, and **Taíno Divers** (see **Snorkeling and Scuba Diving,** above) offers excursions to give you a closer look.

◪ NIGHTLIFE

It's inadvisable to surf at night, so Rincón has a hopping nightlife scene in winter, the height of surfing season. Because most partiers are on vacation, weeknights can be as exciting as weekends. During the summer, things are relatively quiet, but you can still find a mix of locals and surfers hanging out. Even nightlife is a bit of a misnomer, since it's quite common to find people chilling with a Medalla beer at 11am. Cheers to the surfing life.

Puesta del Sol Inn and Restaurant, Rte. 413 Km 2.8 (☎823-2787). One of the few places to get your groove on in Puntas. The night starts off slow, with a few people playing pool ($0.50) downstairs or sipping drinks ($2.50-4) at the bar, then crescendoes to a 2-story dance party with fluorescent lights and loud rock, pop, and reggaeton. Occasionally hosts sponsored concerts, drawing a Puerto Rican and foreign crowd. F-Su live music 11pm. Cover for monthly music show $3. Open daily noon-2am. MC/V.

Tamboo Bar & Seaside Grill (☎823-8550), at Beside the Pointe Guest House (p. 282). Everyone knows where Tamboo is, and if you're looking for the crowd, you're sure to end up here at some point in the night. Surfers sit on the large wooden patio watching people try their luck at Sandy Beach. Open-mike jam sessions on M night and live bands F-Sa nights pump up the energy and draw a mix of locals and tourists. Beer $2-3. Mixed drinks $4-6. Happy hour daily 7-9pm. Open daily 11am-last customer. MC/V.

Rock Bottom Bar and Cafe (☎605-5351), adjoining Casa Verde Vacation Rentals (p. 282), is an upstairs surfer bar replete with dozens of broken and graffitied boards, a wrap-around mahogany bar, open-air seating, and righteous surfers mixing up strong drinks. Every night is a different drink special, including Tu night 2 for 1 rum punch, W night $3 margaritas, and Sa night spin the wheel every half hour for a drink special. Beer $2-3. Piña coladas $5. Open 5pm-midnight.

Calypso Cafe (p. 284), on the road to the lighthouse. Every day surfers, locals, and wanderers gather at this tropical outdoor bar to sit on the patio and watch the sun drop down over María's Beach while enjoying Happy hour specials (daily 5-7pm; rum punch and Corona $2.50). Live music during the winter Sa 10pm. Beer and mixed rum drinks $2.75-3. Open daily 11am-last customer. MC/V.

Brisas, at the intersection of Rte. 413 and the road to Rincón Surf and Board, below Ocean Tribe. Expat waiters and waitresses from Rock Bottom and Tamboo end the night here with local friends. Pool tables dominate the dim red room. Surfing slide shows W and live music weekends during the winter. Beer $2-3. Mixed drinks $3-4. Open Tu-W and Su 7pm-midnight, Th-Sa 7pm-2am. Cash only.

NORTHWEST

LA RUTA PANORÁMICA

The Central Mountains are the heartland of Puerto Rico, both geographically and culturally. In the home of the *jíbaro*, or mountain farmer, boys still trot their Spanish mounts along mountain lanes. For over 100 mi., the series of the roads known as La Ruta Panorámica (The Panoramic Route) twists through this region—ascending mountains, descending into valleys, and offering easy access to luscious expanses of jungle. Sudden vistas of forested peaks appear around the bends and coffee-plantations-turned-*paradores* overlook quiet valleys. You can go miles without seeing a fast-food restaurant, the stars are visible at night, and locals tend to respond to you in Spanish. Lodging is generally divided between upscale hotels and camping, meaning that travel here can be either extremely cheap or comfortably classy, depending on your preference.

Still, in some ways, the Ruta Panorámica is less than idyllic. Trash, including quite a few abandoned cars, litters the roads, and stray or abandoned dogs loudly assert their ownership as cars drive by. Mountain towns under constant construction still suffer from traffic jams on weekends and holidays. The winding mountain roads range from narrow to tiny, with frequent washouts, and Puerto Ricans accustomed to the area feel no need to go slow. It's best to honk your horn as you drive around blind curves and avoid driving on the Ruta Panorámica at night or during an afternoon rainstorm. For those who can accept its imperfections, a drive through the island's mountains is an incomparable way to experience the remnants of pre-industrial Puerto Rico.

HIGHLIGHTS OF LA RUTA PANORÁMICA

VOLUNTEER With forest conservation groups at **Las Casas de La Selva** (p. 292).

DESCEND into the depths of the **Cañón de San Cristóbal** near Aibonito (p. 294).

ASCEND the island's highest peak at **Reserva Forestal Toro Negro** (p. 299).

UNCOVER the secrets of Taíno culture amid the numerous *batey* fields at Utuado's **Parque Indígena Caguana** (p. 304).

EXPLORE the Tanamá River along an eerie 700 ft. rock tunnel near **Utuado** (p. 304).

RESERVA FORESTAL CARITE

Carite's proximity to the capital makes it one of the most visited nature reserves on the island. During the summer months, hundreds of *sanjuaneros* trek over the hills to picnic in the cool subtropical forest or feast on the tasty *lechón* (roast pig) at one of Guavate's famous *lechoneras*. The best examples of these roadside grills/dance halls are on Rte. 184 along Km 27-8. Inside the forest, Puerto Ricans relax at picnic tables and swimming holes at one of three recreation areas. Visitors can explore the reserve under the guidance of the knowledgeable staff at the privately run Casas de la Selva (see **Accommodations and Camping,** below), but it is not advisable to hike alone deep in the forest, as there are few marked trails; the DRNA has not been able to maintain established trails in the face of hurricane damage and funding shortages. From September to May, the reserve sees few visitors and makes an excellent place to camp on a trip across the island.

◨◪ TRANSPORTATION AND PRACTICAL INFORMATION

The only way to reach Bosque Estatal Carite is by car. From San Juan or Ponce take Hwy. 52 south to Exit 32, then hop on Rte. 184 southbound. Driving along La

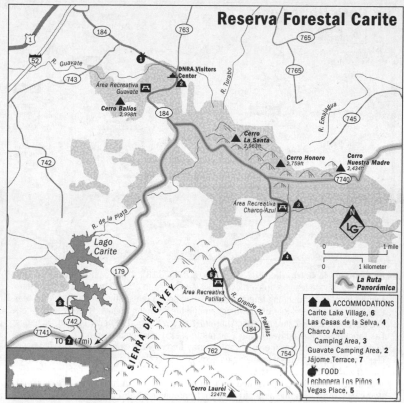

Reserva Forestal Carite

ACCOMMODATIONS
Carite Lake Village, 6
Las Casas de la Selva, 4
Charco Azul
  Camping Area, 3
Guavate Camping Area, 2
Jájome Terrace, 7

FOOD
Lechonera Los Piños 1
Vegas Place, 5

Ruta Panorámica from the east, take Rte. 7740 to Rte. 184; from the west, take Rte. 179 to Rte. 184. Rte. 184 runs directly through the forest and contains most of the forest's points of interest. The DRNA office is located in the northwest corner near Cayey, directly before the *lechoneras*. To reach the popular **Charco Azul Recreation Area,** follow Rte. 184 southeast to Km 16.6. La Ruta Panorámica follows Rte. 179 out of the forest toward **Lago Carite,** which is located near a separate section of forest southwest of the main reserve. Drivers should be aware that Puerto Rican drivers often use the whole road when taking tight mountain turns and may pose a threat to traffic in the opposite lane.

Visitors Center: The DRNA office, Rte. 184 Km 27.5 (☎ 747-4545 or 747-4510), at the northwest corner of the park. Open M-F 7am-2pm.

Hours: Charco Azul Recreation Area open daily 9am-5pm. Guavate Recreation Area open M-F 9am-4:30pm, Sa-Su 8am-5pm.

Supplies: All visitors should bring mosquito repellent, bottled water, toilet paper, and any food they may want. There are no supplies in the park.

ACCOMMODATIONS AND CAMPING

The unique lodging options in and around Bosque Estatal Carite are sharply divided between upscale lodges and camping sites.

La Ruta Panorámica

Las Casas de la Selva, Rte. 184 Km 15.9 (☎839-7318), 1 mi. past Charco Azul. This 1000-acre private reserve opened over 25 years ago in an effort to promote reforestation and protect the surrounding forest. Campers can set up tents either under a shelter near the lodge or in the middle of the forest among the crooning *coquís*. Renting a tent gets you access to the kitchen, bamboo showers, and bathroom. The newly built rustic cabin, Las Tabonucos, offers privacy, with 2 air mattresses, a hammock, and a fan. Las Casas is quieter and further from the road than nearby Charco Azul campsites, and visitors will likely get to meet volunteers working on ecological projects, or even volunteer themselves (see **Constructive Conservation,** p. 294). Meals and guided hikes available at reasonable prices. Wi-Fi $3. Reservations required or the gate will be closed. Tent space $10; dome tent rental with thin air mattress $25. Las Tabonucos $50 per night, $80 per weekend night, $45 per night for 5 or more days. Tax included. Cash only. ❶

Jájome Terrace, Rte. 15 Km 18.6 (☎738-4016), where Rte. 741 and Rte. 15 meet, near the town of Jájome. Well-decorated, quiet rooms, a popular restaurant, and a remarkable view extending all the way to the Caribbean. All 10 rooms have views of the mountains, the town of Salinas, or the sea. No TVs or phones, just ample room for relaxation in the garden and wicker chairs. Breakfast included. Popular restaurant open Th 11am-6pm, F-Sa 11am-10pm, Su 11am-8pm. Downstairs double with A/C $107; upstairs quads $125. Tax included. AmEx/MC/V. ❹

Carite Lake Village (☎763-2950). From San Juan, follow directions to Carite, then take Rte. 184 to Rte. 179, to Rte. 742 Km 2. The huge Carite Lake Village looks a bit like a misplaced Alpine retreat, with over 50 peach-and-white steep-roofed villas surrounding Lago Carite. The undecorated, concrete 2-story villas come with bathroom, a full kitchen, a living room, and 3 upstairs bedrooms. Restaurant, swimming pool, basketball court, playground, and boat ramp round out the gated vacation community. 6 person max. Check-in 1pm. Check-out 11am. Reservations required. Villas M-Th and Su $82, F-Sa $164. Tax included. MC/V. ❸

Charco Azul Camping Area, Rte. 184 Km 16.6, on the east side of the road, across from the day-use picnic area. Popular with families for its accessibility and the swimming hole 10min. up an asphalt walkway. Bathrooms (bring your own toilet paper), trash cans, and fire pits. Reservations and a DRNA permit ($4) required (p. 291). ❶

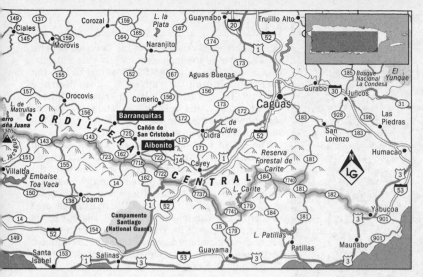

Guavate Camping Area, Rte. 184 Km 27.3, just south of the Visitors Center with parking across the road. Walk through the green wood entryway. Hillside camping area with rocky tent sites right next to a stream and the roadside; easy access to a peaceful and scenic spot. Bathrooms (bring your own toilet paper), covered picnic tables, and an outdoor shower. Reservations and a DRNA permit ($4) required (p. 291). ❶

FOOD

What could make *sanjuaneros* leave their homes at 3am to brave the strenuous drive to Puerto Rico's central mountains? Roast pig, of course. *Lechón*, as it's called, is a staple in Puerto Rico. On Rte. 184, just north of the DRNA center in the small town area known as Guavate, curious visitors can choose from a long row of *lechoneras*, where whole pigs roast in the windows. If it's a holiday, expect long lines as families load up on food for the beaches and nearby water holes. Most of the open-air *cafeterías* open only for the weekend crowds, but local favorite **Lechonera Los Piños ❶**, Rte. 184 Km 27.7, opens daily at 4am to lines of hungry customers. A full meal with *lechón*, rice, side, and drink goes for $7. Live music on weekends competes with the live music from every other *lechonera* on the block, contributing to the festive atmosphere. A pool table and bar in back provide the entertainment for smaller crowds after dark. (☎286-1917 or 489-7578. Live traditional music Sa 3pm. Live merengue Su 2pm. Open daily 4am-9pm. Bar open until 10pm. AmEx/MC/V; min. $5, $0.25 charge.)

The DRNA maintains several **recreation areas** throughout the park. The best are at **Charco Azul,** across the road from the campground, where a dozen covered picnic tables are spread throughout a large area surrounded by the river. Facilities include pit toilets, trash cans, and picnic tables, but no water. The largest picnic area, **Área Recreativa Guavate,** on Rte. 184 about one mile south of the Visitors Center, has countless picnic tables. Facilities include fire pits, trash cans, water, and bathrooms. Beverages of various kinds are sold at **Área Recreativa Patillas,** at the southern extremity of the Bosque. Local José keeps a family-friendly bar there called **Vegas Place ❷,** across the concrete bridge and near the main waterhole. A friendly crowd of locals sips beers in manmade swimming holes in the slow-moving river next to the road. The bar does not have regular hours or a phone number, but José lives upstairs and opens up most afternoons.

CONSTRUCTIVE CONSERVATION

Puerto Rico's much-needed economic development often comes at the expense of its unique natural resources. The Tropic Ventures Foundation, through its research station at the private rainforest reserve called **Las Casas de la Selva**, is working to prove that economic growth and environmental conservation need not always be at odds. Adjoining the government-run Reserva Forestal de Carite, the reserve is run entirely by volunteers who pay their own lodging expenses. Part of a large network of similar operations in unique biospheres around the world, Las Casas' goal is to develop eco-friendly forestry methods as an economically viable alternative to slash-and-burn logging and monoculture farming. Volunteers test out a forestry technique studied by the British Institute of Ecotechniques that involves planting and harvesting limited stands of valuable hardwood trees. The hope is that this method of utilizing Puerto Rico's natural wood resources will prove to be profitable while having a low impact on the surrounding forest.

Las Casas de la Selva is located at Rte. 184 Km 15.9, Patillas. ☎839-7318. Volunteers pay $15 per day for their tent platform lodgings and food and have the opportunity to take part in ongoing research projects. To get involved, check out the website at www.eyeontheforest.co or call to reserve a campsite.

ⓘ HIKING

Serious hikers should head to **Las Casas de la Selva** (p. 292), where the managers can provide information about hikes or guides for longer treks into the forest, including the rugged six-hour journey through Hero Valley. Only experienced hikers should attempt this trek, on which 60 ft. precipices lead down to a boulder-filled river. Hikes can be tailored to the visitor's experience level.

The DRNA maintains the **Vereda Charco Azul** trail (8min.), a short paved path that leaves from the Charco Azul camping area across the road from the parking area and follows a creek through beautiful forest surroundings. The path ends in a little pond good for wading. In the summer, this trail can become overcrowded with families, but in the winter it offers a serene glimpse of the nature reserve. Longer trails are not well maintained by the DRNA due to continual hurricane damage and understaffing. Check with the DRNA office for current conditions.

SIREN SIGNALS. Police, ambulances, and other emergency response vehicles always drive with their lights flashing. You don't need to pull over unless the lights are accompanied by a siren. If you're unsure, turn off your radio and open the window to make sure you're not missing the siren.

AIBONITO

¡Ay, bonito! (Oh, pretty!) exclaimed the Spaniards upon seeing this mountain hamlet. Or so the legend goes. More likely the town's name came from the native Taíno word *Atibonicu*, meaning "River of the Night," but the Spanish expression is still applicable today. With scenic vistas, roadside *cafeterías*, and cool mountain air, it's no wonder that Aibonito is the vacation home of choice for *sanjuaneros*. The town center pays homage to its Spanish roots with a historic church and a plaza built in the tradition of a small Spanish town. Every June, the town celebrates the Flower Festival (p. 296), one of the largest such festivals in the world. For hikers, Aibonito serves as a trailhead for expeditions into the Cañón de San Cristóbal.

⌐ TRANSPORTATION. From San Juan, take Hwy. 52 to Cayey, and then take Rte. 1 south to Rte. 7722. From Rte. 7722, turn right on Rte. 722 or Rte. 162, both of which lead directly into town. **Públicos** (☎735-1375) from Aibonito go to: Barranquitas (25min., $2);

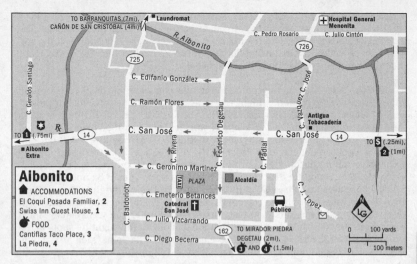

Cayey (30min., $2); and Coamo (30min., $2). **Taxis** (☎735-7144) gather on the plaza across from the Alcaldía, but it might be faster to call.

■**↗ ORIENTATION AND PRACTICAL INFORMATION.** Most routes from out of town retain their numerical signage in town, but local streets can be harder to identify, and many run one-way. The main street, **Route 14** (C. San José), runs one block north of the plaza and is usually clogged with traffic. From the Ruta Panorámica, **Route 162** goes directly into the city center, passes the plaza, and then intersects Rte. 14. Rte. 725 and Rte. 726 originate at Rte. 14 and then head north towards Barranquitas. Rte. 722 intersects with Rte. 14 just east of the city center. The city center is weldable, but most sights lie outside of town. The **Alcaldía** on the main plaza has some tourist and historical information. (☎735-3871. Open M-F 8am-4pm, Sa 9am-2pm.) **Bunco Popular** is at the intersection of Rte. 14 and Rte. 722. (☎735-3681 or 735-6191. ATM. Open M-F 8am-4pm, Sa 9am-noon.) The **police station**, C. San José 53, Rte. 14 Km 50.2, is open 24hr. (☎735-2020 or 735-2111.) Next door **Pharmacy Unity**, C. San José 51, sells pharmaceuticals. (☎735-4747 or 735-2241. Open M-Sa 8am-9pm, Su 9am-9pm. AmEx/MC/V.) The largest medical center in the area is **Hospital General Mennonite**, Rte. 726 Km 0.5, a block up the road from the intersection of C. Rosary and C. Clinton. (☎735-8001 or 735-8002. 24hr. emergency room. Open daily 10am-8pm.) The **post office**, C. Agency Lopez 20, does not have General Delivery. (☎735-4071. Open M-F 8am-4:30pm, Sa 8am-noon.) **Postal Code:** 00705.

↑ ACCOMMODATIONS. Aibonito is one of the few mountain towns that has accommodations within walking distance of the plaza. The best deal is the **Swiss Inn Guest House ❷**, Rte. 14 Km 49.3, west of the plaza, just before the cemetery. The guesthouse sits above an out-of-business beauty salon, so don't be misled by the "for sale" sign out front—just buzz at the bottom of the right-hand stairs and the friendly owner will let you in. An assortment of basic rooms with tiled floors have either two twin beds or one queen and are connected to a common room with a long balcony. The owner speaks both English and Spanish and offers discounts for longer stays. (☎735-8500. Common fridge, TV, and microwave. $55 per night for 1 night, $50 per night for 2 nights, $45 per night for the week. During the Flower Festival $75 for 1 night or $50 per night for the week. AmEx/MC/V.) For chain motel-like uniformity, try **El coquís**

Posed Familiar ❸, Rte. 722 Km 7.3. All rooms include private bath, cable TV, telephone, kitchenette with fridge and microwave, and a balcony overlooking a parking lot. The hotel is located on the second floor of a shopping center, so if nobody is at the second-floor reception, ask at the first-floor pharmacy. (Check-in 1pm. Check-out 11am. 1 double bed $80; 2 double beds $90. Tax included. AmEx/MC/V.)

◘ **FOOD.** A few days in the central mountains can leave you desperate for food other than *comedy corolla*, which is the only option for miles on end. For groceries try **Aibonito Extra**, C. San José 96, Rte. 14 Km 50.3. (☎735-7979. Open M-Sa 7am-9pm, Su 11am-5pm. MC/V.) While cheap local and fast-food places are found near the town center, Aibonito's most distinctive eateries line the Ruta Panorámica. Locals recommend **La Pedro ❹**, Rte. 7718 Km 0.7. The fresh seafood and expansive mountaintop views produce a rare dining experience. (☎735-1034. Entrees $7-25. Su buffet $14. Open W-Th and Su noon-7pm, F-Sa noon-10pm. D/MC/V.) **Conclaves Taco Place ❷**, at Rte. 722 and Rte. 162, on the Ruta Panorámica, provides a Mexican twist to the roadside menu. Their specialty is fajitas, but everything on the menu is fast, tasty, and less than $11. On weekends, a local crowd gathers for drinks and music, making this one of few nightlife spots in the mountains. (☎735-8870. Karaoke F. Live dance music Sa 3pm. Open M-W 11am-9:30pm, Th 11am-midnight, F-Sa 11am-1:30am, Su 11am-10pm. MC/V.)

◙ ▓ **SIGHTS AND FESTIVALS.** Complete with waterfalls, 500 ft. cliffs, and several ecological zones, the impressive 5½ mi. ▓**Cañón de San Cristóbal** is the jewel of Puerto Rico's central mountains. Located between Aibonito and Barranquitas, the canyon was used for years as the local garbage dump. In the early 1970s, local citizens protested this state of affairs, and in 1974, the Association of Environmental Control ordered that the canyon be protected. Now, the private Fideicommissa de Conservación de Puerto Rico (Conservation Trust of Puerto Rico) has assumed control of the area, reforesting it and using it for research purposes. The best way to experience the canyon is by hiking into the basin. However, locals warn that nobody should attempt the descent into the canyon without a guide; several visitors have been killed hiking into the canyon alone. The Fideicomiso recommends going with Dr. Samuel A. Oliveras Ortiz (☎857-2094 or 647-3402), a Barranquitas geographer and historian who offers tours tailored to each participant's interests and abilities ($40 per person). At least one trek usually leaves every weekend, unless it rains, in which case it is too dangerous to enter the canyon.

Private property surrounds most of the canyon, but non-hikers can still catch glimpses of its waterfalls and forbidding cliffs. From Aibonito, take Rte. 725 to approximately Km 5.5, then turn right just after the elementary school. Follow the road through the residential area until it heads uphill, and the canyon will be on the right. You can also try any of the roads leading downhill before the intersection with Rte. 162. If you tell locals that you're interested in seeing the canyon, most should be able to point out the best viewing spot. A good view of the canyon is available from the Fideicomiso office in **Barranquitas** (p. 297). The **Mirador Piedra Degetau**, Rte. 7718 Km 0.7, is worth a stop. The lookout tower has great views of the island—on a clear day you can see San Juan, El Yunque, the Caribbean, and the Atlantic. (Covered picnic tables and bathrooms. Open W-Su 9am-6pm. When M is a public holiday, open M and Th-Su 9am-6pm. Free.)

Aibonito blossoms during the last 10 days of June, during the annual **Festival de las Flores (Flower Festival)**. Started in 1969, the festival has grown from a small event put on by a few plant lovers to a large production drawing people from all over Puerto Rico. Locals display their homegrown flowers, farmers compete for the prizes of best garden and best plant, vendors hawk food, and musicians perform traditional mountain tunes. (For more information, call ☎735-4070 or try the mayor's office at ☎735-3871.)

BARRANQUITAS

Barranquitas is a typical mountain town, perched on the edge of a steep hill in the forest. Originally built as a trade stop between the north and south of the island, the town has a charm quite its own, meriting an afternoon's exploration. The recently renovated plaza's wrought-iron benches, gazebo, and fountains set a stylish tone for the birthplace of Luis Muñoz Rivera—politician, journalist, and ostensibly the most important man in the island's history (see **History,** p. 54). His home is preserved here as a museum, and the town center's other attractions also tend towards the historical. Similar in size to Aibonito, Barranquitas also offers access to the Cañón de San Cristóbal.

⊏ TRANSPORTATION. From the west, continue on Rte. 143 after it leaves the Ruta Panorámica, then turn left on Rte. 162. Coming from Aibonito, skip the Ruta Panorámica and take Rte. 14 to Rte. 162. Alternatively, coming from the east on the Ruta Panorámica, turn right on Rte. 143, then take a left onto Rte. 162, which leads into town. **Taxis** (☎ 857-0508) and the occasional **público** congregate around the plaza in front of the Alcaldía, but there is no regular public transportation to surrounding towns. A taxi to Aibonito, which has regular *públicos*, costs $15.

◧⌗ ORIENTATION AND PRACTICAL INFORMATION. Coming into town, Rte. 162 becomes C. Muñoz Rivera, the main street, which passes the Alcaldía and the plaza before intersecting Rte. 156, which leads east. Remember that going downhill will always lead east. Continue east along Rte. 156 to find fast food and the suburbs. **Casa Museo Joaquín de Rojas,** on C. Ubaldino Font, behind the church, does double duty as a tourist office and a small museum. The staff answers questions and distributes maps. (☎ 857-2065. Open M-F 8am-4:30pm with a break for lunch.) **Banco Santander,** Rte. 156 Km 16 (C. Barceló 60), 1½ blocks downhill from the plaza, exchanges American Express Travelers Cheques and has an **ATM.** (☎ 857-2355. Open M-F 8:30am-4pm.) For groceries, head to the **Grande** supermarket in the San Cristobal Plaza on Rte. 156, a quarter mile past the intersection with Rte. 152. (☎ 857 1144. Open M-Sa 7am-9pm, Su 9am-6pm.) The **police station,** Ave. Villa Universitaria 2 (☎ 857-2020 or 857-4400), down the hill at the intersection of Rte. 156 and Rte. 719 across from the Shell gas station, is open 24hr. **Farmacia del Pueblo,** C. Muñoz Rivera 27, is across the street from the Alcaldía. (☎ 857-3035. Open M-Sa 7:30am-6pm. MC/V.) The **Centro de Medicina Primaria de Barranquitas,** Rte. 156 Km 16.4, about a quarter mile downhill from the police station just before the intersection with Rte. 152, is the main hospital. (☎ 857-5923. Open M-F 6am-4:30pm. Emergency room open 24hr.) The sleek, modern **Biblioteca Municipal** on C. Susana Maldonado, across the plaza from the church, has several new computers with unreliable **Internet access.** (☎ 857-6661. Open M-F 8am-4:30pm.) Head uphill to find the **post office,** C. Muñoz Rivera 41. (☎ 857-3020. General Delivery. Open M-F 8am-4:30pm, Sa 8am-noon.) **Postal Code:** 00794.

⌗◨ ACCOMMODATIONS AND FOOD. The beautiful **Hacienda Margarita ❸,** about 15min. from town, is the more scenic of the two accommodations in the area. The peaceful mountain retreat sits on the very edge of a hill, offering incredible views of the valley below. Sparkling rooms come with TV and A/C, and the pool is a nice place to relax on a clear night. To get there, head east on Rte. 156 past the Shell Station, then turn left on Rte. 152. Drive all the way up the hill, then at Km 1.7, turn right directly before the wooden restaurant. Passing all the driveways, take your first left at the fork, then take another left just before a sign for the hotel. Continue to the end of the residential road, following the signs. (☎ 857-4949. Check-in noon. Check-out noon. 1 double bed $75; 2 double beds $85. MC/V.) **Niaian Guest House ❷,** at Km 57.0 on Rte. 143 west of town, is conveniently located for travelers on their way west to Bosque Estatal de Toro Negro. There is no sign, but look for a long yellow building with a yel-

Barranquitas

🔺 ACCOMMODATIONS
Niaian Guest House, **2**
Hacienda Margarita, **5**
🍴 FOOD
Cafetería El Senioral, **1**
Cafetería Plaza, **3**
El Criollito, **4**

low and green fence. Brightly lit rooms with kitchenettes, tiled floors, TV, A/C, queen bed, and small balconies overlooking the mountains make this a pleasant place to stay. (☎857-1240 or 553-8976. $60 per day. MC/V.) Of the many inexpensive *cafeterías* surrounding the plaza, **Cafetería Plaza ❶**, C. Muñoz Rivera 34, is the most welcoming. The rush of construction workers, businesspeople, and police officers fills it in the morning, but the crowd thins out during the day. It serves a variety of breakfast and lunch foods—from burritos to sandwiches to pizza to ice cream. (☎857-3475. Breakfast $1-3. Entrees $1-6. Open M-Sa 6:30am-4pm.) For a more relaxed breakfast, head to **Cafetería El Senioral ❶**, on C. Barcelo, a block up from the plaza at the corner of C. Torres. (Breakfast $3-4, sandwiches $4. Open M-Sa 8am-5pm. Cash only.) Outside of town, just before the turn for Hacienda Margarita, is a good example of the roadside *cafeterías*. **El Criollitos ❶** serves local seafood dishes for $6-15. It also has a bar, juke-box, and TV. (☎857- 5426. Open Tu-Th 11am-5pm, F-Su 11am-midnight. MC/V.)

🄶 **SIGHTS.** Luis Muñoz Rivera, famous for negotiating Puerto Rican auton-omy from Spain just before the US invaded in 1898 (see **History,** p. 54), domi-nates the town's cultural attractions. The **Mausoleo Familia Muñoz,** on C. El Parque, contains a quiet courtyard and monuments to the Muñoz clan. Inside, a small exhibit contains biographical information as well as an impressive mural depicting Muñoz Rivera's life. If the building is closed, ask someone in the office on the left side of the building to open it. (Open Tu-F 8:30am-4:20pm. Free.) Down C. Muñoz Rivera toward the plaza is the **Casa Museo Luis Muñoz Riv-era,** where Muñoz Rivera's birthplace has been reconstructed with much of the original furniture. (☎857-0230. Open Tu-Sa 8:30am-4:30pm. $1.)

Tours of 🖼**Cañón de San Cristóbal** leave from neighboring **Aibonito** (p. 294), but the best views are found in Barranquitas at the office of the **Fideicomiso de Con-servación** (Conservation Trust); head east on Rte. 156 and then turn right at Km 17.7. Continue to the end of the street, turn left on C. A, and drive to the end. The office, which provides brochures on the canyon and the Fideicomiso, is on the right after the road becomes a narrow one-lane path. (☎857-3511. Normally open M-F 8am-3:45pm, but call ahead to see if anyone is around as the staff does conservation work at several different sites.)

On the road from Barranquitas to Bosque Forestal Toro Negro, another government-constructed viewpoint rivals **Mirador Degetau** (p. 296) for the best view of the ocean. **Mirador Villalba-Orocovis**, Rte. 143 Km 39.3, makes a nice stop for those driving the Ruta Panorámica. The viewpoint has covered picnic tables, bathrooms, a play area, a basketball court, a small restaurant, and of course the panoramic view—on a clear day it is possible to see the Caribbean, the Atlantic, Ponce, Embalse Toa Vaca, and the islands off the southern coast. (☎867-6111. Open W-Su 9am-6pm, when M is a holiday open M and Th-Su 9am-6pm. Free.)

RESERVA FORESTAL TORO NEGRO

Toro Negro marks the high point of the island—literally. The reserve encompasses Cerro Punta (4930 ft.), the highest mountain in Puerto Rico, and some of the most impressive views on the Ruta Panorámica. Most visitors stick to the popular Área Recreativa Doña Juana, which contains several short trails and a public campground. Island-spanning views and solitude reward visitors who make their way to the less developed western half of the forest.

AT A GLANCE

AREA: 6945 acres.

CLIMATE: Cool and moist. Averages 67-75°F. Rainy season Apr.-Dec.

HIGHLIGHTS: Summitting Cerro Punta, reveling in views of the distant Caribbean.

FEATURES: Waterfalls, acres of isolated palm forest, the island's tallest peak.

GATEWAYS: La Ruta Panorámica, Jayuya, Adjuntas, Ponce (p. 201).

CAMPING: Public camping at Los Viveros camping area. Campers must obtain a DRNA permit ($4) in advance (p. 299).

FEES: None.

⊏⚹ TRANSPORTATION AND PRACTICAL INFORMATION

You must drive if you want to visit Reserva Forestal Toro Negro. From San Juan take Hwy. 22 to Barceloneta and then take Rte. 140 south past Florida to Rte. 141. Turn left on Rte. 144 in Jayuya and right on Rte. 149, which will run into Rte. 143. From Ponce, take Hwy. 123 north, exit onto Rte. 143, and drive east

Almost all sights lie along **Route 143,** which runs directly through the forest as La Ruta Panorámica. The only other important road, **Route 149,** overlaps briefly with Rte. 143 just west of the Doña Juana Recreation Area and runs north-south between Manatí and Juana Diaz. Toro Negro is Puerto Rico's most remote reserve, with only the small towns of Jayuya and Villalba nearby.

Visitors Center: The **DRNA** office, Rte. 143 Km 32.4 (☎867-3040), west of Área Recreativa Doña Juana, distributes info and a hand-drawn trail map. Open daily 8am-4pm. Guards at the police office next door can help when the DRNA office is unattended.

Hours: Área Recreativa Doña Juana is open daily 9am-5pm.

Supplies: All visitors should bring mosquito repellent, bottled water, and food. There are no supplies in the park; the only "restaurant" open regularly doubles as a gas station.

⛺ CAMPING

There are no hotels around Toro Negro, but several locals along Rte. 149 north of the forest advertise guesthouses, usually only available for weekend use.

These are generally rustic two-bedroom cabins with enough room for large families. Most include a kitchen, a bathroom, and several beds, but no sheets or dishes. Visitors will find more options in nearby Jayuya. The most economical and idyllic accommodation in Toro Negro is a campground. The DRNA maintains **Los Viveros camping area ❶**, Rte. 143 Km 32.5, just east of the office down a short paved road. This large field surrounded by Doña Juana Creek has covered picnic tables, fire pits, trash cans, and bathrooms. Several trails start here. You must get a DRNA permit ($4) in advance (p. 299).

🍴 FOOD

The best option in Toro Negro is to bring your own food and picnic. Almost all of the rental cabins have kitchens, and **Área Recreativa Doña Juana** has an attractive picnic area with fire pits and 10 covered tables. There are also a couple of *comida criolla* options. Despite its name, **Las Cabañas de Doña Juana ❶**, Rte. 143 Km 30.5, is actually a restaurant specializing in charcoal-grilled meats. The "cabañas" are covered concrete picnic tables that allow patrons to experience the surrounding mountains. (☎ 867-3981. Everything on the menu under $6. Open Sa-Su and holidays 8am-6pm; summer also open F.) If Las Cabañas is closed, try **Terraza y Gasolinera Divisoria ❶**, at the intersection of Rte. 143 and Rte. 149. The small *comida criolla* counter is also stocked with snack food, juice and water. (☎ 847-1073. Meals under $5. Open daily 7am-8pm. MC/V.)

🌄 SIGHTS

On the eastern side of the reserve, **Doña Juana Waterfall,** Rte. 149 Km 41.5, cascades 120 ft. over a rocky cliff just next to the road. This is one of the most accessible waterfalls on the island, and after rainfall it is certainly one of the most impressive.

The western portion of Toro Negro has not been developed for tourism, but that just means you'll have the best views on the island to yourself. West of the intersection with Rte. 149, Rte. 143 continues ascending until it follows the ridge of Puerto Rico's tallest peaks. Almost all of the mountains have radio towers and roads leading to the top. Traveling east to west, you first pass **Cerro Maravillas** (3880 ft.) at the intersection of Rte. 143 and Rte. 577. Although it is by no means the tallest, this peak is well known as the site of one of the most infamous murders in Puerto Rican history (see **Terror and Tragedy,** p. 59). Two small white crosses still mark the gravesites. Continue past two more radio-towered mountaintops to reach the road up to **Cerro Punta,** the tallest mountain in Puerto Rico. The mountain is distinguishable by the gravel area at the base and the incredibly steep paved road winding up the side. Get to the observation platform early (at the top, past both radio towers), before the clouds roll in, and you'll be rewarded with the best view on the island. While signs at some of the radio stations seem to warn visitors off, the local DRNA rangers say that it is legal to visit the summits, and the workers there are friendly, if a bit surprised to see visitors.

🥾 HIKING

Some of the longer and more popular trails are listed below; for a complete list, visit the DRNA office. These trails are often old unpaved roads, so they are accessible to hikers of most abilities.

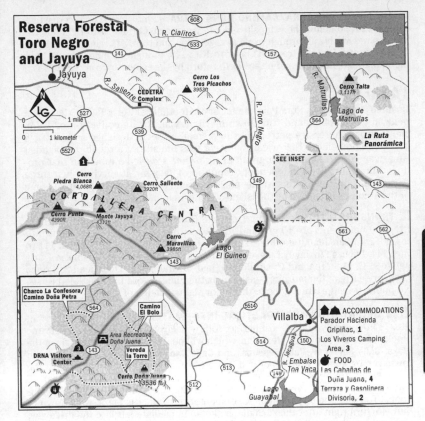

Reserva Forestal
Toro Negro
and Jayuya

CAMINO EL BOLO. *(2¾ mi.)* This is the longest trail in Toro Negro, and viewpoints are perfect for a picnic lunch. The trail begins across the street from the Visitors Center; walk through the parking lot and continue on the rocky road leading uphill. After about 15min. you reach a flat grassy path along the ridge of the mountain with great views to the south. When you come to the paved road, turn left to continue along the path. Vereda La Torre crosses this trail and leads uphill to another viewpoint. El Bolo ends farther east on Rte. 143. It is possible to make a circle by coming back along the road, but given the blind turns and narrow roads, it's easier to return via the same path.

VEREDA LA TORRE. *(2 mi.)* The trailhead is located at the Área Recreativa Doña Juana; the path leads up to an observation tower with stellar views, and is an easy, shady climb. From the picnic tables, follow the grass path uphill past valleys full of ferns and palm trees. The trail gets slightly rougher as you progress, but the path is always easy to follow. After 20min., the trail comes to what looks like an old service road, which is actually Camino El Bolo. Turn left and walk about five minutes past the short stretch of concrete to reach the second half of La Torre, which leads to the stone observation tower.

CHARCO LA CONFESORA/CAMINO DOÑA PETRA. *(1 mi.)* From Los Viveros, take the paved road below the campsites. When you reach a bridge, turn right and follow the red mud trail through tropical vegetation and rows of orange trees. Eventually Camino Doña Petra leads back to Rte. 143, though it's quite a walk back along the road, and it would be easier to return by the same way you came.

JAYUYA

Located 30min. off La Ruta Panorámica at the foothills of Cerro Punta, the tallest peak in the whole island, this town merits a visit for its collection of Taíno sights, from impressive petroglyphs to a small museum designed as a *cemí*, a Taíno religious icon. Historically, Jayuya was the site of a revolution against American control. In 1950, a group of *nacionalistas* led a rebellion that produced the short-lived independent republic of Jayuya—it survived just three days. Today the town offers a quiet place to spend the night at the spiritual home of the Taínos, surrounded by the island's highest mountains.

⊟ TRANSPORTATION. Coming from the Ruta Panorámica, detour north on Rte. 140 between Toro Negro and Adjuntas, then take Rte. 144 straight into town. From San Juan, take Rte. 123/Hwy. 10 to Utuado, then follow Rte. 111 to Rte. 144. **Públicos** in Jayuya leave from the parking lot next to Mueblería Doris between C. Figueros and C. Guillermo, just off the plaza. They head to Ponce ($4) very early in the morning—ask locals the night before for scheduled times. No public transportation goes to the major sights outside of town.

⊞🛈 ORIENTATION AND PRACTICAL INFORMATION. Coming into town, Rte. 144 deposits you on C. Guillermo; follow it through town and veer left one block before the "Do Not Enter" sign, which will put you on C. Figueres right at the plaza. **Calle Guillermo, Calle Figueros,** and **Calle Canales,** the three main streets in town, run parallel to each other and the latter two border the plaza. Most of the major sights are on Rte. 144 as it continues south out of town. **Banco Popular,** C. Guillermo Esteves 84, has an ATM. (☎828-4120. Open M-F 8am-4pm, Sa 9am-noon.) To reach the **police station,** C. Cementerio 1, from the plaza, walk down C. Barceló, turn right after the Alcaldía, make an immediate left into the driveway, and walk uphill. (☎828-2020 or 828-3600. Open 24hr.) Across the street, the **hospital,** C. Cementerio 2, has a 24hr. emergency room. (☎828-3290 or 828-0905. Open M-F 8am-4:30pm.) The **university library** on C. Figueras across the plaza from the church offers free **Internet access.** (☎828-2824, ext. 1759. Open M-F 7:30am-4:30pm.) The **post office,** C. Canales 15, has General Delivery. (☎828-3010. Open M-F 7:30am-4:30pm, Sa 7:30am-11:30pm.) **Postal Code: 00664.**

🖪🖪 ACCOMMODATIONS AND FOOD. **Parador Hacienda Gripiñas ❸,** on Rte. 527, was originally a 19th-century coffee plantation and retains the charm of an old country house, with wooden porches and rocking chairs from which you can enjoy an incredible mountain landscape, a cool breeze, and the smell of fresh flowers. Carpeted rooms have cable TV and air-conditioning. Steep weekend prices include dinner and breakfast at the hotel restaurant, while weekday prices without meals are more budget friendly, making this a good deal for mid-week travelers. (Take Rte. 144 east to Rte. 527, then follow the green signs. ☎828-1717 or 828-1718; www.haciendagripinas.com. 2 swimming pools. Check-out 11am. Singles M-Th and Su $75, F-Sa $98; doubles $85/126. AmEx/MC/V.) Those who want to stay in town have one choice—**Hotel Posada Jayuya ❸,** C. Guillermo Esteves 49. The back entrance is accessible from C. Libertad, parallel to C. Guillermo Esteves, right near the bridge. Wicker furniture, TV, and bar in the lobby give way to neat, tile-floored rooms. Textured murals decorate the walls. (☎828-7250. Small pool. Fridge, TV, and A/C. Su breakfast included. Doubles $69. Extra person $10. AmEx/MC/V.)

Jayuya proper doesn't offer many dining options beyond one or two *panaderías*. Just outside of town, the restaurant at **Parador Hacienda Gripiñas ❸** has a wonderful view over a peaceful valley. Its prices may be high, but this *mesón gastronómico* creates an exceptional dining experience—its glass-ceilinged central room holds a tree in the middle, growing upward from the courtyard below. Dishes include traditional seafood and steak options. (Entrees $11-22. Open daily 8am-10pm.) **Tainy Cafe's ❶** is a small roadside sandwich stand with sandwiches that are anything but small, making it a good place to get a bite to eat just outside of Jayuya on Rte. 539 Km 0.2. (☎828-3353. Sandwiches $5.)

◙ ❀ SIGHTS AND FESTIVALS. The **CEDETRA (Development and Labor Center)** complex, Rte. 144 Km 9.3, holds a variety of Taíno artifacts and contemporary *artesanía* work. Constructed in 1989, the bulbous **Museo El Cemí** was designed to look like a *cemí*, a Taíno religious image carved in stone. Don't worry if the building looks a little amorphous—there are at least 20 different theories about what the *cemí* was designed to look like. Inside, visitors will find Taíno artifacts and replicas, including an *espátula vomita*, a spatula that the Taíno people used to induce vomiting before they took hallucinogenic drugs. (☎828-4618. Open M-F 9:30am-4pm, Sa-Su 9am-3pm. $1, under 15 $0.50.) Completely unrelated but on the same property, **Museo Casa Canales** housed one of Jayuya's most important families. Built in the late 19th century by Don Rosario Canales Quintero, the town's first mayor, the house also served as a residence for his son Nemesio Canales Rivera, a legislator and humorist who aided in the legal emancipation of women. Don Rosario's daughter Blanca Canales, the leader of the revolution of October 30, 1950, also resided there. The house was abandoned while she served her prison term, but in the early 1990s CEDETRA painstakingly reconstructed it in its original form (☎828-4094. Open Sa-Su 10am-5pm. $1, under 12 $0.50.) The nondescript building in back holds the **CEDETRA exhibition hall** and a small *artesanía* souvenir shop. (Open T-Sa 10am-4pm.) The kiosks across the path provide a venue for **local artisans** to sell their work on weekends and holidays. Finally, near the kiosks, the **Museo de Café** displays coffee-related antiques. Despite the extensive work put into the CEDETRA complex, the most impressive sight lies about 1 mi. down the road. **La Piedra Escrita**, Rte. 144 Km 7.7, is a huge rock in the middle of the creek covered with Taíno petroglyphs. A new wood ramp leads down to the rock, which locals use as a diving board into the surrounding creek.

Within the city center, yet another cultural monument honors the island's Taíno heritage. From the plaza, hike up the steep staircase to reach a bust of the *cacique* Jayuya (Jayuya Taíno chief). Behind the bust, the small locked building contains the **Puerto Rican Indian tomb,** the bones of a Taíno man lying on a bed of dirt accumulated from each of the island's 78 municipalities. Unfortunately, the monument is often locked and difficult to see. Behind the tomb, the Puerto Rican Department of Culture maintains a small **cultural center,** C. San Felipe 25, with an assortment of antiques, broken Taíno artifacts, and reproductions. (☎828-2220. Spanish only. Open M-F 8am-noon and 1-4:30pm. Free.)

Jayuya's largest festival is the annual **Festival Nacional Indígena** (National Indigenous Festival), which is celebrated over three to five days in mid-November and includes food, music, games, and several large historical exhibitions. The festival focuses on Taíno culture with indigenous dances, *batey* (a ritual ball game), and reproductions of an indigenous town. Check at CEDETRA for details.

UTUADO

Utuado's highlights are its rich Taíno roots and forward-thinking eco-development of its natural surroundings. The town reflects its colonial history, with a Spanish central plaza and American fast-food joints on the outskirts. More than a main attraction itself, Utuado serves as an excellent base for heading out into the neighboring mountains. Park the car, throw on your boots, and get ready to experience the adventurous side of Puerto Rico's rainforest.

🖪🗹 TRANSPORTATION AND PRACTICAL INFORMATION. *Públicos* leave early in the morning for Arecibo (45min., $2) from Av. Esteves and C. Israel Malaret Juarbe. The city center is divided by a river. Rte. 123 becomes **Avenue Esteves** and goes through town; at the Plaza Mercado, turn right to hit the town plaza. On the other side of the river, Rte. 111 runs parallel to the river and becomes **Avenue Fernando Luis Rivas. Tourist information** and hand-drawn maps are available at the **Centro de Arte, Cultura y Turismo,** C. Doctor Cueto 10, as you enter town from Rte. 123 from the south, a few blocks from the plaza. **Banco Popular,** C. Doctor Cueto 93, is before the tourist info center, heading away from the plaza. (☎894-2700. 24hr. ATM. Open M-F 8am-4pm, Sa 9am-noon.) The **police station** is on C. Sampson, at the corner of the plaza uphill from the main church. (☎894-3022. Open 24hr.) The **CDT** (Centro de Diagnóstico y Tratamiento), at C. Betances 2, acts as the local hospital; it is down from the police station behind the main church on the plaza. (☎894-2288. Open 24hr.) Free **Internet** is available only during the school year at the **Biblioteca Pública** across the street from the Centro de Arte, Cultura y Turismo. (Open M-F 8am-4pm, Sa 9am-3pm.) The **post office,** Av. Fernando Luis Rivas 41, is on Rte. 111, at the third traffic light up from the intersection with Rte. 123. (☎894-2490. General Delivery. Open M-F 8am-4:30pm, Sa 8am-noon.) **Postal Code:** 00641.

🖪🗗 ACCOMMODATIONS AND FOOD. If you just want a place to crash, look no further than **Hotel Riverside ❶,** Av. Fernando Rivas 1, at the intersection of Rte. 111 and Rte. 123, above a Chinese restaurant. This tiny hotel is connected to the owner's house and has no signs, but its small rooms manage to fit a fridge and a TV, and the price is right. (☎216-3279. A/C. Doubles $40; 6-person room $60. Cash only.) For lakefront luxury, visitors should head to **Los Piños Lake Resort ❸,** at the intersection of Rte. 140 and Rte. 613, on the picturesque Lago Caonillas. The recently renovated villas contain a sitting room with sleeper sofa, kitchen, and bedroom with queen bed. The resort has its own restaurant and bar open Friday to Sunday. Classical music or jazz concerts liven things up twice a month. (☎894-3481 or 894-3464. $75, better view $85. Extra person $15. AmEx/MC/V.) For groceries head to **Econo,** on Rte. 111 about 0.7 mi. past the post office. (Open daily 7am-9pm.) In town, there are plenty of *cafeterías* and fast-food joints, but to take advantage of Utuado's natural surroundings, head out of town to **Jungle Jane's Restaurant ❹,** on Rte. 612 just off Rte. 140, at the remote Casa Grande Mountain Retreat. This *mesón gastronómico* serves breakfast and dinner in a former coffee plantation. Candlelit tables on a balcony overlooking the forest with *coquís* chirping in the background create a romantic mood. (Entrees $12-25. Open daily 8-10:30am and 6-9pm. AmEx/D/MC/V.) Ravenous adventurers will appreciate the diversity of the menu (*mofongo*, spaghetti, pizza), the quick service, and reasonable prices at **La Familia ❷,** Rte. 111 Km 12. (☎894-7209. Entrees $6-15. Open M and W-Th 11am-9pm, F-Sa 11am-11pm, Su 1-10pm. MC/V.)

🖸 SIGHTS. Utuado is surrounded by natural wonders and historic sites on a prodigious scale. The island's largest cave system, the most extensive Taíno site, and the world's biggest telescope are all accessible from this one small town. If you really want to explore the area and get up-close with nature, then head to ■Tanamá **Expeditions.** Owner Roberto was born and raised in the mountains and knows every rock, river, and trail. Today he leads exhilarating hiking excursions along subterranean rivers, through the overgrown bamboo forests of the **Tanamá Trail,** and to the enormous **Arecibo Observatory.** These trips require good physical health and sturdy shoes, but Roberto provides specialized equipment, lunch, and even a place to stay the night before. Trips range from 3½ to 7hr. and include a combination of different trails, but the highlight is certainly the famous bamboo trail and tubing through the 700 ft.-long Arco Cave ($78, including lodging.) The more adventurous can arrange for a two-day journey that includes traversing a bioluminescent cave and hiking the Tanamá Trail ($250, check with owner about necessary camping equipment). All tours include **free lodging** (shared basic rooms with bathrooms or camping space) at the owner's house and a filling lunch. (Continue past Parque Caguana to Rte. 111 at about Km 15.3, turn left on Rte. 602 and follow signs to the office at Km 1.3. ☎894-7685 or 201 9174; www.puertoricoadventures.com. Cash only.)

Parque Indígena Caguana is the largest site of Taíno ruins on the island, which leads archaeologists to believe that it once served as a social, religious, or ceremonial center. Supposedly the Taínos came down the Río Tamaná, then chose to settle in this spot when they saw that the surrounding mountains had the shape of their religious icon, the *cemí*. The site contains several *batey* courts, a ritual handball game that had major religious significance. Carbon-dating techniques suggest that the first settlement here took place as early as 1200. The **Institute of Culture** maintains the site today, which means that it has much better infrastructure than other Taíno sights, and friendly workers frequently provide unofficial, free guided tours. Even without a tour, it's enjoyable to wander around the picturesque botanical garden and *batey* courts as you attempt to identify the petroglyphs in the rocks. A museum explains the basics of Taíno culture. (Rte. 111 Km 12.3, west of Utuado. ☎894-7325 or 894-7310. Open daily 8:30am-4:20pm. $2, ages 6-12 $1, under 6 and over 60 free.)

ADJUNTAS

Because Adjuntas is situated in the central mountains, visitors might expect it to be a quiet town; however, during the day *"La cuidad del gigante dormido"* (the city of the sleeping giant) is wide awake and full of life. This fruit- and coffee-exporting town has not developed much tourist infrastructure, but has affordable accommodations and unique eateries. It is also a gateway to the Bosque Estatal de Guilarte and home to one of the most successful ecological activism projects in Puerto Rico.

▐ TRANSPORTATION. From Jayuya, take Rte. 123 south into town, where it becomes **Calle Doctor Barboza** and leads to the plaza. From the Ruta Panorámica, Rte. 123 north becomes C. Rodulfo Gonzalez, which runs one-way along the plaza. These two roads run the length of the town and are perpetually clogged with traffic due to ongoing construction on the plaza. It's best to park near the plaza and walk around town. San Joaquín is the Catholic Church on the plaza and is a good landmark. If you're facing the church, you're facing south.

▐ PRACTICAL INFORMATION. The **Oficina de Turismo** is in the library and has information on the town and its history. The friendly staff can also direct you around town. (Open M-F 8am-noon and 1-4:30pm.) Visitors will find an **ATM** at the **Banco Popular** on C. San Joaquín on the plaza. (☎829-2120. M-F 8am-4pm, Sa 9am-noon.) **Police** are available 24hr. at C. San Joaquín just off the right-hand side of the plaza, facing the church, in the small green building (☎829-7800). The **hospital, Centro de Diagnóstico y Tratamiento (CDT),** C. Doctor Fendini 4, is two blocks east of the plaza. (☎829-2860. 24hr. emergency room.) Free **Internet** is available at the **public library** on C. César Gonzalez; go past the police station and take a right. (☎829-5039. M-Th 8am-8pm, F 8am-4:30pm, Sa 10am-1:30pm.) The **post office,** C. Luis Muñoz Rivera 37, is a block up from the northeast corner of the plaza. (☎829-3740. M-F 8am-4:30pm, Sa 8am-noon.) **Postal Code:** 00601.

Ⲅ Ⲥ ACCOMMODATIONS AND FOOD. The cheaper of the only two accommodation options is the **Hotel Monte Río ❸,** C. César Gonzalez 18, just past the library, at the end of the road. It offers a pool, bar, and simple rooms with bed and futon. (☎829-3705. TV. A/C. Lunch buffet $6. Rooms with bed and futon $50; larger rooms with balconies $65-88. Extra person $10.) The much more elaborate **Parador Villas Sotomayor ❸,** Rte. 123 Km 37.6, a few hundred meters up Rte. 522 from Rte. 123, is a popular vacation destination. Villas with bedroom, bathroom, and kitchenette are spread around a grassy area with basketball and tennis courts and a swimming pool. (☎829-1717 or 829-1774. TV. A/C. Horse rental $25 per hr. Bicycle rental $5 per hr. Doubles $85; more for multiple bedrooms.) The resort also has a small **campground ❶** with barbecue pit, water spigots, bathrooms, and showers. ($35 including access to pool. Extra person $5.)

On the northeast corner of the plaza, **Esquina de la Amistad ❶,** C. Rodfulo Gonzalez 56, bakes daily *pan de hogaza* (homestyle bread) that draws customers from the whole region. (Pastries $0.50-0.70. Bread $1-2. Open daily 5:30am-11pm.) Old men smoke their cigars at **La Playita Coffee House ❷,** Rodulfo Gonzalez 3, marked by the sign *"Lechonera La Playita,"* around the corner from Casa Pueblo. A bar, back patio, and a couple of pool tables round out the relaxed atmosphere. (☎316-9095. *Comida criolla* entrees $5-10. Open M and W-Su 9am-midnight.) If you really want your fill of delicious *comida criolla,* head to **Hotel Monte Río ❷** for their all-you-can-eat $6 lunch buffet. One meal here is all you may need for the day. (Open daily 11am-2pm.) **Lucy's Pizzeria ❶,** on the right corner of the plaza, facing the church, offers a taste of the States, with pizza and sandwiches. (☎829-1555. Sandwiches $1.50-3. Sm/M/L/XL pizzas, $5/7.50/9/11. Open daily 10am-10pm. MC/V.) If you're wondering where the delicious smell is coming from, follow your nose to **Sun Hill's Fried Chicken ❷,** on C. Rodulfo Gonzalez, one block away from the plaza. The closest thing to fast food in the mountains, the lunchtime crowd moves through quickly, enjoying chicken and various side dishes. (☎829-1952. Open M-Sa 10am-9pm, Su 11am-7pm. Cash only.) The **Villas Sotomayor ❸** also has a restaurant serving *comida criolla.* (Breakfast $3-5. Lunch entrees $9-13. Dinner entrees $9-22. Open daily 8-10am and noon-10pm.)

ⓖ SIGHTS. 🏠**Casa Pueblo,** C. Rodulfo Gonzalez 30, is the epicenter of Puerto Rico's ecological activism movement (see **In the People's House,** p. 307). The museum includes displays on the group's community projects—ranging from the 15-year struggle to prevent open-pit mining in the town's watershed to more recent studies on Puerto Rican rainforests. A collection of butterflies and various agricultural experiments fills the backyard. The gift shop sells the group's coffee, **Café Madre Isla,** which pays for the entire operation's expenses. Large groups can call ahead about volunteering for a weekend at the plantation. (☎829-4842. Coffee $6 per lb.; you can try some in the small kitchen. Open daily 8am-4:30pm. Free.)

Southwest of Adjuntas, the Ruta Panorámica winds through **Bosque Estatal de Guilarte,** a protected area composed of six distinct units of land, created in 1935 to preserve several different river areas throughout the central mountains. Visitors coming from the east first pass Lago Garzas (Rte. 131 Km 7.7), a popular **fishing** spot. Farther west, the official forest entrance is marked by a patrol unit at the intersection of Rte. 131 and Rte. 518. Drive up the hill across from the office to reach the DRNA office, which provides information about the forest and nearby

swimming holes. The **Área Recreativa**, at the end of a short path from the DRNA office, has a *mirador* (scenic overlook) with superb views of the surrounding valley. (☎829-5767. Open M-F 8am-3:30pm, Sa-Su 9am-3:30pm.) The only **marked trail** in the forest is *Camino al cerro* (Pig Road), a slippery 30min. path leading up to the peak of **Monte Guilarte**. The trailhead is 75 ft. from the guard station, next to a private driveway across from a ramshackle roadside eatery near the dead end of Rte. 131. Don't hike if it is raining, since the trail becomes a continuous creek bed and a little rain at the base may mean a downpour at the summit. There are two sheltered rest stops along the trail, and the summit is just past the metal handrails. To make use of the wilder eastern segment of the forest, visitors will need to arrange a trip with either the DRNA officer or another local guide, as those trails date to before the reserve was established and require local knowledge. The highlight of Guilarte is its exceptional **cabins ❶**. Guilarte has bathrooms, rustic showers, trash cans, running water, and fire pits. To stay here you must have a DRNA permit and a reservation. (Call the DRNA offices in either Mayagüez or Ponce, ☎844-4660 or 844-4051. Cabins $20, bedding not provided.)

MARICAO

The remoteness and rugged terrain of this coffee-producing town have preserved its old-fashioned feel. Possibly the only town on the main island without any fast-food restaurants, Maricao offers a rare glimpse of what many Puerto Rican towns used to be like. The town's largest festival, the **Fiesta del Café** (Coffee Festival) is in mid-February, and includes traditional music, coffee samples, drama shows, *artesanía*, and folkloric dances.

⛏ 🚹 ORIENTATION AND PRACTICAL INFORMATION. To get to the main plaza from the west, take Rte. 120 into town. Cross the small bridge, pass the intersection with Rte. 410, and head up the hill. At the post office and bank, turn right to reach the plaza. Tourist information is available at the **Oficina de Relaciones Públicas** in the Alcaldía on the plaza. (☎838-2290. Open Aug.-June M-F 8am-4:30pm.) A 24hr. **ATM** is available at the **Banco Popular** on C. Luis Zuzuarregui, across the street from the post office. (Open M-F 8am-3:30pm.) There is a small **police** substation in the purple building on the plaza, but the main police station, Luchetti 14, is located on the outskirts of town. (☎838-2020 or 838-2035. Open 24hr.) Across the street from the police is the **hospital**, Av. Luchetti

GIVING BACK

IN THE PEOPLE'S HOUSE

When a group of mining companies came to Puerto Rico looking to dig in the region around Adjuntas, a local civil engineer put his foot down. Alexis Massol González founded **Casa Pueblo** (The People's House) to organize a series of door-knocking campaigns, concerts, and demonstrations. Over a period of 15 years these convinced González's neighbors, and eventually the whole of Puerto Rico, that digging over a dozen mile-wide pit mines in the collective water source would be a big mistake. In 1995, the organization succeeded in overturning the mining plans, but it was for González's continued work with Casa Pueblo that he received the Goldman Environmental Prize in 2002. Recently, the organization secured government protection for over 50,000 acres of forest, spanning a tract between Adjuntas and Barranquitas. Casa Pueblo divides its activities between promoting public education, protesting environmental abuses, and taking part in ecological research studies. The organization is funded entirely by the sales of its coffee, Café Isla Madre, and accepts volunteer groups on weekends for various projects.

(More information is available at www.casapueblo.org or C. Rudulfo González 30 in Adjuntas. ☎829-4842. Open daily 8am-4:30pm.)

9. (☎838-2100. Open 24hr.) To get to the police station and hospital, take Rte. 120 through town; they are just past the baseball field. The **post office**, C. Luis Zuzuarregui 9, is near the church. (☎838-3605. General Delivery available. Open M-F 7:30am-4pm, Sa 8am-noon.) **Postal Code:** 00606.

◪◻ ACCOMMODATIONS AND FOOD. ◪**Parado Hacienda Juanita ❹**, Rte. 105 Km 23.5, is an attractive mountain *parador*. To reach it, take Rte. 120 east of town, then turn onto Rte. 105. This 19th-century coffee plantation centers on a lush courtyard garden; the grounds include a swimming pool, tennis court, game room with ping pong and billiards, and restaurant with a collection of farming instruments on display. (☎838-2550; www.haciendajuanita.com. Cable TV. Wi-Fi. Singles $80, with breakfast and dinner $102; doubles $96/133. Tax included. AmEx/MC/V.) It's possible to camp or stay in concrete cabins at the private **Monte de Estado ❶**, Rte. 120 Km 13.0, which borders on the Bosque Estatal de Maricao and is operated by the CPN. Families vacation here and make use of the pool, playground, bathrooms, running water, and grills near the cabin. Because no camping is allowed in the nearby state forest, staying here is pricey. Budget travelers would do better to bring some friends and split a cabin. (☎873-5632. Office open daily 8am-4:30pm. Campsites $50, up to 12 people per site; cabins $65, up to 6 people.)

Even travelers not staying at Hacienda Juanita can enjoy the idyllic setting and stylish dining room the *parador*'s **La Casona de Juanita ❸**. Like most *mesones gastronómicos*, this restaurant serves succulent *comida criolla* on a back porch that makes you feel like you're sitting in the middle of the forest. (Entrees $9-18. Wine $20-180. Open M-Th and Su 8am-9pm, F-Sa 8am-10pm.) Those passing through town can grab a quick bite to eat at **El Buen Café ❶**, on the plaza. This is the type of place where locals congregate to discuss weather, politics, and the mistakes of the Spanish-American War over drinks. There is no written menu, but you shouldn't pay more than $5-6 for a sandwich or a plate of *comida criolla*. (☎838-4198. Open M 6am-3pm, Tu-W 6am-10pm, Th-Su 6am-midnight. MC/V.)

◪ SIGHTS. Maricao is a magnet for birdwatchers from around the world, as many species of birds take a break along their annual migratory route in the **Bosque Estatal de Maricao** between November and March. DRNA officers at the Visitors Center, Rte. 120 Km 16.2, can direct visitors to one of three trails. Serious hikers will want to inquire with the DRNA office in San Juan (p. 96) to arrange a private guide for longer hikes on unmaintained trails in the forest. (☎838-1040 or 838-1045. M-F 7am-2:30pm, Sa-Su 8am-3:30pm.) Half a mile up from the Monte del Estado campsite, visitors can stop at the ◪**Torre de Piedra**, a small rock tower built in the late 1930s by the Civilian Conservation Corps. On a clear day, you can see the south coast, most of the central mountains, and all the way to Mayagüez. (Open 8am-4pm. Free.) Maricao is also known for providing seed fish for the island's artificial lakes. **Los Viveros Fish Hatchery,** Rte. 410 Km 1.7, raises fish in several large pools to populate artificial lakes around the island. From the east, turn right at the sign for Los Viveros and continue to the end of Rte. 410. Fishing is not allowed, but visitors can check out the different water systems and try to count the fish as they dart away. (☎838-3710. Open Th-Su 8:30-11:30am and 1-3:30pm. Free.) **La Gruta San Juan Bautista,** Rte. 410 Km 0.3, a tiny waterfall with a Catholic shrine, makes for a nice stop on the way to Los Viveros.

APPENDIX

CLIMATE

The biggest climatic variations in Puerto Rico are between the mountainous areas (represented below by Barranquitas) and the coastal plains. In general, Puerto Rico's weather is beautiful year-round.

Avg. Temp. (°C/F) Avg. Precipitation (mm)	January			April			July			October		
	°C	°F	mm	°C	°F	mm	°C	°F	mm	°C	°F	mm
Arecibo	23.8	74.8	120.7	24.7	76.5	14.8	26.9	80.4	111.8	26.5	79.7	142.8
Barranquitas	20.2	68.4	83.9	21.7	71.1	105.7	23.7	74.7	99.9	23.2	73.8	216.4
Fajardo	24.3	75.7	94.1	25.6	78.1	106.2	27.7	81.9	147.5	27.0	80.6	215.1
Mayagüez	23.8	74.8	56.7	24.9	76.8	141.5	26.5	79.7	261.3	26.2	79.2	255.9
Ponce	24.4	75.9	25.3	25.6	78.1	54.3	27.7	81.9	67.2	26.9	80.4	150.8
San Juan	25.0	77.0	75.3	26.3	79.3	94.9	28.1	82.6	145	27.7	81.9	139.9

MEASUREMENTS

Puerto Rico generally uses the metric system. The basic unit of length is the **meter (m)**, which is divided into 100 **centimeters (cm)**, or 1000 **millimeters (mm)**. One thousand meters make up one **kilometer (km)**. Fluids are measured in **liters (L)**, each divided into 1000 **milliliters (mL)**. A liter of pure water weighs one **kilogram (kg)**, divided into 1000 **grams (g)**, while 1000kg make up one metric **ton.**

1 in. = 25.4mm	1mm = 0.039 in.
1 ft.= 0.30m	1m = 3.28 ft
1 yd. = 0.914m	1m = 1.09 yd.
1 mi. = 1.609km	1km = 0.62 mi.
1 oz. = 28.35g	1g = 0.035 oz.
1 lb. = 0.454kg	1kg = 2.205 lbs.
1 fl. oz. = 29.57ml	1ml = 0.034 fl. oz.
1 gal. = 3.785L	1L = 0.264 gal.

SPANISH QUICK REFERENCE

PRONUNCIATION

Spanish pronunciation is pretty straightforward; Puerto Rican Spanish is a bit more complicated. Puerto Ricans have a notoriously strong accent and tend to speak very rapidly. Some also have a tendency to drop off the ends of words—for example, "buenos días" becomes "buen día." In Spanish, each **vowel** has only one pronunciation: *a* ("ah" as in father); *e* ("eh" as in pet); *i* ("ee" as in feet); *o* ("oh" as in oat); *u* ("oo" as in boot); *y*, by itself, is pronounced the same as the Spanish *i* ("ee"). Most **consonants** are pronounced the same as in English. Important exceptions are *j*, pronounced like the English "h" in "hello," and *ñ*, pronounced like the "ny" in "canyon." *Ll* theoretically sounds like the English "y" in "yes," but in Puerto Rican Spanish it frequently comes out like "s" as in "pleasure." *R* at the beginning of a word or *rr* anywhere in a word is trilled. *H* is always silent. *G* before *e* or *i* is pronounced like the "h" in "hen"; elsewhere it is pronounced like the "g" in "gate." *X* has a bewildering variety of pronunciations: depending on dialect and word position, it can sound like English's "h," "s," "sh," or "x." *B* and *v* are often pronounced somewhere in between a "b" and a "v."

Spanish words receive stress on the syllable marked with an accent ('). In the absence of an accent mark, words that end in vowels, "n," or "s" usually receive stress on the second-to-last syllable. For words ending in all other consonants, stress falls on the last syllable. The Spanish language has masculine and feminine nouns, and gives a gender to all adjectives. Masculine words generally end with an "o": for example, *él es un tonto* (he is a fool). Feminine words generally end with an "a": for instance, *ella es bella* (she is beautiful). Pay close attention—slight changes in word ending can have drastic changes in meaning. For instance, when receiving directions, watch for the distinction between *derecho* (straight) and *derecha* (right).

LET'S GO SPANISH PHRASEBOOK

ESSENTIAL PHRASES

ENGLISH	SPANISH	PRONUNCIATION
Hello.	Hola.	OH-la
Goodbye.	Adiós.	ah-dee-OHS
Yes/No.	Sí/No.	SEE/NO
Please.	Por favor.	POHR fa-VOHR
Thank you.	Gracias.	GRAH-see-ahs
You're welcome.	De nada.	DEH NAH-dah
Do you speak English?	¿Habla inglés?	AH-blah een-GLESS
I don't speak Spanish.	No hablo español.	NO AH-bloh ehs-pah-NYOHL
Excuse me.	Perdón.	pehr-DOHN
I don't know.	No sé.	NO SAY
Can you repeat that?	¿Puede repertirlo?	PWEH-deh-reh-peh-TEER-lo

SURVIVAL SPANISH

ENGLISH	SPANISH	ENGLISH	SPANISH
Good morning.	Buenos días.	I'm sick/fine.	Estoy enfermo(a)/bien.
Good afternoon/evening.	Buenas tardes/noches.	I'm fine, thanks.	(Estoy) bien, gracias.
How are you?	¿Cómo está?	Is the store open/closed?	¿La tienda está abierta/cerrada?
What's up?	¿Qué pasa?/¿Qué tal?	How much does it cost?	¿Cuánto cuesta?
What is your name?	¿Cómo se llama?	That is very cheap/expensive.	Es muy barato/caro.

ENGLISH	SPANISH	ENGLISH	SPANISH
I don't understand.	No entiendo.	Do you accept traveler's checks?	¿Acepta cheques de viaje?
Again, please.	Otra vez, por favor.	I'm hungry/thirsty.	Tengo hambre/sed.
What (did you just say)?	¿Cómo?/¿Qué?	I'm hot/cold.	Tengo calor/frio.
Can/Could you speak more slowly?	¿Puede/Podría hablar más despacio?	I want/would like...	Quiero/Quisiera...
How do you say (beer) in Spanish?	¿Cómo se dice (cerveza) en español?	It's/That's fine.	Está bien.
Who?	¿Quién?	Let's go!	¡Vámonos!
When?	¿Cuándo?	What?	¿Cómo?
Why?	¿Por qué?	Because...	Porque...
Where?	¿Dónde?	Stop/That's enough.	Basta.
Where is (the bathroom)?	¿Dónde está (el baño)?	Maybe/Perhaps.	Tal vez.
Where can I make a phone call?	¿Dónde puedo hacer una llamada de teléfono?	Look!/Listen!	¡Mira!

YOUR ARRIVAL

ENGLISH	SPANISH	ENGLISH	SPANISH
I am from (the US/ Europe).	Soy de (los Estados Unidos/Europa).	What's the problem, sir/ madam?	¿Cuál es el problema, señor/señora?
I have nothing to declare.	No tengo nada para declarar.	I lost my baggage/passport.	Se me perdió mi equipaje/pasaporte.
Please do not detain me.	Por favor no me detenga.	I don't know where (the drugs) came from.	No sé de dónde vinieron (las drogas).

GETTING AROUND

ENGLISH	SPANISH	ENGLISH	SPANISH
How do you get to (the público station)?	¿Cómo se puede llegar a (la terminal de guaguas públicas)?	Could you tell me what time it is?	¿Podría decirme qué hora es?
Does this público go to (Río Piedras)?	¿Va este guagua para (Río Piedras)?	Which way is the cockfight?	¿Dónde está la pelea de gallos?
How long does the trip take?	¿Cuánto tiempo dura el viaje?	Where can I check email?	¿Dónde se puede chequear el correo electrónico?
Please let me off at (the zoo).	Por favor, déjeme en (el zoológico).	I would like to rent (a car).	Quisiera alquilar (un coche).
What bus line goes to...?	¿Cuál línea de autobuses tiene servicio a...?	How much does it cost per day/week?	¿Cuánto cuesta por día/ semana?
I am going to (the airport).	Voy para (el aeropuerto).	Are there student discounts available?	¿Hay descuentos para estudiantes?
Where is (Fortaleza) street?	¿Dónde está la calle (Fortaleza)?	On foot.	A pie.
How near/far from here?	¿Qué tan cerca/lejos está de aquí?	I'm lost.	Estoy perdido(a).

DIRECTIONS

ENGLISH	SPANISH	ENGLISH	SPANISH
(to the) right	a la derecha	(to the) left	(a la) izquierda
straight ahead	derecho	turn (command form)	doble
next to	al lado de/junto a	across from	en frente de/frente a
near	cerca (de)	far from	lejos de
above	arriba	below	abajo
traffic light	semáforo	corner	esquina
street	calle/avenida	block	cuadra

ON THE ROAD

ENGLISH	SPANISH	ENGLISH	SPANISH
car	carro, auto, coche	public bus/van	guagua
stop	pare	slow	despacio
lane (ends)	carril (termina)	yield	ceda
entrance	entrada	seatbelt	cinturón de seguridad
exit	salida	(maximum) speed	velocidad (máxima)
(narrow) bridge	puente (estrecho)	dangerous (curve)	(curva) peligrosa
(narrow) lane	carril (estrecho)	parking	estacionamiento, parking
toll (ahead)	peaje (adelante)	dead-end street	calle sin salida
authorized public buses only	transporte colectivo autorizado solamente	only (traffic only in the direction of the arrow)	solo
slippery when wet	resbala mojada	rest area	área de descansar
danger (ahead)	peligro (adelante)	do not park	no estacione
do not enter	no entre	do not turn right on red	no vire con luz roja
north	norte	south	sur
east	este	west	oeste

ACCOMMODATIONS

ENGLISH	SPANISH	ENGLISH	SPANISH
Is there a (cheap) hotel around here?	¿Hay un hotel (económico) por aqui?	Are there rooms available?	¿Tiene habitaciones libres?
Do you have any singles/ doubles?	¿Tiene habitaciones sencillas/dobles?	I am going to stay for (four) days.	Me voy a quedar (cuatro) días.
I would like to reserve a room.	Quisiera reservar una habitación.	I'll take it.	Lo tomo.
Can I see a room?	¿Puedo ver una habitación?	I need another key/ towel/pillow.	Necesito otra llave/ toalla/almohada.
Are there cheaper rooms?	¿Hay habitaciones más baratas?	The toilet/shower/sink is broken.	El baño/la ducha/el lavabo está roto.

ENGLISH	SPANISH	ENGLISH	SPANISH
Do they come with fans/kitchen/windows?	¿Vienen con abanicos/cocinas/ventanas?	My bedsheets are dirty.	Mis sábanas están sucias.
(The cockroaches) are biting me.	(Las cucarachas) me están mordiendo.	Dance, cockroaches, dance!	¡Bailen, cucarachas, bailen!

EATING OUT

ENGLISH	SPANISH	ENGLISH	SPANISH
breakfast	desayuno	lunch	almuerzo
dinner	comida/cena	drink (alcoholic)	bebida (trago)
dessert	postre	Bon appetit!	¡Buen provecho!
fork	tenedor	knife	cuchillo
spoon	cuchara	cup	copa/taza
napkin	servilleta	Do you have hot sauce?	¿Tiene salsa picante?
Where is a good restaurant?	¿Dónde está un restaurante bueno?	Table for (two), please.	Mesa para (dos), por favor.
Can I see the menu?	¿Podría ver la carta/el monú?	Do you take credit cards?	¿Aceptan tarjetas de crédito?
This is too spicy.	Es demasiado picante.	Disgusting!	¡Guácala!/¡Qué asco!
I would like to order (the eel).	Quisiera (el congrio).	Do you have anything without meat?	¿Hay algún plato sin carne?
Delicious!	¡Qué rico!	The check, please.	La cuenta, por favor.

EMERGENCY

ENGLISH	SPANISH	ENGLISH	SPANISH
Help!	¡Socorro!/¡Ayúdame!	Call the police!	¡Llame a la policía!
I am hurt.	Estoy herido(a).	Leave me alone!	¡Déjeme en paz!
It's an emergency!	¡Es una emergencia!	They robbed me!	¡Me han robado!
Fire!	¡Fuego!/¡Incendio!	They went that-a-way!	¡Fueron por allá!
Call a clinic/ambulance/doctor/priest!	¡Llame a una clínica/una ambulancia/un médico/un padre!	I need to contact my embassy.	Necesito comunicar con mi embajada.
I will only speak in the presence of a lawyer.	Solo hablaré con la presencia de un abogado.	Don't touch me!	¡No me toque!

MEDICAL

ENGLISH	SPANISH	ENGLISH	SPANISH
I feel bad/better/worse/fine.	Me siento mal/mejor/peor/bien.	Call an ambulance.	Llame para una ambulancia.
I have a headache/stomachache.	Tengo dolor de cabeza/estómago.	It hurts here.	Me duele aquí.
I'm sick/ill.	Estoy enfermo(a).	I think I'm going to vomit.	Creo que voy a vomitar.
What is this medicine for?	¿Para qué es esta medicina?	I haven't been able to go to the bathroom for (four) days.	No he podido ir al baño en (cuatro) días.

ENGLISH	SPANISH	ENGLISH	SPANISH
Where is the nearest hospital/doctor?	¿Dónde está el hospital/doctor más cercano?	I have a cold/a fever/diarrhea/nausea.	Tengo gripe/una calentura/diarrea/náusea.
I'm allergic to...	Soy alérgico(a)...	Here is my prescription.	Aquí está la receta médica.

INTERPERSONAL INTERACTION

ENGLISH	SPANISH	ENGLISH	SPANISH
Pleased to meet you.	Encantado(a)/Mucho gusto.	This is my first time in Puerto Rico.	Esta es mi primera vez en Puerto Rico.
What is your name?	¿Cómo se llama?	My name is...	Me llamo...
Where are you from?	¿De dónde es?	I am going to the club.	Voy al club.
I love you.	Te quiero.	I have a boyfriend/girlfriend/spouse.	Tengo novio/novia/esposo(a).
How old are you?	¿Cuántos años tiene?	I'm (twenty) years old.	Tengo (veinte) años.
Do you have a light?	¿Tiene fuego?	I'm gay/bisexual.	Soy gay/bisexual.
No more (rum) for me.	No más (ron) para mi.	Do you come here often?	¿Viene aquí a menudo?
What's wrong?	¿Qué te pasa?	Would you like to go out with me?	¿Quiere salir conmigo?

NUMBERS, DAYS, AND MONTHS

ENGLISH	SPANISH	ENGLISH	SPANISH	ENGLISH	SPANISH
0	cero	21	veintiuno	yesterday	ayer
1	uno	22	veintidós	last night	anoche
2	dos	30	treinta	weekend	fin de semana
3	tres	40	cuarenta	morning	mañana
4	cuatro	50	cincuenta	afternoon	tarde
5	cinco	60	sesenta	night	noche
6	seis	70	setenta	month	mes
7	siete	80	ochenta	year	año
8	ocho	90	noventa	early/late	temprano/tarde
9	nueve	100	cien	January	enero
10	diez	1000	mil	February	febrero
11	once	Monday	lunes	March	marzo
12	doce	Tuesday	martes	April	abril
13	trece	Wednesday	miércoles	May	mayo
14	catorce	Thursday	jueves	June	junio
15	quince	Friday	viernes	July	julio
16	dieciseis	Saturday	sábado	August	agosto
17	diecisiete	Sunday	domingo	September	septiembre
18	dieciocho	today	hoy	October	octubre
19	diecinueve	tomorrow	mañana	November	noviembre
20	veinte	day after tomorrow	pasado mañana	December	diciembre

SPANISH GLOSSARY

abajo: below
abanico: fan
adelante: ahead
aduana: customs
aeropuerto: airport
agencia de viaje: travel agency
agua: water
aguas termales: hot springs
ahora: now
ahorita: in just a moment
a la orden: at your service
al gusto: as you wish
alcaldía: mayor's office
amigo/a: friend
área de descansar: rest area
arriba: above
artesanía: arts and crafts
artesano: artisan
auto: car
avenida: avenue
ATH: ATM
bahía: bay
balneario: public beach
barato(a): cheap
béisbol: baseball
biblioteca: library
boletería: ticket counter
boleto: ticket
bomba: African-influenced music popular in Loíza
bonito(a): pretty, beautiful
Boricua: an affectionate term for a Puerto Rican
Borikén: Taíno name for Puerto Rico
borracho(a): drunk
bosque estatal: state forest
buen provecho: bon appetit
bueno(a): good
buena suerte: good luck
buenos días/buenas tardes/ buenas noches: good morning/ afternoon/evening
burro: donkey
caballero: gentleman
caballo: horse
cafetería: a small, informal restaurant
cajeros: cashiers
calle: street
cambio: change
camino: path, road, track
camión: truck
campo: countryside
capilla: chapel
caro(a): expensive
carretera: highway
carril: lane
carro: car
casa: house
casado(a): married
cascada: waterfall
catedral: cathedral
ceda: yield
centro: city center

centro vacacional: government-sponsored vacation center
cerca: near, nearby
cerro: hill
cheques de viaje: traveler's checks
chico(a): boy/girl
cigarillo: cigarette
cine: movie theater
cinturón de seguridad: seatbelt
ciudad: city
coche: car
cocina criolla: Puerto Rican food
coliseo: coliseum, stadium
colmado: small store
comedor: dining room
comida criolla: regional dishes
comida típica: traditional Puerto Rican food dishes
con: with
consulado: consulate
cordillera: mountain range
CPN: *Compañia de Parques Nacionales* (National Parks Company)
correo: post office
cuadra: street block
cuatro: four, or a traditional Puerto Rican instrument similar to a guitar
cuba libre: rum and coke
cuento: story, account
cueva: cave
curva: curve
damas: ladies
derecha: right (direction)
derecho: straight
despacio: slow
dinero: money
disco: dance club
doblar: to turn
DRNA: Departamento de Recursos Naturales y Ambientales
dulce: sweet
edificio: building
embajada: embassy
embotellada: bottled
emergencia: emergency
entrada: entrance
español: Spanish
esquina: corner
estacionar: to park
estadio: stadium
este: east
estrecho: narrow
estrella: star
extranjero: foreign/foreigner
farmacia: pharmacy
feliz: happy
fiesta: party, holiday
finca: farm, ranch
friaje: sudden cold wind
fumar: to smoke
gobierno: government

gordo(a): fat
gracias: thank you
gratis: free
gringo: American (sometimes derogatory)
guagua: van
hacienda: ranch
hola: hello
hombre: man
iglesia: church
impuestos: taxes
independentistas: supporters of the Puerto Rican independence movement
inglés: English
isla: island
izquierda: left (direction)
jarra: 1-liter pitcher
jíbaro: a man from the countryside
ladrón: thief
lago/laguna: lake
lancha: launch, small boat
larga distancia: long distance
lavandería: laundromat
lejos: far
lento: slow
librería: bookstore
luz: light
mal: bad
malecón: seaside boardwalk
maleta: luggage, suitcase
mar: sea
máxima: maximum
mercado: market
mesón gastronómico: traditional restaurant endorsed by the Puerto Rican Tourism Company
mirador: an observatory or lookout point
muelle: dock
museo: museum
música (folklórica): (folk) music
nada: nothing
naranja: orange
nevera: refrigerator
niño(a): child
norte: north
nueces/nuez: nuts/nut
Nuyorican: someone of Puerto Rican descent living in New York
obra: work of art, play
oeste: west
oficina de turismo: tourist office
panadería: bakery
parada: a bus or train stop (in San Juan "parada" is an old trolley stop that no longer exists; however, the term is still used for giving directions)
pare: stop
parque: a park (recreational)
pasaporte: passport

peaje: toll
pelea de gallos: cockfight
peligroso(a): dangerous
playa: beach
plena: a form of Puerto Rican music that originated in sugar plantations around Ponce
población: population
policía: police
por favor: please
públicos: public vehicles
pueblo: town
puente: bridge
puerta: door
puerto: port
reloj: watch, clock
río: river
ropa: clothes
sabor: flavor
salida: exit
salsa: sauce; a type of music and dance
santos: small hand-carved wooden religious figurines
seguro: insurance
semáforo: traffic light
semana: week
Semana Santa: Holy Week
sexo: sex
sí: yes
sin salida: dead end
SIDA: AIDS
solo/solamente: only
soltero(a): single, unmarried
supermercado: supermarket
sur: south
Taínos: The indigenous people of Puerto Rico
tarifa: fee
termina: ends
tiburón: shark
tienda: store
tiple: traditional Puerto Rican instrument similar to a guitar
turismo: tourism
turista: tourist
valle: valley
vejigante mask: a colorful mask with horns used during *carnaval* festivals
velocidad: speed
vereda: trail, path
vino: wine
virar: to turn
volcán: volcano
zoológico: zoo

ACCOMMODATIONS GLOSSARY

aire acondicionado: air conditioning (A/C)
baño: bathroom
barrio: neighborhood
cabaña: cabin
cama: bed
cama de matrimonio: double bed

cama sencilla: single bed
cuarto: room
cuenta: bill, check
desayuno: breakfast
estacionamiento: parking
habitación: room
parador: "country inn" endorsed by the Puerto Rican Tourism Company
piscina: swimming pool
sábanas: sheets
sala: room
ventana: window

FOOD GLOSSARY

acerola: West Indian cherry
aguacate: avocado
ajo: garlic
a la plancha: grilled
alcapuria: meat-filled fried plantains
almejas: clams
amarillos: sweet, fried plantains
arepas: corn dough patties, sometimes filled with meat, cheese, or vegetables
arroz: rice
arroz con dulce: sweet rice pudding
asada: roast
asopao: stew, thick soup
atún: tuna
avena: oatmeal
bacalaíto: flat fritter fried in codfish oil
batidas: smoothies or milkshakes made from fresh fruit
bistec empanado: breaded Spanish steak
bistec/bistek/biftec: beefsteak
bocaditos: appetizers (at a bar)
café: coffee, cafe
caldo: soup, broth, or stew
camarón: shrimp
cangrejo: crab
carne: red meat
carrucho: conch
cerveza: beer
chapín: trunk fish
chicharrón: bite-sized pieces of meat
chillo: red snapper
china: orange
chuletas: pork chops
churrasco: breaded steak
coco: coconut
empanadilla: stuffed fritter
empanado: breaded
encebollado: with onions
ensalada: salad
flan: egg custard
fresa: strawberry
frijoles: beans
frito: fried
fruta: fruit

gandules: green pigeon peas
guanábana: soursop
guayaba: guava
guayaba con queso: guava with cheese
guineo: banana
habichuelas: beans
helado: ice cream
hervido(a): boiled
hielo: ice
huevo: egg
huevo frito: fried egg
jamón: ham
juey: crab
jugo: juice
langosta: lobster
leche: milk
lechón: roast pork
lechuga: lettuce
limber: frozen fruit juice
mantequilla: butter
manzana: apple
mayonesa: mayonnaise
mariscos: seafood
mofongo: mashed plantain typically filled with meat
mojo: traditional sauce with garlic, lemon, and olive oil
ostiones: oysters
pan: bread
pana: breadfruit
pan mallorca: sweet bread
panqueques: pancakes
parcha: passion fruit
parilla: grilled (as meat)
pavo: turkey
pechuga de pollo: chicken breast
pera: pear
pescado: fish
picante: spicy
pinono: fried plantain wrapped around ground beef
piña: pineapple
plátano: banana
pollo: chicken
pulpo: octopus
queso: cheese
queso suiza: Swiss cheese
refrescos: refreshments, soft drinks
sándwich: sandwich
sorullito: fried corn sticks
té: tea
tembleque: coconut milk custard
tocineta: bacon
tomate: tomato
tortilla española: Spanish omelette
tostadas: toast with butter
tostadas francesas: French toast
tostones: dry, fried plantains
trago: mixed drink/shot
tres leches: sweet, moist cake
vegetales: vegetables

INDEX

INDEX

GET CONNECTED & SAVE WITH THE HI CARD

An HI card gives you access to friendly and affordable accommodations at over 4,000 hostels in over 60 countries, including across Central America. Members also receive complementary travel insurance, members-only airfare deals, and thousands of discounts on everything from tours and dining to shopping, communications and transportation.

Join millions of HI members worldwide who save money and have more fun every time they travel.

 Hostelling International USA

ABOUT LET'S GO

NOT YOUR PARENTS' TRAVEL GUIDE

At Let's Go, we see every trip as the chance of a lifetime. If your dream is to grab a machete and forge through the jungles of Costa Rica, we can take you there. If you'd rather bask in the Riviera sun at a beachside cafe, we'll set you a table. We write for readers who know that there's more to travel than sharing double deckers with tourists and who believe that travel can change both themselves and the world—whether they plan to spend six days in Mexico City or six months in Europe. We'll show you just how far your money can go, and prove that the greatest limitation on your adventures is not your wallet, but your imagination.

BEYOND THE TOURIST EXPERIENCE

To help you gain a deeper connection with the places you travel, our fearless researchers scour the globe to give you the heads-up on both world-renowned and off-the-beaten-track attractions, sights, and destinations. They engage with the local culture only to emerge with the freshest insights on everything from local festivals to regional cuisine. We've also opened our pages to respected writers and scholars to hear their takes on the countries and regions we cover, and asked travelers who have worked, studied, or volunteered abroad to contribute first-person accounts of their experiences. In addition, we increased our coverage of responsible travel and expanded each guide's Beyond Tourism chapter to share more ideas about how to give back while on the road.

FORTY-EIGHT YEARS OF WISDOM

Let's Go got its start in 1960, when a group of creative and well-traveled students compiled their experience and advice into a 20-page mimeographed pamphlet, which they gave to travelers on charter flights to Europe. Four and a half decades later, we've expanded to cover six continents and all kinds of travel—while retaining our founders' adventurous attitude toward the world. Laced with witty prose and total candor, our guides are still researched and written entirely by students on shoestring budgets, experienced travelers who know that train strikes, stolen luggage, food poisoning, and marriage proposals are all part of a day's work.

THE LET'S GO COMMUNITY

More than just a travel guide company, Let's Go is a community. Our small staff comes together because of our shared passion for travel and our desire to help other travelers see the world the way it was meant to be seen. We love it when our readers become part of the Let's Go community as well—when you travel, drop us a postcard (67 Mt. Auburn St., Cambridge, MA 02138, USA), send us an e-mail (feedback@letsgo.com), or post on our forum (http://www.letsgo.com/connect/forum) to tell us about your adventures and discoveries.

For more information, visit us online: www.letsgo.com.

MAP INDEX

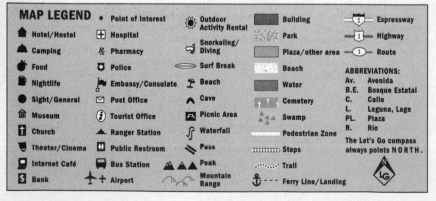

MAP LEGEND

- Point of Interest
- Hotel/Hostel
- Camping
- Food
- Nightlife
- Sight/General
- Museum
- Church
- Theater/Cinema
- Internet Café
- $ Bank

- Hospital
- Pharmacy
- Police
- Embassy/Consulate
- Post Office
- Tourist Office
- Ranger Station
- Public Restroom
- Bus Station
- Airport

- Outdoor Activity Rental
- Snorkeling/Diving
- Surf Break
- Beach
- Cave
- Picnic Area
- Waterfall
- Pass
- Peak
- Mountain Range

- Building
- Park
- Plaza/other area
- Beach
- Water
- Cemetery
- Swamp
- Pedestrian Zone
- Steps
- Trail
- Ferry Line/Landing

- Expressway
- Highway
- Route

ABBREVIATIONS:
Av.   Avenida
B.E.   Bosque Estatal
C.   Calle
L.   Laguna, Lago
PL.   Plaza
R.   Río

The Let's Go compass always points NORTH.